A Bibliography of
EARLY SECULAR
AMERICAN MUSIC

A Bibliography of

EARLY SECULAR

AMERICAN MUSIC

(18th Century)

By

Oscar George Theodore Sonneck

REVISED AND ENLARGED BY

William Treat Upton

With a Preface to the Da Capo Edition by
IRVING LOWENS
Library of Congress
Music Division

Da Capo Press
NEW YORK
1964

A Da Capo Reprint Edition

*Da Capo Press wishes to express its appreciation to
the Library of Congress, whose cooperation made this
unabridged reprint edition possible.*

Library of Congress Catalog Card Number: 64-18992

Da Capo Press
227 West 17th Street
New York, N.Y. 10011

Printed in the United States of America

Preface to the Da Capo
Edition

$\mathcal{A}$T 2:30 ON THE AFTERNOON OF JULY 6, 1905, the Bibliographical Society of America held its first meeting in the parlor of the Portland (Ore.) Hotel. The first paper read to those there assembled was one by Oscar George Theodore Sonneck (1873-1928), Chief of the Music Division of the Library of Congress, dealing with the bibliography of American music. "When the invitation reached me," Sonneck told his listeners, "I hesitated at first to accept. Not that I lacked interest in the theme — on the contrary — but I felt very much like the student who was called upon to describe a vacuum. Indeed, worse, for a vacuum represents at least an ingeniously positive accomplishment in a negative direction, whereas the present vacuum of the bibliography of American music impresses me as a very negative accomplishment in a positive direction."[1] Sonneck was the first person who seriously tried to fill this bibliographical vacuum, and the volume to which these paragraphs serve as a third preface is the direct descendant of his *Bibliography of Early Secular American Music*, which was ready for publication in 1902.

As a matter of fact, Sonneck probably won his position as Chief of the Library's Music Division (a position which he built into one of the most strategically important posts in the entire range of American musical life) because of this very bibliography. According to history, a virtually unknown 28-year-old scholar walked unheralded into the office of Herbert Putnam, then Librarian of Congress, one day early in 1902 and tried to persuade him that the United States Government should bring out a comprehensive bibliography of American music, the manuscript of which he held in his hand. This was a pretty fantastic idea in the days just after Theodore Roosevelt had succeeded to the presidency and, not unexpectedly, the young man did not accomplish the impossible. Sonneck's path-breaking bibliography ultimately appeared in 1905 in an edition of 200 copies, neatly

---

[1] "The Bibliography of American Music," *Proceedings of the Bibliographical Society of America*, I, 1 (1904-5), 50.

turned out for the author (who footed the bill himself) by the Washington printer, H. L. McQueen. But he did have an even bigger success than he bargained for — he impressed Putnam with his vision, intelligence, background, and ability. This is the way the Librarian of Congress (who later became his close personal friend) related the story at the funeral services held for Oscar Sonneck on November 1, 1928:

Among the groups of material that I encountered at the Library, when I went there thirty years ago, was one of music: some 250,000 compositions, all the result of copyright; and a very meagre representation of the literature.

What was to be our duty to it, and to the subject generally? I swiftly satisfied myself that there *was* a duty, positive and appealing; that music, as one of the noblest of the arts — most penetrating, most influential — had a rightful claim to recognition from the National Government; and that the fervor for it among our people was certain to develop a zeal for exact knowledge and understanding promising studies and research which the National Library might foster as could no other institution.

The duty, then, was to develop the collection on the scholarly side, and to assure a scholarly conduct of it.

But for both of these the indispensable, indeed the prerequisite, was the *man* with the adequate learning and the necessary qualities. The combination required was complicated. He must be a specialist in the subject matter, thoroughly grounded through studies abroad; yet he must, if possible, have some familiarity with our American ways, some sympathies, some faith in what we might do in music — some appreciation of what we had already done. He must be familiar with the technique of music as an art, yet prefer to pursue it as a science: the history of it, the theory, the philosophy, even the bibliography. He must be young, for the task would be long; and personally industrious, for his staff would be small. And he must have the urge to gather and interpret for the benefit of others, which is the requisite in a library.

The combination in one person of all these qualifications seemed scarcely credible. Yet I shaped them, and waited.

I waited three years. Then one day (in 1902) there strolled into my office a young man who introduced himself as Oscar Sonneck, and his interest as music. He had under his arm a packet of manuscript which he proffered to me — without recompense — for publication by the government.

The explanation of it — very simple and modest — induced me to draw from him the facts of his career: that, born in Jersey City [on October 6, 1873], he had been educated at Kiel and Frankfurt and Heidelberg and Munich, specializing in music, which he had pursued further in studies in Italy; that his particular interest was on the historical, philosophic, and critical side; that for several years preceding he had been writing criticisms and reviews, during the last two, however, concentrating upon the preparation of this manuscript. And the manuscript proved to be "A Bibliography of American Music in the Eighteenth Century"!

Providence, you see, had intervened: do you wonder I thought it?

I talked to him of the task with us, asked him if he would consider it. He thought it might interest him. There were some adjustments — of our roll — involved for which I had to look to the Appropriation Committees in Congress.

---

[2] Herbert Putnam, "Remarks ... at the Funeral Services [of O. G. Sonneck]," *Musical Quarterly*, XV, 1 (January 1929), 1-2.

I sought them, describing the opportunity, and, very frankly, the man himself. They were granted; and he came.[2]

Sonneck looked upon bibliography with rather mixed feelings. "Bibliographical work is fascinating for him who happens to be afflicted with the disease," he wrote. "It is stupid work in the eyes of him who is not, but it becomes useful work in the eyes of even the scoffers if circumstances compel them to depend upon a piece of bibliographic work well done."[3]

Needless to say, he himself was severely afflicted with bibliographomania, the germ of which he caught as a pioneer in the untrod jungle of 18th-century American music history. He had no choice in the matter since he was convinced that before he could complete a definitive study of our music during that period, it would be "necessary, of course, first to form a bibliographical basis for the work."[4] No one else had done it for him, and as a conscientious historian, he had to do it for himself. Thereafter, the crucial importance of the "bibliographical basis" for scholarly research was one of the main tenets of his philosophy. This fact, together with his friendship with Putnam and his association with the Library of Congress, resulted in the practical realization of what had begun as a wild dream— the issuance of a long series of music bibliographies *as official publications of the United States Government.* The red, bound volumes, well known (and thoroughly used) by librarians and music scholars throughout the world, fill a good-sized shelf. They are a living monument to Sonneck's memory — and it is a measure of the quality of his workmanship as a bibliographer to note that even though many are now more than half a century old, none is yet completely superseded — even in 1964.

Thanks in large part to Sonneck's own effort as bibliographer-musicologist, interest in the serious investigation of early American music history mushroomed during the 1920's and the 1930's. It was becoming more and more evident that the 1905 *Bibliography of Early Secular American Music,* while still quite useful, was no longer a truly adequate guide to a growing field. New discoveries had been made, and John Tasker Howard's fine comprehensive history, *Our American Music* (New York, 1929), had enormously stimulated further basic research. A revision of Sonneck's *Bibliography* was clearly indicated. The man who stepped forward in the mid-1930's to bring the work up to date was William Treat Upton (1870-1961), an elder contemporary of Sonneck's who devoted his years of retirement (after having served as a respected pedagogue at the Oberlin College and Conservatory from 1893 to 1936) to a new career. Dr. Upton was educated at Oberlin; he studied piano with Leschetizky in Vienna from 1896 to 1898. All his years of teaching were spent at his Alma

[3] "The History of Music in America—a Few Suggestions," *Papers and Proceedings of the Music Teachers' National Association,* XI (1916), 52.

[4] *PBSA*, op. cit., 54.

Mater, but while he was busily instructing budding piano virtuosos, he gradually developed a strong interest in the history of American music. Dr. Upton himself tells of this aspect of his intellectual growth:

I first began published writing as music critic for the *Oberlin Alumni Magazine,* 1915-1918, followed by similar service for the *Oberlin Review* (college undergraduate periodical) from 1918 to 1936, at which time I retired from active teaching.

Through this long continued service as writer of critiques on all important musical events connected with Oberlin College and Conservatory I found myself increasingly interested in the matter of writing for a larger audience and so gradually drifted into a fairly continuous contribution of articles to musical magazines, here and abroad — this paralleling my regular teaching as Professor of Pianoforte in Oberlin Conservatory.

Beginning the publication of these magazine articles soon after the first World War, I was naturally interested in taking stock of the contemporary American musical scene, and found that at that time the American composer was expressing himself more fully through the song form than through any other medium, with the result that I became intensely interested in that particular phase of American music, as is clearly shown in the list of contributions made to various magazines during the 1920's. This series of articles finally culminated in the publication in 1930 of *Art Song In America — A Study in the Development of American Music.* (A *Supplement,* bringing it up to later date, was issued in 1938.)

Through the research necessary to the opening chapters of this work my interest became centered upon our earlier musical development, particularly before the Civil War, i.e., the first half of the 19th century, and that period still so little known, though recently more and more studied, has been my predominant interest ever since, resulting in the biography of Anthony Philip Heinrich (1781-1861), published in 1939 (its publication made possible through an award from the Sonneck Memorial Fund in the Library of Congress — the first award made by this Fund) and [my] plan for a study of the life of William Henry Fry (1813-1864).

The carrying out of this latter plan has been delayed by three years spent in the preparation of a long overdue revision and enlargement of Oscar G. Sonneck's invaluable *Bibliography of Early Secular American Music* (1905). In this revised form the *Bibliography* has been increased to more than triple its original size and its contents made more readily accessible through numerous indexes.

This work has been of the greatest interest to me and has served to complete a certain cycle in my writing. I seem to have progressed in reverse — having begun with this present 20th century, then working my way back through the 19th (late and early), finally emerging in those important later decades of the 18th century — the 1780's and '90's.[5]

How Upton viewed the importance of what must have seemed to many no more than sheer drudgery is made plain in a letter he wrote in response to a request from President Ernest H. Wilkins of Oberlin for a statement of the work he proposed to undertake upon the completion of his revision of the Sonneck *Bibliography*:

---

[5]Cited from an unpublished draft-statement of his plans (dating from around 1943) to begin intensive work on what was to be his last major contribution to American music history, a biography of the mid-19th-century composer-journalist, William Henry Fry. In the William Treat Upton Papers, Music Division, Library of Congress.

As this revision draws towards its close I am becoming more and more conscious that the value of Sonneck's work (and even more in its enlarged form) is showing itself in many ways not clearly realized at its inception. Of course its more obvious value lies in the picture it presents of 18th-century music publishing in America, and also in its practical service as a comprehensive finding list for such of this published material as is still extant in various libraries and private collections in the United States. But to the student of early American culture, particularly in the field of music, it has a far deeper and more vital significance. For here one begins to sense a certain perspective, a clearer, better proportioned view of the culture of the time.[6]

Dr. Upton's work on the Sonneck *Bibliography* was entirely a labor of love. His major recompense for the three years of his life he lavished upon it turned out to be the satisfaction he got from seeing the job well done, and from seeing the handsome volume encompassing the results of his work published (with the aid of a grant from the Sonneck Memorial Fund) by the Music Division of the Library of Congress in 1945. In recognition of his achievement, in 1946 Oberlin conferred upon him an honorary degree of Doctor of Music (seldom has it been more doggedly earned) with a citation that read, in part:

His unflagging enthusiasm, his superb scholarship, his precision of form and expression are illustrated in every page of this reference work. Mr. Upton has picked up the voice of America in the 18th century and early 19th century and has made live again . . . makers of music that time had covered with darkness. He too has heard "America singing."[7]

After Dr. Upton's death, the Assistant Chief of the Music Division in the Library of Congress, Edward N. Waters, put into words the esteem in which he was held by those who came to know him in his later years:

I should like to say that never have we had a scholar studying here for whom we entertained more respect and affection. He seemed like a colleague rather than a client, and we watched the progress of his research and writing with a warm and personal interest. When each of his books appeared, we were almost as proud as he was, for we witnessed the industry, meticulousness, and integrity that went into them. He made a great contribution to learning, and we derived a deep satisfaction from providing materials and assistance.[8]

The Sonneck-Upton *Bibliography,* released by the Government Printing Office is a small edition, was a rare bargain, and as a consequence, it very quickly went out of print. Within a decade, it had become a much sought item in the antiquarian book market, frequently commanding as much as five times its original price when copies could be found at all. Unfortunately, a further reprint by the Library of Congress proved unfeasible.

This reprint is, therefore, most welcome. It is doubly welcome at this

---

[6]Letter dated December 14, 1939. Carbon copy in the William Treat Upton Papers, Music Division, Library of Congress.

[7]From the "General Faculty Minutes for March 14, 1961, Oberlin College," p. 3.

[8]From a letter to Professor George O. Lillich of Oberlin College dated March 3, 1961.

particular time because Richard J. Wolfe's eagerly awaited *Bibliography of Secular American Music (1801-1825)* — in essence a supplement to Sonneck-Upton even though dwarfing it in size — is about to be published by the New York Public Library and is expected from the presses this year. Since the Wolfe *Bibliography* will include an appendix listing pre-1800 items not now in Sonneck-Upton, items dated out of Sonneck-Upton, and new or additional locations[9] of items in Sonneck-Upton, it is plain that its appearance will give its venerable parent a new lease on life. Together, the Sonneck-Upton and the Wolfe bibliographies should stand for many years to come as *the* essential source of authentic information about the music published in the United States through 1825.

IRVING LOWENS

Music Division, Library of Congress
Washington, D. C.
January, 1964

[9]A word of caution about the private collections listed on page xv would seem to be called for here. These collections were seen by Dr. Upton more than two decades ago, and (quite naturally) many changes in locations have taken place since then. Some collections have been broken up completely; others have been partly or completely absorbed by institutional or private libraries; new private collections have been amassed; individual items have moved from one collection to another. The reader should remember that page xv gives the leading private collections of the early 1940's, and private locations in Sonneck-Upton should be double-checked against the locations in the appendix to the Wolfe *Bibliography*. It may be assumed that institutional locations are still accurate.

A Bibliography
of Early Secular
American Music

[18TH CENTURY]

BY

Oscar George Theodore Sonneck

Chief of the Division of Music

1902–1917

REVISED AND ENLARGED BY

William Treat Upton

The Library of Congress

MUSIC DIVISION

1945

CONTENTS

THIS REVISED EDITION OF THE BIBLIOGRAPHY HAS BEEN
PUBLISHED WITH THE AID OF A GRANT FROM THE SONNECK
MEMORIAL FUND ADMINISTERED BY THE MUSIC DIVISION IN
THE LIBRARY OF CONGRESS

Preface

THIS bibliography grew out of material collected for a 'History of early secular music in the United States.' The origin of the book, my inexperience in bibliographical matters when I first undertook its compilation, and the fact that it seems to be the first of its kind, will account for such imperfections as it necessarily and involuntarily contains.

I have aimed at a complete collection of titles of secular music and books, pamphlets, essays, etc., relating to secular music—

1. Issued by the American press prior to the nineteenth century and extant in certain libraries to be mentioned;
2. Issued but not extant in these libraries;
3. Written by native or naturalized Americans and extant in manuscript;
4. Written by the same but apparently neither published nor extant.

With these points in view I examined the collections at the following institutions:[1]

American Antiquarian Society.
Boston Athenaeum.
Boston Public Library.
Brown University.
Charleston Library Society.
Harvard University.
Library Company of Philadelphia.
Library of Congress.
Maryland Historical Society.

Massachusetts Historical Society.
New York Historical Society.
Pennsylvania Historical Society.
Pennsylvania University.
Rhode Island Historical Society.
South Carolina Historical Society.
Virginia Historical Society.
Yale University.

I also had access to the famous library of Governor Samuel W. Pennypacker of Philadelphia, to the exceedingly interesting archives of the Hopkinson family in Philadelphia (*Hopk.*), and to the manuscripts of Francis Hopkinson in possession of his descendant, Mrs. Florence Scovel Shinn of New York City.

Special, and perhaps the most important, sources of information I found in our early magazines and newspapers as on file in the libraries enumerated. Not of equal importance but nevertheless of value proved to be the consultation of—

Henry M. Brooks' "Olden time music," Boston, 1888;
William Dunlap's "History of the American theatre," New York, 1832;
Charles Durang's important work on "The Philadelphia stage from 1749 to 1821" (clippings from the Sunday dispatch, Philadelphia, 1855, in *Pa. H. S.*);

---

[1] *I regret that circumstances prevented me from visiting the Newberry Library, Chicago. I also wish to state that since this preface was first written I have added no titles except those which came under my personal supervision at the Library of Congress. While, therefore, my sins of omission may have become more numerous during the last three years, I hope that the book does not really show the wrinkles of age.*

Louis C. Elson's "National music of America and its sources," Boston, 1900, and his "History of American music," New York, 1904;

Charles R. Hildeburn's "Issues of the Press in Pennsylvania" (1685-1784), Philadelphia, 1885–1886, 2 vols.;

Joseph N. Ireland's "Records of the New York stage" (1750–1860), New York, 1866, 2 vols.;

Joseph Sabin's "Dictionary of books relating to America," 1867–1892;

George O. Seilhamer's monumental "History of the American stage" (1749–1797), New York, 1896, 3 vols.;

Isaiah Thomas' "History of Printing in America," 1874, 2d vol.;

Oscar Wegelin's "Early American plays" (1714–1830), New York, 1900, 1905—

and other works known to the student of early Americana in general and of our early music in particular.

Whoever is familiar with these different sources of information will understand the difficulty of my task. In the first place, our libraries are daily purchasing or receiving titles which enter into my theme but which I, for obvious reasons, was unable to examine. In the second place, many of our card-catalogues are under a process of regeneration or reformation which seriously interferes with the work of the student. Finally, it is well-nigh impossible to examine complete and perfect files of all the magazines and newspapers printed in our country during the eighteenth century. Such files do not exist, and the imperfect files extant are so scattered as to oblige the student to travel extensively if he aims at anything like completeness. Unfortunately scientific enthusiasm does not always go hand in hand with a full purse and consequently I found myself obliged to limit my investigations to the principal newspapers as issued in the more important cities and on file in the institutions mentioned.

But a more serious obstacle to completeness resulted from the deplorable lack of interest taken in the history of our early musical life. To some extent this indifference is due to the superficiality and prejudice with which the subject has repeatedly been approached. Historians, popular and unpopular, have steadily (and with surprisingly uncritical methods) guided the public into the belief that a secular musical life did not exist in our country during the eighteenth century. To be sure, these pages throw little more than side-lights on the formative period in our musical history, but possibly they will help to undermine an absurd theory and strengthen the opposite position correctly held by a few writers, as, for instance, Henry Edward Krehbiel.

At any rate, the book should be useful to bibliographers, collectors and dealers, especially if our old families learn that the music collected by their ancestors, lovers of art as well as men of affairs, but which is now stored away in garrets and closets because it is considered as of use to nobody, possesses a commerical and historical value. I am convinced that there are other families besides the Hopkinson family in whom an inherited and traditional love of music has kept such treasures intact, and I am equally sure that families in whom the love of music has died out possess interesting collections of old American (or European) music. Not until these hidden treasures have been examined will the "missing links" be found or completeness be obtained.

When compiling this book, I strictly adhered to the principle of admitting nothing that did not, in my judgment, with certainty come within the general plan. This work of selection had its difficulties. To begin with, where ought we to draw the line between sacred and secular music? Of course, all music intended for church service must be classified as sacred, but we know that American psalmody, etc., of olden times had its place not only in the church but in the homes of the people, in singing-schools, in musical societies, in college and so forth.

This explains why we occasionally find pieces of a decidedly secular flavor in our early psalm-tune collections. In fact, the personality of an Andrew Law or William Billings can not be fully understood without the study of their secular traits and tendencies. We remember, for instance, Billings' tune "Jargon," and ask ourselves in astonishment to what purpose the grim and grotesque bars figure in a collection of sacred music.

At first I intended to collect from the rich literature of early American psalmody those tunes and anthems which impressed me as being of secular conception. But I soon abandoned the pedantic idea and restricted myself to secular music proper. However, a few anthems, etc., with an evident political or personal background have been admitted into the list.

The second difficulty was met with when titles had to be extracted from the old newspapers. For instance, we frequently find advertisements of pantomimes and ballets as "composed by . . ." But experience soon forbade to admit them on the basis of this vague term, for it applied mostly not to the composer of the music but to the composer of the chorographical figures. The titles of such pantomimes were entered only, if the advertisement read "music composed by . . ." or "arranged by . . ." In applying this test I possibly have been too sceptical in certain instances and probably I excluded a few titles which others would have included.

The same remark applies even more strongly to concertos, quartets, and the like. Again, the form of many a newspaper advertisement made it necessary to work with a sceptical method. For instance, "Messrs. Hewitt, Bergman and Philips" advertised in 1793 their third "Subscription Concert" for March 2d at Corre's Hotel, New York, as follows: [2]

Act I.

Sinfonia	Van Hall, M. S.
Song	Mrs. Hodgkinson
Quartetto	Pleyl
Song	Mrs. Pownall
Concerto Violoncello	Mr. Phillips

Act II.

Concerto Violin	Mr. Hewitt
Song	Mrs. Pownall
Overture	Stamitz
Song	Mr. Hodgkinson
Finale	Haydn

It will be noticed how indiscriminately composers and performers are thrown together. Quite in accord with the ideas of the time, the authors of the concertos are not mentioned, the soloist attracting more attention than the composer. But it is equally characteristic of the eighteenth century that, very frequently, the performers would be their own composers and the composers their own performers. Furthermore, it will be seen that James Hewitt was a very active composer. Therefore the question arises, did Mr. Hewitt play a violin concerto of his own composition on said occasion?

We feel inclined to dispel historical doubt in such instances and to confuse probability with certainty. I hope to have succumbed to this temptation seldom, if at all.

In quoting newspaper advertisements, it became necessary to give the address of printers or publishers, a proceeding which might, at first glance, seem unwarranted. But a careful reader will notice upon consultation of the index that it frequently would have been impossible to otherwise approximately ascertain the dates of publication. He will also readily understand my reasons for departing from an author arrangement in favor of a title arrangement.

The titles have been entered in strictly alphabetical order. As many of them are rather vague, especially those of works advertised but not published, frequent cross-references had to be made either in the body of the text or in the index. The latter, being an index to an index, had to be compiled so as to avoid needless repetitions. Attention was therefore paid mostly to names and subjects. Biographical items were added to the names of American composers, or Europeans emigrated to the United States, less in order to furnish biographical data than to show why compositions by certain unknown or forgotten musicians appear in the list.

---

[2] Compare New York daily advertiser, February 26, 1793.

It remains to offer my thanks to all those who, in one way or the other, encouraged and assisted me when compiling this book. I am under great obligations to the officials of all the institutions mentioned, in particular to Mr. Edmund Barton of the American Antiquarian Society; Mr. Wilberforce Eames of the New York Public Library; Dr. Samuel Abbot Green of the Massachusetts Historical Society; Mr. John W. Jordan of the Pennsylvania Historical Society; Mr. Victor H. Paltsits of the New York Public Library; Mr. Herbert Putnam, Librarian of Congress; Mr. A. S. Salley, jun., of the South Carolina Historical Society; Mr. J. Sumner Smith of the Yale University Library, and Mr. Walter R. Whittlesey of the Library of Congress.

I am equally indebted to Governor Samuel W. Pennypacker of Philadelphia; Mr. and Mrs. Edward Hopkinson of Philadelphia; Mrs. Florence Scovel Shinn of New York City, for having so generously given me access to their private collections, and to Mr. Henry Edward Krehbiel of New York City and Mr. James Warrington of Philadelphia for their interest taken in my work.

O. G. SONNECK

New York City, March, 1902.
Washington, D. C., September, 1905.

Preface to the Revised
Edition

TO THOSE of us who have long been engaged in serious study of our early musical development in these United States of America, the name of Oscar George Theodore Sonneck has always been the object of an unique and enduring respect, even veneration.

It would be unthinkable, then, for any one of us to undertake the task of revising one of his works without (as it were) reverently removing the shoes from off our feet, and entering with deep humility into what might well seem to us a consecrated place. True, there was nothing sacrosanct about Sonneck himself—he was intensely human, and could say caustically human things. But so fine was his spirit, so accurate his scholarship, so unflagging his energy, that we who follow him may well feel a becoming modesty in his presence and walk warily before him.

It is entirely in this spirit that I have undertaken the revision and enlargement of his *Bibliography of early secular American music*, and it has been my constant aim to maintain as far as possible the fine simplicity and dignity of the original work. Only such changes and modifications have been adopted as would serve to bring it into somewhat closer conformity with present day bibliographical usage.

The spirit and intent of the original plan have been little (if at all) changed. Its outward form, however, has been considerably altered—notably through the addition of numerous indexes, by means of which it is hoped that the mass of material forming the main body of the work may become more easily accessible, and that each item in turn, instead of forming an isolated unit, may find itself fitted into the general scheme of its own time and place.

In pursuance of this plan the bibliographical section remains as Sonneck had it, except that its non-musical material (such as essays, articles, books, etc.) has been placed elsewhere.

In the limited and highly specialized field of eighteenth century American musical manuscripts but few titles have been added (and those holographs only), as also little of American musical literature of that time. The emphasis remains where Sonneck so definitely placed it—on the actual printed music. In this field—the foundation of the whole work—surprisingly large gains have been made.

Many of these additional issues (acquired from time to time by the Library of Congress) have been noted in the master copy, inter-leaved, in the office of the Chief of the Music Division. These annotations, on the margins as well as on the added leaves, were written by Sonneck himself, his successors as Chief of the Division (Carl Engel, Oliver Strunk, Harold Spivacke) and numerous Division assistants. These notations have been of great value in forming the nucleus of the mass of new material located since the *Bibliography* was originally issued in 1905.

As to the line drawn between secular and sacred music, Sonneck has been followed (*cf.* his Preface, p. vii) except that there have been included in the main body of the work certain additional titles (taken from various collections of psalm and hymn-tunes) which show a "decidedly secular flavor."

It is also an interesting fact that in addition to the quasi-secular items in their collections of sacred music, all succeeding eighteenth century editors of such collections followed Thomas Walter's pioneer work, *The Grounds and Rules of Musick Explained* (Boston, 1721), by including in their own collections similar rules and instructive articles. All this, of course, has its own bearing on secular music as well, and I have made some reference to it in the text. No claim is made, however, to anything more than a passing glance in this direction.

For the better understanding of the *Bibliography* as a whole, the following points should be noted:

Since in most cases the only title available in these early musical imprints is found in the caption, the caption title has furnished copy for almost all entries. For this reason "caption title" is to be everywhere understood, except when a title-page is indicated. The indication of a title-page also signifies the source for the entry, unless a specific note to the contrary is appended.

When an entry is made from a magazine, only the location of that particular copy is given, *e. g.*, DLC (etc.). Other locations are to be found in the *Union list of serials.*

When individual entries are made for all titles in a collection, all locations are given in each case, except in the single instance of *The American musical miscellany,* which contains well over a hundred titles with numerous locations. In this case, therefore, it has seemed wiser to restrict the naming of locations to the main entry.

Sonneck's phrase, "Song with pf. acc." (abbreviated to "Song, pfte. acc.") is retained in preference to the longer, perhaps more exact expression, "Pfte. 2 hds., with interlinear text," primarily because this latter form seems to throw undue emphasis upon the instrumental phase of the composition, as opposed to its more fundamental character as a song. Two staves are understood unless otherwise stated.

Throughout the text of the Bibliography proper, the words "The same" are used to indicate identical title, but not identical imprint. On the other hand,

"The same as preceding" indicates both identical title and identical imprint *i. e.*, presumably, use of identical plate.

When date of an issue is determined from the publisher's address, no explanation of such date is given. (A directory of such publishers as concern us here is found in this volume.)

When date is determined from the publisher's advertisement, such advertisement is given.

When date, otherwise indeterminate, is approximately located by some form of circumstantial or internal evidence (as *e. g.*, a first performance in America of the opera from which a certain song is taken) such evidence is given.

When a publisher's address remains the same for several years (*e. g.*, 1794-97) notation of these limits is considered sufficient, unless a definite or approximate date within these limits is ascertainable. If so, such fact is stated. If these limits cross our boundaries (*e. g.*, 1798-1804) only such imprints are included as seem to be quite definitely of the eighteenth century. This is often a puzzling question—and there is no claim to infallibility in this respect!

When a publisher's address represents one definite year, together with certain months on either side (*e. g.*, late 1797 to February or March 1799) the date is given as 1797–1799, although ca. 1798 is perhaps equally satisfactory. In general, however, *circa* has been avoided as far as possible.

In giving titles, first lines, advertisements, etc., great care has been exercised at all times to preserve the exact spelling of the original, although it has sometimes been difficult to keep to the strait and narrow way between such apostrophic pitfalls as *soldier's* and *soldiers*, *'twas* and *twas*, to say nothing of *walked*, *walkd*, *walk'd* and *wandering*, *wand'ring*, *wandring* (all of these *ad infinitum*). It must be admitted that now and again our steps have faltered here. And if we consider this as treacherous ground, what shall we say of any attempt to cut a clean path through the wild chaotic disorder of eighteenth century capitalization and punctuation—except to state bluntly that it can't be done. That impossiblity has not been attempted.

The various dates of opera performances in the United States as noted in the text have been checked not only with Sonneck's *Early Opera in America* (1915), but also for Philadelphia with *The Philadelphia Theatre in the Eighteenth Century*, by Thomas Clark Pollock (1933) and for New York with George C. D. Odell's *Annals of the New York Stage* (1927–).

In addition to the libraries and private collections that were visited by Sonneck, I add the following—

LIBRARIES

Cornell University.
Free Library of Philadelphia.
Free Library of Philadelphia.[3]
Grosvenor Library [Buffalo].
Huntington Library [San Marino, Calif.].

John Carter Brown Library [Providence].
Newberry Library [Chicago].
New York Public Library.
New York State Library [Albany].
Sibley Music Library [Rochester].

[3] *Edward I. Keffer Collection.*

Harry F. Bruning, San Francisco, Calif.

J. Francis Driscoll, Brookline, Mass.

Mrs. Josephine L. Hughes, Charleston, S. C.

Arthur Billings Hunt, Brooklyn, N. Y.

Matt B. Jones,[4] Newton Center, Mass.

Lester S. Levy, Baltimore, Md.

Josephine A. McDevitt and Edith A. Wright, Washington, D. C.

Elliott Shapiro, New York City.

Malcolm N. Stone, West Englewood, N. J.

Mrs. Clara de Windt, Boston, Mass.

4 *Since deceased.*

My sincere gratitude goes out to all those who helped make these exploratory expeditions such an unqualified pleasure. Truly, library officials and private collectors, too, are a fine and friendly folk; and it has been a great privilege to come into such direct contact with them.

Naturally, my first thought is of the Library of Congress, where I have spent so much of my time—of Doctor Harold Spivacke, of Edward N. Waters—indeed of the entire staff of the Music Division, each and every one. No less, however, to all the others, who in various places, in shorter time, have shown the same spirit of helpfulness. To all of these, too numerous to be named, my hearty thanks.

At this point must be added a very special word of appreciation of the valuable assistance rendered in the final preparation of this work by Mrs. Wilhelmina Andrews Spalding, Assistant in the Music Division of the Library of Congress. To her ready skill and technical knowledge, I am happy to pay sincerest tribute.

And perhaps here is also my opportunity to say that without the untiring and capable assistance of my wife, Lelia Elmore Upton, this work could never have been accomplished.

WILLIAM TREAT UPTON

Washington, D. C.
December, 1943.

Key to Symbols & Abbreviations

LIBRARIES [5]

CSmH	Henry E. Huntington Library, San Marino, Calif.
CtY	Yale University, New Haven, Conn.
DLC	Library of Congress, Washington, D. C.
ICN	Newberry Library, Chicago, Ill.
MB	Boston Public Library, Boston, Mass.
MBAt	Boston Athenaeum, Boston, Mass.
MH	Harvard University, Cambridge, Mass.
MHi	Massachusetts Historical Society, Boston, Mass.
MWA	American Antiquarian Society, Worcester, Mass.
MdHi	Maryland Historical Society, Baltimore, Md.
N	New York State Library, Albany, N. Y.
NBuG	Grosvenor Library, Buffalo, N. Y.
NHi	New York Historical Society, New York, N. Y.
NIC	Cornell University, Ithaca, N. Y.
NN	New York Public Library, New York, N. Y.
NRU–Mus	Sibley Music Library, Eastman School of Music, Rochester, N. Y.
PHi	Historical Society of Pennsylvania, Philadelphia, Pa.
PP	Free Library of Philadelphia, Philadelphia, Pa.
PP–K	———— Edward I. Keffer Collection
PPL	Library Company of Philadelphia, Philadelphia, Pa.
PU	University of Pennsylvania, Philadelphia, Pa.
RHi	Rhode Island Historical Society, Providence, R. I.
RPB	Brown University, Providence, R. I.
RPJCB	John Carter Brown Library, Providence, R. I.
ScC	Charleston Library Society, Charleston, S. C.
ScHi	South Carolina Historical Society, Charleston, S. C.
ViHi	Virginia Historical Society, Richmond, Va.
Hopk.	A Collection of compositions by Francis Hopkinson in the custody of the Library of the University of Pennsylvania

PRIVATE COLLECTIONS

ABHu	Arthur Billings Hunt, Brooklyn, N. Y.
CdeW	Clara de Windt, Boston, Mass.
ES	Elliott Shapiro, New York, N. Y.
HFB	Harry F. Bruning, San Francisco, Calif.
JFD	J. Francis Driscoll, Brookline, Mass.
JLH	Josephine L. Hughes, Charleston, S. C.
LSL	Lester S. Levy, Baltimore, Md.
MBJ	Matt B. Jones,[6] Newton Center, Mass.
MNSt	Malcolm N. Stone, West Englewood, N. J.
McD–W	Josephine A. McDevitt and Edith A. Wright, Washington, D. C.

An asterisk before a title indicates that no published copy of such title has been located.

---

[5] *The symbols used in this book to locate the various libraries and collections conform to those used in the Union Catalog of the Library of Congress.*

[6] *Since deceased.*

ABBREVIATIONS

BM Cat.   Catalogue of printed music published between 1487 and 1800 now in the British Museum. By W. Barclay Squire. London, 1912.
Eitner   Quellen-Lexikon der Musiker und Musikgelehrten. Leipzig, 1900.
Evans   American bibliography by Charles Evans, Chicago. 1903–34.
Fétis   Biographie universelle des musiciens. Deuxième édition. Paris, 1883.
Grove   Dictionary of music and musicians. 4th ed. London, 1940.
Moore   Complete encyclopaedia of music. Boston, 1854.

A Bibliography

A SON ALTESSE ROYALE Madame Elizabeth de France, soeur du Roi.   Philadelphia, Sold by H. & P. Rice, No. 50 Market street.   Price 20 cents.   Les
paroles par M. de Curt.   Misique [!] de M. Martini [1794]   2–3 p.   31 cm.

Song, pfte. acc.   Three staves.
First line: Ce regard plein de bien veillance.   McD–W

Advertised in May, 1794, "Philadelphia, printed for Shaw & co."   Undoubtedly this issue.   (*Cf. The waggoner* (Dibdin) with identical imprint, also
advertised as published in May, 1794.)   Concerning this piece and a "Ronde
chanté à la reine" we read:

> Les suivans sont tirés d'une collection publiée à Londres par M. Curt, au
> profit de l'honourable infortune.

A-TY'D-Y-NOS.   A favorite Welch song.   New York, Printed & sold by J.
Hewitt, No. 23 Maiden Lane.   Price 25 cents.   [1799–1800] 1 l.   32 cm.

Song, pfte. acc., followed by arr. for flute.
First line: Fain would some with vows persuade me.   ES, NN

———— The same as preceding.
(*In* A collection of new & favorite songs.   [A] Philadelphia [ca. 1800]   p.
[199])   HFB

*ABROAD AND AT HOME.
Opera by William Shield (1796).   The "principal songs . . . adapted for
the pianoforte" were advertised as published by Geo. Gilfert, New York, in
November, 1797.

AN ABSTRACT OF GEMINIANI'S ART of playing on the violin, and of another book of instructions for playing in a true taste on the violin, German
flute, violoncello and the thorough bass on the harpsichord, with some additions.   Containing the most necessary rules to attain to a perfection on
those instruments.   Boston, New-England, Printed by John Boyles.   1769.
14 p.   Sm. 4º.   RPJCB

THE ACCOMPLISH'D MAID.   A new comic opera as it is performed at the
Theatre Royal in Covent-Garden.   The music by Signior [!] Niccolo Piccini.
[Verse] Philadelphia, Printed and sold by Robert Bell in Third-street, 1777.
61, [3] p.   20 cm.

Libretto.
Half-title; t.-p., verso blank; dramatis personae, p. [5]; text, p. [7]–61; "Table
of the songs," p. [62]; list of old and new books, p. [63]–[64].   DLC

[1]

[ACROSS THE DOWNS THIS MORNING] Sung by Mrs. Hodgkinson in No song, no supper.

(*In* Young's vocal and instrumental musical miscellany. Philadelphia [1793–95] p. 4)

Song, pfte. acc., followed by arr. for German flute.
Title from first line.
In No. 1, 1793.   DLC, ES, HFB, Hopk.

[ACROSS THE DOWNS THIS MORNING] Sung by Mrs. Oldmixon in the opera of No song, no supper.

(*In* The gentleman's amusement, ed. by R. Shaw. Philadelphia [1794–96] p. 24)

Melody only, flute (or violin) with accompanying text.
Title from first line.
In No. 3, 1794.
No song, no supper, by Stephen Storace.   DLC, PHi

ADAMS AND LIBERTY.

Song written by Thomas Paine in 1798, when a war with France seemed imminent; like *The Star spangled banner*, set to the tune of *To Anacreon in heaven*, the authorship of which is generally ascribed to John Stafford Smith, although this authorship has never been absolutely established. Paine's poem beginning, "Ye sons of Columbia who bravely have fought," appeared in *The Philadelphia monthly magazine*, May, 1798, p. 286–287. It was first advertised as a song in June, 1798:

> Adams and liberty, the Boston patriotic song. Written by Thomas Paine, A. M. . . . set to music as was lately sung at the Massachusetts Charitable Society with the most unbounded applause . . . Just published and for sale by W. P. and L. Blake, at the Boston Book Store, No. 1, Cornhill . . .

Probably identical with the undated:

ADAMS AND LIBERTY. The Boston patriotic song. Written by Thomas Paine, A. M. [Boston, Thomas and Andrews, June, 1798] 2 p. 37½ cm.

Below caption a manuscript note, presumably in the handwriting of Thomas himself: Boston, Printed by Thomas & Andrews.
Undoubtedly the first edition.
Song, pfte. acc.
First line: Ye sons of Columbia who bravely have fought.
Printed from movable type.   MWA

That the song was printed from the press of Thomas & Andrews appears from the following advertisement in *The Columbian centinel*, May 30, 1798:

> Adams and liberty. On Friday morning will be published from the press of Thomas & Andrews and sold at all the book-stores, the Boston Patriotic Song called Adams and Liberty . . . (*See* L. C. Elson's *History of American music*, 1904 and 1925, p. 151)

——— The same as preceding, but without manuscript note.

         JFD, MB, MWA, NN

[2]

A second edition:

ADAMS AND LIBERTY. The Boston patriotic song. Written by Thomas
Paine, A. M. Second edition—corrected. [Boston] Sold by Linley & Moore,
No. 19 Marlborough street, where may be had The Green Mountain farmer,
a new patriotic song. Price, 25 cents each [1798–99] 2 p. 39½ cm.

At foot of p. 2, design of music, flowers, musical instruments.
Song, pfte. acc.
First line same as preceding.
Printed from movable type.
The Green Mountain farmer was advertised as published in October, 1798.

DLC

In November, 1800, P. A. von Hagen advertised as "just published":
Adams and liberty, as altered by Thomas Paine, esq., A. M., and sung at
the theatre by Mr. Story with universal applause on the President's
birthday.

This probably refers to:

ADAMS AND LIBERTY. The Boston patriotic song. Written by Thomas
Paine, A. M. Third edition corrected. Boston, Printed & sold by P. A. von
Hagen & co. at their pianoforte warehouse, No. 3 Cornhill, where also may be
had the new published songs just received from London, viz., Honest Colin,
How tedious alas are the hours, Lillies & roses, Come buy my wooden-ware,
The little singing girl, Monseer Nong Tong Paw, Megen Oh! Oh! Meegen Ee,
Young Jemmy is a pleasing youth, As forth I rang'd the banks of Tweed, The
favorite song in the Stranger & the Answer. Likewise, Adams & Washington
& To arms, Columbia, written by Thomas Paine, A. M. The music composed
by P. A. von Hagen, jun. Also a great variety of single songs & lessons & an
elegant assortment of the verry [!] best kind of pianofortes, flutes, haut-boys,
clarinetts, bassoons, trumpets, French horns, violins, bass viols & guitars.
Also the best violin & bass viol strings just received from Naples & other
musical articles of superior quality [1799–1800] [2] p. 34 cm.

Below imprint: For the pianoforte, German flute, or violin.
Song, pfte. acc.
First line same as preceding.
Sonneck says, "Published between May, 1799, and November, 1800," but
more probably in 1799. This in spite of the above advertisement.

MB, MH, NRU–Mus

In the meantime, the song was advertised in August, 1798, as "just published
and for sale at Wm. Howe's wholesale and retail warehouse, 320 Pearl street,
New York":

ADAMS AND LIBERTY. The Boston patriotic song. Written by Thomas
Paine, A. M. Price 25 cents. New York, Printed & sold by W. Howe, organ
builder & importer of all kinds of musical instruments, No. 320 Pearl street
[1798] [3] p. 32½ cm.

Imprint at foot of p. [2].
Song, pfte. acc. Arr. for two flutes or violins, p. [3].
First line same as preceding.

MB

ADAMS AND LIBERTY. By T. Paine.
  (*In* The American musical miscellany. Northampton, 1798. p. 211–218)

    Melody and bass, with accompanying text.
    First line same as preceding.   DLC (etc.)

    This reprint in the *American musical miscellany* is reproduced by Mr. L. C.
    Elson in his book *The National music of America and its sources*, 1900 and
    1924, p. 183–190.

ADAMS AND LIBERTY. Written by Thomas Paine, A. M.   Price 25 cents.
  New York, Printed & sold at J. Hewitt's Musical repository, No. 131 William
  street [1798–99] [2] p.   32½ cm.

    Imprint at foot of p. [2].
    Song, pfte. acc.
    First line same as preceding.   McD–W, LSL

———— The same as preceding.
  (*In* A collection of new & favorite songs.   [A] Philadelphia [ca. 1800] p. [16]–
  [17])   HFB

ADAMS AND LIBERTY. New York, Printed & sold by G. Gilfert at his
  Musical magazine, No. 177 Broadway [1798–1801]   [2] p.   32 cm.

    In caption, engraved circular portrait of Adams.
    Song, pfte. acc.
    First line same as preceding.   CSmH, DLC, JFD, MWA

ADAMS AND LIBERTY. The Boston patriotic song.   Written by Thomas
  Paine, A. M.   [New York, ca. 1799]   [2] p.   33 cm.

    At foot of p. [2]: New York, Engraved by W. Pirsson.
    Song, pfte. acc.
    First line same as preceding.
    In DLC copy the word "Adams" has been cut out of title.
    W. Pirsson first noted in New York ca. 1798.   DLC

    Probably identical with the above is a copy at NN with the same title and the
    supplied imprint [New York, Printed & sold by W. Howe, 1798].   This copy
    lacks the words "New York, Engraved by W. Pirsson" at the foot of p. [2],
    but as that page has very evidently been trimmed, it is quite likely that these
    words were originally there.   Granting this, but noting that an authentic
    Howe imprint with quite different format has been located, it seems open to
    question that this is another Howe issue.

———— Boston patriotic song.   Tune, Anacreon in Heaven.
  (*In* New [American] patriotic songs, added to a collection of songs by C.
  Dibdin.   Philadelphia, 1799.   p. 315–317)

    Words only.
    First line same as preceding.   DLC, MWA, NHi, NN, RPJCB

    It is interesting to note that the original song *To Anacreon in heaven* was sung
    in America as early as June 3, 1793, by Mr. West at his benefit in New York.

[4]

ADAMS & WASHINGTON. A new patriotic song. The music composed by
P. A. von Hagen, jr. Boston, Printed & sold by P. A. von Hagen, jr. & co. at
their Musical magazine, No. 62 Newbury street, where also may be had the
new patriotic songs of Washington & independence, Hail, patriots all, Our
country is our ship, The ladies' patriotic song. Also a great variety of single
songs, lessons, and an elegant assortment of pianofortes, flutes, haut-boys,
clarinetts, bassoons, trumpets, French horns, violins and other musical articles
of superior quality [1798–99] [2] p. 31½ cm.

Song, with chorus, pfte. acc.

First stanza:
    Columbia's brave friends with alertness advance
    Her rights to support in defiance of France . . .
    To volatile fribbles we never will yield,
    While John's at the helm, and George rules the field.

Published between May, 1798, and March, 1799.
                                DLC, ES, MB, MH, MWA, NRU–Mus

ADAMS MARCH. Boston, Printed & sold at P. A. von Hagen & cos. imported pianoforte warehouse, No. 3 Cornhill, and to be had at G. Gilfert,
New York [1799–1800] 1 l. 32½ cm.

Below imprint: For the pianoforte, German flute or violin.
Pfte. 2 hds.
Published probably in 1799.   ES, JFD, LSL, McD–W, MH, RPJCB

*ADDRESS TO THE LADIES of Charleston, set to music by Mrs. Pownall.
Mrs. Pownall was to sing this song as "Pink" in the comedy of *The young
Quaker* at the City theatre in Charleston, S. C., on February 16, 1796.

ADDRESSED TO MISS D. by a lady, both of Boston.
    (*In* [Unidentified collection (beginning with "A lesson")] Boston [?] ca.1800.
    p. 5–6)

Song, pfte. acc.
First line: The fair Eliza's living grace.   MHi

ADESTE FIDELES. The celebrated Portuguese hymn for Christmas Day.
With an English translation.
    (*In* The musical journal for the pianoforte, ed. by B. Carr. Baltimore
    [1800] v. 2, no. 29, p. 12)

Chorus. Two staves.
First lines: Adeste fideles.—Hither ye faithful.   DLC, ES, NN

[ADESTE FIDELES] Portugueze [!] hymn on the Nativity.
    (*In* The musical journal for the flute or violin. Baltimore [1800] no. 11, p. 24)

Two parts. For flutes or violins (or flute and violin) with accompanying text.
Title from first line.   DLC

THE ADIEU. Alternative title of *Anna*, by James Hook.

ADIEU, ADIEU MY ONLY LIFE. Alternative title of *The soldier's adieu*,
by Charles Dibdin.

ADIEU SWEET GIRL. Taken from the Children of the Abbey, by Maria Regina Roche. The music by R. Chateaudun. Philadelphia, Printed and sold by G. Willig, No. 185 Market Street [1798–1804] [2] p. 33 cm.

Song, pfte. acc. Three staves.
First line same as title.
Regina Maria Roche's *Children of the Abbey* was published in England in 1798. Chateaudun has been traced in Philadelphia as late as 1799.
This issue probably 1798–99.   MWA, NN

ADIEU THOU DREARY PILE. Philadelphia, Printed for A. Reinagle; I. Aitken, sculp. [1789] [2] p. 34½ cm.

Imprint at foot of p. [2].
Song, pfte. acc.
First line same as title.   C de W, McD–W

Advertised in March, 1789, as "just published and sold by Thomas Dobson," Philadelphia, among other "songs and pieces arranged for the pianoforte or harpsichord by Alexander Reinagle."

———— The same as preceding, but with pagination.
(*In* [A collection of favorite songs, arr. by A. Reinagle. Philadelphia, 1789 (?)] p. 23–24)   ES

ADIEU TO ALL MY HEART HOLDS DEAR.
(*In* Nine new songs, by I. B. Gauline. Philadelphia [ca. 1800] p. 15–16)

Song, pfte. acc.
First line same as title.
I. B. Gauline: John B. Gauline.   ES, MdHi

ADIEU TO OLD ENGLAND. Alternative title of *Dear Mary*.

[ADIEU! YE VERDANT LAWNS AND BOW'RS]
See The select songster. New Haven, 1786. p. 20.

ADMIRAL JARVIS'S WALTZ. [n. p., ca. 1800] [2] p. 33 cm.
Pfte. 2 hds.   DLC, JFD

ADMIRAL NELSON'S MARCH.
(*With* A favorite new German waltz, arr. by I. C. M. [New York] I. and M. Paff [ca. 1800])

Pfte. 2 hds.
I. C. M., initials of John C. Moller.   DLC, MWA, NN

*THE ADOPTED CHILD, or The baron of Milford Castle.
Originally composed by Thomas Atwood (1795), this "musical drama, the music entirely new and composed" by P. A. von Hagen, probably the elder, was to be performed "for the last time" at the Haymarket theatre in Boston, on June 5, 1797.

ADVICE TO THE FAIR. A new song set to music. (Written during the late war)
(*In* The Boston magazine, December 1783. Opposite p. 73)

Song, pfte. acc.
First line: If you're not too proud for a word of advice.   DLC (etc.)

[6]

ADVICE TO THE FAIR.
(*In* The songster's assistant, ed. by T. Swan. Suffield [ca. 1800] p. 31–32)

Song, pfte. acc.
First line same as preceding.   CtY, MB

ADVICE TO THE LADIES, Composed by J. Hewitt.
(*In* Six songs by Mrs. Pownall and J. Hewitt. New York [1794] p. 12)

Song, pfte. acc.
First line: No more along the daily mead.   ES

———— The same as preceding.
(*In* A collection of new & favorite songs [A] Philadelphia [ca. 1800] p. [198] numbered 12).   HFB

*ADVICE TO THE LADIES of Boston.
Song. "Composed and to be sung by Mrs. Pownall" at a concert in Boston, on July 22, 1794.

THE AGREEABLE SURPRISE. A comic opera in two acts. As it is performed at the theatres in London and Dublin. By John O'Keeffe, esq., author of the Poor soldier, &c. New York, Printed and sold by W. Morton, opposite Coffee house, and by Berry and Rogers, No. 35 Hanover square, 1786. 38, [1] p. 17½ cm.

Libretto.
Title-page. Verso, dramatis personae; text, p. [3]–38; advertisment, p. [39]
          MWA

THE AGREEABLE SURPRISE. A comic opera in two acts as it is performed at the theatres in Philadelphia and New York. By Mr. O'Keefe.
From the press of Mathew Carey, May 27, 1793. 32 p. 12 mo.

Libretto.   NN

THE AGREEABLE SURPRISE. A comic opera, in two acts. By John O'Keefe, esq. The music by Dr. Arnold. As performed at the Theatre in Boston. Printed at the Apollo press, in Boston, by Belknap and Hall, for William P. Blake, No. 59 Cornhill, and William T. Clap, No. 90 Newbury street, 1794. 33 p. 18½ cm.

Libretto.   MB, MWA, RPJCB

AH CAIRA.
See Ça ira.

AH CAN I CEASE TO LOVE HER. Composed by Mr. Storace. Philadelphia, Printed for Carr & co., at their Musical repository, No. 136 High street.
(*In* The favorite songs from the Pirates, by S. Storace. Philadelphia [1793] p. (5).)

Song, pfte. acc., followed by arr. for flute.
First line: In childhood's careless happy day.
Title forms last line of each stanza.   HFB

———— Separate issue of preceding, 1793.   DLC, Hopk., LSL, PHi

AH CAN I CEASE TO LOVE HER.
(*In* The musical repertory. Boston [1796] No. II, p. 20)
Song, pfte. acc., followed by arr. for flute.
First line same as preceding. DLC

[AH DELIA] A pastoral. Written by Metastasio. Translated and adapted to the original air.
(*In* The musical repertory. Boston [1796] No. II, p. 28–29)
Song, pfte. acc.
Title from first line: Ah Delia see the fatal hour. DLC

AH DELIA! see the fatal hour. .Composed by F. Kotzwara. New York, Printed and sold by G. Gilfert, No. 177 Broadway [1798] [2] p. 32 cm.

Song, pfte. acc.
First line same as preceding. DLC

Advertised as published among other "favorite songs for the pianoforte or harpsichord" in November, 1798, by George Gilbert at his music store, 177 Broadway, Apollo's Head," New York.

AH DELIA see the fatal hour.
(*In* The American musical miscellany. Northampton, 1798. p. 86–88)

Melody only, with accompanying text.
First line same as preceding. DLC (etc.)

AH! DELIA. Sung by Mrs. Hodgkinson with applause. Composed by Dr. G. K. Jackson. Printed for the author. Copyright secured.
(*In* New miscellaneous musical work, by Dr. G. K. Jackson [n. p., ca. 1800] p. 15–16)

Song, pfte. acc. Three staves.
First line same as preceding. DLC, MWA

———— Separate issue of preceding, ca. 1800. MWA

AH HOW HAPLESS IS THE MAIDEN. Sung by Mrs. Oldmixon and Mrs. Hodgkinson in the Spanish barber, at the Philadelphia and New York theatres. And by Miss Broadhurst at the Concerts. Published by request. Composed by B. Carr.
(*In* The musical journal for the pianoforte, ed. by B. Carr. Baltimore, 1800. v. 1, nos. 19 and 21. p. 41–48)

At head of title: No. 19 of a Musical journal for the pianoforte. Vocal section.
At top of p. 45: No. 21 of a Musical journal for the pianoforte. Vocal section.
Song, pfte. acc.
First line same as title.
The Spanish barber, by Samuel Arnold.
DLC, ES, LSL, McD–W, NN, NRU–Mus

[AH HOW NEEDLESS IS EXPRESSION] Song set to musick by a gentleman in the County of Worcester.
(*In* The Massachusetts magazine. Boston, November, 1789. p. 727–728)
Song, pfte. acc.
Title from first line. DLC (etc.)

AH HOW SWEET were those moments of love.
  (*In* Nine new songs, by I. B. Gauline. Philadelphia [ca. 1800] p. 9–10)

  Song, pfte. acc.
  First line same as title.
  I. B. Gauline: John B. Gauline.   ES, MdHi

[AH LOVELY APPEARANCE OF DEATH]
  (*In* The rural harmony, by Jacob Kimball, jun. Boston, 1793. p. 57–58)

  Three-part chorus. Open score.
  Title from first line.   DLC, MB, MH, MWA

[AH MARY SHALL THY HEART. A new song. Composed by Pleyel
  Philadelphia, Printed & sold by G. Willig, No. 185 Market street [1798–1804.
  1 l. 32½ cm.

  Song, pfte. acc.
  First line same as title.   PP–K

AH! ONCE when I was a very little maid. A favorite air. Sung in the farce
  of Fast asleep. Composed by Mr. Attwood. Price 25 cents. New York,
  Printed & sold at J. Hewitt's Musical repository, No. 131 William street
  [1798] [2] p. 32 cm.

  Imprint at foot of p. [2].
  Song, pfte. acc. Arr. for flute, p. [2].
  First line same as title.
  Advertised at Baltimore in June, 1798, as "just published" among "new
  songs sung at the theatres New York."   MWA

*AH'S ONE TO JACK.
  Advertised as "just published and for sale at Wm. Howe's Wholesale and
  retail warehouse, 320 Pearl street," New York, in August, 1798. Probably
  refers to *All's one to Jack,* by Charles Dibdin.

AH SEEK TO KNOW. A favorite song. Composed by J. C. Bach. Arranged
  for the pianoforte by A. Reinagle.
  (*In* A collection of favorite songs, arr. by A. Reinagle. Philadelphia [1789 ?]
  p. 1–4)

  Song, pfte. acc.
  First line same as title.
  At foot of p. 4: Philadelphia, Sold by H. Rice, Market street. J. Aitken,
  Sculpt.   DLC

——— Separate issue of preceding, ca. 1789.   ES

*AH! SEEK TO KNOW IT.
  Advertised as published among other "favorite songs for the pianoforte or
  harpsichord" in November, 1798, by "George Gilbert, at his music store,
  177 Broadway, Apollo's Head," New York.

[9]

[AH! TELL ME SOFTLY BREATHING GALE] The favorite duett. Sung by Mrs. Oldmixon and Miss Broadhurst in The Prize. Price 20 cents. Philadelphia, Printed at Carr & cos Musical repository [1794] 2 p. 32 cm.

Title from first line.
Duet, pfte. acc.
Stephen Storace's *The prize* was first performed in Philadelphia, May 26, 1794, with Mrs. Oldmixon and Miss Broadhurst in the cast.   ES

AH! TELL ME SOFTLY BREATING [!] GALE. A favorite duett. Pr. 1-6. New York, Printed and sold by G. Gilfert & co. [1794-96] [2] p. 33½ cm.

Duet, pfte. acc. Two and three staves.
First line same as title.   JFD

AH WELADAY [!] MY POOR HEART. Sung by Mrs. Martyr in the Follies of a day.
(*In* The gentleman's amusement, ed. by R. Shaw. Philadelphia [1794-96] p. 18)

Melody only, flute (or violin) with accompanying text.
First line: To the winds, to the waves, to the woods I complain.
In No. 2, 1794.
The follies of a day, by William Shield.   DLC, PHi

AH WELL A DAY POOR ANNA. A favorite song. Sung at Vauxhall Gardens. (25 cts.) Printed by B. Carr & sold at his Musical repository's, Philadelphia & N. York & by J. Carr, Baltimore [1796] [3] p. 31½ cm.

Song, pfte. acc. Arr. for guitar, p. [3].
First line: Fair Anna lov'd a rustic boy.
Advertised as published in February, 1796.   CtY, DLC, MWA

AH WELLADAY POOR ANNA. A favorite new song. New York, Published and sold by G. Gilfert & Co., No. 209 Broadway, near St. Pauls [1795] [2] p. 33½ cm.

Song, pfte. acc. Arr. for German flute, p. [2].
First line same as preceding.   DLC

AH WERE [!] ARE FLED THOSE HOURS.
(*In* Nine new songs, by I. B. Gauline. Philadelphia [ca. 1800] p. 13-14)

Song, pfte. acc. Three staves.
First line: Ah where are fled those hours.
I. B. Gauline: John B. Gauline.   ES, MdHi

AH WHY ENVEIL THAT PANTING BREAST. Written and composed by a gentleman of this city. Printed by G. Willig, No. 185 Market st., Philadelphia [1798-1804] 1 l. 33½ cm.

Song, pfte. acc.
First line same as title.   NRU-Mus

AH WHY MUST WORDS.
(*In* The American musical miscellany. Northampton, 1798. p. 74-76)
Melody only, with accompanying text.
First line same as title.   DLC (etc.)

AH WILL NO CHANCE [!] of clime. A favorite song. Published by G. Willig, 165 Market st., Philadelphia [1795–97]   1 l.   32½ cm.

Song, pfte. acc.
First line same as title.
See also "Hope told a flatt'ring tale."   MWA

AIR. By Pleyel.
(*In* The Philadelphia pocket companion for guittar or clarinett [Philadelphia, 1794]   v. 1, p. 6–7)

Melody only, with accompanying text.
First line: Why turns my Jen her head away.   MWA

—— The same.
(*In* Elegant extracts for the German flute or violin. Philadelphia [1798] bk. 3, p. 12)

Melody only, flute or violin.   16 measures.   DLC, NN

AIR. Shield.
(*In* The musical journal for the flute or violin. Baltimore [1800] no. 10, p. 20)

Duet for flutes or violins (or flute and violin).   DLC

AIR BY HAYDN.
See Evening amusement, p. 23.

AIR DES DEUX SAVOYARDS. Varié pour deux flutes par F. Devienne.
(*In* The gentleman's amusement, ed. by R. Shaw. Philadelphia [1794–96] p. 7–9)

For two flutes. Two staves.
In No. 1, April 1, 1794.   DLC, PHi

AIR IN THE CRITIC.
See Evening amusement, p. 21.

AIR. In the Pirates.
See Ever remember me.

AIR IN THE RECONCILIATION. A comic opera by Peter Markoe.
(*In* The universal asylum. Philadelphia, June, 1790. p. 383–384)
Song, pfte. acc. (Tune: In infamy)
First line: Truth from thy radiant throne look down.
Two more airs from Markoe's libretto are given in the same number:

Why sleeps the thunder in the skies.   Tune: "The Birks of Indernay" [!]
The birds who wing their way through air. Tune: "The bird that hears."
                                                              DLC (etc.)

A FAVORITE AIR in the pantomine of *Oscar and Malvina.*
(*In* The musical repertory. Boston [1796] No. I, p. (5).)
Pfte. 2 hds.

Oscar and Malvina, by William Reeve.   DLC, MB

—— Separate issue of preceding, ca. 1796.   NRU-Mus

[11]

A FAVOURITE AIR GROTESQUE OR WALTZ. Composed by Mazzinghi. New York, Publish'd at J. & M. Paffs music store, Broad Way [1799–1803] [2] p. 33 cm.

Pfte. 2 hds.
Foot of p. [2]: Air grotesque.   JLH   (mutilated)

THE ALBION, the pride of the sea. Sung with universal applause by Mr. Denman. The words by Dr. Houlton.
(In A collection of favorite songs, by Mr. Hook. New York [1799–1801] bk [2] p. 12–13)

Song, pfte. acc.
First line: My boys would you know how our ship got her name.   DLC

*ALGERINE CAPTIVE.
Song by Raynor Taylor. Made part of his "olio . . . entirely new," which was to be performed at Philadelphia, on February 1, 1794.

ALKNOMOOK. The death song of the Cherokee Indians. New York, Printed & sold by G. Gilfert, No. 177 Broadway. Likewise to be had at P. A. von Hagen's music store, No. 3 Cornhill, Boston [1799–1801] 1 l. 31½ cm.

Song, pfte. acc.
First line: The sun sets at night and the stars shun the day.   MWA

Reprint to be found attached to the Dunlap Society's edition (1887) of Royall Tyler's comedy *The contrast*, Philadelphia, 1790. The song (between p. 10 and 11) occurs in Act I, Scene 2. On p. x, of his introduction, Mr. Thomas McKee wrote:

> The illustration to the song of Alknomook is from music published contemporaneously with the play. This song had long the popularity of a national air and was familiar in every drawing room in the early part of the century.

But the NewYork directories and newspaper advertisements render it impossible that the music was published contemporaneously with the play (1790) as G. Gilfert appears at the address given in the imprint from 1797–1801 only. Furthermore, P. A. von Hagen resided at No. 3 Cornhill, Boston, not earlier than 1799. Therefore, the song was published 1799 to 1801. A copy of *Alknomook* (given as *Alkmoonok*) will also be found (p. 464) in Sonneck's monograph on *Early American Operas* (Sammelbände d. Int. Mus. Ges., 1905, p. 428–495), where he contends that the words were not original with Tyler as Mrs. Julia Hatton used them in her libretto to the opera *Tammany*, 1794, as "altered from the old Indian song."

Further interesting discussion of this subject is to be found in *The musical antiquary*, London, April, 1912. Vol. III, p. 166–170, 235.

———— Indian chief.
(In The Philadelphia songster, ed. by A. Aimwell [pseud.] Philadelphia, 1789. p. 8)

Melody only, with accompanying text.
First line: The sun sets in night.   NN

—— The Indian chief.
(*In* The American musical miscellany.   Northampton, 1798.   p. 114–115)

Melody only, with accompanying text.
First line: The sun sets at night and the stars shun the day.   DLC (etc.)

—— The Indian chief. [n. p., 179– ?] 1 l.   21 x 25 cm.

At top of page: The Indian chief [printed].
Below title, music (two staves), ms.
Below this, "Original ode" with nine stanzas.
First line: In a chariot etherial [!] from regions of light.
Same tune as "Indian chief" in *The Philadelphia songster*, and "Death song
of the Cherokee Indians" [Alknomook] but with different text.   MB

ALL FOR PRETTY POLLY.   A new song.   Sung by Mr. Denman.   New
York, Printed & sold by G. Gilfert, No. 177 Broadway.
(*In* A collection of favorite songs, by Mr. Hook.   New York [1799–1801]
bk. [1], p. 8–9)

Song, pfte. acc.
First line: They tell me I have grown too proud.   DLC

*ALL ON BOARD OF A MAN OF WAR.
Advertised March 22, 1797, as to be published in a few days by "G. Gilfert at
his Musical Magazine, No. 177 Broadway," New York.

ALLEGRETTO.
See A collection of airs . . . arr. by J. Willson.

ALLEMANDE.
(*In* [Unidentified collection of instrumental and vocal music] New York,
Hewitt & Rausch [1797] p. 10)

Pfte. 2 hds.   DLC

—— The same as preceding.
(*In* A collection of new & favorite songs.   [A] Philadelphia [ca. 1800] p. [91]
numbered 10)   HFB

ALLO.   From Oscar and Malvina.
(*In* The gentleman's amusement, ed. by R. Shaw.   Philadelphia [1794–96]
p. 67)

Melody only, flute (or violin).   Twelve measures.
In No. [8], 1796.
Oscar and Malvina, by William Reeve.   DLC, PHi, PP–K

ALLOA HOUSE.
(*In* The American musical miscellany.   Northampton, 1798.   p. 21–23)

Melody only, with accompanying text.
First line: The springtime returns.
Composed by James Oswald.   DLC (etc.)

[13]

ALMIGHTY GOD WHOSE HEAV'NLY POW'R. [New York] Sold at I. and M. Paffs [ca. 1800] 1 l. 32 cm.

> At head of title: Hymn Ordinary.
> Imprint at foot of page.
> Song, pfte. acc.
> First line same as title.   MWA

ALONE BESIDE A STREAM. Boston, Printed & sold by P. A. von Hagen & cos. Musical magazine, No. 3 Cornhill. And to be had at G. Gilfert, No. 177 Broadway, New York. Where may be had the Funeral dirge on the death of General Washington & Come buy my daffodillies [ca. 1799] [2] p. 32 cm.

> Song, pfte. acc.
> First line same as title.   ES, LSL, MB, RPJCB

ALONE BY THE LIGHT OF THE MOON. A favorite song. Composed by Mr. Hook. New York, Printed for G. Gilfert & co., No. 209 Broadway, near St. Pauls. Where may be had a great variety of single songs, lessons. all kinds of musical instruments, strings, &c. [1795] [2] p. 33 cm.

> Song, pfte. acc. Arr. for German flute, p. [2].
> First line: The day is departed.   JFD, MWA, NN

———— The same. New York, Printed & sold by G. Gilfert & co., No. 177 Broadway [1796] [2] p. 29 cm.

> Song, pfte. acc. Arr. for German flute or guitar, p. [2].
> First line same as preceding.
> Advertised as published, 1796.   DLC, JFD, LSL, MB, MWA, RPJCB

ALONE BY THE LIGHT OF THE MOON. Boston, Printed & sold by P. A. von Hagen, Junior & co., at their imported pianoforte warehouse, No. 62 Newbury street [1798–99] [2] p. 31 cm.

> Song, pfte. acc. Arr. for German flute or "guittar," p. [2].
> First line same as preceding.   ES, JFD, MB, RPJCB

———— The same.

> (*In* The American musical miscellany. Northampton, 1798. p. 71–73)

> Melody only, with accompanying text.
> First line same as preceding.   DLC (etc.)

———— The same.

> (*In* Elegant extracts for the German flute or violin. Baltimore [1794] bk. 1, p. 22–23)

> Melody only, flute or violin, with accompanying text.
> First line same as preceding.   DLC, NN

ALTHO' HEAV'N'S GOOD PLEASURE. Jn the favorite opera of Amintas. Compos'd by Sigr. Giordani.
(*In* A collection of favorite songs, divided into two books. Arr. by A. Reinagle [1789?] bk. 1, p. 11)

> Song, pfte. acc.
> First line same as title.   CdeW, DLC, ES, Hopk.

AMANDA.
See Two new favorite *Cotillions*.

AMERICA. A new march. Composed by H. Gram of Boston, 1791.
(*In* The Massachusetts magazine. Boston, July, 1791. p. 448–449)

Open score. Three parts.
H. Gram: Hans Gram.   DLC (etc.)

AMERICA AND BRITTANNIA [!]. Peace. A new march. Composed by R.
Taylor (and so arranged as to harmonize perfectly with Washingtons march
played both together). Philadelphia, Published & sold at G. Willig's Musical
magazine [n. d.] [2] p. 32½ cm.

In center of title, design of America and Britannia with the eagle and the lion.
Pfte. 2 hds. Three staves with the melody of "Washinton's [!] march"
at top.   DLC, PP–K

Although several different issues of the *Washington's march* here incorporated
appeared under the above imprint during the 1790's (one of them containing
also a *Quick step* by R. Taylor) there is still an argument for the later date
181–, which has sometimes been assigned. It seems, however, that the earlier
date, 179–, should come nearer the truth.

AMERICA, COMMERCE & FREEDOM. Sung by Mr. Darley, junr., in the
ballet pantomine of the Sailors landlady. Composed by A. Reinagle. Philadelphia. Printed at Carr's Musical repository. Price 20 cents [1794] [2] p.
32 ½ cm.

Song (with chorus), pfte. acc.
First line: How blest the life a sailor leads.
Advertised as published October, 1794, among "new songs, never published
in America."   CdeW, CtY, DLC, McD–W, NN

———— The same as preceding, except Baltimore, instead of Philadelphia, in
imprint.   MWA

———— The same.
See Evening amusement, p. 24.

AMERICA DISCOVERED, OR TAMMANY, the Indian chief.
See Tammany, or the Indian chief.

*AMERICAN ACADEMY OF COMPLIMENTS, or the Complete American
secretary. With a collection of the newest songs. Wilmington, Printed by
Peter Brynberg. 1797.

*THE AMERICAN COCK ROBIN, or A choice collection of English songs,
both old and new, being such as are generally esteemed, and agreeable to the
North-American taste. New-York: Printed and sold by John Holt, at the
Exchange, 1764.

[15]

AMERICAN HARMONY. Containing a variety of airs suitable for divine worship on Thanksgivings, ordinations, Christmas, fasts, funerals and other occasions. Together with a number of psalm tunes in three and four parts. The whole intirely [!] new. By Oliver Holden, teacher of music in Charlestown. [Verses] Published according to Act of Congress. Printed typographically at Boston by Isaiah Thomas and Ebenezer T. Andrews, Faust's statue, No. 45 Newbury street, 1792. 32 p. 13 x 22 cm.

Title-page; preface, p. [2]; music, p. 3-32.
Three and four-part choruses. Open score.
The most important secular numbers are: Ode on music. Words by Thaddeus M. Harris, p. 3-4; Ode on music. Words by Mr. Pope, p. 13-17.
                                        CSmH, CtY, DLC, MH, MHi

THE AMERICAN HERO. A Sapphick ode by Nath. Niles, A. M.

First line: Why should vain mortals tremble at the sight of. Evidently to be sung to *Bunker Hill, A Sapphick ode*, appearing on p. 8 of Andrew Law's *A select number of plain tunes adapted to congregational worship* (q. v.)
This text is found only in certain copies.   CSmH, CtY

*THE AMERICAN IN LONDON. A musical entertainment. Performed at the New theatre, Philadelphia, March 28, 1798.
Advertised, March 28, 1798, with "music composed and adapted by Mr. Carr."

*THE AMERICAN LADIES POCKETBOOK for 1798.
Advertised January 17, 1799 as "just published by William Y. Birch, 17 South Second st.," Philadelphia. Contains "new country dances, songs, &c."

*THE AMERICAN MOCK-BIRD. A collection of the most familiar songs now in vogue. New-York: 1760. 12 mo.

*THE NEW AMERICAN MOCK-BIRD. A collection of the best songs on different subjects. New-York: Printed by Hugh Gaine, 1761.

THE AMERICAN MUSICAL MAGAZINE. Published in monthly numbers, intended to contain a great variety of approved music. Carefully selected from the works of best American and foreign masters. Vol. I. New Haven, Published & sold by Amos Doolittle & Daniel Read. [May, 1786–September, 1787] 48, [2] p. 28½ x 23½ cm.

Title-page, verso blank; "Contents of Vol. I," p. [50].
There are twelve numbers of four pages each, only the secular numbers being listed here:

   No. 1. The seasons moralized, p. 3-6.
   No. 4. The pastoral nymph, p. 15.—The morning, p. 16-17.—Sweet echo, p. 17-18.—Fischer's minuit [!], p. 18.
                        Cty, MBJ, ICN (lacks t.-p. and p. [49]-[50])

THE AMERICAN MUSICAL MISCELLANY. A collection of the newest and most appoved [!] songs, set to music. [Verses] Printed at Northampton, Massachusetts, by Andrew Wright, for Daniel Wright and Company. Sold by them, and by S. Butler, in Northampton; by I. Thomas, jun., in

Worcester; by F. Barker, in Greenfield; and by the principal booksellers in Boston.—1798. xii, [13]–300 p. 16 cm.

Title-page, verso blank; dedication, "To all true lovers of song in the United States of Columbia . . . the Publishers," p. [iii]; p. [iv] blank; "To the public," p. [v]–vi; contents, p. [vii]–xii; "The American musical miscellany. Being a collection of the most approved songs and airs, both old and new," p. [13]–300.

In certain copies, p. 31–32 are misplaced, following p. 28 instead of p. 30. In the "Contents" the intended alphabetical arrangement has not been carried out correctly and

"Awful hero, Marlbro' rise"
"Hark notes melodious fill the air"
"Spanking Jack was so comely"

are missing. The collection contains one hundred and eleven songs, numbered I–CXI. The music is printed from movable type. The majority of the pieces show words and tune only, but several are set for two, three, and four voices. The arrangement generally is such as to allow an accompaniment on the pianoforte *unisono* with the voice or voices. In the two-part songs the right hand plays the tune and the left a simple bass, as in many other collections of the time, but with this difference that the basses are not figured. In some instances short preludes or postludes are found.

CSmH, CtY, DLC, ICN, MB, McD–W, MH, MHi, MWA, NBuG, NHi, NN, NRU–Mus, RPB, RPJCB

As the preface throws light upon the object and method of the editors, it may follow:

> The editors of the American Musical Miscellany present the public with the following collection of songs, accompanied with notes: And whenever they have found the same words of a song sung in different tunes, (which is not unfrequently the case) they have endeavoured to select such notes as, in their opinion, were best adapted to the words; but whether they have, in every instance, been happy in the selections, will be determined by the connoisseurs in the science of music. Great care has been taken that the work should be accurate; and an able master employed to inspect and correct the music. The great proficiency which, within a few years past, has been made in the various branches of this science, and the facility with which the lovers of Music, now read notes to which they have not been accustomed, has induced the editors to believe this work would at least be acceptable to the public.

> Their aim has been to cull, from a great variety of ancient songs, such as have been, at all times, generally approved; and have endeavoured to avoid such as would give offence to the delicate ear of chastity itself.

> —— A general preference has been given to American productions, and perhaps nothing will more effectually exhibit the progress of the human mind in the refinements which characterize the age, than the songs, which from general consent, are now in vogue.

The collection contains the following individual "songs" (known either by titles or by first words):

p. 13–16   The lucky escape. (Words and tune.)

[19]

p. 245–246   The life of a beau. (Words and tune with bass, followed by *unisono* chorus with bass.)

247–249   A new song for a serenade. By D. George. (Words, "Rise my Delia," and tune with bass.)

249–252   Friendship—by Bidwell. (Words and tune with bass.)

252–254   Nobody. (Words and tune.)

254–256   The dispairing [!] damsel. (Words and tune.)

256–258   Death or victory. (Words and tune.)

258–259   Oh! Say simple maid. A duet in the comic opera of Incle and Yarico. (Words and tune.)

260–263   Tom Tackle. (Words and tune.)

263–264   The charms of nature. (Words and tune with bass.)

265–267   Polly Ply. (Words and tune.)

268–270   Tho' Bacchus may boast of his care killing bowl. (Words and tune.)

271–273   Strew the sweet roses of pleasure between. (Words and tune with bass.)

274–277   Washington. Set to music by S. Holyoke. (Words, "When Alcides, the son of Olympian Jove," and tune with bass.)

278–284   How cold it is. A winter song. (Words and 3-part chorus.)

285–286   A shape alone let others prize. Set to music by H. Gram. (Words and tune with bass.)

287–291   Bright dawns the day. A hunting song. Set to music by a student of the University of Cambridge. (Words and recitative with bass followed by "Song" with bass.)

291–292   Winter. (Words and tune.)

293–294   Song in the Spoil'd child. (Words, "Since then I'm doom'd," and tune.)

295–296   Ye mortals whom fancies. (Words and tune.)

297–300   On music. (Words, "To music be the verse addrest," and 3-part chorus.)

*THE AMERICAN MUSICAL MISCELLANY.

Under this heading the following advertisement appeared in the *Columbian centinel*, Boston, February 6, 1799:

A collection of the newest and most approved songs. This collection contains among a great number of the best songs in the English language; a large variety of the late Federal American songs, suited to the true spirit of the times. The music is prefixed to each song. Price one dollar . . . Just published and for sale by W. P. and L. Blake at the Boston Book Store, No. 1 Cornhill.

This was obviously identical with the American musical miscellany of 1798.

*AMERICAN ROBIN. A collection of new songs. New York, 1774.

AMERICAN SERENADE. The words by Mrs. Jackson. Composed by Dr. G. K. Jackson. Printed for the author. Copyright secured.
(*In* New miscellaneous musical work by Dr. G. K. Jackson [n. p., ca. 1800] p. 8)

Song, pfte. acc.
First line: Bring your vows to Cupid's shrine.   DLC, MWA

[20]

THE AMERICAN SOLDIER. Written by a gentlemen [!] in Queen Ann's County. Music by J. B. Gauline. Printed by G. Willig, No. 185 Market street, Philadelphia [1798–1804] [2] p. 30½ cm.

Song, pfte. acc.
First line: Thou country unkind yet so dear.   MdHi

THE AMERICAN SOLDIER. Music by J. B. Gauline. Printed by G. Willig, No. 185 Market street, Philadelphia [1798–1804] [2] p. 30½ cm.

Song, pfte. acc.
First line same as preceding.   NN

THE AMERICAN SONGSTER. Being a select collection of the most celebrated American, English, Scotch and Irish songs. New York, Printed for Samuel Campbell, No. 44, Hanover Square, and Thomas Allen, No. 16 Queen street, 1788. xii, 204 p. 14½ cm.

Title-page, verso blank; preface, p. iii–iv; index, p. v–xii; the words of 227 songs, p. 1–204. Contains no music, but frequently the names of the tunes to which the songs were to be sung are mentioned.
                    MWA, NN (lacks p. 11–14), RPB
The preface begins:
    To the lovers of music in the United States of America.
    Ladies and Gentlemen.
    It has been a subject of considerable regret that a Collection of the best modern songs not only the productions of America, but likewise those of Britain has never before appeared on this continent . . .

RPB possesses also an edition of this collection, dated 1803. It contains 204 p., but neither index nor dedication.

*THE AMERICAN SONGSTER, being a collection of the most celebrated ancient and modern songs. Portsmouth: Printed by John Melcher, 1790.

*AMERICAN SONGSTER: Being a select collection of the most celebrated American, English, Scotch, and Irish songs. Boston: Sold by Wm. Spotswood, No. 55, Marlborough-street, 1795.

THE AMERICAN SONGSTER; or Federal museum of melody and wit. In four parts, containing a collection of much admired songs, selected from the writings of various English and American authors. Baltimore: Printed and sold by Warner & Hanna, No. 2 North Gay street, 1799. 245, [7] p. 16°.

    Part I. "American patriotic songs." (p. 3–35)
    Part II. "Irish patriotic songs". (p. 36–72)
    Part III. "Dibdin's songs." (p. 73–180)
    Part IV. "Favorite songs from various gardens cull'd." (p. 181–245)
    Index (p. [246]–[251] at end)

The collection contains no music, but frequently the names of the tunes to which the songs were to be sung are mentioned.   RPB

—— The same, 1800.   DLC, NHi, NN

*THE AMERICAN TAR, or the Press gang defeated.
This ballet, "founded on a recent fact at Liverpool . . . the music entirely new & composed by R. Taylor," was given under the direction of William Francis at the New Theatre in Philadelphia, June 17, 1796.

*AMERICAN TRUE BLUE or the Naval volunteer.
An "interlude of song, dialogue, and dance . . . the whole to conclude with the admirable song of the United Volunteers by Mr. Fox," was performed at the New Theatre in Philadelphia, April 3, 1799.

*AMERICANA AND ELUTHERIA; or a new tale of the Genii.
Under this title was to be performed at Charleston, S. C., February 9, 1798, an anonymous "new musical and allegorical masque, never yet printed or performed." A brief description is given in Sonneck's monograph on *Early American Operas* (Sammelbände d. Int. Mus. Ges. 1904–1905). Wegelin mentions as dedicated to Thomas Jefferson:

> Americana; or, A new tale of the Genii. Being an allegorical mask in five acts. Baltimore, 1802. 128 p. 8vo.

AMERICAN'S LAMENTATION FOR WASHINGTON.
(*In* The easy instructor, or A new method of teaching sacred harmony, by William Little and William Smith [n. p., ca. 1802] p. 89–91)

Three-part chorus. Open score.
First line: Moan ye sons of America, for your chief is gone.   DLC

AMIDST THE ILLUSIONS. A favorite song. Sung by Miss Broadhurst in the New York Old City Concert. Composed by W. Shield. New York, Printed and sold at G. Gilfert & cos. Musical magazine, No. 209 Broadway [1795] 3 p. 33½ cm.

Song, pfte. acc.
First line: Amidst the illusions that o'er the mind flutter.
                                                        DLC, MWA

AMIDST THE ILLUSIONS. From Hartford bridge, or the Skirts of a camp. Sold at Carr's Musical repository's, Philadelphia & N. York & by I. Carr, Baltimore. Price 25 cents. [1796] [2] p. 33½ cm.

Song, pfte. acc.
First line same as preceding.
Hartford bridge, by William Shield.
                        CdeW, CtY, DLC, ES, LSL, MWA, NN, PHi

AMIDST THE ILLUSIONS. Sung by Miss Broadhurst.
(*In* The gentleman's amusement, ed. by R. Shaw. Philadelphia [1794–96] p. 68–69)

Melody only, with accompanying text.
First line same as preceding.
In No. [9], 1796.   DLC (incomplete), PHi, PP-K

Advertised and published "as sung by Miss Broadhurst" in February, 1796.

AMINTOR, or the Arcadian shepherdess, by Raynor Taylor.
See Amyntor.

THE AMOROUS SONGSTER. Compared with this vigorous volume, The frisky songster is a lifeless chap. New York, Printed for the Sporting club, 1800. 96 p. 13 × 6½ cm.

Title-page, verso blank; text, p. [3]–96.
Words only.   NBuG

L'AMOUR INTERROGE PAR UN BERGER. Composed by R. Taylor.
(*In* The musical journal for the pianoforte, ed. by B. Carr. Baltimore [1800] v. 2, no. 27. p. (7)–(8).)

Song, pfte. acc.
First line: Cupid rambling once astray   DLC, ES, LSL, MdHi, NN

AMYNTA.
(*In* The Philadelphia pocket companion for guittar or clarinett [Philadelphia, 1794] v. I, p. 10–12)

Melody only, with accompanying text.
First line: My sheep I neglected.   MWA

AMYNTOR. A pastoral song. Composed by R. Taylor. Philadelphia, Printed for the Author, No. 96 North Sixth street; and sold at Carr's Musical repository's Market street, Philadelphia; William street, New York, and at I Carr's music store, Market st., Baltimore. (Price ¼ of a dollar) [1795] [2] p. 33 cm.

Song, pfte. acc.
First line: What tho' the blooming genial year.
                                        DLC, HFB, LSL, MWA, PP–K

This "pastoral song" was to be sung at "Taylor's musical performance . . . The whole of the music original and composed by Mr. Taylor" in Annapolis, on January 20, 1793. The song under the title, *Amintor*, by R. Taylor, was for sale at "Carr's Musical Repositories, Philadelphia, and William street, New York . . . " in March, 1795.

*THE ANCIENT TIPLERS.
This song was to be sung in Raynor "Taylor's musical performance . . . the whole of the music original and composed by Mr. Taylor," at Annapolis, on February 28, 1793.

AND A FOR LOVE OF ME. A favorite Scots song. New York, Printed & sold by J. Hewitt, No. 131 William street. Price 25 cents.
(*In* A collection of new & favorite songs. [A] Philadelphia [ca. 1800] p. [22]–[23])

Song, pfte. acc. Arr. for "guittar" or German flute, p. [23].
First line: Last midsummer morning.
Originally issued 1797–99.   HFB

AND A FOR LOVE OF ME. Boston, Printed & sold by P. A. von Hagen & co. at their warranted imported pianoforte ware house, No. 3 Cornhill; and to be had at G. Gilfert, New York. Where may be had Come, come, my love to the window, come, sung with universal applause in the play of Count Benyowsky. Also the new favorite songs of No, not yet, Come buy my

[23]

daffodilles, Honest Colin, Tranquil pleasures never cloy, the much admired song in the play of the Stranger & Answer to this song. [1799–1800] [2] p. 32 cm.

Below imprint: For the pianofortes, German flute, or violin.
Song, pfte. acc.
First line: Last midsummer morning I gang'd to the fair.
Count Benyowsky, produced in New York, April 1, 1799.
This issue published probably in 1799. MB, RPB

AND HEAR HER SIGH ADIEU! A favorite song sung in the opera of the Shipwreck. Comoposed [!] by Dr. Arnold. New York, Printed & sold by J. Hewitt at his Musical repository, No.131 William street; sold also by B. Carr, Philadelphia & J. Carr, Baltimore [ca. 1798] [2] p. 33 cm.

Song, pfte. acc.
First line: On board the Valliant we set sail.
Title forms last line of second stanza.
DLC, LSL, McD–W, MWA, NN, RPJCB

―――― The same as preceding.
(*In* A collection of new & favorite songs. [A] Philadelphia [ca. 1800] p. [52]–[53]) HFB

―――― On board the Valiant. A favorite song. Sung by Master Welch in the opera of the Shipwreck. New York, Printed by W. Howe . . . No. 320 [Pearl street] [1798] [2] p. 32½ cm.

Song, pfte. acc. Arr. for flute, p. [2].
First line same as title. NRU–Mus

Advertised in August, 1798, as "just published and for sale at Wm. Howe's wholesale and retail warehouse, 320 Pearl street," New York.

AND STREW THE SWEET ROSES of pleasure between. A favorite song. The musick composed by Mr. Hook.
(*In* The Massachusetts magazine. Boston, November, 1791. p. 709–710)

Song, pfte. acc.
First line: If life's a rough path as the sages have said. DLC (etc.)

ANDANTE.
(*In* [Moller & Capron's monthly numbers] The fourth number [Philadelphia, 1793] p. 29)

Pfte. 2 hds. NN

ANDANTE D'HAYDN.
(*In* The musical journal for the pianoforte, ed. by B. Carr. Baltimore [1800] v. 1, no. 16, p. (29)–(32))

At head of title: No. 16 of A musical journal for the pianoforte.
Instrumental section.
Pfte. 2 hds. DLC, ES, LSL, McD–W, MdHi, NN, NRU–Mus, PP–K

―――― The same as preceding, but with added imprint: Baltimore, Printed & sold at Carr's music store, No. 36 Baltimore street. [181–]
DLC, McD–W, NBuG, NN

ANDANTE D'HAYDN. With added imprint as above, and also, below title: Printed and sold at Carr's music store, Baltimore [181–]   DLC

—— The same.
(*In* The musical journal for the flute or violin. Baltimore [1800] nos. 20, 22, 24. p. 38–47)

Duet for flutes or violins (or flute and violin).
At top of p. 41: No. 22 of A musical journal for the flute or violin. Instrumental section.
At top of p. 45: No. 24 of A musical journal for the flute or violin. Instrumental section.
At foot of p. 47: End of Vol. 1.   DLC

ANDANTINO.
See A collection of airs . . . arr. by J. Willson, p. 2–7.

ANDANTINO. Tiré de Boccherini.
(*In* The musical journal for the pianoforte, ed. by B. Carr. Baltimore [1800] v. 1 no. 8. p. (13)–(16).)

At head of title: No. 8 of A musical journal for the pianoforte. Instrumental section.
Pfte. 2 hds.   DLC, ES, McD–W, MdHi, NN, NRU–Mus

ANDRÉ'S GHOST. The poetry from a late publication. Set to musick by E. Mann of Worcester.
(*In* The Massachusetts magazine. Boston, December, 1789. p. 794)

Song, pfte. acc.
First line: From visions of eternal day.
E. Mann: Elias Mann.   DLC (etc.)

ANGELS EVER BRIGHT AND FAIR. Sung at the funeral ceremonies in honor to the memory of the late General Washington. New York, Printed & sold by G. Gilfert, No. 177 Broadway [1800] 1 l. 32 cm.

Song, pfte. acc.
First line same as title.   NN

THE ANGLER. From the German of Göthe. Composed by Reichardt.
(*In* The musical journal for the pianoforte, ed. by B. Carr. Baltimore [1800] v. 1 no. [17]. p. (40).)

Song, pfte. acc.
First line: In gurgling eddies roll'd the tide.
Reichardt: Johann Friedrich Reichardt.   DLC ES LSL NN NRU–Mus

—— The same.
(*In* The musical journal for the flute or violin. Baltimore [1800] no. 19, p. 38–39)

Melody only (flute or violin) with accompanying text.
First line same as preceding.   DLC

ANNA. A new song. The music composed by P. A. von Hagen. Boston. Printed & sold at P. A. von Hagen's imported pianoforte warehouse, No. 3 Cornhill, and at No. 4 Old Massachusetts Bank, Head of the Mall. Also at G. Gilferts warehouse, N. York; David Vintons Providence; W. R. Wilder Newport; B. B. Macanulty, Salem; E. M. Blunt, Newburyport; Isaac Stanwood, Portsmouth, and E. A. Jenks, Portland. (Entered according to law) [n. d.] [2] p. 31 cm.

Song, pfte. acc. Arr. for guitar or clarinet, p. [2].
First line: The morning was fair and the hamlet look'd gay.
Sonneck notes that "the composer probably was P. A. von Hagen, junior."
Published probably after 1800. DLC, ES, LSL, MB, MH, RPB

ANNA.
(*In* The Philadelphia songster, ed. by A. Aimwell [pseud.] Philadelphia, 1789. p. 9)

Melody only, with accompanying text.
First line: Shepherds I have lost my love. NN

———— Shepherd I have lost my love. [n. p., n. d.] p. 14 33 cm.

Song, pfte. acc.
First line same as title. ES

ANNA, OR THE ADIEU. Composed by Mr. Hook. New York, Printed for and sold by I. C. Moller's musical store, No. 58 Vesey street [1797] [2] p. 32 cm.

Song, pfte. acc.
First line: When the sails catch the breeze. DLC, ES, MB, McD–W, MWA, NN
———— The same as preceding.
(*In* A collection of new & favorite songs. [A] Philadelphia [ca. 1800] p. [142]–[143]) HFB

ANNA'S URN.
(*In* The Philadelphia songster, ed. by A. Aimwell [pseud.] Philadelphia, 1789. p. 15–16)

Melody only, with accompanying text.
First line: Encompassed in an angels frame. NN

ANNA'S URN.
(*In* The American musical miscellany. Northampton, 1798. p. 224–227)
Duet. Two staves.
First line: Encompass'd in an angel's frame. DLC (etc.)

ANNE HATHEAWAY [!] by Dibdin.
(*In* Elegant extracts for the German flute or violin. Philadelphia [1798] bk. 3, p. 8)

Melody only, flute or violin, with accompanying text.
First line: Would ye be taught ye feather'd thronge [!]. DLC, NN

ANNIVERSARY DIRGE. Words by the Rev. T. M. Harris.
(*In* Sacred dirges [Oliver Holden] Boston [1800] p. 20-21)

Recitative, air (or duet) and chorus.
First line: Is this the anniversary so dear.

CSmH, DLC, ICN, MB, MH, MHi, MWA, NHi, NN, RPB

ANSPACHER.
See Twenty-four American country *Dances*, p. 24.

THE ANSWER [Without music]
See The select songster. New Haven, 1786. p. 44.

ANSWER TO THE FAVORITE SONG in the Stranger. Boston, Printed &
sold at P. A. von Hagen & co's Musical magazine, No. 3 Cornhill & by
G. Gilfert, New York [1799] 1 l. 31 cm.

Below imprint: For the pianoforte, German flute or violin.
Song, pfte. acc.
First line: Poor suff'ring soul thy woe worn beast.
Advertised in *Columbian centinel*, July 3, 1799 as "this day" published by
P. A. von Hagen and Son. ES, JFD, MB, MWA, RPJCB

ANSWER TO THE MALE COQUETT.
(*In* Nine new songs, by I. B. Gauline. Philadelphia [ca. 1800] p. 7-8)

Song, pfte. acc.
First line: Why thus do you treat us with scorn and disdain.
I. B. Gauline: John B. Gauline. ES, MdHi

*ANTHEM AND ODE, by Benjamin Yarnold.
We read in the *South Carolina gazette*, February 13-20, 1762:

PROPOSAL for printing by subscription an *Anthem*, an *Ode* for voices and
instruments, composed by Benjamin Yarnold, organist of St. Philip's
Charles Town, South Carolina, being the same that was performed before
the Ancient Fraternity of Free Masons, at the installation of the Hon.
Benjamin Smith, Esq., Grand Master in South Carolina.

That each Subscriber, on his receiving an engraved copy of each from
London shall pay, or order to be paid, the sum of seven pounds current
money, into the hands of Mr. Robert Wells, or Peter Timothy.

The anthem probably was identical with a Masonic anthem performed at
Charleston on December 27, 1857, "St. John the Evangelist's Day," at
St. Michael's Church, "suitable to the occasion, set to music by Brother
Benjamin Yarnold . . . sung and played by several masterly hands."

Whether the two compositions were published Sonneck was unable to
ascertain. Still not known.

AN ANTHEM. Designed for Thanksgiving Day. But proper for any publick
occasion. By William Cooper. [Verse] Published according to Act of

Congress. Printed at Boston by Isaiah Thomas and Ebenezer T. Andrews. Faust's Statue, No. 45 Newbury street, [°1792]. 16 p. 13½ x 22 cm.

Title-page, verso blank; preface, p. [3]; p. [4] blank; music and text, p. 5–16. Four-part chorus. Open score.
First line: The Lord hath done great things for us.
Copyright entry, February 22, 1792. District of Massachusetts.
This appears to be the earliest American copyright of an individual piece of music—not a collection. DLC

AN ANTHEM FROM THE 114th PSALM.
(*In* [A volume of songs, etc., composed or copied by Francis Hopkinson. 1759–60] p. 180–181)

Three-part chorus. Open score.
First line: What aileth thee, oh thou sea.
Below the initials "F. H." in upper left hand corner is the date "1760."
Composed by Francis Hopkinson. DLC

AN ANTHEM ON PEACE.
See A hymn on peace, by A. Wood.

AN ANTHEM SUNG IN TRINITY CHURCH at the celebration of St. John's Day, June 24, 1793, by the Episcopal charity children, accompanied with the organ. Composed by Brother Low.
(*In* New York magazine or Literary repository. June, 1793. p. 377)

Words only.
First line: From the seat of bliss above. CSmH (etc.)

TWO ANTHEMS for three and four voices. Composed in an easy and familiar stile [!], adapted for the use of singing societies. By William Selby, professor of music in Boston, New England. Price four shillings lawful money. To be sold at the Author's house in Boston, and most of the booksellers and printers on the continent. [179– ?] 9 l. 21 x 31½ cm.

For mixed chorus. Open score.
First lines: O be joyful in the Lord.—O praise the Lord all ye nations.
Presumably from *Apollo, and the Muse's musical compositions*, by William Selby (*q. v.*) DLC

*ANTHEMS IN FOUR PARTS, with symphonies by William Selby.
See Apollo, and the Muses musical compositions.

*THE APOLLO; being a collection of such English songs as are most eminent for poetical merit. To which is added, a table of first lines with the author's names annexed. Philadelphia: Printed by William Spotswood, Front-street, between Market and Chestnut-streets, 1789.

THE APOLLO; being a collection of English songs; including a collection of Masonic songs, anthems, odes, preludes, prologues, epilogues, toasts, &c. Philadelphia: Printed by William Spotswood, 1791. [4], 164 p. 16 x 19 cm.
MWA, RPB

APOLLO: being a collection of English songs including a selection of Masonic songs, anthems, odes, preludes, prologues, epilogues, toasts, etc. A new

[28]

edition with additions.   Philadelphia: Printed by William Spotswood, 1793.
[9], 164 p., front.   16 x 9 cm.

Title-page, verso blank; table of first lines, p. 3–[8]; Masonic toasts, p. [9];
text, p. 1–164.

Tunes are mentioned for the *Masonic songs* (p. 144–152) only.

MH, PPL, RPJCB

Advertised in January, 1793, among "new books.   American editions.   For
sale by William Spotswood. . . . "

*APOLLO, and the Muse's musical compositions, by William Selby.   In the
Columbian centinel, Boston, June 16, 1790, appeared:

> Proposals for printing by subscription APOLLO, AND THE MUSE'S
> MUSICAL COMPOSITIONS, by William Selby, organist of the Stone
> Chapel, in Boston, Massachusetts, in six numbers.   Dedicated (by per-
> mission) to Mrs. L. Mason of Boston.

> Consisting of anthems in four parts, with symphonies for the organ—
> Voluntaries or fuges for the organ or harpsichord—Sonatas or lessons for the
> harpsichord or pianoforte, also, transposed for the German flute and guitar—
> A piece with variations for the harpsichord or pianoforte, in concert with
> the violin and guittar—A concerto for the organ or harpsichord, with
> instrumental parts—A sonata for two violins and violoncello.

CONDITIONS

> 1st. That each number will be neatly engraved and printed on Royal
> Quarto, to be delivered one every two months, until the whole is completed.

> 2d. That the price of the numbers will be three Dollars, one-third to be
> paid on the delivery of the first number, and the remainder on the delivery
> of the last.

> 3d. As soon as 200 copies are subscribed for, they will be put in hand.
> Those who subscribe for six sets, shall have a seventh gratis.

> 4th. With the last number will be given a list of subscribers—Those who
> chose to have their names inserted will be pleased to send them to the
> several places where subscriptions are taken in.

> Subscriptions are taken in at Isaiah Thomas's Office, Worcester—also
> at the Book-store of said Thomas & Co. in Boston; at the Post Office—at
> the Author's house in Court Street, Boston—and by most of the book-
> sellers and printers on the continent.

The same proposals, with slight changes, appeared in the *Columbian centinel*,
for October 12, 1791.   Sonneck was unable to ascertain whether the collection
was published, but it seems probable that *Two anthems for three and four
voices*, composed . . . by William Selby (*q. v.*) were taken from this collection.   Probably also music listed in [*Unidentified collection (beginning with
"A lesson")*] (*q. v.*)

*APOTHEOSIS OF FRANKLIN, or his reception in the Elysian Fields.
This "grand allegorical finale" by Audin, jun., "with a new set of decorations
. . . new dresses, and new musical grand overture, agreeable to the subject,
executed by the first musicians" was to be performed at the City Theatre,
Charleston, S. C., on April 22, 1796.

[29]

ARABELLA. Boston, Printed & sold by P. A. von Hagen, junior & co's, No. 62 Newbury street [1798–99] [2] p. 33 cm.

Song, pfte. acc. Arr. "for Germ. flute, violin, guittar, &c.," p. [2].
First line: Say have you seen my Arabel. RPJCB

*ARABELLA, THE CALEDONIAN MAID.
Advertised in March, 1795, as "published and to be had at G. Willig's Musical magazine, No. 165 Market street," Philadelphia.

THE MUCH ADMIRED SONG OF ARABELLA, THE CALEDONIAN MAID. With an harp accompaniment New York, Printed for G. Gilfert & co., No. 191 Broadway [1795] [2] p. 33½ cm.

Song, harp acc. Arr. for flute or "guittar," p. [2].
First line: Say have you seen my Arabel. DLC, JFD, NN, RPJCB

Advertised in April. 1795, as "published and to be had of G. Gilfert & co., at their Musical magazine, No. 121 [191] Broadway," New York.

———— The same. New York, Printed and sold by G. Gilfert, No. 177 Broadway [1797–1801] [2] p. 32½ cm.

Song, harp acc.
First line same as preceding. Mutilated copy in DLC

———— The Caledonian maid. Written by Peter Pindair, esquire. Composed by I. Moulds. Printed for and sold by B. Carr at his Musical repository's Market st., Philadelphia & William street, New York. And at I. Carr's, Market st., Baltimore. (Price 20 cents) [1794–97] [2] p. 31½ cm.

Song, pfte. acc. Arr. for German flute, p. [2].
First line: Oh say have you my Mary seen.
Text, a paraphrase of the preceding—the music similar but not identical.
I. Moulds: John Moulds. DLC, ES, JFD, McD–W, MWA, RPJCB

———— The Caledonian maid.
(*In* The gentleman's amusement, ed. by R. Shaw. Philadelphia. [1794–96] p. 37)

Melody only, flute (or violin) with accompanying text.
First line: Oh say have you my Mary seen.
In No. 5, March 1, 1795. DLC, PHi

———— The Caledonian maid.
(*In* Elegant extracts for the German flute or violin. Philadelphia [1798] bk. 3, p. 14–15)

Melody only, flute or violin, with accompanying text.
First line same as preceding. DLC, NN

*THE ARABS OF THE DESERT, or Harlequin's flight from Egypt. This "entire new pantomine olio, taken from the Arabian Night Entertainments with a new overture and music composed by Mr. Reinagle," was to be performed at the New Theatre, Philadelphia, on April 13, 1799.

*ARCADIA, or the Shepherds wedding.
This "dramatic pastoral as it is performed at the Theatre Royal. By the
Rev. Mr. Lloyd. The music composed by [John] Stanley," was advertised
in December, 1762, as "just printed and sold by Andrew Stuart, at the
Bible in Heart, in Second street," Philadelphia.

THE ARCHERS, or Mountaineers of Switzerland. An opera in three acts.
As performed by the Old American Company in New York. To which is
subjoined a brief historical account of Switzerland, from the dissolution of
the Roman Empire to the final establishment of the Helvetic Confederacy by
the battle of Sempach. New York, Printed by T. & J. Swords, No. 99 Pearl
street—1796. viii, [9]–94, [1] p. 21 cm.

Libretto.
Half-title and title-page; preface, p. [v]–vi; prologue, p. [vii]-viii; "characters,"
p. viii; text, p. [9]–78; historical account, p. [79]–94; errata, p. [95].
Half-title and "errata," p. [95], are lacking in some copies.   CSmH, CtY,
        DLC, MB, MH, MWA, NHi, NN, PHi, PPL, PU, RPB, RPJCB

The book was written by William Dunlap, who in the preface, signed "W.
Dunlap. New York, April 10th, 1796," remarked:

> In the summer of the year 1794, a dramatic performance, published in
> London, was left with me, called "Helvetic Liberty." I was requested to
> adapt it to our stage. After several perusals, I gave it up, as incorrigible;
> but pleased with the subject, I recurred to the history of Switzerland, and
> composed the piece now presented to the public.

The archers, sometimes called the first American opera, belongs to the class of
English ballad-opera. It was first performed on April 18, 1796. The music
was composed by Benjamin Carr and seems to be lost, except "A fragment"
(There lived in Altdorf City fair) in the *Second book of Elegant extracts*, published in Philadelphia in 1796, and possibly the "Archers march" in *Military
amusement*, 1796, which is listed in the index as "March in the Archers;"
a "Rondo from the overture . . . arranged for the pianoforte," printed in
1813, as No. 7 of *Carr's musical miscellany in occasional numbers;* and the air
"Why, huntress, why," to be found in No. 39 of *The Musical journal for the
pianoforte*, 1801.

For a detailed description of the opera and further historical details see
Sonneck's monograph on *Early American operas* (Sammelbde. d. Int. Mus.
Ges., 1904–5). Also his *Early opera in America* (1915).

ARCHERS MARCH.
See Military amusement, p. 15.

ARE YE FAIR AS OP'NING ROSES. A favorite song as sung by Sigra. Storace
in the musical entertainment of My grandmother. Composed by Stephen
Storace. Philadelphia, Published by G. Willig, No. 165 Market street
[1795–97] [2] p. 34 cm.

Song, pfte. acc.
First line same as title.
My grandmother performed in Philadelphia, April 27, 1795.   ES, NN, PU

———— The same. Philadelphia, Published by G. Willig, No. 185 Mark. St. [1798-1804] [2] p. 33 cm.

Song, pfte. acc.
First line same as preceding.   DLC, MWA

THE ARETHUSA. Sung by Mr. Story at the Federal Street theatre in the Lock and key with the greatest applause. Boston, Printed & sold by P. A. von Hagen at his imported pianoforte & music ware house, No. 3 Cornhill [ca. 1800] [2] p. 33 cm.

Song, pfte. acc. Arr. for German flute or violin, p. [2].
First line: Come all ye jolly sailors bold.
Lock and key, by William Shield.
This issue published possibly as early as 1799.   JFD, MNSt, NRU-Mus

ARIA ALLA TEDESCA. Arranged as a rondo by Dussek.
(*In* The musical journal for the pianoforte, ed. by B. Carr.
Baltimore [1800] v. 2, no. 26, p. (2)-(4).)

At head of title: Decr. 8, 1800. Musical journal, No. 26. Instrumental section.
Pfte. 2 hds.   DLC, ES, LSL, NN

———— Separate issue of preceding, ca. 1800.   NN, PP-K

ARIA CON VARIAZIONE. Composed by Haigh.
(*In* The musical journal for the pianoforte, ed. by B. Carr. Baltimore [1800] v. 1, no. [2]. p. (2)-(4).)

At head of title: Subscribers are respectfully informed that the numbers of the Instrumental Section are to be kept seperate [!] from the vocal.
Pfte. 2 hds.
Haigh: Thomas Haigh.   DLC, ES, MdHi, NN, NRU-Mus, PP-K

ARIA CON VARIAZIONE. By T. Haigh.
(*In* The musical journal for the flute or violin. Baltimore [1800] no. 2, p. 2-4)

Duet for flutes or violins (or flute and violin).   DLC

*ARIADNE ABANDONED BY THESEUS in the Isle of Naxos.
"A piece in one act, never performed in America, called Ariadne abandoned by Theseus in the Isle of Naxos" was advertised for performance on April 26, 1797, at New York. We further read that, "Between the different passages spoken by the actors will be full orchestra music, expressive of each situation and passion. The music composed and managed by [Victor] Pelisier."
Was this perhaps an altered version of G. Benda's melodrama?

ARISE MY FAIR. Boston, Printed & sold at P. A. von Hagen's imported pianoforte warehouse, No. 3 Cornhill. Sold also by G. Gilfert, New York; D. Vinton, Providence; W. K. Wilder, Newport; B. B. Macanulty, Salem; E. M. Blunt, Newburyport; I. Stanwood, Portsmouth & A. Jenks, Portland [ca. 1800] [2] p. 31½ cm.

Song, pfte. acc.
First line: The cheerful spring begins today.
Published possibly as early as 1799.   DLC, ES, MB

[32]

Same text, but not identical with [*The cheerfull spring begins today*]. "A new favorite song" in The first number of [*Moller & Capron's monthly numbers*]. Philadelphia, 1793.

AROUND THE BRIM of the inspiring goblet.   A favorite new song. The words by P. Derrick.   Publish'd by G. Willig, 165 Market st. [1795–97] 1 l.   31½ cm.

Song, pfte. acc.
First line same as title.   MWA

[AS BRINGING HOME THE OTHER DAY]
See The select songster.   New Haven, 1786.   p. 24.

AS FORTH I RANG'D THE BANKS OF TWEED.   Composed by Mr. Hook.   Boston, Printed & Sold at P. A. von Hagen, junr. & cos. Musical magazine, No. 3 Cornhill.   Also by G. Gilfert, New York.   Where also may be had the new song of Young Jemmy is a pleasing youth.   Also a great variety of warranted imported pianoforte, flutes, hautboys, bassoons, trumpets, French horns, violins, guitars, fifes & other musical articles of superior quality [1799]   [2]   p.   31½ cm.

Song, pfte. acc.   Arr. for German flute, p. [2].
First line same as title.   JFD, MB, MWA, RPJCB

This "new song" was advertised in May, 1799, as "published by P. A. von Hagen & co. . . . No. 3 Cornhill," Boston.   The P. A. von Hagen here mentioned is evidently the same as the P. A. von Hagen, junr. of the above imprint.

AS LATE BY LOVE.   By Corri.   Philadelphia, Printed by G. Willig, Mark. street, No. 185 [1798–1804]   [2] p.   33 cm.

Song, pfte. acc.
First line same as title.
Corri: Domenico Corri.   DLC, MWA

AS PENDANT O'ER THE LIMPID STREAM.   Composed by F. Kotzwara. New York, Printed & sold by G. Gilfert, No. 177 Broadway [1798]   [2] p. 34 cm.

Song, pfte. acc.
First line same as title.
Advertised in November, 1798, as just published by "George Gilbert, at his music store, 177 Broadway, Apollo's Head," New York.   JFD

[AS WRAPT IN SLEEP I LAY] The Scotch air in the comic opera of the Pirates.   Philadelphia, Printed for Carr & co., at their Musical repository, No. 136 High street.   Where may be had, all the newest music, reprinted from European publications; likewise an elegant assortment of piano fortes guittars, flutes, violins and other musical articles of superior quality. (*In* The favorite songs from the Pirates, by S. Storace.   Philadelphia [1793] p. (8)–(9).)

Song, pfte. acc.   Arr. for the German flute and for the "guittar," p. (9).
Title from first line.   HFB

—— Separate issue of preceding, ca. 1793.   DLC

[33]

*ASK WHY A BLUSH. Glee for three voices by Raynor Taylor.
This glee figured on a concert program which was to be performed at Philadelphia, on April 3, 1800.

ASTERIA'S FIELDS. By a lady of Philada.
(*In* [Moller & Capron's Monthly numbers] The third number [Philadelphia, 1793] p. 21–22)

Song, pfte. acc.
First line: As o'er Asteria's fields I rove. DLC, PHi

ASTLEY'S HORNPIPE.
(*In* The gentleman's amusement, ed. by R. Shaw. Philadelphia [1794–96] p. 29)

Melody only, flute (or violin).
In No. 4, February 1, 1795. DLC, PHi

—— The same.
See Evening amusement, p. 22.

AT MORNING DAWN THE HUNTERS RISE. A favorite hunting song. Composed by S. F. Rimbault. New York, Engrav'd printed and publish'd by I. and M. Paff, No. 127 Broadway [1799–1803] [2] p. 30 cm.

Song, pfte. acc.
First line same as title. McD–W, NBuG, NN

AT THE DEAD OF THE NIGHT. Sung by Mr. Johnstone in Zorinski. Sold at Carr's Musical repository's, Philadelphia & N. York and B. Carr, Baltimore. (Price 12 c⁺ˢ) [n. d.] 1 l. 32 cm.

Song, pfte. acc.
First line same as title.
Zorinski, by Samuel Arnold was first performed in America in 1797; in New York, March 23, 1798.
Above issue probably late in 1797.
Most unusual is the "B. Carr, Baltimore," in imprint. Apparently a misprint for "J." DLC

AUF DER LÜFTE HEIL'GEN WEBEN. Quartetto di Wolf.
Ms. parts for two violins, viola fondamento, flauto, soprano, alto, tenore, basso, preserved in the library of the Philharmonic Society, Bethlehem, Pa. (Sonneck).

AULD ROBIN GRAY. A favorite Scots air. Sung by Miss Broadhurst. Price 25 cents. New York, Printed & sold at J. Hewitt's Musical repository, No. 131 William street. Sold also by B. Carr, Philadelphia & J. Carr, Baltimore.
(*In* A collection of new & favorite songs. [A] Philadelphia [ca. 1800] p. [138]–[139])

Song, pfte. acc.
First line: Young Jammie [!] lov'd me weel and ask'd me for his bride.
Originally issued 1797–99. HFB

*AULD ROBIN GRAY, or Jamie's return from America.
An altered version of Samuel Arnold's "new pastoral opera," 1794, was advertised for performance at the New Theatre, Philadelphia, on May 4, 1795, as "never performed here . . . the new music, with a Scotish medley overture, by Mr. [Alexander] Reinagle."

THE AVIARY. A collection of three elegant sonnets. Entitled The linnetts, The goldfinch, and The nightingale. Composed by Mr. Hook. Price 62 cents. Printed & sold at B. Carr's Musical repository, Philadelphia; J. Carr's, Baltimore, and J. Hewitt's, New York [1798] 7 p. 33 cm.

Ornamental title-page.
Contents: The linnetts, p. (2)–(3).—The gold finch, p. (4)–(5).—The nightingale, p. (6)–(7).   JFD, LSL, NN (lacks last page)

Advertised in *Porcupine's gazette*, Philadelphia, January 22, 1798, to be published in the following week at "Carr's Musical repository."

[THE AVIARY. A collection of sonnets by James Hook] New York, Published by I. and M. Paff, No. 127 Broadway [1799–1803] 30½ cm.

Contents: No. 1. The thrush.—No. 2. The linnetts.—No. 3. The gold finch.— No. 4. The robin red breast.—No. 5. The nightingale.—No. 6. The lark.— No. 7. The black bird.—No. 8. The cuckoo.

Imprint and collective title supplied from *The cuckoo* and certain other individual numbers.
Published probably in 1800 or soon after.   NN (complete set)

For locations other than NN see under individual titles.

AWAY WITH MELANCHOLY. By Mozart. Price 25 cts. New York, Printed and sold by J. C. Moller [179–] [2] p. 33½ cm.

Duet, pfte. acc. Three staves.
First line same as title.
Adapted from Finale of Act I, *Die Zauberflöte.*   JFD

AWAY WITH MELANCHOLY. By Mozart. Printed & sold at B. Carr's Musical repository, Philadelphia; J. Carr's, Baltimore & J. Hewitt's, New York. (25 cents) [1797–99] [2] p. 32½ cm.

Duet, pfte. acc. Three staves.
First line same as preceding.   DLC, ES, LSL, McD–W, MdHi, NN, NRU–Mus

AWAY WITH MELANCHOLY. Philadelphia, Published and sold at G. Willig's music store [179–] 1 l. 32 cm.

Duet, pfte. acc.
First line same as preceding.   MWA

———— Merrily sings. L'allegro. Canzonetta VII. Air or duett. New York, Printed & sold by G. Gilfert, No. 177 Broadway [1797–1801] p. 20–22. 32 cm.

Duet, pfte. acc. Four staves.
English and Italian text.

First lines: Away with melancholy.—Non piu melanconia.
Imprint crowded under title and in very small type, apparently added to an earlier (English ?) plate. Reprint from some unidentified collection. DLC

BACHELORS HALL.
See Batchelors hall.

THE BACHELOR'S SONG. Music by F. C. Schaffer. [n. p., 179–] [2] p 31½ cm.

Song, pfte. acc.
First line: A bachelor leads an easy life. MB, MH

BALLAD. In Caernarvon castle.
(*In* The Philadelphia pocket companion for guittar or clarinett [Philadelphia, 1794] v. 1, p. 28)

Song, melody only.
First line: Ah woe is me. Shou'd cuddy be.
Caernarvon castle, by Thomas Attwood. MWA

THE BALLAD SINGER'S PETITION. In No song no supper [Philadelphia] Publish'd by G. Willig, 165 Market s⸸ [1795–97] 1 l. 32 cm.
Song, pfte. acc.
First line: With lowly suit and plaintive ditty.
No song no supper, by Stephen Storace. CdeW

THREE BALLADS. Viz. The new somebody, Mary will smile, and Poor Richard. Composed by B. Carr. Op. 2. Price 62 cents. Or in seperate [!] sheets at 25 cents each. Copyright securr'd [!] according to law. Printed and sold at B. Carr's Musical repository, Philadelphia; J. Carr's, Baltimore & J. Hewitt's, New York. Just published, Three canzonetts by Haydn. And shortly will be published Musical bagatelles or Six little ballads selected from some late English publications [°1799] 7 p. 33 cm.

DLC copy has ms. note on title-page: No. 232. Title page of Three ballads. Deposited 17th of May, 1799, by Benjamin Carr, as author.
Songs, pfte. acc.
Contents:—The new somebody, p. 2–3.—Mary will smile, p. 4–5.—Poor Richard, p. 6–7.
Advertised for sale by J. Carr, Baltimore, in August, 1799, among "music lately published."
JFD (complete) DLC (incomplete, title-page and p. 2 only)

*THE BALTIMORE SONGSTER. Baltimore, Sold by J. Keatinge. 1794.

*THE BALTIMORE SONGSTER, or festive companion. A choice and approved collection of songs, interspersed with many originals and the patriotic song of Hail, Columbia! Second edition. Baltimore, Printed for Henry S. Keatinge. 1798.

THE BANKS OF KENTUCKE.
See Sky lark.

[36]

THE BANKS OF THE DEE.
(*In* The American musical miscellany. Northampton, 1798. p. 34–38)

Melody only, with accompanying text.
First line : 'Twas summer and softly the breezes were blowing.   DLC (etc.)

THE BANKS OF YARROW. Sung by Miss Bertles.   Vauxhall.
(*In* A collection of favorite songs, divided into two books.   Arr. by A.
Reinagle.   Philadelphia [1789 ?]   bk. 2, p. 4–5)

Song, pfte. acc.   Arr. for German flute, p. 5.
First line: The morn was fair, soft was the air.   CdeW, DLC,   PU

THE BASTILE.   Composed in the French taste by Elfort.   Philadelphia,
Printed for S. R. Bader; J. Aitken, sculpt.   [179– ?]   11 p.   32½ cm.

Imprint at foot of page.
Pfte. 2 hds.   DLC. NN

*THE BASTILE, a favorite sonata by Elfort.
Thus advertised in December, 1793, as published by "B. Carr & Co.
Musical Repository, No. 122 South side of Market street. . . . Printed singly,"
Philadelphia.

BATCHELORS [!] HALL.   By Dibdin.
(*In* Young's vocal and instrumental musical miscellany. Philadelphia.
[1793–95]   p. 5)

Song, pfte. acc.
First line: To Batchelor's Hall we good fellows invite.
From *The oddities*, by Charles Dibdin.
In No. 1, 1793.   DLC, ES, HFB, Hopk.

BATCHELORS [!] HALL.
(*In* The American musical miscellany.   Northampton, 1798.   p. 42–44)

Melody only, with accompanying text.
First line same as preceding.   DLC (etc.)

———— Bachelors Hall.
(*In* Elegant extracts for German flute or violin.   Baltimore [1794] bk. 1, p.
34–35)

Melody only, flute or violin, with accompanying text.
First line: To Bachelors hall we good fellows invite.   DLC, NN

THE BATTLE OF GEMMAPPE.   A sonata for the forte piano by F⁸. Devienne. New York, Printed for G. Gilfert & co. at their Musical magazine.
No. 177 Broadway [1796]   13 p.   31 cm.

Title page.
Pfte. 2 hds.
Battle of Jemappes, November 6, 1792.   MB

THE BATTLE OF HEXHAM.   Alternative title of *The days of old*, by Samuel
Arnold.

[37]

THE BATTLE OF PRAGUE. A favourite sonata for the pianoforte or harpsichord. Philadelphia, Printed for I. C. Moller; C. S., sculpt. [ca. 1793] 7 p. 31½ cm.

Imprint at foot of p. 7.
Pfte. 2 hands.
Composed by Franz Kočzwara.   MB, NN

———— The same as preceding, except that below title has been added: Publish'd by G. Willig, Market street.
Probably issued between 1795 and 1800.   DLC, PP–K

———— The same as preceding, with the above addition below title and also a substitution of "G. Willig" for "I. C. Moller" in imprint at foot of p. 7.
Probably issued between 1795 and 1800.   NN, PU

"C. S., sculpt." is very indefinite. Possibly reference is made to "Charles Shipman, advertised as an engraver on copper plate in the *New York Mercury* of May 16, 1768." (Quoted from William Dunlap's *History of the arts of design in the United States*, 1918 ed.)

THE BATTLE OF PRAGUE. Selected and adapted for a flute and violin or for one or two flutes or violins, by B. Carr. Price 38 cents. Printed and sold at B. Carr's Musical repositories in New York and Philadelphia, and by J. Carr, Baltimore.
(*In* The gentleman's amusement, ed. by R. Shaw. Philadelphia [1794–96] p. (83)–(86).)

Below imprint: N. B. If a flute plays the 2d where double notes occur, the uppermost are to be play'd and if a violin as they are printed except in a few instances small notes are mark'd purposely for that instrument.
In No. 11, 1796.   PHi, PP–K

THE BATTLE OF PRAGUE. A favorite sonata for the piano forte or harpsichord. Price 8 sh. New York, Printed and sold at I. C. Mollers musical store [179–] 7 p. 33 cm.

Pfte. 2 hds.
Probably issued between 1796 and 1800.   McD-W, RPJCB

THE BATTLE OF PRAGUE. A sonata for the pianoforte or harpsichord. Price 1 dollar. New York, Printed by G. Gilfert, No. 177 Broadway [1797–1801] 1 p. l., 8 p. 31½ cm.
Pfte. 2 hds.   NN

THE BATTLE OF PRAGUE. A favorite sonata for the piano forte. Composed by F. Kotzwara. Philadelphia, Printed for B. Carr Musical repository, High street; I. Carr, Baltimore & I. Hewitt, Musical repository, No. 131 William street, New York [ca. 1798] 1 p. l., 8 p. 32 cm.

Title-page with design of cannon, flags, drum, &c.
Pfte. 2 hds.   DLC, LSL, McD-W

LSL copy contains two additional pages giving:

 Catalogue of favorite songs . . . Printed and sold at B. Carr's Musical repositories, Philadelphia and New York, & J. Carr's Baltimore.

This list embraces 195 songs.

THE BATTLE OF PRAGUE. A favourite sonata for the piano forte or harpsichord. Philadelphia, Printed for A. Reinagle; J. Aitken, sculpt. [179–?] 7 p. 32½ cm.

Imprint at foot of p. 7.
Pfte. 2 hds.
Sonneck gives this rather vague date, and there seems no way of clarifying it.   DLC, MB

Kočzwara's popular piece as "adapted for a full band by J. G. C. Shetky" was probably first played at the New Theatre, Philadelphia, on June 23, 1794, thus analyzed:

1. Slow march. 2. Word of command, and first signal of cannon. 3. Bugle horn for the cavalry and second signal cannon. 4. Trumpet call. 5. Attack, cannonade, musketry, light-horse advancing, heavy artillery, etc., etc. Trumpet of recall. 6. Cries and groans of the wounded and dying. 7. Trumpet of victory. 8. Grand march. 9. Turkish music. 10. General rejoicing—"Go to bed Tom" and finale.
(Some copies read "Go to bed home.")

THE BATTLE OF THE KEGS.
See Liberty songs, p. 2–4.

THE BATTLE OF TRENTON. A sonata for the piano forte. Dedicated to General Washington. New York, Printed & sold by James Hewitt at his Musical repository, No. 131 William street; B. Carr, Philadelphia & J. Carr, Baltimore. Price [illegible] [1797] 1 p. l., 2–14 p. 33 cm.

Title-page richly embellished with portrait of Washington, Goddess of Liberty with cap on spear, flags, drums, etc.
Pfte. 2 hds.
Composed by James Hewitt, who has introduced into his score the music of *Washington's march* and *Yankee Doodle.*   CSmH, DLC, MNSt, NN

Advertised in *Minerva*, New York, August 23, 1797, as published by J. Hewitt at his "Musical repository, 131 William st."

THE BEAUTIES OF FRIENDSHIP. A favourite song by W. A.
(*In* The Massachusetts magazine. Boston, September, 1792. p. 583)

Melody and bass, with accompanying text.
First line: Young Myra is fair as Spring's early flower.   DLC (etc.)

THE BEAUTIES OF FRIENDSHIP.
(*In* The American musical miscellany., Northampton, 1798. p. 222–224)

Melody and bass, with accompanying text.
First line same as preceding.   DLC (etc.)

*BEAUTIES OF MUSIC.
The following advertisement appeared in the *Columbian centinel*, June 26, 1799:

BEAUTIES OF MUSIC. Just published by William Norman and sold at his Bookstore, No. 75 Newbury Street, or nearly opposite the sign of the Lamb Tavern, Boston.

No. 1 of the Beauties of music, being a collection of songs, airs, dances, marches, reels, duets, rondos, trios, etc. adapted to the violin and German flute—taken from a late London edition. N. B. This work with some additions will be continued in numbers 'till the whole is complete.

THE BEAUTIES OF SPRING.
(*In* The songster's assistant, ed. by T. Swan. Suffield [ca. 1800] p. 9)

Song, pfte. acc.
First line: Flocks are sporting, doves are courting.   MB

BEAUTY. A favorite sonnet. Composed by the celebrated Ignace Pleyel. Also just published Pleyels Sonnet to Time. New York, Sold by I. and M. Paff, No. 127 Broadway [1799–1803] [2] p. 33 cm.

Song, pfte. acc.
First line: What is beauty but a flow'r.   RPJCB

THE BEDFORDSHIRE MARCH.
See Compleat tutor for the fife . . . p. 13.

THE BEE.
(*In* The American musical miscellany. Northampton, 1798. p. 182–183)

Melody and bass, with accompanying text.
First line: As Cupid in a garden stray'd.   DLC (etc.)

THE BEECH TREE'S PETITION. The words by Campbell. The music by R. Taylor. Copyright secured. Philadelphia, Published & sold at G. Willig's Musical magazine [ca. 1800] [2] p. 31 cm.

Caption vignette, design of tree and woodman.
Song, pfte. acc.
First line: O leave this barren spot to me.
DLC, LSL, MWA, NBuG, PHi, PP

THE BEGGAR BOY. [New York, I. and M. Paff, No. 127 Broadway, 1799–1803] [2] p. 33 cm.

At head of title: No. 7. Ladies musical journal.
Song, pfte. acc.
First line: Of you happy stranger, I supplicate bread.
On p. [2]: Federal waltz. (For pfte. 2 hds.)
Composed by William Horsley (?).
Ladies musical journal, 1799–1803, from which above imprint is supplied.
DLC, NBuG

THE BEGGAR GIRL. [New York, I. and M. Paff, No. 127 Broadway, 1799–1803] [2] p. 32½ cm.

At head of title: No. 6. Ladies musical journal.
Song, pfte. acc.
First line: Over the mountain and over the moor.
Composed by H. Piercy.
On p. [2]: The Prince of Wales's waltz. (For pfte. 2 hds.)
Ladies musical journal, 1799–1803, from which above imprint is supplied.
DLC, NBuG

THE BEGGAR GIRL. A favorite song or duett. By H. Piercy. [n. p., n. d.]
p. (6)–(8). 32 cm.

> Song, or duet, pfte. acc. Three staves.
> First line same as preceding.
> Probably a Carr imprint, 179–. *cf. *Elegant extracts.*　　　　DLC, MdHi

BEGONE DULL CARE. A favorite duett. Printed and sold by J. Carr
music store, Baltimore. Price 25 cents. [ca. 1796] [2] p. 31½ cm.

> Duet, pfte. acc. Three staves.
> First line same as title.
> Approximate date suggested by the fact that a similar issue is listed in the
> *British Museum Catalogue* as [1795 ?] and also that J. Carr seems to have
> begun publishing music in 1796 (Sonneck).　　　　McD–W

——— The same as preceding, except that at lower right hand margin of p. [1]
and [2] respectively, appear the letters BD1 and BD2, implying perhaps a
somewhat later issue.　　　　MdHi

[BEGONE DULL CARE] Duett for two mandora's [!]
(*In* The Philadelphia pocket companion for guittar or clarinett [Philadelphia,
1794] v. 1, p. 8–9)
Duet. Two staves.
Title from first line.
Mandora: a member of the lute family, related to the mandolin.　　　　MWA

LA BELLE ANNETTE.
See Twenty-four American country *Dances*, p. 13.

LA BELLE CATHERINE with variations (In wich [!] is introduced the favorite
air of the Yellow hair'd lady) for the harpsichord or piano forte.
(*In* [Moller & Capron's monthly numbers] The second number [Philadelphia,
1793] p. 9–12)

> At head of title: The 2d number.
> Pfte., or harpsichord, 2 hds.　　　　DLC, NN

LA BELLE CATHERINE. Adapted with variations (in which are introduced
the favorite air of the Yellow hair'd laddie) for the piano forte by Domenico
Corri. New York, Printed & sold by G. Gilfert, No. 177 Broadway [1797–
1801] 4 p. 33½ cm.

> Pfte. 2 hds.　　　　DLC, NN

LA BELLE FRENE [IRÈNE ?]
See Twenty-four American country *Dances*, p. 9.

THE BELLES ABOUT THE FLAT BUSH.
See Twenty-four American country *Dances*, p. 12.

BELLEISLE [!] MARCH.
See Military amusement, p. 20.

THE BELLISLE MARCH.
See Compleat tutor for the fife . . . p. 15.

THE BELLS. Composed by R. Taylor.
> Ms. 2 p. in G. maj. added to a miscellaneous volume which contains Brown's
> Rondos and other music printed before 1800.　　　　Hopk.

[41]

THE BELLS OF SCOTLAND.
See Manuscript collection of hymns, songs, etc. (45).

BEN & MARY. By T. Dibdin.
(*In* The musical journal for the flute or violin. Baltimore [1800] no. 11, p. 22–23)

Melody only, flute or violin, with accompanying text.
First line: The decks were clear'd. DLC

BEN BACKSTAY. A favorite new song. Composed by Mr. Dibdin. Philadelphia, Sold by H. & P. Rice, No. 50 Market st., between Front and Second streets. Price 10 cents.
(*In* The gentleman's amusement, ed. by R. Shaw. Philadelphia [1794–96] p. 6)

Song, pfte. acc., followed by arr. for flute.
First line: Ben Backstay lov'd the gentle Anna.
In No. 1, April 1, 1794. DLC, PHi

—— Separate issue of preceding advertised in May, 1794, as "published . . . Philadelphia, Printed for Shaw & co." LSL

—— The same as preceding. Fourth page, numbered 6, of a detached portion (p. 3–6) from above collection. NN

[BENEATH A WEEPING WILLOW'S SHADE] Song III.
(*In* Seven songs, by F. Hopkinson. Philadelphia [1788] p. 3–4)

Song, pfte. acc.
Title from first line. DLC, Hopk., MB, McD–W

BENEATH THE HONORS, &c.
(*With* Hark from the tombs, &c. By Samuel Holyoke. Exeter [1800] p. 6–12)

For mixed chorus. Three staves.
First line same as title.
Composed by Samuel Holyoke in memory of Washington, and performed at Newburyport, January 2, 1800. CSmH, DLC, MH

BENEVOLENT TAR. Alternative title of *The purse.*

THE BETTER SORT, or the Girl of spirit. An operatical comical farce. [Verses, followed by elaborate monogram I T & Co.] Printed at Boston by Isaiah Thomas and company. Sold at their bookstore, No. 45 Newbury street, and at said Thomas's bookstore in Worcester, 1789. 50, [1] p. 20½ x 13 cm.
Libretto.
Title-page, verso blank; preface, p. [iii]–iv; prologue, p. [v]–vii; persons of the drama, p. [viii]; text, p. [ix]–50; index to songs, p. [51].
Author unkown. NHi

THE BIRD.
See The select songster. New Haven, 1786. p. 43.

[THE BIRDS WHO WING THEIR WAY THROUGH AIR]
See Air in the Reconciliation.

[42]

THE BIRKS OF INVERMAY. New York, Printed & sold at J. Hewitts Musical repository, No. 23, Maiden Lane.
(*In* A collection of new and favorite songs. [A] Philadelphia [ca. 1800] p. [162])

Song, pfte. acc.
First line: The smiling morn, the breathing Spring.   HFB

———— Separate issue of preceding, 1799–1800.   DLC

THE BIRKS OF INVERMAY.
See The select songster. New Haven, 1786. p. 47–48.

THE BLACK BIRD. A favorite new song. Composed by Mr. Hook. New York, Printed & sold by G. Gilfert, No. 177 Broadway [1797–1801] [2] p. 31 cm.

Song, pfte. acc.
First line: 'Twas on a bank of daisies sweet.   MWA

THE BLACK BIRD. Composed by Mr. Hook.
(*In* [Unidentified collection of instrumental and vocal music. New York] Hewitt & Rausch [1797] p. 17–18)

Song, pfte. acc.
First line same as preceding.
Followed on p. 18 by *Independent rangers quick march*. (For pfte.) DLC, ES

———— Separate issue of preceding, ca. 1797.   NN

———— The same as preceding.
(*In* A collection of new & favorite songs. [A] Philadelphia [ca. 1800] p. [112]–[113])   HFB

THE BLACK BIRD. Selected for [!] the aviary, a collection of sonnets.
Also just published

No. 1. The thrush.	No. 4. The robin red breast.
No. 2. The linnets.	No. 5. The Nightingale.
No. 3. The goldfinch.	No. 6. The lark.

and No. 8. The cuckoo.

New York, Sold by I. and M. Paff, No. 127 Broadway [1799–1803] [2] p. 30½ cm.

At head of title: No. 7.
Imprint at foot of p. [2].
Song, pfte. acc.
First line: Woud [!] you know true enjoyment.   ES, NN

*BLACK BIRD SONGBOOK.
Advertised in *The Pennsylvania gazette*, July 13, 1769, by "William Woodhouse, book-binder and stationer in Front-street, near Chestnut street, and partly opposite Mr. John Bayly, Goldsmith, Philadelphia. Where merchants, shopkeepers and others may be furnished with . . . Wood Lark and Black Bird song books . . . "

[43]

THE BLEAK WIND WISTLES [!] o'er the main.
(*In* Young's vocal and instrumental musical miscellany. Philadelphia [1793–95] p. 8–9)

Song, pfte. acc.
First line: The bleak wind whistles o'er the main.
From *The highland reel*, by William Shield.
In No. 1, 1793.   DLC, ES, HFB, Hopk

THE BLEEDING HERO. A favourite song. Composed by Sigr. Giordani.
New York, Printed & sold at J. & M. Paff's musical store, No. 127 Broad Way [1799–1803] [2] p. 30½ cm.

Song, pfte. acc.
First line: Gentle river, gentle river, lo thy streams are stain'd with gore.
                                                        DLC, NN

A BLESSING ON BRANDY & BEER. A favorite song in the comic opera of the Magician no conjurer. Composed by Mr. Mazzinghi.
(*In* The musical repertory. Boston [1796] No. I. p. (6)–(7))

Song, pfte. acc.
First line: When one's drunk not a girl but looks pretty.
In MB copy, after title, "Pr. 25ᶜᵗ." This is in different type. Apparently added later.   DLC, MB

————— Separate issue of preceding, ca. 1796.   JFD

THE BLEW BIRD.
See Manuscript collection of hymns, songs, etc. (44).

*THE BLOCKHEADS, or, Fortunate contractor. An opera in two acts. As it was performed at New York. New York printed. London reprinted for G. Kearsley, 1782. p. v–43, 2 pl. 8vo.

Entry taken from Wegelin. This counter-farce to Burgoyne's *Blockade* is attributed to Mrs. Mercy Warren (1728–1814). Born in Barnstaple, Massachusetts; died at Plymouth, Massachusetts.

BLOSSOM LOVELIEST FLOWER. A new song. Composed by Schulz.
Philadelphia, Published by G. Willig, No. 185 Market street [1798–1804] 1 l. 32 cm.

Song, pfte. acc.
First line same as title.   CSmH, PHi, PP-K

BLUE BEARD, or Female curiosity.
Michael Kelly's opera (1798), libretto by George Colman, the younger, was performed "with accompaniments by Mr. [Alexander] Reinagle" at the New Theatre in Baltimore, June 10, 1799.
Songs in Blue Beard were for sale in August at J. Carr's music store under "music lately published" which does not necessarily imply that they were published at Baltimore. They appeared under the following imprint: Printed and sold by B. Carr, Philadelphia, I. Hewitt, New York and J. Carr, Baltimore. (*See* A collection of new & favorite songs. [C] [From the opera of Blue Beard].)

Wegelin mentions:
Blue Beard; or Female curiosity. A dramatic romance in three acts. New York, 1803. 48 p. 18mo. Another edition. New York, 1806. 16mo.

THE VERY POPULAR AND BEAUTIFUL SCOTCH BALLAD sung by Mrs. Oldmixon called *The Blue Bell of Scotland.* As lately revived in England by Mrs. Jordan and sung by her with the most unbounded applause.
(*In* The musical journal for the piano forte, ed. by B. Carr. Baltimore [1800] v. 2, no. 25, p. (2)–(4))
At head of title: Dec. 1, 1800. No. 5 of The musical journal—Vocal section—Being the commencement of the second volume. Which will be completed in 24 numbers.
Song, pfte. acc.
First line: Ah! where and ah! where is your Highland laddie gone.
On p. (4), a more elaborated version (three staves): The Blue Bell of Scotland. With an accompanyment for the harp or piano forte. N. B. The superior effect that will be produced by those who can sing one part and play the other as here adapted will make an apology unnecessary for the reinserting it in this form.   DLC, ES, LSL, McD–W, NN

—— The same as preceding, but without title page and p. (4), ca. 1800.
                                                                                 DLC, MdHi
THE BLUE BELL OF SCOTLAND. A favorite Scotch ballad. Sung by Mrs. Oldmixon in St. David's Day. Philadelphia, Printed & sold by G. Willig, No. 185 Market st. [ca. 1800] 1 l. 32½ cm.
Song, pfte. acc.
First line: Ah where and ah where is your Highland laddie gone.
Sonneck dates this imprint, ca. 1798. But all authorities (including *BM Cat.*) seem to agree that this song was first published in London in 1800. Its prompt appearance in America is attested by its inclusion in Carr's *Musical journal for the pianoforte* under date of Dec. 1, 1800, as noted above.
                                                                       DLC, LSL, PHi, PP-K

THE BLUE BELL OF SCOTLAND. A favorite ballad. As composed and sung by Mrs. Jordan at the Theatre Royal, Drury Lane. New York, Printed & sold at G. Gilfert's music store, No. 177 Broadway. And to be had of P. A. von Hagen, No. 3 Cornhill, Boston [ca. 1800] [2] p. 29 cm.
Song, pfte, acc.
First line: Oh where and oh where is your Highland laddie gone.
                                                                          DLC, ES, JFD, NN

THE BLUE BELL OF SCOTLAND. A favorite Scotch ballad. Boston, Printed & sold at P. A. von Hagen's piano forte warehouse, No. 3 Cornhill [ca. 1800] 1 l. 31 cm.
Song, pfte. acc.
First line: Ah where and ah where is your Highland laddie gone.
                                                            DLC, ES, LSL, MB, NN, RPJCB

THE BLUE BELL OF SCOTLAND. Philadelphia, Published by G. Willig [ca. 1800] p. 12. 32 cm.
Song, pfte. acc.
First line same as preceding.   NBuG

BLUE EYED MARY.
See Manuscript collection of hymns, songs, etc. (47).

BLYTHE COLLIN.
See Mrs. Pownall's adress [!].

THE BOATMAN.   A favorite Scotch song.   Composed by Mr. Barthelemon.
New York, Printed and sold by G. Gilfert, No. 177 Broadway [1797–1801]
1 l.   31½ cm.

Song, pfte. acc.
First line: Ye gales that gently wave the sea.
Mr. Barthelemon: François Hippolyte Barthélemon.   MWA

BONNIE WILLY.   The music by Mr. Taylor.   The words by Mr. C. Harford
Philadelphia, Published by G. Willig, No. 185 Market street [1798–1804]
[2] p.   32½ cm.

Song, pfte. acc.
First line: My Willy is the finest lad.
Presumably "Mr. Taylor" refers to Raynor Taylor.
A song, *Bonny Will*, was sung in Boston, April 23, 1795.

NRU–Mus, PP–K

BONNY CHARLEY.   A favorite new Scotch song.
(*In* Young's vocal and instrumental musical miscellany.   Philadelphia
[1793–95] p. 21)

Song, pfte. acc.
First line: O dearly do I love to rove.
Composed by James Hook.
In No. 3, 1793.   DLC, Hopk.

BONNY CHARLY.   A favorite Scotch song.   25 cents.   New York, Publis'd [!]
by I. and M. Paff at their music warehouse, No. 127 Broadway.   Where may
be had London made pianofortes, grand and small.   Also every article in the
musical line for sale upon reasonable terms.   [1799–1803]   [2] p.   30 cm.

Song, pfte. acc.
First line same as preceding.
Sung in New York, July 4, 1798.   NN

BONNY CHARLEY.   [n. p., n. d.]   p. 141–142.   34½ cm.
Song, pfte. acc.
First line same as preceding.
Published probably 179–.   ABHu

BONNY LEM OF ABERDEEN, as a contry [!] dance.
(*In* Young's vocal and instrumental musical miscellany.   Philadelphia
[1793–95] p. 7)

Pfte. 2 hds., followed by directions for dancing.
Possibly title should read "Jem," instead of "Lem."
In No. 1, 1793.   DLC, ES, HFB, Hopk.

BONNY MARY.   Printed by G. Willig, No. 185 Market st., Philadelphia [1798–
1804]   1 l.   34 cm.

Song, pfte. acc.
First line: How sweet that season of the year.   NRU–Mus

[46]

A BOOK OF SONGS, for the piano forte or harpsichord, composed by M. A. Pownall and J. Hewitt.

Proposals for publishing the above were advertised in the *N. Y. Daily advertiser*, May 11, 1793, as follows:

Music. Flatter'd by the unbounded applause which the songs of the Primrose Girl, Jenny of the Glen, etc. have met with in this city and Philadelphia, M. A. Pownall and J. Hewitt, are induced to publish them (with four others entirely new) arranged for the Harpsichord and Pianoforte. A work which they hope will do credit to themselves and give satisfaction to those Ladies and Gentlemen who will please to honour them by becoming subscribers.

CONDITIONS

This work will consist of the following pieces:
1st. Rosette's celebrated "La Chasse."
2d. 7 Ballads composed by M. A. Pownall and J. Hewitt.
3d. A Duet for two voices.

TERMS OF SUBSCRIPTION

Twelve shillings, one dollar to be paid at the time of subscribing and the remainder on delivery of the work.
Non subscribers sixteen shillings.

Subscriptions received by J. Hewitt. No. 72 Courtlandt street. May 9.

The "Rosette" above undoubtedly refers to Francesco Antonio Rosetti (Franz Anton Roessler) 1750–1792.

Sonneck adds that No. 3 seems to have been the piece performed at the second "City concert," New York, January 9, 1794, under the title, "Duet for 2 voices, 'How sweet is the breath of morn,' Mrs. Pownall and Mr. Capron."

Sonneck's thoroughly reasonable conjecture as to the *Duet for two voices* proves nevertheless mistaken. We find it to be the well known *Canzonet* by William Jackson of Exeter, "Time has not thin'd my flowing hair," as noted below immediately following the six songs.

The same proposals appeared in the *Federal gazette*, Philadelphia, September 9, 1793, with these alterations:
1. Rostette instead of Rosette.
2. 6 ballads instead of 7.
3. Mrs. Pownall instead of M. A. Pownall.
4. "Subscriptions received by Mrs. Pownall at the theatre, and at Messrs. Carr & Co's Musical Repository, No. 136 Highstreet. Phil. Sept. 3."
5. One dollar instead of twelve shillings.

The following advertisement appeared in the *N. Y. Daily Advertiser* for March 29, 1794:

New Music. Just published a book of songs, for the pianoforte or harpsichord, composed by M. A. Pownall and J. Hewitt: Song of the waving willow, and the celebrated French national air La Carmagnole; to be had of J. Hewitt, Greenwich street near the battery.

The collection as finally published is as follows:

[47]

SIX SONGS FOR THE HARPSICHORD or piano forte, composed by Mrs. Pownall and J. Hewitt. To which are added and selected Rossetti's celebrated La chasse and a Duet for two voices. Price two dollars. New York, Printed for Mrs. Pownall and J. Hewitt and appointed to be sold at Mr. Mathew Carey's store, No. 118 High street, Philadelphia [1794] 19 p. 32 cm.

Title-page; music, p. 1 (verso of t.-p.)–19.
Contents: La chasse, p. 1–8.—Jemmy of the Glen, p. 9–10.—A rural life, p. 11.—Advice to the ladies, p. 12.—Straw bonnet, p. 13–14.—Lavinia, p. 15.—The primrose girl, p. 16.—Canzonet, p. 17–19.
ES (complete), HFB (lacks p. 12–15)

A BOOK OF TWELVE SONGS, by Alexander Juhan.
See A Set of six sonatas.

BOSTON PATRIOTIC SONG. Alternative title for *Adams and liberty.*

BOSTON'S MARCH. Boston, Printed & sold at P. A. von Hagen & cos. imported piano forte warehouse, No. 3 Cornhill. And to be had at G. Gilfert, New York [1799–1800] 1 l. 31½ cm.

Pfte. 2 hds., followed by arr. for German flute or violin.
Published probably 1799. ES, LSL, MB

*BOURVILLE CASTLE, or The Gallic orphans.
This play by John Blair Linn, of New York, "a popular poet of the day" (Ireland) was advertised for first performance at New York, on January 16, 1797, with "music composed and compiled" by Benjamin Carr. "Accompaniments" by Victor Pelissier.

In Boston, *Bourville castle* was to be acted on October 27, 1797, with music by Arne and Pelissier's orchestral accompaniments.

BOW WOW WOW, As sung by Mr. Hooke at the Anacreontic society. [n. p., n. d.] [2] p. 33 cm.

Song, pfte. acc.
First line: Sit down neighbours all and I'll tell a merry story.
BM Cat. gives imprint: [New York ? 1783 ?] MB

THE NEW BOW WOW.
See Evening amusement, p. 17.

THE BRANDEWINE.
See Twenty-four American country *Dances*, p. 22.

*BRAVOURA SONG, with variations on the violin, composed by Mr. Boullay.
This song with violin obbligato was performed in a concert at Philadelphia, on July 4, 1796.

BRAYS OF BALENDINE.
See The select songster. New Haven, 1786. p. 21–22.

BRIDE BELLS.
See Evening amusement, p. 27. (Lacking in DLC copy)

BRIGHT CHANTICLEER.
See Old Towler.

[48]

BRIGHT DAWNS THE DAY. A hunting song. Set by a student of the University at Cambridge.
(*In* The Massachusetts magazine. Boston, March, 1789. p. 188–189)

Melody and bass, with accompanying text.
First line same as title. DLC (etc.)

BRIGHT DAWNS THE DAY. A hunting song. Set to music by a student of the University at Cambridge.
(*In* The American musical miscellany. Northampton, 1798. p. 287–291)

Melody and bass, with accompanying text.
First line same as title. DLC (etc.)

BRIGHT PHOEBUS. A favorite hunting song. Composed by Mr. Hook. New York, Printed & sold at J. Hewitt's Musical repository, No. 131 William street. Sold also by B. Carr, Philadelphia, & J. Carr, Baltimore [1797–99] [2] p. 34 cm.

Song, pfte. acc.
First line: Bright Phoebus has mounted the chariot of day.
DLC, ES, JFD, MB, McD–W, MH, NN

—— The same as preceding.
(*In* A collection of new & favorite songs. [A] Philadelphia [ca. 1800] p. [76]–[77]) HFB

—— The same.
(*In* A collection of favorite songs, arr. by A. Reinagle. Philadelphia [1789 ?] p. 11–12)

Song, pfte. acc.
First line same as preceding.
At foot of p. 12: J. Aitken, sculpt.
Sung in Boston as early as October 9, 1788. DLC

—— The same. Philadelphia, Printed and sold by G. Willig, Mark. street, No. 185 [1798–1804] [2] p. 32 cm.

Song, pfte. acc.
First line same as preceding.
Probably published about 1798. DLC, RPJCB

BRIGHT PHOEBUS.
(*In* The American musical miscellany. Northampton, 1798. p. 96–98)

Melody only with accompanying text.
First line same as preceding. DLC (etc.)

[BRIGHT SOL AT LENGTH] A song. The words from a British publication. Set by Philo-Musico.
(*In* The Massachusetts magazine. Boston, February, 1790. p. 123–124)

Song, pfte, acc.
Title from first line. DLC (etc.)
See also *Lovely Stella.*

THE BRITISH MUSE [Melody only]
See The select songster. New Haven, 1786. p. 45.

BROTHER SOLDIERS ALL HAIL. A favorite new patriotic song in honor of Washington. To which is added a toast written & composed by F. Hopkinson, Esqr. Price 37 cents. Printed and sold at B. Carr's musical repository, Philadelphia; J. Carr's Baltimore & J. Hewitt's, N. York [1799]   4 p.   31 cm.

Portrait of Washington mounted in caption. Around portrait: Heav'n has lent him in love to mankind to add a new grace to the earth.
Below imprint: Pianoforte, guittar and clarinett.
Song with chorus, pfte, acc. Arr. for flute or violin, p. 4.
First line same as title.
On p. 4: A toast. Written and composed by Fras. Hopkinson, Esqr.
Song, pfte. acc.
First line: 'Tis Washington's health, fill bumper all round.

ABHu, DLC, LSL, MB, NN

MB copy lacks portrait. In DLC, LSL and NN copies, price has been changed from 32 to 37 cents, the figure 7 being in ink.
On March 25, 1799, Benjamin Carr, Philadelphia, advertised as just published:

> Brother soldiers all hail, new patriotic song in honor of Washington, ornamented with an elegant likeness of the General, to which is added a Toast written and composed by F. Hopkinson, esq.—Price 37 cents.

BROWN'S MARCH.
(In Twelve favorite pieces, arr. by A. Reinagle.   Philadelphia [1789 ?]   p. 3)
Pfte. 2 hds.
At foot of p. 3: J. Aitken, sculqt [!].

DLC

THE BUD OF THE ROSE. A favorite song in Rosina.
(In The Columbian magazine.   Philadelphia, November, 1789.   Between p. 676 and 677)
Song, pfte. acc.
First line: Her mouth which a smile.
Composed by William Shield.

DLC (etc.)

———— Her mouth which a smile. In Rosina.
(In A collection of favorite songs, divided into two parts. Arr. by A. Reinagle.   Philadelphia [1789 ?]   bk. 2, p. 9)
Song, pfte. acc.
First line same as title.
Rosina, by William Shield.

CdeW, DLC, PU

BUNKER HILL. A Sapphick ode.
See A select number of plain tunes . . . by Andrew Law.

THE BUONA FIGUILIOLA [!]
See Twenty-four American country Dances, p. 4.

BUONAPARTE'S GRAND MARCH. New York, Printed & sold at J. Hewitt's Musical repository, No. 23 Maiden Lane [1799–1800] 1 l.   31½ cm.
Pfte. 2 hds.

DLC, JFD, LSL, NN

BUONAPARTES MARCH. New York, Printed & sold by G. Gilfert, No. 177 Broadway [1797–1801] 1 l.   31½ cm.
Pfte. 2 hds.

DLC, MB, McD–W

BUONAPARTE'S MARCH. Composed by C. Kalckbrenner [!] Boston. Printed
& sold by P. A. von Hagen & co., at their Musical magazine, No. 3.
Cornhill [1799–1800] 1 l.   31 cm.
Pfte. 2 hds.
Published probably in 1799.   ES, JFD, LSL

BUONAPARTE'S MARCH, called "The Mantuane," and "Buonaparte's
march," called "The Pyrenees."
See Three new marches.

BURBANKS MARCH.
See Manuscript collection of hymns, songs, etc. (41).

BURGOYNE'S DEFEAT.
See Liberty songs, p. 5–6.

BURR'S GRAND MARCH.
(*With* Ground ivy. Composed by Daniel Marshal. New York, J. and M.
Paff [ca. 1800])
Pfte. 2 hds.   DLC

BY BABY BUNTING. By Hook.
(*In* The musical journal for the flute or violin. Baltimore [1800] no. 19,
p. 40)
Two parts. For flutes or violins (or flute and violin) with accompanying text.
First line same as title.   DLC

[BY THIS FOUNTAIN'S FLOW'RY SIDE] Belville.
(*In* Miscellaneous and incomplete [?] collection. Philadelphia, G. Willig
[ca. 1795] p. 5–6)
Duet, pfte. acc. Followed by chorus.
Title from first line.
Part of Finale, Act I of *Rosina*, by William Shield.   DLC

CA IRA.
(*In* The Philadelphia pocket companion for guittar or clarinett [Philadelphia,
1794] v. 1, p. 29)
Melody only, guitar or clarinet.   MWA

CA IRA.
(*With* President's march [Philip Phile] Philadelphia, 1793–94)
Pfte. 2 hds.   DLC, MdHi, MNSt, NN, PP–K, RPJCB

———— Ah caira [!]
(*In* The gentleman's amusement, ed. by R. Shaw. Philadelphia [1794–96]
p. 37)
Melody only, flute (or violin).
In No. 5, March 1, 1795   DLC, PH

———— The same.
See Evening amusement [1796] p. 21.   DLC

[51]

*THE CALEDONIAN FROLIC.
The ballet-master Francis' "much admired ballad dance" of "The Caledonian frolic" was to be performed at New York, on May 20, 1795, "with a new overture and music adapted to the piece" by Benjamin Carr. The pantomime was "composed" by Francis in 1794 for performance in Philadelphia.

THE CALEDONIAN HUNT.
(*In* The gentleman's amusement, ed. by R. Shaw. Philadelphia [1794-96] p. 81)

Melody only, flute (or violin).
Followed by "The fife hunt."
In No. 10, ca. 1796. PHi, PP-K

THE CALEDONIAN HUNT with variations. Printed & sold by Dr. G. K. Jackson, Boston [ca. 1800?] [3] p. 29 cm. (apparently trimmed)

Pfte. 2 hds. PP-K

THE CALEDONIAN LADDY. Printed for B. Carr & sold at his Musical repositorys in Philadelphia & New York & by I. Carr, Baltimore.
(*In* The favorite songs, by Mr. Hook. Philadelphia [1794-95] p. 2-3)

Song, pfte. acc. Arr. for "guittar," p. 3.
First line: Blithe Sandy is a bonny boy.

McD-W, MdHi, MWA, NN

———— Separate issue of preceding, ca. 1796. DLC, LSL, RPJCB

———— The same as preceding.
(*In* A collection of new & favorite songs. [A] Philadelphia [ca. 1800] p. [28]–[29]) HFB

THE CALEDONIAN LADDY. A new Scotch song. Composed by Mr. Hook. New York, Printed for and sold at I. C. Moller's musical store, No. 58 Vesey street [1797] 1 l. 27½ cm. (trimmed)

Song, pfte. acc., followed by instrumental arr.
First line same as preceding. NN

THE CALEDONIAN LADDY. A Scotch song. Composed by Hook. Printed by G. Willig, Philadelphia [ca. 1800] 1 l. 30 cm.

Song, pfte. acc.
First line same as preceding.
Sung in Philadelphia in 1800. NN

THE CALEDONIAN LADDY. Composed by Mr. Hook. Printed and sold by R. Shaw at his music store, South Fourth street, Philadelphia (Price 25 cents) [n. d.] [2] p. 34 cm.

Song, pfte. acc.
First line same as preceding.
Published possibly as early as 1800. DLC, ES, MB, McD-W, RPJCB

THE CALEDONIAN MAID.
See Arabella, the Caledonian maid.

[52]

*THE CALEDONIAN MUSE.
We read in the *Federal gazette*, Baltimore, April 13, 1798: Just published and for sale at J. Carr's Music store, Gay-street. A new edition of the CALEDONIAN MUSE, with additions, being a collection of one hundred and thirty Scotch Songs, Reels, Strathspays, and ancient and modern, adapted for the voice, pianoforte and violin, most of them in compass of the German flute, with a dissertation on the Scotch music, and a glossary, embellished with a beautiful title plate, engraved by Edwin, describing the infancy of Scotch music, price bound, 6 dollars, unbound, 5 dollars and 40 cents.

CALL FREEDOM TRIUMPHANT.
See Freedom triumphant.

CALM THE WINDS. Sung in the opera of the Turnpike gate. Composed by J. Mazzinghi. New York, Printed & sold at J. & M. Paff's musical store, No. 127 Broadway [1799–1803] 3 p. 31 cm.

Song, pfte. acc.
First line same as title.
Probably not published until after 1800, as the first American performance of *The turnpike gate* seems to have been in New York in 1801. NN

*THE CAMP.
Song. Advertised at New York in August, 1798, as "just published."

CAN I MY COMELY TURK FORGET.
See Chica cho.

CANCHERIZANTE. A song to be sung forwards & then backwards beginning at the last note & ending with the first. Composed by Dr. G. K. Jackson. Printed for the Author. Copyright secured.
(*In* New miscellaneous musical work, by Dr. G. K. Jackson [n. p., ca. 1800] p. 9)

Song, pfte. acc.
First line: The groves, the plains, the nymphs. DLC, MWA

——— Separate issue of preceding, ca. 1800. MWA

A CANTATA. The Nightingale, by R. Taylor.
See The Nightingale.

CANZONET. Jackson.
(*In* Six songs by Mrs. Pownall and J. Hewitt. New York [1794] p. 17–19)

Duet, pfte. acc. Three staves.
First line: Time has not thin'd my flowing hair.
Composed by William Jackson of Exeter. ES, HFB

——— Separate issue of preceding, ca. 1794. DLC, McD-W, NN

——— The same as preceding.
(*In* A collection of new & favorite songs. [A] Philadelphia [ca. 1800] p. [128]–[130] numbered 17–19) HFB

[53]

CANZONET. Adapted to one voice. Composed by W. Jackson.
(*In* A collection of favorite songs, divided into two books. Arr. by A. Reinagle. Philadelphia [1789 ?] bk. 2, p. 22–23)

Song, pfte. acc.
First line: Time has not thin'd my flowing hair. CdeW, DLC, PU

CANZONETT. By Jackson of Exeter.
(*In* The musical journal for the flute or violin. Baltimore, [1800] no. 5, p. 10–12)

Duet for flutes or violins (or flute and violin) with accompanying text.
First line: Love in thy eyes forever plays. DLC

CANZONETT. With an accompanyment.
(*In* The Philadelphia pocket companion for guitar or clarinet [Philadelphia, 1794] v. 1, p. 34–37)

Song, guitar or clarinet acc.
First line: Soft music let my humble lay.
Composed by Richard Suett (*BM Cat.*) MWA

*CANZONETTI, composed by a lady of Philadelphia.
Sonneck assigns this title to the First of Moller and Capron's Monthly numbers, but it has been impossible to locate it there.

THREE OF THE MOST ADMIR'D CANZONETTS by Haydn. Viz., The mermaids song, The knitting girl & My mother bids me bind my hair. Price 62 cents. Or in single sheets at one quarter dollar each canzonett. Printed and sold at B. Carr's musical repository, Philadelphia; J. Carr's, Baltimore & J. Hewitts, New York. Shortly will be published Three ballads composed by B. Carr & Musical bagatelles or Six little ballads selected from some late English publications [1799] 7 p. 32 cm. NN (Lacks p. 7)

Advertised in August, 1799, Baltimore, as for sale at J. Carr's music store among "music lately published."

*CAPOCCHIO AND DORINNA.
This "mock Italian opera . . . dressed in character . . . consisting of recitative, airs and duets," was to be performed in Annapolis, Md., January 20, 1793, at Raynor "Taylor's musical performance . . . the whole of the music original and composed by Mr. Taylor."

CAPTAIN MONEY'S MARCH.
See Compleat tutor for the fife . . . p. 15.

CAPTAIN OAKER'S WHIM.
See Twenty-four American country *Dances*, p. 11.

CAPT. O'BLUNDER. By Swan.
(*In* The songster's assistant, ed. by T. Swan. Suffield [ca. 1800] p. 35–36)
Song, pfte. acc.
First line: Wherever I'm going and all the day long. CtY, MB

CAPTAIN REED'S, or the Third Regiment of Guards march.
See Compleat tutor for the fife . . . p. 19.

CAPT. TRUXTON, or Huzza for the Constellation. Sung by Mr. Tyler at the Theatre with the greatest applause. New York, Printed & sold at J. Hewitts Musical repository, No. 131 William street. Sold also by B. Carr, Philadelphia & J. Carr, Baltimore. Price 25 cents [1799] [2] p. 32 cm.

Song, pfte. acc.
First line: Ye jovial tars now lend an ear.

From internal historical evidence (battle between the *Constellation* and *Insurgente*, February 9, 1799) to be dated not earlier than March, 1799.

DLC, MNSt

——— The same as preceding.

(*In* A collection of new & favorite songs. [A] Philadelphia [ca. 1800] p. [20]–[21])   HFB

——— Huzza for the Constellation. Sung by Mr. Fox at the Theatre. Printed & sold at B. Carr's Musical repository, Philadelphia; J. Carr's, Baltimore & J. Hewitt's, N. York (Price 32 cts.) Secured according to law. [1799] 3 p. 30½ cm.

Vignette of fighting ships above title.
Song, pfte. acc.   Arr. for flute or violin, p. 3.
First line: Come join my hearts in jovial glee.
Alternative title of *Capt⁹ Truxton*. Music essentially identical. Different text.
Advertised in March, 1799, to be published shortly by Benjamin Carr.

Gilbert Fox (1776–1807 ?) actor, singer, engraver.

DLC, ICN, LSL, MdHi

THE CAPTIVE. New York, Printed for and sold at J. C. Moller's musical store, No. 58 Vesey street [1797] [2] p.   32½ cm.

Song, pfte. acc.
First line: Be hush my soul, for heav'n prepare.
Composed by John Percy (*BM Cat.*)   DLC

*THE CAPTIVE OF SPILBERG.
This "favorite romance" was advertised in June, 1799, as published by "P. A. Von Hagen, jun. and Co. Musical Magazine.   No. 3 Cornhill," Boston.

CAPTIVITY.   A ballad supposed to be sung by Marie Antoinette during her confinement. Composed by Storace. Price 20 cents. Philadelphia, Printed for Carr & co., at their Musical repository, No. 136 High street [1793] [2] p. 32½ cm.

Song, pfte. acc.   Arr. for flute, p. [2].
First line: My foes prevail, my friends are fled.

DLC, HFB, LSL, McD-W, MWA

THE CAPTURE.   A favorite song in the Pirates. Composed by S. Storace. Philadelphia, Printed at Carr & co's Musical repository, No. 136 High street. (*In* The favorite songs from the Pirates, by S. Storace.   Philadelphia [1793] p. (10)–(12).)

Song, pfte. acc.
First line: Scarcely had the blushing morn.   HFB

——— Separate issue of preceding, 1793.   DLC, Hopk.

[55]

THE CAPTURE. A favorite song in the Pirates.
(*In* The Musical repertory. Boston. [1796–97] No. III, p. 45–47)

Song, pfte. acc.
First line same as preceding.
The pirates, by Stephen Storace.   DLC (lacks p. 47)

—— Separate issue of preceding (complete, p. 45–47), ca. 1796.   ES

LA CARMAGNOLE. Price 25 cents. Philadelphia, Printed at Carr & co's
Musical repository [1794] [4] p. 31 cm.

Song, pfte. acc. Followed by arr. for "guittar."
First line: Le cannon vient de re'sonner.

This famous song of the French Revolution was advertised in June, 1794, as
published by "Carr & Co. Musical Repository, No. 122 Market Street."
           DLC, PU

LA CARMAGNOLE. New York, Printed for James Hewitt. Pr. 2/. [ca.
1794] [2] p. 33½ cm.

Song, pfte. acc., French text.
First line: Madame Veto avait promis.   MWA

Advertised in New York, March 29, 1794, as "just published . . . the
celebrated French national air, La Carmagnole to be had of J. Hewitt,
Greenwich street, near the Battery."

—— Carmagnole.
See Evening amusement [1796] p. 18.

CARO BENE. Del Sigr. Sarti. Philadelphia, Printed for A. Reinagle.I. Aitken,
sculpt.
(*In* A collection of favorite songs, arr. by A. Reinagle. Philadelphia [1789?]
p. 21–22)

Imprint at foot of p. 22.
Song, pfte. acc.
First line same as title.   DLC

—— Separate issue of preceding (without pagination), 1789(?).
           DLC, ES, NN
The DLC copy is contained in a volume of vocal and instrumental music once
belonging to Nellie Custis.

THE FAVORITE CAROL. Sung in the Adopted child, a muscal [!] drama.
New York, Printed for G. Gilfert & co. at their Musical magazine, No. 177
Broadway [1796] 1 l. 31½ cm.

Song, pfte. acc. Three staves.
First line: Thro' forests drear I once did stray.
The adopted child, by Thomas Attwood, first performed in New York, May
23, 1796.   MWA

*THE CASTLE OF OTRANTO. Altered from "The Sicilian romance." Music
and accompaniments by Victor Pelissier.

This version of William Reeve's "celebrated musical romance" (1794) was
advertised for performance at New York on November 7, 1800.

[56]

THE CASTLE SPECTRE. A drama in five acts. By M. G. Lewis, esq., M. P. author of The Monk, &c., now performing with unbounded applause at the Theatre in Boston. Sold at the bookstore, No. 56 Cornhill [1798] 70 p. 17 cm.

Libretto.
Title-page. Verso, dramatis personae; text, p. [3]–70.   MWA

THE CASTLE SPECTRE. A drama in five acts. By M. G. Lewis, esq., M. P. Author of "The monk," &c. As performed with unbounded applause at the theatres in Boston, Salem, Printed for Bernard B. Macanulty, 1799. 92 p. 19½ cm.

Libretto.
Title-page; dramatis personae, p. [2]; text, p. [3]–92. Whether Michael Kelly's music for *The Castle spectre* was used at all in these American perform-ances we do not know.   CSmH, DLC, MWA, RPB, RPJCB

A CATCH FOR THREE VOICES.
(*In* The Philadelphia songster, ed. by A. Aimwell [pseud.] Philadelphia, 1789. p. 5)

Melody only, with accompanying text.
First line: How great is the pleasure.   NN

A CATCH FOR THREE VOICES. Suitable for three ladies.
(*In* The Massachusetts magazine. Boston, April, 1792. p. 267)

Melody only, with accompanying text.
First line: If 'tis joy to wound a lover.   DLC (etc.)

*THE CAVE OF ENCHANTMENT, or, The Stockwell wonder.
With "music selected and composed by Mr. [John] Bentley" this "superb pantomine entertainment never before attempted in this city" was performed at New York, on August 25, 1785.

CEASE A WHILE YE WINDS TO BLOW. A favorite rondo by Sr. Bach [Phila-delphia] Publish'd by G. Willig, 165 Market st. [1795–97] [2] p. 30½ cm.

Song, pfte. acc.
First line same as title.
Sonneck adds: Composed by Raynor Taylor, the song was sung at a concert, Philadelphia, June 6, 1798.
Sr. Bach: Johann Christian Bach.   DLC, ES

A CELEBRATED DUETT IN ARTAXERXES.
See Fair Aurora.

THE CELEBRATED MARCH IN BLUE BEARD.
See The celebrated *March* in Blue Beard.

THE CELEBRATED OVERTURE TO LODOISKA.
See The celebrated *Overture* to Lodoiska.

A CENT'RY AGO. A favorite song.
(*In* A collection of favorite songs, by Mr. Hook. New York [1799–1801] bk. [1] p. 6–7)

Song, pfte. acc.
First line: Tother day as I sat by the green willow tree.   DLC

CHANTONS L'HYMEN. Cambini.
(*In* The Musical journal for the flute or violin. Baltimore [1800] no. 10, p. 18–19)

Duet for flutes or violins (or flute and violin). DLC

CHARITY.
See Favorite *Cotillions.*

*THE CHARMER. Being a select collection of English, Scotch and American songs, including the modern; with a selection of favorite toasts and sentiments. Philadelphia: Printed and sold by W. Spotswood, Front-street, between Market and Chesnut-streets, 1790.

THE CHARMING CREATURE. Set by H. J.
(*In* The Massachusetts magazine, Boston, April, 1790. p. 253–254)

Song, pfte. acc.
First line: As 'tother day in harmless chat. DLC (etc.)

———— The same.
(*In* The American musical miscellany. Northampton, 1798. p. 176–178)

Melody and bass, with accompanying text.
First line same as preceding.
Reprinted in Henry M. Brooks' *Olden time music,* Boston, 1888. p. 153–154.
DLC (etc.)

THE CHARMS OF FLOREMEL.
(*In* The songster's assistant, ed. by T. Swan. Suffield [ca. 1800] p. 16)

Song, pfte. acc.
First line same as title. MB

*THE CHARMS OF MELODY. A new collection of songs. Philadelphia: Printed for Thomas Seddon, 1788.

*THE CHARMS OF MELODY: A choice collection of the most approved songs, catches, duets, &c. Philadelphia: Printed for Mathew Carey, 1794.

Advertised November 28, 1794.

THE CHARMS OF MUSIC.
(*In* Nine new songs, by I. B. Gauline. Philadelphia [ca. 1800] p. 1–2)

Song, pfte. acc.
First line: Breathe soft fair maid.
I. B. Gauline: John B. Gauline. ES, MdHi

THE CHARMS OF NATURE (Being a solution of Thec. Ha!, R. M. sofna Ture, published last month) Set by Philo-musico.
(*In* The Massachusetts magazine. Boston, March, 1790. p. 189)

Melody and bass, with accompanying text.
First line: The cheek enros'd with crimson dye. DLC (etc.)

THE CHARMS OF NATURE.
(*In* The American musical miscellany. Northampton, 1798. p. 263–264)

Melody and bass, with accompanying text.
First line same as preceding. DLC (etc.)

[58]

LA CHASSE. Allegro. Del Sigr. Campioni.
(*In* Twelve favorite pieces, arr. by A. Reinagle. Philadelphia [1789 ?] p. 1–2)

Pfte. 2 hds.
Sigr. Campioni: Carlo Antonio Campioni.
Performed at William Brown's benefit concert, Philadelphia, February 13, 1787.   DLC

—— Separate issue of preceding, without pagination, 1789.   CdeW

This is presumably the edition advertised in March, 1789, among other "songs and pieces arranged for the pianoforte or harpsichord by Alexander Reinagle" as "just published and sold by Thomas Dobson," Philadelphia.

LA CHASSE. Rossette [!] Adapted by J. Hewitt.
(*In* Six songs, by Mrs. Pownall and J. Hewitt. New York [1794] p. 1–8)

Pfte. 2 hds.
On p. 5: A la chasse. Allegro.
Rossette: Francesco Antonio Rossetti.   ES, HFB

LA CHASSE. A new lesson for the pianoforte. Composed in an easy familiar stile [!] by A. Reinagle. Price 20 cents. Philadelphia, Printed at Carr & cos. Musical repository [ca. 1794] [2] p. 33 cm.

Pfte. 2 hds.
At foot of p. [1]: No. 3. Jan. 20, 94.
Advertised in January, 1794, as published by "B. Carr & co. Musical repository, No. 122 Southside Market street," Philadelphia.   ES

—— The same as preceding.
(*In* A collection of new & favorite songs. [A] Philadelphia [ca. 1800] p. [196]–[197])   HFB

LA CHASSE. New York, Printed for P. Weldon [ca. 1800] [2] p. 32 cm.

Pfte. 2 hds.
Both pages marked with "I" at upper left hand corner and middle of lower margin.
Composed by Reinagle.   MWA

FAVORITE LA CHASSE. Composed by I. C. Moller [n. p., ca. 1800] [2] p. 32½ cm.
Pfte. 2 hds.   DLC, NBuG, RPJCB

—— The same [n. p., n. d.] [2] p. 33 cm.

Pfte. 2 hds.
Because of its strong similarity to certain issues of I. C. Moller in New York, particularly as regards its bass clef (*cf.* The President's march), this issue can presumably be ascribed to that publisher and place. Sonneck dates these Moller issues ca. 1800.   DLC

[THE CHEERFULL SPRING BEGINS TODAY] A new favorite song by a lady of Philada.
(*In* [Moller & Capron's Monthly numbers] The first number [Philadelphia. 1793] p. 7)

Song, pfte. acc.
Title from first line.

[59]

The same text but not identical with *Arise my fair*, Boston, P. A. von Hagen [ca. 1800] (*q. v.*)   DLC

THE CHEERING ROSARY. Sung with great applause in the new opera of the Midnight wanderers. Composed by Mr. Shield. Price 20 cents. Philadelphia, Printed at Carr & co's Musical repository [1793] [2] p. 33 cm.

Song, pfte. acc. Arr. for flute, p. [2].
First line: Tho' oft we meet severe distress.
In certain copies, *e. g.*, NN, "20" has been changed to "25" in price given.
Advertised as published in December, 1793.
ABHu, DLC, ES, Hopk., JFD, LSL, MB, McD–W, MdHi, NBuG, NN,
                                                                                                                          RPJCB

THE CHEERING ROSARY. New York, Published by I. and M. Paff, No. 127 Broadway [1799–1803] 1 l. 32½ cm.

Song, pfte. acc.
First line same as preceding.   ABHu, DLC, ES

——— The same. [n. p., 179–?] 1 l. 31½ cm.   NBuG

——— The same.
New York, Printed & sold at J. Hewitt's Musical repository, No. 23 Maiden Lane.
(*In* A collection of new & favorite songs. [A] Philadelphia [ca. 1800] p. [167])   HFB

——— The rosary. A ballad in the comic opera of the Midnight wanderers Composed by Mr. Shield.
(*In* The musical repertory. Boston [1796] No. I, p. (8).)

Song, pfte. acc.
First line same as preceding.   DLC, MB, NRU–Mus

——— Separate issue of preceding, ca. 1796.   ES

——— The rosary.
(*In* The American musical miscellany. Northampton, 1798. p. 98–99)

Melody only, with accompanying text.
First line same as preceding.   DLC (etc.)

The midnight wanderers was first produced in Philadelphia, June 1, 1796.

CHELMER'S BANKS. Sung by Miss Huntley. Composed by R. Taylor.
(*In* Young's vocal and instrumental musical miscellany. Philadelphia [1793–95] p. 36)

Song, pfte. acc.
First line: From Chelmer's banks why flies my swain.
In No. 5, 1793.   DLC, Hopk.

THE CHERRY GIRL. A favorite ballad. Composed by T. Costellow. [Philadelphia] Printed for I. C. Moller, No. 163 North Third street. Where may be had a great variety of new vocal and instrumental music &c. [1793] [2] p. 32 cm.

Song, pfte. acc.
First line: Sweet cowslips I cry.   ES, NBuG

[60]

―――― The same as preceding, except that in the imprint, "I. C. Moller, No. 163 North Third" has been erased and "G. Willig, Market" substituted The original word "Third" is still legible. This altered imprint may be dated 1795–1804, as Willig was located on Market street during those years. However, it is probably nearer 1795 than the later date.   MWA

THE CHERRY GIRL. A favorite song. Composed by T. Costelow. Printed by B. Carr & sold at his Musical repositories, New York & Philadelphia & by I. Carr, Baltimore. Price 20 cents. [ca. 1796] [2] p. 33 cm.

Song, pfte. acc. Arr. for "guittar," p. [2].
First line same as preceding.
Sung in New York, August 1, 1798.   ABHu, DLC, MWA

THE CHESAPEAKE.
See Mr. *Francis's ballroom assistant.*

―――― The Chesapeak [!]
See No. 1 of a new sett of *Cotilions* [!]

CHESTER.
(*In* The singing master's assistant, by William Billings. Boston, 1778. p. 12)

Four-part chorus. Open score.

Text:
   Let tyrants shake their iron rod,
   And Slav'ry clank her galling chains,
   We fear them not, we trust in God,
   New-England's God forever reigns.

   Howe and Burgoyne and Clinton too,
   With Prescott and Cornwallis join'd,
   Together plot our Overthrow,
   In one Infernal league combin'd.

   When God inspir'd us for the fight,
   Their ranks were broke, their lines were forc'd,
   Their Ships were Shatter'd in our sight,
   Or swiftly driven from our Coast.

   The Foe comes on with haughty Stride,
   Our troops advance with martial noise,
   Their Vet'rans flee before our Youth,
   And Gen'rals yield to beardless Boys.

   What grateful Off'ring shall we bring?
   What shall we render to the Lord?
   Loud Halleluiahs let us sing,
   And praise his name on ev'ry Chord.

This was one of the popular war songs of the American Revolution.

                CSmH. DLC, ICN, MB, MH, MHi, MWA

CHICA CHO. Sung by Miss Arnold in Blue Beard. Printed & sold at B. Carr's Musical repository, Philadelphia; J. Carr's Baltimore & J. Hewitt's, New York. (Pr. 12 cent)
(*In* A collection of new & favorite songs. [C] Philadelphia [ca. 1799] p. 8)
Song, pfte. acc.
First line: His sparkling eyes were dark as jet.
Blue Beard, by Michael Kelly. First performance in Philadelphia, May 24, 1799. Miss Arnold as Beda. ABHu, LSL, NN

———— Separate issue of preceding, ca. 1799. ICN, MdHi, RPJCB

———— Can I my comely Turk forget. A favorite song. New York, Printed and sold by G. Gilfert, No. 177 Broadway [1797–1801] [2] p. 32 cm.
Song, pfte. acc.
First line: His sparkling eyes were dark as jet. MWA

THE CHILDREN IN THE WOOD.
Samuel Arnold's popular opera, libretto by Thomas Morton (1793), was advertised for performance at Philadelphia on November 24, 1794, as "a new musical piece in two acts, never acted in America . . . with accompaniments and additional songs" by Benjamin Carr.

In March, 1795, was advertised:

THE CHILDREN IN THE WOOD. A musical piece in two acts. With the additions and alterations, as performed by the Old American Company. New York. Printed at the Columbian Press, by Robertson and Gowan, for Benjamin Gomez, bookseller and stationer, No. 97, Maiden-Lane, 1795. 57, [2] p., front. 17 cm.
Libretto.
Frontispiece: Children in the woods. Scolex, sc. Mr. Hodgkinson as Walter and Mr. Lee as Oliver.
Title-page, verso blank; dramatis personae, p. 3; text, p. [5]–57; advertisement, Benjamin Gomez, p. [59].
DLC, NN, PU (lacks front.), RPB, RPJCB

The overture to the opera was advertised in March, 1795, as "published and to be had at G. Willig's Musical Magazine, No. 165 Market street," Philadelphia.

THE CHILDREN IN THE WOOD. A musical piece in two acts. With the additions and alterations, as performed at Boston. Boston, Printed at the office of Jno. and Jos. N. Russell, Quaker Lane. Sold at the Boston bookstore, No. 59 Cornhill [1795] 30, [1] p. 12 mo.
Libretto. CtY, MWA

THE CHILDREN IN THE WOOD. A musical piece, in two acts. With the additions and alterations, as performed in Boston. Boston, Printed and sold at the office of Jno. and Jos. N. Russell, Quaker Lane; also sold at the several bookstores in town [n. d.] 30 p. 16 cm.
Libretto.
Sonneck says, "Published, as may be inferred from the *dramatis personae* on p. 3, in 1796." But Evans (29115) gives the date 1795. MWA, RPB

[62]

THE CHILDREN IN THE WOOD. A musical piece in two acts. With the additions and alterations as performed at Boston. Boston, Printed at the office of Jno. and Jos. N. Russell, Quaker Lane. Sold at John West's Book store, No. 75 Cornhill [n. d.] 30 p. 12 mo.

Libretto.
Title-page, verso blank; 1 l.; text, p. [5]–30.
Published probably 1795–96.   JFD

*THE CHILDREN IN THE WOOD. A musical entertainment as performed at the Theatre. Boston, Printed and sold by Alexander Martin at the printing office over Major Hawes's shop, Quaker-Lane. 1795.

Not located.

See also "Songs, duets and chorusses, of the Children in the Wood" (words only).

A CHOICE COLLECTION OF FREE MASONS SONGS.
See A choice *Collection* of Free Masons songs.

CHORUS SUNG BEFORE GEN. WASHINGTON as he passed under the triumphal arch raised on the bridge at Trenton, April 21th [!] 1789. Set to music and dedicated by permission to Mrs. Washington by A. Reinagle. Price ½ dollar. Philadelphia. Printed for the Author, and sold by H. Rice, Market street. C. Tiebout, sculp. [1789] 2 p. l., 4 p. 32½ cm.

Title-page, verso blank; text and narrative, headed *chorus*, second p. l.; music, p. 1–4. Recto of second p. l., recto of p. 1, and verso of p. 4, blank.
At foot of p. 4: I. Aitken, sculpt.
Three-part chorus, pfte. acc. Open score.
First line: Welcome Mighty Chief once more.   DLC

Sonneck comments.:

Copies of the original seem to be extremely scarce. I failed to trace the piece in any of the libraries visited.

A startling query: Was this the chorus really sung before Washington on Trenton bridge? For the following reasons I believe not:

1. In the printed title a distinction may be read between *"chorus sung,"* which seems to mean "words sung" and *"set to music."*

2. They were sung before Washington on April 21, whereas Reinagle's composition was advertised in the *Pennsylvania packet*, Philadelphia, December 29, 1789, as "just published." An unusual interval between performance and publication!

3. The "plan" of the New York Subscription Concert, September 22, 1789, as advertised in the *Daily advertiser*, September 15, contains this passus:

"After the first act, will be performed a *chorus, to the words* that were sung as Gen. Washington passed the bridge at Trenton.—The music NOW composed by Mr. Reinagle."

4. Reingle's piece is engraved for "2 voice. 1 voice. 3 voice." with pf. acc. apparently reduced from orchestral acc. The 3. voice stands in the

[63]

bass clef and the whole is composed for either a mixed chorus or a 3-part male chorus; at any rate certainly not for female voices only. But the *Sonata*, as the orginal chorus was called in all the contemporaneous newspaper accounts, was sung *"by a number of young girls,"* and of a band or orchestra assisting on the occasion and accompanying the singers no mention is made.

The inference is plain. If therefore, Reinagle's music was not sung on April 21, 1789, whose was? This leads to Philip Phile and his problematic connection with the origin of "Hail Columbia."

(For particulars *see* Sonneck's *Critical notes on the origin of Hail Columbia*, Sammelbände d. Int. Mus. Ges. 1901–2. In this connection reference should also be made to Sonneck's *Report on the Star-spangled Banner, Hail Columbia [etc.]*, 1909,) p. 62 f.)

Reverting to the matter of the Chorus, Sonneck has written in the margin of his own copy of the *Bibliography* as follows:

Dr. C. E. Godfrey found that in *The New Jersey Journal*, Elizabeth, N. J., May 6, 1789, a correspondent under date of May 6, 1789, says that the tune was (Handel's) "See the conquering hero comes." *See* Godfrey's article "Washington's Reception by the Ladies of Trenton," *Trenton Sunday Advertiser*, December 29, 1912. The words and music fit perfectly. G. arranged the piece, acting on my suggestion, according to Chrysander's version.

The following interesting note is to be found in *The American Songster*, Providence, 1807, p. 269 (MWA, NBuG, RPB):

When President Washington arrived in the City of Trenton, in New Jersey, on his way to New York, a Triumphal Arch was erected, and elegantly decorated by the Ladies of Trenton. Upon his coming under the Arch, he was met by Twelve Young Ladies dressed in white, arranged on each side of the Arch, with each a basket of Flowers, which, while they strewed them before him, a Band of Music played a popular air—which occasioned the following stanzas:
The beauties of Flora delightfully blooming, the ladies of Trenton arranging, display'd; [etc.]

This "popular air" is supposed to have been Philip Phile's *President's March*, later used as the tune for *Hail Columbia*. Could this tune, after all, have been what was sung as well as played?

——— The same as preceding, except that it has on verso of p. 4: Faederal march (pfte. 2 hds.). *Chorus* lacks 2 p.l.   CdeW, McD–W

[CHORUSES FROM THE MILITARY GLORY OF GREAT BRITAIN]
Introductory chorus (Allegro) Triumphant fame ascends the skies.
Chorus 2 (Allegro): Gallia's sons shall vaunt no more.
Chorus 3d (Largo): Propitious Powers who guard our state.
Chorus 4th (Piu allegro): Glory, triumph, vict'ry, fame forever crown Britannia's name.
Chorus 5th (Tune of Chorus 3d): While mountains poise the balanced globe.

As to James Lyon's possible authorship of these Choruses, *cf.* Sonneck: *Francis Hopkinson . . . and James Lyon*, p. 129–130.

CSmH, CtY, DLC, NN, PHi, Princeton U, RPB

[64]

A CHRISTMAS HYMN. The words by Mr. Harrison and composed by Mr. Page. New York, Printed by James Harrison at his music warehouse in [108] Maiden Lane, where may be had the greatest variety of new songs and music of all kinds [1794] [2] p. 32 cm.

Song, pfte. acc. Arr. for guitar, p. [2].
First line: See the morning star appear. ES

Advertised in December, 1794, as "published by James Harrison . . . 108 Maidenlane," New York, "A Christmas hymn. Composed by Mr. Page, adapted for the harpsichord, pianoforte, harp, violin, German flute and guitar."

CLEMENTI'S GRAND WALTZ. Philadelphia, Printed for G. Willig and sold at his Musical magazine [179– ?] 1 l. 31½ cm.

Pfte. 2 hds.
Clementi: Muzio Clementi. Hopk., NN

*CLIO AND EUTERPE, a collection of celebrated songs and cantatas, set to musick by the most approved masters. With thorough bass for the harpsichord, and transposition for the German flute; containing near 600 airs.

Thus advertised in October, 1763, in *Rivington's New York gazette* as published. It is remarked that

It would exceed the usual limits of an advertisement to give the titles of the songs in this place, but the public may depend upon finding all the best modern English and Scots compositions, and such as are the favourites of all lovers of musick.

THE CLOCK OF LOMBARDY, or the Surrender of Milan to General Buonaparte. Capriccio for the forte piano. Composed and published by Sigʳ Trisobio. For sale by the Author at No 66 North Front Street, Philadelphia. Price one dollar [1796–98] 1 p. l., 10 p. 32 cm.

Title-page (printed, with elaborate border), verso blank; music (p.1– 10) engraved.
Pfte. 2 hds.
Consists of twelve descriptive episodes.
Milan surrendered in May, 1795. CdeW

If one wishes to study the published output of Filippo Trisobio—that itinerant Italian musician of whom so little is actually known—he will find most, if not all of this material (with the exception of the *Scuola del canto*, published "For the Author" in London in 1795 [*BM Cat.*] and also mentioned by Eitner) in one of two volumes formerly belonging to Nellie Custis and now in Mrs de Windt's possession. There are other copies of a few of these issues scattered about, but here we find all ten of them together. Of these, *Fair Aurora* seems most certainly to have been engraved in England. Its general appearance and particularly its figured bass, bear clear testimony to this fact. *Water parted from the sea, Did not tyrant custom guide me,* and certain other issues, although they lack any figured bass, seem more English than American. Trisobio's imprint rarely conforms to the rest of the plate and one is tempted to think that many of these plates were originally brought from England and the imprint added here. *Pour bien juger une maitresse,* while similar to the others in general style is distinctly inferior in workmanship and quite apparently was engraved in the United States. *A poor little gypsy*, even without its full Philadelphia imprint, would be recognized as a typical American issue of its period. *The clock of Lombardy*, with its peculiar combination of printed title-page and engraved music, is definitely a local issue—at least as far as its title-page is concerned. The similarity of *Par sa legéreté* to *La marmotte* justifies the assumption that they are both Trisobio issues. In short, we find Trisobio's publications almost as vague and indefinite as his own wanderings.

We note that after Trisobio's death in 1798, G. Willig acquired at least some of his plates (*cf. Fair Aurora*).

THE CLOSE OF THE YEAR.
(*In* Harmonia Americana, by Samuel Holyoke. Boston, 1791. p. 56)

Three-part chorus with treble solo. Open score, four staves.
First line: So fly our months and years.
CSmH, DLC, ICN, MB, MH, MWA, NHi, NN, RPJCB

COLD STREAM or Second Regiment of Guards march.
See Compleat tutor for the fife . . . p. 18.

THIRD COLDSTREAM MARCH.
See Military amusement, p. 12–13.

COLINET AND PHEBE.
See The select songster. New Haven, 1786. p. 41–42.

A COLLECTION OF AIRS for three or two performers on the piano forte.
Selected and arranged by J. Willson. [New York] Sold by J. & M. Paff, Broadway & J. Hewitt's, Maiden Lane [1799–1803] 15 p. 33 cm.

Title-page; music, p. 2–15.
Pfte., four or six hds.
Contents: No. 1, Andantino, p. 2–7.—No. 2, Grazioso, p. 8–11.—No. 3, Allegretto, p. 12–15. NN

*A COLLECTION OF CONTRA DANCES, containing a hundred and forty fashionable figures. Hanover: Printed by Dunham and True, 1796.

A COLLECTION OF CONTRA DANCES of late, approved, and fashionable figures. Walpole [N. H.] Printed at the Museum press. And sold at the Walpole bookstore, 1799. 12 p. 17½ cm. MWA

*A COLLECTION OF COUNTRY DANCES. By Mons. St. Vellum, a French dancing master. Walpole, Newhampshire: Printed by Isaiah Thomas and David Carlisle, jun., 1795.

*A COLLECTION OF COUNTRY DANCES and cotillions with their proper figures for the pianoforte and violin, price 75 cents.

Advertised by J. Carr, Baltimore, in September, 1797, among "music lately published."

A COLLECTION OF FAVORITE SONGS. Arranged for the voice and pianoforte by A. Reinagle. Book [ ]. Philadelphia, Printed for A. Reinagle. [1789 ?] 1 p. l., 22 p. 32½ cm.

Title-page, verso blank; music, p. 1–22; recto of p. 1 and verso p. 22, blank.

On title-page, in blank space after the word *Book*, there appears what seems to be a faintly distinguishable ms. Roman numeral, II.

At foot of p. 4: Philadelphia, Sold by H. Rice, Market street.

At foot of p. 4, 6, 8, 10, 12, 20, 22: I. Aitken. Sculpt.

At foot of p. 18: John Aitken. Sculpt.

At foot of p. 20, 22: Philadelphia, Printed for A. Reinagle.

Probably printed by Thomas Dobson in 1789, as two songs in this collection, *In vain fond youth,* and *The soldier tir'd* are advertised in March, 1789, as included among other "songs and pieces arranged for the piano forte or harpsichord by Alexander Reinagle . . . just published and sold by Thomas Dobson at the Stone House in Second street," Philadelphia.

Contents:

p. 1–4 Ah seek to know. A favorite song. Composed by I. C. Bach. Arranged for the piano forte by A. Reinagle.

5–6 The tear. A favorite song. Composed by J. Hook. Sung by Mrs. Leaver at Vauxhall.

7–8 Ma chere amie. A favorite song. Written by a lady and set to music by Mr. Hook.

9 The streamlet. A favorite new song in the Woodman. Composed by W. Sheild [!]

10 Sylvia. A favorite canzonett. Composed by T. Billington.

11–12 Bright Phoebus. A favorite hunting song. Composed by Mr. Hook.

13 [What med'cine can soften the bosom's keen smart] A favorite song in the Chaplet. Composed by Dr. Boyce.

14–16 The soldier tir'd. Compos'd by Dr. Arne.

17–18 [For tenderness form'd] A favorite song in the Heiress. Composed by Sigr. Paesiello.

19–20 In vain fond youth. Sung by Mrs. Stuart at Vauxhall.

21–22 Caro bene. Del Sigr. Sarti.   DLC

[A COLLECTION OF FAVORITE SONGS. Arranged for the voice and pianoforte by A. Reinagle. Book [ ] Philadelphia, Printed for A. Reinagle, 1789 (?)] 25 p. 32½ cm.

Title-page lacking. Recto of p. 1 blank.

At foot of p. 4: Philadephia [!] Sold by H. Rice, Market street. I. Aitken. Sc.

At foot of p. 10, 16: I. Aitken. Sculp [t].

At foot of p. 12, 18, 20, 24, 25: Philadelphia. Printed for A. Reinagle. I. Aitken. Sculpt. [Sometimes abbreviated]

Contents:

p. 1–4 Come Hope thou queen of endless smiles. A favorite song composed by Dr. Arnold. Arranged for the piano forte by A. Reinagle.

5 The request.

6–9 [lacking]

[67]

    10 [last page of unidentified song]
 11–12 If 'tis joy to wound a lover.   Dr. Arnold.
 13–14 My soul is thine sweet Norah.   A favorite song sung by Mr
       Jonstone in Love in a camp or Patrick in Prusia [!]. Arranged
       for the piano or harpsichord by A. Reinagle.
 15–16 The rose. A favorite song in the opera of Selima and Azor.
       Composed by T. Linley.
 17–18 Tantivy hark forward huzza.   The favorite hunting song sung
       by Mrs. Iliff at Vauxhall.
 19–20 Was I a shepherd's maid.
 21–22 Shou'd he think of another.   Sung by Miss Leary at Vaux Hall.
 23–24 Adieu thou dreary pile.
    25 I'll think of Willy far away.   Sung by Miss Leary at Vauxhall.
                                                                    ES

     It becomes quite evident that in (or about) 1789, Reinagle issued four
different collections of music, engraved for him by John Aitken and printed
by Thomas Dobson.   Of these four collections, Sonneck, when preparing
his *Bibliography* knew but one, and that one only in part—namely, Book I
of *A collect on of favorite songs, divided into two books* (*cf.* following entry).
Somewhat later, as indicated in Sonneck's ms. marginal notes, the Library
of Congress acquired Book II of this same work.   In another marginal
note, Sonneck states that the Library had obtained still another collection
printed for Reinagle (*cf.* preceding entry), and expresses his surprise that
neither of these additional collections seems to conform to Dobson's advertisement (quoted in preceding entry) of "Songs and pieces arranged . . . by
Alexander Reinagle."   Sonneck gives the following nine titles, taken from
the advertisement, with the comment that only one of them (actually two
songs, however) had appeared in either of these more recently acquired
collections:

     Tis not the bloom on Damon's cheek
     In vain fond youth you would conceal
     Tantive [!] hark forward
     My soul is thine sweet Norah
     The soldier tir'd
     Adieu thou dreary pile
     Overture to the new opera of Marian
     Ouverture La Schiava
     La chasse

Still later, the Library of Congress secured a copy of *Twelve favorite pieces.*
Arranged for the piano forte or harpsichord by A. Reinagle (*q. v.*).   This
collection, issued in similar fashion, includes the three instrumental compositions listed above.

In the meantime, individual issues of the remaining six songs appeared,
most of them unpaged.   And it was not until this present *Revision* of Sonneck
had gone to press that this latest collection was located, containing three
of these six songs.   Since two of these same six songs had already appeared
in one of the other collections, as also the three instrumental numbers,
there remains but one song, "Tis not the bloom on Damon's cheek," outside
any of these Reinagle collections.   And of course it may be that this song
originally appeared in the still missing portion of this collection (p. 6–9).

As to the contents of this rare collection, we note that all its songs have been met with elsewhere, save only "Shou'd he think of another," a song hitherto quite unknown.

From the above discussion it seems clear that Reinagle gave up any possible plan of issuing a mixed collection of "songs and pieces" and instead of this decided on a volume of "songs" and a volume of "pieces," the former of which has now at long last made its appearance.

Whether this collection may have been issued as Book I of *A collection of favorite songs . . . arranged by A. Reinagle* (*cf.* preceding entry) we cannot tell, since we lack the title-page. But until such title-page shall be found, internal evidence seems to justify the similar (supplied) title as given, and also, presumably, its designation as *Book I*.

A COLLECTION OF FAVORITE SONGS, divided into two books containing most of the airs in the Poor soldier, Rosina, &c., and the principal songs sung at Vaux Hall. The basses rendered easy and natural for the piano forte or harpsichord by Alexr. Reinagle. Book I. Philadelphia, Printed for A. Reinagle, of whom may be had a collection of Scotch tunes with variations for the piano forte or harpsichord. Also piano fortes of the best makers in London. J. Aitken, scu. [1789?] 1 p. l., 20 p. 32 cm.

Title page, verso blank; p. [1] blank; music, p. 2–20.

Contents:

p. 2 Drink to me only.
3 Farewell ye green fields.
4 I've kiss'd and I've prattled. Rosina.
5 When William at eve. Rosina.
6–7 The twins of Latona. Poor soldier.
8 How happy the soldier.
9 May I never be married.
10 Norah the theme of my song.
11 Altho' heav'n's good pleasure. In the favorite opera of Amintas. Compos'd by Sigr. Giordani.
12 The spring with smiling face. Poor soldier.
13 My friend and pitcher. Poor soldier.
14 How imperfect is expression.
15 A rose tree. Poor soldier.
16 Out of my sight or I'll box yours ears. Duetto.
17 Johnny and Mary.
18–19 Ye sluggards. Hunting song.
20 Good morrow to your night cap. Poor soldier.

——— The same. Bk. I [i. e. II] 1 p. l., 24 p. 32 cm.

Title-page, verso blank; p. [1] blank; music, p. 2–24.

Contents:

p. 2–3 May. A favourite pastoral. Sung by Miss Leary. Vauxhall.
4–5 The banks of Yarrow. Sung by Miss Bertles. Vauxhall.
6–7 The tartan plaiddie. Scotch song. Sung by Miss Leary. Vauxhall.
8 Let's seek the bow'r of Robin Hood.

[69]

9 Her mouth which a smile. In Rosina.
10–11 Sweet Poll of Plymouth.
11 The morn returns in saffron drest. In Rosina.
12–13 Laughing song. Sung by Miss Poole. Vauxhall.
14–15 Dear gentle Kate. Sung by Mr. Incledon. Vauxhall.
16–17 Henry cull'd the flowret's bloom. Rosina.
18–19 The friend and the lover. Vauxhall.
20 When bidden to the wake or fair. Rosina.
21 My heavy heart. A favorite Scotch song. Sung by Miss Bertles. Vauxhall.
22–23 [Time has not thin'd my flowing hair] Canzonet. Adapted to one voice. Composed by W. Jackson.
24 Music is the voice of love. Sung by Miss Bertles. Vauxhall.

Book I   DLC (lacks p. 9–10), ES, Hopk.
Book II (given on title-page as Book I, but really Book II)
                                         DLC, PU
Books I and II (complete)   CdeW

The above work is undated, but published probably before 1800, and possibly as early as 1789, for we read in the *Pennsylvania packet*, March 3, 1789:

Just published and sold by Thomas Dobson . . . songs and pieces arranged for the piano forte or harpsichord by Alexander Reinagle.

Evans (21420) gives date 1788.

A COLLECTION OF FAVORITE SONGS sung at Vauxhall gardens. Composed by Mr. Hook. Book [ ]. Price 1ᵈ¹. New York, Printed & sold at G. Gilfert's piano forte warehouse, No. 177 Broadway [1799–1801] 1 p.l., 17 p. 33cm.

Title-page, verso blank; music, p. 2–17; p. [1] and verso of p. 17, blank.
At top of title page, an elaborate vignette, showing Vauxhall gardens surrounded by various figures. A group of musical instruments underneath.
Below vignette: G. Gilfert's pianoforte warehouse, No. 177 Broadway.
In title, after the word "Book", manuscript note: 1st.
In Book [I], full caption title and imprint at head of each song.
In DLC copy, page 17 is repeated.

Contents:
p. 2–3 The men are all rovers alike. A new song. Sung by Miss Howells.
4–5 Thou'rt gone awa frae me Mary. A favorite Scotch song. Sung by Mr. Dignum.
6–7 A cent'ry ago. A favorite song. Sung by Mrs. Franklin.
8–9 All for pretty Polly. A new song. Sung by Mr. Denman.
10–11 I love to speak my mind. A new song. Sung by Miss Sims.
12–13 Fair Anna that dwells by the Tyne. A new song. Sung by Mr. Dignum.
14–15 I'll be married to thee. A new song. Sung by Mrs. Franklin.
16–17 He's stole my heart from me. A new Scotch song. Sung by Miss Sims.

———— The same. Book [II] 18 p.
Title page wanting; p. [1] blank; music, p. 2–18.
No individual imprints as in Bk. I, titles only being given.

Contents:

p. 2–3 How handsome is my sailor lad. A new Scotch song. Sung by
Mrs. Franklin.
4–5 Mary of Sunbury Hill. A new song. Sung by Mr. Dignum.
6–7 When once by the clear gliding stream. A new song. Sung by
Master Gray.
8–9 Dilly dally, shilly shally. A new song. Sung by Miss Sims.
The words by Dr. Houlton.
10–11 O give me the lass that I love. A new song. Sung by Mr. Dignum.
12–13 The Albion, the pride of the sea. Sung with universal applause
by Mr. Denman. The words by Dr. Houlton.
14–15 When the merry bells. A new song. Sung by Miss Howells.
The words by Bragshaw, junr. esqr.
16–18 Maidens listen I'll discover. A new song. Sung by Mrs. Cooke.

Because of the Von Hagen imprint (3 Cornhill) on one of the songs in the
first book, we know that the collection could not have been published before
1799. The Gilfert imprint makes it not later than 1801.

Book [I] Book [II] DLC

Title-page only of this [second] book is found in the collection of J. Francis
Driscoll. Identical with t.-p. of [first] book, except that after the word
"Book," a manuscript note, "2d." Also the added figures "180" followed
by manuscript "3." This apparent date "1803," however, is misleading
(as shown above) unless we have here once more the use of an old plate
with later additions.

A COLLECTION OF NEW & FAVORITE SONGS. [A] Price [blank] Printed
& sold by B. Carr, Philadelphia; I. Hewitt, New York & J. Carr, Baltimore.
Where may be had all the newest musical productions [ca. 1800] [212] p.
34 cm.

Title-page, verso blank; music, p. [3]–[212].

Title enclosed in semi-circular spray of leaves and blossoms.

Below this spray: Price [blank]

Continuous pagination supplied; p. 2, 154, 212 blank. Such compositions
as were originally paged retain this pagination in addition to what is supplied.

Contents:

p. [3]–[5]   Hark the goddess Diana.
[6]–[7]   Columbia & liberty.
[8]–[9]   Green Mountain farmer.
[10]–[11]   Let Washington be our boast.
[12]–[13]   New Yankee Doodle.
[14]–[15]   Federal constitution & liberty forever.
[16]–[17]   Adams & liberty.
[18]–[19]   Mansion of Peace.
[20]–[21]   Capt. Truxton, or Huzza for Constellation.
[22]–[23]   And a for love of me.
[24]–[25]   'Twas in the solemn midnight hour.
[26]–[27]   Oh had it been my happy lot.
[28]–[29]   Caledonian laddy.

[71]

[30]–[31]	How can I forget.
[32]–[33]	Favorite ballad of the poor black boy.
[34]–[35]	Lash'd to the helm.
[36]–[37]	Little sailor boy.
[38]–[39]	Lillies & roses.
[40]–[41]	Crops.
[42]–[43]	Galley slave.
[44]–[45]	I have a silent sorrow here.
[46]–[47]	Little Sally.
[48]–[49]	How happy was my humble lot.
[50]–[51]	Sweet Myra of the vale.
[52]–[53]	And hear her sigh adieu.
[54]–[55]	Oh since I've found you.
[56]–[57]	When the shepherd asks my hand sir.
[58]–[59]	Come, come love to the window come.
[60]–[61]	If a body loves a body.
[62]–[63]	Now's the time to sing & play.
[64]–[65]	Rosline Castle.
[66]–[67]	Young Willy for me.
[68]–[69]	The Linnets.
[70]–[71]	Dear Mary, or Adieu to old England.
[72]–[73]	Unfortunate sailor.
[74]–[75]	Hare hunt.
[76]–[77]	Bright Phoebus.
[78]–[79]	Tho' you think by this to vex me.
[80]–[81]	May day morn.
[82]–[83]	Hey dance to the fiddle & tabor.
[84]–[85]	Whither can my William stray.
[86]–[87]	There's the pretty girl I love.
[88]–[89]	Hoot awa ye loon.
[90]–[91]	My Bonny Lowland laddie.
[92]–[93]	Where's the harm of that.
[94]–[95]	What can a lassy do.
[96]–[97]	'Tis all a test.
[98]–[99]	Straw bonnet. Composed by Mrs. Pownall.
[100]–[101]	Meg of Wapping.
[102]–[103]	I'm in haste.
[104]–[105]	When the old heathen gods.
[106]–[107]	Pretty lad.
[108]–[109]	Jemmy of the glen. Words and music by Mrs. Pownall.
[110]–[111]	O dearly I love somebody.
[112]–[113]	Black bird [and] Independent rangers.
[114]–[115]	Girl of my heart [and] Fife hunt.
[116]–[117]	Talacoy.
[118]–[119]	Lisbia.
[120]–[121]	Of plighted faith so truly kept.
[122]–[123]	Favorite fishing duett.
[124]–[125]	Ellen.
[126]–[127]	The tear.
[128]–[130]	Canzonet—Jackson.
[131]–[133]	The female cryer.
[134]–[135]	The kiss.

[136]–[137] Owen, a favorite Welch air.
[138]–[139] Auld Robin Gray.
[140]–[141] Lucy, or Selim's complaint [and] Nancy.
[142]–[143] Anna, or The adieu.
[144] Primrose girl.
[145]–[147] Gather you rosebuds.
[148] Ellens fate deserves a tear.
[149]–[151] Hark forward Tantivy huzza.
[152] Rural life.
[153]–[154] Wampum belt—Composed by Hewitt.
[155] My native shore.
[156]–[157] Negro philosophy.
[158] The girl with a cast in her eye.
[159] Queen Mary's lamentation.
[160]–[161] Patent coffin.
[162] The Birks of Invermay.
[163] Poor Mary.
[164]–[165] Hail Liberty.
[166] From thee Eliza I must go.
[167] The cheering rosary.
[168]–[169] Morning is up.
[170] Crazy Jane.
[171] Streamlet.
[172]–[173] Where Liffey rolls its silver streams.
[174] Flower of Yarrow.
[175] Sweet transports.
[176]–[177] To arms Columbia.
[178] Within a mile.
[179] Shipwrecked boy.
[180]–[181] The waggoner.
[182] How shall I my fair discover.   Composed by Hewitt.
[183] Young Henry loved his Emma well.
[184]–[185] The tinker.
[186] Tho' Prudence may press me.
[187] When bidden to the wake or fair.
[188]–[189] No good without an exception.
[190] Two bunches a penny primroses.
[191] Moll in the Wad.
[192]–[193] A new patriotic song.
[194] Oh the moment was sad.
[195] Lavinia.
[196]–[197] La chasse.
[198] Advice to the ladies.
[199] A-tyd-y-nos.
[200]–[201] He loves his winsome Kate.
[202] Poor sailor boy.
[203] Johnny & Mary.
[204]–[205] Sing old rose [and] Burn the bellows.
[206] A favorite song translated from the Irish.
[207] Some time ago.
[208]–[210] Minuetto—Composed by Saliment.
[211] Prithee fool be quiet.

One is tempted to date this unique and interesting collection as definitely 1800, since so much of its material is known to have been issued before or during that year. But there are certain items not to be so easily and confidently placed.

Nevertheless, the most logical and determining factor in fixing the date has seemed to be the song *'Twas in the solemn midnight hour. Sung with great applause by Miss E. Westray in the Sighs, or the Daughter*. As this work of Prince Hoare's was given but twice in America (April 16 and 18, 1800) and we know from advertisements in the New York *American citizen and general advertiser* of these same dates that Miss Westray sang at both performances, it becomes evident that the collection could not have been issued before April 16, 1800, presumably not much later.

The very great value of the collection, lies in the fact that it presents a much jumbled but still representative portion of the publishing activities of the Carr family and its affiliates in America throughout the important years of Benjamin Carr's leadership—from early 1794 up to 1800, the year in which he finally withdrew. Thus it lacks only the Carr & Co. issues of 1793 to make its representation complete.

In this respect it is unique and would seem to have been compiled by either Carr or Hewitt—not for general publication, but to serve as just such a personal record. HFB

The same title-page. [B] Separate issues, each with its own imprint. Unpaged [1797–99] 15 l. 32½ cm.

Title-page, verso blank.
Contents: Toll, toll the knell [Storace].—The little sailor boy [B. Carr].—The willow [Storace].—The death of poor Cock Robin [Master Walsh].—Ellen arise [B. Carr].—Comely Ned that died at sea [Dibdin].—What are the boasted joys of love [Shield].

On t.-p. of PU copy, after the word "Price," ms. note, in pencil: $1.50.
McD–W (incomplete), PU

The same title-page. [C] On t.-p., ms. note: From the opera of Blue Beard. [ca. 1799] 8 p. 30½ cm.

Contents: Pit a pat, p. 2–3.—Tink a tink, p. 4–5.—When pensive, p. 6–7.—Chica cho, p. 8.

Blue Beard, by Michael Kelly, was first performed in Philadelphia, May 24, 1799.
On t.-p. of one NN copy, after the word "Price," ms. note: 75/100
ABHu, LSL, McD–W, NN

A COLLECTION OF SONGS selected from the works of Mr. Dibdin. To which are added, the newest and most favourite American patriotic songs. Philadelphia: Printed by J. Bioren for H. & P. Rice, and sold by J. Rice, Baltimore. 1799. 1 p. l., 328, x p. 16½ cm.

Title-page, verso blank. Songs, p. [1]–328; index, p. [i]–x. Words only, with frequent indications of the particular entertainment, opera, etc., from which the songs are taken.

"New [American] patriotic songs" (words only) contained in the above:

p. [313]–314 Song adapted to The President's march. [Hail Columbia happy land]

314–315 The New York patriotic song. Called The federal constitution boys and liberty forever. [Poets may sing of their Hellicon streams]

315–317 Boston patriotic song. Tune, Anacreon in heaven. [Ye sons of Columbia who bravely have fought]

317–318 Song. [Our country is our ship, d'y'see]

318–319 Song. [Come all grenadiers whom your country invites]

319–320 Song. Tune, President's march. [Lo! I quit my native skies]

320–321 Song. Tune, Yankee Doodle. [Columbians all, the present hour]

321–322 Song. Tune, Hearts of oak. [Whilst Europe is wrapt in the horrors of war]

322–323 Song. [Come genius of our happy land]

323–325 Ode for the 4th of July, 1798. [There's Ichabod has come to town]

226 [326] Our country's efficiency! Tune, To Anacreon in heaven,
–328 &c. [Ye sons of Columbia, determined to keep]

Advertised January 17, 1799, as "just published."
RPJCB copy lacks index.   DLC, MWA, NHi, NN, RPJCB

*A COLLECTION OF THE NEWEST and most approved songs.
In preparation and will speedily be ready for delivery a collection of the newest and most approved songs now singing both in London and America amongst which are those much admired songs of Mr. Dibdin's, the Rara Avis, Roses and Lilies, Virtue, and the Lamplighter with a number of others, one of which is intended to be published each week. Each song will contain three pages of music adapted to the piano forte and harpsichord, violin, German flute and guitar. Price 1 s. The first song will be ready for delivery in a few days by the subscriber at his store, No. 38 Maiden-Lane, where subscriptions will be received from those who approve of his proposal . . . Amongst which [issues] will be those admired variations of Rosline Castle & Malbrouk, with a few favorite songs, to form one handsome volume folio with 30 pages of music intended as an entertaining set of lessons for the above instruments, to be delivered to the subscribers at one dollar each: as part of the plates are already finished it will be printed as soon as a sufficient number of subscribers appear, by the public's most obedient
                                                            JAMES HARRISON

The above advertisement appeared in the *Weekly museum*, New York, July 13, 1793.

Apparently no prints from these "already finished" plates have survived.

*A COLLECTION OF THE NEWEST and most fashionable country dances and cotillions. The greater part by Mr. John Griffith, dancing master in Providence.

Thus advertised in May, 1788, as "published and to be sold by the printer hereof," John Carter, Providence, R. I.

*A COLLECTION OF THE NEWEST COTILLIONS and country dances, principally composed by John Griffiths, dancing master. To which is added; instances of ill manners, to be carefully avoided by youth of both sexes. Printed and sold at Northampton, Massachusetts. (Price nine pence) [1788] 12 p. 12 mo. [Evans 21121]

*A COLLECTION OF THE NEWEST COTILLIONS, and country dances. To which is added, instances of ill manners, to be carefully avoided by youth of both sexes. By John Griffiths. Greenfield: Printed by Thomas Dickman, 1794.

A COLLECTION OF THE NEWEST COTILLIONS and country dances. To which is added, a variety of modern songs. Also, rules for conversation and instances of ill manners: to be carefully avoided by both sexes. Worcester, Massachusetts, 1800. 36 p. 24°. NN

Advertised by Isaiah Thomas & Son, Worcester, in August, 1800, as published.

A CHOICE COLLECTION OF FREE MASONS SONGS. To which is added Solomon's Temple, an oratorio. Providence, Printed by John Carter, at the printing office at Shakespears Head. 1779.

Words only.
Advertised in June, 1779, as "just published and now selling at the Printing Office [of John Carter] at Shakespear's Head," Providence, R. I. RHi

*FAVOURITE COLLECTION OF AIRS, marches, minuets, etc. by H. B Victor.
See Compleat instructor for the violin, by the same author.

*JEMMY CARSON'S COLLECTION [OF BALLADS ?] Philadelphia: Printed by Andrew Steuart, 1762.

[MISCELLANEOUS AND INCOMPLETE [?] COLLECTION] Philadelphia, Printed for and sold by G. Willig, Nr° 165 Market street [1795–97] 11 p. 23 x 32½ cm.

Title-page missing; recto of p. 1, blank; music, p. 1–11. At foot of p. 4: C. S. Sculpt.
Contents: The overture to Rosina, p. 1–4.—[By the fountain's flow'ry side] Belville, p. 5–6.—A. favorite. song [Indulgent pow'rs if ever], p. 7–8.—The wedding . day . A . favourite . song, p. 9–10 .—A . favourite . French . song [Vous l'ordonné je me serai connoitre], p. 10.—Ella and Edwin, p. 11. DLC

*A NEW AND SELECT COLLECTION of the best English, Scots and Irish songs, catches, duets, and cantatas, in the true spirit and taste of the three different nations—Being an attempt to improve upon others in the true spirit of social mirth and good fellowship—With a collection of the various sentiments and hob-nobs in vogue. New York, Printed and sold by James Rivington. 1780.

Thus advertised under the heading "A Song book," in Rivington's *Royal gazette*, New York, June 17, 1780, as "this day . . . published." It is remarked that

No pains have been spared to render this publication as complete as possible, by a judicious selection of the materials, thus furnishing novelty to gratify the taste of all sorts of readers; 'tis hoped the public will afford a favourable reception to the compiler's labours.

Price of these three hundred and fifty four songs, neatly bound in red, only one dollar. To be had of the printer.

[UNIDENTIFIED COLLECTION (beginning with "A lesson")] Boston [?] ca. 1800 11 p.

Songs and a composition for piano.
Contained in a volume of tracts.
Probably published before 1800.

Contents: A lesson, p. 1–3.—Sylvia, p. 4.—Addressed to Miss D., by a lady, both of Boston, p. 5–6.—Ode, p. 7–8.—In Acis and Galatea, p. 9–11.

MHi

Sonneck (*Early Concert-life*, p. 272) suggests that this collection may well be the work of William Selby—a portion of his *Apollo and the Muse's musical compositions* (*q. v.*).

[UNIDENTIFIED COLLECTION of instrumental and vocal music. New York] Printed for Hewitt & Rausch [1797] 2–25 p. 32 cm.

Title-page missing.
In lower margin, p. 2–9, 11, 13, 16, 18–19, 22, 24–25: Printed for Hewitt & Rausch.

Contents:
p. 2–7 The celebrated overture to Ladoiska [!] Composed by Kreutzer.
  8 The Wampum belt [Song] Composed by James Hewitt.—The rangers cotillon [!] [For pfte.]
  9–10 My bonny lowland laddie. A favorite Scotch song. Composed by Mr. Hook.
  10 Allemande [For pfte.]
  11–12 The girl of my heart [Song] Composed by Mr. Hook.
  12 Fife hunt [For pfte.]
  13 Ellen's fate deserves a tear [Song]
  14–16 Hark forward tantivy huzza [Song] Composed by Mr. Hook.
  17–18 The blackbird [Song] Composed by Mr. Hook.
  18 Independent rangers quick march [For pfte.]
  19 How shall I my pain discover [Song] Composed by James Hewitt.
  20–22 Gather your rosebuds. Composed by Mr. Hook. Adapted for one two or three voices.
  23–24 The crops. A favorite song. Composed by Mr. Hook.
  25 The shipwreck'd boy. [Song] DLC, ES

We know from advertisements that the partnership between James Hewitt and Frederick Rausch was in existence as early as March 10, 1797. Apparently dissolved ca. August, 1797.

COLLEGE HORNPIPE.
See Evening amusement, p. 15.

COLLIN AND BETSEY.
See The select songster, New Haven, 1786. p. 29.

[77]

*COLLIN'S ODE ON THE PASSIONS, to be spoken by Mr. Hodgkinson. With music representative of each passion, as performed at the Anacreontic Society, composed by J. Hewitt.

Thus advertised for performance at a concert in New York, on June 11, 1795. John Hodgkinson (1767–1805). Stage name of John Meadowcraft, born near Manchester, England. Actor of extraordinary ability and versatility, a very gifted singer and not without talent as playwright. Famous on the English stage before he, in 1792, settled in the United States. He soon became joint-manager with Hallam of the Old American Company. After a career of triumphs, he died of yellow fever in a tavern near Bladensburg, Maryland, just outside of Washington.

COLUMBIA. A new country dance. By Philo-Musico.
(*In* The Massachusetts magazine. Boston, February, 1790. p. 125)

Pfte., melody only. Single staff. 8 measures. DLC (etc.)

COLUMBIA. A song. Composed and set to music by Mr. T. Dwight.
(*In* The American Museum, Philadelphia, June, 1787, p. 566)

Words only. First line: Columbia, Columbia, to glory arise. DLC (etc.)

COLUMBIA. By Dr. Dwight.
(*In* The American musical miscellany. Northampton, 1798. p. 207–211)

Melody and bass, with accompanying text.
First line: same as preceding. DLC (etc.)

COLUMBIA AND LIBERTY. A new patriotic song. Written by Mr. Davenport. The music by Dr. Arne. New York, Printed & sold at J, Hewitt's musical repository, No. 131 William street. Sold also by B. Carr. Philadelphia & J. Carr, Baltimore. Copyright secured. Price 25 cents. (*In* A collection of new & favorite songs. [A] Philadelphia [ca. 1800] p. [6]–[7])
Song, pfte. acc.
First line: When Britain with despotic sway.
The original issue was entered in copyright records for Massachusetts, October 27, 1798. HFB

——— The same as preceding, but without music.
(*In* The American museum. Philadelphia, June, 1787, p. 566) DLC (etc.)

THE COLUMBIAN HARMONY. Containing the rules of psalmody together with a collection of sacred music. Designed for the use of worshiping assemblies & singing societies. By Joseph Stone and Abraham Wood. Published according to Act of Congress. Engraved by J. Allen. [n. p., n. d.] viii, 112 p. 13½ x 23 cm.

Title-page, verso blank. Rules of psalmody, p. iii-vii; index, p. viii; music, p. 1–112.
At foot of p. viii: Joel Allen, sculpt.
At foot of p. 9: E. Ruggles, junr. Sculpt.
At foot of p. 112: Engraved by E. Ruggles, jun.
For mixed chorus. Open score. Four staves.
Contains more secular and semi-religious numbers than most collections of this sort. Among them:

Music descending on a silent cloud, by Wood, p. 9.
Sweet muse descend and bless ye shade, by Wood, p. 17.
Sleep, downy sleep, come close my eyes, by Babcock, p. 22.
Swift as the sun revolves ye day, by Wood, p. 40.
Our term of time is seventy years, by Stone, p. 48.
Farewell honour's empty pride, by Stone, p. 55.
An elegy on the death of a young lady, by Wood, p. 68–71.

The *Elegy* is the most important of the above, and is written for treble solo, three-part and four-part chorus. Open score.
First line: Ye virgin souls whose sweet complaint.

The Columbian harmony was probably published in 1793, as its copyright was recorded, Massachusetts, September 13, 1793. DLC, NN

THE COLUMBIAN SONGSTER. Being a select collection of genuine songs. From the press of Thomas and Waldo, Brookfield, Massachusetts, 1795. 36 p. 14½ cm. MH, MWA

*THE COLUMBIAN SONGSTER, containing a great variety of melodious and entertaining songs. Boston, Printed by E. Russell, and sold near Liberty-pole. 1795.

THE COLUMBIAN SONGSTER, a jovial companion: Being a collection of two hundred and twenty choice songs, selected from various volumes and detached parcels—of which near fifty are American productions. Mirth, love and sentiment are here happily blended, the chaste to the chastest ear unoffended. From Greenleafs Press. New York, 1797. viii, 232 p. 16 cm.

Contains no music, but frequently the tunes are mentioned to which, especially the patriotic songs were to be sung. MB, NHi, RPB

THE COLUMBIAN SONGSTER AND FREEMASON'S POCKET COMPANION. A collection of the newest and most celebrated sentimental, convivial, humourous, satirical, pastoral, hunting, sea and masonic songs, being the largest and best collection ever published in America. Selected by S. Larkin. Portsmouth: New-Hampshire, Printed by J. Melcher, for S. Larkin, at the Portsmouth book-store, 1798. x, 11–216, 70, [2] p. 18 cm.

Title-page, verso blank; preface, p. [iii]–[iv]; index, p. [v]–x; songs, p. 11–216.

Freemason's pocket companion has separate title page and special paging.

Verso t.-p. blank; songs, p. [3]–70; index, p. [71]–[72].
Words only, tunes frequently indicated.
Advertised in April, 1798, as "published, price 1 dollar, neatly bound and lettered, sold by F. Larkin, No. 47 Cornhill," Boston. DLC

Freemason's pocket companion, issued separately. RPB

THE COLUMBIAN SONGSTER. Being a large collection of fashionable songs for gentlemen & ladies. In a series of numbers. Printed by Nathaniel Heaton, jun. [Wrentham, Mass.] 1799. 7 v. 14½ cm.

Nos. I–VI, each 36 p.; no. VII, Masonic songs, p. [1]–24; toasts and sentiments, p. [25]–30; contents [i]–vi.

[79]

173 songs, words only.   Tunes sometimes mentioned in *Masonic songs.*
DLC, NBuG (lacks p. 1–4 of No. VII), NHi, NN, NRU–Mus   RPB

[COLUMBIANS ALL, THE PRESENT HOUR]   Song.   Tune, Yankee Doodle.
(*In* New [American] patriotic songs, added to a collection of songs by C.
Dibdin.   Philadelphia, 1799.   p. 320–321)

Words only.
Title from first line.   DLC, MWA, NHi, NN, RPJCB

*COLUMBIA'S BOLD EAGLE, a patriotic song, words by a gentleman of
Salem.   Music by Mr. Graupner.

Was to be sung at a concert in Salem, Mass., on June 25, 1799.

COLUMBIA'S GUARDIAN SLEEPS IN DUST.
(*In* Sacred dirges [Oliver Holden] Boston [1800]   p. 12–13)

Trio [?] and three-part chorus.   Open score.
First line: What mournful strains invade our ears.
CSmH, DLC, ICN, MB, MH, MHi, MWA, NHi, NN, RPB

[COLUMBIA'S SONS IN SONG PROCLAIM]   A song composed and sung
by Jonathan M. Sewell at a civic festival in Portsmouth, N. H.

Words printed in *Aurora* (Philadelphia), April 21, 1795.
Title from first line.   DLC (etc.)

COLUMBUS, OR THE DISCOVERY OF AMERICA.   An historical play.
As performed at the Theatre Royal, Covent Garden, London.   By Thomas
Morton, of the Honourable Society of Lincoln's Inn.   Boston, Printed and
sold by William Spotswood, sold also by H. & P. Rice, Philadelphia, 1794.
2 p.l., 52, [3] p.   16½ cm.

Title-page.   Advertisement and dramatis personae, p. [ii]; prologue, p.
[iii]–[iv]; text, p. [1]–52; epilogue, p. [53]–54.   "Plays, American editions
for sale by William Spotswood, Boston," p. [55] DLC, MB, MWA, NN, PU

The play was performed with incidental music composed by Alexander
Reinagle at the New Theatre, Philadelphia, on January 21, 1797; with
incidental music composed by James Hewitt in New York, on May 15, 1799;
with incidental music composed by P. A. von Hagen, probably the elder,
at the Federal Street Theatre, Boston, for the first time on February 17.
1800.   Reinagle's music "in the historical play of Columbus, composed and
adapted for the piano-forte, flute, or violin" was copyrighted, Pennsylvania,
February 22, 1799.   However, no copy of this music has been located,
although "Indian march of the much admeired [!] American play caled
(!) Columbus" (paged 16) may prove to be a reprint from this collection.

[COME ALL GRENADIERS]   Song.
(*In* New [American] patriotic songs, added to a collection of songs by C.
Dibdin.   Philadelphia, 1799.   p. 318–319)
Words only.

Title from first line.   DLC, MWA, NHi, NN, RPJCB

[80]

COME BLUSHING ROSE. [Philadelphia] Publish'd by G. Willig, Nro. 163 North Third street [1794–95] 1 l. 31½ cm.

Song, pfte. acc.
First line same as title.
Composed by Ignaz Pleyel.   DLC, MWA, PHi

———— Same as preceding, except that the imprint has been partially erased and altered to read: 165 Market street [1795–97]   PU

*COME BLUSHING ROSE.
Song. Advertised in April, 1795, as published by "G. Gilfert & co., at their Musical Magazine, No. 121 Broadway," New York.

COME BUY MY DAFFODILLIES. A favorite song. Boston, Printed & sold by P. A. von Hagen & co., No. 3 Cornhill, also by G. Gilfert, N. York. Where may be had a general assortment of warranted imported piano fortes, &c. For the pianofortes [!], German flute or violin. [1799–1800] [2] p. 32 cm.

Song, pfte. acc.
First line: 'Twas in the blooming month of May.
Probably published in 1799.   JFD, MB, N, RPJCB

COME BUY MY WOODEN WARE. A favorite song. Boston, Printed & sold at P. A. von Hagen, junr. & cos. Musical magazine, No. 55 Marlboro' street. Also by G. Gilfert, New York,   Where may be had

Lillies & roses.   Adams & Washington.
The little singing girl.   The much admired Song in the Castle
Mounseer Nong Tong Paw.   spectre.

For te [!] piano forte, German flute or violin. [1799] [2] p. 31½ cm.

Song, pfte. acc.
First line: Thy influence love I needs must own.
Advertised, May, 1799, as a "new song."   MWA, RPB

COME, COME MY LOVE TO THE WINDOW COME. A favorite duett. Sung by Mrs. Oldmixon & Mr. Jefferson in the play of Count Benyowsky. The words by W. Dunlap, esqr. The air is the celebrated Pas Russe. New York, Printed & sold by J. Hewitt at his Musical repository, No. 23 Maiden Lane. Sold also by B. Carr, Philadelphia & J. Carr, Baltimore. Price 25 cents. [1799–1800] [2] p. 32 cm.

Duet, pfte. acc. Arr. for flute and for "guittar," p. [2].
First line same as title.   MH, MWA

———— The same as preceding.
    (In A collection of new & favorite songs. [A] Philadelphia [ca.1800] p. [58]–[59])   HFB

Count Benyowski was performed with Mrs. Oldmixon and Mr. Jefferson in the cast in New York, April 1, 1799.

COME FAIR ROSINA COME AWAY] Song I.
    (In Seven songs, by F. Hopkinson. Philadelphia [1788] p. 1)

Song, pfte. acc.
Title from first line.   DLC, Hopk., MB, McD-W

COME GENIUS OF OUR HAPPY LAND. A favorite patriotic song. Composed by H. C. Printed & sold at B. Carr's Musical repository, Philadelphia; J. Carr's, Baltimore & J. Hewitt's, New York (12 cts.) [1797–99] 1 l. 33 cm.

Song, pfte. acc.
First line same as title.
H. C., probably Henry Capron.   DLC, LSL

[COME GENIUS OF OUR HAPPY LAND] Song.
(In New [American] patriotic songs, added to a collection of songs by C. Dibdin. Philadelphia, 1799. p. 322–323)

Words only.
Title from first line.   DLC, MWA, NHi, NN, RPJCB

COME HOLY GHOST. A hymn for Whit Sunday. The words from No. 202, United Brethren Hymn Book and Fr. Rausch. New York, Printed & sold by Gilfert & co., No. 209 Broadway, near St. Pauls and at No. 165 Market street, Philadelphia [1795] [2] p. 33 cm.

Two vocal parts, pfte. acc.
First line: Come Holy Ghost, come Lord our God.   JFD, MWA

COME HOPE, thou queen of endless smiles. A favorite song. Composed by Dr. Arnold. Arranged for the pianoforte by A. Reinagle. Philadephia[!] Sold by H. Rice, Market street. I. Aitken, sc. [1789] 4 p. 33½ cm.

Imprint at foot of p. 4.
Song, pfte. acc.
First line same as title.   ES, McD–W, NN

—––– The same as preceding.
(In [A collection of favorite songs, arr. by A. Reinagle. Philadelphia, 1789 (?)] p. 1–4)   ES

COME NOW ALL YE SOCIAL POW'RS.
(In The American musical miscellany. Northampton, 1798. p. 40–41)

Melody only, with accompanying text.
First line same as title.   DLC (etc.)

COME ROUSE BROTHER SPORTSMAN.
(In The American musical miscellany. Northampton, 1798. p. 150–152)

Melody only, with accompanying text.
First line same as title.
Composed by James Hook.
Sung in New York as early as July 14, 1769.   DLC (etc.)

COME SMILING HOPE. A favorite song. Sung in the new opera of Abroad and at home. New York, Printed and sold by G. Gilfert, No. 177 Broadway [ca. 1798] 1 l. 31½ cm.

Song, pfte. acc.
First line same as title.
William Shield's opera, Abroad and at home, was first performed in New York, November 10, 1797.

MWA

COME SWALLOW YOUR BUMPERS, ye tories and roar.
See Parody parodized.

COMELY NED THAT DIED AT SEA. By Dibdin. Price 25 cents. Printed
and sold at B. Carr's Musical repository, Philadelphia; J. Carr's, Baltimore & J. Hewitts, N. York [1797–98] [2] p. 31½ cm.

Song, pfte. acc. Arr. for two flutes or "guittars," p. [2].
First line: Give ear to me both high and low.
Advertised, January, 1798, as "just published." DLC, NN

———— Also (*In* A collection of new & favorite songs. [B] Philadelphia, [1797–
1799] no paging) McD–W, PU

THE COMPANION: being a selection of the beauties of the most celebrated
authors in the English language in prose and verse [Two lines from Aken-
side] Printed by Nathaniel and Benjamin Heaton for Joseph J. Todd. Providence, at the Sign of the Bible and Anchor. 1799. viii, [9]–280 p. 14½ cm.

Contains on p. 253–280, "Fashionable songs for the year 1798."[Words only]
These include the patriotic songs, "Adams and Liberty," "Hail Columbia,"
"The Federal Constitution and the President forever."
DLC, MWA, RHi. RPB, RPJCB

*THE COMPLEAT INSTRUCTOR FOR THE FLUTE.

*THE COMPLEAT INSTRUCTOR FOR THE GUITAR.

*THE COMPLEAT INSTRUCTOR FOR THE HARPSICHORD.
All three by H. B. Victor, 1778. *See*:

*THE COMPLEAT INSTRUCTOR FOR THE VIOLIN. By H. B. Victor.
Advertised in the *Pennsylvania ledger* for April 4, 1778, as

Just published, and now selling by I. Norman, Engraver, opposite the
old Workhouse, in Third-street, Mr. Victor's new composition of music
for the violin, with compleat instructions for learning to obtain a proficiency: Price One Dollar.

N. B. Mr. Victor intends publishing three other books (viz) for German
flute, guitar and harpsichord, by subscription . . .

Sonneck took the titles from the proposals for publishing the book, which
appeared in the *Pennsylvania ledger* for January 31, 1778, and read:

Now publishing by Subscription A NEW COMPOSITION OF MUSIC
consisting of four separate books, viz.

The Compleat Instructor for the violin, flute, guitar and harpsichord.
Containing the easiest and best method for learners to obtain a proficiency;
with some useful directions, lessons, graces, etc. by H. B. VICTOR.

To which is added, A favourite collection of airs, marches, minuets, etc.
now in vogue; with several useful pieces for two violins, etc. etc.

Also, a dictionary explaining such Greek, Latin, Italian and French words,
as generally occur in music.

[83]

CONDITIONS

I. The composer of this work intends printing it in four separate books; as it is possible the whole together may not suit every subscriber, he gives them the opportunity of chusing [!] four books of either sort.

II. The price to subscribers will be twenty shillings (non subscribers twenty-five), one Dollar advance at the time of subscribing, the remainder to be paid when the work is compleat and delivered.

III. Three weeks after fifty subscribers have approved of these conditions, the book for the violin will be published; the others will be published every three weeks after, till the whole is compleat.

IV. An elegant, new and original frontispiece, in the present tastes will be given.

V. Subscriptions are received by H. B. Victor, musician; by Robert Bell, printer and bookseller, in Third-street; by Nichola Brooks, at his picture and dry good store in Second street; by Samuel Delap, bookseller, the corner of Chestnut and Third street, by Narius Montillius, at his stationary shop near the Coffee house; and by I. Norman, engraver, opposite the old Work-house in Third-street.

The same book, under the title of "New and complete instructions for the violin . . . By H. B. Victor," was advertised as published in the *Royal Pennsylvania gazette*, April 7, 1778.

THE COMPLEAT TUTOR; for the fife, containing ye best & easiest instructions for learners to obtain a proficiency. To which is added a choice collection of ye most celebrated marches, airs, etc. Properly adapted to that instrument, with several choice pieces for two fifes. Philadelphia. Price 62½ cents. Printed for & sold by George Willig. No. 12 South Fourth Street Philada. Where also may be had a great variety of other music, musical instruments, strings, etc. etc. [ca. 1805] 1 p.l., 30 p., front. 26 cm.

Title-page, verso blank. "Instructions for the fife" for fingering; on the gamut, on time, etc., p. 1–7; music, p. 8–30.

Contents:

p. 8 Foot march with 8 divisions; troop.
   9 Doublings of the troop; Doublings; Taptoo.
  10 The Reveilly; the General; To Arms; Troop or assembling; troop.
  11 The Scotch reveilly; The General; The Drums call; The Dead March; The Singling of a troop by Mr. Weidman.
  12 Lord Loudon's Grenadiers march; The Turk's march; The Train or artillery Grenadiers march.
  13 The Coronation march; The Second Grenadiers march; The Wiltshire march; The Bedfordshire march.
  14 March of the Thirty-fifth Regiment [for two fifes].
  15 Bellisle march [for two fifes]; The Retreat; Captain Money's march.
  16 The new Coldstream march; The Marquis of Granby's or 1st Troop of Horse Grenadiers march; The Gloucestershire march; The Militia march.
  17 The Warwickshire march; The Lincolnshire march; The Light Horse march.
  18 Cold stream or Second Regiment of Guards march [for two fifes].

19 Captain Reed's or the Third Regiment of Guards march [for two fifes]; The Dukes march.
20 The Duke of Glousters march as performed before his majesty at the review in Hyde Park [for two fifes]; The Essex march.
21 Presidents march; Washingtons march; Stoney Point.
22 Jefferson's march; Life let us cherish; Roslin castle.
23 The Prince of Wales's march; Prince Ferdinand march; Pioneers march.
24 The Dorsetshire march [for two fifes]; March in Scipio.
25 Grenadiers march; Count Brown's march; Lord Camarthen's march.
26 Grano's march [for two fifes]; Cumberland march.
27 White Joke; Cotillion; Merrily dance the Quaker; Lady's breast knot.
28 The Philadelphia Association Quick march; Yankee Doodle; The Sette in Queen Mab; Lovely Nancy.
29 The Georgia Grenadiers march by Mr. Alexander; Heymakers dance; Guardian angels; Corellis Gavot.
30 The Congress [for two fifes].   PHi

As George Willig appears at "No. 12 South Fourth Street" for the first time in the Philadelphia city directory of 1805, the *Compleat Tutor* possibly was printed in this form as early as 1805. But there can be little doubt that the book was originally published during the second half of the eighteenth century (Sonneck).

We find on close examination, for instance, that
1. p. 21–22 have been interpolated. The original page 21 has clumsily been changed into p. 23; p. 22 into 24, etc.
2. The engraving of these two plates differs from that of the others.
3. Most of the pieces are English. The interpolated pages, however, are American airs, as "The President's march"; "Washington's march"; "Stoney Point"; "Jefferson's march."

Apparently the *President's march*, etc. were added for selling purposes, and in order to destroy to some extent the pronounced English character of the book. That it was Americanized with this object in view appears from the engraved plate. It shows a Hessian soldier playing a fife in front of a fort from the flagpole of which the American stars and stripes are flowing. The helmet of the Hessian shows the word "Liberty" instead of the Hessian coat of arms. Apparently these were rubbed out and the word "Liberty" was inserted instead. It is equally evident that the "Stars and Stripes" have been added. The plate is by *Norman*, an early American engraver, and can be traced back to Revolutionary times, as Mr. Jordan of the Pennsylvania Historical Society informed Sonneck. These facts and the tune of "The Philadelphia Association" (p. 28) render it probable that the book was originally published during the Revolution.

Probably, before being "doctored," it was identical with:

*A COMPLEATE TUTOR FOR THE FIFE, comprehending the first rudiments of music and of that instrument in an easy, familiar method. To which is annexed besides the fife duty, and the usual collection of lessons, airs on marches, in the English edition, a variety of new favourite ones never before printed.

Thus advertised in the *Pennsylvania gazette* for July 3, 1776, as "just published and to be sold by Michael Hillegas."

[85]

PLEYEL'S CELEBRATED CONCERTANTE. Adapted for the piano forte. New York, Printed and sold by J. & M. Paff, Broadway [1799–1803] 9 p. 33 cm.

Pfte. 2 hds.
At foot of p. 9: Engd. by W. Pirsson. ABHu, MWA

CONCERTOS.
Sonneck says:
> In the eighteenth century it was customary for virtuosos to play concertos of their own composition, but it was also customary not to mention the composer if a virtuoso did not play a concerto of his own. As I had to rely upon programs as printed in the newspapers it was therefore impossible, except in the very few instances mentioned to settle the problem whether our early virtuosos played concertos of their own or not, but I am convinced that our early virtuosos such as Capron, Bentley, Moller, Reinagle, Taylor, Brown, Graupner, etc., had many more concertos to their credit than have been entered here.

*CONCERT VIOLIN [by Raynor] Taylor.
Thus advertised for performance in Philadelphia on April 21, 1796, by George Gillingham at a concert, the program of which consisted chiefly of Taylor's compositions.

*A CONCERTO FOR THE ORGAN OR HARPSICHORD by William Selby
See Apollo, or, The Muse's musical companion.

A CONCERTO FOR THE PIANO FORTE or harpsichord. Composed by Sr. Giordani. Op. XIV. Pr. 8ª. Philadelphia, Printed for I. C. Moller, No. 163 North Third street, between Vine and New street. Where may be had a great variety of the newest vocal and instrumental music, etc. [1793–94] p. [29]–35. 33½ cm.

Title-page.
Caption title, p. 30: Concerto V.
Pfte. (or harpsichord) 2 hds. DLC, NN

*CONCERTO ON THE CLARINET, composed and executed by Mr. Gautier.
Thus announced on the program of a concert given at Philadelphia, December 1, 1795.

*CONCERTO ON THE CLARINET, composed and performed by Mr. Shaffer [F. Schaffer, F. C. Sheffer].
Thus announced on the program of a concert given at Boston, April 2, 1798.

*CONCERTO ON THE IMPROVED PIANOFORTE, with the additional keys.
Composed by [Alexander] Reinagle.
Thus announced for performance by Miss Broadhurst, the celebrated opera singer, at the end of the opera "The Woodman" on June 18, 1794, at the New Theatre, Philadelphia.

*CONCERTO-PIANO FORTE, Mr. Moller, was advertised to be played at the fifth city concert under the direction of Messrs. Reinagle and Moller at Mr. Oeller's Hotel, Philadelphia, January 14, 1792.

*CONCERTO VIOLINCELLO   [!]   composed and to be performed by Mr. Demarque. Thus announced on the program of a concert given at Baltimore on July 15, 1795.

*CONCERTO VIOLONCELLO—Phillips.
Thus announced on the program of the first of the twelve concerts given by "Messrs. Hewitt, Gehot, Bergman, Young and Philips" on October 4, 1792, at New York, as to be played by the composer.

*GERMAN FLUTE CONCERT with solos, composed by Giovanni Gualdo.
Was to be performed in Philadelphia, on November 16, 1769, at a "concert directed by Mr. Gualdo after the Italian method."

*VIOLIN CONCERTO by Giovanni Gualdo.
"A new violin concerto with solos, composed by Mr. Gualdo," was to be performed on November 16, 1769, in Philadelphia, at a "concert . . . directed by Mr. Gualdo after the Italian method."

*VIOLIN CONCERTO by Mr. Phile.
A "Violin concerto by Mr. Phile, of New York," (Philip Phile's name standing under "Authors,") was announced in the "Syllabus" of the First Uranian Concert, given on April 12, 1787, at Philadelphia.

THE CONGRESS.
March. *See* Compleat tutor for the fife . . . p. 30.

CONNECTICUT.
See United States country *Dances*, p. 7.

THE CONQUEST OF BELGRADE.   A sonata for the harpsichord or piano forte by Schroetter.   New York, Printed for G. Gilfert & co., at their Musical magazine, No. 191 Broadway [1795]   11 p.   31½ cm.

Title-page ornamented with wreath, eagle, shield, globe, lyre, etc.   In MB copy there is pasted on t.-p.:   To be sold at P. A. von Hagen jun. and cos. Musical magazine, No. 62 Newbury street, Boston, where may be had . . .

Pfte. 2 hds.

Advertised in April, 1795, as "published and to be had of G. Gilbert & Co., at their Musical Magazine, No. 121 Broadway," New York. *BM Cat.* gives as probable composer, J. H. Schroeter, or H. B. Schroeder. *Eitner* gives Johann Samuel Schröter (Schröder).   MB

CONSONANCE.   An anthem.   Words from Dr. Byles.
(*In* The psalm-singer's amusement, by William Billings, Boston, 1781. p. 81–89)
Four-part chorus.   Open score.
First line: Down steers the Base with grave majestic air.
                                        CSmH, DLC, ICN, MB, MHi

THE CONSTELLATION.
See Mr. *Francis's ballroom assistant.*
See No. 1 of a new sett of *Cotilions* [!]

THE CONSTITUTION.
See Mr. *Francis's ballroom assistant.*
See No. 1 of a new sett of *Cotilions* [!]

[87]

CONTENT—A pastoral. By Mr. Cunningham.
(*In* The universal asylum. May, 1791. p. 342–344)

Song, pfte. acc.
First line: O'er moorlands and mountains.   DLC (etc.)

THE CONTENTED COTTAGER. A favorite new song. New York, Printed
and sold by G. Gilfert & co., No. 177 Broadway [1796] [2] p. 31 cm.

Song, pfte. acc.
First stanza repeated with melody in higher key, p. [2].
First line: My Collin is the kindest lad.
Composed by Edward Frith.   NN, RPJCB

THE CONTENTED COTTAGER. A favorite new song. Price 25 cts. New
York, Printed and sold at J. C. Moller's musical store [1796–1803] [2] p
32½ cm.

Song, pfte. acc. Arr. in higher key, p. [2].
First line same as preceding.
Probably published about 1796.   DLC, McD–W

THE CONTENTED DWARF. A favorite romance by Shield. Published by
G. Willig, 185 Market st., Philadelphia [1798–1804] 1 l. 32½ cm.

Song, pfte. acc.
First line: Ah! tell me why should silly man.   DLC

THE CONTENTED SHEPHERD. Composed by Hook. New York, Printed
& sold by J. & M. Paff, No. 127 Broadway [1799–1803] [2] p. 30½ cm.

Song, pfte. acc.
First line: By the side of a mountain.   ES, NN

A NEW CONTREDANCE. By H. Capron.
(*In* [Moller and Capron's monthly numbers] The third number. [Phila-
delphia, 1793] p. 22)
Pfte. 2 hds.   DLC, NN, PHi

THE CONVENT BELL. A favorite song. Sung by Miss Broadhurst at the
Old city concert. New York, Printed & sold by G. Gilfert & co., No. 209
Broadway near St. Pauls [1795] 1 l. 32½ cm.

Song, pfte. acc.
First line: When waken'd by the convent bell.
Composed by Thomas Attwood.   DLC, LSL, MWA

THE CONVENT BELL. A favorite song. New York, Printed & sold by G.
Gilfert, No. 177 Broadway [1797–1801] 1 l. 32½ cm.

Song, pfte. acc.
First line same as preceding.   DLC

COOLUN. A celebrated Irish air.
(*With* The thrifty wife, by J. Hook. New York [1798] p. [2])
Song, pfte. acc.
First line: Oh! the hours I have pass'd in the arms of my dear.
                                                        MWA, NRU–Mus

[88]

CORELLIS GAVOT.
See Compleat tutor for the fife . . . p. 29.

THE CORONATION MARCH.
See Compleat tutor for the fife . . . p. 13.

CORYDON'S GHOST. By Dr. N. Dwight.
(*In* The American musical miscellany. Northampton, 1798. p. 228–230)

Two parts, treble voices, with accompanying text. Two staves.
First line: What sorrowful sounds do I hear. DLC (etc.)
Sonneck suggests that "N. Dwight" should have read "T. Dwight."

*COT PLESS HER.
Song. Advertised in March, 1797, as to be published "in a few days" by "G. Gilfert at his Musical Magazine, No. 177 Broadway," New York.

COTILLION.
See Compleat tutor for the fife . . . p. 27.

COTILLION MINUET. Composed by Mr. Sicard.
(*With* The President of the United States' march, by Mr. Sicard. Philadelphia [1789 ?])
Melody only. DLC

QUADRILL OR DOUBLE COTILLION. As danced by the scholars of Mr. Francis.
(*In* Mr. *Francis's ballroom assistant.* Philadelphia, ca. 1800. p. 15)
Pfte. 2 hds.
Composed or arranged by A. Reinagle. JFD, McD–W

——— The same as preceding. Second page, numbered 15, of a detached leaf from above collection. DLC

COTILLIONS AND COUNTRY DANCES. Selected and arranged with figures by Alexr. Dupouy. For the use of his cotillion parties. Price $1.75 cts. Philadelphia, Published and sold at G. Willig's Musical magazine [n. d.] 18 p. 33½ cm.

Title-page.
Music (pfte. 2 hds.) with directions for dancing, p. 2–18.
Thirty-four dances, without title except Nos. 31–34: The three graces, Sarah's fancy, The morning star, The four graces. DLC, NBuG

There was a certain Dupuy, an orchestral player, in New York, 1798–99; a Dupuis, apparently a French horn player, in New York, 1797. Whether these are identical, and the same as our Alexr. Dupouy, we do not know. That he here appears as a probable dancing master is not at all inconsistent. Published probably ca. 1800.

FAVORITE COTILLIONS. Introduced by P. L. Duport. For the piano forte, harp, clarinett, flute and flagelet [!]. New York, Engrav'd and publish'd by I. and M. Paff [ca. 1800 ?] [2] p. 32½ cm.

Pfte. 2 hds.
At foot of p. [1], "No. I. The signal" (with directions for dancing) followed by "Copyright secured."
At top of p. [2], "No. II. The polle" (with directions for dancing).
ABHu, NBuG, NN

FAVORITE COTILLIONS . . . With identical title and imprint, all separate sheets [2] p. each:

At foot of p. [1], "No. III. Lespagnol . . ."
At top of p. [2], "No. IIII. The rose . . ."

At foot of p. [1], "No. V. Hope . . ."
At top of p. [2], "No. VI. Faith . . ."

At foot of p. [1], "No. VII. Charity . . ."
At top of p. [2], "The two friends, No. VIII . . ."

At foot of p. [1], "No. VIIII [!] The waltz cotillion . . ."
At top of p. [2], "No. X. A menuit [!], composed by P. L. Duport, Professor of dancing . . ."

"Copyright secured" appears on all except the last. However, no such record has been found.

ABHu (complete), NN (complete), NBuG (VII and VIII)

Duport seems to have been particularly active in New York ca. 1798-1801.

MARINE COTILLIONS.
See Mr. *Francis's ballroom assistant.*

NO. 1 OF A NEW SETT OF COTILIONS [!] With figures called after the American navy. Composed by Mr. P. Langrin Duport, Professor of dancing from Paris and original composer of cadriels [!] New York, Printed for the Author & copyright secured. Rollinson Sct. [n. d.] 1 p.l., 20 p. 26 x 17 cm.

Title-page, verso blank; recto p. 1 blank; music (melody only) with directions for dancing, p. 1–20.
At foot of t.-p., signature of composer: P. L. Duport.

Contents:
p. 1–2 The Eagle
    3–4 The Constitution
    5–6 The President
    7–8 The Constellation
    9–10 The Essex
    11–12 The Merrimack
    13–14 The Chesapeak [!]
    15–16 The Herald
    17–18 The Experiment
    19–20 The Enterprise

DLC copy bound with Duport's *United States country dances,* copyright November 3, 1800, and presumably published about the same time. William Rollinson, engraver in America ca. 1780–1842.   DLC

TWO NEW FAVORITE COTILLIONS. The music and figures composed and introduced by P. L. Duport, Professor of dancing. Printed and sold at Carr's music store, Baltimore. [n. d.] [2] p. 32½ cm.

At lower r. h. corner each page: D. C.
Pfte. 2 hds.
Amanda, p. [1]; Rosedale, p. [2]. Each followed by directions for dancing.
Published probably ca. 1800 or 180-.   McD–W

THE COTTAGE BOY. A favorite song. New York, Printed and sold bv
G. Gilfert, No. 177 Broadway [1797–1801] [2] p. 33½ cm.

Song, pfte. acc.
First line: Morn shook her locks.
Sung in Philadelphia as early as February 2, 1793.   DLC, JFD, MWA

THE COTTAGE IN THE GROVE. Sung by Mr. Tyler. Composed by Mr.
Hook. Printed & sold by Carr at his Repository's, Philadelphia & N. York.
And by I. Carr, Baltimore (20 cts.) [1794–97] [2] p. 33 cm.

Song, pfte. acc.
First line: Now wanton gales perfume the glade.
The cottage of the grove, sung by Joseph Tyler, New York, November 15,
1796.   CtY, DLC, LSL, MWA, NRU–Mus, RPJCB

THE COTTAGE IN THE GROVE. A favorite song. Boston, Printed & sold
by P. A. von Hagen & co. at their warranted piano forte ware house, No. 3
Cornhill and G. Gilfert, New York. Where also may be had the much
admired songs of Come buy my daffodillies and No not yet [1799–1800]
[2] p. 33 cm.

Below imprint: For the piano fortes, German flute or violin.
Song, pfte. acc.
First line same as preceding.
Published probably in 1799.   NBuG, RPJCB

THE COTTAGE IN THE GROVE. A favorite new song. New York, Publish'd
for P. Weldon. 25 cents. [ca. 1800] 2 p. 30½ cm.

Song, pfte. acc.
First line same as preceding.   DLC, LSL

*THE COTTAGE OF THE MOOR.
This "very favorite ballad" was advertised in October, 1800, as "published
at Chalk's Musical Repository and Circulating Library, No. 57 North Third
Street," Philadelphia. Probably identical with:

THE COTTAGE ON THE MOOR. A favorite song in the pantomime of Niobe.
Composed by Sanderson. Written by Mr. Cross. Philadelphia, Printed &
sold by G. Willig, No. 185 Market st [1798–1804] [2] p. 33 cm.

Song, pfte. acc.
First line: My mam is no more and my dad in his grave.
Sanderson: James Sanderson.   DLC, JFD, MWA, PHi

This title was advertised in the *Federal gazette,* Baltimore, in November 1800,
as "just published." Whether reference is made to this imprint or the following one is uncertain. It seems likely, however, that both should be dated ca.
1800.
The cottage on the moor was sung by Joseph Tyler in New York, July 16, 1799.

THE COTTAGE ON THE MOOR. A favorite ballad. Composed by J.
Sanderson. [n. p., ca. 1800] [2] p. 30½ cm.

Song, pfte. acc.
First line same as preceding.   DLC, MdHi

THE COTTAGE ON THE MOOR. A favorite new song. New York, Published by P. Weldon [ca. 1800] [2] p. 32 cm.

Song, pfte, acc. Arr. for Ger. flute, p. [2].
First line same as preceding. DLC

THE COTTAGER.
(*In* The American musical miscellany. Northampton, 1798. p. 128–129)

Two parts (treble) with accompanying text. Two staves.
First line: As on a lonely hill I stray'd.
BM Cat. assigns this song to William Wheatley. DLC (etc.)

THE COTTAGER'S DAUGHTER. Printed & sold at B. Carr's Musical repository, Philadelphia; J. Carr's Baltimore & J. Hewitt's, New York. (Price 25 cents) [1797–99] [2] p. 32½ cm.

Song, pfte. acc. Arr. for "guittar," p. [2].
First line: Ah tell me ye swains have you seen my Pastora.
ABHu, LSL, McD–W, MdHi, NN

THE COTTAGER'S DAUGHTER. Boston, Printed & sold by P. A. von Hagen, junr. & co., No. 3 Cornhill. Also by G. Gilfert, New York [ca. 1800] 1 l. 32 cm.

Song, pfte. acc.
First line same as preceding. DLC, MWA, NN

THE COTTAGER'S DAUGHTER. New York, Sold by I. and M. Paff, No. 127 Broadway [1799–1803] [2] p. 32½ cm.

Below title: Arranged for the piano forte, violin, or flute.
Imprint at foot of p. [2].
At head of imprint (pasted on), "New York, Sold at S. Terrett's music store, No. 320 Pearl street" [1804–05].
Song, pfte. acc.
First line same as preceding.
Sung in New York as early as 1798. MB, McD–W

THE COTTAGER'S DAUGHTER. Philadelphia, Printed and sold by G. Willig, Mark. street, N. 185 [1798–1804] 1 l. 31½ cm.

Song, pfte. acc.
First line same as preceding.
The cottager's daughter was sung by Joseph Tyler in New York, June 13, 1798, and May 22, 1800. DLC, NN, NRU–Mus

COUNT BROWN'S MARCH.
See Compleat tutor for the fife . . . p. 25.

COUNTRY DANCES.
See Country *Dances*.

COURT ME NOT TO SCENES OF PLEASURE. Sung by Miss Broadhurst. Printed & sold at Carr's Musical repository's, Philadelphia & N. York & by I. Carr, Baltimore (20 cts.) [1794–97] [2] p. 33½ cm.

Song, pfte. acc.
First line same as title.
Sung by Miss Broadhurst in New York, January 21, 1796.
CtY, DLC, ES, LSL, MdHi

[92]

COURTEOUS STRANGER. The favorite polonaise. Sung by Miss Broadhurst in Zorinsky.
(*In* The Musical journal for the piano forte, ed. by B. Carr, Baltimore [1800]
v. 1, no. [7], p. (14)–(16).)

Song, pfte. acc.
First line: Courteous stranger, now free from danger.
Samuel Arnold's opera *Zorinski* (with Miss Broadhurst in the cast) was first
performed in New York, March 23, 1798.

DLC, ES, LSL, MdHi, NN, NRU–Mus, PP–K

——— The same.
(*In* The musical journal for the flute or violin. Baltimore [1800] no. 7,
p. 14–16)

Melody only, flute or violin, with accompanying text.
First line same as preceding. DLC

CRAZY EMMA. The words by a lady of Queen Ann's county. Music by
J. B. Gauline. Printed by G. Willig, No. 185 Market street, Philadelphia
[1798–1804] [2] p. 33½ cm.

Song, pfte. acc.
First line: When far from thee by adverse fortune drove.

CSmH, DLC, MdHi

CRAZY HENRY TO CRAZY JANE. Composed by Thos. Welch. Boston,
Printed & sold at P. A. von Hagen's imported piano forte & music warehouse, No. 3 Cornhill [ca. 1800] 3 p. 32 cm.

Song, pfte. acc.
First line: As frantic Henry his morning ramble took.
Possibly as early as 1799. ES, LSL, NBuG

CRAZY JANE. The original ballad. The words by G. M. Lewis, esqr. The
music by John Davy. New York, Printed & sold by G. Gilfert, No. 177
Broadway. Also by P. A. von Hagen & co., No. 3 Cornhill, Boston [1799–
1800] [2] p. 31 cm.

Song, pfte. acc. Arr. for German flute, violin, clarinett and "guittar," p. [2].
First line: Why fair maid in ev'ry feature.

DLC, ES, LSL, MH, NRU–Mus, RPJCB

CRAZY JANE. A favorite song. Boston, Printed & sold at P. A. von Hagen's
music store, No 3 Cornhill. And to be had of G. Gilfert, No. 177 Broad
Way, New York [1800] 1 l. 29½ cm.

In lower margin, at the right: July 1800.
Song, pfte. acc.
First line same as preceding.
Composed by John Davy. JFD

"The much admired song of Crazy Jane" was advertised in November, 1800,
as "just published" by P. A. von Hagen, No. 3 Cornhill. On November 29,
we read:

"This day published . . . Henry's return, or the sequel to Crazy Jane,"
and on December 23, "N. B. Next week will be published The Death of
Crazy Jane."

[93]

CRAZY JANE. A favorite song. The words by Mr. Lewis, esqr. Set to music by Miss Abrams. Philadelphia, Printed and sold by G. Willig, No. 185 Market st. [ca. 1800] [2] p. 32½ cm.

Song, pfte. acc.
First line same as preceding.
Miss Abrams: Harriet Abrams. DLC, ES, MWA, NRU–Mus

CRAZY JANE. Sung by Mrs. Hodgkinson. [n. p., n. d.] 1 l. 32½ cm.
Song, pfte. acc.
First line same as preceding.
This setting is neither that of Miss Abrams nor of John Davy. It is presumably the one sung by Mrs. Hodgkinson in New York, June 13, 1800. Probably published ca. 1800. DLC, MB, MH, RPJCB

CRAZY LAIN. Written by a gentlemen [!] in Kent county. Music by J. B. Gauline. Philadelphia, Printed by G. Willig, No. 185 Market Street [1798–1804] [2] p. 30½ cm.

Song, pfte. acc.
First line: O come Louisa lovely fair. MdHi

THE CRICKET. A favorite song. Composed by Dr. G. K. Jackson. Sung by Miss Brett with applause. Printed for the Author, Copyright secured. (*In* New miscellaneous musical work, by Dr. G. K. Jackson [n. p., ca. 1800] p. 1–2)

Song, pfte. acc.
First line: Little inmate full of mirth. DLC, MWA

——— Separate issue of preceding, ca. 1800. DLC, MWA

THE CROPS. A favorite song. Composed by Mr. Hook.
(*In* [Unidentified collection of instrumental and vocal music. New York] Hewitt & Rausch [1797] p. 23–24)

Song, pfte. acc.
First line: Ye nymphs & swains attend my strains. DLC, ES

——— The same as preceding.
(*In* A collection of new & favorite songs. [A] Philadelphia [ca. 1800] p. [40]–[41]) HFB

*THE CROPS.
Song. Advertised in March, 1797, as to be published "in a few days" by "G. Gilfert at his Musical Magazine, No. 177 Broadway," New York.

THE CUCKOO. Selected from The Aviary. A collection of sonnets.
Also just published:

No. 1.	The thrush.	No. 4.	The robin red breast.
No. 2.	The linnets.	No. 5.	The nightingale.
No. 3.	The gold finch.	No. 6.	The lark.

and No. 7. The blackbird.
New York, Sold by I. and M. Paff, No. 127 Broadway [1799–1803] [2] p. 32½ cm.

At head of title: No. 8.
Imprint at foot of p. [2].

Song, pfte. acc.
First line: Now the sun is in the West.
Composed by James Hook.   ABHu, DLC, JFD, NN, RPJCB

———— Separate issue of preceding, but without imprint, ca. 1800.   JFD, MB

CUMBERLAND MARCH.
See Compleat tutor for the fife . . . p. 26.

CUPID BENIGHTED.   Sung by Mrs. Jordan in the new comedy of the Wedding day. New York, Printed for G. Gilfert & co., No. 209 Broadway, near St. Pauls [1795] 1 l. 31½ cm.

Song, pfte. acc.
First line: In the dead of the night.
Tune adapted from "At the dead of the night" from Samuel Arnold's *Zorinski*.   After first line, text entirely different.
Mrs. Inchbald's comedy *The wedding day* had its American première in Philadelphia, May 22, 1795.   JFD, MWA

———— The same.   New York, Printed & sold by Geo. Gilfert, No. 177 Broadway [1797–1801] 1 l.   34 cm.

Song, pfte. acc.
First line same as preceding.   JFD, RPJCB

CUPID BENIGHTED.
(*In* The musical journal for the piano forte, ed. by B. Carr. Baltimore [1800]   v. 1, no. 3, p. (8).)

Song, pfte. acc.
First line same as preceding.   DLC, ES, MdHi, NN, NRU–Mus

CUPID BENIGHTED.
(*In* The musical journal for the flute or violin. Baltimore [1800] no. 3, p. 8)

Melody only, flute or violin, with accompanying text.
First line same as preceding.   DLC

———— In the dead of the night. A favorite song. Sung by Mrs. Jordan at the Theatre Royal Drury Lane in the comedy of the Wedding day. [n. p., n. d.] [2] p.   34 cm.

Song, pfte. acc.   Arr. for "guittar," p. [2].
First line same as title.
This is perhaps the issue advertised in February, 1796, as "published . . . printed and sold by Benjamin Carr at his Musical Repository, No. 131 William-street," New York.   MH

CYMRO OBLE, or the Welch [!] question.
(*In* Young's vocal and instrumental musical miscellany. Philadelphia [1793–95] p. 17)

Pfte. 2 hds. (sixteen measures) followed by directions for dancing.
In No. 2, 1793.   DLC, HFB, Hopk.

CYNTHIA'S COTTAGE. A new favorite serenade. Philadelphia, Printed by G. Willig, No. 165 Market street. The words by Mr. Derrick. [1795–97] 1 l. 30½ cm.

Song, pfte. acc.
First line: When at night the village swains.
Sonneck gives date as 1795. DLC, LSL, MWA, PP, PU

DAMON AND CLORA [A duet in canon form].
See The select songster, New Haven, 1786. p. 5–7.

DAMON & CLORA. A favorite dialogue. Price 25 cents. Philadelphia, Printed at Carrs Musical repository [1794] 4 p. 32 cm.

Duet in canon form, pfte. acc. Three staves.
First lines: Turn fair Clora.—Go false Damon.
At foot of p. [2]: This may be play'd as a duett by two flutes or guittars.
Composed by Henry Harington.
On p. 4: The reconciliation. Being a sequel to Damon and Clora. Composed by R. Taylor.
Advertised in October, 1794, as published among "new songs, never published in America." DLC, Hopk., LSL

*THE DANAIDES. Pantomime by Quenet. Music by Victor Pelissier. Performed by the Old American Company at the Southwark Theatre, Philadelphia, October 8, 1794, and in New York, January 3, 1795. Seilhamer speaks of it as "very popular" (v. 3, p. 102).

DANCE FOR WALTZING. [Philadelphia] Publish'd by G. Willig, Market st., No. 165 [1795–97] [2] p. 33½ cm.

Pfte. 2 hds.
Contains not *one*, but *six* short waltzes. DLC, JFD, NN, PP-K

DANCE TUNES, ETC., by Pierre Landrin Duport.
This autograph collection, now in the Library of Congress, containing about seventy airs for dancing (jigs, sarabandes, cotillions, etc.) or marching, bears dates from 1783–1834. Several of the earlier tunes were written in Boston and New York. Their titles are entertaining, not alone on account of Duport's orthography. The dances composed until 1800 are the following:

No. 4. English dance; Jig to pleas Miss Hall, Boston, 1793
No. 8. Compose in New Jersey 1790
No. 11. Allemand belong to the May at Boston 1794
No. 11*. Air favôry of Miss Gair at Boston 1793
No. 14. Menuit & Gavôtte. belong to Miss K. Henne & performd by Her. Composed By P. L. D. in New York 1800
No. 15. Franch Contre-Dance-Call Convention belong to the May at Boston 1794
No. 19. Grand Jig for A Ballet at Boston 1796
No. 24. Grand Contre-Dance La Clement belong to a quadreil at Boston in 1786
No. 25. Sarabande. Made for a Quadreill at Boston in 1794
No. 29. English Dance. Composed for Miss Burr at New York 1797 Cotillion Mr. Rizzio. Compose at New York 1798
No. 30. Miss Burr faverette New York 1799

[96]

No. 31. Miss Charch's fancy New York 1798
No. 35. Fancy Menuit with figure Dance by Two young Ladies in the presance of Mrs. Washington in 1792. Philada.
No. 39. Franch Milôdy may be Dance as a Cotillion made at Boston 1793
No. 40. Fancy Menuit Dance before Genl. Washington 1792
Nos. 43 and 44. Minuetto & Gavott Compos'd by Alxr. Reinagle Esqr. The Marige of 84   Made in Boston 1796.   The return to New York in 1797   DLC

FAVORITE COUNTRY DANCE. Compos'd by Dibdin.
(*With* [Say how can words a passion feign] by S. Storace.   Philadelphia [ca. 1795])

Melody only.   ES, LSL, NN

COUNTRY DANCES:
Speed the plough, Philadelphia medley, The lucky hit, The stranger, The secret, Virginia Reel.
See Mr. *Francis's ballroom assistant.*

TWENTY FOUR AMERICAN COUNTRY DANCES as danced by the British during their winter quarters at Philadelphia, New York & Charles Town.   Collected by Mr. Cantelo Musician at Bath, where they are now dancing for the first time in Britain, with the addition of Six favorite minuets now performing this present spring season 1785.   Price 5 s.   London. Printed by Longman & Broderip, No. 26 Cheapside & 13 Hay Market . . . 31 p. of music.   8°.   oblong.

Formerly in possession of Governor Samuel W. Pennypacker of Philadelphia.
Present location unknown.
Of the six minuets, four were written by Cantelo.
The dances are written for treble and bass.

Contents:
p. 1 The Hamiltonian—Lady Amelia Murray's choice. (By the Hon. C. G.).
    2 The Monckton—or British white feathers. (Hon. C. G.).
    3 Lady George Murray's reel.
    4 La Buona Figuiliola—Lady Jean Murray's Dance (from Piccini).
    5 The Fair Emigrant—or Mrs. Dawsons delight. (Hon. C. G.).
    6 General Abercromby's reel or the Light Bob. (Hon. C. G.).
    7 The Walton (Capt. W.).
    8 Mrs. Lt. Col. Johnson's reel—(Hon. C. G.).
    9 La Belle Frene—(Austrian Dance).
   10 Mrs. S. Douglas' reel. (Royal Navy) Hon. C. G.
   11 Capt. Oaker's whim. (33d regt.).
   12 The Belles about the Flat Bush—(a Village on Long Island so called).
   13 La Belle Annette.
   14 The Yager horn.
   15 How imperfect is expression (Capt. O–).
   16 The Heredetary prince.
   17 Laurel Hill.
   18 The Munichhausen.

[97]

19 The Moment—or the victory.
20 The St. George (Capt. Baker's choice).
21 L'Escapade.
22 The Brandewine.
23 The Donop—Lady Mary Murray's fantaisie.
24 The Anspacher.

Cantelo, "musician at Bath" was with the British Army in Philadelphia'
New York and Charles Town.

TWENTY-FOUR FASHIONABLE COUNTRY DANCES for the year 1799,
with their proper figures as performed at court, & Bath, and all public
assemblys. London, printed, Boston, reprinted and sold by W. Norman
[1799 ?] 7 l. obl. 4to.

With music.
In original wrappers. NN

UNITED STATES COUNTRY DANCES. With figures also accompaniments
for the piano forte. Composed in America by Mr. P. Landrin Duport,
Professor of dancing from Paris & original composer of cadriels [!] New
York, Printed for the author. Copyright secured. Price 1 dol. & fifty
cents. Roberts, Sc. [n. d.] 1 p. l., 20 p. 26 x 17 cm.

Title-page, verso blank; recto p. 1 blank; music (pfte. 2 hds.) with directions
for dancing (except first and last numbers) p. 1–20.
At foot of t.-p., signature of composer: P. L. Duport.
At foot of p. 20: Engraved by Wm. Pirsson, No. 417 Pearl Street, New York.

Contents:

p. 1–2 Washington's minuet and gavott.
3 No. 1. Vermont. French country dance.
4 No. 2. New Hampshire. Allemande.
5 No. 3. Massachusetts hop.
6 No. 4. Rhode Island jigg.
7 No. 5. Connecticut.
8 No. 6. New York.
9 No. 7. New Jersey.
10 No. 8. Pennsylvania.
11 No. 9. Delaware.
12 No. 10. Maryland.
13 No. 11. Virginia.
14 No. 12. Kentucky. French country dance.
15 No. 13. North Caroline jigg.
16 No. 14. Tennessee.
17 No. 15. South Carolina.
18 No. 16. Georgia. French country dance.
19–20 Duport's hornpipe.

Copyright recorded November 3, 1800.
Published probably in 1800.
John Roberts, engraver, in America 1793–1803.
William Pirsson was at 417 Pearl street, New York, ca. 1797–1801. DLC

DANS VOTRE LIT.   Sung by Mr. Marshall in Patrick in Prussia.
(*In* The gentleman's amusement, ed. by R. Shaw.   Philadelphia [1794–96].
p. 69)

At foot of page, "From the overture."   Duet for flutes (or violins) or flute
and violin.

Melody only, flute (or violin) with accompanying text.
First line: Dans votre lit that bright parterre.
In No. [9], ca. 1796.
Love in a camp, or Patrick in Prussia, by William Shield.   PP–K

———— The same as preceding.   First page, numbered 69, of a detached portion
of above collection.   PHi

DANS VOTRE LIT.
See Evening amusement [1796]   p. 22.

DARBY'S RETURN.   A comic sketch, as performed at the New York theatre,
November 24, 1789, For the Benefit of Mr. Wignell.   Written by William
Dunlap.   New York.   Printed by Hodge, Allen and Campbell and sold at
their respective Bookstores and by Berry and Rogers.   1789.   14, [2] p.
23½ cm.

Libretto.
Title-page.   To the public, p. 3; characters, p. 4; text, p. [5]–14.   An etch-
ing precedes the t.-p. representing "Mr. Wignell in the character of Darby,"
signed "Wm. Dunlap del. et fect."
                                    CSmH, MB, MBAt, NN, PU, RPB

A fac-simile reprint of this once popular comic operatic sketch is contained in
the publications of the Dunlap Society for 1899, in P. L. Ford's *Washington
and the theatre.*   Printed also in the *New York magazine* January, 1790, p.
47–51.

DARBY'S RETURN.   A comic sketch.   As performed at the New York and
Philadelphia Theatres.   Written by William Dunlap.   Philadelphia, Printed
and sold by Enoch Story.   1791.   12 p.   16½ cm.

Libretto.
On t.-p., between title and imprint, an elaborate monogram "E S"; verso
t.-p. blank; "To the public" and cast of characters, p. [3].   CtY

THE DAUPHIN.
See The select songster, New Haven, 1786.   p. 52–53.

———— The same.
(*In* The   songster's assistant, ed. by T. Swan.   Suffield [ca. 1800]   p. 27–28.]
Song, pfte. acc.
First line: Ye sons of Mars attend.   MB

THE DAWN OF HOPE.   Set by H. J.
(*In* The Massachusetts magazine.   Boston, May, 1791.   p. 313.)
Song, pfte. acc.
First line: A dawn of hope my soul revives.   DLC (etc.)

[99]

THE DAY OF GLORY.
See Manuscript collection of hymns, songs, etc. (49).

*THE DAYS OF OLD, or The battle of Hexham. An opera by George Colman, jun. Author of Inkle and Yarico, Mountineers, &c. Boston, Printed at the Apollo Press, by Joseph Belknap for William P. Blake, 1795.
Libretto.

THE DAYS OF OLD, or The battle of Hexham. A comedy in three acts. As performed at The Theatre in Boston. Boston, Printed by John and Jos. N. Russell and sold at their printing chamber over Maj. Hawes's workshops, Quaker Lane (Price 20 cents) [1796] 44 p. 12 mo.
Libretto. MWA, NBuG

With "orchestra accompaniments entirely new, composed by Mr. [P.' A.] van Hagen [senior], leader of the band," this "historical, tragic, comic opera" was to be performed at the Hay Market Theatre in Boston, on January 25, 1797.

*DE TOUT MON COEUR, by Raynor Taylor.
This song was advertised in February, 1798, as "by B. Carr, at his Repository Market street . . . republished . . . with many of the same author."

THE DEAD ALIVE, or The double funeral. A comic opera. In two acts. With additions and alterations. As performed by the Old American Company in New York: with universal applause. By John O'Keefe, Esquire; author of the Poor Soldier, Agreeable Surprise, and twenty four other dramatic pieces. With an account of the author. New York: Printed by Hodge, Allen and Campbell; and sold at their respective book-stores. 1789. 1 p. l., iv, [7]-46, [2] p. 18 cm.

Libretto to Samuel Arnold's opera (1781).
Title-page, verso blank; "An account of John O'Keefe, Esquire," p. [i]-iv; list of actors in the play, p. iv; text, p. [7]-46; advertisements and list of recent publications, p. [47]-[48]. Certain copies lack p. [47]-[48].
CtY, DLC, MB, NHi, NIC, NN, PHi

DEAD MARCH.
See Military amusement, p. 22.

DEAD MARCH.
See Compleat tutor for the fife . . . p. 11.

DEAD MARCH.
(*In* New miscellaneous musical work, by Dr. G. K. Jackson [n. p., ca. 1800] p. 18)
Pfte. 2 hds. DLC, MWA

DEAD MARCH & MONODY. Performed in the Lutheran Church, Philadelphia on Thursday, the 26 December 1799, being part of the music selected for funeral honours to our late illustrious cheif [!] General George Washington. Composed for the occasion and respectfully dedicated to the Senate of the United States by their obet. humble servt. B. Carr . . . Printed by J. Carr, Baltimore. Copyright secured. [1799–1800] [2] p. 36 cm.

Imprint at foot of p. [2].
Dead march (pfte. 2 hds.), p. [1].

[100]

Monody. Sung by Miss Broadhurst, p. [1]–[2].
First line: Sad are the tidings rumuour [!] tells.
"Dead march. Adapted for two flutes, violins, clarinetts or guittars," p. [2].
"Monody. Adapted for two voices, flutes, violins, clarinetts or guittars," p. [2].
PHi copy has portrait of Washington mounted in title. Other copies lack this portrait.
This rare and impressive piece must have been published either very late in December, 1799, or early in January, 1800, for J. Carr, in Baltimore, advertised it for sale on January 13, 1800. CSmH, DLC, ES, LSL, PHi

DEAR ANNA. A new song. The words by George Heyl, and set to music by A. Reinagle. [Philadelphia] Printed and sold by G. Willig, Market street, No. 185 [1798–1804] 1 l. 32½ cm.

Song, pfte. acc.
First line: Dear Anna repine not the Gods bid us scorn. DLC, PP-K

DEAR GENTLE KATE. Sung by Mr. Incledon. Vauxhall.
(In A collection of favorite songs, divided into two books. Arr. by A. Reinagle. Philadelphia [1789?] bk. 2, p. 14–15)

Song, pfte. acc.
First line: Dear gentle Kate, oh! ease my care. CdeW, DLC, PU

DEAR IS MY LITTLE NATIVE VALE. A favorite song. Composed by Hook. Printed & sold at B. Carr's Musical repository, Philadelphia; J. Carr's, Baltimore & J. Hewitt's, New York. (32 cts.) [1797–99] 3 p. 30 cm.

Song, pfte. acc.
First line same as title. ABHu, LSL, McD-W, MdHi

DEAR LITTLE COTTAGE MAID.
(In Elegant extracts for the German flute or violin. Philadelphia [1796] bk. 2, p. 8–9.)

Melody only, flute or violin, with accompanying text.
First line: From place to place I travers'd long.
Composed by James Hook. DLC, NN

———— The same.
(In The American musical miscellany. Northampton, 1798. p. 170–172)

Melody only, with accompanying text.
First line same as preceding. DLC (etc.)

DEAR LITTLE COTTAGE MAIDEN. Sung with great applause at Vauxhall Gardens. Sold at Carr's Musical repository's, Philadelphia & N. York and by J. Carr, Baltimore. Price 20 cents [1796] [2] p. 32½ cm.

Song, pfte. acc. Arr. for guitar, p. [2].
First line: From place to place I travers'd long.
Advertised as published in March, 1796. CtY, MWA

[101]

DEAR MARY, OR ADIEU TO OLD ENGLAND. Price 25 cents. New York, Printed & sold at J. Hewitt's Musical repository, No. 131 William street. Sold also by B. Carr, Philadelphia & J. Carr, Baltimore [1797–99] ⟍ [2] p. 33 cm.

Imprint at foot of p. [2].
Song, pfte. acc.
First line: Farewel [!] to old England, thy white cliffs adieu.
Composed by Michael Arne.   DLC, MB, MH

────── The same as preceding.
(In A collection of new & favorite songs. [A] Philadelphia [ca. 1800] p. [70]–[71].)   HFB

────── The same as preceding, but with additional imprint at foot of p. [1]:
Sold by Wm. Howe, No. 320 Pearl street, N. York [1797–98]   NRU–Mus

DEAR NANCY I'VE SAIL'D THE WORLD ALL AROUND, or the pretty brunette.
See Then say my sweet girl can you love me, or The pretty brunette.

DEAR WALTER.   Alternative title of Dorothy Dump, by Samuel Arnold.

DEAR WANDERER.   A song in the opera of the Midnight wanderers.
(In The musical repertory.   Boston.   [1796] No. I. p. (16).)

Song, pfte. acc.
First line: Dear wand'rer, O whither thy steps shall I trace.
The Midnight wanderers, by William Shield.   DLC

────── The same.   Second page, numbered (16), of a detached leaf from above collection, 1796.   JFD

────── Separate issue of preceding.   Verso blank.   ca. 1796.   MB

DEAR WHITELANDS ADIEU.   By a young lady only fourteen years of age leaving Whitelands School.   New York, Printed for G. Gilfert & co., at their Musical magazine, No. 177 Broadway [1796] 1 1. 34 cm.

Song, pfte. acc.
First line: Vacation approaches with sadness I learn.   JFD, MWA

[DEAR YANKOO WHITHER DOST THOU STRAY]   Sung by Mrs. Oldmixon.
(In The volunteers, by A. Reinagle.   Philadelphia [1795] p. 11–12)

Song, pfte. acc.
Title from first line.
Sung by Mrs. Oldmixon in Philadelphia in what were apparently the only performances of The volunteers, January 21 and 26, 1795.   DLC

THE MUCH ADMIR'D DEATH AND BURIAL OF COCK ROBIN.   Composed by Dr. Arnold.
(In The Musical journal for the piano forte, ed. by B. Carr.   Baltimore [1800] v. 1, no. [5].   p. (10)–(12).)

Song, pfte. acc.
First line: Who kill'd poor Robin.
                    DLC, ES, McD–W, MdHi, NN, NRU–Mus, PP–K

THE DEATH OF ANNA. A favourite ballad. Sung by Mr. Incledon. Written by John Bayley, esqr. Composed with an accompaniment for the harp or piano forte by Reginald Spofforth. Pr. 30 ct. [1799] p. 81–83. 31 cm.

Song, pfte. (or harp) acc.
First line: Oh hear a poor and shepherds tale.
Verso of p. 83 blank. Evidently a separate issue from No. VI of *The Musical repertory.* Boston, 1799.   DLC

THE DEATH OF CRAZY JANE. A favorite new song. Composed with an accompaniment for the piano forte. By Reginald Spofforth. New York, Printed & sold at G. Gilfert's Music store, No. 177 Broadway [1797–1801] 2 p. 32½ cm.

Song, pfte. acc. Three staves.
First line: O'er the gloomy woods resounding.
Published probably ca. 1800.
First London edition, 1799.   McD–W

THE DEATH OF CRAZY JANE. Boston, Printed and sold at P. A. von Hagen & co. imported piano forte & music warehouse, No. 3 Cornhill [1800] 1 l. 31 cm.

Song, pfte. acc.
First line same as preceding.   JFD, LSL, MB, NRU–Mus, RPB

Advertised December 23, 1800: N. B. Next week will be published The Death of Crazy Jane.

THE DEATH OF CRAZY JANE. An admir'd sequel to the favorite ballad of Crazy Jane. Composed by an amaeteur [!]
(*In* The Musical journal for the piano forte, ed. by B. Carr. Baltimore [1800] v. 2, no. 27. p. (5)–(6).)

At head of title: Decr. 15, 1800. Journal No. 27. Vocal.
Song, pfte. acc.
First line: In awful gloom the tufted grove.   DLC, ES, LSL, MdHi, NN

DEATH OF GENERAL WOLFE.
See General Wolfe.

*THE DEATH OF MAJOR ANDRE and Arnold's treachery, or West Point preserved. Composed by a citizen of Philadelphia. "The music selected from the most celebrated French and English matters [!]"

Performed at Lailson's Circus, Philadelphia, May 14, 1798.

THE DEATH OF POOR COCK ROBIN. Composed and sung by Master Walsh of Drury Lane Theatre. Price 25 cents. Printed and sold at B. Carr's Musical repository, Philadelphia; J. Carr's, Baltimore and J. Hewitt's, New York. [2] p. 32½ cm.

(*In* A Collection of new & favorite songs. [B] Philadelphia [1797–99] no paging)

Song, pfte. acc.
First line: Here, here, here lies Cock Robin.   PU

[103]

———— Separate issue of preceding, 1798.   DLC, LSL, PP–K, NI'

Advertised in January, 1798, as published "at Carr's Musical Repository."

DEATH OR VICTORY.
(*In* The American musical miscellany. Northampton, 1798. p. 256–258
Melody only, with accompanying text.
First line: Hark the din of distant war.
From *The wags*, by Charles Dibdin.   DLC (etc.

———— The same.
(*In* Elegant extracts for the German flute or violin. Baltimore [1794] bk. 1
p. 30–31.)

Melody only, flute or violin, with accompanying text.
First line same as preceding.   DLC, NN

THE DEATH SONG OF AN INDIAN CHIEF. Taken from "Ouâbi" ar
Indian tale in four cantos, by Philenia, a lady of Boston.   Set to musick by
Mr. Hans Gram, of Boston.
(*In* The Massachusetts magazine, Boston, March, 1791. On fly-lea
between p. 180–181)

For tenor voice with orch. acc.
This setting of Mrs. Sarah Wentworth Morton's song was the first orchestra
score published in the United States, so far as Sonneck was able to discover.
The (not very valuable) piece is scored for strings, two clarinets, and two
E-flat horns. The words begin:

Rear'd midst the war empurpled plain
What Illinois submits to pain!   DLC (etc.)

DEATH SONG OF THE CHEROKEE INDIANS. Alternative title of
Alknomook.

THE DECLARATION OF INDEPENDENCE. A poem: accompanied by
odes, songs &c. adapted to the day. [Two lines from] Thomson. By a
citizen of Boston.   Printed at Boston [by Isaiah Thomas and E. T. Andrews]
Faust's Statue, No. 45 Newbury street. 1793. 24 p. 8vo

Words only.
Dedicated to John Hancock.
"A citizen of Boston": George Richards. MBAt, MHi, MWA, NHi, RPJCB

Reprinted in an edition of fifty copies in New York in 1870.

DELAWARE.
See United States country *Dances*, p. 11.

DELIA.
See The select songster. New Haven, 1786. p. 15.

DELIA. A new song by H. Capron.
(*In* [Moller & Capron's monthly numbers] The second number [Philadelphia, 1793] p. 14–15)
Song, pfte. acc.
First line: Soft pleasing pains unknown before.   DLC

[104]

———— The same. Printed and sold by G. Willig, No. 185 Market st., Philadelphia [1798–1804] p. 14–15.

Reprint of the preceding.
Moller & Capron were at 163 North Third street, Philadelphia, in 1793. George Willig took over their business in November, 1794, or thereabouts, remaining until 1795, when he moved to 165 Market street—later to 185. It is perfectly natural then that we find Willig printing from Moller & Capron plates.   DLC, NHi, PP–K

THE DELIGHTS OF WEDDED LOVE. Written & Sung by Mrs. Melmoth. (*In* Four songs from an unidentified collection, ed. by B. Carr. New York, ca. 1795] p. [1])

Song, pfte. acc.
First line: Mark my Alford all the joys.   NN

———— Separate issue of preceding, ca. 1795.   MWA

Sung by Mrs. Melmoth in Samuel Arnold's opera, *The children in the wood*, January 2, 1795, in New York.

See also Songs, duets, and choruses of *The children in the wood*.

THE DEMOCRATIC SONGSTER: Being a collection of the newest and most admired Republican songs, interspersed with many originals. To which is added, some of the most admired French airs. Baltimore: Printed for Keatinge's Book Store Market-street. [To be continued monthly] 1794. 36 p. Advertised as "printed by James Angell for George Keatinge."
                                                                                    DLC, MH

*THE DEMOLITION OF THE BASTILE [!] on the harpsichord or piano forte by Mr. Berkenhead.

Advertised in the *Columbian centinel* (Boston) January 28, 1795, to be performed in concert on following January 31.

Although it is not clear from the program whether this composition was composed or merely played by Mr. Berkenhead, Sonneck understands it to be an original composition.

*DERMOT AND KATHLEEN (pantomime based on Shield's *Poor soldier*) "composed" by Mr. Byrne, the company's pantomimest, was performed in Philadelphia, December 7, 1796. Both Mr. and Mrs. Byrne were members of the company, coming from London in the fall of 1796. The word "composed" does not refer to the music of the production.

THE DESERT PLAINS.
See The select songster. New Haven, 1786. p. 19.

THE DESERTER, a comic opera in two acts, as performed at the theatre, New York, with universal applause. By Mr. C. Dibdin. New York: Printed for Samuel Campbell, bookseller, No. 44, Hanover square, corner of the Old-slip. 1787. 31, [1] p. 17 cm.

Libretto.
Title-page; dramatis personae, p. [2]; text, p. [3]–31; advertisement, p. [32].
                                        CSmH, DLC, NHi, NIC, NN, PPL

THE DESERTER. A comic opera. In two acts. By C. Dibdin. As performed at the Boston theatre. Boston, W. P. Blake, 1795. 34 p. 8°.

Libretto.
Advertised in December, 1795, as published by Wm. P. Blake at the Bostor Book Store, No. 59 Cornhill." ICN, NN

———— The same. 2d. Boston ed. Boston, Printed for L. Blake. 1796. 32 p. MH

The opera was to be performed at New York, on May 19, 1795, "with new accompaniments by Messrs. [Victor] Pelisier and [Benjamin] Carr."

THE DESPAIRING DAMSEL.
See The select songster. New Haven, 1786. p. 8–9.

———— The dispairing [!] damsel.
(In The American musical miscellany. Northampton, 1798. p. 254–256)

Melody only, with accompanying text.
First line: 'Twas when the seas were roaring. DLC (etc.)

THE DESPONDING NEGRO. A favorite song. Price 20 cents. Philadelphia, Printed for Carr & co. at their music store, No. 136 High street. Where may be had all the newest music reprinted from European publications. Likewise an elegant assortment of piano fortes, guittars, flutes, violins and other musical articles of the first quality. [1793] [2] p. 31½ cm.

Song, pfte. acc. Arr. for German flute, p. [2].
First line: On Africk's wide plains.
BM Cat. ascribes this song to William Reeve, in The evening brush.
Advertised in August, 1793, as "printed singly and sold at Carr & cos. Musica repository, No. 136 High street."
ES, HFB, LSL, McD–W

THE DESPONDING NEGRO.
(In Elegant extract for the German flute or violin. Baltimore [1794] bk. 1. p. 16–17.)

Melody only, flute or violin, with accompanying text.
First line: On Afric's wide plains.
DLC copy lacks p. 16. DLC, NN

———— The same.
(In The American musical miscellany. Northampton, 1798. p. 166–168)

Melody only, with accompanying text.
First line same as preceding. DLC (etc.)

*LES DEUX CHASSEURS ET LA LAITIÈRE.
An adaptation of this opera (by Duni, L. Piccini, Goblain ?) was thus advertised for performance at the New theatre, Baltimore, August 22, 1795:

A pantomine ballet, in one act, composed and under the direction of Mons. Lege, from the Italian theatre at Paris, called LES DEUX CHASSEURS ET LA LAITIÈRE with the original music, the accompaniments by Mr. De Marque.

[106]

DE'IL TAK THE WARS. A favorite Scotch song. New York, Printed & sold by G. Gilfert, No. 177 Broadway [1797–1801] 1 l. 34 cm.

Song, pfte. acc.
First line: Fy on the wars that hurried Willie from me.

JFD, MWA

THE DEVIL WILL HAVE HIS OWN. Alternative title of *Harlequin, Dr. Faustus.*

DEVONSHIRE CUT.
(*In* The songster's assistant, ed. by T. Swan. Suffield [ca. 1800] p. 23–24)

Song, pfte. acc.
First line: When I drain the rosy bowl.

MB

A DIALOGUE ON PEACE, an entertainment, given by the senior class at the anniversary commencement, held at Nassau Hall, September 28th, 1763. Philadelphia. Printed by William Bradford. 1763. 27 p. 19½ cm.

Title-page, verso blank; introductory ode, p. 3; dialogi personae, p. [4]; dialogue, p. 5–24; an ode, p. 25–27.
This *Dialogue on peace* contains the following music (engraved): A setting for solo and chorus of the Introductory Ode, between p. [4]–5, (text on p. 3); a setting for solo and chorus of An Ode, between p. 26–27, (text, p. 25–27). In this final Ode (p. 25–27), five of the six sections are set to music taken from *The military glory of Great Britain* (1762), the same plates being used. The text is completely altered in each case, as is shown conspicuously in the old plate. There are also a few changes in the music to fit the declamation of the new text—there might well have been more!

The musical setting of the remaining section of the final Ode, and all of the Introductory Ode seems to be new.

If, as seems likely, James Lyon composed the music for *The Military glory of Great Britain*, then it is safe to assume that he is responsible for that of *A dialogue on peace.*

DLC, PPL, RPB

DIBDIN'S FANCY.
(*In* Young's vocal and instrumental musical miscellany. Philadelphia [1793–95] p. 30)

Pfte. 2 hds. Eight measures. Followed by directions for dancing.
In No. 4, 1793.

DLC, HFB, Hopk.

DIBDIN'S FANCY.
(*In* Elegant extracts for the German flute or violin. Philadelphia [1798] bk. 3, p. 23)

Melody only, flute or violin.

DLC NN

DIBDIN'S MUSEUM, being a collection of the newest and most admired songs. Philadelphia. Printed by R. Aitken, No. 22, Market Street. For Joseph Charless. 1797. 72 p. 15½ cm.

Title-page, verso blank; songs (words only), p. [3]–72.

PPL

[107]

DID NOT TYRANT CUSTOM GUIDE ME. Giordani. And published by M.
Trisobio [Philadelphia, 1796–98] 3 p. 32 cm.

Song, pfte. acc. Three staves. Voice part on middle staff.
First line same as title.   CdeW

DILLY DALLY, SHILLY SHALLY. A new song. Sung by Miss Sims. The
words by Dr. Houlton.
(*In* A collection of favorite songs, by Mr. Hook. New York [1799–1801]
bk. [2] p. 8–9)

Song, pfte. acc.
First line: A mountain maid, both rich and fair.   DLC

———— Separate issue, paged [8] and 9, with added imprint at top of p. [8].
                                                                        NRU–Mus

*DING DONG BELL, or The Honeymoon expired, being the courtship and
wedding of Ralph and Fan.

This song made part of an "*Olio* . . . entirely new" by R. Taylor, which was
to be performed in Philadelphia, on February 1, 1794.

DIOGENES SURLY AND PROUD.
(*In* The American musical miscellany. Northampton, 1798. p. 100–102)

Melody only, with accompanying text.
First line same as title.   DLC (etc.)

A DIRGE. Words by Mrs. Rowson of Medford.
(*In* Sacred dirges [Oliver Holden] Boston [1800] p. 15–17)

Recitative, air and chorus.
First line: Peace to his soul, the fatal hour is past.
                CSmH, DLC, ICN, MB, MH, MHi, MWA, NHi, NN, RPB

A DIRGE, OR SEPULCHRAL SERVICE, commemorating the sublime virtues
and distinguished talents of General George Washington. Composed at the
request of the Mechanics Association of Boston. (Words by Anthony
Pasquin esq.) 4 p. 21 x 26 cm.
(*With* Sacred dirges, 2d. issue. By Oliver Holden. Boston, 1800)

Recitatives, airs, choral responses.
First line: Lo sorrow reigneth.
Composed by Oliver Holden.
Anthony Pasquin, pseud. for John Williams.   MWA, NN

Under the title of "New funeral music" the dirge was advertised in February, 1800, as "just published price 12½ cents by Thomas and Andrews,"
Boston.

On February 26, appeared an account of the "Sepulchral service." According
to this, it was "written at the request of the board of trustees for the occasion,
by J. M. Williams, Esq. and set to music by Mr. Oliver Holden."

It was composed as a cantata. The first "Solemn Recitative" began: Lo!
sorrow reigneth, and the nation mourns.

[108]

DIRGE FOR GENERAL WASHINGTON. Composed by Dr. G. K. Jackson.
Printed for the Author. Copyright secured.
(*In* New miscellaneous musical work, by Dr. G. K. Jackson. [n. p., ca.
1800] p. 17-18)

Song, pfte. acc. Three staves.
First line: Mourn, mourn all ye winds.
Followed by "Dead march," p. 18.   DLC, MWA

—— Separate issue of preceding, ca. 1800.   Harv. Mus. Assn.

THE DISAPPOINTED LOVER.
See The select songster. New Haven, 1786. p. 13-14.

THE DISAPPOINTMENT: or, the Force of credulity. A new American comic
opera of two acts. By Andrew Barton Esq. [Verses]. New York: Printed
in the year 1767. v, [4], 10-58 p. 16½ cm.

Libretto.
Title-page, verso blank; preface, p. [iii]-v; p. [6] blank; prologue p. [7];
dramatis personae p. [8]; text p. [9]-56; epilogue p. [57]-58; errata, foot of
p. 58.   DLC, MB, NN, PHi, PPL

Distinctly a libretto for a ballad-opera, and probably the first written in
our country. The coarse, but very witty and clever libretto contains
eighteen songs with the names of the "Airs" to which the words were to be
sung. Air IV is "Yankee Doodle," a fact which overthrows all theories that
connect the musical history of our jolly patriotic song with the War of the
Revolution.

The "local piece," written as the author informs us in the preface in derision
of the "foolish and pernicious practice of searching after supposed hidden
treasure," was to be performed by the American Company at Philadelphia,
on April 20, 1767, but it was withdrawn, "personal reflections" rendering it
"unfit for the stage." However, the public had ample opportunity for
satisfying its curiosity as to the "personal reflections," for the libretto was
advertised in the *Pennsylvania chronicle*, April 20-27, 1767, as:

> Just published and to be sold at Samuel Taylor's, bookbinder, at the corner
> of the Market and Water Streets, price one shilling and sixpence.

Mr. Seilhamer and others claim that Andrew Barton is a pseudonym for Col.
Thomas Forrest of Germantown, who died in 1828 at the age of 83. This
supposition is based upon circumstantial evidence, in particular on the fact
that the copy at the Ridgway branch of the Library Company of Philadelphia
contains an ink-memorandum on the title page reading "by Col. Thomas
Forrest of Germantown," followed by a half faded sign in form of an "S"
which looked to Sonneck like a question mark. The arguments favoring
Forrest's authorship are not at all convincing and Sonneck advised librarians
to enter the libretto under Barton. For a critical examination of the matter
and for a detailed description of "The Disappointment" *see* Sonneck's monograph on "Early American operas" (*Sammelbände d. Int. Mus. Ges.* 1904-5).

A second, altered, edition of "The Disappointment" appeared in 1796,
under the title:

THE DISAPPOINTMENT, or the Force of credulity. A new comic-opera in three acts. By Andrew Barton, Esq. Second edition, revised and corrected with large additions by the author. [Verses.] Philadelphia. Printed for and sold by Francis Shallus, No. 40, Vinestreet. 1796. iv, [3], 8–94 p., 1 1. 17 cm.

Libretto.
Title-page. On verso t.-p: Copyright secured according to Act of Congress.
Preface, p. [iii]-iv; prologue p. [v]; dramatis personae, p. [vi]; text, p. [7]–94; epilogue, p. [95].
Copyright recorded May 23, 1796.   MB, MHi, NHi, NN, PHi, PU, RPB

In this edition the "Airs" to the songs are omitted; the language has become less coarse; and the transformation into an opera of three acts has occasioned many additions, but it must be said that this first American opera libretto, if we except James Ralph's doubtful "Fashionable Lady" (London, 1730), has lost a good deal of its brilliancy and wit by the surgical operation.

THE DISH OF TEA, or Ladies answer to the "Pipe tabac." [New York, I. and M. Paff, No. 127 Broadway, 1799–1803] [2] p. 32 cm.

At head of title: No. 10. Ladies musical journal.
Song, pfte. acc.
First line: Drowsy mortals, time destroying.
Composed by Pierre Gaveaux (BM Cat.)
Imprint supplied from Ladies musical journal.   DLC

THE DISPAIRING [!] DAMSEL.
See The despairing damsel.

DISTRESS ME WITH THESE TEARS NO MORE. Composed by W. Shield. Philadelphia, Printed and sold by R. Shaw, No. 13 South Fourth street. Pr. 25cs. [n. d.] [2] p. 31 cm.

Song, pfte, acc. Arr. for German flute, p. [2].
First line same as title.
Published possibly as early as 1800.   ES, MB

*DIVERTIMENTI, OR FAMILIAR LESSONS for the pianoforte by Raynor Taylor. Thus advertised at Philadelphia, on May 1, 1797:

DIVERTIMENTI, or familiar lessons for the pianoforte, to which is prefixed a Ground for the Improvement of Young Practitioners, composed by R. Taylor, music professor, Philadelphia, published this day (price two dollars) and printed for the author, No. 96 North Sixth Street, and sold at Carr's Musical Repositories, Philadelphia and New York . . .

Probably Taylor's "Divertimento," which was to be performed at a concert in Philadelphia, on April 21, 1796, belonged to this set.

DIVERTIMENTO.
(In The Philadelphia pocket companion for guittar or clarinett [Philadelphia, 1794] v. 1, p. 38–40)

Melody only, guitar or clarinet.   MWA

3 DIVERTIMENTOS.   By B. Carr.
(*In* the musical journal for the piano forte, ed. by B. Carr.   Baltimore [1800]
v. 1, no. [18].   p. (34)–(36).)

Pfte., 2 hds.   DLC, ES, LSL, NN, NRU-Mus

*GRAND DIVERTISMENT in the Temple of Liberty, taken from the cele-
brated ballet called Warriors welcome home.   The overture and music
compiled by Mr. Reinagle "in which is introduced a number of Irish and
Scot airs."
Performed in Philadelphia, March 28, 1796.

*THE DOCTOR & APOTHECARY.
Advertised for performance at the City Theatre, Charleston, S. C., on April
26, 1796, for the benefit of Mr. Bergman, with "the music selected by
Storace, the orchestra accompaniments composed by Mr. Bergman."   Probably a pasticcio made from Dittersdorf's famous opera.

DON JUAN; or the Libertine destroyed.   A grand pantomimical ballet, in two
parts.   As performed with great applause by the Old American Company
at the theatre in Southwark.   First American edition.   Philadelphia: From
the press of Mathew Carey.   Dec. 22, 1792.   12 p.   16½ cm.

Libretto.   CSmH, MB

The libretto was advertised in the *Columbian centinel*, Boston, December 12,
1795, "with the songs, etc., as performed last evening at the theatre" as
"published and for sale by Wm. P. Blake, at the Boston Bookstore, No. 59,
Cornhill."
In the same number appeared another advertisement to the effect that the
libretto was "published and for sale at John West's Bookstore, No. 75
Cornhill," but as Blake was publishing quite a number of librettos just
then, it was probably he who published the libretto to "Don Juan."   This
was probably the pasticcio made from Mozart's immortal opera and performed at London about the time of his death (Sonneck).   Perhaps more
likely the pantomime-ballet by Delpini—music by W. Reeve with adaptation from Gluck.

DONALD OF DUNDEE.   A new song.   Sung by Miss Milne.   New York,
Printed for G. Gilbert & co., No. 209 Broadway, near St. Pauls, where may
be had a great choice of music and musical instruments of the very first
quality, as also piano fortes let out on hire, and if purchased within three
months the hire abated [1795]   12–13 p.   33½ cm.

Song, pfte. acc.
First line: Young Donald is the blithest lad.
Separate issue from some unidentified collection.   DLC

DONNA DONNA DONNA DELLA.   A favorite song.   Composed by Mr.
Hook.   New York, Printed & sold at J. Hewitt's Musical repository, No. 131
William street.   And at B. Carr's, Philadelphia and J. Carr's, Baltimore
[1797]   [2] p.   33½ cm.

Caption very elaborate.
Song, pfte. acc.
First line: When Cupid first his trade began.
"Donna Dellay" advertised as "just published by Mr. Hewitt . . ."
May 30, 1797.   DLC, NN

[111]

THE DONOP.
See Twenty-four American country *Dances*, p. 23.

DOROTHY DUMP. Sung by Mr. Hodgkinson in the Children in the wood.
(*In* The gentleman's amusement, ed. by R. Shaw. Philadelphia [1794-96]
p. 36)

Melody only, flute (or violin) with accompanying text.
First line: There was Dorothy Dump.
In No. 5, March 1, 1795. DLC, PHi

Mr. Hodgkinson sang in the first American performance of Samuel Arnold's
opera *The children in the wood*, New York, December 26, 1794.

DOROTHY DUMP. Sung by Mr. Hodgkinson in the Children of the wood.
Price 12 cents. Printed for B. Carr at his Musical repositorys in New York
& Philadelphia and by J. Carr, Baltimore.
(*In* [Four songs from an unidentified collection, ed. by B. Carr. New York,
ca. 1795] p. [4])

Song, pfte. acc.
First line same as preceding. NN

—— Separate issue of preceding, ca. 1795. LSL

—— Dear Walter. Sung by Mr. Hodgkinson in the opera of the Children in
the wood. New York, Printed for G. Gilfert & co., No. 191 Broadway [ca.
1795] 1 l. 33 cm.

Song, pfte. acc.
First line same as preceding. JFD

Advertised in January, 1795, among "new songs adapted to the pianoforte,
just published at G. Gilfert & Co. Musical Magazine."

—— Walter's sweethearts. A comic song in the opera of the Children in the
woods.
(*In* The musical repertory. Boston. [1796] No. I, p. (9).)

Song, pfte. acc.
First line same as preceding.
In MB copy, after title, "Pr. 12 cᵗ." This is in different type, apparently
added later. DLC, MB, NRU–Mus

DORSETSHIRE MARCH.
See Compleat tutor for the fife . . . p. 24.

*THE DOUBLE DISGUISE, or, the Irish chambermaid.
James Hook's "musical piece (never acted in America), the accompanyments by Mons. Pelisier," was advertised for performance at New York,
on April 29, 1795.

THE DOUBLE FUNERAL. Alternative title of *The dead alive*, by Samuel
Arnold.

DOUBLINGS OF THE TROOP.
See Compleat tutor for the fife . . . p. 9.

DOWN THE BURN & THRO' THE MEAD.
See Johnny and Mary.

*DR. ROGERSON'S ANTHEM, sacred to the memory of his Excellency John
Hancock, Esq., late Governor and Commander in Chief of the Commonwealth of Massachusetts.

Thus advertised in October, 1793, as "for sale by Thomas and Andrews,
Faust's Statue, No. 45 Newbury Street, Boston."

THE DREAM. Written by Mrs. Ann Julia Hatton. Price 20 cents. Philadelphia, Printed at Carr & cos. Musical repository [1794] [2] p. 32½ cm.

Song, pfte. acc. Arr. for the "guittar," p. [2].
First line: The other day by sleep oppress'd.   DLC, NN

Advertised as "new music," June 5, 1794. Attributed to Dibdin by Sonneck.
Apparently confused with the song of the same name in Dibdin's *Will of the
wisp* ("Twas a hundred years ago").

THE DREAM. Composed by Sigr. D'on [!] Giovanni Paisiello. Philadelphia,
Printed & sold by G. Willig, No. 185 Market street [1798–1804]. 2–4 p.
32 cm.

Song, pfte. acc.
First line: Oft to my heart the airy sprite.   DLC, PP–K

DRIMENDOO. A much admir'd ancient Irish air. As sung with great applause by Mrs. Melmouth. To which are adapted some verses written by
Miss Owenson. [n. p., ca. 1800?] 3 p. 33½ cm.

Song, pfte. acc. Three staves.
On p. 3, simplified version of first stanza. Two staves.
First line: Oh farewell dear Erin.   LSL

[DRINK TO ME ONLY] Glee for three voices. Words by Ben Johnson.
(*In* The Philadelphia songster, ed. by A. Aimwell [pseud.] Philadelphia,
1789. p. 14)

For three voices. Open score.
First line: Drink to me only with thine eyes.   NN

DRINK TO ME ONLY.
(*In* A collection of favorite songs, divided into two books. Arr. by A.
Reinagle. Philadelphia [1789?] bk. 1. p. 2)

Song, pfte. acc.
First line same as preceding.
At foot of page, arr. for higher voice.   CdeW, DLC, ES, Hopk.

DRINK TO ME ONLY WITH THINE EYES.
(*In* Young's vocal and instrumental musical miscellany. Philadelphia
[1793–95] p. 45)

Song, pfte, acc.
First line same as title.
In No. 6, 1794.   ABHu, DLC, Hopk.

DRINK TO ME ONLY WITH THINE EYES.   [n. p., n. d.]   1 l.   31½ cm.

At head of title: Glee.
Three voices, pfte. acc.   Four staves.
First line same as title.
Between second and third stanzas, engraved design of grapes, ribbon, &c.
Enclosing figures 2, 3 and 4, small wreaths.
At foot of page: 201.
The figures 201 (apparently a plate number), the excellence of the engraving,
the four staves, point to a later date.   But the irregular printing, the pre-
dominant use of the long "s", the general appearance, suggest eighteenth
century.   DLC, JFD, MB, MWA, NBuG

THE DRUMMER.   In the Prisoner.
(*In* The Philadelphia pocket companion for guittar or clarinett [Philadelphia,
1794] v. 1, p. 2–3)

Melody only (guitar or clarinet) with accompanying text.
First line: How charming a camp is.   MWA

———— How charming a camp is.   A favorite song in the Prisoner.   Printed
and sold at G. Willig's Musical magazin [!] No. 165 Market street, Philadelphia.   Pr. 18 cts. [1795–97]   [2] p.   31½ cm.

Song, pfte. acc.   Arr. for guitar or flute, p. [2].
First line same as title.   PHi, PP–K, PU

———— [How charming a camp is] Sung by Mrs. Bland in the opera of the
Prisoner.
(*In* The gentleman's amusement, ed. by R. Shaw.   Philadelphia [1794–96]
p. 56–57)

Melody only, with accompanying text.
First line same as preceding.
In No. 7, May 1, 1796.   PHi, PP–K

The first American performance of *The prisoner*, by Thomas Attwood, was
at Philadelphia, May 29, 1795.

*THE DUENNA: A comic opera.   Philadelphia; Printed and sold by James
Humphreys, jun. and Valentine Nutter, New York, 1779.

Sheridan's libretto to Thomas Linley's comic opera (1775) was advertised
in March, 1779, as "just published by James Humphreys, jun. and Valentine
Nutter," New York.   The publishers "thought it needless to say anything
more in favour of this celebrated performance than that it had a run of
sixty-two nights last winter in London."

On March 13, 1795, "The Duenna, or, Double elopement" was to be performed at Charleston, S. C., "with the original overture and proper accompanyments to the songs for every instrument in the orchestra, composed by
Mr. Bradford, of this city."

*DUET ON THE HARMONICA, accompanied with the violin, by Mr. Pick.
John Pick was to perform this at a concert, Boston, August 24, 1792.

DUETT FOR TWO VOICES.
See Canzonet (Time has not thin'd my flowing hair) by William **Jackson** of
Exeter.

[114]

DUETT FOR TWO MANDORA'S.
(*In* The Philadelphia pocket companion for guittar or clarinett [Philadelphia, 1794] v. 1, p. 8–9)   MWA

*DUETTI, arranged for the pianoforte and clarinet, by Mr. Moller.
These duets by John Christopher Moller were to be performed at the third City Concert, Philadelphia, December 29, 1792.

DUETTO, HOFFMEISTER.
(*In* The gentleman's amusement, ed. by R. Shaw. Philadelphia [1794–96] p. 11–13.)

Duet for flutes.
Duetto: Andante con variatione (two staves) p. 11; Allegretto (flauto primo, p. 12, flauto secondo, p. 13).
In No. 2, May, 1794.   DLC (lacks p. 13), PHi

DUETTO, PLEYEL.
(*In* The gentleman's amusement, ed. by R. Shaw. Philadelphia [1794–96] p. 26–27)

Duet for flutes (or violins).
Introducing variations on melody known as "Pleyel's Hymn."
In Nos. 3 and 4, 1794–95.   DLC, PHi

———— The same as preceding. Second page (numbered 26) of a detached leaf from above collection.   NN (incomplete)

DUETTO BY MOZART.
(*In* The gentleman's amusement, ed. by R. Shaw. Philadelphia [1794–96] p. 74)

Duet for flutes (or violins). Two staves.
In No. [9], [ca. 1796].   DLC, PHi, PP–K

A DUETTO FOR TWO FLUTES. Composed by Willm Pirsson. Pr. 1/6.
Printed for B. Carr at his Musical repository's in New York & Philadelphia.
(*In* The gentleman's amusement, ed. by R. Shaw. Philadelphia [1794–96] p. (90)–(91).)

Duet (for two flutes).
In Nos. 11 and 12 [ca. 1796].   PHi, PP–K

———— The same as preceding (incomplete). Apparently a portion of some separate issue (unpaged).

First page only.
On recto, the last part of Harington's duet, *How sweet in the woodlands*, arr. for two guitars. ca. 1796.   NN

DUETTO. Selected and arranged from that beautiful composition of Handel "As steals the morn" in his "L'Allegro il Penseroso."
(*In* The musical journal for the flute or violin. Baltimore [1800] no. 16 p. 29–32)

At head of title: No. 16 of A Musical journal for the flute or violin. Instrumental.
Duet for flutes or violins (or flute and violin).   DLC

[115]

SIX EASY DUETTS for two violins or flute and violin. Composed & dedicated to Mr. C. Moore by I. Hewitt. Printed & sold at J. Hewitt's Musical repository, No. 131 Wm. St. N. York & B. Carr Philadelphia [ca. 1798] 6 p, 37 cm.
Title page. Music, p. 2–6.

Separate parts for "violino ou flauto primo" and "violino secondo" with identical title-page as above. At foot of p. 6 of second violin part: Engraved by W. Pirsson Nº. 24 Rutgers Street.
I. Hewitt: James Hewitt.

NRU–Mus

THREE DUETTS for two performers on one harpsichord or pianoforte. Composed by Theodore Smith. [Philadelphia] Printed for I. C. Moller, No. 163 North Third street between Vine and New street. Where may be had a great variety of the newest vocal and instrumental music, &c., &c., &c. [1793] 13 p. 32 cm.
Title-page. Music, p. [2]–13.
Harpsichord (or pfte.), 4 hds.

NN

——— The same, except that "G. Willig, No. 185 Market street between 4th and 5th street" has been substituted for the original address. This latter dates: 1798–1804.

DLC, Hopk

DUKE OF GLOSTER'S MARCH.
See Military amusement p. 13.

——— The duke of Glousters march.
See Compleat tutor for the fife . . . p. 20.

THE DUKE OF YORKS MARCH.
See Evening amusement p. 23.

——— Duke of York's march.
See Military amusement p. 8–9.

——— The Duke of York's march. New York, Sold at J. Paff's Music store, Broadway [1798] [2] p. 33½ cm.

Pfte. 2 hds. Arr for flute, p. [2].

MWA

——— The Duke of Yorcks' march. Printed and sold, Philadelphia, by G• Willig, Mark. st., N. 185 [1798–1804] 1 l. 33 cm.

Pfte. 2 hds.

DLC, MWA, NRU–Mus, RPJCB

——— The Duke of York's march. Printed and sold, Philadelphia, by G. Willig, Market street, No. 185 [1798–1804] 1 l. 33 cm.

Pfte. 2 hds.

MB, PPL

——— Duke of York's march. Philadelphia, Published and sold at G. Willig's Musical magazine [ca. 1800] 1 l. 33½ cm.

Pfte. 2 hds.

DLC, NBuG

DUKE OF YORK'S TROOP.
See Military amusement, p. 10–11.

THE DUKE'S MARCH
See Compleat tutor for the fife . . . p. 19.

DUNCAN GRAY. A favorite Scotch song. Written by Burns. The bass
accompanyment by R. Taylor. To which is added a short glossary of the
Scotch words that occur in the song. Price 25 cents. Printed and sold at
B. Carr's Musical repository, Philadelphia; J. Carr's, Baltimore and J.
Hewitt's, New York [1797–99]   [2] p.   31½ cm.
Song, pfte. acc.
First line: Duncan Gray came here to woo.
Glossary at foot of p. [2].   DLC, MWA

DUO.
   (In The musical journal for the flute or violin. Baltimore [1800]   no. 6,
   p. 10–12)
   Duet, flutes or violins (or flute and violin).
   Composed by Pleyel.   DLC

DUPORT'S HORNPIPE.
   See United States country Dances, p. 19–20.

THE DUSKY NIGHT.
   (In The American musical miscellany.   Northampton, 1798.   p. 23–25)
   Melody only, with accompanying text.
   First line: The dusky night rides down the sky.   DLC (etc.)

THE EAGLE.
   See No. 1. of a new sett of Cotilions.

AN EASY AND FAMILIAR LESSON . . . by R. Taylor.
   See An easy and familiar Lesson . . . by R. Taylor.

*AN EASTER HYMN by Dr. Arnold adapted for the pianoforte.
   Thus advertised in April, 1795, as "published and to be had of G. Gilfert &
   Co. at their Musical Magazine, No. 121 Broadway," New York.

THE EASY INSTRUCTOR, or a new method of teaching sacred harmony,
   containing the rudiments of music on an improved plan wherein the naming
   and timing the notes are familiarized to the weakest capacity. Likewise,
   an essay on Composition with directions to enable any person with a tolerable
   voice to take the air of any piece of music at sight and perform it by word
   without singing it by note.   Also the transposition of Mi, rendering all the
   keys in music as easy as the natural key whereby the errors in composition
   and the press may be known.   Together with a choice collection of psalm
   tunes and anthems from the most celebrated authors in Europe with a number
   composed in Europe & America entirely new, suited to all the metres sung
   in the different churches in the United States.   Published for the use of
   singing societies in general, but more particularly for those who have not
   the advantage of an instructor.
   The above title entry in the copyright record for Pennsylvania, June 15, 1798,
   was signed by Edward Stammers and William Little.
   No such issue has been as yet discovered, the earliest known edition having
   been copyrighted December 10, 1802, by William Little, and signed on the
   title-page by William Little & William Smith.   This book, which may have
   been published before its copyright date, contains two titles of interest to
   us, viz., Federal ode (Hail Columbia) and American's lamentation for Washington (q. v.)   DLC

THE ECHO: OR, COLUMBIAN SONGSTER, being a large collection of the most celebrated, modern poetical writings, of different authors.—Second edition. Brookfield: (Massachusetts) From the press of E. Merriam. Sold by him in Brookfield, and by Dan Merriam in Worcester. 1800. MH

THE ECHO, OR FEDERAL SONGSTER. Being a large collection of the most celebrated, modern poetical writings of different authors. First edition [double line] Brookfield (Massachusetts) From the press of E. Merriam & co. Sold by them in Brookfield and by G. Merriam in Worcester [November 13, 1789] 248 p. 24 mo.

With an appendix, of Masonic songs. A collection of the most celebrated cotillions and country dances. Toasts and sentiments. [No music included.] On MWA copy, the date "1798," is written in. This date seems accurate in spite of the supplied date given above (Evans 33663) as both Merriams appear in 1798. Neither of them in 1789. MWA

THE ECHOING HORN.
(*In* The American musical miscellany. Northampton, 1798. p. 28–29.)

Melody only, with accompanying text.
First line: The echoing horn calls the sportsman abroad.
From *Thomas and Sally*, by Thomas A. Arne. DLC (etc.)

EDWIN AND ANGELINA, or the Banditti. An opera in three acts. New York, Printed by T. & J. Swords, No. 99 Pearl street. 1797. 72 p. 20 cm.

Libretto.
Title-page. On verso t.-p.: Copyright secured according to law. Dedication (signed E. H. Smith) "To Reuben and Abigail Smith, Litchfield, Connecticut. My dear parents . . . ," p. [3]; preface, p. [5]–6; "Persons of the drama," p. [7]; text, p. [9]–72.

CtY, DLC, MB, MHi, NHi, NN, PPL, PU, RPB

The preface, dated "New York, Feb. 15, 1797," informs us that the author conceived the piece in 1791 as a drama in two acts, presented it in 1793 to the managers of the "Old American Company," and converted it, after it had been accepted in June, 1794, into the opera, in its present form. The work is based upon Goldsmith's "Edwin and Angelina," the second, third, fifth and sixth songs in the third act being almost literal quotations.

Elihu Hubbard Smith's book was composed by Victor Pelissier and had its first and last performance on December 19, 1796, at New York. For a detailed description *see* Sonneck's monograph on "Early American operas" (*Sammelbände d. Int. Mus. Ges.* 1904–5), also his *Early Opera in America*, p. 100.

Two songs from Pelissier's opera are found in his *Columbian melodies*, published for the author by George Willig, Philadelphia, ⁰1811, viz., "Few are the joys," p. 5–7, and "The bird when summer charms no more," p. 55–57. Copies of *Columbian melodies* are found at the Library of Congress, the Maryland Historical Society and perhaps elsewhere.

Elihu Hubbard Smith was born in Litchfield, Conn. in 1771; died in New York, 1798, of yellow fever contracted from a patient. Graduate of Yale, physician and author.

[118]

EDWY AND ELGIVA. Sung by Mrs. Merry in the tragedy of that name written by Chas. Jared Ingersoll, junr., esqr. The music by A. Reinagle. Printed by G. Willig, No. 185 Market street, Philadelphia [1798–1804] [2] p. 32½ cm.

At head of title: Copyright secured.
Song, pfte. acc.
First line: Bleak sweeps the wind. McD–W, PP–K

Dunlap's reference to the performance of *Edwy and Elgiva* (p. 285 of his *History of the American Theatre*, New York, 1832) is indefinite. But the inference is that it was performed at Philadelphia in the season 1800–1801. Mrs. Merry was in the cast.

AN EGYPTIAN AIR. Arranged as a rondo by T. H. Butler. Philadelphia, Published by G. Willig [179–?] p. 14–15. 33 cm.

Pfte. 2 hds.
T. H. Butler: Thomas Hamley Butler. MWA, NN

AN EGYPTIAN AIR. Arranged as a rondo for the piano forte by T. H. Butler. Price 25 cents. Philadelphia, Published and sold by G. Willig [179–?] [2] p. 32 cm.

Pfte. 2 hds. MNSt, MWA, NN

*ELEGANT EXTRACTS.
That there was another collection of *Elegant extracts* besides the one listed below, of entirely different format (ca. 32 cm. instead of small oblong) and in two books instead of three, becomes evident through the discovery of the three following reprints from such a collection: *Overture to Rosina*, p. (34)–(37), whose title is preceded by the words "Elegant extracts. Book the 2ᵈ;" *Overture to The Lady of the manor*, with the words at foot of p. (32): "End of book the 1st;" *Together let us range the fields*, with the words at foot of p. (64): "End of book the 2ᵈ."

The similarity in these phrases, the identity in format, the use of parentheses about the page numbers at top center of page — all these seem to make the identification complete.

On this basis it is possible to reconstruct a part of each of the two books.

BOOK I

p. (22)–(23) No flow'r that blows.
  (24)–(25) Sweet passion of love.
  (26) Had I a heart.
  (27)–(32) Overture to the Lady of the manor.

BOOK II

p. (34)–(37) Overture to Rosina.
  (62)–(64) Together let us range the fields.

Not so definitely established as the above, but still possible:
p. (6)–(8) The beggar girl.
  (14)–(16) Still the lark finds repose.
  (42)–(43) Light as thistle down moving.

[119]

The type of pagination points rather clearly to Carr as publisher. The best we can do for date, however, is 179–. It is entirely possible that some confusion exists in the advertisements given by Sonneck for the other *Elegant extracts* (see below) and that reference is made to this issue in some of them.

ELEGANT EXTRACTS FOR THE GERMAN FLUTE or violin, selected from the most favorite songs &c, sung in the theatres and public places. Book 1. Price 1 dollar. Baltimore, Printed & sold by I: Carr at his Music store, Market street, and by B: Carr at his Musical repository's, Market street, Philadelphia & William st., New York [1794]   36 p.   17 x 23½ cm.

Title-page, numbered 1; music, p. 2–36.

In "Book 1" on t.-p., figure 1 is given in ink.

Contents:

    p. 2–3 Heaving the lead.
        4–5 The race horse.
        6–8 Poor Jack.
          9 The streamlet that flow'd.
   10–11 Nothing like grog.
   12–13 Whither my love.
   14–15 Sweet lillies of the valley.
   16–17 The desponding Negro.
   18–19 The sweet little girl that I love.
   20–21 The sailor boy capering ashore.
   22–23 Alone by the light of the moon.
   24–25 My heart is devoted dear Mary to thee.
   26–28 The lucky escape.
      29 The mansion of peace.
   30–31 Death or victory.
   32–33 The sailors consolation.
   34–35 Bachelors Hall.
      36 The lullaby.

                     DLC (lacks p. 15–16), NN (lacks t.-p. and p. 2)

Advertised in June, 1794, as published by "Carr & co., Musical repository, No. 122 Market street."

BOOK THE SECOND OF ELEGANT EXTRACTS for the German flute or violin. Selected from the most favorite songs sung at the theatres and other public places. Printed for & sold by Carr at his Musical repositorys, Philadelphia and New York, and by J. Carr, Baltimore. Price one dollar [1796] 32 p.   17 x 23½ cm.

Title-page, numbered 1; index to second book, p. 2; music, p. 3–32. After index: N. B. Any of the above songs may be had singly at the publishers who have always for sale a great variety of new songs.

Contents:

    p. 3–5 Tom Tackle.
        6–7 A sailor lov'd a lass.
        8–9 Dear little cottage maid.
   10–11 The soldiers adieu.
      12 Oh say simple maid.
      13 One kind kiss.

[120]

14-15 My native land.
  16 Lucy Gray of Allendale.
  17 Homeward bound.
18-19 The galley slave.
  20 E're around the huge oak.
  21 Fresh and strong the breeze is blowing.
22-23 When Lucy was kind.
24-25 Poor Tom Bowling.
26-27 Jack's fidelity.
28-29 Then say my sweet girl can you love me.
30-31 From night till morn.
  31 A fragment sung by Mrs. Hodgkinson in the Archers [There liv'd
     in Altdorf city fair]
  32 I sigh for the girl I adore.   DLC, NN

Advertised in August, 1796, as "printed by J. Carr, Music Store, No. 6 Gay Street, Baltimore, and B. Carr's Musical Repositories, Market St reet Philadelphia and William Street, New York."

THE THIRD BOOK OF ELEGANT EXTRACTS for the German flute or violin, from the most favorite songs sung at the theatres and other pubilc places, among which are several of Dibdin's and some of the most favorite sung at the Philadelphia Vauxhall. Printed & sold at B Carr's music store, Philadelphia; J. Carr's Baltimore & J. Hewitt's, New York. Price one dollar [1798] 32 p. 17 x 23½ cm.

Title-page, verso paged 2; music, p. 2-31; index, p. 32.

Contents:

p. 2-3 Lovely Nan, by Dibdin.
    4 Within a mile of Edinboro' town.
    5 A smile from the girl of my heart, in the Woodman.
 6-7 Sweet lavender.
    8 Anne Hatheaway [!], by Dibdin.
    9 The little gipsey.
10-11 Old Towler.
  12 Primroses.
  12 Air, by Pleyel.
  13 No 'twas neither shape nor feature.
14-15 The Caldonian maid.
  16 Sweet Martindale.
  17 A favorite duett. [In thee each joy possessing]
  18 The sailors journal.
  19 When nights were cold.
  20 The smile of benevolence.
  21 Lucy or Selim's complaint.
22-23 When Nicholas.
  23 Dibdin's fancy.
  24 Little Ben.
  25 Tom Trueloves knell.
26-27 I never lov'd any dear Mary but you.
  28 The Irishman.
29-30 Home's home, by Dibdin.
       DLC, NN (lacks p. 31-32, and p. 25-26 occur between p. 28-29)

[121]

Advertised in June, 1798, as published.
NN copies bound in one volume. DLC copies bound in one volume and followed by "Military amusement" and "Evening amusement."

AN ELEGY ON THE DEATH OF A YOUNG LADY. By Wood.
(*In* The Columbian harmony [n. p., 1793] p. 68–71)

For treble solo, three and four-part chorus. Open score.
First line: Ye virgin souls whose sweet complaint.
Composed by Abraham Wood. DLC, NN

ELEMENT OF LIQUID BEAUTY. Composed by Mr. Shield. Price 20 cents.
Philadelphia, Printed at Carr's Musical repository [1794] [2] p. 33 cm.

Song, pfte. acc. Arr. for flute and for "guittar," p. [2].
First line same as title.
From *The travellers in Switzerland*.

Advertised in October, 1794, as published at Carr's Musical Repository, Philadelphia, among "new songs, never published in America."

ELLA AND EDWIN. Publish'd by G. Willig, 165 Market street.
(*In* [Miscellaneous and incomplete [?] collection] Philadelphia, G. Willig [ca. 1795] p. 11)

Song, pfte. acc.
First line: See beneath yon bow'r of roses.
Composed by Edward Bailey. DLC

────── Separate issue of preceding. Page no. changed to "9", ca. 1795.
MWA

ELLEN AND I. An admired new song. Composed by Mr. Hook. [Philadelphia] Published by G. Willig, Market st., No. 165 [1795–97] 1 l. 31½ cm.

Song, pfte. acc.
First line: In Spring when sweet cowslips. MWA, PP–K

ELLEN ARISE. A ballad. Written by J. E. Harwood. Composed by B. Carr. As sung at the Philadelphia and New York theatres by Mrs. Oldmixon & Mrs. Hodgkinson. Price 25 cents. Printed and sold at B. Carr's Musical repository, Philadelphia; J. Hewitts, New York, and at J. Carr's, Baltimore. Entered according to law [ᵒ1798] [2] p. 36 cm.

Song, pfte. acc. Arr. for "guittar," p. [2].
First line: See from yon cottage window plays.
In LC copy (verso, p. [2]) ms. note: No. 200. Title of "Ellen arise &c."
(Music) Deposited 22d. Jan, 1798, by Benj, Carr as author & prop.
ABHu, DLC, ICN (incomplete), JFD, LSL

────── The same.
(*In* A collection of new & favorite songs. [B] Philadelphia [1797–99] no paging) McD–W, PU

In the Edward I. Keffer collection at the Free Library of Philadelphia there is an excellently preserved holograph of this song.

[122]

*ELLEN OF THE DEE.
(*In* The musical repertory, Boston. [1799] No. VI)

No. VI, advertised August 31, 1799, as "just published," has never been located.

ELLEN, THE RICHMOND PRIMROSE GIRL. Price 25 cents. Printed and sold at B. Carr's Musical repositories, Phildaelphia and New York & J. Carr's, Baltimore [1797] [2] p. 29½ cm.

Song, pfte. acc.
First line: Near bow'ry Richmond, Thames's pride.
Composed by Reginald Spofforth.
Apparently the song advertised in September, 1797, by J. Carr, Baltimore, among "songs lately published."

DLC, JFD, LSL, MB, McD–W, MdHi, MWA

—— The same as preceding.
(*In* A collection of new & favorite songs. [A] Philadelphia [ca.1800] p. [124]–[125])

HFB

ELLEN, THE RICHMOND PRIMROSE GIRL. New York, Printed and sold by G. Gilfert, No. 177 Broadway [1797–1801] [2] p. 32½ cm.

Song, pfte. acc.
First line same as preceding.

DLC, MWA, NBuG

—— The same.
Boston, Printed & sold at P. A. von Hagen, junior & cos. Musical magazine, No. 62 Newbury street [1798–99] [2] p. 32 cm.

Below imprint: For the piano forte, German flute or violin.
Song, pfte. acc.
First line same as preceding.

DLC, ES, JFD, MB, NN

ELLEN THE RICHMOND PRIMROSE GIRL. A favorite song. Boston, Printed & sold at P. A. von Hagen & co., Musical magazine, No. 62 Newbury st. [1798–99] [2] p. 33 cm.

Below imprint: For the piano fortes, German flute or violin.
Song, pfte. acc.
First line same as preceding.

JFD

ELLEN, THE RICHMOND PRIMROSE GIRL. As sung by Mr. Incledon with universal applause at the Public Readings, Free Mason Hall. Written by Wm. Pearce, esqr. The music by Reginald Spofforth. Pric [!] 30 cents. Baltimore, Printed and sold by C. Hupfeld and F. Hammer, No. 173 Mark: street [179–] 2–4 p. 32½ cm.

Below imprint: (No. 6)
Song, pfte. acc.
First line same as preceding.

PHi

ELLEN'S FATE DESERVES A TEAR.
(*In* [Unidentified collection of instrumental and vocal music. New York] Hewitt & Rausch [1797] p. 13)

Song, pfte. acc.
First line: In life's fair morn a maiden gay.
Title is the last line of each stanza.

DLC, ES

ELLEN'S FATE DESERVES A TEAR.
(In A collection of new & favorite songs. [A] Philadelphia [ca. 1800] p.
[148])   HFB

*———— The same.
(In The musical repertory. Boston. [1799] No. VI)

No. VI, advertised August 31, 1799, as "just published," has never been
located.

ELOISA'S COMPLAINT.
See The select songster. New Haven, 1786. p. 17.

*THE ELOPEMENT, or Harlequin's tour through the Continent of America.
This "entire new local pantomime . . . the music composed and selected by
Mr. De Marque," was to be performed at the New Theatre in Philadelphia,
on June 29, 1795.

THE EMIGRANT. New York, Printed & sold at J. & M. Paff's music store,
No. 127 Broadway [1799–1803] 4 p. 32½ cm.

Song, pfte. acc. Three staves.
First line: Memory source of sweet employ.
Composed by James Hook.   McD–W

EMMA. A pastoral. Worgan. New York, Sold at I. and M. Paff's, No. 127
Broadway [1799–1803] p. 3–4. 32½ cm.

At head of title: (No. 2) Ladies musical journal.
Imprint at foot of p. 4.
Song, pfte. acc.
First line: Come Emma dear and live with me.
Composed by James Worgan, the Younger.   DLC

*EMMA'S PLAINT.
Song. Advertised in September, 1797, by J. Carr, Baltimore, among "songs
lately published."

THE ENGLISH NAVAL DANCE. For the pianoforte. New York, Sold by
I. and M. Paff [n. d.] [2] p. 32 cm.

Imprint at foot of p. [1].
Pfte. 2 hds.
At foot of p. [2], "Quick step." 12 measures.
                                                DLC, BS, NBuG, NN, RPJCB

———— The same as preceding, but with imprint: New York, Published by
John Paff.   NN

Sonneck has dated this first imprint as ca. 1800. It is difficult to say whether
the second should be considered as earlier (1798) or later (1811–1817).

THE ENGLISH NAVAL DANCE. New York, Printed & Sold by P. Erben
[n. d.] [2] p. 31½ cm.

Imprint above title.
Pfte. 2 hds.
Song, pfte. acc., "Johnny and Mary," on recto of p. [1].
Probably issued after 1800.   NBuG

[124]

*AN ENGLISH SONG, by James Hewitt.
Was to be sung by Miss Broadhurst in Philadelphia at a concert on May 28, 1799.

[ENRAPTUR'D I GAZE WHEN MY DELIA IS BY]   Song IV.
(*In* Seven songs, by F. Hopkinson.   Philadelphia [1788] p. 5).
Song, pfte. acc.
Title from first line.   DLC, Hopk., MB. McD-W

THE ENTERPRISE.
See No. 1 of a new sett of *Cotilions.*

AN ENVIOUS SIGH.   A favorite song, for the piano forte.   Set to music by
   J. Fowler.   New York, Sold by J. & M. Paffs, Broad Way [1799-1803]
   [2] p.   31½ cm.
Song, pfte. acc.
First line same as title.   McD-W

[ERE AROUND THE HUGE OAK]   Sung by Mr. Darley in the Farmer.
   (*In* The gentleman's amusement, by R. Shaw.   Philadelphia [1794-96]
   p. 5)
Melody only, flute (or violin), with accompanying text.
Title from first line.
In No. 1, April 1, 1794.
The farmer, by William Shield, with John Darley in the cast, was performed
at Philadelphia, March 12, 1794.   DLC, PHi

——— The same as preceding.   On third page, numbered "5" of a detached
portion (p. 3-6) from above collection.   NN

ERE AROUND THE HUGE OAK.   Price 12 cents [n. p., n. d.]   1 l.   33 cm.
Song, pfte. acc.
First line same as title.
This is quite evidently the issue advertised in March, 1796, as published
"at Carr's Musical Repository, William street," New York.
                                                DLC, LSL, MWA, McD-W, MdHi, PP-K

ERE AROUND THE HUGE OAK.
   (*In* Elegant extracts for the German flute or violin.   Philadelphia [1796] bk.
   2, p. 20)
Melody only, with accompanying text.
First line same as title.   DLC, NN

ERE AROUND THE HUGE OAK.   A song in the opera of the Farmer.   Com-
   posed by Mr. W. Shield.
   (*In* The musical repertory.   Boston [1796-97] No. III, p. 39)
Song, pfte. acc.
First line same as title.   DLC

ERE AROUND THE HUGE OAK.   A favorite song taken from the Farmer.
   Price 12 cents.   New York, Publish'b [!] for P. Welbon [Weldon] No. 76
   Chamder [!] street. [ca. 1800]   1 l.   33 cm.
Song, pfte. acc.
First line, same as title.
Our imprint shows a strange conglomeration of *b's* and *d's!*   DLC

[125]

[ERE BRIGHT ROSINA MET MY EYES] A favorite song. Shield.
(*In* The universal asylum. Philadelphia, February, 1791. p. 119–120)
Song, pfte. acc.
Title from first line.   DLC (etc.)

ERE SORROW TAUGHT MY TEARS TO FLOW. Boston, Printed & sold by
P. A. von Hagen at his imported piano forte & music warehouse, No. 3
Cornhill. Also by G. Gilfert, New York [ca. 1800] [2] p. 32 cm.

Below imprint: For the voice, piano forte, guittar, violin, clarinett & German flute.
Song, pfte. acc.
First line same as title.
Published possibly 1799.   JFD, RPJCB

L'ESCAPADE.
See Twenty-four American country *Dances*, p. 21.

L'ESPAGNOL.
See Favorite *Cotillions*.

THE ESSEX.
See No. 1 of a new sett of *Cotilions*.

THE ESSEX MARCH.
See Compleat tutor for the fife . . . p. 20.

EUGENES MARCH.
See Military amusement, p. 23.

THE EVANGELICAL HARMONY. Containing a great variety of airs suitable for Divine Worship besides a number of favourite pieces of music selected from different authors. Chiefly original. To which is prefixed a concise introduction to the grounds of music. By Daniel Belknap, author of The Harmonist's Companion. Published according to Act of Congress. Printed typographically at Boston for the Author by Isaiah Thomas and Ebenezer T. Andrews. Faust's statue, No. 45 Newbury street. Sept. 1800. vi, [7]–79, [1] p. 13 x 21 cm.

Title-page. Preface, p. [ii]; subscribers' names, p. [iii]; introduction to the grounds of music, p. [iv]-vi; music, p. [7]–79; index, p. [80].
Two, three or four-part choruses. Open score.

Secular numbers:

    Summer ("How soon alas must summer's sweets decay"), p. 9.
    Autumn (" 'Twas Spring, 'Twas Summer all was gay"), p. 10.
    Winter ("Now clouds the wintry skies deform"), p. 11.
    Disconsolation ("As on some lonely building's top"), p. 30.
    Milton ("When verdure clothes the fertile vale"), p. 31.
    East Needham ("The little hills on ev'ry side"), p. 46.
    Funeral ode ("Deep resound the solemn strain"), p. 65.
    A view of the Temple—a Masonic ode ("Sacred to heav'n behold the dome appears"), p. 66–68.

All the above are by Belknap himself except "Disconsolation," by Stone. "Summer" and "A view of the Temple" appeared also in Belknap's *Harmon-*

ist's companion, Boston, October 1797.   The most important of these secular numbers are: Funeral ode, p. 65· A view of the temple—a Masonic ode, p. 66–68.   CtY, DLC, ICN, MB, MHi, MWA, RPJCB

[EVENING] SONNET III.
(*In* The hours of love, by J. Hook.   Philadelphia [ca. 1794] p. 6–7)

Song, pfte, acc.   Arr. for Ger. flute or "guittar," p. 7.
First line: E'er night assumes her gloomy reign.   DLC, JFD LSL

EVENING.   Printed & sold by G. Willig, Philadelphia [1795–97] p. 6–7.
24½ x 34 cm.

At head of title: E'er night assumes her.
At head of first score: Sonnet III.
At foot of p. 6: I. Burger, sct., No. 207 Queen str.
At foot of p. 7: C. Tiebout, sculp., N. Y.
Song, pfte. acc.   Arr. for German flute or "guittar," p. 7.
First line same as preceding.
Apparently a separate issue from some Willig publication of James Hook's *The hours of love*.
Although Sonneck dated this issue as ca. 1800, its striking similarity in format to Willig's *Miscellaneous . . . collection*, 1795–97, makes it practically certain that it should be given this earlier date.
In addition to "Evening," similar Willig issues of "Morning" and "Noon" have been located.   DLC

EVENING.   149 psalm.
(*With* Hymn.   On Death [New York, ca. 1800] p. 2)

At foot of page: Expressly arranged for the voice and pianoforte.
First line: O praise ye the Lord.
Song followed by: Interlude.   To be played at the end of each verse. MWA

EVENING AMUSEMENT.   Containing fifty airs, song's duett's, dances, hornpipe's, reel's, marches, minuett's, &c., &c., for 1 and 2 German flutes or violins.   Price 75 cents.   Printed & sold at B. Carr's Musical repositories, Philadelphia and New York & J. Carr's, Baltimore [1796] [1], 14–32 p. 15½ x 23 cm.

Title-page, verso numbered 14; music, p. 14–31; index, p. 32.   At head of p. 14: Lest the Purchaser should think, by the number, of the first page, the work imperfect, and the preceding Pages wanting; he is assur'd. of its being perfectly complete. the Paging, being, only "a private arrangement, of the publishers." [Four pages are incorrectly numbered: 19, 17, 20, 18. p. 27–28 are lacking.]
Unless otherwise noted, all titles are for melody only, single staff.

Contents:

p. 14 Le Reveil du Peuple.
        God save great Washington. [Tune, *God save the King*]
        Stoney Point.
        What a beau your Granny was.
    15 When the rosy morn appearing.   As a duett. [Two staves]
        College hornpipe.
        Fishers hornpipe.

[127]

p. 16 Soldiers joy.
Plow boy.
Roslin Castle.
Savage dance.
19 General Washingtons march.
The rose tree.
The white cockade.
17 The new bow wow.
Thou soft flowing Avon.
Money musk.
20 The highland reel.
When bidden to the wake or fair.
Haydns minuet.   [From *Overture* by Haydn, *q. v.*ⱼ
18 Yanke [!] Doodle.
Tho Prudence.
Carmagnole.
Russian dance.
21 The Kentucky volunteer.
Air in the Critic.
Ah caira.
22 The Marseilles hymn.
Dans votre lit.
Astleys hornpipe.
23 The Duke of Yorks march.
Air by Haydn.
24 America, commerce and freedom.
Mrs. Frasers strathspay.
The Irish washer woman.
25 Scots air from the Highland reel. [Shelty's song, "Boys when I
play, cry oh crimini,' by Shield]
French tune.
March in the Battle of Prague.
Finale to Inkle and Yarico.
26 [How happily my life I led] Sung by Mr. Darley in No song no
supper [by Storace.   Melody only, for flute or violin, with
accompanying text.   Lacks closing measures]
27–28 [Lacking]
29 Malbrook.
Spencers fancy.
Mrs. Casey.
Madrigal.
30–31 Martini's march in Henry the IV.   [Two staves]
31 Minuet de la cour.   [Two staves]

The Index (p. 32) lists for p. 27–28 (lacking in this copy) the following:

p. 27 Bride bells.
La Storace.
28 O dear what can the matter be.
Slow march.   DLC

From another copy loaned for an exhibit in the Library of Congress, we learn
that p. 27 and p. 28 actually contained:

[128]

p. 27 Closing measures of [How happily my life I led]
La Storace.
St. Brides bells.
28 O dear what can the matter be. Duetto [Two staves]

Nowhere in the volume is found the "Slow march" listed in the index.

Advertised in August, 1796, as "printed by J. Carr, Music Store, No. 6 Gaystreet, Baltimore, and B. Carr's Musical Repositories, Market street, Philadelphia, and William-street, New York."

EVER REMEMBER ME. From the opera of the Pirates.
(*In* The gentleman's amusement, ed. by R. Shaw. Philadelphia [1794–96]
p. 56)

Melody only, flute (or violin) with accompanying text.
First line: When you shall hear the sound of joy.
Title forms part of last line of each stanza.
In No. 7, May 1, 1796.
The pirates, by Stephen Storace.   PHi, PP–K

———— Air. In the Pirates.
(*In* The Philadelphia pocket companion for guittar or clarinett [Philadelphia,
1794] v. 1, p. 32–33)

Melody only, with accompanying text.
First line: When you shall hear ye sound of joy.   MWA

EVERYBODY'S MARCH. For the harp & piano forte. Composed by H. B.
Schroder. Dedicated to James K. Paulding, esqr. New York, Printed &
sold at J. & M. Paff's musical store, No. 127 Broadway [1799–1803] [2] p.
32 cm.

Pfte. 2 hds.
"Everybody's quick march," p. [2].
At foot of p. [2]: N. B. These marches may be had for a military band.
Schroder: Schroeder.   DLC, MWA

EVERYBODY'S QUICK MARCH.
(*With* Everybody's march, by H. B. Schroder. New York [1799–1803]
p. [2])

Pfte. 2 hds.   DLC, MWA

AN EXERCISE, CONTAINING A DIALOGUE AND ODE. On occasion of
the peace. Performed at the public commencement in the College of Philadelphia, May 17th, 1763.

Words only.
This "Exercise" is contained in Nathaniel Evans' "Poems on several
occasions . . . Printed by John Dunlap, in Market Street, 1772."
We are informed that the *Ode* was "written by Paul Jackson, A. M."
It was intended for solo-voice and chorus.   DLC

[129]

AN EXERCISE CONTAINING A DIALOGUE AND ODE. On the accession of His present gracious Majesty, George III. Performed at the public commencement in the College of Philadelphia, May 18th, 1762. Philadelphia. Printed by W. Dunlap, in Market Street; 1762. 8 p. 24½ cm.

Title-page, verso blank; text, p. [3]–8.
At foot of p. 8, advertisement of "Science. A poem by Francis Hopkinson, esq."   NN, PHi, PPL

The Ode was "written and set to music" by Francis Hopkinson, in whose "Miscellaneous essays and occasional writings" (1792) it is contained in vol. III, p. 83–88 of the "Poems on several subjects." It is there stated that the dialogue was written by the Rev. Mr. Duché.

AN EXERCISE CONTAINING A DIALOGUE AND ODE. Sacred to the memory of His late gracious Majesty, George II. Performed at the public commencement in the College of Philadelphia, May 23, 1761. The Ode written and set to music by Francis Hopkinson, esq., M. A., in said College. Philadelphia: Printed by W. Dunlap, in Market Street, 1761. 8 p. 20 cm.

Title-page, verso blank; dialogue, p. [3]–5; Ode, p. 6–8.   PHi

The dialogue was written by Rev. Dr. Smith, as we are informed by Francis Hopkinson, in whose "Miscellaneous essays and occasional writings" the ode stands in vol. III, p. 77–82, of the "Poems on several subjects."

AN EXERCISE CONTAINING A DIALOGUE and two odes. Performed at the public commencement in the College of Philadelphia, May 20th, 1766. Philadelphia: Printed by W. Dunlap, in Market Street, 1766. 8 p. 21½ cm.

Title-page, verso blank; text, p. [3]–8.   PHi

In the Pennsylvania gazette, June 5, 1766, we read, "Exercise . . . written chiefly by one of the candidates, Thomas Hopkinson, B. A. . . ." Consequently the author was not, as is frequently stated, the father of Francis Hopkinson, but his younger brother Thomas. It is highly probable that Francis Hopkinson composed the odes though Sonneck found no reference thereto. The odes were "sung by the two Master Banksons, accompanied by the organ."

AN EXERCISE, CONTAINING A DIALOGUE and two odes. Performed at the public commencement in the College of Philadelphia, November 17, 1767. Philadelphia. Printed by William Goddard, In Market Street [1767] 8 p. 21½ cm.

Title-page, verso blank; text, p. [3]–8.   PHi

According to the Pennsylvania gazette, November 19, the exercise was "written in Verse by Mr. Thomas Coombe, B. A." and the "Ode, set to music, was sung by Mr. John Bankson." The composer is not mentioned.

AN EXERCISE CONTAINING A DIALOGUE and two odes set to music for the public commencement, in the College of Philadelphia, May 17th, 1775. Philadelphia. Printed by Joseph Crukshank, in Market Street, between Second and Third Streets. 1775. N. B. The following Lines are chiefly collected from former exercises of a like nature, and were hastily thrown together to supply the place of another exercise laid aside. But as they are suitable to the present occasion, it is hoped they will be acceptable. 8 p. 8°.   PU

THE EXPERIMENT.
See No. 1 of a new sett of *Cotilions.*

THE FADED LILLY! OR LOUISA'S WOE. Composed by R. Taylor.
(*In* The musical journal for the pianoforte, ed. by B. Carr, Baltimore [1800]
v. 1, no. [23], p. (52).)

Song, pfte. acc.
First line: O lilly! why so droops thy head.
R. Taylor: Raynor Taylor.   DLC, ES, LSL, NN, NRU–Mus

FAEDERAL MARCH.
See under Federal.

FAIR ANNA THAT DWELLS by the Tyne. A new song. Sung by Mr.
Dignum. New York, Printed & sold at G. Gilfert's music store, No. 177
Broadway.
(*In* A collection of favorite songs, by Mr. Hook. New York [1799–1801]
bk. [1] p. 12–13)

Song, pfte. acc.
First line: How sweet are the meadows in spring.   DLC

———— Separate issue of preceding, ca. 1800.   DLC

FAIR AURORA. Composed by Dr. Arne and published by Mr. Trisobio [Phila-
delphia, 1796–98] [2] p. 34 cm.

At head of title: A celebrated duett in Artaxerxes.
Duet, pfte. acc. Three staves. Figured bass.
First line: Fair Aurora, prithee stay.
Sung by Miss Huntley and Raynor Taylor in Philadelphia, April 21, 1796.
Mr. Trisobio: Filippo Trisobio.   CdeW, DLC, ES, NN

———— The same as preceding, except that in the imprint "Mr. Trisobio" has
been erased and "G. Willig" substituted. ca. 1799.   McD–W, PP–K

THE FAIR EMIGRANT.
See Twenty-four American country *Dances,* p. 5.

*FAIR LUNA, a pastoral by Raynor Taylor.
Was to be sung at Annapolis, Md., on February 28, 1793, in "Taylor's musical
performance . . . the whole of the music original and composed by Mr.
Taylor."

FAIR MARIA OF THE DALE. A favorite song. New York, Printed for
G. Gilfert & co. at their Musical magazine, No. 177 Broadway [1796] 1 l.
33½ cm.

Song, pfte. acc.
First line: 'Tis not the tint of ruby hue.   DLC, NBuG

*FAIR MARY.
Song. Advertised in March, 1797, as to be published "in a few days" by
"G. Gilfert at his Musical Magazine, No. 177 Broadway."

FAIR ROSALE. A favorite song. Sung by Miss Westray at the New Theatre. New York, Printed and sold by G. Gilfert, No. 177 Broadway [1797–1801] [2] p. 32½ cm.

Song, pfte. acc. Arr. for German flute, p. [2].
First line: On that lone bank where Lubin dy'd [!].
Melody by Charles Dignum *(BM Cat.)*

DLC, ES, PP–K, RPJCB (flute part trimmed off)

Apparently identical with *Fair Rosaline*, sung by Miss Westray in New York, June 24, 1799.

FAIR ROSALE. Price 25 cents. New York, Printed for S. Howe & sold at her music ware-house, No. 320 Pearl street [n. d.] [2] p. 32 cm.

Song, pfte. acc. Arr. for flute, p. [2].
First line: On that lone bank where Lubin died.
Published possibly as early as 1799. DLC, ES

FAIR ROSALE. A favorite song. New York, Printed and sold by I. and M. Paff, No. 127 Broadway [1799–1803] [2] p. 30½ cm.

Imprint at foot of p. [1].
Song, pfte. acc. Arr. for flute, p. [2].
First line same as preceding. ES, NN

FAIR ROSALIE. Harmonized by Mr. Webbe. [n. p., ca. 1800] 3 p. 32 cm.

Trio (Canto 1mo·, Canto 2mo·, Basso). Open score.
First line same as preceding.
Possibly an English publication. MB

THE FAIRIES. A favorite song. Composed by Dr. G. K. Jackson.
(In New miscellaneous musical work, by Dr. G. K. Jackson. [n. p., ca. 1800] p. 19)

At foot of page: Copyright secured. Printed for the author.
Song, pfte. acc.
First line: All in a lonely mossy cell. DLC, MWA

FAIRY REVELS. Canzonetta by Mozart. Price 32 cents. Printed and sold at B. Carr's Musical repository, Philadelphia; J. Carr's, Baltimore & J. Hewitt's, New York [1797–99] 3 p. 32½ cm.

Song, pfte. acc.
First line: Hark the raven flaps his wing. McD–W

FAITH.
See Favorite *Cotillions.*

THE FAITHFUL TAR. A much admired song. Written by F. Offley. Composed by W. R. Sale. New York, Printed & sold at J. and M. Paff's music store, 127 Broadway [1799–1803] [2] p. 31½ cm.

Song, pfte. acc. Arr. for flute, p. [2].
First line: With downcast look and fault'ring [!] heart. DLC

FAITHLESS DAMON.
(In The songster's assistant, ed. by T. Swan. Suffield [ca. 1800] p. 34–35]
Song, pfte. acc.
First line: Faithless Damon turn'd a rover. MB

FAL LAL LA. The favorite Welsh air. Sung by Mrs. Seymour. Price 20 cents. Printed at Carr's Musical repositories [n. p., 1797] [2] p. 34 cm.

Song, pfte. acc. Arr. for flute, p. [2].
First line: A shepherd lov'd a nymph so fair.
Music identical with "Fal la lal" in *The Cherokee*, by Stephen Storace, but text is different. NN

Sung by Mrs. Seymour in New York, June 28, 1797.
Advertised in September, 1797, by J. Carr, Baltimore, among other "songs lately published."

FAL LAL LA. The favorite Welch air, sung by Mrs. Bland in the Cherokee. New York, Printed and sold by G. Gilfert, No. 177 Broadway [1797] [2] p. 33 cm.

Song, pfte. acc.
First line: A sheperd [!] wander'd we are told.
In DLC copy, lower part of p. [2] is trimmed off. DLC

Under title of *Tal lal la*, advertised in January, 1797, as "just published by G. Gilfert at his Musical magazine, No. 177 Broadway," New York.

———— Welch air in the Cherokee [Stephen Storace].
(*In* The gentleman's amusement, ed. by R. Shaw. Philadelphia [1794-96] p. (87).)

Melody only, with accompanying text.
First line: A shepherd wander'd we are told.
In No. 11, 1796. PHi, PP–K

———— The little bird. From the opera of the Cherokee. [n. p., n. d.] 1 l. 32 cm.

Song, pfte. acc., followed by arr. for "guittar."
First line: A shepherd once had lost his love.
Apparently an early Carr imprint, ca. 1794–97.
The original text as given in the score of the opera, except that it appears there without title. DLC, ES

THE FAN.
See The select songster. New Haven, 1786. p. 40.

FAR FAR AT SEA. A favorite ballad. Sung by Mr. Incledon. Composed by C. H. Florio. New York, Publish'd by J. & M. Paff, Broadway [1799– 1803] [2] p. 31½ cm.

Song, pfte. acc.
First line: 'Twas at night when the bell had toll'd twelve.
McD–W, MWA, N, RPJCB

FAR O'ER THE SWELLING WAVES. A new song. Composed by Mr. Hook. New York, Printed & sold by G. Gilfert, No. 177 Broadway, and to be had at P. A. von Hagen's music store, Boston [1798–1801] [2] p. 34 cm.

Song, pfte. acc.
First line same as title. JFD, MWA

FARE THEE WELL FOR EVER. A favorite song. Price 25 cents Printed and sold at Carr's music store, Baltimore [179–?] [2] p. 32½ cm.

Song, pfte. acc.
First line: Tho' 'tis fruitless to regret thee. McD–W

[FAREWELL YE FRIENDS OF EARLY YOUTH] A favourite song in the opera of Amyntas. Giordani.
(*In* The universal asylum. Philadelphia, September, 1790. p. 191–192)

Song, pfte. acc.
Title from first line. DLC (etc.)

FAREWELL YE GREEN FIELDS.
(*In* A collection of favorite songs, divided into two books. Arr. by A. Reinagle. Philadelphia [1789 ?] bk. 1, p. 3)

Song, pfte. acc.
First line same as title.
Composed by Samuel Howard *(BM Cat.)* CdeW, DLC, ES, Hopk

———— The same.
See The select songster. New Haven, 1786. p. 37–38.

THE FARMER. A comic opera. In two acts. As performed with great applause, by the Old American Company at the theatre in Southwark. By John O'Keefe, esq. First American edition. Philadelphia: From the press of Mathew Carey. Dec. 14, 1792. 40, [2] p. 17 cm.

Libretto to Shield's opera (1787).
Title-page; dramatis personae, verso t.–p.; text, p. [3]–40; advt., p. [41]–[42].
MB, NN

THE FARMER. A comic opera in two acts. As performed in the New theatre in Chestnut street. By John O'Keefe, esq. Phila., Printed by Mathew Carey. 1794. 12 p. 12 mo.

Libretto. PPL

THE FARMER. A comic opera. In two acts. By John O'Keefe, esq. As performed at the theatre in Boston. Printed at the Apollo Press, in Boston by Belknap and Hall, for William P. Blake, No. 59 Cornhill and William T. Clap, No. 90, Newbury street. 1794. 35 p. 17½ cm.

Libretto.
Title-page. Dramatis personae, p. [2]; text, p. [3]–35.
MWA, PHi, RPJCB

THE FASHIONABLE LADY, or Harlequin's opera. In the manner of a rehearsal, as it is perform'd at the theatre in Goodman's Fields. Written by Mr. Ralph. London: Printed for J. Watts, at the printing office in Wild Court near Lincoln's Inn Fields. 1730 (Price 1 s. 6 d.) [viii], 94 p. 16 cm.

Libretto.
Title-page, verso blank. DLC, MB, NN, PU, RPB, RPJCB

RPJCB has also in manuscript the original publisher's agreement between Ralph and Watts for the publication of the above title, dated 1720.

This opera is a grotesque and coarse, but brilliant parody of ballad-operas, or

more correctly, of those ballad-operas which imitated Gay-Pepusch's famous "Beggar's opera" without wit or sense. Though not the prototype of English Harlequin-operas and speaking pantomimes, "The fashionable lady" was one of the earliest of the kind. All airs are given in the libretto with their music and under their original name. The book has been entered here because James Ralph is said to have been born in Pennsylvania about 1700. Should this supposition be proved, then "The fashionable lady" and not Andrew Barton's "The disappointment" (Philadelphia, 1767) would be the first opera (libretto) produced by an American. For a description and further particulars *see* Sonneck's monograph on "Early American operas" [*Sammelbände d. Int. Mus. Ges.* 1904–05].
James Ralph (ca. 1695–1762). Born probably in what is now New Jersey, died in England. Mentioned by B. Franklin in his autobiography, with whom he went to London. Here he became a journalist of talent, but his pen was at the command of the highest bidder. None of his plays seems to have met with lasting success.

FASHIONABLE SONGS FOR THE YEAR 1798.
(*In* The companion . . . Providence, 1799. p. 253–280)
Words only.
Patriotic songs included: Adams and Liberty, Hail Columbia, The Federal constitution and the President forever.   DLC, MWA, RHi, RPB, RPJCB

THE FASHIONS. Sung with universal applause by Mrs. Graupner at the Boston theatre. Boston, Printed & sold by P. A. von Hagen & co. Musical magazine, No. 3 Cornhill & G. Gilfert, New York [n. d.] [2] p. 32 cm.
Song, pfte. acc.
First line: Ye ladies who listen to fashions gay voice.
Published probably 1799.   ES, MB, MH, RPJCB

FATHER AND MOTHER AND SUKE. Written and composed by Mr. Dibdin and sung by him in his new entertainment called Castles in the Air. Price 25 cents.   Baltimore, Printed and sold by C. Hupfeld and F. Hammer, No. 173 Mark. street [179–] 4 p. 33 cm.
Below imprint: (No. 5.)
Song, pfte. acc. Three staves, voice part on middle staff.
Arr. for two flutes, p. 4.
First line: Says my father, says he one day to I.
Castles in the air first produced in 1793.
Father and mother and Suke, sung by Mr. Sully in Philadelphia, May 4, 1797; by Joseph Jefferson in New York, June 28, 1798. Published probably ca. 1797–98.   DLC, ES

A FAVORITE AIR in the pantomime of Oscar and Malvina.
See A favorite *Air in* . . . Oscar and Malvina.

THE FAVORITE AIR. WHEN THE HOLLOW DRUM.
See When the hollow drum.

THE FAVORITE BALLAD of the Poor black boy.
See The poor black boy.

THE FAVORITE CAROL. Sung in the Adopted child.
See The favorite *Carol.* Sung in the Adopted child.

FAVORITE COTILLIONS. Introduced by P. L. Duport.
See Favorite *Cotillions* . . . P. L. Duport.

FAVORITE COUNTRY DANCE. Composed by Dibdin.
See Favorite country *Dance* . . . Dibdin.

A FAVORITE DUETT.
See [In thee each joy possessing]

THE FAVORITE DUETT OF TINK A TINK.
See Tink a tink.

THE FAVORITE DUETT sung by Mrs. Oldmixon and Miss Broadhurst in
the Prize.
See [Ah! tell me softly breathing gale]

THE FAVORITE DUETT sung in the opera of the Children in the wood.
See [Young Simon in his lovely Sue]

THE FAVORITE FISHING DUETT.
See The favorite *Fishing duett.*

THE FAVORITE GERMAN WALTZ.
See The favorite *German waltz.*

A FAVORITE HUNTING SONG.
See [Hark, hark from the woodlands]

FAVORITE LA CHASSE. Composed by I. C. Moller.
See Favorite *La Chasse* . . . Moller.

A FAVORITE LESSON for the piano forte. Shuster.
See A favorite *Lesson* . . . Shuster.

THE FAVORITE MARCH in Feudel [!] times.
See The favorite *March* in Feudel [!] times.

THE FAVORITE MARCH in Pizzarro.
See The favorite *March* in Pizzarro.

THE FAVORITE MARCH in Ramah Droog.
See The favorite *March* in Ramah Droog.

A FAVORITE MINUET. Composed by G. C. Schetkey.
See A favorite *Minuet* . . . Schetkey.

A FAVORITE MOVEMENT for the piano forte by Vanhal.
See A favorite *Movement* . . . for the piano forte.

THE FAVORITE NEW FEDERAL SONG.
See Hail Columbia.

A FAVORITE NEW GERMAN WALTZ.
See A favorite new *German waltz.*

THE FAVORITE OVERTURE to Lodoiska.
See The favorite *Overture to Lodoiska.*

FAVORITE RONDO. By Garth.
See Favorite *Rondo* . . . Garth.

[136]

HE FAVORITE RONDO BASQUE.
See The favorite *Rondo Basque.*

. FAVORITE RONDO for the piano forte.   Composed by D. Steibelt.
See A favorite *Rondo* for the piano forte . . . D. Steibelt.

FAVORITE RONDO in the Gipsy style.   Composed by Dr. Haydn.
See A favorite *Rondo* . . . Haydn.

HE FAVORITE SERENADING GERMAN WALTZ.
See The favorite *Serenading German waltz.*

. FAVORITE SONATA.   By Niccolai.
See A favorite *Sonata* . . . Niccolai.

. FAVORITE SONATA for the pianoforte . . . Composed by Jos^h. Willson.
See A favorite *Sonata* . . . Jos^h. Willson.

FAVORITE SONG [Indulgent pow'rs if ever]
See [Indulgent pow'rs if ever]

FAVORITE SONG.   Shield.
See [Ere bright Rosina met my eyes]

FAVORITE SONG.   The musick composed by Mr. Hook.
See [If life's rough path]

FAVORITE SONG.   Translated from the Irish.
See [Thou dear seducer of my heart]

FAVORITE SONG by H. Capron.
See [Softly as the breezes blowing]

FAVORIT [!] SONG by Mr. Bach.
See [No twas neither shap [!] nor feature]

A FAVORITE SONG from the Agreeable surprise.
See [My Laura will you trust the seas]

A FAVORITE SONG from the Woodman.
See [When first I slipp'd my leading strings]

A FAVORITE SONG in the Heiress.
See [For tenderness form'd]

THE FAVORITE SONG OF NANCY, OR THE SAILOR'S JOURNAL.
See Nancy, or the sailor's journal.

THE FAVORITE SONGS from the last new opera called the Pirates, composed by S. Storace.
See The favorite *Songs from* . . . the Pirates, composed by S. Storace.

THE FAVORITE SONGS in the opera of [The haunted tower]
See The favorite *Songs in* . . . [The haunted tower]

THE FAVORITE SONGS sung at Vauxhall Gardens.   Composed by Mr. Hook.
See The favorite *Songs sung at Vauxhall Gardens.*   Composed by Mr. Hook.

THE FAVORITE SONGS sung in the Shipwreck.
See The favorite *Songs sung in the Shipwreck.*

A FAVOURITE AIR grotesque or waltz.
See A favourite *Air* grotesque or waltz.

A FAVOURITE FRENCH SONG.
See [Jai perdu mon Euridice]

A FAVOURITE FRENCH SONG.
See [Vous l'ordonné]

A FAVOURITE PATRIOTIC SPANISH WALTZ.
See A favourite *Patriotic Spanish waltz.*

A FAVOURITE RONDO. Composed by F. Staes.
See A favourite *Rondo* . . . F. Staes.

A FAVOURITE SONG in No song, no supper.
See [From aloft the sailor looks around]

A FAVOURITE SONG in the opera of Amyntas.
See [Farewell ye friends of early youth]

*THE FAVOURITE SONGS in the Wild goose chase.
See The wild goose chase.

FEAST OF MERRIMENT; a new American jester. Being a most curious collection of witty jests—merry stories—smart repartees—droll adventure—funny
jokes—wise sayings—anecdotes—waggeries—whims—puns—bon mots—and
laughable tricks, many of which were never before published. To which are
added a clever collection of curious epitaphs, humorous epigrams—amorous
and facetious songs—conundrums—toasts—sentiments, &c, &c. Compiled
principally for the amusement of long winter evenings—to expel care—drown
grief—create mirth—and give the reader a light heart and chearful [!]
countenance. By well-fed Domine Doublechin, esq. Burlington: Printed
by I. Neale, for Neale and Kammerer, jun., No. 24, North Third street,
Philadelphia. 1795. [132] p. 12 mo.   DLC

THE FEDERAL CONSTITUTION & LIBERTY FOREVER. A new patriotic
song, Written by Mr. Milns & sung with great applause by Mr. Williamson.
The music adapted by Mr. Hewitt. New York, Printed & sold at J. Hewitt's
Musical repository, No. 131 William street; sold also by B. Carr, Philadelphia
& J. Carr, Baltimore. Price 25 cents. [1798] [2] p. 32½ cm.

Caption vignette, design with eagle, shield, flags, etc.
Song, pfte. acc. Arr. for flute, p. [2].
First line: Poets may sing of their Helicon streams.
Introduces tunes of *Yankee Doodle* and *Washington's march.*
In ICN copy, p. [2] precedes p. [1].   ES, ICN, LSL, NHi, NN, NRU–Mus

———— The same as preceding.
(*In* A collection of new & favorite songs. [A] Philadelphia [ca. 1800] p. [14]–
[15])   HFB

This is undoubtedly the song advertised as follows:

The Federal Constitution and the President forever, written by Mr.
Millns and adapted by Mr. J. Hewitt to the joint tunes of Washington's
March and Yankee Doodle.

[138]

This "new patriotic song" was to be sung "for the first time" at the theatre in New York, after the play on May 16, 1798.

The words are to be found in the *Philadelphia monthly magazine*, May 1798, on p. 285–6, beginning, "Poets may sing of their Helikon streams." Also in *New [American] patriotic songs added to a collection of songs by C. Dibdin*, Philadelphia, 1797, p. 314–315.

The expression, "The Federal constitution and the President forever," occurs as the last line of the second stanza.

FŒDERAL MARCH. As performed in the grand procession in Philadelphia the 4th of July, 1788. Composed and adapted for the pianoforte, violin or German flute by Alex. Reinagle.
(*In* Twelve favorite pieces, arr. by A. Reinagle. Philadelphia [1789?] p. 16)

At left of caption, a pole with Liberty cap.
Pfte. 2 hds.   DLC

—— The same as preceding, except that it is unpaged and appears on verso of p. 4 of "Chorus sung before Gen. Washington."   McD–W

—— Separate issue of the same, 1788–89.   ES, NN

A facsimile was printed in the *Public ledger*, Philadelphia, Monday morning, October 10, 1898, with the following foot-note:

"FACSIMILE OF THE FEDERAL MARCH." Composed by Alexander Reinagle for the great parade given on the Fourth of July, 1788, in honor of the Ratification of the Federal Constitution by ten of the States. It will be played before the President by the bands in the military parade on October 27. The reproduction is from the only known copy of the march, which is owned by Judge Samuel W. Pennypacker.

*FEDERAL MINUET.
See New constitution march.

FEDERAL ODE.
See Hail Columbia.

THE FEDERAL OVERTURE. As performed at the theatres in Philadelphia and New York. Selected and compose [!] by B. Carr. Price half dollar. Printed and sold at B. Carr's Musical repositorys, Philadelphia and New York and J. Carr, Baltimore [1794] 7 p. 32½ cm.

Pfte. 2 hds.
Makes use of *President's march, Yankee Doodle* and other melodies.   ES

At the Cedar Street Theatre, Philadelphia, on September 22, 1794, "The band" was to "play a New Federal Overture, in which is introduced several popular airs; Marseilles hymn; Ça ira; O dear what can the matter be; Rose tree; Carmagnole; President's march; Yankee Doodle, etc. Composed by Mr. Carr."

This Federal overture by B. Carr "as performed at the Theatre, Cedar Street, for the piano forte" was advertised in Dunlap and Claypoole's *American daily advertiser*, Philadelphia, for November 24, 1794, as for sale at Carr's Musical Repository, Philadelphia.

[139]

In the *Daily advertiser*, New York, December 13, 1794, Hallam and Hodgkir son announce the opening of the theatre on December 15, with the opera o Love in a village. "End of the second act the grand new orchestra will pla a piece called The Federal overture, composed by Mr. Carr."

Also advertised in March, 1796, as "adapted for one or two flutes or violins and "published at Carr's Musical Repository, William Street," New York Presumably this refers to a re-issue of the "Medley duetto adapted for tw German flutes" in *The gentleman's amusement*, p. 42–45.

*FEDERAL OVERTURE, composed by Mr. Von Hagen, sen.
Was to be played at the Haymarket Theatre, Boston, on October 25, 1797

*NEW FEDERAL OVERTURE. Composed by Mons. Leaumont.
Was to be played at the New Theatre, Providence, R. I., on September 21 1795.

THE NEW FEDERAL OVERTURE. Selected and composed by James Hewitt Arranged for the piano forte, flute, and violin. Price 75 cents. New York Printed for the Author and sold at B. Carr's Musical repositories [n. d. 8 p. 32 cm.

Pfte. 2 hds.
Makes use of *Yankee Doodle, President's march, Washington's new march Ça ira* and other melodies.
Sonneck assigns this to the year 1797.   DLC, Es

THE FAVORITE NEW FEDERAL SONG.
See Hail Columbia.

FEDERAL WALTZ.
(*With* The beggar boy. Ladies musical journal, No. 7 [New York, 1799–1803])
Pfte. 2 hds.   DLC, NBuG

THE FEDERALS MARCH.
See Manuscript collection of hymns, songs, etc., p. 50.

THE FEMALE CRYER. A favorite song. Written by a lady. Sung at Vaux Hall Gardens. Composed by Mr. Hook. New York, Printed & sold by G. Gilfert, No. 177 Broadway [1797] 3 p. 29½ cm.
Song, pfte. acc.
First line: Oh yes, Oh yes, I've lost my heart.   JFD
Advertised in March, 1797, as to be published "in a few days."

THE FEMALE CRYER. Sung at Vauxhall. Composed by Mr. Hook. Price 25 cents. Printed & sold at B. Carr's Musical repositories, Philadelphia and New York & J. Carr's, Baltimore.
(*In* A Collection of new & favorite songs. [A] Philadelphia [ca. 1800] p. [131]–[133] numbered [1]–3)
Song, pfte. acc.
First line same as preceding.
At foot of respective pages: Cryer 2, Cryer 3.   HFB
As "sung by Miss Broadhurst at Bush Hill," Philadelphia, the song was advertised on November 4, 1797, as "this day . . . published at Carr's Musical Repository."

[140]

ERNANDO. The much admired romance in the opera of Lodoiska. Composed by Kreutzer. [New York] Sold by I. and M. Paff, No. 127 Broadway [1799–1803] [2] p. 33 cm.

Imprint at foot of p. [2].
Song, pfte. acc. Arr. for flute, p. [2].
First line: Adieu my Fernando.
Kreutzer: Rudolph Kreutzer. NN

'HE FESTIVAL OF MIRTH, and American tar's delight: a fund of the newest humorous, patriotic, hunting, and sea songs. With a variety of curious jests, bon mots, entertaining and witty anecdotes, &c. New-York; Printed for Thomas B. Jansen & co., No. 248 Pearl-street. 1800. 12 p. incl. front. 15 cm.

Words only. DLC (incomplete), MB

'IDELE. A favorite song.
(*In* The Massachusetts magazine, Boston, November, 1790. p. 701)

Song, pfte. acc.
First line: To fair Fidele's grassy tomb. DLC (etc.)

THE FIELDS THEIR WONTED HUES RESUME. The celebrated air. Sung by Mrs. Bland in the opera of the Cherokee. The words by Peter Pindar, esqr. Composed by Ditters. New York, Printed and sold by G. Gilfert & co., No. 209 Broadway, near St. Pauls [1795] [2] p. 34 cm.

Song, pfte. acc. Arr. for German flute, p. [2].
First line same as title.
Not found in score of *The Cherokee*, by Stephen Storace. Probably interpolated.
Ditters: Carl Ditters von Dittersdorf. JFD

THE FIELDS THEIR WONTED HUES RESUME. Sung in the opera of the Cherokee. New York, Printed & sold by G. Gilfert, No. 177 Broadway [1797–1801] 1 l. 34 cm.

Imprint at foot of page, followed by "Hill, sculpt" . . . (illegible).
Song, pfte. acc., followed by arr. for German flute.
First line same as title. JFD

THE FIFE HUNT.
(*In* The gentleman's amusement, ed. by R. Shaw. Philadelphia [1794–96] p. 81.)

Melody only, flute (or violin). 12 measures.
In No. 10, ca. 1796. PHi, PP–K

FIFE HUNT.
(*In* [Unidentified collection of instrumental and vocal music. New York] Hewitt & Rausch [1797] p. 12)

Pfte. 2 hds. DLC

———— The same as preceding.
(*In* A collection of new & favorite songs. [A] Philadelphia [ca. 1800] p. [115]) HFB

*LA FILLE A SIMONETTE composed with variations by Mr. Daguetty fo:
two violins and bassoons.
Was to be played "by Messrs. Daguetty, Duport and Brunette" at :
"Grand Concert," Savannah, Ga., on August 18, 1796.

FINALE.
(In The volunteers, by A. Reinagle. Philadelphia [1795 ?] p. 20)
Trio [?], pfte. acc.
First line: Then haste the laurel wreaths entwine.   DL(

FINALE. In the pantomine of Oscar and Malvina.
(In The musical repertory. Boston. [1796–97] No. III, p. 44)
Chorus [?], pfte. acc.
First line: When the battle's rage is ended.
Oscar and Malvina, by William Reeve.   DL(

——— The same as preceding. Fourth page, numbered 44, of a detached portion of above collection.   DLC

——— Separate issue from above collection, 1796–97.   JFD, LSL, MWA

*A FINALE, "SPRING," or Mirth and innocent festivity by Raynor Taylor.
Was to be sung by Miss Huntley and Raynor Taylor in Philadelphia, April
21, 1796, at a concert consisting chiefly of compositions by Taylor

FINALE TO INKLE & YARICO.
(In The gentleman's amusement, ed. by R. Shaw. Philadelphia [1794–96]
p. 73)
Melody only, flute (or violin). Sixteen measures.
In No. [9], ca. 1796.
Inkle and Yarico, by Samuel Arnold.   DLC, PHi, PP–K

FINALE TO INKLE AND YARICO.
See Evening amusement, p. 25.

THE FIRST NUMBER. Printed and sold by Moller & Capron.
See [Moller & Capron's monthly numbers]

FISCHERS MINUIT [!]
(In The American musical magazine. New Haven, 1786. p. 18)
Melody only.
Fischer: Joh. Christian Fischer.   CtY, ICN, MBJ

FISHERS MINUET. With new variations. Sold at Carr's Repository's, Phila-
phia, New York & Baltimore.
(In The gentleman's amusement, ed. by R. Shaw. Philadelphia [1794–96]
p. 34–35)
Flute (or violin) with bass. Two staves.
In Nos. 4 and 5, February and March, 1795.
Fisher's minuet, same as Fischers minuet.   DLC, PHi

FISCHERS MINUET. With variations by W. Mozart. Printed and sold at
Carr's Music store, Baltimore. Price 1 dolʳ [ca. 1800] 9 p. 31½ cm.
Pfte. 2 hds.
PP–K copy mutilated by trimming.   NN, PP–K

[142]

FISHERS HORNPIPE.
See Evening amusement, p. 15.

FISHERS SECOND MINUET. For the German flute or harpsichord.
(In The gentleman's amusement, ed. by R. Shaw. Philadelphia
[1794–96] p. 35)
Harpischord, 2 hds., or flutes with bass. Two staves.
In No. 5, March 1, 1795. DLC

THE FAVORITE FISHING DUETT. Sung in the pantomine of Don Juan
comp⁴ by Mr. Reeve. New York, Printed & sold at J. Hewitt's Musical
repository, No. 131 William street. Sold also by B. Carr, Philadelphia and
J. Carr, Baltimore. Price 25 cents. [1797–99] [2] p. 32 cm.

Duet, pfte. acc. Second page, three staves.
First line: Thus for men the women fair. ES, NN

———— The same as preceding.
(In A collection of new & favorite songs. [A] Philadelphia [ca. 1800] p.
[122]–[123]) HFB

*THE FLITCH OF BACON, or, the Matrimonial prize.
This "celebrated comic opera . . . music by Shields" (1778) . . . "with
new grand Orchestra Accompanyments, by Mr. Pelisier," was advertised
for performance at New York, on March 7, 1796.

THE FLOWER GIRL. New York, Printed & sold by G. Gilfert, No. 177
Broadway [1798] [2] p. 31½ cm.

Song, pfte. acc.
First line: In povertys garb tho' 'tis true I'm array'd.
Advertised in November, 1798, by "George Gilbert [!]" as "just published."
The "new song" The flower girl was sung by Miss Broadhurst in Philadelphia
at her Benefit, December 11, 1798. MWA

THE FLOWER OF YARROW. A favorit [!] song. Composed by Mr. Hook.
[New York] Printed for Hewitt and Rausch [1797] 1 l. 27½ cm.

Imprint at foot of page.
Song, pfte. acc.
First line: Say have you seen young Sandy fair. DLC, ES

———— The same as preceding.
(In A collection of new & favorite songs. [A] Philadelphia [ca. 1800] p. [174])
HFB
THE FLOWING BOWL.
See The select songster. New Haven, 1786. p. 62–64.

THE FLOWING CANN [!] As sung by Mr. Hodgkinson in No song, no supper.
(In Young's vocal and instrumental musical miscellany. Philadelphia
[1793–95] p. 48–49)

Song, pfte. acc.
First line: A sailor's life's a life of woe.
In No. 6, 1794.
This song is from The oddities by Charles Dibdin, and was sung by John
Hodgkinson in Stephen Storace's No song no supper, New York, February
15, 1793. ABHu, DLC, Hopk.

[143]

——— The same as preceding (incomplete). Second page, numbered 48, of a detached leaf from above collection. On p. 47, *The request*. PHi

——— The same. Philadelphia, Published by J. Young. I. Aitken, Scult., ca. 1793. 1 l. 32 cm.

Imprint at foot of page.
Song, pfte. acc. First line same as preceding. McD-W

THE FLOWING CAN. By Dibdin. Price 25 cents. Philadelphia, Printed at Carr & cos. Musical repository [1794] [2] p. 32½ cm.

Song, pfte. acc.
First line same as preceding. LSL, McD-W

Advertised in February, 1794, as published by "B. Carr & Co. Musical Repository, No. 122 South Side Market Street" Philadelphia.

THE FLOWING CAN.
(*In* The American musical miscellany. Northampton, 1798. p. 17–20)
Melody only, with accompanying text.
First line same as preceding. DLC (etc.)

FŒDERAL MARCH. *See under* Federal.

FOLLY OF THE SPANIARDS. A favorite lesson with variations. New York, Printed & sold at J. & M. Paff's Musical store, No. 127 Broadway [1799–1803] 4 p. 33 cm.

Pfte. 2 hds. ES, NBuG

FOOT MARCH WITH 8 DIVISIONS.
See Compleat tutor for the fife . . . p. 8.

[FOR TENDERNESS FORM'D] A favorite song in the Heiress. Composed by Sigr. Paesiello.
(*In* A collection of favorite songs, arr. by A. Reinagle. Philadelphia [1789?] p. 17–18)

Song, pfte. acc. Title from first line.
At foot of p. 18: John Aitken, Sculpt.
BM Cat. states that this is an adaptation by Thomas Linley, the Elder, of the air, "Saper bramate" from Paisiello's opera *Il barbiere di Siviglia*.
The heiress, a play by Gen. John Burgoyne, was first performed in Philadelphia, April 4, 1789. DLC

FOR TENDERNESS FORM'D. Printed at B. Carr's Musical repositories, Philadelphia & New York & J. Carr's, Baltimore (Price 12 cents) [1794–97] 1 l. 32½ cm.

Song, pfte. acc.
First line same as title. DLC, MdHi, MWA, NRU-Mus, PHi

FOR TENDERNESS FORM'D. A favorite song in the Heiress. For the piano forte or harp. Composed by Paesiello. Philadelphia, Printed & sold by R. Shaw, No. 13 South Fourth street. Price 25cs. [n. d.] [2] p. 31½ cm.

Song, pfte. acc. Three staves, voice part on middle staff.
First line same as title.
Sonneck's date, ca. 1800. DLC, JFD

[144]

THE FORCE OF CREDULITY. Alternative title of *The disappointment*, by Andrew Barton.

*LA FORET NOIRE.
This "serious pantomime . . . originally performed at the theatre in Paris," was advertised for performance at the Chestnut Street Theater, Philadelphia, on April 26, 1794, with "the overture etc, entirely new, composed by Mr. Reinagle." A theatrical advertisement in the *Federal intelligencer*, Baltimore, November 18, 1794, mentions the "overture *and music*" as composed by Alexander Reinagle.

As "last new celebrated pantomime . . . with new music" by Victor Pelissier, the piece was performed at New York, on March 30, 1795.

FOREVER FORTUNE.
(*In* The American musical miscellany. Northampton, 1798. p. 175–176)

Melody only, with accompanying text.
First line: Forever fortune wilt thou prove.   DLC (etc.)

FORGET ME NOT. A favorite song. Composed by Mozart [n. p., n. d.] [2] p. 31½ cm.

Song, pfte. acc.
First line: Forget me not when friends & fortunes smiling.
This song was not composed by Mozart, but by Georg Lorenz Schneider (*Eitner*).
The watermark makes it probable that it was issued by J. and M. Paff, No. 127 Broadway, 1799–1803.   NN

FORTUNATE CONTRACTOR. Alternative title of *The blockheads*.

THE FORTUNATE ROAM. A pastoral. Set to musick by M. F.
(*In* The Massachusetts magazine, Boston, May, 1792. p. 332)

Song, pfte. acc.
First line: Oer moorlands and mountains rude barren and bare.
Text essentially the same as the first two (eight line) stanzas of *Content*.
Music entirely different.   DLC (etc.)

FOUR BALLADS. Three from Shakespear and one by Harwood. Composed & respectfully inscribed to Mrs. Hodges by Benjamin Carr. Pr. ½ a dollar. Philadelphia, Printed & sold by Carr & co. at their Musical repository, No. 122 Market street [1794] 9 p. 31 cm.

Title-page; music, p. 2–9.
Songs, pfte. acc.
Contents: When icicles hang by the wall, p. 2–3.—Take, oh! take those lips away, p. 4–5.—Tell me where is fancy bred, p. 6–7.—When nights were cold, p. 8–9.
Advertised in June, 1794, as published.   DLC

FOUR EXCELLENT NEW SONGS.
See Four excellent new *Songs*.

[FOUR SONGS FROM AN UNIDENTIFIED COLLECTION]
See [Four *Songs* from an unidentfied collection]

*THE FOURTH OF JULY, or Temple of American independence.
Advertised for performance at New York on July 4, 1799, as "a splendid,
allegorical, musical drama, never exhibited . . . music" by Victor Pelissier.

THE FOWLER. A favorite song by the celebrated Mr. Mozart. Printed and
sold at G. Willig's Musical magazin [!] No. 165 Market street, Philadelphia
[1795-97] [2] p. 33 cm.

Song, pfte. acc. Arr. for guitar, p. [2].
English and German text.
First lines: I am a fowler brisk and gay.—Der vogel fänger bin Ich ja.
From *The magic flute.*
Sonneck date, 1795.   ABHu, DLC, PP-K, RPJCB (mutilated)

A FRAGMENT. Sung by Mrs. Hodgkinson in the Archers.
See [There liv'd in Altdorf city fair]

MR. FRANCIS'S BALLROOM ASSISTANT. Being a collection of the most
admired cotillions and country dances with their proper figures annexed.
Including a variety of marches, minutes [!], reels, gavots, hornpipes, &c.
The music composed and selected and the whole arranged as lessons for the
piano forte by Mr. Reinagle. The work to consist of eight numbers to be
published every other week. Price to subscribers, 25 cents. To non-subscribers, 37½ cents. [n. p., n. d.] 17 p. 32 cm.

Title page. At head of title: (No. 1)
On verso of t.-p., "To the subscribers and the public in general . . ." Signed,
"William Francis, Balletmaster to the New Theatre, Philadelphia & Baltimore."
Pfte. 2 hds.

Contents:

p.   3 No. 1. Marine cotillions. United States.
     4 The Constellation.
     5 Country dance. Speed the plough.
     6 No. 2. Francis's ballroom assistant. Grand march in Alexander the
       great. The music by A. Reinagle.
   7-8 The Constitution. The Chesapeake. The Virginia reel.
     9 Country dance. Philadelphia medley.
    10 No. 3. Francis's ballroom assistant. The music by A. Reinagle.
       Minuit as danced at the theatres Philadelphia & Baltimore.
 11-12 Gavotta. The Maryland hornpipe. Master Harris's Strathspey.
    13 Country dance. The lucky hit. Miss Smith's waltz.
    14 No. [4]. Francis's ballroom assistant. The music by A. Reinagle.
       The new President's or Jefferson's march. As performed at
       the theatres, Philadelphia and Baltimore.
    15 Quadrill or double cotillion. As danced by the scholars of Mr.
       Francis.
    16 Mr. Francis' Strathspey. As introduced in the pantomime of
       Aladdin or the Wonderful lamp.
    17 Country dance. The stranger. The secret.

At end of p. 17:

N. B. The country dances of the Stranger and the Secret were introduced
to the public by Mr. Francis in the year of 1800, but never published.

Apparently published in Philadelphia shortly after 1800.   It is quite evident
that No. [4] could not have been issued before 1801.   Title-page is entirely
different from remaining pages in both paper and type.   McD-W

────── The same as preceding.   Lacks title-page.   On p. 3, imprint: Philadelphia,
Printed by G. Willig, Market st., No. 185 [1798–1804]
At head of caption: Copyright secured.   DLC (p. 14–15), JFD

MR. FRANCIS' STRATHSPEY.   As introduced in the pantomine of Aladdin
or the Wonderful lamp.
(*In* Mr. *Francis's ballroom assistant.*   Philadelphia, ca. 1800.   p. 16)

Pfte. 2 hds.
Composed or arranged by A. Reinagle.   JFD, McD-W

FREE MASONS MARCH.   Composed by Mr. Dubois.   Arranged for the piano
forte by Mr. Genin.   [Philadelphia] Published by G. Willig, Market street,
No. 185 [1798–1804]   1 l.   33 cm.

Pfte. 2 hds.   DLC, McD-W, PPL

THE FREEMASONS MONITOR or Illustrations of Masonry; in two parts
   Part I. containing illustrations of the degrees of Entered apprentice; Fellow
   craft; Master Mason; Master mark Mason; Passing the chair, Most excellent
   master; Royal arch Mason; Knights templars & Knights of Malta; with the
   charges of each degree.   Also a sketch of the history of Masonry in America.
   Part II. containing an account of the ineffable degrees of Masonry, viz. Secret
   master; Perfect master; Illustrious secretary; Provost and Judge; Intendants
   of the building; or Master in Israel; Elected knights; Elected grand master;
   Illustrious knights; or Sublime knights elected; Grand master architects;
   Knights of the ninth, or royal arch; Grand elect, perfect and sublime, or
   ultimate degree of Masonry; together with the history and charges appertaining
   to each degree.   By a Royal arch Mason, K. T. K. of M. &c. &c.   Printed at
   Albany [by Fry and Southwick ?] for Spencer and Webb and sold at their book
   store in Market-street. 1797.   [12], 284 p.   12 mo.

   With an appendix of Masonic songs.   Reprinted as No. 1 of the publications
   of the Masonic Historical Society of New York, in 1899.   53d New York
   District copyright, issued to Spencer and Webb, as proprietors, 12 September,
   1797.
   cf. Evans 33173.   MBAt, MWA, RPJCB

*THE FREE MASONS POCKET BOOK, being a curious collection of original
   Masonic songs, never before published, calculated for all the degrees of
   Masonry.   To which is added a toast applicable to each song.   Humbly
   dedicated to the brethren in general.   *Sit lux, et lux fuit.*   This collection is
   by far the greatest masterpiece of any thing of the kind hitherto attempted.
   The songs adapted to the different officers, are inimitable and truly sublime.
   To be had of the printer.

   Thus advertised in the *Royal gazette*, New York, July 3, 1782, as "just published at Lewis and Horner, No. 17, Hanover Square.   Price, four shillings."
   Probably the collection contained no music.

FREE MASON'S POCKET COMPANION, by S. Larkin.
   See Columbian songster, 1798.

[147]

FREEDOM.
(*In* The songster's assistant, ed. by T. Swan. Suffield [ca. 1800] p. 18–19)

Song, pfte. acc.
First line: Come all ye young lovers who wan with dispair [!]   MB

FREEDOM TRIUMPHANT. A new song. Printed by B. Carr and sold at his Musical repositories, New York & Philadelpª and by I. Carr, Baltimore. Price ¼ dollar [1796]   2–3 p.

Song, with chorus, pfte. acc.
First line: Unfold Father Time, thy long records unfold.
Tune: Anacreon in heaven.   HFB

Careful search through DLC, MWA and NHi files of the New York papers for April, 1793, has failed to show the source of Sonneck's original notation:

> *Freedom triumphant*, a new song.   Advertised in April, 1793, by "B. Carr, No. 131 William Street" New York, as "just published."

In point of fact, it seems quite certain that the date 1793 is an error and that Sonneck's further notation, *"Call freedom triumphant.* 'New song' advertised in April, 1796, as 'just published' by B. Carr, No. 131 William Street," is correct for both forms of the title.

This deduction is of importance, for it would seem to be upon this supposed issue in 1793 that Sonneck must have based his statement that Carr began publishing in New York in 1793, before forming "Carr & Co." in Philadelphia in that same year.   Later research has shown that Carr opened his New York branch either late in 1794, or early in 1795.

A FRENCH MARCH.
(*With* Presidents march [P. Phile] Boston, P. A. von Hagen, jr. & co. [1798–1799]   p. [2])

Pfte. 2 hds.   MB

NEW FRENCH MARCH "LE REVIEL [!] DU PEUPLE."
See Military amusement [1796], p. 2.

A FAVOURITE FRENCH SONG.
See [Jai perdu mon Euridice]

See also [Vous l'ordonné je me serai connoitre]

FRENCH TUNE.
See Evening amusement, p. 25.

FRESH AND STRONG THE BREEZE IS BLOWING.   In Inkle and Yarico
[n. p., n. d.]   1 l.   32½ cm.

Song, pfte. acc.
First line same as title.
Apparently a Carr imprint, 1794–97.
Inkle and Yarico, by Samuel Arnold.   DLC, MB, McD–W

Possibly the issue advertised in February, 1796, under the title *Strong the breeze is blowing* as "published and sold by Benjamin Carr," New York.

FRESH AND STRONG THE BREEZE IS BLOWING.   Printed and sold at
Carr's music store, Baltimore.
(*In* Linley's assistant for the piano forte.   Baltimore [1796]   p. 22)

Song, pfte. acc.
First line same as title.   MdHi

———— The same as preceding.   Second page, numbered 22, of a detached leaf
from above work.   1796.   DLC

———— The same.
(*In* Elegant extracts for the German flute or violin.   Philadelphia [1796]
bk. 2, p. 21)

Melody only, flute or violin, with accompanying text.
First line same as preceding.   DLC, NN

———— The same.   Philadph., Printed by C. Hupfeld & sold by G. Willig, No. 185
Market street [1798–1804]   [2] p.   34 cm.

Song, pfte. acc.
First line same as preceding.   ABHu, PP–K

FRESH AND STRONG.
(*In* The American musical miscellany.   Northampton, 1798.   p. 125–127)

Two parts, with accompanying text.   Two staves.
First line same as preceding.   DLC (etc.)

FREUT EUCH DES LEBENS.   Alternative title of *Life let us cherish*, by Hans
Georg Nägeli.

THE FRIEND AND THE LOVER.   Vauxhall.
(*In* A collection of favorite songs, divided into two books.   Arr. by A.
Reinagle.   Philadelphia [1789?]   bk. 2, p. 18–19)

Song, pfte. acc.
First line: I'm told by the wise ones a maid I shall die.   CdeW, DLC, PU

THE FRIENDLESS BOYS TALE.   The music by W. F. Crouch.   New York,
Printed & Sold by J. & M. Paff, Broadway [1799–1803]   [2] p.   33 cm.

Song, pfte. acc.
First line: I am a poor youth in a distant land.
In lower right hand corner of p. [2]: W. P. [Probably Wm. Pirsson].   NN

FRIENDSHIP: the words from Dr. Watts' lyric poems—set to music by the Rev.
James Lyon.

Thus advertised in the syllabus of Andrew Adgate's First Uranian Concert,
Philadelphia, April 12, 1787.   The hymn as found in John Stickney's *Gentleman and lady's musical companion* is as follows:

FRIENDSHIP.
(*In* The gentleman and lady's musical companion, by John Stickney, Newbury-Port, 1774.   p. 17–22)

Four-part chorus.   Open score.
First line: Friendship, thou charmer of the mind.
Composed by James Lyon.   DLC, ICN, MB

[149]

It appears as transcript prefixed to DLC copy of Lyon's "Urania" on p. 13; and in Elias Mann's "Massachusetts collection of sacred harmony" (Boston, 1807), p. 170–174. Quoted also with historical notes in Sonneck's book on *Francis Hopkinson . . . and James Lyon* (1905).

FRIENDSHIP. Words by Mr. Bidwell of Connecticut. Tune: The British muse.
(*In* The Philadelphia songster, ed. by A. Aimwell [pseud.] Philadelphia, 1789. p. 12–13)
Two parts.
First line: Friendship to ev'ry gen'rous mind.   NN

FRIENDSHIP. By Bidwell.
(*In* The American musical miscellany. Northampton, 1798. p. 249–252)
Melody and bass, with accompanying text.
First line: Friendship to ev'ry willing mind.   DLC (etc.)

FRIENDSHIP. An ode. By B. B.
See The select songster. New Haven, 1786. p. 46.

FRIENDSHIP.
(*In* The harmony of Maine, by S. Belcher. Boston, 1794. p. 47)
Four -part chorus. Open score.
First line: How pleasant 'tis to see.
                   CtY, DLC, ICN, MB, MHi, MWA, MN

FRIENDSHIP. By Mr. Swan.
(*In* The songster's assistant, ed. by T. Swan. Suffield [ca. 1800] p. 15)
Song, pfte. acc.
First line: Hard is the fate of him who loves.   CtY, MB

FRIENDSHIP, LOVE & WINE. A round. The poetry by Mr. Ball. Adapted to the three celebrated national waltzes. Philadelphia, Published and sold at G. Willig's Musical magazine [n. d.] [2] p. 30 cm.
Three parts, with pfte. acc. Five staves.
First line: Sweet is the lay where thy praise is accorded.
The three waltzes are: German.—Hungarian.—Tyrolese.
Published probably ca. 1800.   NBuG

THE FROG AND MOUSE. A satire on Italian plays.
See The select songster. New Haven, 1786. p. 56–58.

[FROM ALOFT THE SAILOR LOOKS AROUND] A favourite song in No song, no supper. Storace.
(*In* Young's vocal and instrumental musical miscellany. Philadelphia [1793–95] p. 16–17)
Song, pfte. acc.
Title from first line.
In No. 2, 1793.   DLC, Hopk.

FROM NIGHT TILL MORN. A favorite duett.
(*In* Young's vocal and instrumental musical miscellany. Philadelphia [1793–95] p. 10)
Duet, pfte. acc. Three staves. Followed by arr. for guitar or flute.

First line: From night till morn I take my glass.
Probably by William Shield.
In No. 1, 1793. DLC, ES, HFB, Hopk.

—— Separate issue of preceding (without page number) ca. 1793. DLC

FROM NIGHT TILL MORN. A duetto for two flutes.
(*In* Elegant extracts for the German flute or violin. Philadelphia [1796] bk. 2, p. 30–31)
Two flutes, with accompanying text.
First line same as title. DLC, NN

FROM THE OVERTURE.
(*In* The gentleman's amusement, ed. by R. Shaw. Philadelphia [1794–96] p. 69)
Duet for flutes or violins (or flute and violin).
In No. [9], ca. 1796.
Overture to Shield's *Love in a camp, or Patrick in Prussia.* PP–K

FROM THEE ELIZA I MUST GO. New York, Printed & sold at J. Hewitt's Musical repository, No. 23 Maiden Lane [1799–1800] 1 l. 31½ cm.
Song, pfte, acc.
First line same as title. DLC, McD–W

—— The same as preceding.
(*In* A collection of new & favorite songs. [A] Philadelphia [ca. 1800] p. [166]) HFB

—— The same.
[New York] Publish'd by J. and M. Paff. Of whom may be had the Maid of the rock, the Pleasures of reflection, the Unfortunate sailor, the Cottage on the moor. [n. d.] [2] p. 30½ cm.
Song, pfte. acc. Arr. for German flute, p. [2].
First line same as preceding.
Published possibly as early as 1799. DLC, ES, JFD

—— The same [n. p., n. d.] p. 10. 33 cm.
Song, pfte. acc.
First line same as preceding.
Apparently separate issue from some unidentified collection.
Published probably ca. 1800. NBuG
Sung in New York as early as 1797.

FUGE, OR VOLUNTARY.
(*In* [Unidentified collection (beginning with "A lesson")] Boston [?] [ca. 1800] p. 12–14)
Pfte. (or organ) 2 hds.
Contained in a volume of tracts. MHi

A FUNERAL ANTHEM. Chiefly from the book of Isaiah.
(*In* Sacred dirges [Oliver Holden] Boston [1800] p. [5]–11)
Three-part chorus. Open score.
First line: The sound of the harp ceaseth. CSmH, DLC, ICN, MB, MH, MHi, MWA, NHi, NN, RPB

[151]

FUNERAL DIRGE. Adopted for & play'd by the Alexandria band at the funeral of Genl. Geo. Washington. By I. Decker. Price 25 cts. [Alexandria, 1799 ?] 1 1. 30½ cm.

Below title: Engr'd by A. Lynn.
Pfte. 2 hds. LSL

A. Lynn was probably Adam Lynn, who at that time had a jeweler's shop in Alexandria, Virginia. The combination of jeweler and engraver was far from uncommon in those days.

FUNERAL DIRGE on the death of General Washington as sung at the Stone Chapel. The music composed by P. A. von Hagen, organist of said church. Boston, Printed & sold at P. A. von Hagen & cos. Musical magazine, No. 3 Cornhill and to be had of G. Gilfert, New York. (Enter'd according to law) [1800] 1 1. 33 cm.

Song, pfte. acc.
First line: Assembled round the patriot's grave.
Composed by P. A. von Hagen, Sr. (Sonneck), although advertised as "Jr."
Advertised in January, 1800, as "just published." CSmH, LSL

A FUNERAL ELEGY on the death of General George Washington. Adapted to the 22d. of February. By Abraham Wood. Printed at Boston by Thomas & Andrews, Jan. 1800. 8 p. 14 x 22 cm.

Title-page.
On verso of t.-p. the same urn as shown in O. Holden's *Sacred dirges.* The urn bears the inscription; "G. W. Born Feb. 22, 1732. Died at Mount Vernon, Dec. 14, 1799. Aged 68." At base of urn, "The just shall be had in everlasting remembrance."
Certain copies have greenish grey paper cover with cover title: Funeral elegy for the 22d. February. Published according to Act of Congress. Price 20 cts. single—1 doll. 25 cts. per dozen.

Four parts. Open score.
First line: Know ye not that a great man hath fall'n today.
CSmH, DLC, MH, MWA, NHi, NN, RPB, RPJCB

A FUNERAL HYMN. Translated from the German by the Reverend C. G. Peter, Minister of the United Brethrens Church in New York, Sung by the choir of said church at the funeral of Miss Sally Ten Brook. New York, Printed for G. Gilfert & co., at their Musical magazine, No. 177 Broadway [1796] 1 1. 31½ cm.

Song, pfte. acc.
First line: Tranquil is Deaths happy slumber.
Black border around entire page. MWA

A FUNERAL HYMN. For the words see page 19.
(*In* Sacred dirges [Oliver Holden] Boston [1800] p. 23)

Air (trio?). Three staves.
First line: Up to thy throne, Almighty King, we raise our streaming eyes.
CSmH, DLC, ICN, MB, MH, MHi, MWA, NHi, NN, RPB

FUNERAL ODE. P. M. Words by J. Lane. Music by Belknap.
(*In* The evangelical harmony, by Daniel Belknap. Boston, Sept. 1800. p. 65)

Four-part chorus. Open score.
First line: Deep resound the solemn strain.
Apparently in memory of Washington.

CtY, DLC, ICN, MB, MHi, MWA, RPJCB

GAILY LADS. A favorite sea song. The words by Colonel Humphreys.
Philadelphia, Published by G. Willig, No. 185 Market street [1798–1804]
1 l. 33 cm.

Song, pfte. acc.
First line: Gaily lads our friends are leaving. NRU–Mus

GAILY LADS. A favorite sea song. The words by Colonel Humphreys.
Set to music by a gentleman of this city. Philadelphia, Published by
G. Willig, No. 185 Market street [1798–1804] 1 l. 31½ cm.

Song, pfte. acc.
First line same as preceding. MWA

THE GALLEY SLAVE. Price 20 cents. Philadelphia, Printed at Carr's
Musical repository [1794] [2] p. 32½ cm.

Song, pfte. acc.
First line: Oh think on my fate.
From *The purse, or Benevolent tar*, by William Reeve.

ABHu, CdeW, DLC, ES, JFD, MB, MWA, McD–W, NN, RPJCB

Advertised in October, 1794, as published at Carr's Musical Repository,
Philadelphia, among "new songs, never published in America."

—— The galley slave.
(*In* Elegant extracts for the German flute or violin. Philadelphia [1796] bk. 2,
p. 18–19)

Melody only, flute or violin, with accompanying text.
First line same as preceding. DLC, NN

THE GALLEY SLAVE. A song in the opera of the Purse.
(*In* The musical repertory. Boston [1796–1797] No. III, p. 37)

Song, pfte. acc.
First line same as preceding. DLC

—— Separate issue of preceding, 1796–97. LSL, MWA

THE GALLEY SLAVE. New York, Printed & sold by J. Hewitt at his
Musical repository, No. 131 William street. Sold also by B. Carr, Philadelphia & J. Carr, Baltimore. Price 25 cents. [1797–99] [2] p. 32½ cm.

Song, pfte. acc.
First line same as preceding. MB, MWA, NHi, NN, RPJCB

—— The same as preceding.
(*In* A collection of new & favorite songs. [A] Philadelphia [ca. 1800] p.
[42]–[43]) HFB

—— The same.
(*In* The American musical miscellany. Northampton, 1798. p. 66–68)

Melody only, with accompanying text.
First line same as preceding. DLC (etc.)

[153]

THE GALLEY SLAVE. Philadelphia, Printed and sold by G. Willig, Mark, street, N. 185 [1798-1804] [2] p. 33½ cm.

Song, pfte. acc.
First line same as preceding. DLC, McD-W, MNSt, NBuG, NN, PP-K

—— The same. Boston, Printed & sold at P. A. von Hagen & co's imported piano forte ware house, No. 3 Cornhill. Also by G. Gilfert, New York [ca. 1800] [2] p. 32 cm.

Song, pfte. acc.
First line same as preceding.
Published probably 1799. DLC, ES, JFD, RPJCB

GALLIA'S SONS SHALL VAUNT NO MORE.
Chorus. See Military glory of Great Britain.

THE GARLAND.
(In [A volume of songs, etc. Composed or copied by Francis Hopkinson. [1759-60] p. 111)

Song, pfte. acc.
First line: The pride of ev'ry grove I chose.
Composed by Francis Hopkinson.
The first bars are quoted in Sonneck's book on *Francis Hopkinson . . . and James Lyon* (1905). DLC

GARNER'S AIR.
See The instrumental assistant, p. 76.

GATHER YOUR ROSEBUDS. Composed by Mr. Hook.
(In [Unidentified collection of instrumental and vocal music. New York] Hewitt & Rausch [1797] p. 20-22)

Below title: Adapted for one, two or three voices.
Song, pfte. acc.
First line: Gather your rosebuds while you may. DLC, ES

—— Separate issue of preceding. ca. 1797. ES

—— The same as preceding.
(In A collection of new & favorite songs. [A] Philadelphia [ca. 1800] p. [145]-[147]) HFB

GAVOTTA.
See Mr. *Francis's ballroom assistant*, p. 11.

*GAY STREPHON, a comic song.
Was to be sung at Annapolis, Md., on January 20, 1793, in Raynor "Taylor's musical performance . . . the whole of the music original and composed by Mr. Taylor."

GENERAL ABERCROMBY'S REEL.
See Twenty-four American country *Dances*, p. 6.

GEN. GREEN'S MARCH.
See The instrumental assistant, p. 61.

GENERAL KNOX'S MARCH.
See The instrumental assistant, p. 52.

—— The same.
See Military assistant, p. 6.

*GENERAL PINCKNEY'S MARCH. Composed by Mons. Foucard.
This "new march" was to be played at Charleston, S. C., on February 9, 1799, in the course of "a new occasional fete, consisting of dancing, dialogue and song, called The Charleston celebration, or the Happy return."

GENERAL WASHINGTON'S MARCH.
See Washington's march.

GEN. WAYNE'S MARCH.
See The instrumental assistant, p. 42.

GENERAL WAYNE'S NEW MARCH.
See Military amusement, p. 18.

GENERAL WOLFE. (A new song. Engrav'd for the Pennsylvania magazine. J. Smither, sculp.) Set to music by a gentleman of this country, the words by Atlanticus.
(*In* The Pennsylvania magazine, March, 1775, opposite p. 134)

Song, pfte. acc.
First line: In a mould'ring cave where the wretched retreat.   DLC (etc.)

—— The death of General Wolfe.
See The select songster. New Haven, 1786. p. 54–55.

—— Death of General Wolfe. [Words only]
See Four excellent new *Songs*. New York, 1788.

GENERAL WOLFES MARCH.
See Military amusement, p. 19.

GENTLE AIR. Composed by Dr. G. K. Jackson. Printed for the Author. Copyright secured.
(*In* New miscellaneous musical work, by Dr. G. K. Jackson. [n. p., ca. 1800] p. 20)

At head of title: Glee.
Three parts. Open score.
First line: Gentle air thou breath of lovers.   DLC, MWA

GENTLE LOVE. A favorite ballad. Composed by J. Fisin. New York, Printed & sold by George Gilfert, No. 177 Broadway [1797–1801]   [2] p.   32½ cm.

Song, pfte. acc.
First line: Gentle love this hour befriend me.
J. Fisin: James Fisin.   DLC

THE GENTLE SHEPHERD. By Mr. Swan.
(*In* The songster's assistant, ed. by T. Swan. Suffield [ca. 1800] p. 8)
Song, pfte. acc.
First line: Tell me my lovely shepherd.   CtY, MB

THE GENTLE SHEPHERD: A Scots pastoral comedy, by Allan Ramsay. A new edition, with the songs, carefully corrected. [Verses]   Philadelphia: Printed for Robert Campbell, No. 40 South Second-street. 1795. iv, [5]–72 p. 20 cm.
Libretto.   NHi

*THE GENTLE SHEPHERD, a comic opera. "The favorite Scots pastoral by Allan Ramsey . . . With the original airs—the accompaniments by Mr. Reinagle." Performed in Philadelphia, April 16, 1798.

THE GENTLE SWAN. Composed by F. Kotzwara. New York, Printed and sold by G. Gilfert, No. 177 Broadway [1798] [2] p. 29 cm.

Song, pfte. acc. Arr. for guitar, p. [2].
First line: The gentle swan with graceful pride. JFD

Advertised in November, 1798, as "just published" by "George Gilbert, at his Music store, 177 Broadway, Apollo's Head," New York.

GENTLE ZEPHYR. A new song. Written by the author of Anna. The music composed by P. A. von Hagen. Boston, Printed & sold at P. A. von Hagen's piano forte ware house, No. 4 Old Massachusetts Bank, Head of the Mall & at the Music store, No. 3 Cornhill. Also at G. Gilferts warehouse, N. York; David Vinton's, Providence; W. R. Wilder, Newport; B. B. Macanulty, Salem; E. M. Blunt, Newbury-Port; Isaac Stanwood, Portsmouth; and E. A. Jenks, Portland [n. d.] 1 l. 32 cm.

Song, pfte. acc.
First line: Charming pleasing unseen wand'rer.
Sonneck notes that "the composer probably was P. A. von Hagen, junior." Published probably after 1800. DLC, LSL, MB, N

THE GENTLEMAN AND LADY'S MUSICAL COMPANION. Containing a variety of excellent anthems, tunes, hymns, &c. Collected from the best authors with a short explanation of the rules of musick. The whole corrected and rendered plain. By John Stickney [verses] Printed and sold by Daniel Bayley in Newbury-Port. Sold also by John Boyle, Henry Knox, John Langdon, Nicholas Bowes, Thomas Leverett and Cox and Berry in Boston, and Mascoll Williams in Salem, Smith and Coit in Hartford. Price eight shillings. 1774. 9, [3], 212 p. 12 x 19½ cm.

Title-page, verso blank; a short explanation, p. 3–9; alphabetical table of tunes and anthems, p. [10]–[11]; music, p. 1–212.
Four-part chorus. Open score.
Most important secular numbers: Friendship, p. 17–22; Sapphick ode, p. 47–48. DLC, ICN, MB

THE GENTLEMAN'S AMUSEMENT, a select collection of songs, marches, hornpipes, etc. No. 1. Price 1 dollr. Properly adapted for the flute, violin & patent flageolet. New York, Sold at J. Paff's, Broadway.

Nos. 2 and 4 (the latter called Book 4) with title changed to *The gentlemen's amusement*, and with other slight changes on title-page, are also published by John Paff, New York. No. 3 has never been located.

These three issues are bound together in one volume at MWA and are also found at CtY and RHi.

Sonneck notes that for various reasons it seems unlikely that any of these known issues appeared before 1800, though he suggests that possibly No. 1 was issued in 1798, as John Paff was alone on Broadway in 1798 and not again until 1811. A careful study of the contents of No. 1, however, shows

[156]

that it too was not issued until after 1800. The determining factor is the somewhat cryptic title on p. 28, "Spring from the wood deamond," which unquestionably refers to "Spring," a part of the popular *Pageant of the Seasons* in M. G. Lewis's *The wood demon* (also given as *The wood daemon*) with music by M. Kelly and M. P. King. Since this was first produced in 1807, reaching America in 1808, an eighteenth century date for this imprint seems impossible.

For this reason no further description of these volumes is given. They are included here because of the importance given them by Sonneck in the original issue of the *Bibliography*.

THE GENTLEMAN'S AMUSEMENT. A selection of solos, duetts, overtures, arranged as duetts, rondos & romances from the works of *Pleyel, Haydn, Mozart, Hoffmeister, Fischer, Shield, Dr. Arnold, Saliment,* etc. Several airs, dances, marches, minuetts & Scotch reels. Sixty four select songs from the favorite operas & Dibdins latest publications with some general remarks for playing the flute with taste and expression and a dictionary of musical terms. The whole selected, arranged & adapted for one, two, & three German flutes or violins by *R. Shaw* of the theatre, Charlestown, & *B. Carr.* Forming the cheapest, and most compleat, collection ever offerd to the public; the contents being selected from the best authors, and what, purchased in any other manner would amount to more than three times the price. Price bound six dollars. Unbound five dollars or in 12 single number at 50 cents each. Printed for the editors and sold at B. Carr's Musical Repositories, Philadelphia and New York and J. Carr's, Baltimore [1794–96] 98 p. 32½ cm.

Title-page, verso blank; music, p. 3–(93); "Some general remarks on playing the flute with taste and expression," followed by six examples, p. (94)–(95); "complete index," p. (96)–(97); "A short dictionary of musical terms," p. (98), numbered also 32.

Of this important publication, DLC has the first seventy-seven pages, with certain omissions; PP–K has the remainder, almost complete; PHi lacks only some ten pages. So that taken together, we possess in this (as it were) combined volume almost the entire work. In point of fact only two pages are wanting. Of these two pages the contents of p. 53 are still unknown. From a separate issue we learn that p. 54 contained: [*Say how can words a passion feign*] q. v., and *Favorite country dance compos'd by Dibdin.*

To sum up more exactly: DLC lacks p. 13–16, 45–48, 53–56, 69–72, (77)–(98). PP–K lacks p. [1]–54, (97)–(98); it lacks also separate leaf giving violoncello part of Geo. Ed. Saliment's *Minuetto* for flute and violoncello. PHi lacks p. 49–58, and separate leaf with 'cello part.

Page numbers from 3–75 are in corner without parentheses; from 76 to 98, in centre and with parentheses.

It will be noted that the work contains several items (songs with pianoforte accompaniment, etc.) which do not conform to the general pattern of "one, two, & three German flutes or violin," and that each of these exceptional items bears its own individual imprint. The natural assumption that these were published earlier, as separate issues, and then later incorporated into the work has been verified by a careful comparison of the various dates of

[157]

issue. That there is still some apparent inconsistency is evident from the fact that some of these earlier separate issues show the pagination given in the completed collection. This, however, could easily be accounted for through the imposition of the later page numbers upon the original plates.

Undated, but in the *New York daily advertiser*, May 8, 1794, appeared the following advertisement:

To be continued monthly. On Tuesday the 1st of April, 1794, was published, No. 1, OF THE GENTLEMAN'S AMUSEMENT, or Companion for the German flute. Arranged and adapted by *R. Shaw* of the New Theatre.

CONTAINING

The President's march, for two German flutes.
The Triumph of fame, and I traversed Judah's barren sands, as sung by Mrs. Warrel and Miss Broadhurst in the opera of Robin Hood.
Air des deux Savoyards, varié pour deux flutes, par *F. Deviane.*
Yeo, yeo, sung by Mrs. Marshall in the Spoil'd child.
Ere around the huge oak; sung by Mr. Darley in the Farmer.
Two favourite strathspey reels introduced in the Caledonian Frolic, by Mr. *Francis.*
Patty Clover, from the Opera of Marian.
Stoan Lodge.
Ben Backstay, written, composed and sung by Mr. Dibdin.

Each number will be correctly and uniformly engraved, at the end of the year to form one handsome volume: at which time will be given, (to subscribers only), a general title and index, and also, Instructions and examples for playing the German flute with expression and taste, calculated for performers who have made some progress on this instrument.

Price to subscribers 3 s. Any subscriber not approving of the first number, will have the subscription returned.

Philadelphia subscriptions taken in by Carr & Co., No. 122, Mr. Rice, No. 50 Market street, Mr. Shaw, No. 81 North Sixth street, and Mr. Priest, No. 157 Mulberry street, and by Mr. Harrison, No. 108 Maidenlane, New York.

The contents of the first number as given in this advertisement correspond with p. 3–10 of the titles copied. But there the pieces are arranged as follows:

p. 3 The Presidents march.
    Two favourite strathpey reels introduced by Mr. Francis in the Caledonian frolick.
  4 Patty Clover from the opera of Marian. [When little on the village green]
4–5 Sung by Miss Broadhurst in the opera of Robin Hood. [I travers'd Judah's barren sand]
  5 Sung by Mr. Darley in the Farmer. [Ere around the huge oak]
  6 Ben Backstay. A favorite new song composed by Mr. Dibdin. Philadelphia, Sold by H. & P. Rice, No. 50 Market st., between Front & Second streets. Price 10 cents. [Ben Backstay lov'd the gentle Anna]
7–9 Air des deux Savoyards. Varié pour deux flutes par F. Devienne

p.   9 Sung by Mrs. Marshall in the Spoil'd child.   [I am a brisk &
     sprightly lad]
     Stour lodge.
    10 Sung by Mrs. Warrell in the opera of Robin Hood.   [The trump
     of fame]
 11-18 constituted the second number, for a footnote on p. 18 reads,
     "To be continued in No. 3." This number, DLC copy incomplete,
     contains on
 11-13 Duetto.   Hoffmeister.
     "Andante con variatione" and "Allegretto."
 14-15 No good without an exception.   Written and composed by Charles
     Dibdin for his new entertainment called Castles in the air.   (20
     cents)   Sold by B. Carr at the Musical repository; H. & P. Rice,
     No. 50 Market st., Philadelphia; by J. Rice, bookseller, Baltimore
     and by J. Harrison, No. 108 Maiden lane, New York.   [The
     world's a good thing]
    16 Henry's cottage maid.   Pleyle [!]
 16-17 Sung by Mrs. Marshall in the Highland reel.   [Tho I am now a
     very little lad]
    17 Grand march from the opera of the Prisoner.   *Mozart.* [!]
    18 Ah weladay my poor heart.   Sung by Mrs. Martyr in the Follies
     of a day.
     Scotch medley in the Overture to the Highland reel.
     To be continued in No. 3.

This second number was advertised in May, 1794, as containing:

Tho' I am now a very little lad from the Highland reel, sung by Mrs.
Marshall with universal applause.
Duetto for two German flutes, composed by Hoffmeister.
Henry's cottage maid, composed by Pleyel.
Grand march from the opera "the Pirates," composed by Moyard [!]*
No good with out an exception, composed by Dibdin.
Scotch medley, from the Ouverture to the Highland reel.*
"Ah, well a day, my poor heart"—sung by Mrs. Montyre in "the Follies
of a day."

Those tunes marked with an * are adapted to be played with one or two
German flutes *ad libitum*.

Each number will be correctly and uniformly engraved, . . ,

P. 19–26 constitute the third number, also published in 1794, as will become
clear from the advertisement of the fourth.

It contains on
p.   19 The continuation of the Scotch medley.
    20 Sung by Mrs. Shaw in the opera of No song no supper.   [Go
     George, I can't endure you]
    21 The Je ne scai quoi.   A favorite ballad sung by Mrs. Oldmixon
     in Robin Hood.   [Your wise men all declare]
 22-23 The lucky escape.   Written and composed by Dibdin.   (20 cents)
     Philadelphia, Sold at Carr's Musical repository & by H. & P.
     Rice, No. 50 Market street.

p. 24 Sung by Mrs. Oldmixon in the opera of No song no supper.
[Across the downs this morning]
General Washingtons march.
24–25 Sung by Miss Broadhurst, Mrs. Oldmixon & Mr. Marshall in the
Critic. [I left my country and my friends]
25 Sung by Mr. Marshall in the Woodman. [The streamlet that
flow'd round her cot]
26 Duetto. Pleyel. [first part]

In Dunlap's *Daily American advertiser* for January 19, 1795, "R. Shaw,
No. 44 Seventh near Mulberry street" advertised under "The Gentleman's
Companion for the flute":

. . . in a few days will be published, the fourth number of the Gentleman's
Companion for the flute; price 50 cents, to subscribers 40 cents; to be had
as above; at Mr. Carr's music store, and at Messrs. Rice's bookstore,
No. 50 Market street.

Evidently the *Gentleman's amusement* by Shaw and the above are identical.
The publication of the fourth number of the collection was advertised in
New York, February 21, 1795, as follows:

New Music. On the first of February was published, No. 4, to be continued monthly, of the *Gentleman's Companion.* For the German flute
or violin.

The advertised contents are the same as they appear on p. 27–34. [Footnote:
"Continued in No. 5"]

p. 27 Continuation of Pleyel's Duett.
28 Sung by Mr. Carr in the opera of the Haunted tower. [My
native land]
28–29 O Dear what can the matter be.
29 The Gipsy's song introduced in the Maid of the mill by Mrs.
Oldmixon. [The fields were gay and sweet]
Astleys Hornpipe.
30–31 When seated with Sal. A favorite sea song sung by Mr. Harwood
in the Purse or Benevolent tar. Sold at Carr's Musical
repository's, Philadelphia, N. York & Baltimore. (Price ⅙ of
a Dollar)
32 The waxen doll. Sung by Miss Solomon in the Children in the
wood. [When first I slip'd my leading strings]
32–33 The indigent peasant. [Tho the muses neer smile]
33 Romance by Haydn.
34 Fishers minuet. With new variations. Sold at Carr's Repository's, Philadelphia, New York & Baltimore. Price ⅙ dollar.
[Continued in No. 5]

In a N. B. to the advertisement of the fourth number we read:

N. B. In the course of this work will be inserted the favourite songs,
duetts, etc., for the operas and musical pieces performed at the theatres
in New York, Philadelphia and Baltimore . . . On the first of March
will be published No. 5, in which will be begun the Federal overture, for
two flutes, and concluded in No. 6 . . .

Therefore p. 35–42 constitute No. 5, containing on

p. 35 Var. 3. of Fishers minuet, and Fishers second minuet for the German flute or harpsichord.

36 Dorothy Dump. Sung by Mr. Hodgkinson in the Children in the wood. [There was Dorothy Dump]

36–37 Sung by Mrs. Marshall in the Purse or Benevolent tar. [When a little merry he]

37 The Caledonian maid. [Oh say have you my Mary seen] Ah caira.

38–39 The waggoner. Written and composed by Dibdin. (20 cents) Philadelphia, Sold by H. P. Rice, 50 Market st. between Second and front streets. [When I comes to town]

40 Sung by Mrs. Warrell in the Haunted tower. [Tho pity I cannot deny]

40–41 Sung by Mr. Incledon in the new opera called Sprigs of laurel. [When night, & left upon my guard]

41 Sung by Mr. Francis in the Haunted tower. [Now all in preparation] Quick march from the Battle of Prague.

42–43 A medley duetto adapted for two German flutes from the Federal overture. Selected & composed by B. Carr. [Continued in the sixth number on pp. 44–45]

Advertisements of numbers 6, or 8–12 have not been found, but it appears that number seven was not issued before May, 1796, for we read in the *Minerva*, New York, April 23, 1796, in an advertisement of "B. Carr, No. 131 William street":

On the first of May will be published No. 7 of the Gentleman's amusement for the flute or violin. The subscribers to the above work are respectfully informed that such arrangements are now made as to prevent any disappointment respecting the delivery of the numbers of every month.

The contents on p. 44–98 (with gaps) are as follows:

p. 44 Continuation of Federal overture.

45 Conclusion of Federal overture.

46–47 The Highland laddie. Introduced by Mrs. Warrell in the Highland reel. (20 cents) Sold by Carr & co., at their Musical repository, No. 122 High st. and by H. & P. Rice, No. 50 Market street. [The Lowland lads think they are fine]

48 Poor black boy. From the Prize. Sung by Miss Broadhurst and by Mr. Carr. [You care of money ah care no more]

48–49 Lullaby. From the opera of the Pirates.

49 Sung by Mrs. Marshall in the comedy of She wou'd & she wou'd not. [Ye chearful virgins] The village maid.

50–51 A medley duetto adapted from the overture to the Children in the wood. Composed by Dr. Arnold.

52 Sung by Miss Solomons in the character of Tom Thumb. [That petty fogging Grizzle] Sung by Mrs. Oldmixon in the Purse or Benevolent tar. [How sweet when the silver moon]

p. 53 (Missing from all three copies. Contents unknown.)

54 (Missing from all three copies: [Say how can words a passion feign] *and* Favorite country dance compos'd by Dibdin.)

55 Within a mile of Edinbourgh. Introduced & sung by Miss Broadhurst in the musical farce called My grandmother. Price 12 cents.

56 Ever remember me. From the opera of the Pirates. [When you shall hear the sound of joy]
Sung by Mrs. Bland in the opera of the Prisoner. [How charming a camp is]

57 Sung by Mr. Bates in Tom Thumb the Great. [We kings who are in our senses]

58–59 Rondo by Haydn.

59 Sung by Mrs. Warrell at the New theatre. Pastorale: [Were I oblig'd to beg my bread]

60 Sung by Miss Solomons in the Prisoner. Attwood. [Tears that exhale]

60–61 Sung by Mrs. Oldmixon in the Prize or 2.5.3.8. [Oh dear delightfull skill]

61 Winsome Kate. Compos'd by Mr. Hook. [Young Sandy's gone to kirk I ken]

62–64 The vetrans. Written for the new entertainment called Great news or a Trip to the Antipodes. Charles Dibdin. Sold at Carr's Musical repository's, Philadelphia, New York & Baltimore. Price 20 cents. [Dick Dock a tar at Greenwich]

64 Sung by Mrs. Oldmixon in the Noble peasent [!] [When scorching suns]

65 Sung by Miss Broadhurst in the Prisoner. [Young Carlos sued a beauteous maid]
Sung by Mr. Marshall In the Quaker. [I lock'd up all my treasure]

66 Happy tawny Moor. A favorite duett from the Mountaineers. For two flutes. [Oh, happy tawny Moor]

67 Neighbour Sly. Dibdin. [The passing bell was heard]
Allo. From Oscar and Malvina.

68–69 Amidst the illusions. Sung by Miss Broadhurst.

69 Dans votre lit. Sung by Mr. Marshall in Patrick in Prussia. Followed by "From the Overture."

70–71 Ronde. Chantee a la reine par Monseigneur le Dauphin. Philadelphia, Sold by H. & P. Rice, No. 50 Market street. Price twenty cents. Les paroles par M. de Curt. Musique de M. Martini. [L'amour ici nous rassemble]

72 The way worn travellers. For two flutes.

73 The jolly gay pedlar from Oscar and Malvina. [I am a jolly gay pedlar]

74 Duetto by Mozart.

75–(77) Minuetto with eight Variations for the flute and violoncello composed by Geo. Ed. Saliment. Printed by B. Carr & sold at his Musical repositories, New York & Phila^a. Price ½ dol. [On a separate unpaged leaf, the violoncello part]

p. (78)–(79) Lovely Nan. Written and composed by Mr. Dibdin. Price
20 cents. Printed & Sold at B. Carr's Musical repositories
in New York and Philadelphia & by J. Carr, Baltimore.
[Sweet is the ship]
(80)–(81) Sigh no more ladies. For three German flutes or violins.
(81) The Caledonian hunt.
The fife hunt.
(82) Loose were her tresses seen.
When nights were cold. Introduced in the Children in the
wood.
(83)–(86) The Battle of Prague. Selected and adapted for a flute and
violin, or for one or two flutes or violins, by B. Carr. Price
38 cents. Printed and sold at B. Carr's Musical repositories in New York and Philadelphia and by J. Carr, Baltimore.
(87) Whilst happy in my native land. Sung by Mr. Darley in the
Patriot.
Welch air in the Cherokee. [A shepherd wander'd we are
told]
(88)–(89) Lucy or Selim's complaint. A favorite song composed by Mr.
Hook. Published at B. Carr's Musical repositories, Philadelphia, New York & J. Carr's, Baltimore. Price one
quarter dollar. [Night o'er the world her curtain hung]
(90)–(91) A duetto for two flutes composed by Willm. Pirson. Pr. 1/6.
Printed for B. Carr at his Musical repository's in New York
& Philadelphia.
(92)–(93) The tinker. A favorite comic song in Merry Sherwood.
Published at B. Carr's Musical repositories, Philadelphia,
New York & J. Carr's, Baltimore. Price 20 cents. [My
father is a tinker]
(94)–(95) "Some general remarks on playing the flute with taste and
expression."
(96)–(97) "A complete index to the Gentlemans Amusement."
(98) paged "A short dictionary of musical terms." [cf. A new assistant
also 32   for the piano forte . . . by F. Linley]

THE GENTLEMAN'S AMUSEMENT, or Companion for the German flute
. . . by R. Shaw.
See Gentleman's amusement, a selection.

THE GENTLEMAN'S COMPANION for the flute . . . by R. Shaw.
See Gentleman's amusement, a selection.

GENTLEMEN AND LADIES' COMPLETE SONGSTER. Alternative title
of The skylark.

GEORGIA. French country dance.
See United States country Dances, p. 18.

GEORGIA GRENADIERS MARCH, by Mr. Alexander.
See Compleat tutor for the fife . . . p. 29.

GERMAN FLUTE CONCERT with solos, composed by Giovanni Gualdo.
See Concertos.

[163]

GERMAN WALTZ. No. 3 & 4. New York, Printed & sold at G. Gilfert's Piano forte warehouse, No. 177 Broadway [ca. 1800] 1 l. 34½ cm.

Pfte. 2 hds. NRU–Mus

THE FAVORITE GERMAN WALTZ. [n. p., n. d.] 1 l. 31½ cm.

Pfte. 2 hds.
Published probably ca. 1800. NN

A FAVORITE NEW GERMAN WALTZ. Arranged for the piano forte, flute or violin. By I. C. M. [New York] Sold by I. and M. Paff, 127 Broadway [1799–1803] [2] p. 32½ cm.

Pfte. 2 hds. (Flute or violin)
Imprint at bottom of p. [2].
"Admiral Nelson's march," p. [2].
I. C. M.: John Christopher Moller. DLC, MWA, NN

SIX FAVORITE GERMAN WALTZEN [!]
(*In* The musical journal for the pianoforte, ed. by B. Carr. Baltimore [1800] v. 1, no. [14], p. (26)–(28).)

Pfte. 2 hds. DLC, ES, LSL, NN, NRU–Mus

———— Separate issue of preceding, ca. 1800. DLC

———— The same.
(*In* The musical journal for the flute or violin. Baltimore [1800] no. 14, p. 25–28)

At head of title: No. 14 of a musical journal for the flute or violin. Instrumental section.
Melody only, flute or violin. DLC

THE GHOST OF CRAZY JANE. Written and composed by a lady. New York, Printed & sold at J. & M. Paff's musical store, 127 Broadway [1799–1803] [2] p. 32 cm.

Song, pfte. acc. Arr. for flute or "guittar," p. [2].
First line: The evening of a summer's day.
Published probably ca. 1800. DLC, NN

THE GIPSY. A new ballad. The words by Peter Pindar. Composed by J. Fisin. New York, Printed & sold by G. Gilfert, No. 177 Broadway [1797–1801] [2] p. 32½ cm.

Song, pfte. acc.
First line: A wand'ring gipsy, sirs, am I.
J. Fisin: James Fisin. DLC, MWA

*THE GIPSY
(*In* the musical repertory, Boston [1799] No. VI)

No. VI, advertised August 31, 1799, as "just published." Has never been located.

THE GIPSY'S SONG. Introduc'd in the Maid of the mill, by Mrs. Oldmixon (*In* The gentleman's amusement, ed. by R. Shaw. Philadelphia [1794–96] p. 29)

Melody only, flute (or violin) with accompanying text.
First line: The fields were gay and sweet the hay.
In No. 4, February 1, 1795. DLC, PHi

————— The same.
(*In* Young's vocal and instrumental musical miscellany. Philadelphia [1793–95] p. 58)

Song, pfte. acc.
First line same as preceding.
In No. 8, 1795. DLC, Hopk.

—————The same as preceding. Second page, numbered 58, of a detached leaf from above collection. ES, NN

The maid of the mill, by Samuel Arnold, with Mrs. Oldmixon in the cast, was performed in Philadelphia, May 16, 1794.

THE GIRL OF MY HEART. Composed by Mr. Hook.
(*In* [Unidentified collection of instrumental and vocal music. [New York] Hewitt & Rausch [1797] p. 11–12)

Song, pfte. acc.
First line: How sweet is the breeze at eve's modest hour. DLC, ES

————— Separate issue of preceding, 1797–99. DLC

————— The same as preceding.
(*In* A collection of new & favorite songs. [A] Philadelphia [1800] p. [114]–[115]) HFB

*————— The girl of my heart.
(*In* The musical repertory. Boston [1799] No. VI)

Advertised but not located.

*————— The same.
Advertised in March, 1797, as to be published "in a few days" by "G. Gilfert at his Musical magazine, No. 177 Broadway," New York.

THE GIRL OF SPIRIT. Alternative title of *The better sort.*

THE GIRL WITH A CAST IN HER EYE. New York, Printed & sold by J. Hewitt, No. 23 Maiden Lane. Price 12½ cents [1799–1800] 1 l. 30½ cm.

Song, pfte, acc.
First line: I sigh for a damsel that's charming and fair. DLC

————— The same as preceding.
(*In* A collection of new & favorite songs. [A] Philadelphia [ca. 1800] p. [158]) HFB

[GIVE ME THY HEART AS I GIVE MINE] A new song. Words and music by F. H., Esqr.
(*In* The Columbian magazine, August, 1789. Between p. 490 and 491.)

Song, pfte. acc.

[165]

First line as above.

F. H., Esqr.: Francis Hopkinson.

First bars quoted in Sonneck's book on "Francis Hopkinson . . . James Lyon" (1905), p. 111.   DLC (etc.)

*GLEE.

A "new glee, for four voices composed by William Pirston [Pirsson ?] and sung at the Columbian Anacreontic Society" was advertised in April, 1796, as published by "B. Carr, No. 131 William st.," New York.

GLEE FOR THREE VOICES.

See Drink to me only.

A GLEE FOR WHICH A MEDAL WAS CONFERRED on the author by the New York Anacreontic Society on the 8th of June, 1797.

(*In* Pelissier's Columbian melodies. Philadelphia, 1811. p. 73–76)

At head of title: Mr. Pelissier has published in this number the following, his prize medal glee, at the repeated solicitation of several of his subscribers.
At foot of p. 73: Copyright secured.
Open score, three parts.
First line: Silent, silent nymph.
While not published until 1811, this title is included because of the date of the award—1797.   DLC

*NEW GLEE. Written by Mr. Harwood and set to music by R. Taylor. Advertised to be given at Mrs. Oldmixon's benefit in Philadelphia. July 2, 1795.

GLIDE GENTLY ON THOU MURM'RING BROOK. Translated from an Italian canzonetta. Composed by Wm. Pirsson. New York, Engrav'd & published by W. Pirsson, No. 417 Pearl street & sold at ye music shops. Pr. 25 cents [1799–1801] [2] p. 33 cm.

Song, pfte. acc. Arr. for "guittar", p. [2].
First line same as title.   CtY, DLC, NN

GLORY TRIUMPH VICT'RY FAME. Chorus.

See Military glory of Great Britain.

THE GLOUCESTERSHIRE MARCH.

See Compleat tutor for the fife . . . p. 16.

GO GENTLE ZEPHYR, ETC. A celebrated duet.

(*In* The universal asylum. Philadelphia, January, 1791. p. 55–56).

Duet, pfte. acc.
First line same as title.   DLC (etc.)

[GO, GEORGE, I CAN'T ENDURE YOU] Sung by Mrs. Shaw in the opera of No song no supper.

(*In* The gentleman's amusement, ed. by R. Shaw. Philadelphia [1794–96] p. 20)

Song, pfte. acc.
Title from first line.
In No. 3, 1794.
Stephen Storace's *No song, no supper* with Mrs. Shaw in the cast was performed at Philadelphia, June 6, 1794.   DLC, NN, PHi

GO LOVELY ROSE THY STATION CHOOSE. The music by H. Capron. Words by Edward Atkins. Philadelphia, Printed & sold by G. Willig. No. 185 Market street [1798–1804] 1 l. 32½ cm.

Song, pfte. acc.
First line same as title. PP–K

GO WITH YOU ALL THE WORLD OVER. The much admired dialogue duett in the Surrender of Calais.
See Pauvre Madelon.

GOD SAVE AMERICA.
(*In* The Philadelphia songster, ed. by A. Aimwell [pseud.] Philadelphia, 1789. p. 3–4)

Melody and bass with accompanying text. Two staves.
First line: God save America free from tyrannic sway.

One of the early appearances of the melody of "God save the King" set to an American text. NN

———— The same.
See The instrumental assistant, p. [25]. (Without text)

———— God save great Washington.
See Evening amusement, p. 14. (Same tune, without text)

The first appearance of this tune in America to other text than "God Save the King", is probably in James Lyon's *Urania*, Philadelphia, 1761, p. 190, where it appears under the title *Whitefields*. First line: Come thou almighty King.

THE GOLD FINCH.
(*In* The aviary. A collection of three sonnets by J. Hook. Philadelphia [1798] p. (4)–(5).)

Song, pfte. acc. Arr. for flute or "guittar," p. (5).
First line: The gold finch swells his little throat. JFD, LSL, NN

————The gold finch. Hook. Also just published
No. 1. The thrush.　　No. 4. The robin red breast.
No. 2. The linnets.　　No. 5. The nightingale.
and No. 6. The lark.
New York, Sold by I. and M. Paff, No. 127 Broadway [1799–1803] [2] p. 30½ cm.

At head of title: Selected from The Aviary, a collection of sonnets. No. 3. Imprint at foot of p. [2], followed by "3."
Song, pfte. acc.
First line same as preceding. ES, NN

GOLDEN DAYS OF GOOD QUEEN BESS.
(*In* The American musical miscellany. Northampton, 1798. p. 89–93)

Melody only, with accompanying text.
First line: To my muse give attention. DLC (etc.)

THE GOLDEN DAYS WE NOW POSSESS. A sequel to the favorite song (
Good Queen Bess. To the foregoing tune.
(*In* The American musical miscellany. Northampton, 1798. p. 93–95)

Words only.
First line: In the praise of Queen Bess.
The foregoing tune: The golden days of good Queen Bess. DLC (etc.

GOOD MORROW TO YOUR NIGHT CAP. Poor soldier.
(*In* A collection of favorite songs, divided into two books. Arr. by A
Reinagle. Philadelphia [1789 ?] bk. 1, p. 20)

Song. pfte. acc.
First line: Dear Kathlean you no doubt find.
Poor soldier, by William Shield. CdeW, DLC, ES, Hopk

GOOD NIGHT. A favorite song in the new opera of the Captive of Spilberg
Composed by I. L. Dussek. Printed and sold by R. Shaw (Importer c
music and musical instruments) Market street, No. 92, Baltimore [1798–180(
1 l. 27 cm. (trimmed)

Song, pfte. acc.
First line: In poor one's ne'er let envy rise. LSL, NI

—— The same as preceding, except that instead of 92 Market street, Baltimore
the imprint gives Shaw's address as "No. 13 South Fourth stre. Philadelphia"
and adds "Price 12 cents." Otherwise the plates are identical.
This later issue was probably after 1800. DLC, ES, McD-W, MI

The captive of Spilberg (or *Spilburg*) by J. L. Dussek and Michael Kelly, wa
first performed in November, 1798, but seems not to have reached Americ:
until after 1800.

GRACEFUL MOVE.
(*In* The Philadelphia songster, ed. by A. Aimwell [pseud.] Philadelphia
1789. p. 11)

Melody only, with accompanying text.
First line: When first I saw thee graceful move.
Composed by Signora —— Galli (*BM Cat.*) NN

—— The [!] graceful move.
(*In* The American musical miscellany. Northampton, 1798. p. 158–159)

Song, pfte. acc. Three staves.
First line same as preceding. DLC (etc.)

GRANBYS MARCH.
See Military amusement p. 12.

—— The Marquis of Granby's, or 1st troop of horse grenadiers march.
See Compleat tutor for the fife . . . p. 16.

GRAND DIVERTISMENT in the Temple of liberty.
See Grand *Divertisment* in the Temple of liberty.

GRAND MARCH from the opera of the Prisoner. Mozart.
See Grand *March* from the opera of the Prisoner. Mozart.

GRAND MARCH IN ALEXANDER THE GREAT.
See Grand *March* in Alexander the Great . . . A. Reinagle.

THE GRAND SPY.
See Manuscript *Collection* of hymns, songs, etc. (42)

THE GRAND TROOP.
See Manuscript *Collection* of hymns, songs, etc. (48)

GRANO'S MARCH.
See Compleat tutor for the fife . . . p. 26.

THE GRASSHOPPER. Set by E. Mann of Worcester.
(*In* The Massachusetts magazine, Boston, December, 1790. p. 766)

Song, pfte. acc.
First line: Little insect that on high. DLC (etc.)

THE GRASSHOPPER.
(*In* The American musical miscellany. Northampton, 1798. p. 64–66)

Two parts, with accompanying text.
First line same as preceding. DLC (etc.)

THE GRATEFUL LION. Alternative title of *Harlequin shipwreck'd.*

*GRAY MARE'S THE BEST HORSE.
This "dramatic proverb (performed in London with great applause being a
burletta)" was to be performed in Raynor "Taylor's musical performance
. . . The whole of the music original and composed by Mr. Taylor" at
Annapolis, Md., on January 20, 1793. It consisted of

A breakfast scene, a month after marriage, a duet.
The Mock wife in a violent passion.
A Father's advice to his son in law.
Giles the countryman's grief for the loss of a scolding wife.
The Happy miller.
Dame Pliant's obedience to her husband.
The Obedient wife determined to have her own way, a duet.
New married couple reconciled, a duet.
Finale, All parties happy, a duet.

GRAZIOSO.
See A collection of airs . . . arranged by J. Willson, p. 8–11.

THE GREEN MOUNTAIN FARMER. A new patriotic song. Written by
Thomas Paine, A. M. The music & accompaniments by the celebrated
Shield. Boston, Printed & sold by Messrs. Linley & Moore, No. 19 Malbro'
street [1798] [2] p. 34 cm.

Song, pfte. acc.
First line: Blest on his own paternal farm.
At foot of p. [2], "Copyright secured." [October 27, 1798]
Advertised as published in October, 1798.
LSL, MB, MWA, NBuG, NRU–Mus

THE GREEN MOUNTAIN FARMER. A new patriotic song. Written by
Thomas Paine, A. M. The music by Shield. New York, Printed & sold

at J. Hewitt's Musical repository, No. 121 [i. e. 131] William street. Sold also by B. Carr, Philadelphia & J. Carr, Baltimore. Price 25 cents. Copywright secured [ca. 1798] [2] p. 33 cm.

Song, pfte. acc.
First line same as preceding.   McD–W, PP–K

———— The same as preceding.
In A collection of new & favorite songs. [A] Philadelphia [ca. 1800] p. [8]–[9])   HFB

THE GREENWICH PENSIONER. Alternative title of *Twas in the good ship Rover*, by Charles Dibdin.

GRENADIERS MARCH.
See Compleat tutor for the German fife . . . p. 25.

GROUND IVY. Price 20 cents. Printed and sold at Carr's Musical repositories in New York and Philadelphia and J. Carr's, Baltimore [1796] [2] p. 32 cm.

Song, pfte. acc. Arr. for flute, p. [2].
First line: Last April morn as forth I walk'd.   ABHu

Advertised in March, 1796, among "new editions of . . . favorite songs some of which never before published in America . . . At Carr's Musical Repository, William Street," New York.

GROUND IVY. Composed by Daniel Marshal. New York, Printed & sold at J. & M. Paff's musical store, No. 127 Broadway [1799–1803] [2] p. 32 cm.

Song, pfte. acc.
First line: Near yonder hamlet in the vale.
"Burr's grand march," p. [2].
Music not identical with preceding.   DLC

THE GROUNDS AND RULES OF MUSICK EXPLAINED, or An introduction to the art of singing by note. Fitted to the meanest capacities by *Thomas Walter*, M. A. Recommended by several ministers. Let everything that hath breath praise the Lord. Psal. 150: 6. Boston, Printed by J. Franklin for S. Gerrish, near the Brick Church in Cornhill. 1721. 1 p. l., iv, 24, [16] p. 10 x 15½ cm.

Title-page, verso blank. Preface, p. i–iv; "Some brief and very plain instructions for singing by note," p. 1–24; music, [16] p.

Three part chorus. Open score. Diamond shaped notes.
This is the first edition.
                        MBJ, MH, MHi, NN (complete, except 3 p. photostat)

GUARDIAN ANGELS.
See Compleat tutor for the fife . . . p. 29.

See also Four excellent new *Songs*.

*GUITAR COMPOSITIONS by Mr. Cassignard.
"Several pieces of his compostition on the guitar" were to be performed by "Mr. Cassignard, amateur," at a concert in Philadelphia, on May 29, 1792.

HAD I A HEART. From the Duenna. Irish air of Gramachree [n. p., 179–] p. (26). 32 cm.

Song, pfte. acc.
First line same as title.
The duenna, by Thomas Linley.
"Had I a heart" was sung in Philadelphia as early as 1789, also in 1792. Probably a Carr imprint. *cf. *Elegant extracts.* NRU–Mus

HAIL! AMERICA, HAIL!
(*In* The American musical miscellany, Northampton, 1798. p. 122–125)
Melody only, with accompanying text, followed by "Choro grando."
First line: Hail, America hail, unrival'd in fame. DLC (etc.)

HAIL COLUMBIA.

The poem was written in 1798 by Joseph Hopkinson at the request of his friend, the actor, Gilbert Fox, who wished to draw a full house for his benefit by having some stirring words adapted to the "President's march."

From Joseph Hopkinson's own account of the history of his poem (in a letter to the Wyoming Bard, Wilkesbarre, Pa., August 24, 1840) we know that his object was "to get up an American spirit which should be independent of, and above the interests, passion and policy of both belligerents"; that is to say, of the Federalists and Anti-Federalists. Therefore, "Hail Columbia" was intended as a patriotic and *not* as a political song, and indeed the poem contains no party allusions whatsoever. This and the fact that the poem was adapted to the popular "President's march" soon gained a wide-spread popularity for the song, and thus "Hail Columbia" in a surprisingly short time became a national song.

It was first advertised in *Porcupine's gazette,* April 24, 1798, as follows:

MR. FOX'S NIGHT. On Wednesday evening, April 25. By desire will be presented (for the second time in America) a play, interspersed with songs, in three acts, called the *Italian Monk* . . . after which an entire new song (written by a citizen of Philadelphia) to the tune of the "President's march" will be sung by Mr. Fox; accompanied by the full band and the following *Grand Chorus:* Firm united let us be . . .

Only two days afterwards the first reference to the publication of the song was printed. We read in the same paper on April 27:

On Monday afternoon will be published at Carr's Musical Repository, the very favourite New Federal Song; written to the tune of the "President's march" by J. Hopkinson, Esq. and sung by Mr. Fox, at the New Theatre with great applause, ornamented with a very elegant portrait of the President. (Price 25 cents.)

Interesting as it might be, it seems inadvisable here to concern ourselves with the spirited discussion over the chronological sequence of the earliest imprints of "Hail Columbia" (The favorite new Federal song) begun by Louis C. Elson in his *National music of America* (1900) and in his *History of American music* (1904) and carried on by Sonneck in this *Bibliography* and various succeeding volumes, and by Charles Henry Hart in the pages of *The Pennsylvania magazine of history and biography.* Particularly as this whole early discussion now seems somewhat beside the point, as copies of the

[171]

authentic first edition, not located by any one of these writers, have since been found.

However, for sake of the record and because of the inherent value of the discussion itself, we note (in addition to the original edition [1905] of the present work) the following:

Sonneck's *Report on The star-spangled banner, Hail Columbia, America Yankee Doodle* (1909), p. 43–72.
(This chapter is invaluable as a study of the subject in all its phases.)

Hart's " 'Hail Columbia' and its first publication. A critical inquiry.'
Reprinted from *The Pennsylvania magazine of history and biography* for April, 1910.
(Contains facsimile of copy with Washington's portrait [oval].)

Hart's supplementary article on "The first edition of Hail Columbia,' in the same magazine for January, 1912.

Sonneck's article "The first edition of 'Hail Columbia,' " reprinted from the same magazine (1916) in his *Miscellaneous studies in the history of music* (1921), p. 180–189.

One fact seems now fully established, viz., that the advertisement quoted above is correct in stating that its issue (unquestionably the first) was "ornamented with a very elegant portrait of the President" [i. e. John Adams]. We now know that it really was Adams' portrait, and after all these years it still remains an "elegant," clean cut miniature. On the other hand, Sonneck's theory that Washington's portrait appeared at about the time of his appointment as Commander-in-Chief (July 3, 1798) seems entirely tenable, although his supposition that the legend underneath the portrait, "Behold the Chief who now commands," appeared first with Washington's portrait has been disproved. The fact that these Washington portraits (like that of Adams) were mounted on the finished imprint, and not engraved on the original plate, renders it more understandable that they should appear in such different forms.

The NN and PHi copies show entirely different portraits; and Hart speaks of seeing three other copies, all different. It seems reasonable, then, to consider these various imprints bearing the Washington portrait as a second issue. The issue with the eagle engraved on the plate in place of a mounted portrait probably came next; followed perhaps almost immediately by that with a portrait of Washington mounted directly below the engraved eagle.

It is quite evident that all these impressions were made from the same plate; that this plate was engraved for Carr; and that all these issues appeared probably during 1798.

THE FAVORITE NEW FEDERAL SONG. Adapted to the President's march. Sung by Mr. Fox. Written by J. Hopkinson, Esqr. For the voice, piano forte, guittar and clarinett [Philadelphia, B. Carr. 1798] [2] p. 31½ cm.

In caption, portrait of John Adams (circular) mounted, and lower half encircled by engraved legend: Behold the Chief who now commands.
Song, pfte. acc. Arr. for flute or violin, p. [2].
First line: Hail Columbia, happy land.
Unquestionably the first issue.

[172]

Published April 30, or May 1, 1798 (Sonneck).
ABHu, DLC, ES, LSL, PHi, CdeW (lacks part of p. [2] with arr. for flute
or violin)

—— The same as preceding, except that a portrait has been removed.
Legend still present. Presumably the missing portrait is that of Adams
(as above). It is possible, however, that one of the various Washington
portraits had been used—particularly the one of identical size and shape with
that of Adams. (This appeared in a somewhat later issue and is there placed
immediately under the engraved eagle.) 1798. DLC, McD–W, NRU–Mus

In DLC copy lower half of p. [2] is cut off.

—— The same as preceding, except that in caption is mounted portrait of
Washington (after Joseph Wright) slightly oval, apparently taken from engraved title-page of Hewitt's Battle of Trenton. Legend still present.

Published probably ca. July 3, 1798, the date of Washington's appointment
as Commander-in-Chief (Sonneck).   PHi (Baker collection)

—— The same as preceding, except that in caption is portrait of George
Washington (circular, mounted in somewhat larger square).
Legend not showing. Portrait is of Stuart type.

Published probably ca. July 3, 1798.   NN

—— The same as preceding, except in caption an American eagle with shield
and sunrays (engraved). No legend. 1798.
                    ABHu, CSmH, DLC, ES, LSL, MNSt, NN

—— The same as preceding, except in caption, portrait of Washington (Stuart
type) mounted directly under shield and eagle as above (engraved). No
Legend. 1798.   DLC

Of one further issue known to Hart, with portrait of Washington (circular)
of Stuart type mounted above the legend, thus differing from the three
already discussed, the present whereabouts is unknown.

The supplied imprint, common to all these issues, is based upon the above
quoted advertisement of Carr's Musical Repository.

"A grand allegorical pantomimical ballet dedicated to the · President of
the United States by Mr. Francisque" was performed at Philadelphia, June
1, 1798. Advertised in Aurora (Philadelphia) to contain a new American
song to the tune of the President's March. Quite evidently this was Hail
Columbia.

—— The Presidents march. A new Federal song. Published by G. Willig,
Market street, No. 185, Philadelphia [1798–1804] [2] p. 33½ cm.

Song, pfte. acc., with chorus.
First line: Hail Columbia, happy land.
Followed on p. [2] by Yankee Doodle (song, pfte. acc.).
                    DLC, MNSt, NHi, PP–K, PP–L
Probably published in 1798, particularly as such a song was advertised in the
Federal gazette, Baltimore, June 25, as among "new music. Just published."

Sonneck adds: The words "new Federal song" render it almost certain
that the piece was published in 1798.

—— Hail Columbia. Death or Liberty. A favorite new Federal song, adapted to the Presidents March. Boston, Printed & sold at P. A. Von Hagen, jun. & cᵒs, Musical magazine, Nᵒ 62, Newbury street [1798] [2] p. 33 cm.

In caption, eagle with shield. In its beak a ribbon inscribed "E pluribus unum."
Below imprint: For the Voice, Piano Forte, Guittar, Clarinett, Violin and Flute.
Song, pfte. acc. Arr. for flute or violin, p. [2].
First line same as preceding.
Advertised in the *Columbian centinel* (Boston), May 30, 1798. DLC

—— Hail Columbia. A patriotic song. Sung by Mr. Williamson with universal applause at the New York Theatre. New York, Printed & sold by G. Gilfert, No. 177 Broadway [1798–1801] [2] p. 33 cm.

Song, pfte. acc.
First line same as preceding.
Sung by Mr. Williamson in New York "at the end of the play," May 4, 1798, and repeated May 18. JFD

It seems likely that both the above issues (the first under the new title, "Hail Columbia") were published ca. May, 1798.

Mr. Williamson also sang Hail Columbia at the Ranelagh Garden, New York, July 4, 1798; Mr. Tyler "and full chorus" at the New City Tavern, New York, July 24, 1798. Referring to this latter performance Sonneck adds:

> What a hold Joseph Hopkinson's hastily written lines set to the "President's march" . . . were speedily gaining on the public may be inferred from the fact that Mr. Adde's "grand" benefit at Columbia Garden on Sept. 4th, concluded with this our first really national hymn. (*Early concert life in America*, p. 242)

[HAIL COLUMBIA, HAPPY LAND] Song. Adapted to the President's march.
(*In* New [American] patriotic songs, added to a collection of songs by C. Dibdin. Philadelphia, 1799. p. [313]–314)

Words only.
Title from first line. DLC, MWA, NHi, NN, RPJCB

FEDERAL ODE [HAIL COLUMBIA HAPPY LAND]
(*In* The easy instructor, or A new method of teaching sacred harmony, by William Little and William Smith [n. p., ca. 1802] p. 85–86)

DLC h as copy of complete t.-p. entered for copyright June 15, 1798. As far as we know, the book itself was not published until 1802 (copyright, New York, December 10, 1802).
On p. 85–86 of this edition we find the above version of *Hail Columbia*, given on two staves—for treble and bass.

Whether there was an earlier edition, as yet undiscovered, and whether this earlier edition may have contained this *Federal ode* we do not know. We do know, however, that such an issue was possible, as the song was advertised to be published within a few days of its first performance (by Gilbert Fox in Philadelphia, on April 25, 1798).

That this 1802 edition is not an identical reprint of a possible 1798 issue is evident from the fact that it contains *American's lamentation for Washington*, beginning "Moan ye sons of America, for your chief is gone," which obviously could not have appeared in 1798.

All of which goes to show that in all probability we have here the first edition, delayed in its publication until 1802.

Under the title of "Hail Columbia" the song was advertised in August, 1798, among "patriotic and other favorite songs" as "just published and for sale at Wm. Howe's wholesale and retail warehouse, 320 Pearl street," New York. No such issue has been located.

As a broadside without music (6 p. 20 x 12 cm. NN) "Hail Columbia" was printed (evidently in Philadelphia) under the title of:

Song adapted to the President's march sung at the theatre by Mr. Fox, at his benefit. Composed by Joseph Hopkinson, Esq. Printed by J. Ormrod, 41, Chestnut street.

No further editions with music seem to have been issued before 1800. The reason for this may be that it was hardly necessary to reprint a song of which the words rapidly became and of which the music was already common property.

For a discussion of the music to which Joseph Hopkinson's text was set, *see* President's march.

HAIL HAPPY WARBLER. Sung by Mrs. Harrison with the greatest applause at the Vocal concerts and musical festivals. Composed by Mr. Harrison. New York, Sold by I. & M. Paff [179–?] [2] p. 33½ cm.

Song, pfte. acc.
First line: O'er hill and valley, dell and glade.
Composed by Samuel Harrison, and first published in London, 1794 ? (*BM Cat.*) NN

HAIL LIBERTY. Sung by Mr. Darley, Junr. at the Vauxhall Gardens, Philadelphia and in the Patriot. Price 25 cents. [Philadelphia] Printed and sold at B. Carr's Musical repository; J. Carr's, Baltimore and J. Hewitt's, New York (1797] 2 p. 30½ cm.

Song, pfte. acc.
First line: Hail Liberty, supreme delight. NN, PHi

As "Sung by Mr. Darley, junr. at Bush Hill," Philadelphia, advertised in November, 1797, as published "at Carr's Musical Repository."

——The same as preceding.
(*In* A collection of new & favorite songs. [A] Philadelphia [ca. 1800] p. [164]–[165]) HFB

HAIL PATRIOTS ALL. A favorite patriotic song composed by Mr. $ $ $. New York, Printed & sold by G. Gilfert, No. 177 Broadway. Where may be had Hail Columbia, Adams & Liberty, Washington & Independence and Ladies patriotic song [ca. 1798] [2] p. 32 cm.

Song, pfte. acc. Arr. for German flute, p. [2].
First line same as title. MNSt

[HAIL! SONS OF FREEDOM! HAIL THE DAY] Patriotic song. Composed by a citizen of Lancaster for a special occasion on July 4, 1794. Tune: Marseilles hymn.

Words only.
Title from first line.
Printed in Dunlap and Claypoole's *American daily advertiser*, Philadelphia, August 2, 1794.   DLC (etc.)

THE HAMILTONIAN.
See Twenty-four American country *Dances*, p. 1.

HANDELS MARCH.
See Military amusement, p. 23.

HANDLE'S [!] CELEBRATED WATER MUSIC. [New] York, Published by S. Terret, No. 320 Pearl [street] [1804–05]   2 p.   31½ cm.

Pfte. 2 hds.
Imprint is pasted on. The words "New" and "street" have been scratched away. Although no original imprint shows under this later one, it is probable that the plate belonged to William Howe at this same address, which would date this issue as eighteenth century, possibly as early as 1797. DLC

HANDLE'S [!] WATER MUSIC. New York, Printed & sold by G. Gilfet [!] No. 177 Broadway [1797–1801]   [2] p.   32 cm.

Pfte. 2 hds.   DLC, JFD, MB, NN, RPJCB

Both of the above issues contain material not included in authentic editions of *Handel's Water music*, viz., an *Arioso* of thirty two measures which follows the opening section. In the Terret issue it appears without title.

THE HAPPY DREAMER. A ballad. Philadelphia, Printed and sold by G. Willig, Mark: street, No. 185 [1798–1804]   [2] p.   33 cm.

Song, pfte. acc.
First line: Blest were the hours in which I stray'd.   ES

*THE HAPPY RENCONTRE, or Second thoughts are best.
This "cantata" was "composed and sung by Mrs. Pownall" at a concert, Boston, July 22, 1794.

*THE HAPPY SHEPHERD AND SHEPHERDESS, a pastoral duet by Raynor Taylor.
Was to be sung in "Taylor's musical performance . . . the whole of the music original and composed by Mr. Taylor" at Annapolis, Md., January 20, 1793.

HAPPY TAWNY MOOR. A favorite duett. Sung by Mrs. Oldmixon & Mr. Harwood in the Mountaineers. Published at B. Carr's Musical repositories, New York & Philadelphia & J. Carr's, Baltimore. Price 25 cents. [ca. 1796] [2] p.   33 cm.

Duet, pfte. acc. Two and three staves. Arr. for "guittar," p. [2].
First line: Oh happy tawny moor.
Mrs. Oldmixon and John E. Harwood first appeared in Samuel Arnold's *The mountaineers* in Philadelphia, April 18, 1796.   MdHi (guitar part torn)

[176]

—— The same as preceding, but with an additional page, numbered 66. This page is identical with page 66 of *The gentleman's amusement*, except that the words, "For two flutes" are added below the title. The date would therefore seem to be ca. 1796. DLC, MWA, PHi

HAPPY TAWNY MOOR. A favorite duet from the Mountaineers.
(*In* The gentleman's amusement, ed. by R. Shaw. Philadelphia [1794–96] p. 66)

Duet for flutes or violins, or flute and violin, with accompanying text. Two staves.
First line same as preceding.
In No. [8], ca. 1796. DLC, PHi, PP–K

HAPPY TAWNY MOOR. A favorite duett. New York, Printed by G. Gilfert, No. 177 Broad Way [ca. 1797] 1 l. 33½ cm.

Duet, pfte. acc. Two and three staves.
First line same as preceding. DLC, MWA

THE HAPPY WEDDING.
(*In* The songster's assistant, ed. by T. Swan. Suffield [ca. 1800] p. 25–27)

Song, pfte. acc.
First line: Now the happy knot is ty'd. MB

HAPPY WERE THE DAYS. In the new opera of Ramah Droog. Printed and sold by R. Shaw (Importer of music and musical instruments) Market street, No. 92, Baltimore. Price 25 cents [1798–1800] [2] p. 33½ cm.

Song, pfte. acc. Arr. for flute, p. [2].
First line same as title.
Ramah Droog, by Joseph Mazzinghi, was first produced in 1798. LSL

—— The same as preceding, except that the imprint reads, "No. 13 South Fourth street Philadelphia," therefore to be dated possibly after 1800.
DLC, McD–W

THE HARE HUNT. New York, Printed & sold at J. Hewitt's Musical repository, No. 131 William street; B. Carr, Philadelphia & J. Carr, Baltimore. Price 25 cents [1797–99] [2] p. 31½ cm.

Song, pfte. acc.
First line: Since Zeph'rus first tasted the charms of coy Flora. LSL, NN

—— The same as preceding.
(*In* A collection of new & favorite songs. [A] Philadelphia [ca. 1800] p. [74]–[75]) HFB

HARK AWAY TO THE DOWNS. A favourite hunting song. Price 6d [Carr, Philadelphia, 1797] [2] p. 32½ cm.

Song, pfte. acc.
First line: Hark, hark my brave boys.
At end of seventh stanza, p. [2]: J. Carr.
Advertised in November, 1797, as "published at Carr's Musical Repository," Philadelphia. ICN, NN

—— The same as preceding, but without "Price 6d." MdH

[177]

HARK ELIZA'S TUNEFUL VOICE.
(*In* The favorite scngs, by Mr. Hook. Philadelphia [1794–95] p. 10)
Song, pfte. acc.
First line same as title. McD–W, MdHi, MWA, NN

HARK FORWARD TANTIVY HUZZA. Composed by Mr. Hook.
(*In* [Unidentified collection of instrumental and vocal music. New York]
Hewitt & Rausch [1797] p. 14–16)
Song, pfte. acc.
First line: To pleasure let's raise the heart chearing [!] song. DLC, ES

—— Separate issue of preceding, 1797–99. DLC

—— The same as preceding.
(*In* A collection of new & favorite songs. [A] Philadelphia]ca. 1800] p. [149]–
[150]) HFB

*—— Hark forward. Song.
Advertised March 22, 1797, as to be published "in a few days" by "G.
Gilfert at his Musical Magazine, No. 177 Broadway," New York.

HARK FROM THE TOMBS, &C. And Beneath the honors, &c. Adapted
from Dr. Watts and set to music by Samuel Holyoke, A. M. Performed at
Newburyport, 2d. January, 1800. The day on which the citizens unitedly
expressed their unbounded veneration for the memory of our beloved Washington. Copyright secured. Exeter, Printed by H. Ranlet [1800] 1 p. l.,
12 p. 14 x 22½ cm.

On p. l.: To be performed at the Brattle street Church, on Wednesday,
February 19, 1800:

Ode I, From Vernon's mount behold the hero rise.

Ode II, That matchless form, which aw'd the world. [Words only]

Title-page with ornamental border; music, p. 2–12.
For mixed chorus. Three staves.
First lines same as titles.
Copyright, January 21, 1800.
Certain copies lack p. 1. CSmH, DLC, MH

[HARK, HARK FROM THE WOODLANDS] A favorite hunting song.
(*In* [Moller & Capron's Monthly numbers] The first number [Philadelphia,
1793] p. 6)
Song, pfte. acc.
Title from first line. DLC

HARK THE GODDESS DIANA. A favorite duett. Sung by Messrs. Hodgkinson & Williamson at the Anacreontic Society. New York, Printed &
sold at J. Hewitt's Musical repository, No. 131 William street. Sold also
by B. Carr, Philadelphia & J. Carr, Baltimore. Price 31 cents. [1797–99]
3 p. 32½ cm.

Duet, pfte. acc. Three staves.
First line: Hark the goddess Diana calls out for the chace [!].

[178]

Composed by Reginald Spofforth. *cf. Encyclopedia of Music,* John W. Moore. Boston, 1854.
The Columbian Anacreontic Society of New York was founded ca. 1795, with John Hodgkinson as President. The society was still in existence in 1800.

CtY, DLC, ES, MB, McD–W, MdHi, MWA, NN, PP–K

———— The same as preceding.
(*In* A collection of new & favorite songs. [A] Philadelphia [ca. 1800] p. [3]–[5])

HFB

HARK THE GODDESS DIANA. Duett. New York, Sold at J. Paff's store, Broadway [1798] [2] p. 32 cm.

Duet. Three staves.
First line same as title.

MBuG, NHi

HARK THE LARK AT HEAV'NS GATE SINGS.
(*In* Young's vocal and instrumental musical miscellany. Philadelphia [1793–95] p. 38 and 40)

Song, pfte. acc. Arr. for flute, p. 40.
First line same as title.
In No. 5 [1793].

DLC, Hopk.

*HARLEQUIN DR. FAUSTUS, or The devil will have his own.
Performed in Philadelphia, June 3, 1796. Advertised in *Aurora*, Philadelphia, of the same date as introducing *A dance of the furies.*
"The music of this scene and an introductory symphony by R. Taylor."

*HARLEQUIN EVERYWHERE. Alternative title of *The witches of the rocks.*

*HARLEQUIN PASTRY COOK.
This "new pantomime, as. performed . . . at Paris . . . with entire new music by Mr. [Victor] Pellisier" was given at Philadelphia, on November 21, 1794.

*HARLEQUIN SHIPWRECK'D, or the Grateful lion.
This "new pantomime" was performed at Philadelphia, on January 2, 1795, with "the music compiled by Mr. De Marque from Pleyel, Gretri [!], Giornowicki [!], Giordani, Shields, Reeves, Moorehead, etc. The new music by Mr. [Alexander] Reinagle."

*HARLEQUIN'S FLIGHT. Alternative title of *The Arabs of the desert.*

*HARLEQUIN'S INVASION.
This "speaking pantomime, written by the late David Garrick," was performed for the first time at Philadelphia, on June 12, 1795, "with the original music, the accompaniments by Mr. Gillingham, with an entire new medley overture by Mr. [Alexander] Reinagle."

THE HARMLESS SHEPHERD.
See The select songster. New Haven, 1786. p. 49–50.

HARMONIA AMERICANA. Containing a concise introduction to the grounds of music with a variety of airs suitable for divine worship and the use of musical societies. Consisting of three and four parts. By Samuel Holyoke, A. B. Printed at Boston, typographically by Isaiah Thomas and Ebenezer

[179]

T. Andrews. At Faust's statue, No. 45 Newbury street. 1791. Sold at their bookstore, by said Thomas at his bookstore in Worcester, and by the booksellers in town and country. 119, [1] p. 13 x 22½ cm.

Title-page, verso blank; subscribers' names, p. [3]; preface, p. [4]; a concise introduction to the grounds of music, p. [5]–16; music, p. 17–119; index, p. [120].

Three (or four) part chorus. Open score.

Contains two secular numbers: The scatter'd clouds are fled at last, p. 43–45; The close of the year [So fly our months and years], p. 56.

CSmH, DLC, ICN, MB, MH, MWA, NHi, NN, RPJCB

THE HARMONIST'S COMPANION. Containing a number of airs suitable for divine worship, together with an anthem for Easter and a Masonic ode never before published. Composed by Daniel Belknap, teacher of music in Framingham [Verse] Published according to Act of Congress. Printed typographically at Boston by Isaiah Thomas and Ebenezer T. Andrews, Faust's statue, No. 45 Newbury street, Oct., 1797. 31, [1] p. 13 x 21 cm.

Title-page; preface, p. [2]; music, p. [3]–31; index, p. [32].

Principally for four-part chorus. Open score.

Most important secular number: A view of the temple—A Masonic ode, p. 29–31. DLC, MWA

*HARMONY MUSIC, Phile.

A piece, thus announced on the program, was to conclude the last concert for the season at Gray's Gardens, Philadelphia, October 16, 1790. The real title of Philip Phile's composition, evidently for wind instruments, is not given.

THE HARMONY OF MAINE. Being an original composition of psalm and hymn tunes of various metres suitable for divine worship. With a number of fuging [!] pieces and anthems. Together with a concise introduction to the grounds of musick and rules for learners. For the use of singing schools and musical societies. By S. Belcher, of Farmington, County of Lincoln, District of Maine [Verses] Published according to Act of Congress. Printed typographically at Boston by Isaiah Thomas and Ebenezer T. Andrews. Sold by them at Faust's statue, No. 45 Newbury street, and by said Thomas in Worcester. Sold also by the booksellers in town and country. 1794. 103, [1] p. 12½ x 22 cm.

On verso of t.-p. is an elaborate design of musical instruments and flowers. Also verses, "On musick."

Preface, p. [3]; musical terms, p. [4]; introduction to the grounds of musick and rules for learners; p. [5]–16; music, p. 17–103; index to the musick, p. [104].

Secular numbers: Transition [When snows descend and robe the fields], p. 29.—Invitation [Child of the summer, charming rose], p. 30–32.—Heroism [Why should vain mortals], p. 35.—The lilly [Peaceful and lowly in their native soil], p. 36.—Content [I'm not concern'd to know], p. 42.—Friendship [How pleasant 'tis to see], p. 47.—Spring [The scattr'ed clouds are fled at last], p. 63–64.—The power of musick. Words by Stoddard [Hark some soft swell], p. 84–90. CtY, DLC, ICN, MB, MHi, MWA, NN

The above collection has been so fully described because it stands almost alone among its contemporaries in being written "for the use of singing schools and musical societies." Hence its unusually numerous secular items, as noted above. Among the most important of these: Spring, p. 63–64; The power of musick, p. 84–90.

THE HAUNTED TOWER, a comic opera, in three acts. As performed by the Old American Company. Written by Mr. Cobb. Philadelphia. Printed by Thomas Bradford, No. 8, South Front street. 1794. 1 p. l., 57 p. 17 cm.

Libretto by Cobb to Stephen Storace's opera (1789).
Half-title: The haunted tower.
Title-page; dramatis personae, p. [2]; text, p. [3]–57.   DLC, MB, PHi, PU
The opera was to be given at New York, January 7, 1795, with "the music by Mr. Storace, and the accompaniments by Mr. [Victor] Pelisier."

*HAY DAY MORN. New song. Composed by Mr. Hook.
Advertised in *Minerva*, New York, May 30, 1797, as just published by James Hewitt and for sale at his Musical Repository, William Street.

HAYDN'S CELEBRATED ANDANTE for the pianoforte.
(*In* Twelve favorite pieces, arr. by A. Reinagle. Philadelphia [1789?] p. 13–14)

Pfte. 2 hds.
In lower margin of p. 14: John Aitken, Sculpt.
From Symphony No. 26 (*Pohl*).   *cf.* Overture by Haydn.   DLC

———— The same as preceding but unpaged.   ca. 1789.   DLC

HAYDN'S GRAND OVERTURE.
See Overture by Haydn.

HAYDN'S MINUET.
See Evening amusement, p. 20.

HAYDN'S 3 CANZONETTS.
See Three . . . *Canzonetts* by Haydn.

HE LOVES HIS WINSOME KATE.
See Winsome Kate.

HE SLEEPS IN YONDER DEWY GRAVE.   A favorite song.   Composed by I. W. Callcott.   New York, Printed & sold by G. Gilfert, No. 177 Broadway. Where may be had: Ah seek to know, The gentle swan, As pendant o'er the limpid stream, Tell me fairest, tell me true, Ah Delia, see the fatal hour, When Lelia on the plain appears.   Composed by Kotzwara, author of The battle of Prague, O wou'd I ne'er had seen thee, The village recruit, P & T, The duel, Chelsea reach, Still the lark finds repose, The flower girl, The woodman's fair daughter, The rose, a moral song, To the copse lead along & Overture to the opera of Blue Beard.   [1798]   [2] p.   32½ cm.

Song, pfte. acc.
First line: While o'er thy cheek desponding.
I. W. Callcott: John Wall Callcott.   McD–W
Advertised in November, 1798, as "just published" by "George Gilbert, at his Music store, 177 Broadway, Apollo's Head," New York.

HE SLEEPS IN YONDER DEW'Y [!] GRAVE. Callcot, M. B. As now singing at the nobilitys public and private concerts in London with the greatest applause. New York, Sold at I. and M. Paff's music store, No. 127 Broadway [1799–1803] [2] p. 32½ cm.

At head of title: (No. 1) Ladies musical journal.
Imprint at foot of p. [2].
Song, pfte. acc. Arr. for Ger: flute, p. [2].
First line same as preceding. DLC

HE'S STOLE MY HEART FROM ME. A new Scotch song. Sung by Miss Sims. New York, Printed & sold by G. Gilfert, No. 177 Broadway. (*In* A collection of favorite songs, by Mr. Hook. New York [1799–1801] bk. [1], p. 16–17)

Below imprint: Written by Mr. Upton.
Song, pfte. acc.
First line: Young Jemmy is a bonny boy. DLC

——— Separate issue of preceding, 1799–1801 DLC

HE STOLE MY TENDER HEART AWAY.
(*In* The American musical miscellany. Northampton, 1798. p. 50–51)

Melody only, with accompanying text.
First line: The fields were green, the hills were gay. DLC (etc.)

THE HEART THAT HAS NE'ER TASTED SORROW. A favorite song. Sung in the new opera of Abroad and at home. New York, Printed & sold by G. Gilfert, No. 177 Broadway [1797–98] 1 l. 31½ cm.

Song, pfte. acc.
First line same as title.
Abroad and at home, by William Shield, first performed in America in Philadelphia, January 27, 1797; in New York, November 10, 1797. MWA

THE HEAVING OF THE LEAD. A favorite sea song. Composed by Mr. Shield. Price 20 cents. Philadelphia, Printed for Carr & co., at their Musical repository, No. 136 High street. Where may be had all the newest music, reprinted from European publications. Likewise an elegant assortment of piano fortes, guittars, flutes, violins and other musical articles of superior quality. [1793] [2] p. 32½ cm.

Song, pfte. acc. Arr. for German flute, p. [2].
First line: For England when with fav'ring gale.
From *The Hartford bridge.*

Advertised in August, 1793, among other "new songs, printed singly . . . printed and sold at Carr & Co. Musical Repository, No. 136 High street."
ABHu, DLC, HFB, LSL, MdHi, MWA, PP

HEAVING THE LEAD. A favourite new song.
(*In* Young's vocal and instrumental musical miscellany. Philadelphia [1793–95] p. 33–34)

Song, pfte. acc. Arr. for flute, p. 33.
First line: For England here with fav'ring gales.
In No. 4 [1793]. DLC, Hopk.

[182]

THE HEAVING OF THE LEAD.
(*In* Elegant extracts for the German flute or violin. Baltimore [1794] bk. 1, p. 2–3)

Melody only, flute or violin, with accompanying text.
First line: For England when with fav'ring gale.
NN copy lacks p. 2.   DLC, NN

HEAVING THE LEAD.
New York, Printed for G. Gilfert, No. 177 Broadway [1797–1801] 1 l. 31½ cm.

Song, pfte. acc.
First line same as preceding.   MWA, RPJCB

THE HEAVING OF THE LEAD.
(*In* The American musical miscellany. Northampton, 1798. p. 140–141)

Melody only, with accompanying text.
First line same as preceding.   DLC (etc.)

HEAVING THE LEAD.   A favorite new song. [New York] Sold at I. and M. Paffs music warehouse, No. 127 Broadway. 12 cents. [1799–1803] 1 l. 30½ cm.

Song, pfte. acc.
First line: For England here with fav'ring gales.   NN

THE HEAVING OF THE LEAD.   A favorite song. Composed by Mr. Shield in the Hartford bridge. [n. p., n. d.] 72–73 p. 31 cm.

Song, pfte. acc. Arr. for flute, p. 73.
First line: For England when with fav'ring gale.
Evidently a reprint from some unidentified collection, ca. 179–.   MB

THE HEAVY HOURS.
(*In* The American musical miscellany. Northampton, 1798. p. 38–39)

Melody only, with accompanying text.
First line: The heavy hours are almost past.
Composed by William Jackson of Exeter.   DLC (etc.)

[THE HEAVY HOURS ARE ALMOST PAST] Song.
(*In* The universal asylum. Philadelphia, June, 1791. p. 414–415)

Song, pfte. acc.
Title from first line.   DLC (etc.)

HEIGHO.   In the new opera of the Captive of Spilberg. Composed by I. L. Dussek.   Printed and sold by R. Shaw, Importer of music and musical instruments, Market street No. 92, Baltimore. Price 12 cents. [1798–1800] 1 l.   32 cm.

Song, pfte. acc.
First line: I lov'd so many maidens fair.   DLC, ES, LSL

HELEN.
See Mark my Alford.

[183]

HENRY AND MARIA. Printed and sold at Carr's music store, Baltimore [ca. 1800] [2] p. 33 cm.

Song, pfte. acc.
First line: The drums resound, the trumpets call.
BM Cat. lists a song "Henry & Maria" by James Hook.   DLC

HENRY CULL'D THE FLOW'RET'S BLOOM. Rosina.
(In A collection of favorite songs, divided into two books. Arr. by A. Reinagle. Philadelphia [1789?] bk. 2, p. 16–17)

Song, pfte. acc.
First line same as title.
Rosina, by William Shield.   CdeW, DLC, PU

———— Separate issue of preceding, ca. 1789.   DLC

HENRY'S ADIEU. Composed by T. Costellow. New York, Printed by G. Gilfert & co., No. 191 Broadway [1794–95] [2] p. 33 cm.

Song, pfte. acc.
First line: Now Henry has left me to plough the salt sea.   JFD

*HENRY'S ADIEU.
Advertised in March, 1795, as "published and to be sold at G. Willig's Musical Magazine, No. 165 Market street," Philadelphia.

HENRY'S COTTAGE MAID.
(In Young's vocal and instrumental musical miscellany. Philadelphia [1793–95] p. 28)

Song, pfte. acc.
First line: Ah where can fly my soul's true love.
In No. 4 [1793].
Composed by Ignaz Pleyel.   DLC, Hopk.

HENRY'S COTTAGE MAID. By Pleyel. Price 20 cents. Philadelphia, Printed at Carr & cos. Musical repository [1794] [2] p. 33 cm.

Song, pfte. acc. Arr. for "guittar," p. [2].
First line same as preceding.   ABHu, DLC, ES, LSL, McD–W, MWA,

Advertised February 3, 1794, as "this day" published.   NRU–Mus

HENRY'S COTTAGE MAID. Pleyle.
(In The gentleman's amusement, ed. by R. Shaw. Philadelphia [1794–96] p. 16)

Melody (flute or violin) with accompanying text.
First line same as preceding.
In No. 2, May, 1794.
Pleyle: Ignaz Joseph Pleyel.   PHi

HENRY'S COTTAGE MAID. A favorite song. Composed by Pleyel. New York, Printed for G. Gilfert & co. at their Musical magazine, No. 177 Broadway [1796] 1 l. 31½ cm.

Song, pfte. acc.
First line same as preceding.   MWA, NN, RPJCB

HENRY'S COTTAGE MAID. Published by G. Willig, Market street, No. 185 [1798–1804] 1 l., numbered 3. 32½ cm.

Song, pfte. acc.
First line same as preceding.   DLC, JFD, RPJCB

HENRY'S COTTAGE MAID. A favorite song. Composed by Pleyel. Pr. 12 cts. [n. p., n. d.] p. 76. 31 cm.

Song, pfte. acc.
First line same as preceding.
Evidently a reprint from *The musical repertory*, Boston [No. V, 1799].
                                          JFD, MB, NBuG, RPJCB

HENRY'S COTTAGE MAID. [New York] Sold by I. and M. Paff [n. d.] 1 l. 32½ cm.

Song, pfte. acc.
First line same as preceding.
Published possibly as early as 1799.   ABHu, DLC, ES

HENRY'S COTTAGE MAID. [n. p., n. d.] 1 l. 31½ cm.

Song, pfte. acc.
First line same as preceding.
Published probably 179–.   NBuG

HENRY'S DEPARTURE. Composed by W. P. R. Cope. New York, Engrav'd & published by I. & M. Paff [n. d.] [2] p. 30½ cm.

Song, pfte. acc.
First line: With grief opprest and heaving sighs.
Very unusual typography. Text in large capitals.
Published possibly as early as 1799.   NBuG, NN

HENRY'S RETURN. The sequel to Crazy Jane. Written by Mr. Rannie. Composed & respectfully dedicated to the Honble Miss Fraser of Saltoun. By John Ross of Aberdeen. New York, Printed & sold at G. Gilfert's music-store, No. 177 Broadway [ca. 1800] [2] p. 32½ cm.

Song, pfte. acc.
First line: A coward to love and manly duty.   McD–W

HENRY'S RETURN. The sequel to Crazy Jane. Boston, Printed & sold at P. A. von Hagen & co. imported piano forte & music warehouse, No. 3 Corn-hill [1800] [2] p. 33 cm.

Song, pfte. acc.
First line same as preceding.   JFD, LSL, MB, NRU–Mus

Advertised, November 29, 1800, as "this day published."

HER ABSENCE WILL NOT ALTER ME.
(*In* The American musical miscellany. Northampton, 1798. p. 147–149)

Melody only, with accompanying text.
First line: Though distant far from Jessy's charms.   DLC (etc.)

HER MOUTH WHICH A SMILE. Alternative title of *The bud of the rose.*

[185]

HER MUCH LOV'D LITTLE SAILOR BOY.
See The little sailor boy.

THE HERALD.
See No. 1 in a new sett of *Cotilions* [!].

[HERE BENEATH OUR LOWLY COTT] Sung by Miss Broadhurst & Mr. Darley, Junr.
(*In* The volunteers, by A. Reinagle. Philadelphia [1795] p. 4)
Duet, pfte. acc.
Title from first line.   DLC

HERE'S THE PRETTY GIRL I LOVE. Composed by Mr. Hook. New York, Printed & sold at J. Hewitt's Musical repository, No. 131 William st. Sold also by B. Carr, Philadelphia & J. Carr, Baltimore. Pr. 25 cts. [1798] [2] p. 32½ cm.

Song, pfte. acc.
First line: Jack Oakham was a gallant tar.   DLC, ES, MB, NN (mutilated)

Advertised as published in January, 1798.
Probably identical with issue advertised in December, 1797, as "published at Carr's Musical Repository, Market Street," Philadelphia.

—— The same as preceding.
(*In* A collection of new & favorite songs. [A] Philadelphia [ca. 1800] p. [86]–[87])   HFB

THE HEREDETARY [!] PRINCE.
See Twenty-four American country *Dances*, p. 16.

THE HERMIT.   [Philadelphia] Published by G. Willig, 165 Market st. [1795–97] 3 p.   32 cm.

Song, pfte. acc.
First line: At the close of the day when the hamlet is still.   NBuG

THE HERMIT.
(*In* The American musical miscellany. Northampton, 1798. p. 204–207)
Melody and bass, with accompanying text.
First line: At the close of the day, when the hamlet was still.   DLC (etc.)

HERO AND LEANDER.
(*In* The American musical miscellany. Northampton, 1798. p. 219–221)
Melody and bass, with accompanying text.
First line: Leander on the bay at Hellespont.   DLC (etc.)

HEY DANCE TO THE FIDDLE & TABOR.   A dialogue in the Lock and key. Sung by Mr. & Mrs. Hodgkinson.   New York, Printed & sold at J. Hewitt's Musical repository, No. 131 William Street.   Sold also by B. Carr, Philadelphia & J. Carr, Baltimore.   Price 25 cts. [1797–99] [2] p.   31   cm.
Duet, pfte. acc.
First line same as title.
The lock and key, by William Shield.
                                    DLC, JFD, MdHi, MWA, NN (incomplete)

—— The same as preceding.
(*In* A collection of new & favorite songs. [A] Philadelphia [ca. 1800] p. [82]–[83])   HFB

HEY DANCE TO THE FIDDLE & TABOR. A dialogue in the Lock and key.
Sung by Mrs. & Mr. Hodgkinson. Pr. 25 cts. [n. p., n. d.] p. 94–95.

Song, pfte. acc.
First line same as title.
Apparently separate issue from Norman's *Musical repertory*, Boston, No. VI
[1799].   McD–W

HEYMAKERS [!] DANCE.
See Compleat tutor for the fife . . . p. 29.

HIGH O'ER THE GRAVE WHERE MARY SLEEPS. A favorite ballad.
Composed by John Ross. New York, Printed & sold at G. Gilferts piano
forte ware house, No. 177 Broadway. And to be had of P. A. von Hagen,
No. 3 Cornhill, Boston. And G. Willig, No. 185 Market street, Philadelphia [ca. 1800] [2] p. 33 cm.

Song, pfte. acc.
First line same as title.   DLC, JFD, McD–W

THE HIGHLAND BELLE. Alternative title of *Moggie*, by R. Taylor.

THE HIGHLAND LADDIE. Introduced by Mrs. Warrell in the Highland
reel. (20 cents) [Philadelphia] Sold by Carr & co. at their Musical repository, No. 122 High St., and by H. & P. Rice, No. 50 Market street.
(*In* The gentleman's amusement, ed. by R. Shaw. Philadelphia [1794–96]
p. 46–47)

At head of first score: Flute.
Song, pfte. acc. Arr. for guitar, p. 47.
First line: The lowland lads think they are fine.
In No. 6, 1795–96.
Sung by Mrs. Warrell in William Shield's *Highland reel*, Philadelphia,
April 4, 1794.   PHi

—— Separate issue of preceding, 1795–96.   JFD, LSL, MWA

THE HIGHLAND QUEEN. By Swan.
(*In* The songster's assistant, ed. by T. Swan. Suffield [ca. 1800] p. 30–31)

Song, pfte. acc.
First line: No more my songs shall be, ye swains.   CtY, MB

THE HIGHLAND REEL: a comic opera, in three acts. As performed with
universal applause, at the Theatres royal, London and Dublin: And, at the
theatre, New York, by the Old American Company. By John O'Keeffe, Esq.
New York. Printed by John Harrisson, (Yorick's Head) No. 3, Peck Slip,
1794. 72 p. 16½ cm.

Libretto to William Shield's opera (1788).
Title-page, verso blank; dramatis personae, p. [3], text, p. [5]–72.
Certain copies have frontispiece.   CSmH, MH, NN, PHi

[187]

THE HIGHLAND REEL. A comic opera, in three acts, by John O'Keeffe, Esq. [Printer's mark] Philadelphia, Printed and sold by E. Story, Fourth near Chestnut st. (No. 36), 1794. 55 p. 17½ cm.

Libretto. MWA
Title-page, verso blank; p. [3] blank; The Characters, p. [4]; text, p. [5]–55.

THE HIGHLAND REEL: A comic opera in three acts. As performed with universal applause, at the Theatre-Federal-Street. By John O'Keeffe, Esq. Boston. Printed for Wm. P. and L. Blake at the Boston Book-Store Cornhill. 1797. 68, [3] p. 17 cm.

Libretto.
Title-page; dramatis personae, p. [2]; text, p. [3]–68; "Song," p. [69]; advertisements, p. [70]–[71].

On p. [69]:
> The following Song, written by Mrs. Rowson, was substituted for the Original p. 58. "A Soldier is the noblest name, Enroll'd upon the lists of fame."

On p. 58 we find:

AIR SERGEANT

Old England, great in arts and arms,
For manly worth and female charms.

CSmH, CtY, MB, MH, MWA, NN, PPL

THE HIGHLAND REEL.
See Evening amusement, p. 20.

THE HILL TOPS. A new hunting song.
(In The royal American magazine. Boston, April, 1774. Opposite p. 151)
At head of page engraved hunting scene, signed J. C.
Song, pfte. acc.
First line: Now the hill tops are burnished with azure and gold. DLC (etc.)

A HINDUSTANI GIRL'S SONG. Tis thy will and I must leave thee. Adapted by Mr. Briggs [!] New York, Printed and sold by I. and M. Paff, No. 127 Broadway [1799–1803] [2] p. 31½ cm.
Song, pfte. acc.
First line: Tis thy will and I must leave thee.
Mr. Briggs: Edward Smith Biggs. McD–W

HIS MAJESTY'S REVIEW of the volunteer corps of London, &c., &c. In Hyde Park, June 4th, 1799. A sonata for the piano forte. Composed by Joseph Michele. New York, Printed and published by John & M. Paff, No. 127 Broadway [1799–1801] 11 p. 31½ cm.
Pfte. 2 hds.
At foot of p. 11: Engraved by W. Pirsson, No. 417 Pearl street [1799–1801]
NN

HITHER MARY. Sung with universal applause at Vauxhall Gardens, 1793. Composed by Mr. Hook. Price 20 cents. Philadelphia, Printed at Carr & cos. Musical repository [1793] [2] p. 33 cm.
Song, pfte. acc. Arr. for "guittar," p. [2].
First line: Hither, hither Mary, hither, hither come!
DLC, ES, MWA, NBuG

Advertised in December, 1793, as "published . . . printed singly" by "B. Carr & Co. Musical Repository, No. 122 South side of Market street," Philadelphia.

*THE HOBBIES, a favorite song, written and sung by Mr. Williamson, at the Heymarket Theatre.
Thus advertised in July, 1797, in the *Columbian centinel*, Boston, as "published . . . to be had at the book stores . . ."

THE HOBBIES.
   (*In* The American musical miscellany. Northampton, 1798. p. 84–86)

   Melody only, with accompanying text.
   First line: Attention pray give while of hobbies I sing.   DLC (etc.)

HOLY NATURE, HEAV'NLY FAIR. A favorite song. Translated from the German. By Mr. Schulz. New York, Printed & Sold by G. Gilfert, No. 177 Broadway [1797–1801] 1 l. 34 cm.

   Song, pfte. acc.
   First line same as title.   JFD

HOME'S HOME, BY DIBDIN.
   (*In* Elegant extracts for the German flute or violin. Philadelphia [1798] bk. 3, p. 29–30)

   Melody only, flute or violin, with accompanying text.
   First line: I've thought and I've said it.
   From *Great news*, by Charles Dibdin.   DLC, NN

HOMEWARD BOUND.
   (*In* Elegant extracts for the German flute or violin. Philadelphia [1796] bk. 2, p. 17)

   Melody only, flute or violin, with accompanying text.
   First line: Come loose ev'ry sail to the breeze.
   Composed by Michael Arne (*BM Cat.*)   DLC, NN

HOMEWARD BOUND. Price 20 cents. Printed and sold at B. Carr's Musical repositories in New York and Philadelphia & J. Carr's, Baltimore [1797] [2] p. 32 cm.

   Song, pfte. acc. Arr. for flute and guitar, p. [2].
   First line same as preceding.   CtY

   Advertised in September, 1797, Baltimore, among other "songs lately published."

HOMEWARD BOUND.
   (*In* The American musical miscellany. Northampton, 1798. p. 202–204)

   Melody only, with accompanying text.
   First line same as preceding.   DLC (etc.)

HONEST COLIN. A favorite ballad. Boston, Printed & sold at P. A. von Hagen & co. Musical magazine, No. 3 Cornhill & G. Gilfert, N. York, where also may be had an elegant assortment of warranted imported piano fortes &

the latest published songs just received from London [ca. 1800] 1 l. 30 cm.

Below imprint: For the piano fortes, German flute, or violin.

Song, pfte. acc.

First line: The evening fair in purple drest.

Published probably in 1799. DLC, MB

HONEST COLIN. A favorite ballad. Price 25 cts. New York, Printed for and sold at J. C. Moller's musical store [n. d.] 2 p. 33 cm.

Song, pfte. acc.

First line same as preceding.

Sonneck dates this issue ca. 1800. DLC, ES

THE HONEYMOON EXPIRED. Alternative title of *Ding dong bell*, by Raynor Taylor.

HOOT AWA YE LOON. A favourite Scots song. Composed by Mr. Hook New York, Printed & sold at J. Hewitt's Musical repository. No. 131 William. str. Price 25 cents. [1797–99] [2] p. 33 cm.

Song, pfte. acc. Arr. for flute, p. [2].

First line: When weary Sol gang'd down the West. DLC

——— The same as preceding.

(*In* A collection of new & favorite songs. [A] Philadelphia [ca. 1800] p. [88]–[89]) HFB

HOPE.

See Favorite *Cotillions*.

HOPE THOU SOURCE OF EV'RY BLESSING. Composed by the celebrated Pleyel. New York, Printe [!] and sold by G. Gilfert & co., No. 209 [Broadway] near St. Pauls [1795] 1 l. 31½ cm.

Song, pfte. acc.

First line same as title. JFD, MWA, RPJCB

HOPE TOLD A FLATT'RING TALE.

(*With* When the hollow drum, by Samuel Arnold. Philadelphia [ca. 1797])

Song, pfte. acc.

First line: Ah, will no change of clime. NN, PP–K

THE HOST THAT FIGHTS FOR LIBERTY. Sung with great applause by Mrs. Seymour. Composed by Victor Pelissier. Printed and sold at Carr's music store, Baltimore. [n. d.] [2] p. 30 cm.

Song, pfte. acc.

First line: Arm, arm ye brave and nobly join.

Published probably ca. 1800. McD–W

THE HOURS OF LOVE. A collection of sonnets. Containing Morning, Noon, Evening & Night. Properly adapted for the voice, harpsichord, violin, German flute or guitar. Composed by James Hook. Printed for Carr & co. Musical repository's, Philadelphia & Baltimore [ca. 1794] 1 p. 1., 9 p. 32 cm.

Tiele-page, verso blank; p. 1, blank.

Contents:—Sonnet I [Morning], p. 2–3.—Sonnet II [Noon], p. 4–5.—Sonnet III [Evening], p. 6–7.—Sonnet IV [Night], p. 8–9.

DLC, ES, JFD, LSL, RPJCB

Inasmuch as the firm of Carr & Co. presumably ceased to exist in the fall of 1794, and the Baltimore establishment under Joseph Carr was founded sometime in that same year, it seems reasonable to date this imprint as given above. Evans' date of 1799 seems quite impossible, as we know of no such firm as Carr & Co. at that time.

HOW BLEST HAS MY TIME BEEN.
(*In* The American musical miscellany. Northampton, 1798. p. 161–162)

Melody only, with accompanying text.
First line same as title. DLC (etc.)

Note by Sonneck:
Song by Moore. Comp. A select collection of English songs. London, 1783, III. Song LXV.

HOW CAN I FORGET. Sung by Miss Broadhurst. Price 20 cents. Printed at B. Carr's Musical repositorys in New York & Philadelphia [1796] [2] p. 31½ cm.

Song, pfte. acc.
First line same as title.
Appears in the score of Shield's opera, *Marian*, as composed by Paisiello.
DLC, ES, LSL, McD–W, MWA
——— The same as preceding.
(*In* A collection of new & favorite songs. [A] Philadelphia [ca. 1800] p. [30]–[31]) HFB

Sung by Miss Broadhurst at a concert in New York, January 12, 1796. Advertised in February, 1796, as published.

HOW CHARMING A CAMP IS. Alternative title of *The drummer*. by Thomas Attwood.

HOW CHEERFUL ALONG THE GAY MEAD. The much admired Hymn of Eve. Address'd to Spring. Philadelphia, Printed for B. Carr [179–] [2] p. 34 cm.
Song, pfte. acc. Three staves.
First line same as title.
Composed by B. Thomas (*BM Cat.*) JFD

HOW COLD IT IS. A winter song.
(*In* The Massachusetts magazine. Boston, February, 1789. p. 122–124)
Three-part chorus, with text. Open score.
First line: See now the blust'ring Boreas blows. DLC (etc.)

——— The same.
(*In* The American musical miscellany. Northampton, 1798. p. 278–284)
Three-part chorus with text. Open score.
First line same as preceding. DLC (etc.)

HOW D'YE DO. An echo song. Sung at Vauxhall Garden. Composed by Mr. Hook. New York, Printed & sold by G. Gilfert, No. 177 Broadway [1797] [2] p. 31½ cm.
Song, pfte. acc. Partly three staves.
First line: 'Twas in the green meadows so gay. MWA

[191]

Advertised in March, 1797, among other "new songs for the piano forte" as "just published by G. Gilfert. At his Musical Magazine, No. 177 Broadway," New York.

HOW D'YE DO. Boston, Printed & sold by P. A. von Hagen, Junior & cos., at their Music Magazine, No. 62 Newbury st! [1798–99]   [2] p.   31½ cm.

Song, pfte. acc.
First line same as preceding.   ES, LSL, MB, N

HOW D'YE DO. An eccho [!] song.   Sung at Vauxhall Gardens.   Composed by Mr. Hook.   Printed & sold by G. Willig, Market street, No. 185, Philadelphia [1798–1804]   [2] p.   32½ cm.

Song, pfte. acc.   Partly three staves with voice on middle staff.
First line same as preceding.   NN, PP

HOW GAILY ROLL'D THE MOMENTS ON.   A favorite new Scotch song. Sung by Mrs. Frankin [!]   New York, Printed & sold by G. Gilfert & co. No. 177 Broadway, where may be had a general assortment of fine tuned piano fortes and other musical articles of superior quality [1796]   [2] p. 31½ cm.

Song, pfte. acc.
First line same as title.   MWA

HOW HANDSOME IS MY SAILOR LAD.   A new Scotch song.   Sung by Mrs. Franklin.
(In A collection of favorite songs, by Mr. Hook.   New York [1799–1801] bk. [2] p. 2–3)

Song, pfte. acc.
First line same as title.   DLC

———— Separate issue of preceding, 1797–1801.   DLC

[HOW HAPPILY MY LIFE I LED]   Sung by Mr. Darley in No song no supper.
See Evening amusement [1796], p. 26.
Title from first line.

Mr. Darley sang in Stephen Storace's No song, no supper in Philadelphia, April 4, 1796.

HOW HAPPY THE SOLDIER.
(In A collection of favorite songs, divided into two books.   Arr. by A. Reinagle, Philadelphia [1789?]   bk. 1, p. 8)

Song, pfte. acc.
First line same as title.
From The poor soldier, by William Shield.   CdeW, DLC, ES, Hopk.

———— The same.
(In The American musical miscellany.   Northampton, 1798.   p. 115–116)

Melody only, with accompanying text.
First line same as preceding.   DLC (etc.)

HOW HAPPY WAS MY HUMBLE LOT. A favorite ballad. Sung by Mrs. Oldmixon & Miss Broadhurst. Composed by J. Hewitt. New York, Printed & sold by J. Hewitt, No. 23 Maiden lane. Price 25 cents. [1799–1800] [2] p. 32 cm.

Imprint at foot of p. [2].
Song, pfte. acc. Arr. for flute and for "guittar," p. [2].
First line same as title. DLC, JFD

—— The same as preceding.
(In A collection of new & favorite songs. [A] Philadelphia [ca. 1800] p. [48]–[49]) HFB

HOW IMPERFECT IS EXPRESSION.
See The select songster. New Haven, 1786. p. 34.

—— The same.
(In A collection of favorite songs, divided into two books. Arr. by A. Reinagle. Philadelphia [1789?] bk. 1, p. 14)

Song, pfte. acc.
First line same as title. CdeW, DLC, ES, Hopk.

HOW SHALL I MY PAIN DISCOVER. Composed by James Hewitt.
(In [Unidentified collection of instrumental and vocal music. New York] Hewítt & Rausch [1797] p. 19)

Song, pfte. acc.
First line same as title. DLC, ES

—— The same as preceding.
(In A collection of new & favorite songs. [A] Philadelphia [ca. 1800] p. [182]) HFB

HOW SWEET IN THE WOODLANDS. Printed for Carr & sold at his repository's, Phila² and N: York & by I: Carr, Baltimore (20 cts.) [1794–97] [2] p. 32½ cm.

Duet, pfte. acc. Three staves. Arr. for two guitars, p. [2].
First line same as title.
At foot of first page: N. B. This is a good duett for two flutes, the second taking the small upper notes when below the compass.
Composed by Henry Harington.
Certain copies, e. g., ABHu, have 25 instead of 20 in price given.
ABHu, CdeW, DLC, ES, LSL, MWA, NN

HOW SWEET IN THE WOODLANDS. A favorite duett, Composed by Harrington. New York, Sold at I. Paffs, Broadway [1798] [2] p. 33 cm.

Duet, pfte. acc. Three staves.
First line same as title. RPJCB

HOW SWEET IN THE WOODLAND [!] Published by G. Willig, No. 185 Market st., Philada. [1798–1804] 1 l. 34 cm.

Song, pfte. acc.
First line same as title. DLC, ES, RPJCB

How sweet in the woodlands was sung in America as early as 1792, in Philadelphia.

———— The pursuit. Duetto. Set by a student of the University at Cambridge. (*In* The Massachusetts magazine, Boston. January, 1789. p. 59–61)

Duet. Voice parts only. Two staves.
First line: How sweet through the woodlands.
Words practically identical with the preceding. The music a free rendering of Harington's composition. Rhythmically almost identical throughout, with the first four measures a strict inversion of the original. DLC (etc.)

*HOW SWEET IS THE MORNING. Duet by Benjamin Carr.
This duet was to be performed at a concert, Philadelphia, April 3, 1800.

HOW SWEET THE LOVE THAT MEETS RETURN. A favorite song. Sung by Mrs. Kennedy. Composed by Mr. Hook. [n. p., n. d.] [2] p. 31½ cm.

Song, pfte. acc.
First line: When first I ken'd young Sandy's face.
Published probably 179–. MH

[HOW SWEET WHEN THE SILVER MOON] Sung by Mrs. Oldmixon in the Purse, or Benevolent tar.
(*In* The gentleman's amusement, ed. by R. Shaw. Philadelphia [1794–96] p. 52–53)

Song, pfte. [?] acc.
Title from first line.
DLC copy incomplete, p. 53 lacking.
In No. 7, May, 1796.
Mrs. Oldmixon sang in William Reeve's *The purse, or Benevolent tar*, January 7, 1795, at Philadelphia. DLC, PHi

HOW TEDIOUS ALAS! ARE THE HOURS. A favorite song. Boston, Printed & sold at P. A. von Hagen & cᵒˢ Musical magazine, No. 3 Cornhill. Also by G. Gilfert, New York. Where also may be had the new patriotic song To arms Columbia. Written by Thomas Paine. The music composed by P. A. von Hagen, jun. [1799] [2] p. 31½ cm.

Below imprint: For the piano forte, German flute or violin.
Song, pfte. acc.
First line same as title. MWA

Advertised in *Columbian centinel* (Boston) July 3, 1799 as "this day" published by P. A. von Hagen and Son.

*HUMMING BIRD, or Collection of fashionable songs. Philadelphia: Printed by Henry Taylor. 1791.

(Advertised in the sale of Henry Taylor's estate, as "one half finished.")

*THE HUMMING BIRD, or; New American songster; embellished with a copper plate frontispiece.

Thus advertised in October, 1798, as "published and for sale by William Spotswood, No. 22 Marlboro st.," Boston.
See also Evans 33013.

[194]

*HUMMING BIRD, or New American songster . . . With modern toasts and sentiments.

Advertised in *Aurora*, Philadelphia, April 18, 1799, as just published and for sale at Mathew Carey's store.

It is probable that both the above advertisements refer to:

THE HUMMING BIRD; or, New American songster; with modern toasts and sentiments. Boston: Printed and sold by Spotswood & Etheridge. 1798.

NHi

*HUNTING CANTATA by Raynor Taylor.

This cantata was to be sung in "Taylor's musical performance . . . the whole of the music original and composed by Mr. Tayor [!]" at Annapolis, Md., on February 28, 1793. Possibly identical with:

*A HUNTING SONG by Raynor Taylor.

This song was to be sung in an "olio, entirely new" and composed by Taylor in Philadelphia, February 1, 1794.

HUNTING SONG. By Mr. Swan.

(*In* The songsters assistant, ed. by T. Swan. Suffield [ca. 1800] p. 3–7)

Song, pfte. acc.
First line: The morning is charming.

CtY, MB

HUNTING SONG. By Swan.

(*In* The songster's assistant, ed. by T. Swan. Suffield [ca. 1800] p. 20–21)

Song, pfte. acc.
First line: When Phoebus the tops of the hill does adorn.

CtY, MB

HUNTING SONG. Set by Mr. Hans Gram.

(*In* The Massachusetts magazine, Boston. June, 1789. p. 388–390)

Song, pfte. acc.
First line: When the orient beam first pierces the dawn.

DLC (etc.)

A HUNTING SONG. Set to music by Mr. Roth of Philadelphia.

(*In* The universal asylum and Columbian magazine, April, 1790. p. 254–256)

Song, pfte. acc.
First line: Ye sluggards who murder your lifetime in sleep.
Mr. Roth: Philip Roth.

DLC (etc.)

This is almost word for word and note for note the same as "Hunting song, sung by Mr. Vernon at Vauxhall," p. 4–5 of "*A collection of favourite songs* sung at Vauxhall by Mr. Vernon and Mrs. Weichsel. Composed by James Hook, Bk II. 1768. Pr. 1–6. Published according to Act of Parliament and entered at Stationer's Hall. London, Printed for C. and S. Thompson, No. 75 St. Paul's Church yard."

This seems to dispose of Roth's authorship rather completely.

—— Ye sluggards. Hunting song.

(*In* A collection of favorite songs, divided into two books. Arr. by A. Reinagle. Philadelphia [1789?] bk. 1, p. 18–19)

Song, pfte. acc.
First line same as preceding.
The same song as preceding.

CdeW, DLC, ES, Hopk.

[195]

*HUNTING SONG.   Set to music by W. S. Morgan.
This "new hunting song" was to be sung at a concert in Boston, on May 17, 1771.

HURLY BURLY.   A favorite sailor's song.   From Haydn's 2d Book of Canzonetts.
(*In* The musical journal for the flute or violin.   Baltimore [1800]   no. 21, p. 42–44)

Melody only, flute or violin, with accompanying text.
First line: High on the giddy bending mast.   DLC

HUSH EV'RY BREEZE.
See [Noon]   Sonnet II . . . Hook.

[HUSH, HUSH SUCH COUNSEL DO NOT GIVE]   Song in the Haunted tower
A new opera.
(*In* The universal asylum, Philadelphia.   August, 1790.   p. 129–130)

Song, pfte. acc.
Title from first line.
Appears in score of Stephen Storace's opera *The haunted tower*, but is there ascribed to Sarti.   DLC (etc.)

HUZZA FOR LIBERTY.   Composed by Dr. G. K. Jackson.   Printed for the Author.   Copyright secured.
(*In* New miscellaneous musical work, by Dr. G. K. Jackson [n. p., ca. 1800] p. 4)

At head of title: Song.
Song, pfte. acc.
First line: Come lads your glasses fill.   DLC, MWA

HUZZA FOR THE CONSTELLATION.
See Capt. Truxton.

HYMEN'S EVENING POST.   Sung by Mr. Darley, Junr. at the Vauxhall Gardens, Philadelphia.   Printed and sold at B. Carr's Musical repository, Philadelphia; J. Carr's, Baltimore and J. Hewitt's, New York [1797]   3 p. 32 cm.

Song, pfte. acc.
First line: Great news, great news I'm hither sent.
In lower margin p. 2 and 3: H: Ev^g P:
Composed by James Hook (*BM Cat.*)   LSL, MB, NN

Under the title of "Hymen's evening post, or Great news . . . sung by Mr. Darley, junr. at Bush Hill" the song was advertised in November, 1797, as "published at Carr's Musical Repository," Philadelphia.

*——— The same.
Advertised in March, 1797, as to be published "in a few days" by "G. Gilfert at his Musical magazine, No. 177 Broadway," New York.

[196]

A HYMN. Written by the Rev. J. S. J. Gardner, at the request of the Committee of Arrangements in Boston.
(*In* Sacred dirges [Oliver Holden] Boston [1800]   p. 18–19)
Air ("instrumental bass") and chorus, four parts.   Open score.
First line: And is th' illustrious chieftain dead.

CSmH, DLC, ICN, MB, MH, MHi, MWA, NHi, NN, RPB

HYMN.   On death.   [New York]   Sold by I. and M. Paff [n. d.]   2 p.   31½ cm.

Imprint at foot of p. 2.
Hymn, pfte. acc.
First line: Great God thy energy impart.
Followed on p. 2 by "Evening."
Published possibly as early as 1799.   MWA

A HYMN ON PEACE.   [Worcester, 1784]   8 l.   ca. 19 x 25 cm.

Unbound, size of leaves varies.
Imprint supplied by Sonneck.
Four-part chorus.   Open score.
First line: Behold array'd in light, and by divine command.
In lower margin of p. 1: Aᵐ Wood, author.
Composed by Abraham Wood.   MB

Under the title "An anthem on peace.   Composed by Abraham Wood," advertised in September, 1784, as "just published . . . sold by him at his house in Northborough, and at the Printing Office in Worcester."

HYMNS [By George Richards]   Composed on the death of Gen Washington; and sung, at the Universal meeting-house, Portsmouth, N. H., January, 1800.   Printed at The United States Oracle press, by Charles Peirce No. 5, Daniel-street.   1800.   [4] p.   19 cm.

Title-page with ornamental border.
"By George Richards" handwritten in ink.   NHi

[I AM A BRISK AND SPRIGHTLY LAD]   Sung by Mrs. Marshall in the Spoil'd child.
(*In* The gentleman's amusement, ed. by R. Shaw.   Philadelphia [1794–96] p. 9)

Melody only, flute (or violin) with accompanying text.
Title from first line.
In No. 1, April 1, 1794.   DLC, PHi

[I AM A BRISK AND SPRIGHTLY LAD]   Sung by Mrs. Jordan in the Spoil'd Child.
(*In* [Two songs]   Sung by Mrs. Jordan in the Spoil'd Child [n. p., ca. 1800] p. [2])

At head of title: Act 2d.
Song, pfte. acc., followed by arr. for German flute.
Title from first line.   DLC

I'M AS SMART A LAD AS YOU'D WISH TO SEE. Sung by Miss Simms in the musical entertainment the Mouth of the Nile. New York, Printed & sold by G. Gilfert, No 177 Broadway.
(*In* [The mouth of the Nile, by T. Attwood. New York, ca. 1799] p. 8–9)

Below imprint: Attwood.
Song, pfte. acc.
First line same as title.   NRU–Mus

I'M IN HASTE. Composed by Mr. Hook. New York, Printed for James Hewitt & sold at his Musical repository, William str^t; at B. Carr's, Phila & at J. Carr's, Baltimore [1797] [2] p. 33 cm.

Song, pfte. acc. Arr. for "guittar," p. [2].
First line: As 'cross the fields the other morn.   DLC, MWA, NN, RPJCB

Certain copies, e. g. DLC, have ms. note after imprint: 25 cts.
Advertised May 30, 1797, as "just published," *Minerva*, New York.

———— The same as preceding.
(*In* A collection of new & favorite songs. [A] Philadelphia [ca. 1800] p. [102]–[103])   HFB

I'M IN HASTE. A favorite song. By P. A. van Hagen, junior. New York, Printed for G. Gilfert, No. 177 Broadway [1797–1801] 1 l. 33 cm.

Song, pfte. acc.
First line same as preceding.   DLC, JFD, MWA, NRU–Mus

I ASK NOT THY PITY. A favorite canzonet with an accompaniment for the piano forte or harp. Composed by John Ross. New York, Sold by I. and M. Paff, No. 127 Broadway [1799–1803] [3] p. 31½ cm.

Imprint at foot of p. [3].
Song, pfte. acc. Three staves.
First line same as title.   McD–W

I BLUSH IN THE DARK. A favorite song. Composed by Giordani. Printed & sold at B. Carr's Musical repository in New York & Philadelphia, & J. Carr's, Baltimore. Price 12 cents. [1796] 1 l. 32 cm.

Song, pfte. acc., followed by arr. for flute.
First line: Was there ever a spark so confounded as I.   MWA

Advertised in March, 1796, as published "at Carr's Musical Repository, William Street," New York.

I FELT THE COMMAND AND OBEY'D WITH A SIGH. A favorite canzonet. Composed by J. Fisin. New York, Printed & sold at J. and M. Paff's music warehouse, No. 127 Broadway [1799–1803] [2] p. 31½ cm.

Song, pfte. acc.
First line: On the brink of the beach.
J. Fisin: James Fisin.   ES

———— The same. [n. p., n. d.] [2] p. 32 cm.
Song, pfte. acc.
First line same as preceding.   DLC

HAVE A SILENT SORROW HERE. Sung with great applause in the Stranger. The words by R. B. Shiridan [!] Esq⁲ The air by the Dutchess of Devonshire. New York, Printed & sold at J. Hewitts Musical repository, No. 131 William street. Sold also by B. Carr, Philadelphia & J. Carr, Baltimore. Price 25 cents. [1798–99] [2] p. 33½ cm.

Song, pfte. acc. Arr. for flute, p. [2].
First line same as title.
Georgiana (Spencer) Cavendish, Duchess of Devonshire.
First American performance of *The stranger*, New York, December 10, 1798.

DLC, LSL, McD–W, NRU–Mus

——— The same as preceding.
(*In* A collection of new & favorite songs. [A] Philadelphia [ca. 1800] p. [44]–[45])   HFB

HAVE A SILENT SORROW HERE. A favorite song. Sung by Mrs. Bland in the play of the Stranger. The words by R. B. Sheridan, Esq⁲ The air by Her Grace the Dutchess of Devonshire. New York, Printed & sold by G. Gilfert, No. 177 Broadway, and to be had at P. A. von Hagen's, Boston [1798–1801] [2] p. 31½ cm.

Song, pfte. acc. Arr. for German flute, p. [2].
First line same as title.
First London edition, 1798. (*BM Cat.*)   DLC, MWA

[I HAVE A SILENT SORROW HERE] The favorite song in the Stranger. Boston, Printed & sold at P. A. von Hagen & co., Musical magazine, No. 3 Cornhill; also by G. Gilfert, N. York, where also may be had the answer of this song and the greatest variety of warranted imported piano fortes of superior quality [1799] 1 l. 31 cm.

Below imprint: For the piano forte, G. flute or violin.
Song, pfte. acc.
Title from first line.
Composed by the Duchess of Devonshire.

ES, MB, MWA, N, RPJCB

Advertised in *Columbian centinel*, July 3, 1799 as "this day" published by P. A. von Hagen and Son.

[I HAVE A SILENT SORROW HERE] The much admir'd song in the Stranger. Sung with great applause by Mrs. Merry. The words by R. B. Sheridan, Esq⁲ The air by A. Reinagle. Price 25 cents. Printed and sold at B. Carr's Musical repository, Philadelphia; J. Carr's, Baltimore; J. Hewitt's, New York, &c. [ca. 1799] [2] p. 32½ cm.

In lower margin of p. [2]: Seccur'd [!] according to law.
Song, pfte. acc. Arr. for flute and for "guittar," p. [2].
Title from first line.
Mrs. Merry appeared in the first Philadelphia performance of *The stranger*, April 1, 1799.

DLC, ES, ICN, LSL, McD–W, MWA, NN, NRU–Mus, PHi, PP–K, PP–L

(In PHi copy arr. for "guittar" has been torn off)

[199]

I'VE KISS'D AND I'VE PRATTLED. Rosina.
(*In* A collection of favorite songs, divided into two books. Arr. by .
Reinagle. Philadelphia [1789?] bk. 1, p. 4)

Song, pfte. acc.
First line same as title.
Rosina, by William Shield.   CdeW, DLC, ES, Hop▮

I'VE LOST MY HEART TO TEDDIE. Composed by Mr. Hook. Ne▮
York, Printed and sold by G. Gilfert & co., at their Musical magazine, N▮
209 Broadway and to be had at No. 165 Market street, Philadelphia. Like▮
wise an assortement [!] of fine toned piano fortes [1795] [2] p. 31½ cm.

Song, pfte. acc.
First line: Young teddy [!] is an Irish lad.   JFD, MW.

I KNOW NOT WHY. A favorite ballad. Composed by T. Castellow [!] Ne▮
York, Printed and sold by G. Gilfert & co., No. 191 Broadway [1794-9▮
[2] p. 33½ cm.

Song, pfte. acc. Arr for German "flutte" or guitar, p. [2].
First line: One summer's eve I chanc'd to stay.
T. Castellow: Thomas Costellow.   JFD, LSL, RPJC▮

[I LOCK'D UP ALL MY TREASURE] Sung by Mr. Marshall in the Quake▮
(*In* The gentleman's amusement, ed. by R. Shaw. Philadelphia [1794-9▮
p. 65)

Melody only, flute (or violin) with accompanying text.
Title from first line.
In No. [8], ca. 1796.
Mr. Marshall sang in Dibdin's *The Quaker*, May 13, 1795, at Philadelphia
                                                          DLC, PHi, PP-▮

I LOVE THEM ALL. Sung by Mr. Darley, Sen. at the Vauxhall Gardens
Philadelphia. Printed & sold at B. Carr's Musical repository, Philadelphia
J. Carr's, Baltimore & J. Hewitts, New York. (Price 25 cents) [1797] 2 p
30½ cm.

Song, pfte. acc.
First line: Some men with rapture view no cheeks.
In lower r. h. corner, p. 2: I love them all 2.   DLC, N▮

Advertised in November, 1797, as "published at Carr's Musical Repository,'
Philadelphia.

I LOVE TO SPEAK MY MIND. A new song. Sung by Miss Sims. New
York, Printed & sold by G. Gilfert, No. 177 Broadway.
(*In* A collection of favorite songs, by Mr. Hook. New York [1799-1801▮
bk. [1] p. 10-11)

Song, pfte. acc.
First line: Tho' I am in my teens I have lovers in great plenty.   DLC

—— Separate issue of preceding, ca. 1800.   DLC

I NEVER LOV'D ANY DEAR MARY BUT YOU. Composed by Mr. Hook.
New York, Printed at G. Gilfert & cos. Musical magazine, No. 209 Broadway,

[200]

where may be had all the newest music reprinted from European publications. Likewise an ellegant [!] assortment of piano fortes and other musical articles of superior quality [1795] [2] p. 33½ cm.

Song, pfte. acc. Arr. for higher key, p. [2].
First line: You tell me dear girl that I'm given to rove.
Title forms last line of first stanza.   JFD

NEVER LOV'D ANY DEAR MARY BUT YOU. Sung by Mr. Darley, jun. at Vauxhall.
(*In* Elegant extracts for the German flute or violin. Philadelphia [1798] bk. 3, p. 26–27)

Melody only, flute or violin, with accompanying text.
First line same as preceding.   DLC, NN

NEVER LOV'D ANY DEAR MARY BUT YOU. A favorite song. Composed by Hook. The words by a lady. Philadelphia, Sold by G. Willig, No. 185 Market st. [1798–1804] [2] p. 32½ cm.

Song, pfte. acc.
First line same as preceding.
Sung by Joseph Tyler in New York, June 10, 1797.
Published probably in 1798.   PP–K

NEVER WOULD BE MARRIED. A favorite song. New York, Printed & sold by Gilfert & co., No. 177 Broadway. Where may be had a general assortment of fine tuned pianofortes and other articles of superior quality [1796] [2] p. 30½ cm.

Song, pfte. acc.
First line: When I had scarcely told sixteen.   DLC, NN

I NEVER WOULD BE MARRIED. Boston, Printed & sold by P. A. von Hagen, junior & cos. at their Musical magazine, No. 62 Newbury street [1798–99] [2] p. 32½ cm.

Song, pfte. acc.
First line same as preceding.   MB, N, RPJCB

I NEVER WOULD BE MARRIED. A favorite song. [n. p., n. d.] [2] p. 31½ cm.
Song, pfte. acc.
First line same as preceding.
Probably published 179–.   LSL, PP–K

I RISE WITH THE MORN. A favorite ballad. As sung by Mrs. Jordan in the new comedy of Indiscretion. Philadelphia, Printed & sold by G. Willig, No. 185 Market st. [1798–1804] 1 l. 31 cm.

Song, pfte. acc.
First line same as title.
Published probably ca. 1800.   MWA

I SIGH FOR THE GIRL I ADORE.
(*In* The favorite songs, by Mr. Hook. Philadelphia [1794–95] p. 7)

Song, pfte. acc.
First line: When fairies trip round the gay green.
Title from last line of each stanza.   McD–W, MdHi, MWA, NN

I SIGH FOR THE GIRL I ADORE.
(*In* The favorite songs in the opera of [The haunted tower, by S. Storace
New York [1795–96]   p. 6)

Song, pfte. acc.
First line same as preceding.
Composed by James Hook.   Perhaps sometimes interpolated in the opera—
or possibly just included by mistake.   ABH

——— Separate issue of preceding, paged 6 in upper left hand corner, paged 7 in
upper right hand corner.   Apparently this same plate was used in *The favorite*
songs in [*The haunted tower*] as page 6 and in *The favorite songs, by Mr. Hook*
as p. 7.   1795–96.   DLC, ES

——— The same.
(*In* Elegant extracts for the German flute or violin.   Philadelphia [1796]   bk.
2, p. 32)

Melody only, flute or violin, with accompanying text.
First line: When faires [!] trip round the gay green.   DLC, NN

——— The same.
(*In* The American musical miscellany.   Northampton [1798]   p. 159–161)

Melody only, with accompanying text.
First line: When faries [!] trip round the gay green.   DLC (etc.)

I SOLD A GUILTLESS NEGRO BOY.   A sentimental ballad.   Composed by
Mr. Moulds.
(*In* The musical repertory.   Boston [1796]   No. I, p. (14)–(15).)

Song, pfte. acc.
First line: When thirst of gold enslaves the mind.   DLC, NRU–Mus

——— The same as preceding.   Detached leaf from the above collection.
Followed on p. (15) by *Moorish march.*   1796.   McD–W

I SOLD A GUILTLESS NEGRO BOY.
(*In* The American musical miscellany.   Northampton, 1798.   p. 81–84)

Melody only, with accompanying text.
First line same as preceding.   DLC (etc.)

——— The Negro boy.   Sung by Mr. Tyler.   Price 25 cents.   Printed at B.
Carr's Musical repositories [n. p., 1796]   [2] p.   33 cm.
Song, pfte. acc.   Arr. for flute, p. [2].
First line same as preceding.   DLC, ES, MWA

As "sung by Mr. Tyler . . . from Inkle and Yarico," Samuel Arnold's opera,
advertised in February, 1796, as "published . . . Printed and sold by Benjamin Carr."

Apparently the advertisement as quoted is inaccurate, as the score of *Inkle*
and Yarico contains no such number.   The song, however, may have been
interpolated in performance of the opera.   Joseph Tyler sang in *Inkle and*
Yarico in New York, February 12, 1796.

STROVE BUT MUCH I FIND IN VAIN. Music by J. B. Gauline. Philadelphia, Printed by G. Willig, No. 185 Market street [1798–1804] [2] p. 32½ cm.

Song, pfte. acc.
First line same as title.
J. B. Gauline: John B. Gauline   DLC

—— The same as preceding except below title: Written by a gentlemen [!] in Queen Ann's County.   MdHi

[THAT ONCE WAS A PLOUGHMAN. Alternative title of *The lucky escape*, by Charles Dibdin.

[I TRAVERS'D JUDAH'S BARREN SAND] Sung by Miss Broadhurst in the opera of Robin Hood.
(*In* The gentleman's amusement, ed. by R. Shaw. Philadelphia [1794–96 p. 4–5)

Melody only, flute (or violin) with accompanying text.
Title from first line.
In No. 1, April 1, 1794.
Miss Broadhurst sang in the first Philadelphia performance of William Shield's *Robin Hood*, March 10, 1794.   DLC, PHi

—— The same as preceding. On second and third pages, numbered "4" and "5" of a detached portion (p. 3–6) from above collection.   NN

I'LL BE MARRIED TO THEE. A new song. Sung by Mrs. Franklin. New York, Printed & sold by G. Gilfert, No. 177 Broadway.
(*In* A collection of favorite songs, by Mr. Hook. New York [1799–1801] bk. [1], p. 14–15)

Below imprint: The words by Mr. Upton.
Song, pfte. acc.
First line: I am teaz'd to death from morn to night.   DLC, JFD

—— Separate issue of preceding, 1799–1801.   DLC, MWA

I'LL DIE FOR NO SHEPHERD, NOT I. Composed by Mr. Hook. New York, Printed & sold by G. Gilfert & co. at their Musical magazine, No. 209 Broadway, near St. Paul's. Where likewise may be had an assortement [!] of fine tuned piano forte [1795] [2] p. 33½ cm.

Song, pfte. acc.
First line: When first on the plain I began to appear.
DLC, JFD, MWA

I'LL DIE FOR NO SHEPHERD, NOT I. Composed by Mr. Hook. New York, Printed & sold by G. Gilfert at his Musical magazine, No. 177 Broadway [1797–1801] [2] p. 33 cm.

Song, pfte. acc.
First line same as preceding.   DLC. JFD

[203]

[I'LL TALK OF ALL MY LOVERS CHARMS]   Sung by Mrs. Marshall &
Mrs. Oldmixon.
(*In* The volunteers, by A. Reinagle.   Philadelphia [1795 ?]   p. 12–13)
Duet, pfte. acc.   Three staves.
Title from first line.   DLC

I'LL THINK OF WILLY FAR AWAY.   Sung by Miss Leary at Vaxhall [!]
Philadelphia, Printed for A. Reinagle; I. Aitken, Sclpt. [1789 ?]   1 l.   34½ cm
Song, pfte. acc.
First line: My love the pride of hill and plain.   McD–W

——— The same as preceding, but with pagination and "Vaxhall" changed to
"Vauxhall."
(*In* [A collection of favorite songs, arr. by A. Reinagle. Philadelphia, 1789 (?)
p. 25)   ES

I WONDER AT YOU.   Alternative title of *The scornful lady*, by Raynor
Taylor.

IF A BODY LOVES A BODY.   Composed by Mr. Hook.   New York,
Printed & sold at J. Hewitt's Musical repository, No. 131 William str
Sold also by B. Carr, Philadelphia & J. Carr, Baltimore.   Pr. 25 cts.   [1797–
98]   [2] p.   32½ cm.
Song, pfte. acc.
First line: A body may in simple way.
                          DLC, ES, LSL, MB, MWA, NN, PP–K

——— The same as preceding.
(*In* A collection of new & favorite songs.   [A] Philadelphia [ca. 1800] p.
[60]–[61])   HFB

Advertised in January, 1798, as "just published by J. Hewitt" but published in December, 1797, if identical with the same song as advertised in
that month as "published at Carr's Musical Repository, Market street,"
Philadelphia.   Undoubtedly identical.

IF TIS JOY TO WOUND A LOVER.   Dr. Arnold.   Philadelphia, Printed
for A. Reinagle; I. Aitken, sculpt.   [ca 1789]   [2] p.   32 cm.
Imprint at foot of p. [2].
Song, pfte. acc.
First line same as title.
Probably printed by Thomas Dobson, on Second street.   CdeW, ES
cf. Catch for three voices.   Suitable for three ladies.

——— The same as preceding, but with pagination.
(*In* [A collection of favorite songs, arr. by A. Reinagle.   Philadelphia, 1789
(?)]   p. 11–12)   ES

IMMORTAL WASHINGTON.   [n. p., n. d.]   1 l.   33 cm.
Song, pfte. acc.
First line: Columbia's greatest glory was her lov'd Chief fair Freedom's
friend.
Published probably early in 1800.   DLC

[204]

HE IMPATIENT LOVER.
(*In* Nine new songs, by I. B. Gauline. Philadelphia and Baltimore [ca. 1800] p. 3-4)

Song, pfte. acc.
First line: Can hope now no pleasure restore.
I. B. Gauline: John B. Gauline.   ES, MdHi

HE IMPUDENT CREATURE stole from me a kiss. I frown'd and was angry. A ballad sung by Mrs. Bland at Vauxhall Gardens with great applause. Composed by T. Costellow. New York, Engrav'd, printed and publish'd by I. and M. Paff, No. 127 Broadway [1799-1803] [2] p. 33 cm.

Song, pfte. acc.
First line: Where a cluster of woodbines had fashion'd a shade.   ES

N ACIS AND GALATEA. By Mr. Handel.
See [Would you gain the tender creature] In Acis and Galatea . . .

N DEAR LITTLE IRELAND. A favorite song. Sung by Mrs. Bland and Mr. Suett in the opera of the Shipwreck. New York, Printed by W. Howe, organ builder and importer of all kinds of musical instruments, No. 320 Pearl street. Price 25 cents. [ca. 1798] [2] p. 34 cm.

Song, pfte. acc.
First line same as title.
The shipwreck, by Samuel Arnold.   JFD

IN DEAR LITTLE IRELAND. A favorite duett. Sung by Mr. Jefferson and Mrs. Oldmixon in the opera of the Shipwreck. New York, Printed and sold by George Gilfert, No. 177 Broadway [ca. 1799] [2] p. 33 cm.

Duet, pfte. acc.
First line same as title.   DLC

Arnold's *Shipwreck* was first performed in New York, with Mrs. Oldmixon and Mr. Jefferson in the company, February 18, 1799.

IN FREEDOM WE'RE BORN. Alternative title of *Liberty song.*

IN MEMORY OF MR. JAMES BREMNER.
A dirge, composed by Francis Hopkinson in memory of James Bremner, who died in 1780. The music to this "Recitative and air" seems to be lost, but the poem is contained in Hopkinson's *Miscellaneous writings,* v. III, p. 184. It begins, "Sing to his shade a solemn strain."

IN MY PLEASANT NATIVE PLAINS. The favourite roundelay. Sung by Miss Sully at the Pantheon. Philadelphia, Printed and sold by G. Willig, Market street, No. 185 [1798-1804] [2] p. 31½ cm.

Song, pfte, acc.
First line same as title.
From *The carnival of Venice,* by Thomas Linley, Sr.
Miss Sully was a member of the company playing at the Pantheon, Philadelphia, in the season of 1796-97.
Also sung by Miss Brett in New York, July 6, 1798.
Probably published ca. 1798.   MWA, PP-K

IN THE COTTAGE.
See Manuscript collection of hymns, songs, etc. (45-46).

IN THE DEAD OF THE NIGHT. Alternative title of *Cupid benighted*, adapted from Samuel Arnold.

IN THE LAND OF HIBERNIA. Printed for B. Carr & sold at his Musical repository in Philadelphia and New York and by J. Carr, Baltimore.
(*In* The favorite songs, by Mr. Hook. Philadelphia [1794–95] p. 8–9)
Song, pfte. acc.
First line same as title.   McD–W, MdHi, MWA, NN

———— Separate issue of preceding, ca. 1794.   DLC

IN THE MIDST OF THE SEA. Sung by Mr. Fawcet in the musical entertainment the Mouth of the Nile. New York, Printed & sold by Gilfert, No. 177 Broad Way.
(*In* [The mouth of the Nile, by T. Attwood. New York, ca. 1799] p. 10–11)
Below imprint: T. Attwood.
Song, pfte. acc.
First line same as title.   NRU–Mus

[IN THEE EACH JOY POSSESSING] A favorite duett.
(*In* Elegant extracts for the German flute or violin. Philadelphia [1798] bk. 3, p. 17)
Duet, flutes or violins (or flute and violin) with accompanying text.
Title from first line.   DLC, NN

IN VAIN DEAR GIRL. Printed & sold by G. Willig, No. 185 Market street. Philadelphia [1798–1804] [2] p. 35 cm.
Song, pfte. acc.
First line same as title.   NRU–Mus

IN VAIN DEAR GIRL. Words by a gentleman of this city. Printed & sold by G. Willig, No. 185 Market street, Philadelphia [1798–1804] [2] p. 32½ cm.
Song, pfte. acc.
First line same as title.   PP–K

IN VAIN FOND YOUTH. Sung by Mrs. Stuart at Vauxhall. Philadelphia, Printed for A. Reinagle; I. Aitken, sculpt.
(*In* A collection of favorite songs, arr. by A. Reinagle. Philadelphia [1789 ?] p. 19–20)
Imprint at foot of p. 20.
Song, pfte. acc.
First line same as title.   DLC

*———— Separate issue of preceding was advertised in March, 1789, among other "songs and pieces arranged for the pianoforte or harpsichord by Alexander Reinagle" as "just published and sold by Thomas Dobson, at the Stone House in Second Street," Philadelphia.

———— Separate issue of preceding with "at Vauxhall" omitted and without pagination. Imprint at foot of p. [2]: Philadephia [!] Printe [!] for A. Reinagle. I. Aitken. Sculpt. Possibly the same as advertised above.
                                                            ES, McD–W

INDEED YOUNG MAN I MUST DENY. Sung by Miss Milne. New York, Printed and sold by G. Gilfert & co. at their Musical magazine, No. 209 Broadway, near St. Pauls, where may be had a great choice of music and musical instm᷊ of the verry [!] first quality as also piano fortes let out on hire & if purchased within three months the hire abated [1795] 12–13 p. 34 cm.

Song, pfte. acc. Arr. for German flute or "guittar," p. 13.

First line: When first young Harry told his tale.   DLC, JFD, MWA

INDEPENDENT AND FREE. From The American tar, or the Press gang defeated. Sung by Mr. Rowson at the New Theatre, Philadelphia. The words by Mrs. Rowson. The music by R. Taylor. [Philadelphia] Printed for the Author, No. 96 North 6th street & sold at Carr's Repository's. (Price 25 cents) [ca. 1796] [2] p. 32½ cm.

Song, pfte. acc.

First line: Come fill your bumpers, fill them high.

The American tar, or The press gang defeated (a ballet "founded on a recent fact at Liverpool") was performed with Mr. Rowson in the cast at Philadelphia, June 17, 1796.   DLC, NRU–Mus

INDEPENDENT RANGERS QUICK MARCH.
    (*In* [Unidentified collection of instrumental [and vocal music. New York] Hewitt & Rausch [1797] p. 18)

Pfte. 2 hds. 16 measures.   DLC

—————— Separate issue of preceding, ca. 1797.
    (*With* The blackbird, by James Hook)   NN

—————— The same as preceding.
    (*In* A collection of new & favorite songs. [A] Philadelphia [ca. 1800] p. [113])
                                                        HFB
INDIAN CHIEF. Alternative title of *Alknomook.*

INDIAN MARCH of the much admeired [!] American play caled [!] Columbus. Arranged for the piano forte. Printed and sold Philadelphia by C. Hupfeld [1797–99] p. 16. 31 cm.

Pfte. 2 hds.

Morton's play *Columbus* with incidental music by Alexander Reinagle was first performed in Philadelphia, January 30, 1797.

Reinagle's music (arr. for pfte.) was copyrighted February 22, 1799. This issue may be a reprint from that collection.   ES, MNSt

THE INDIAN PHILOSOPHER
    (*In* The American musical miscellany. Northampton, 1798. p. 241–244)

Melody and bass, with accompanying text.

First line: Why should our joys transform to pain.   DLC (etc.)

THE INDIGENT PEASANT. A favorite ballad. Sung with great applause by Mr. Darley at Vauxhall. Composed by Mr. Hook. Price 20 cents. Philadelphia, Printed for Carr & cos. Musical repository [1793] [2] p. 33 cm.

Song, pfte. acc. Arr. for flute or "guittar," p. [2].

First line: Tho' the muses ne'er smile by the light of the sun.

Advertised as published in 1793.   DLC, ES, Hopk., NN

THE INDIGENT PEASANT.
   (*In* The gentleman's amusement, ed. by R. Shaw.   Philadelphia [1794–96]
   p. 32–33)

   Melody only, flute (or violin) with accompanying text.
   First line same as preceding.
   In No. 4, February 1, 1795.   DLC, PHi

—— My heart is devoted dear Mary to thee.
   (*In* Elegant extracts for the German flute or violin.   Baltimore [1794]
   bk. 1, p. 24–25)

   Melody only, with accompanying text.
   First line same as preceding.
   Title forms last line of each stanza.   DLC, NN

[INDULGENT POW'RS IF EVER]   A favorite song.
   (*In* [Miscellaneous and incomplete [?] collection]   Philadelphia, G. Willig
   [ca. 1795]   p. 7–8)

   Song, pfte. acc.
   Title from first line.   DLC

INKLE AND YARICO, or the Benevolent maid.
   George Colman, jun's libretto to Samuel Arnold's opera (1787) was adver-
   tised in January, 1793, as "published and sold at Enoch Story's Printing
   Office . . . [Philadelphia] . . . printed on writing paper, containing 66 pages."
   A short synopsis of the libretto was added with the remark that

   This very beautiful and interesting performance is replete with sentiment
   and wit, and will afford much pleasure to the readers.

INKLE AND YARICO.   An opera.   As performed with great applause at the
   Theatre Royal, London.   Philadelphia, Printed and sold at E. Story's office
   in Fourth street.   Nearly opposite the Indian Queen tavern [1793]   66 p.
   16½ cm.

   Libretto.
   On t.-p. at head of imprint elaborate monogram: E. S. "Characters," p. [2];
   text, p. [3]–66.   MWA, PU

INKLE AND YARICO, an opera.   As performed at the theatre in Boston.
   Printed at the Apollo Press in Boston, for William P. Blake, No. 59, Cornhill.
   1794.   60 p.   16½ cm.

   Libretto.
   Title-page; dramatis personae, p. [2]; text, p. [3]–60.
                                                    CSmH, MH, MWA, PPL

   With "orchestra accompaniments by Mr. [Victor] Pelisier" the opera was to
   be performed at New York in February, 1796.

INSTALLATION MARCH.
   See Manuscript collection of hymns, songs, etc. (51).

*INSTRUCTIONS FOR THE STICCADO PASTORALE, with a collection of
airs; Londres(sans date). [By James Bremner]

Thus entered in Fétis *Biographie universelle* on the authority of Forkel and
Lichtenthal. He adds:

Je n'ai trouvé ni ce nom, ni l'ouvrage dans les catalogues Anglais.

Eitner in his *Quellen lexikon* copied Fétis' entry. Sonneck states that he
entered the title here as a clue, though not an American publication and
though James Bremner probably wrote it before he came to America in 1763.

THE INSTRUMENTAL ASSISTANT. Containing instructions for the violin,
German flute, clarionett, bass viol and hautboy. Compiled from late
European publications. Also a selection of favourite airs, marches &c.
Progressively arranged and adapted for the use of learners. By Samuel
Holyoke, A. M. Published according to Act of Congress. Vol. I. Printed
at Exeter, Newhampshire, by H. Ranlet, and sold at his book-store. Sold
also by most of the booksellers in the United States. Price 1 doll. 25 cents
by the 100, 1 doll. 50 cents by the dozen, 1 doll. 75 cents single, sewed in
blue. [n. d.] 79, [1] p. 22 x 27 cm.

Title-page, with ornamental border; Dictionary of musical terms, p. [2];
instructions, explanations, &c., p. [3]–21; introductory lessons, p. 22–24;
airs, marches, &c., p. [25]–79; index and note by the compiler, p. [80].

Instrumental duets and trios. Open score.
Printed from movable type.
Original issue was copyrighted, Massachusetts, August 30, 1800. DLC
copy, with "Vol. I" on t.-p., and bound with Vol. II (1807) may not be the
original issue, as copyright record mentions neither Vol. I nor Vol. II, and
thus would seem to refer to some single issue. However, it is possible that
this first volume is essentially identical with such an issue. On this assumption we list its contents here, but make no individual entries.

Contents:

  p. [25] Serenade.
          God save America.
          Foot's minuet.
      26 Belleisle march.
          March to Boston.
      27 The black cockade.
          Boston march.
      28 Lesson by Morelli.
      29 Marquis of Granby's march.
          Swiss guard's march.
      30 Durham march.
          Quick march.
      31 Capt. Mackintosh's march.
      32 The beauties of fancy.
      33 For there's no luck about the house.
          Dog and gun.
      34 O dear what can the matter be?
          Yankey [!] Doodle.
      35 Staffordshire march.
          Rakes of London.

p. 36 Grano's march
    37 La Choutille cotillion.
       Canada farewell.
 38–39 The wood cutters.
       Handel's clarionett.
    39 British muse.
 40–41 Duke of Holstein's march.
       March in the God of love.
    41 Love's march.
    42 Gen. Wayne's march.
    43 Handyside's march.
       Malbrouk.
 44–45 Count Brown's march.
    45 Prince Eugene's march.
    46 Suffolk march.
       Free Mason's march.
    47 Heathen mythology.
       When first I saw, &c.
    48 Dorsetshire march.
       Felton's Gavot.
    49 Philadelphia march.
 50–51 Duke of Yorks march.
    52 General Knox's march.
    53 Baron Stuben's march.
 54–55 Essex march.
    56 London march.
    57 President's march.
 58–59 Handel's Gavot.
    59 Favorite air.
    60 New German march.
    61 Gen. Green's march.
 62–63 Handel's Water piece.
 63–64 Air in Rosina.
    65 Quick march in Cymon.
 66–67 Col. Orne's march.
    68 Air.
    69 Washington's march.
 70–71 March alla militaire.
    71 Boston quick step.
 72–73 Stamitz's air.
    73 Duettino.
 74–75 Echo.
    75 March in the Water Music.
    76 Garner's air.
 77–79 Sonata.   DLC

INTRODUCTORY CHORUS. Britain's glory . . .
    See Military glory of Great Britain.

*THE INVASION.
    Song by Dibdin. Advertised in August, 1798, as "just published and for sale
    at Wm. Howe's wholesale and retail warehouse, 320 Pearl street," New York.

THE INVITATION. Arranged for the piano forte, flute, or violin. New York, Sold by I. and M. Paff [n. d.] [2] p. 32½ cm.

Imprint at foot of p. [2].
Song, pfte. acc. (flute or violin). Arr. for German flute, p. [2].
First line: Come live with me and be my love.
Composed by George Emrick.
Sonneck's date, ca. 1800.   DLC, RPJCB

THE INVITATION. Words by Shakespear. Music by Geo. Emrick. Philadelphia, Published by G. Willig [n. d.] 1 l. 33 cm.

Imprint at foot of page.
Song, pfte. acc.
First line same as preceding.
Sonneck: ca. 1800.
Christopher Marlowe's well known verses were long attributed to Shakespeare.
                                                                DLC, MWA

THE INVITATION. Written by Mr. J. Lathrop. Set by the author of the "Pursuit" in Magazine No. 1.
(*In* The Massachusetts magazine, Boston, May, 1789. p. 323–324)

Song, pfte. acc.
First line: Come my fair while blooming Spring.   DLC (etc.)

INVOCATION TO CHARITY. A Masonick ode. Words anon. Original. Composed for and performed at the celebration of St. John's Day in Charlestown and suitable for other charitable occasions. The air may be performed as a solo, accompanied with instruments or all parts by the voices alone by omitting the symphonies.
(*In* The union harmony, by Oliver Holden. Boston, 1793. vol. 2, p. 61–65)

Three-part chorus. Open score.
First line: Come Charity, come Charity with goodness crown'd.
Composed by Oliver Holden.   DLC, ICN, MH, MHi, MWA, NN

*THE IRISH CHAMBERMAID. Alternative title of *The double disguise*, by James Hook.

*THE IRISH TAYLOR, or, the Humours of the thimble.
This "burletta in one act . . . with the new grand overture and accompaniments", the composition of the celebrated Mr. [Raynor] Taylor," was to be performed at the City Theatre, Charleston, S. C., on April 7, 1796.

THE IRISH WASHER WOMAN.
See Evening amusement, p. 24.

THE IRISHMAN. Sung by Mr. Darley, junʳ at Vauxhall.
(*In* Elegant extracts for the German flute or violin. Philadelphia [1798] bk. 3, p. 28).

Melody only, flute or violin, with accompanying text.
First line: The turban'd Turk who scorns the world.   DLC, NN

*THE IRON CHEST.
This "favorite new play, interspersed with songs . . . written by George Colman the younger, founded on the celebrated novel of Caleb Williams," was performed at the New Theatre, Baltimore, on June 2, 1797, with "the music and accompanyments by Mr. R. Taylor."

'TIS ALL A JEST. A favourite song. Composed by Mr. Hook. New York, Printed & sold by J. Hewitt, No. 131 William street. Sold also by B Carr, Philadelphia & J. Carr, Baltimore. Price 25 cents.
(*In* A collection of new & favorite songs. [A] Philadelphia [ca. 1800] p. [96]–[97])

Song, pfte. acc. Arr. for "guittar" or German flute, p. [2].
First line: O how I love to play.
In title, letter "J" is reversed.
Original issue, 1797–99.   HFB

'TIS ALL A JEST. A favorite song. Composed by Mr. Hook. Price 25 cts. New York, Printed and sold at I. C. Moller [n. d.] [2] p. 32½ cm.

Song, pfte. acc.
First line same as preceding.
Sonneck gives ca. 1800.   DLC

*'TIS ALL A JOKE.
Song by Raynor Taylor. Was to be sung in his "musical performance . . . the whole of the music original and composed by Mr. Taylor," at Annapolis, Md., on February 28, 1793.

'TIS NO FAULT OF MINE. A favorite song. Composed by Mr. Hook. pr. one quarter doller [!] N. York, Prin'd & solt [!] at G. Gilfert & cos. Musical magazine, No. 191 Broadway, where may be had the new favorite songs Ma belle coquette, Lavender girl & Market lass [1794–95] [2] p. 31½ cm.

Song, pfte. acc.
First line: Young Damon has woot [!] me a monstrous long time.
                                                          JFD, MB, MWA

'TIS NOT THE BLOOM ON DAMONS CHEEK. A favorite rondo. Composed by I. Hook. Philadephia [!] Printed for A. Reinagle; I. Aitken, sculpt. [1789] 3 p. 33½ cm.

Imprint at foot of p. 3.
Song, pfte. acc.
First line same as title.   CdeW, ES, McD–W, NN

Advertised in March, 1789, as "just published and sold by Thomas Dobson, at the Stone House in Second Street," Philadelphia, among "songs and pieces, arranged for the pianoforte or harpsichord by Alexander Reinagle."

'TWAS IN THE GOOD SHIP ROVER, or the Greenwich pensioner. By Dibdin. Price 20 cents. Philadelphia, Printed at Carr's Musical repository [1794] [2] p. 33 cm.

Song, pfte. acc.
First line same as title.
In lower margin of p. [2]: To be had at above new editions of the following favorite songs by Dibdin. Poor Jack, Poor Tom Bowling, Flowing can, Soldiers adieu, Jack at the windlass, Ben Backstay, The watchman, The waggoner, No good without an exception, Sailor's return.
From *The oddities*, by Charles Dibdin.   ABHu, ES, Hopk., LSL

'TWAS IN THE SOLEMN MIDNIGHT HOUR. Sung with great applause by Miss E. Westray in the Sighs, or the Daughter. Composed by J. Hewitt.

New York, Printed & sold at J. Hewitt's Musical repository, No. 23 Maiden lane. Pr. 25 cts.
(*In* A collection of new & favorite songs. [A] Philadelphia [ca. 1800] p. [24]-[25])

Song, pfte. acc. Arr. for flute, p. [25].
First line same as title.
Prince Hoare's *Sighs, or The daughter* was produced in New York, April 16 and 18, 1800, and Miss Westray sang on both occasions. HFB

'TWAS IN THE SULTRY NOONTIDE HOUR. A favorite song. Philadelphia, Printed & sold by G. Willig, No. 185 Market st. [1798–1804] [2] p. 32½ cm.

Song, pfte. acc.
First line same as title. CSmH

['TWAS ON A PLEASANT SUMMERS EVE] Sung by Mrs. Marshall.
(*In* The volunteers, by A. Reinagle. Philadelphia [1798 ?] p. 10)

Song, pfte. acc.
Title from first line. DLC

*IT WAS ONE EVE IN SUMMER WEATHER.
Advertised in March, 1797, as to be published "in a few days" by "G. Gilfert at his Musical Magazine, No. 177, Broadway," New York.

'TWAS PRETTY POLL & HONEST JACK. Alternative title of *Pretty Poll & Honest Jack*, by James Hook.

THE ITALIAN MONK.
Sonneck: Samuel Arnold's opera (1797) was to be performed "for the first time in America" as a "play, interspersed with songs, in three acts," with "the music and accompaniments by Mr. [Alexander] Reinagle" at Philadelphia, on April 25, 1798.

It seems more likely, however, that reference is here made to Boaden's comedy, performed in Philadelphia, April 11 and 25, 1798. *See* [The Italian monk trio].

THE ITALIAN MONK TRIO. Alternative title of [*The mock Italian trio*]

THE ITALIEN [!] MOCK TRIO. Alternative title of [*The mock Italian trio*]

THE ITALIAN SONG.
See Mrs. Pownall's address.

JACK AT THE WINDLASS. By Dibdin. Price 20 cents. Philadelphia, Printed for Carr & co. at their Musical repository, No. 136 High street. Where may be had all the newest music reprinted from European publications. Likewise an elegant assortment of piano fortes, flutes, guittars, violins, and other musical articles of superior quality. [1793] [2] p. 32½ cm.

Song, pfte. acc. Arr. for flute, p. [2].
First line: Come all hands ahoy to the anchor. LSL

Advertised in August, 1793, as "printed singly . . . and sold at Carr & Co's Musical Repository, No. 136 High street," Philadelphia.

JACK CLUELINE. A celebrated sea song. Sung by Mr. Hardinge. Composed by Mr. Moulds. Price 25 cents. Printed & sold at B. Carr's Musical repository, Philadelphia; J. Hewitt's, New York & J. Carr's, Baltimore [1799] [2] p. 32½ cm.

Song, pfte. acc. Arr. for flute, p. [2].
First line: Top sails aback the ship hove to. LSL
Advertised by B. Carr, Philadelphia, as published in March, 1799.

JACK JUNK. Written and composed by Mr. Dibdin. Price 25 cents. Printed and sold at B. Carr's Repositories in New York and Philadelphia and by J. Carr, Baltimore [1794–97] 3 p. 33 cm.

Song, pfte. acc.
First line: 'Twas one day at Wapping.
From *Great News.*
From the prominent position of New York in the imprint, published probably 1795–96. ES

JACK THE GUINEA PIG. A favorite song. Composed by R. Taylor.
(*In* Young's vocal and instrumental musical miscellany. Philadelphia [1793–95] p. 39–40)

Song, pfte. acc.
First line: When the anchor's weigh'd.
Followed on p. 40 by "Hark the lark at heav'n's gate," for flute.
In No. 5, 1793. DLC, Hopk.

JACK'S FIDELITY.
See Polly Ply.

[JAI PERDU MON EURIDICE] A favourite French song.
(*In* Young's vocal and instrumental musical miscellany. Philadelphia [1793–95] p. 29–30)

Song, pfte. acc.
Title from first line: Jai perdu mon euridice [!]
From Orphée et Euridice, by Gluck.
In No. 4, 1793. DLC, Hopk.

JANIZARY'S MARCH.
See Military amusement, p. 7.

JARGON.
(*In* The singing master's assistant, by William Billings. Boston, 1778. p. 102)

Four-part chorus. Open score.

Text:
　　Let horrid Jargon split the Air
　　And rive the nerves asunder;
　　Let hateful Discord greet the Ear
　　As terrible as Thunder. CSmH, DLC, ICN, MB, MHi

In this grotesque composition the music is amply descriptive of the text. Its closing cadence would cause the most rabid modernist to shudder.

JAVOTTE, OR THE MAID OF THE ALPS. Written by John Gretton, Esqr. Composed by Joseph Willson, organist of Trinity church. New York. Sold by I. and M. Paff [n. d.] [2] p. 32 cm.

Song, pfte. acc.
First line: Will you please gentle folks that little Javotte.
Middle of p. [2]: Copyright secured.
Published possibly as early as 1799, probably later.   DLC, NN

THE JE NE SCAI QUOI. A favorite ballad sung by Mrs. Oldmixon in Robin Hood.
(*In* The gentleman's amusement, ed. by R. Shaw. Philadelphia [1794–96] p. 21)

Melody only, with accompanying text.
First line: Your wise men all declare.
From *The siege of Curzola*, by Samuel Arnold.
Robin Hood, by William Shield.
In No. 3, 1794–95.
Mrs. Oldmixon sang in *Robin Hood* in Philadelphia on the occasion of her first appearance in America, May 14, 1794.   DLC, PHi

THE JEALOUS DON. A favorite dialogue and duett in the opera of the Pirates. Philadelphia, Printed for Carr & co. at their Musical repository, No. 136 High street, where may be had all the newest music, reprinted from European publications. Likewise an elegant assortment of guittars, piano fortes, flutes, violins and other musical articles of the first quality.
(*In* The favorite songs from the Pirates, by S. Storace. Philadelphia [1793] p. (13)–(16).)

Duet, pfte. acc. Arr. for "guittar," p. (16).
First line: The jealous don won't you assume when you marry.
The pirates, by Stephen Storace.   HFB

——— Separate issue of preceding, 1793.   ABHu, DLC, ES, MWA

THE JEALOUS DON. A comic duet in the opera of the Pirates. Composed by Sr. Storace.
(*In* The musical repertory. Boston [1796–97] No. III, p. 41–43)

Duet, pfte. acc.
First line same as preceding.   DLC

——— The same as preceding. First three pages, numbered 41–43, of a detached portion of above collection.   DLC

——— Separate issue of preceding, 1796–97.   LSL

JEFFERSON AND LIBERTY.
See Manuscript collection of hymns, songs, etc. (42).

JEFFERSON'S MARCH.
See Compleat tutor for the fife . . . p. 22.

[215]

JEM OF ABERDEEN. A favorite Scotch song. Composed by Mr. Hook.
(*In* The musical repertory. Boston [1796–97] No. III, p. 40–41)
Song, pfte. acc.
First line: The tuneful lavrocks cheer y grove.   DLC

—————— Separate issue of preceding, 1796–97.   LSL

JEM OF ABERDEEN. [n. p., n. d.] 1 l., paged 10. 27 cm.
Song, pfte. acc.
First line: The tunefull lavrocks cheer the grove.   DLC

—————— The same as preceding with added imprint: Printed by G. Willig, Philadelphia.
Published probably 179–.   DLC, LSL, PP–K

*JEMMY CARSON'S COLLECTION [of ballads?] Philadelphia: Printed by
Andrew Steuart, 1762.

JEMMY OF THE GLEN. Words and music by Mrs. Pownall.
(*In* Six songs, by Mrs. Pownall and J. Hewitt. New York [1794] p. 9–10)
Song, pfte. acc.
First line: Where gently flows sweet winding Tay.   ES, HFB

—————— Separate issue of preceding, ca. 1794.   DLC, ES, LSL

—————— The same as preceding.
(*In* A collection of new & favorite songs. [A] Philadelphia [ca. 1800]
p. [108]–[109], numbered 9–10)   HFB

JEMMY OF THE GLEN. Words and musik [!] by Mrs. Pownall. New York,
Printed and sold at I. C. Moller's musical store [n. d.] 2 p. 32½ cm.
Song, pfte. acc.
First line same as preceding.
Possibly published as early as 1796, when Moller first appears in the New
York Directory.   DLC

JEMMY OF THE GLEN. Printed and sold at Carr's music store, Baltimore
[1798] 2 p. 33 cm.
Song, pfte. acc.
First line same as preceding.   DLC
Advertised in April, 1798, as "just published and for sale at J. Carr's music
store, Gay street, Baltimore," under the title of "Jemmy of the glen. Words
and music by the late Mrs. Pownall." Mrs. Pownall died in Charleston,
August 11, 1796.

UN JEU D'ESPRIT. On the word, Idea. A glee for four voices. Composed
by W. Pirsson. And sung at the Columbian Anacreontic society. New
York, Printed by B. Carr & sold at his Musical repositories here & at Philadelphia. [ca. 1795] [2] p. 31½ cm.

Part-song. Open score.
First line: What can force the rending sigh.
The *Columbian Anacreontic Society* was founded in New York ca. 1795 and
apparently functioned until ca. 1798.
(*With* The kiss . . . New York [1797])   ES, NN

[216]

THE JEW BROKER. A favorite song in the new entertainment of the Jew and the Doctor. Sung by Mr. Bernard. Printed and sold by R. Shaw (Importer of music and musical instruments) No. 92 Market St., Baltimore; B. Carr, Philadelphia; T [!] Hewitt, New York. Price 25 cents. [ca. 1800] [2] p. 32½ cm.

Song, pfte. acc.
First line: Ye jobbers, underwriters, ye tribe of pen and ink.
John Bernard played in the first Philadelphia performance of Thomas Dibdin's *The Jew and the Doctor*, December 4, 1799.   LSL

——— The same as preceding except that in the imprint we find "13 South Fourth st., Phiᵃ" instead of "No. 92 Market st., Baltimore." ca. 1800, bu somewhat later than the above.   McD–W, MNS

THE JEW BROKER. A favorite song in the new entertainment of the Jew and the Docter [!] Sung by Mr. Bernard. Price 25 cents. [n. p., ca. 1800?] [2] p. 31½ cm.

Song, pfte. acc.
First line same as preceding.   MB

JOCKEY AND JENNY. Composed by R. Taylor. Philadelphia, Printed for the Author, No. 96 North Sixth street, and sold by B. Carr at his Musical repository, Market st., and by I. Carr, Baltimore (Price ¼ of a dollar) [ca. 1794] [2] p. 32½ cm.

Song, pfte. acc.
First line: Near a shady myrtle bow'r.   DLC, NRU–Mus

This song was to be sung in Raynor "Taylor's musical performance . . . the whole of the music original and composed by Mr. Taylor," at Annapolis, Md., on February 28, 1793.

*JOCKEY AND MOGGY, a comic song by Raynor Taylor.
Ibidem on January 20, 1793.

JOCKEY OF THE GREEN. A favorite Scotch song. Boston, Printed & sold by P. A. von Hagen, No. 3 Cornhill [ca. 1800] [2] p. 32½ cm.

Song, pfte. acc.
First line: Na mair ye bonny lasses gay.
Published probably as early as 1799.
                    ES, JFD, LSL, MB, MH, NBuG, RPJCB

JOHNNY AND MARY.
(*In* A collection of favorite songs, divided into two books. Arr. by A. Reinagle. Philadelphia [1789?] bk. 1, p. 17)

Song, pfte. acc.
First line: Down the burn and thro' the mead.
Composed by William Shield (*BM Cat.*)   CdeW, DLC, ES, Hopk.

——— Separate issue of preceding, ca. 1789.   DLC

JOHNNY AND MARY. New York, Printed & sold at J. Hewitt's Musical repository, No. 131 William street. Sold also by B. Carr, Philadelphia & J. Carr, Baltimore [1797–99] 1 l. 33½ cm.

Song, pfte. acc.
First line same as preceding.   DLC, JFD, NN

[217]

—— The same as preceding.
(*In* A collection of new & favorite songs. [A] Philadelphia [ca. 1800 p. [203])
                                                                HFB

JOHNNY AND MARY. A favorite Scotch song.
(*With* The English naval dance. New York [ca. 1800?])

Song, pfte. acc.
First line: Down the bourne & thro' the mead.   NBuG

JOHNNY WAS A PIPER'S SON. A comic song. Sung by Mr. Hollingsworth
at the Theatre Royal, Manchester. Set to music by Mr. Cheese. Price
25 cents. Baltimore, Printed and sold by C. Hupfeld and F. Hammer
Mark. st., N. 173 [179–] [2] p. 33 cm.

Song, pfte. acc.
First line same as title.   MWA

THE JOLLY GAY PEDLAR. From Oscar & Malvina.
(*In* The gentleman's amusement, ed. by R. Shaw. Philadelphia [1794–96]
p. 73)

Melody only, flute (or violin) with accompanying text.
First line: I am a jolly gay pedlar.
In No. 9, ca. 1796.
Oscar and Malvina, by William Reeve.   DLC, PHi, PP–K

*THE JOLLY HIBERNIAN in full glee; or Complete Irish jester and wits vade-
mecum. Containing a more humorous variety of original stories, comical
bulls, witty repartees, entertaining anecdotes, jests &c. than ever appeared
in the Irish or any other language. To which are added, the facetious history of John Gilpin, and a *new song in praise of St. Patrick*. Philadelphia,
Printed by Henry Taylor, for Robert Campbell. 1790.

Three hundred copies, in sheets, offered at the sale of Henry Taylor's estate
in 1791.

THE JOLLY RINGERS. Composed by Dibdin.
(*In* Young's vocal and instrumental musical miscellany. Philadelphia
[1793–95] p. 60–61)

Song, pfte. acc. Arr. for two flutes, p. 61.
First line: Oft has the world been well defin'd.
In No. 8, 1795.
From *Castles in the air*, by Charles Dibdin.   DLC

THE JOLLY SAILOR.
(*In* The American musical miscellany. Northampton, 1798. p. 163–166)

Four-part chorus. Open score.
First line: When my fortune does frown.   DLC (etc.)

*THE JOVIAL SONGSTER. Philadelphia: Printed and sold by H. Kammerer.
1793.

*JOVIAL SONGSTER. A collection of the most esteemed songs, sung at the
American and English theatres. Fourth edition. Baltimore, Printed for
Henry S. Keatinge. 1798.

[218]

THE JOVIAL SONGSTER. Containing a good collection of songs. Boston, Printed by J. White, near Charles River Bridge. 1800. MWA

*THE JUBILEE.
Garrick's piece with "music by Dibdin, orchestra accompaniments by [Victor] Pelisier" was to be performed at New York, on March 10, 1800.

JULIA SEE. A favorit [!] song. Adapted to the piano forte. By Mr. H. Capron. [n. p., n. d.] 1 l. 34 cm.

Song, pfte. acc.
First line: Julia see the rosy morning.
Published probably at Philadelpha, 179–, or ca. 1800. McD-W

KEEP YOUR DISTANCE. A favorite song. Sung by Miss Broadhurst at the New York Old City Concert. New York, Printed and sold by G. Gilfert & co., No. 209 Broadway, where may be had a general assortment of fine tuned piano fortes &c. [1795] [2] p. 31½ cm.

Song, pfte. acc.
First line: Young Strephon met me on the green.
Composed by James Hook.
Sung by Miss Broadhurst in New York, September 15, 1794.
DLC, MWA, RPJCB

KENTUCKY. French country dance.
See United States Country Dances, p. 14.

THE KENTUCKY VOLUNTEER. A new song. Written by a lady of Philadelphia. Composed by R. Taylor. Price one ·/4 dollar. Philadelphia, Printed & sold at Carr & cos. Musical repository. [1794] [3] p. 33 cm.

Below imprint: N. B. A new song published every Monday.
At foot of p. [1]: Jan. 6. 94. No. 1.
Song, pfte. acc. Arr. for German flute and for the "guittar," p. [3].
First line: Adieu Philadelphia, dear Jenny adieu.
On recto of p. [1], ms. note: No. 51. Title page of the Kentucky volunteer.
Deposited 6th Janʸ 1794. CdeW, DLC, JFD, McD-W

In Dunlap and Claypoole's *American daily advertiser*, Philadelphia, for Wednesday, January 1, 1794, appears the following notice:

NEW MUSIC

B. Carr and Co. inform the public that having settled a correspondence with the principal publishers of music in Britain &c. from whom they are constantly receiving supplies of the newest music—together with several originals in their possession from which they wish to present amateurs with a selection of the most esteemed, they will, for the future, publish *a new song, or piece of music, every Monday*, and by the continuance hope to make their publications a register of fashionable music.

On Monday next will be published, *The Kentucky Volunteer* written by a Lady of Philadelphia, composed by R. Taylor, Professor of music— printed and sold at their Musical Repository, No. 122 South side Market-street, where they have for sale an elegant assortment of grand and small

[219]

Piano Fortes, and all kinds of Musical instruments of the best make, from the first British manufactories.

It is interesting to note that this plan was carried out through five issues, up to February 3, 1794; and that, though very rare, copies of all five have been located. They are as follows:

The Kentucky volunteer, by Raynor Taylor; The poor black boy, by Storace; La chasse, by A. Reinagle; Then say my sweet girl can you love me, or The pretty brunette, by Hook; and finally, Yarrimore, an Indian ballad.

THE KENTUCKY VOLUNTEER.
See Evening amusement [1796] p. 21.

THE KISS. Sung by Mrs. Seymour at the Ladies' Concert. Price 20 cents. New York, Printed by B. Carr and J. Carr, Baltimore [1797 ?] [2] p. 31½ cm.

Song, pfte. acc.
First line: The kiss that he gave when he left me behind.
Composed by James Hook.   DLC, ES, MB, McD–W

We learn from the files of *Minerva*, New York, that Mrs. Seymour sang *The kiss* at the Ladies' Concert sometime during the Spring of 1797, the exact date not given.

———— The same as preceding.
(*With* Un jeu d'esprit, by W. Pirsson. New York (ca. 1797])   ES, NN

———— The same as preceding.
(*In* A collection of new & favorite songs. [A] Philadelphia [ca. 1800] p. [134]–[135])   HFB

———— May I never be married. A favorite song. New York, Printed by G. Gilfert, No. 177 Broadway. Where may be had: How d'ye do, I'm in haste, No, that will never do, The nightingale, Ripe cherries, Three sweethearts I boast, The way to get married, Could I bid the fond passion to cease, The female cryer, Strew the rude crosses of life. [1797–1801] [2] p. 30½ cm.

Song, pfte. acc.
First line: The kiss that he gave when he left me behind.
The present title is a part of the last line of each stanza of *The kiss*.
      DLC, MB, MWA

———— May I never be married.
(*In* A collection of favorite songs, divided into two books. Arr. by A. Reinagle. Philadelphia [1789 ?] bk. 1, p. 9)

Song, pfte. acc.
First line same as preceding.
Pages 9 and 10 are lacking in DLC copy of this collection.   CdeW, ES, Hopk.

KISS ME NOW OR NEVER.
See Mrs. Pownall's address.

KISS MY LADY.
(*With* The yellow hair'd laddie. New York [ca. 1800] p. [2])

Pfte. 2 hds.   DLC

KISSES SUE'D FOR. A favorite song. The words by Shakespear. And music by Mrs. Pownall. New York, Printed for G. Gilfert & co. at their Musical magazine, No. 191 Broadway [1795] [2] p. 33 cm.

Song, pfte. acc. Arr. for two German flutes, p. [2].
First line: Take oh take those lips away.   NN

Advertised in January, 1795, among "New songs adapted to the piano forte just published at G. Gilfert & co. Musical magazine," New York.

*———— The same.
Advertised in March 19, 1795, as "published and to be had at G. Willig's Musical magazine, No. 165 Market street," Philadelphia.

THE KNIGHT OF GUADALQUIVIR. Alternative title of *The Spanish castle.*

THE KNITTING GIRL.
(*In* Three . . . *Canzonetts* by Haydn. Philadelphia [1799] p. 4–5)

Song, pfte. acc.
First line: Hark, Phillis, hark.   NN

———— Separate issue of preceding, ca. 1799.   DLC, ICN, MdHi

THE LABOURER'S WELCOME HOME. A favorite song. Composed by Mr. Dibdin. New York, Printed & sold by G. Gilfert, No. 177 Broad Way [1797–1801] [2] p. 31 cm.

Song, pfte. acc.
First line: The ploughman whistles o'er the furrow.
From Charles Dibdin's *The sphinx,* first produced in 1797.   MWA

*———— The same.
Advertised in August, 1798, as "just published and for sale at Wm. Howe's wholesale and retail warehouse, 320 Pearl street," New York.

THE LABYRINTH OF LOVE. A favorite song by the late Mrs. Pownall. New York, Printed & sold by G. Gilfert, No. 177 Broad Way [ca. 1797] 1 l. 34 cm.

Song, pfte. acc.
First line: Why oh why allmighty passion.
Mrs. Pownall died August 11, 1796.   JFD

THE LAD WHA LILTS SAE SWEETLY. A favorite Scotch song. Sung by Miss Howells at Vauxhall Gardens. Composed by Mr.Hook. New York, Printed & sold at G. Gilfert's piano forte warehouse, No. 177 Broad-Way. And to be had of P. A. von Hagen, No. 3 Cornhill, Boston [ca. 1800] [2] p. 32½ cm.

Song, pfte. acc.
First line: Say lads and lassies ha' ye seen.   DLC

LADIES ANSWER TO THE "PIPE TABAC." Alternative title of *The dish of tea,* by Pierre Gaveaux.

[221]

*THE LADIES' MAGAZINE.
Advertised in *Minerva* (New York) for March 10, 1797:

NEW MUSIC

To be published monthly by subscription by F. Rausch and J. Hewitt a work entitled The Ladies Magazine in which will be introduced sonatas, battle-pieces, songs, duetts, &c., &c., from the most celebrated matters [!] never published in America. Each number will consist of eight pages and with evry twelfth number a title page, index, and list of subscribers will be given. The songs to be arranged for the piano forte and flute. The first number will appear at the beginning of next month. Price to subscribers five shillings—non subscribers seven shillings. To be paid on delivery of each number.

Subscription books are open at J. Hewitt's, No. 40 Gold-street, F. Rausch, 209 Broadway, Carr's Musical Repository, William-street and at Charles Smith's book store, No. 51 Maiden lane.

LADIES MUSICAL JOURNAL.
Ten numbers under the above general title were issued by I. and M. Paff, at 127 Broadway, New York, at about the turn of the century, beginning possibly as early as 1799.

DLC has all but two of these issues.
Imprint is often lacking; when given it is found at foot of page.
Pagination is generally lacking.
Apparently only the earlier numbers belong to the eighteenth century.
All are 32 cm.

The different issues are as follows:

(No. 1)	[2] p.	He sleeps in yonder dewy grave. Callcot.
(No. 2)	p. 3–4	Emma. A pastoral. Worgan.
No. 2	[2] p.	Sweet girl by the light of the moon.
No. 3		[Lacking in DLC]
(No. 4)	p. 7–8	The Persian slave.
(No. 5)	[2] p.	Sonnet to Time.
No. 6	[2] p.	The beggar girl.
		The Prince of Wale's waltz.
No. 7	[2] p.	The beggar boy.
		Federal waltz.
No. 8		[Lacking in DLC]
No. 9	[2] p.	Wully is a bonny lad.
No. 10	[2] p.	The dish of tea.

DLC

THE LADIES PATRIOTIC SONG. Sung by Mrs. Hodgkinson with universal applause at the Columbia gardens. New York, Printed & sold at G. Gilferts Musical magazine, No. 177 Broadway [ca. 1798] [2] p. 31 cm.

In centre of caption an oval engraved portrait of Washington.
Song, pfte. acc. Arr. for "G. flute" or violin, p. [2].
First line: Columbians arise independence proclaim.   ES, MWA
The tune is that of *Washington's march at the Battle of Trenton.*

Sung by Mrs. Hodgkinson at the Columbia Gardens, New York, July 4, 1798.

[222]

LADIES PATRIOTIC SONG. Boston, Printed & sold at P. A. von Hagen & co. imported pianoforte & music warehouse, No. 3 Cornhill [ca. 1800] [2] p. 31½ cm.

Song, pfte. acc. Arr. for German flute or violin, p. [2].
First line same as preceding.
Published probably in 1799.   LSL

LADY COVENTRY'S MINUET with variations by Mr. Bremner.
Piece for the harpsichord, contained in a MS. volume of "Lessons" on p. 112–113. There is no doubt that the composer was James Bremner and not Robert.   Hopk.

LADY GEORGE MURRAY'S REEL.
See Twenty-four American country Dances, p. 3.

LADY WASHINGTON'S FAVORITE.
See Manuscript collection of hymns, songs, etc. (48).

LADY'S BREAST KNOT.
See Compleat tutor for the fife . . . p. 27.

*THE LADY'S MUSICAL MISCELLANY.
Advertised in the Columbian centinel, Boston, April 8, 1797, as:

An entire new work, entitled, The LADY'S MUSICAL MISCELLANY, . . . to be published monthly, in numbers, by P. A. Von Hagen, each number to consist of three songs and pieces of music; with every 12th number a title page index; a list of subscribers will be given. The first number will appear as soon as the subscription is found adequate to the expenses.

Price to Subscribers, One Dollar; non subscribers, 9 d. to be paid on delivery of each number. Subscriptions taken in by Mr. Von Hagen, at the Haymarket Theatre.

Advertised in New York, June 16, 1797, under the same title, but as by P. Aron [!] Hagen, Boston.

We are informed that in the work will be introduced:

Overtures, rondos, songs and duetts, by the most celebrated masters . . . The first number will appear as soon as the subscription is found adequate to the expense.

CONDITIONS

Subscribers to pay one Dollar for each number on delivery.
Subscriptions received at P. Aaron Hagen's Boston; G. Gilfert's Musical Magazine, New York, and at G. Willig's, Philadelphia.

LAFAYETTE. A new song.
(In Young's vocal and instrumental musical miscellany. Philadelphia [1793–95] p. 18)

Song, pfte. acc.
First line: As beside his chereful [!] fire.
In No. 2, 1793.   DLC, HFB, Hopk.

THE LAMPLIGHTER. Written and composed by Mr. Dibdin.
(*In* Young's vocal and instrumental musical miscellany. Philadelphia
[1793–95] p. 19)
Song, pfte. acc.
First line: I'm jolly Dick the lamplighter.
In No. 2, 1793.
From Dibdin's *The oddities*. DLC, HFB, Hopk.

THE LARK. Selected from the Aviary. A collection of sonnets. Hook.
Also just published

No. 1 The thrush.	No. 4 The robin red breast.
No. 2 The linnets.	No. 5 The nightingale.
No. 3 The gold finch.	No. 7 The blackbird.
and No. [blank] The cuckoo.	

[New York] Sold by I. and M. Paff [1799–1803] 3 p. 30½ cm.
At head of title: No. 6.
Imprint at foot of p. 3.
Song, pfte. acc.
First line: Go tunefull bird that glad'st the skies. DLC, ES, NN

LASH'D TO THE HELM. Price 20 cents. Published at B. Carr's Musical
repositories, New York and Philadelphia and J. Carr's Baltimore [1797]
[2] p. 33 cm.
Song, pfte. acc. Arr. for the flute, p. [2].
First line: In storms when clouds obscure the sky.
Composed by James Hook.
Advertised in September, 1797, by J. Carr, Baltimore, among other "songs,
lately published." DLC, LSL, MdHi, NN

———— The same as preceding.
(*In* A collection of new & favorite songs. [A] Philadelphia [ca. 1800] p.
[34]–[35] HFB

LASH'D TO THE HELM. A favorite song. New York, Printed and sold by
G. Gilfert, No. 177 Broadway [1797–1801] [2] p. 32½ cm.
Song, pfte. acc.
First line same as preceding. DLC, NRU–Mus

THE LASS OF HUMBERSIDE. A favorite ballad. Price 20 cents. Printed
by B. Carr [179–] [2] p. 33 cm.
Song, pfte. acc. Arr. for "guittar," p. [2].
First line: In lonely cot by Humberside.
Composed by Jonas Blewitt. ABHu, LSL, McD-W, MWA

THE LASS OF LUCERNE LAKE. Sung in the opera of the Patriot. Com-
posed by Mr. Hewitt. New York, Printed for G. Gilfert & co. [1795] [2] p.
33 cm.
Song, pfte. acc.
First line: Say will you leave your lowland haunts. JFD
Advertised in January, 1795, among "new songs. Adapted to the piano-
forte, just published at G. Gilfert & Co. Musical Magazine," New York.
The patriot, with songs and the overture by James Hewitt was performed in
New York early in June, 1794.

[224]

*——— The same.
Advertised March 19, 1795, in the *Philadelphia gazette* as "this day . . .
published . . . at G. Willig's Musical Magazine, No. 165 Market street."

THE LASS OF RICHMOND HILL. Sung by Mr. Incledon. New York,
Printed & sold by G. Gilfert & co., No. 209 Broadway, near St. Pauls [1795]
1 l. 34 cm.

Song, pfte. acc.
First line: On Richmond hill there lives a lass.
Composed by James Hook.   JFD, MWA

THE LASS OF THE COT. Composed by R. Taylor. Philadelphia, Printed
for the Author, No. 96 North Sixth street, and sold at Carr's Musical repository's, Market street, Philadelphia; William street, New York and at J.
Carr's music store, Market st., Baltimore (Price ¼ of a dollar) [1795] [2]
p. 32½ cm.

Song, pfte. acc.
First line: The meads were all smiling, serene was the day.
Advertised in March, 1795, as just published.   DLC, PP–K

THE LASS OF THE LAKE. Sung by Miss Arnold at Mr. Gillinghams concert. Composed by I. Moorehead. Philadelphia, Printed & sold by R.
Shaw, No. 13 South Fourth street. Where may be had all the new publications &c., violins, flutes, guittars, piano fortes &c. Also sold by J. Carr,
Baltimore & J. Hewitt, New York (Pr. 25 cs.) [n. d.] [2] p. 32 cm.

Song, pfte. acc. Arr. for German flute, p. [2].
First line: At the foot of yon mountain.
I. Moorehead: John Moorehead.
Published possibly as early as 1800.   LSL

THE LASSIES OF DUBLIN.
(*In* The American musical miscellany. Northampton, 1798. p. 117)

Melody only, with accompanying text.
First line: The meadows look cheerful.   DLC (etc.)

LAST ADIEU. A new song. Composed by Mozart. Published & sold by
G. Willig, No. 185 Market st., Philadelphia [1798–1804] 1 l. 32 cm.

Song, pfte. acc.
First line: Stay ye fleeting moments stay.
The music is an arrangement for single voice of a duet in *Die Zauberflöte:*
Könnte jeder brave mann (from Finale of Act I).   DLC, PHi

*LATIN ORATORIO, composed by Trille La Barre.
This "oratorio" (probably a sacred cantata) was to be performed at a "spirit-
ual" concert, Boston, May 31, 1798.

LAUGHING SONG. Sung by Miss Poole. Vauxhall.
(*In* A collection of favorite songs, divided into two books. Arr. by A. Reinagle. Philadelphia [1789 ?] bk. 2, p. 12–13)

Song, pfte. acc.
First line: When Strephon appears how my heart pit-a-pat. CdeW, DLC, PU

*THE LAUNCH, or, Huzza for the Constellation.
This "musical piece, in one act, never yet performed . . . written by John Hodgkinson," was to be given at the Haymarket Theatre, Boston, on September 20, 1797. When the piece was advertised "for the 4th time" (October 23) it was remarked: "the music selected from the best composers, with new orchestra parts by [Victor] Pelisier."

LAUREL HILL.
See Twenty-four American country Dances, p. 17.

THE LAVENDER GIRL. Composed by Mr. Reeve. New York, Printed and sold by G. Gilfert & co., at their Musical magazine, Broadway, No. 191. [1794–95] [2] p. 33 cm.

Song, pfte. acc. Arr. for "guittar," or German flute, p. [2].
First line: Whene'er I view the opening dawn.   MWA

LAVINIA. Composed and sung by Mrs. Pownall.
(In six songs, by Mrs. Pownall and J. Hewitt. New York [1794] p. 15)

Song, pfte. acc.
First line: Why steals from my bosom the sigh.   ES

—— The same as preceding.
(In A collection of new & favorite songs. [A] Philadelphia [ca. 1800] p. [195] numbered 15)   HFB

A LESSON.
(In [Unidentified collection (beginning with "A lesson")] Boston [?] ca. 1800. p. 1–3)
Pfte. 2 hds.   MHi

LESSON by Mr. Jas. Bremner.
Harpsichord piece in B flat major. Contained on p. 114–115 of a MS volume of "lessons," once the property of Francis Hopkinson.   Hopk.

A FAVORITE LESSON for the piano forte. Shuster. Published by J. Carr, Baltimore [ca. 1800] [2] p. 33 cm.
Pfte. 2 hds.   DLC, LSL

AN EASY AND FAMILIAR LESSON for two performers on one piano forte. Composed by R. Taylor. Philadelphia, Printed for the Author, No. 96 North Sixth street. Sold at B. Carr's Musical repository, Market street, and by J. Carr, Baltimore [179–] 2–3 p. 33 cm.

After imprint (at top of p. 3): (Price 1/4 of a dollar)
Pfte. 4 hds.
Published probably 1795–97.   DLC

LET TRUTH AND SPOTLESS FAITH BE THINE. A new song. Composed by Mozart. Printed & sold by G. Willig, No. 185 Market st., Philadelphia [1798–1804] 1 l. 34 cm.

Song, pfte. acc.
First line same as title.
The music is an adaptation of part of the aria in Die Zauberflöte, "Ein mädchen oder weibchen," (Act II, no. 20). The text is entirely new.
                                                CSmH, DLC, PHi, PP-K

[226]

LET'S SEEK THE BOW'R OF ROBIN HOOD.
(*In* A collection of favorite songs, divided in two books.   Arr. by A. Reinagle.
Philadelphia [1789?]   bk. 2, p. 8)

Song, pfte. acc.
First line same as title.   DLC, PU

LET WASHINGTON BE OUR BOAST. Sung with great applause at The
Theatre at the conclusion of the Ode to the memory of Gen'l G. Washington.
The words written & music selected by Mr. Hodgkinson. New York,
Printed & sold at J. Hewitt's Musical repository, No. 23 Maiden Lane. Pr.
25 cents. [1800] [2] p. 33 cm.

Song, pfte. acc.   Arr. for "guittar," p. [2].
First line: Let ev'ry patriot hero sage.   CSmH

————The same as preceding.
(*In* A collection of new & favorite songs. [A] Philadelphia [ca. 1800] p.
[10]–[11])   HFB

THE LIBERTINE DESTROYED.   Alternative title of *Don Juan*.

LIBERTY SONG.
   In 1768 John Dickinson (and not Mrs. Mercy Warren, as Louis C. Elson
states in his *History of American music*) wrote "a song for American freedom."
Of the original version, which Dickinson considered "too bold," no copy
seems to be extant.   A second text was published, also in 1768, as a broadside
without music, by Hall and Sellers in Philadelphia as "A new song, to the
tune of Hearts of oak."   The alterations did not affect the opening stanza,
which begins, "Come, join hand in hand, brave Americans all."   The song
soon became known as the "Liberty song," though Edes & Gill's *North
American almanack*, Boston, 1770, still has it without music as "a new song
now much in vogue in North America.   To the tune of 'Heart of oak,' etc."
As a musical piece the "Liberty song" was first published by Mein and
Fleeming in 1768, but no copy seems to have survived.   The advertisement
appeared in the *Boston chronicle*, August 29–September 5, 1768, and reads:

   The new and favourite LIBERTY SONG, *In Freedom we're born etc.*
   Neatly engraved on copper-plate, the size of half a sheet of paper, set to
   music for the voice, and to which is also added, a set of notes adapted to
   the German flute and violin, is just published and to be sold at the London
   Book-store, King street, Boston, Price sixpence lawful single, and four
   shilling's lawful the dozen.

   Mein and Fleeming again published the song, wor 'ʒ and tune, in Bickerstaff's
Boston almanack, 1769, where it stands on the back of the page which contains
Pascal Paoli's portrait, under the title of "The Liberty song.   In Freedom
we're born."   This edition was reproduced in Paul Leicester Ford's "Life
and writings of John Dickinson" in a chapter devoted to the history of the
song. (*Memoirs*, Hist. Soc. Pa., 1895, v. 14, p. 419–432.)

   Dickinson's "Liberty song" aroused the ire of the tories to such a degree that
they parodized it under the title of "The Parody."   This was printed in the
Boston gazette, September 26, 1768, and began, "Come, shake your dull nod-
dles, ye bumkins and bawl."   In turn, Dr. Benjamin Church, as appears
from John Adams' diary, and not Mrs. Mercy Warren, as Lossing and Winsor

[227]

claim, ridiculed "The Parody." His variation of the "Liberty song" (under the title of "The parody parodiz'd, or The Massachusetts liberty song") was published in Edes & Gill's *Almanack* of 1770, immediately following "A new song" [*i. e.* The liberty song]. "The parody parodiz'd" begins, "Come swallow your bumpers, ye tories! and roar." Both songs are without music. In Bickerstaff's *Boston almanack*, for 1770, "The Massachusetts song of liberty" appears with music—again "The heart of oak."

Liberty song:

ABHu, DLC, ES, JFD, LSL, MB, McD–W, MNSt, MWA, RPJCB

Massachusetts song of liberty: DLC, JFD, MB, MHi

LIBERTY SONGS [n. p., 178–?]   8 p.   16½ cm.

Below caption:
   I. Liberty tree.
  II. The battle of the kegs.
 III. Burgoyne's defeat.
  IV. On General Wayne's taking Stony Point.
To which is added the noted song called Roslin Castle.
Words only.

Contents:
p. [1]–2 Liberty tree.   Tune: The gods of the Greeks.
   2–4 The battle of the kegs.
   5–6 On Gen. Burgoyne's defeat.   Tune: Jack a brisk young drummer.
   6–7 On Gen. Waynes taking Stoney Point.   Tune: One night as Ned
        stept into bed.
   7–8 Roslin Castle.   DLC

LIBERTY TREE.
See Liberty songs, p. [1]–2.

LIBERTY'S THRONE.   A new song.   Composed by F. R. New York.   New York, Printed & sold at J. & M. Paff's musical store, No. 127 Broadway [1799–1803]   [2] p.   33½ cm.
Song and chorus, pfte, acc.
First line: When freedom was banish'd from Greece & from Rome.
In lower margin of p. [2]: Copyright secured.
F. R.: Perhaps Frederick Rausch, particularly as he seems to have been associated with J. and M. Paff (at the same address) from 1800 to 1803.   NN

LIFE LET US CHERISH.
(*In* Linley's assistant for the pianoforte.   Baltimore [1796] p. 20)
Song (or duet ?), pfte. acc.
First line same as title.
Composed by Hans Georg Nägeli.   MdHi

———Separate issue of preceding, ca. 1796.   DLC

LIFE LET US CHERISH.   A favorite new song.   The words by Mr. Derrick. Published by G. Willig, No. 185 Market street, Philadelphia.   [1798–1804]   4 p.   33 cm.
Song, pfte. acc., on first page.
First line same as title.
Pages 2–4, the same theme with variations for pfte. 2 hds.

                                      DLC, JFD, MWA, PHi

—— Separate issue of first page, song only, 1798–1804.   DLC, MWA

LIFE LET US CHERISH. A favorite ballad. Composed by Mozart. Arranged also with variations by the same author. New York, Printed & sold by J. and M. Paff, Broadway [1799–1803]   4 p.   33 cm.

Song, pfte. acc., followed by variations for pfte. 2 hds.
First line same as title.
Actually composed by Nägeli.   ABHu, MNSt (two pages only), NN

LIFE LET US CHERISH. Published at P. A. von Hagen & co. imported piano forte warehouse, No. 3 Cornhill, Boston. Also by G. Gilfert, New York. Where may be had the original song of Crazy Jane & the latest European publications. Also the best toned warranted piano fortes, flutes, hautboys, clarinetts, bassoons, trumpets, French horns, serpents and other musical articles of superior quality [1800]   1 l.   32 cm.

Song, pfte. acc.
First line same as title.   N
Apparently the issue advertised in November, 1800, as "published, at P. A. Von Hagen's Piano Forte Warehouse, No. 3 Cornhill," Boston.

LIFE LET US CHERISH. [n p., n. d.]   3 p.   32 cm.
Variations, pfte. 2 hds.
Published probably ca. 1800.   DLC, RPJCB

LIFE LET US CHERISH.
See Compleat tutor for the fife . . . p. 22.

——The favorite German song Freut euch des lebens. In German and English. New York, Printed & sold by G. Gilfert, No. 177 Broadway [1797–1801]   [2] p.   32½ cm.

Song, pfte. acc.
First lines: Freut euch des lebens.—Taste lifes glad moments.
On p. [2], first column, stanzas 2–7 in German; second column in English.
Music same as preceding.   DLC, McD-W, MWA

—— Snatch fleeting pleasures. A favorite song. Translated from the German. New York, Printed & sold by G. Gilfert, No. 177 Broadway [1797–1801] 1 l. 28½ cm. (trimmed)
Song and chorus, pfte. acc. Two staves.
First line same as title.
Music same as preceding.   NN

—— Snatch fleeting pleasures. Boston, Printed & sold at P. A. von Hagen, Junior & cos. Musical magazine, No. 55 Marlboro street [1799]   1 l.   32 cm.
Song, pfte. acc.
First line same as title.   LSL

THE LIFE OF A BEAU. An English song. Set to musick by a gentleman of Boston.
(In The Massachusetts magazine, Boston, April, 1791, p. 249)
Melody and bass, with accompanying text, followed by chorus.
First line: How brimful of nothing's the life of a beau.   DLC (etc.)

[229]

———— The same as preceding, with simplified title: The life of a beau.
(*In* The American musical miscellany. Northampton, 1798, p. 245–246)

DLC (etc.)

LIGHT AS THISTLE DOWN MOVING. From Rosina. By Shield. [n. p., n. d.] (42)–(43) p. 34 cm.

Song, pfte. acc.
First line same as title.
Probably published by Carr, 179–. *cf. *Elegant extracts.* NN

THE LIGHT HORSE MARCH.
See Compleat tutor for the fife . . . p. 17.

LILLIES AND ROSES. A favorite song. Boston, Printed & sold by P. A. von Hagen, Junr. & co. at theier [!] Musical magazine, No. 55 Marlboro street, and at G. Gilfert's Musical magazine, No. 177 Broadway, Newyork [1799] [2] p. 32½ cm.

Song, pfte. acc.
First line: The father of Nancy a forrester was.
Composed by James Hook.   DLC, JFD, NRU–Mus, RPB

Advertised in May, 1799, as "published at P. A. Von Hagen Jun. and Co's at the Musical Magazine, No. 55, Marlboro' Street," Boston.

———— The same.
Boston, Printed & sold at P. A. Von Hagen junr. & co. at their Musical magazine, No. 55 Marlboro street. Where also may be had the much admired song of the Sailor boy; the same also at G. Gilferts, New York [1799] [2] p. 33 cm.

Song, pfte. acc.
First line same as preceding.   JFD

LILLIES AND ROSES. A favorite song. Composed by Mr. Hook. New York, Printed & sold at J. Hewitt's Musical repository, No. 131 William street. Sold also by B. Carr, Philadelphia & J. Carr, Baltimore. Price 25 cents.
(*In* A collection of new & favorite songs. [A] Philadelphia [ca. 1800] p. [38]–[39])

Song, pfte. acc. Arr. for "guittar," or flute, p. [2].
First line same as preceding.
Original issue 1797–99.   HFB

THE LINCOLNSHIRE MARCH.
See Compleat tutor for the fife . . . p. 17.

LINLEY'S ASSISTANT FOR THE PIANO FORTE.
See New assistant for the pianoforte.

*LINLEY'S SELECTION of country dances and reels, with their proper figures for the pianoforte or violin. Advertised in September, 1797, by J. Carr, Baltimore, among "music lately published."

[230]

HE LINNET. *See* The select songster. New Haven, 1786. p. 23.

'HE LINNET. Composed by Mr. Hook. New York, Printed & sold at J. Hewitt's Musical repository, No. 131 William str. Sold also by B. Carr, Philadelphia & J. Carr, Baltimore. Price 25 cents. [1798] [2] p. 32½ cm.

Song, pfte. acc.
First line: Where wild flow'rs grow & linnets sing.

                                    DLC, ES, MB, McD-W, NN

Advertised in January, 1798, as "just published."
Also advertised in December, 1797, as "published at Carr's Musical Repository, Market street," Philadelphia.
Presumably these are identical.

:HE LINNET. Song. New York, Printed & sold at J. Hewitt's Musical repository, No. 131 William St. Sold also by B. Carr, Philadelphia & J. Carr, Baltimore [1798] [2] p. 34 cm.

Song, pfte. acc.
First line same as preceding.   MB

:HE LINNETS. Boston, Printed & sold by P. A. von Hagen at his imported pianoforte & music warehouse, No. 3 Cornhill. Also by G. Gilfert, New York [ca. 1800] [2] p. 32 cm.

Song, pfte. acc. Arr. for "clarinett or guittar," p. [2].
First line same as preceding.
Published possibly as early as 1799.   DLC, ES, N, RPB, RPJCB

THE LINNETTS.
(*In* The aviary. A collection of three sonnets, by J. Hook. Philadelphia [1798] p. (2)–(3).)
Song, pfte. acc. Arr. for "guittar" or flute, p. (3).
First line: Ye tuneful linnetts bless my care.   JFD, LSL, NN

THE LINNETTS. Published by I. and M. Paff, No. 127 Broadway. Where may be had

        No. 1 The thrush.   No. 4 The robin red breast.
        No. 3 The gold finch. No. 5 The nightingale.
                    and No. 6 The lark.

[1799–1803] [2] p. 32½ cm.

At head of title: Selected from the Aviary, a collection of sonnets. No. 2.
Song, pfte. acc.
First line: Ye tunefull linnets bless my care.   DLC, ES, NN

LIONEL AND CLARISSA: or, The school for fathers. A comic opera, written by Mr. Bickerstaff. Marked with the variations in the manager's book, at the Theatre Royal, in Drury Lane. Philadelphia: Printed by W. W. Woodward, for Mathew Carey, No. 118 Market-street. 1794. 72 p. 16½ cm.

Libretto to Dibdin's opera (1768).
Title-page; Author's note, "The Reader is desired to observe, that the Pas-

sages omitted in the representation at the theatre, are here preserved, an
marked with inverted commas . . . ," p. [2]; Bickerstaff's original adver
tisement, p. [3]; dramatis personae, p. [4], text, p. [5]–72.

MWA, NIC, NN, PPl

Although performed in Philadelphia at irregular intervals (and under variou
names) since 1772, the opera seems not to have reached New York unti
1794 (February 21) and to have had its first performance at Boston, Novem
ber 14, 1796, "with orchestra accompaniments by Mr. Trille Labarre."

LISBIA.   A new canzonet.   Composed by J. C. Graeff.   New York, Printed &
sold at J. Hewitt's Musical repository, No. 23 Maiden Lane.   Pr. 25 cents
[1799–1800]   [2] p.   33½ cm.

Song, pfte. acc.
First line: Lisbia live to mirth and pleasure.
J. C. Graeff: Johann Georg Graeff (BM Cat.)   DL(

———— The same as preceding.
(In A collection of new & favorite songs.   [A] Philadelphia [ca. 1800
p. [118]–[119])   HFl

LISTEN, LISTEN TO THE VOICE OF LOVE.   A favorite new song.   Nev
York, Printed & sold by G. Gilfert & co., No. 209 Broadway, near St. Paul
[1795]   1 l.   33 cm.

Song, pfte. acc.
First line same as title.
Composed by James Hook.   DLC, MWA, Nl

LISTEN, LISTEN TO THE VOICE OF LOVE.   Sung with greatest applaus
at Vauxhall Gardens (Price 20 cents)   Printed for and sold by B: Carr a
his Musical repository's, Market street, Philadelphia & William st., N
York, and by I. Carr, Baltimore [1796]   [2] p.   32 cm.

Song, pfte. acc.   Arr. for flute or guitar, p. [2].
First line same as title.   ABHu, DLC, JFD, LSL, MdHi, MWA, Nl

Advertised in February, 1796, as "published . . . printed and sold b;
Benjamin Carr at his Musical Repository, No. 131 William street," Nev
York.

LITTLE BEN.
(In Elegant extracts for the German flute or violin.   Philadelphia [1798
bk. 3, p. 24)

Melody only, flute or violin, with accompanying text.
First line: Behold your honest little Ben.   DLC, Nl

THE LITTLE BIRD.   Alternative title of Fal lal la, by Stephen Storace.

LITTLE BOY BLEW.   Nursery song for two voices.   Composed by B. Carr
(In The musical journal for the piano forte, ed. by B. Carr.   Baltimore
[1800]   v. 1, no. [9], p. (20)–(21).)

Duet, pfte. acc.   Four staves.
First line: Little Boy Blew come blow me your horn.
                                DLC, ES, LSL, MdHi, NN, NRU–Mus., PP–K

[232]

LITTLE BOY BLEW. Duett by B. Carr.
(*In* The musical journal for the flute or violin. Baltimore [1800] no. 8
[*i. e.* no. 9], p. 20)

Duet for flutes or violins (or flute and violin) with accompanying text. Two
staves.
First line same as preceding. DLC

THE LITTLE COT. A favorite new song. New York, Printed & sold at G.
Gilfert's pianoforte warehouse, No. 177 Broadway. And to be had at P. A.
von Hagen's, No. 3 Cornhill, Boston, and G. Willig, No. 185 Market street,
Philadelphia [ca. 1800] [2] p. 32½ cm.

Song, pfte. acc. Arr. for German flute, p. [2].
First line: I am a very little man. DLC

THE LITTLE FARTHING RUSHLIGHT.
See The rushlight.

THE LITTLE GIPSEY. Price 12 cents. New York, Printed by B. Carr and
J. Carr, Baltimore [1795–96] 1 l. 32 cm.

Song, pfte. acc.
First line: A poor little gipsy, I wander forlorn. DLC, LSL

THE LITTLE GIPSEY. Sung by Miss Broadhurst at Vauxhall.
(*In* Elegant extracts for the German flute or violin. Philadelphia [1798]
bk. 3, p. 9)

Melody only, flute or violin, with accompanying text.
First line: A poor little gipsey, I wander forlorn. DLC, NN

——— A poor little gypsy. Composed by Dr. Arnold and publish'd by Mr
Trisobio Nº 66 Nᵇ Front Sᵗ, Philadelphia [1796–98] 1 l. 32 cm.

At foot of page: Pr 12 cent.
Song, pfte. acc. Three staves.
First line: A poor little gypsy I wander forlorn. CdeW

LITTLE ROBIN RED BREAST; a collection of pretty songs, for children,
entirely new. Printed at Worcester, Massachusetts, by Isaiah Thomas,
MDCCLXXXVII. (Evans 20461)
MWA has a copy dated 1786.

THE LITTLE SAILOR BOY. A ballad. Sung at the theatres & other public
places in Philadelphia, Baltimore, New York, &c. by Messrs. J. Darley,
Williamson, Miss Broadhurst, Mrs. Hodgkinson & Mrs. Oldmixon. Written
by Mrs. Rowson. Composed by B. Carr. Price 25 cents. Printed and sold
at the author's Musical repository, Philadelphia; J. Carr's, Baltimore & J.
Hewitt's, New York. Entered according to law [1798] [2] p. 36 cm.

Song, pfte. acc. Arr. for "guittar," p. [2].
First line: The sea was calm, the sky serene.
On verso of p. [2] in one of DLC copies manuscript note: No. 201. Title of
"The little sailor boy &c." (Music) Deposited 22d. Jan'y, 1798, by Benj.
Carr as author and propr.
ABHu, DLC, ES, JFD, LSL, McD–W, MdHi, MWA, NN, PHi (incomplete),
PP–K, RPJCB

[233]

———— The same as preceding.
(*In* A collection of new & favorite songs. [B] Philadelphia [1797–99] n paging) P

THE LITTLE SAILOR BOY. A favourite ballad. Written by Mrs. Rowsor Composed by B. Carr. Price 25 cents. Enterd [!] according to law. Sol at B. Carr's Musical repository, Philadelphia; J. Carr's, Baltimore & J Hewitt's, New York [1798] [2] p. 33 cm.

Song, pfte. acc. Arr. for "guittar," p. [2].
First line same as preceding. ABH

———— The same as preceding.
(*In* A collection of new & favorite songs. [A] Philadelphia [ca. 1800] p [36]–[37] HF]

Referring to one (or both) of the above items, we have the following: Ad vertised in January, 1798, among "new songs published . . . at Carr' Musical Repository," Philadelphia. Possibly identical with the same song advertised in January, 1798, as "just published, by J. Hewitt, No. 13 William st.," New York.

THE LITTLE SAILOR BOY. A favorite song. Boston, Printed & sold a P. A. von Hagen, Junᵣ & Cos. Musical magazine, No. 3 Cornhill. Als by G. Gilfert, New York. Where also may be had the new song of As fort] I rang'd the banks of Tweed. Also a great variety of warranted piano fortes flutes, hautboys, bassoons, trumpets, French horns, violins, guitars, fifes & other musical articles of superior quality [1799] [2] p. 32½ cm.

Below imprint: For the piano forte, German flute or violin.
Song, pfte. acc.
First line same as preceding. NBuC

THE LITTLE SAILOR BOY. Written by Mrs. Rowson. The melody by ; lady. Boston, Printed & sold at P. A. von Hagen's imported piano fort warehouse, No. 3 Cornhill. Sold also by G. Gilfert, New York; D. Vinton Providence; E. M. Blunt, Newbury Port; W. R. Wilder, Newport; B. B Macanulty, Salem; J. I. Stanwood, Portsm. & A. Jenks, Portland [ca. 1800 [2] p. 30 cm.

Song, pfte. acc. Arr. for "guittar," p. [2].
First line same as preceding.
Published possibly in 1799. DLC, LSL, MB, N, NN, RPB, RPJCE
There is in PP–K a holograph copy of the preceding.

HER MUCH LOV'D LITTLE SAILOR BOY. Words by Mrs. Rowson. Foi Mrs. Mann with the composer's compts. B. Carr.

LITTLE SALLY. A favorite song. Sung in the Shipwreck. Composed by Dr. Arnold. Price 25 cents. New York, Printed & sold at J. Hewitt'i Musical repository, No. 131 William street. Sold also by B. Carr, Philadel phia & J. Carr, Baltimore [1797–99] [2] p. 33½ cm.

Song, pfte. acc. Arr. for "guittar," p. [2].
First line: Come buy, who'll buy. DLC, MWA, NN

[234]

—— The same as preceding.
(*In* A collection of new & favorite songs. [A] Philadelphia [ca. 1800] p. [46]–[47])   HFB

Possibly identical with the same song, advertised in December, 1797, as "published at Carr's Musical Repository, Market street," Philadelphia.

.ITTLE SALLY. Sung by Mrs. Oldmixon in the Shipwreck. New York, Printed and sold by George Gilfert, No. 177 Broadway [ca. 1799] 1 l. 31½ cm.

Song, pfte. acc.
First line same as preceding.

Sung by Mrs. Oldmixon in the first Philadelphia performance of *The shipwreck*, March 2, 1798, and undoubtedly also in the first New York performance, February 18, 1799, as she had become a member of the New York company at this time. No copy of the cast for this performance is available.

                                                      DLC, JFD, MWA, NRU–Mus

:HE LITTLE SINGING GIRL. A new favorite song. Boston, Printed & sold at P. A. von Hagen, junᵗ & cos. Musical magazine, No. 55 Marlboro street & at G. Gilfert's musical store, New York. Also the new songs Come buy my wooden ware, Mounseer Nong Tong Paw, Adams & Washington & Megen Oh Oh Megen EE in the Castle spectre [1799] [2] p. 33 cm.

Song, pfte. acc.
First line: I'm turned of twenty and a maid.
Composed by James Hook.
Advertised in May, 1799.   DLC, JFD, LSL, MWA, N, NN

:HE LITTLE SINGING GIRL. Sung by Mrs. Mountain at Vauxhall Gardens. Composed by Mr. Hook. New York, Printed & sold by S. Howe, No. 320 Pearl street. Price 25 cents. [1799–1800] [2] p. 33 cm.

Song, pfte. acc.
First line same as preceding.   MWA

.ITTLE TAFFLINE, or The silken sash. A favorite song. Sung by Mrs. Marshall. Composed by Storace. Price 25 cents. Printed and sold at B. Carr's Musical repository, Philadelphia; J. Carr's, Baltimore & J. Hewitts, N. York [1798] [2] p. 32½ cm.

Song, pfte. acc.
First line: Should e'er the fortune be my lot.   LSL

Advertised in April, 1798, as "published at Carr's Musical Repository," Philadelphia.

*THE LITTLE YANKEE SAILOR.
This "musical farce, never performed . . . the music selected by the author [?] from Shield, Musslwecet [!], Hook, Dibdin, R. Taylor, etc. The accompaniments by Mr. Gillingham," was to be performed at Philadelphia, on May 27, 1795.

LO! I QUIT MY NATIVE SKIES] Song. Tune, President's march.
(*In* New [American] patriotic songs, added to a collection of songs by C. Dibdin. Philadelphia, 1799. p. 319–320)
Words only.
Title from first line.   DLC, MWA, NHi, NN, RPJCB

LOB UND ANBETUNG DES GOTTMENSCHEN am Tage der Einweihung der neuen Orgel in der Deutsch-Evangelisch-Lutherischen Zions-Kirche in Philadelphia, den 10ten October, 1 [790]. Philadelphia, Gedruckt bey Johanes McCulloch, und zu finden bey David Ott und Heinrich Dickhaut 1790. 1 p. l., 9 p. 15½ x 19½ cm.

Prefatory statement by David Ott, Heinrich Dickhaut, and Friedrich Noltenius, p. [2].
For mixed chorus. Open score.
First line: Sprich sie! Sprich sie, des Donners auf Sina des Donners auf Sina dumpfe.
Composed by David Ott.
DLC copy mutilated. Lower right-hand corner of title page torn.　　DLC

*THE LOCK AND KEY.
This "new musical entertainment," libretto by Prince Hoare, music by William Shield (1796), was to have its first performance at New York, on March 8, 1799, with "orchestra accompanyments" by Victor Pelissier.

LOISA. Composed by J. Fisin. New York, Printed & sold at J. & M. Paff's music store, No. 127 Broad Way [1799–1803] [2] p. 32 cm.

Song, pfte. acc.
First line: The passing bell no longer toll'd.
J. Fisin: James Fisin.　　DLC

LONDON MARCH.
See Military amusement, p. 17.

Perhaps this should be "Loudon" instead of "London." *Cf.* Lord Loudon's grenadiers march in *The compleat tutor for the fife* . . . p. 12.

*LOOSE EVERY SAIL
Song. Advertised in March, 1796, as published "at Carr's Musical Repository, William Street," New York.

LOOSE WERE HER TRESSES. From Collins' Ode on the Passions. [New York] Printed by B. Carr. Price 20 cents. [1796] [2] p. 33½ cm.

At foot of p. [2]: Sold at J. Carrs Music Store, Baltimore.
Song, pfte. acc.
First line same as title.
Composed by Tommaso Giordani.　　ES, LSL, MWA

———— The same as preceding, but without additional imprint at foot of p. [2]
McD-W

"As sung by Miss Broadhurst," advertised in February, 1796, as "published . . . printed and sold by Benjamin Carr," New York.

LOOSE WERE HER TRESSES. From Collins' Ode on the Passions. Composed by Sig. Giordani. [Philadelphia] Publish'd by G. Willig, 165 Market st. [1795–1797] [2] p. 33½ cm.

Song, pfte. acc.
First line same as title.
Probably published ca. 1796.　　DLC, MNSt, MWA, PP-K

LOOSE WERE HER TRESSES SEEN.
(*In* The gentleman's amusement, ed. by R. Shaw. Philadelphia [1794-96] p. 82)

Melody only, flute (or violin) with accompanying text.
First line same as title.
Followed by *When nights were cold.*
In No. 10, ca. 1796. PHi, PP-K

LORD ALEXANDER GORDON'S REEL. Arranged as a rondo for the pianoforte by I. G. C. Schetky.
(*In* The musical journal for the piano forte, ed. by B. Carr. Baltimore [1800] v. 1, no. [10], p. (18)–(19).)

Pfte. 2 hds.
I. G. C. Schetky; Johann Georg Christoff Schetky.

DLC, ES, LSL, MWA, MdHi, NN, NRU–Mus

LORD CAMARTHEN'S MARCH.
See Compleat tutor for the fife . . . p. 25.

LORD LOUDON'S GRENADIERS MARCH.
See Compleat tutor for the fife . . . p. 12.

THE LORD OF THE MANOR. A comic opera as it is performed at the Theatre Royal, Drury-Lane, with a preface by the author. Philadelphia, Printed by William Spotswood, Front street, 1790. xv, [2], 18–71 p. 16 cm.

Libretto to opera by William Jackson of Exeter (1780).
Title-page, verso blank; preface, p. (v)–xv; dramatis personae, p. [16]; text, p. [17]–71. DLC, NIC

THE LORD OF THE MANOR. A comic opera in three acts. As performed with universal applause by The American Company. Philadelphia, Printed and sold by Henry Taylor. 1791. 63 p. 16 cm.

Libretto.
Title-page; dramatis personae, p. [2]; text, p. [3]–63. DLC

LOUIS XVI LAMENTATION.
(*In* The Philadelphia pocket companion for guittar or clarinett [Philadelphia, 1794] v. 1, p. 16–17)

Melody only, with accompanying text.
First line: The awful day approaches fast.
Composed by John A. Stevenson. MWA

LOUISA'S COMPLAINT. From Mrs. Robinson's novel of Nancenza. The music by Krumpholtz. New York, Printed for G. Gilfert & co. at their Musical magazine, No. 191 Broadway [1794–95] [2] p. 32½ cm.

Song, pfte. acc.
First line: In this sad and silent gloom.
Composed by Johann Baptist Krumpholz.
Nancenza: Vancenza. DLC, JFD, NN, NRU–Mus, RPJCB

Also advertised in March, 1795, as "published and to be had at G. Willig's Musical Magazine, No. 165 Market street," Philadelphia. This issue not located.

LOUISA'S WOE. Alternative title of *The faded lilly*, by R. Taylor.

*LOVE AND WAR.
Song. Advertised in November, 1800, as "Published at P. A. Von Hagen's Piano Forte Warehouse, No. 3 Cornhill," Boston.

LOVE FROM THE HEART. Sung by Signr. Storace. Philadelphia, Printed and sold by G. Willig, Market street, No. 185 [1798–1804] [2] p. 33 cm.
Song, pfte. acc.
First line: Love from the heart all its danger concealing. DLC, MWA, PP-K

LOVE IN A VILLAGE. A comic opera. Written by Mr. Bickerstaff. A performed at the New Theatre, in Philadelphia. From the press of M Carey. March 1, 1794. 58, [2] p. 16½ cm.

Libretto to Thomas Arne's opera.
Title-page, verso blank; "Table of the songs with the names of the severa composers. A new overture by Mr. Abel," p. 3; dramatis personae, p. [4] text, p. [5]–58; list of "books printed by Mathew Carey," p. [59]–[60].

DLC, ICN, MWA, NN, PPL, RPJCF

Music for the libretto was composed by Giardini (1757), Abel (1760), Arne (1762), Baildon and Bernard (1763). The advertisement in Dunlap's *Daily American advertiser*, March 1, 1794, may follow as a curiosity:

LOVE IN A VILLAGE. At four o'clock this afternoon will be published (Price twenty cents) By Mathew Carey, No. 118 Market Street . . .

The opera was performed by the Old American Company "with entire new accompaniments by Mr. Pelisier" at the Theatre, Cedar street, Philadelphia, September 24, 1794.

LOVE SHALL BE MY GUIDE. A favorite song. Sung by Miss Milne. Composed by Mr. Hook. New York, Printed & sold at G. Gilfert & cos Musical magazine, No. 209 Broad Way [1795] [2] p. 33 cm.
Song, pfte. acc.
First line: Tho' scarce sixteen by men I'm told. DLC, JFD, RPJCB

LOVE SHALL BE MY GUIDE. A favorite song. Sung by Miss Milne at Vauxhall gardens. Composed by Mr. Hook. New York, Printed for and sold at I. C. Mollers musical store, No. 58 Vesey street [1797] [2] p. 30½ cm.
Song, pfte. acc.
First line same as preceding. NN

LOVE SOFT ILLUSION. A favorite song in the opera of the Castle of Andalusia. The composition of this song by Bertoni. Pr. 25 ct. [n. p., n. d.] 54–55 p. 32 cm.
Song, pfte. acc.
First line: Love soft illusion, pleasing delusion.
Apparently a reprint from *The musical repertory*, Boston [No. IV, 1797–99] *The Castle of Andalusia*, by Samuel Arnold. ES, MB

LOVE, THOU MAD'NING POWER, ETC. A favorite new song by Gluck. (*In* The universal asylum, Philadelphia, October, 1790. p. 272–274)
Song, pfte. acc.
First line same as title. DLC (etc.)

[238]

LOVELY HANNAH. Philadelphia, Published by G. Willig, No. 185 Market st. [1798–1804] [2] p. 34 cm.

Song, pfte. acc.
First line: Ah lovely Hannah do not slight. NRU–Mus

LOVELY HANNAH. The words by a gentleman of this city. Philadelphia, Published by G. Willig, No. 185 Market st. [1798–1804] [2] p. 32½ cm.

Song, pfte. acc.
First line same as preceding. PP–K

THE LOVELY LASS. A new song. Words by Mr. Brown. Set by Mr. Selby. (*In* The Massachusetts magazine, Boston, July, 1790. p. 443–444)

Song, pfte. acc.
First line: O lend dear maid thy patient ear. DLC (etc.)

LOVELY NAN. Written and composed by Mr. Dibdin. Price 20 cents. Printed & sold at B. Carr's Musical repositories in New York and Philadelphia & by J. Carr, Baltimore.
(*In* The gentleman's amusement, ed. by R. Shaw. Philadelphia [1794–96] p. 78–79)

Song, pfte. acc. Arr. for flute, p. 79.
First line: Sweet is the ship that under sail.
In No. 10, 1796. PHi, PP–K

———— Separate issue of preceding, ca. 1796 NN

LOVELY NAN BY DIBDIN.
(*In* Elegant extracts for the German flute or violin. Philadelphia [1798] bk. 3, p. 2–3)

Melody only, flute or violin, with accompanying text.
First line same as preceding. DLC, NN

LOVELY NANCY.
See Compleat tutor for the fife . . . p. 28.

LOVELY NYMPH.
See The select songster. New Haven, 1786. p. 32.

[LOVELY NYMPH NOW CEASE TO LANGUISH]
See The select songster. New Haven, 1786. p. 33.
Text not identical with the preceding.

A LOVELY ROSE
(*In* [Moller & Capron's monthly numbers] The second number [Philadelphia, 1793] p. 13)

Song, pfte. acc., followed by arr. for the German flute.
First line: A lovely rose my Henry brought. DLC

LOVELY SPRING. By Mr. Swan.
(*In* The songster's assistant, ed. by T. Swan. Suffield [ca. 1800] p. 10–11)
Song, pfte. acc.
First line: Lovely Spring is just returning. CtY, MB

[239]

LOVELY STELLA.
(*In* The American musical miscellany. Northampton, 1798. p. 238-241)
Duet, treble voices, with accompanying text.
Instrumental prelude and postlude.
First line: Bright Sol at length by Thetis woo'd. DLC (etc.)

See also [Bright Sol at length].

*LOVE'S PROBATION.
Song. Advertised in August, 1798, among "patriotic and other favourite songs," as "just published and for sale at Wm. Howe's wholesale and retail warehouse, 320 Pearl street," New York.

*LOYAL AND HUMOROUS SONGS.
In the *New York gazette and Weekly Mercury*, October 11, 1779, appeared the following advertisement:

This day will be published, Variety of LOYAL AND HUMOROUS SONGS, On recent Occasions: Birth and Coronation odes, Poems, serious and sarcastical, Martial airs and choruses, Constitutional toasts and sentiments, calculated to promote loyalty and unanimity.

By a Briton in New York; with a Copy of a Letter from E . . . H . . . in London to Dr. Rogers in New York, 1770.

Declaring them the mischief brewing
How some divines contemplate ruin.

To which is added, several favourite old songs, with some new ones, by respectable subscribers, concluding with a *Cantata*, called the *Procession*, with the standard of faction, containing recitatives, airs and songs, characterizing the most violent Persecutors of the New York Loyalists.

The Copies already subscribed for will be delivered as soon after Publication as possible . . .

Evans (16326) notes the publication of the above, printed by Hugh Gaine. New York, 1779.

LUBIN'S RURAL COT.
(*In* The Philadelphia pocket companion for guittar or clarinett [Philadelphia, 1794] v. 1, p. 4-5)

Melody only, with accompanying text.
First line: Returning home across the plain. MWA

THE LUCKY ESCAPE. Written and composed by Dibdin.
(*In* Young's vocal and instrumental musical miscellany. Philadelphia [1793-95] p. 53-54)

Song, pfte. acc.
First line: I that once was a ploughman a sailor am now.
From *Private theatricals*, by Charles Dibdin.
In No. 7, ca. 1794. DLC

[240]

THE LUCKY ESCAPE. Written and composed by Dibdin. (20 cet.
Philadelphia, Sold at Carr's Musical repositary [!] & by H. & P. Rice, No. ‹
Market street.
(*In* The gentleman's amusement, ed. by R. Shaw. Philadelphia [1794–96]
p. 22–23)

Song, pfte. acc.
First line same as preceding.
In No. 3, issued between May, 1794 and February, 1795.　　　　DLC, PHi

———— Separate issue of preceding, ca. 1794.　　　　　　　　　　LSL

THE LUCKY ESCAPE.
　　(*In* Elegant extracts for the German flute or violin.　Baltimore [1794] bk. 1,
　　p. 26–28)

Melody only, flute or violin, with accompanying text.
First line same as preceding.　　　　　　　　　　　　　　　　　DLC, NN

———— The same.
　　(*In* The American musical miscellany.　Northampton, 1798.　p. 13–16)

Melody only, with accompanying text.
First line same as preceding.　　　　　　　　　　　　　　　　　DLC (etc.)

———— I that once was a ploughman.　A favorite song.　Written, composed,
and sung by Mr. Dibdin at his entertainment of the Private theatricals.
(*In* The musical repertory.　Boston [1796–97] No. III, p. 34–35)

Song, pfte. acc.
First line same as title.　　　　　　　　　　　　　　　　　　　DLC

*THE LUCKY ESCAPE, or the Ploughman turned sailor.
　　This "new pantomime dance, composed by Mr. Francis," was performed for
the first time at the New Theatre, Philadelphia, March 14, 1796.　It was
"founded on Dibdin's celebrated ballad of that name.　The music selected
from his most admired songs, and adapted with new accompaniments and
an overture, by Mr. [Alexander] Reinagle."

THE LUCKY HIT.
　　See Country *Dances.*

LUCY GRAY OF ALLENDALE.
　　(*In* The favorite songs, by Mr. Hook.　Philadelphia [1794–95]　p. 6)

Song, pfte. acc.
First line: O have you seen the blushing rose.　　　　　　　　McD–W, NN

———— Separate issue of preceding, ca. 1794–95.　　　　　　　CdeW

—— ——— The same.
　　(*In* Elegant extracts for the German flute or violin.　Philadelphia [1796]
bk. 2, p. 16)

Melody only, flute or violin, with accompanying text.
First line same as preceding.　　　　　　　　　　　　　　　　DLC, NN

[241]

CY GRAY OF ALLENDALE [n. p., n. d.]   p. 37.   32½ cm.
At head of title: Musical Journal, No. 17.   Vocal section.
Song, pfte. acc.
First line same as preceding.   LSL

Since p. 37 is lacking in No. 17 (Vocal section) of Carr's *Musical journal for the piano forte*, Baltimore, 1800, it would seem at first sight that this must be a re-issue of that missing page. This inference, however, proves incorrect (*cf. Waving willow*) and it may be that Carr published an earlier collection of which this formed p. 37 and *Waving willow*, p. 49. This imprint might then be the same as that of *Waving willow*, viz., "Published at B. Carr's Musical repositories, New York & Philadelphia & J. Carr's, Baltimore" and should probably be dated ca. 1796. It is possible, however, that both of these numbers were originally planned for the *Musical journal* (as we know it) but later discarded and issued separately.

LUCY OR SELIM'S COMPLAINT. A favorite song. Composed by Mr. Hook. Published at B. Carr's Musical repositories, Philadelphia, New York & J. Carr's Baltimore. Price one quarter dollar.
(*In* The gentleman's amusement, ed. by R. Shaw. Philadelphia [1794–96] p. (88)–(89).)

Song, pfte. acc.   Arr. for flute and for "guittar," p. (89).
First line: Night o'er the world her curtain hung.

In No. 11, 1796.   PHi, PP–K

———— Separate issue of preceding, ca. 1796.   ABHu, CdeW,
     CSmH, DLC, ES, JFD, LSL, McD–W, MdHi, MWA, PHi, RPJCB
In PHi copy arr. for guitar (p. 89) is torn off.

———— The same.
New York, Printed & sold at J. Hewitt's Musical repository, No. 131 William street. Sold also by B. Carr, Philadelphia & J. Carr, Baltimore. Price 25 cents. [1797–99]   [2] p.   32½ cm.

Song, pfte. acc.
First line same as preceding.
Followed on p. [2] by "Nancy, sung in the opera of the Smugglers," by Thomas Attwood.   ES, MB, PP–K

———— The same as preceding.
(*In* A collection of new & favorite songs. [A] Philadelphia [ca. 1800] p. [140]–[141])   HFB

———— The same. New York, Printed for P. Weldon, No. 76 Chambers street. Price 25 cents [ca. 1800]   2 p.   33½ cm.

Song, pfte. acc.
First line same as preceding.   ES

LUCY OR SELIMS COMPLAINT.
(*In* Elegant extracts for the German flute or violin. Philadelphia [1798] bk. 3, p. 21)

Melody only, flute or violin, with accompanying text.
First line same as preceding.   DLC, NN

[242]

LUCY OR SELIMS COMPLAINT. Boston, Printed & sold by P. A. von
Hagen & co. at their imported piano forte warehouse No. 3 Cornhill.
Also by G. Gilfert, New York [ca. 1799] [2] p. 33½ cm.

Song, pfte. acc. Arr. for "guittar," p. [2].
First line same as preceding. RPB, RPJCB

LULLABY. A favorite ballad in the comic opera of the Pirates. Composed by
Mr. Storace. Philadelphia, Printed for Carr & co., at their Musical repository, No. 136 High street. Where may be had all the newest music reprinted
from European publications. Likewise an elegant assortment of piano
fortes, guittars, flutes, violins and other musical articles of superior quality.
(In The favorite songs from the Pirates, by S. Storace. Philadelphia
[1793] p. (2)–(4).)

Song, pfte. acc. Arr. for German flute, p. (4).
First line: Peaceful slumb'ring on the ocean HFB

———— Separate issue of preceding, 1793.
CtY, DLC, McD–W, MWA, NN, PU

LULLABY. A favorite ballad in the opera of the Pirates.
(In Young's vocal and instrumental musical miscellany. Philadelphia
[1793–95] p. 52)

Song, pfte. acc.
First line same as preceding.
In No. 7, ca. 1794.
At top of page, last stanza of "When first this humble roof I knew" from
The lord of the manor, by William Jackson of Exeter. The first line of this
stanza: Content and peace the dwelling shar'd. DLC

———— Separate issue of preceding, but with page numbered 4, and added imprint at bottom of page: "New York, Published by I. Young & co." Published
probably 1792–93. cf. Young Lubin was a shepherd boy. DLC, FS

The DLC copy forms the verso of: [When a little merry he] A favorite song
sung by Mrs. Marshall in the new musical drama called the Purse. Engraved
& published by J. Young & sold at Carr's Repository's Phila?, N. York &
Baltimore [ca. 1795]

LULLABY. A favorite song in the Pirates. New York, Printed and sold by
G. Gilfert & co., No. 209 Broadway [1795] 1 l. 33½ cm.

Song, pfte. acc.
First line same as preceding. DLC, JFD, PU, RPJCB

LULLABY. From the opera of the Pirates.
(In The gentleman's amusement, ed. by R. Shaw. Philadelphia [1794–96]
p. 48–49)

Melody (for flute or violin) with accompanying text.
First line same as preceding.
In No. 6, 1795–96. DLC (lacks p. 48), PHi (lacks p. 49)

LULLABY. A favorite ballad in the comic opera of the Pirates. Composed by Mr. Storace. Boston, Printed for W. Norman, No. 75 Newbury street. Pr. 20 c⁴ [1796–99] 72–73 p. 32½ cm.

Song, pfte. acc.
First line same as preceding. ES

——— The same as preceding, except that the imprint "W. Norman, No. 75 Newbury" has been erased, and "G. Graupner, No. 6 Franklir [!]" substituted. ca. 1800. DLC, JFD

LULLABY. A favorite song. Sung in the opera of the Pirates. New York, Printed & sold by G. Gilfert, No. 177 Broadway [1797–1801] 1 l. 33 cm.

Song, pfte. acc.
First line same as preceding. DLC, JFD, MWA

LULLABY.
(*In* Elegant extracts for the German flute or violin. Baltimore [1794] bk. 1 p. 36)

Melody only, flute or violin, with accompanying text.
First line same as preceding. DLC, NN

——— The same.
(*In* The American musical miscellany Northampton, 1798. p. 233–234)

Melody only, with accompanying text.
First line same as preceding. DLC (etc.)

——— The same.
Boston, Printed & sold at P. A. von Hagen & cos. Musical magazine, No. 62 Newbury street [1798–99] 1 l. 32 cm.

Song, pfte. acc.
First line same as preceding. ES, LSL, MB, RPB, RPJCB

THE LULLABY OF CORRELLI. Selected from his celebrated 8ᵗʰ Concerto. Composed purposely for the celebration of the Nativity of Our Saviour. N. B. The lullaby is play'd at that part of the celebration where the infant Saviour is suppos'd to be rock'd to slumber by the Virgin Mary.
(*In* The musical journal for the piano forte, ed. by B. Carr. Baltimore [1800] v. 2, no. 28. p. (5)–(8).)

At head of title: Decʳ 22, 1800. Journal No. 28. Instrumental.
Pfte. 2 hds. DLC, ES, LSL, NN

MA BELLE COQUETTE. A favorite song. Composed by Mr. Hook. [Philadelphia] Printed for I. C. Moller, No. 136 North Third street. Where may be had a great variety of the newest vocal and instrumental music [1793] [2] p. 31 cm.

Song, pfte. acc.
First line: Ma belle coquette, ah why disdain.
In Moller's address "136" should be "163." Hopk., PP–K

——— The same as preceding, except that "I. C. Moller, No. 136 North Third" has been erased and "G. Willig, No. 165 Market" has been substituted. 1795–97. DLC, McD–W, NBuG, PU, RPJCB

[244]

MA BELLE COQUETTE. A favorite song. Sung by Mrs. Pownall, Writt
by Mr. Swift. Composed by Mr. Hook. New York, Printed and sold b
G. Gilfert & co. [1794–95] [2] p. 34 cm.

Song, pfte. acc.
First line same as preceding.
For date, cf. 'Tis no fault of mine. DLC, JFD, RPJCB

MA CHERE AMIE. A fvorite [!] song. Written by a lady and set to music
by Mr. Hook.
(In A collection of favorite songs, arr. by A. Reinagle. Philadelphia [1789 ?]
p. 7–8)

Song, pfte. acc.
First line same as title.
In lower margin of p. 8: J. Aitken, Sculpt. DLC

MA CHERE ET MON CHER. Composed by R. Taylor. Philadelphia,
Printed & sold by G. Willig, No. 185 Market street [1798–1804] [2] p.
31½ cm.

Song, pfte. acc.
First line: The day is gone and night is come. PP–K

*MACBETH.
The tragedy was advertised for performance at New York, January 14,
1795, as "written by Shakespeare, music by Locke. With new scenery by
Ciceri and Scotch music between the acts, adapted and compiled by Mr.
[Benjamin] Carr."

MAD PEG BY DIBDIN. Published at B. Carr's Musical repositories, New
York & Philadelphia, & J. Carr's, Baltimore (Price 25 cts.) [ca. 1795–96]
[2] p. 30½ cm.
Song, pfte. acc. Arr. for flute, p. [2].
First line: The gloomy night stalked slow away.
From Will of the wisp. DLC, NN

MADRIGAL.
See Evening amusement, p. 29.

THE MAID OF LODI. The music and words collected by Mr. Shield when
in Italy. Printed and sold at Carr's music store, Baltimore [ca. 1800?]
1 l. 33 cm.

Song, pfte. acc.
First line: I sing the maid of Lodi.

On verso of New York serenading waltz. Philadelphia, Printed for B. Carr.
MWA

THE MAID OF THE ALPS. Alternative title of Javotte, by Joseph Willson.

*THE MAID OF THE MILL.
Samuel Arnold's opera (1765), libretto by Bickerstaff, was advertised for
performance at New York, April 11, 1796, "with new orchestra accompanyments" by Victor Pelissier, and for first performance at Boston, March 5,
1797, "with all the original airs, chorusses, etc. Orchestra accompaniments
by Mons. Leaumont."

1E MAID WITH THE BOSOM OF SNOW. Sung with great applause by
Mr. Hodgkinson at the Philharmonic Society. Composed by J. Mazzinghi.
[n. p., n. d.] [2] p. 32 cm.

Song, pfte. acc. Three staves.
First line: O bright as the morning the maid of the wold.
Probably published in New York, ca. 1799–1800.   DLC, MH

MAIDENS LISTEN I'LL DISCOVER. A new song. Sung by Mrs. Cooke.
The words by Dr. Houlton.
(In a collection of favorite songs, by Mr. Hook. New York [1799–1801]
bk. [2] p. 16–18)

Song, pfte. acc.
First line same as title.   DLC

MAJOR ANDRE.
(In The American musical miscellany. Northampton, 1798. p. 198–199)
Melody only, with accompanying text.
First line: Return enraptur'd hours.   DLC (etc.)

MAJOR ANDRE'S COMPLAINT. Price 12 cents. Philadelphia, Printed at
Carr & co.'s Musical repository [1794] 1 l. 33½ cm.

Song, pfte. acc.
First line: Return enraptur'd hours.
Not identical with "Major Andre." Although the text is essentially the
same, the music is entirely different.
Advertised as published in February, 1794.
                      DLC, ES, JFD, LSL, McD–W, MdHi, RPJCB
MALBROOK.
See Evening amusement, p. 29.

THE MALE COQUETTE.
(In Nine new songs, by I. B. Gauline. Philadelphia [ca. 1800] p. 5–6)
Song, pfte. acc.
First line: From maiden to maiden I rove.
I. B. Gauline: John B. Gauline.   ES, MdHi

THE MANSION OF PEACE.
(In Elegant extracts for the German flute or violin. Baltimore [1794]
bk. 1, p. 29)
Melody only, flute or violin, with accompanying text.
First line: A rose, a rose, from her bosom has stray'd.
The usual recitative, Soft Zephir on thy balmy wing is here omitted.
Composed by Samuel Webbe, Sr.   DLC, NN

THE MANSION OF PEACE. Composed by Mr. Webbe. New York, Printed
& sold at J. Hewitt's Musical repository, No. 131 William street [1797–99]
[2] p. 33½ cm.
Imprint at foot of p. [2].
Song, pfte. acc. Arr. for flute, p. [2].
First line: Soft Zephir on thy balmy wing.   DLC, MB, NN

Probably identical with issue advertised in December, 1797, as "published
at Carr's Musical Repository, Market Street," Philadelphia.

[246]

—— The same as preceding.
(*In* A collection of new & favorite songs.   [A] Philadelphia [ca. 1800] p. [18]–
[19])   HFB

THE MANSION OF PEACE.   Sung by Mr. Chambers at the opening of the
New Theatre. The words by a lady. Composed by Mr. Webbe. Phila-·
delphia, Printed and sold by G. Willig, Market street, No. 185 [1798–1804]
[2] p.   30½ cm.

Song, pfte. acc.
First line: Soft Zephyr on thy balmy wing.   DLC, NN, PP–K, PU

The New Theatre in Philadelphia was opened with concerts early in February,
1793.   Its formal opening as a theatre (delayed because of the yellow fever
epidemic) occurred a year later.

MANUSCRIPT COLLECTION OF HYMNS, songs, etc.   [n. p., n. d.]   10 x 19
cm. This collection contains besides hymns, etc., the tunes of the following
secular pieces:

        p. 41 The Federals march
               Burbanks march
           42 The Grand spy
               Jefferson and liberty
           43 Primrose Hill
               No luck about the house
           44 March to Boston
               Blew bird
           45 The Bells of Scotland
        45–46 In the cottage
           47 Blue eyed Mary
           48 Lady Washington's favorite
               The Grand troop
           49 Day of glory
           50 The Federals march
               The Whippoorwill
               March for Bonaparts imperial guard
           51 Installation march

Though this collection undoubtedly was compiled later than 1800, it figures
here as of importance for the history of popular American 18th century
music (Sonneck).

MARCH.   By Moller.
(*With* The President's march.   By Pheil [!] [n. p., n. d.])
Pfte. 2 hds.
Moller: John C. Moller.   DLC

MARCH by Mr. Jas. Bremner.
Harpsichord piece contained in a MS. volume of "Lessons."
Belonged to Francis Hopkinson's library.   Hopk.

MARCH composed for and dedicated to the United States Marine Corps by a
young lady of Charleston, S. C.   Philadelphia, Published & sold at G. Willig's
Musical magazine [n. d.]   [2] p.   32½ cm.

Pfte. 2 hds.

Published perhaps after 1800.
United States Marine Corps founded 1775.   DLC, NN

MARCH FOR BONAPARTS IMPERIAL GUARD.
See Manuscript collection of hymns, songs, etc. (50).

MARCH IN BLUE BEARD.
(*In* The musical journal for the piano forte, ed. by B. Carr. Baltimore
[1800] v. 1, no. [10], p. (20).)

Pfte. 2 hds.   DLC, ES, LSL, MWA, MdHi, NN, NRU–Mus

——— Separate issue of preceding, 1800   ABHu, MdHi, NN

THE MARCH IN BLUE BEARD. Arranged for two performers on the piano
forte, by R. Taylor. [n. p., n. d.] 2–5 p. 33½ cm.

Pfte. 4 hds.
On lower margins the letter "E."
Published probably ca. 1800.   DLC, RPJCB

THE CELEBRATED MARCH IN BLUE BEARD. For the piano forte, violin
or flute. New York, Sold by I. and M. Paff, No. 127 Broadway [1799–1803]
[2] p. 33½ cm.

Imprint at foot of p. [2].
Pfte. 2 hds. (violin or flute)
Followed by "The favorite march in Feudel [!] Times" (M. Kelly), p. [2].
          DLC

Michael Kelly's *Blue Beard* was first performed in Philadelphia, May 24,
1799; in New York, March 8, 1802.

MARCH IN SCIPIO.
See Compleat tutor for the fife . . . p. 24.

MARCH IN THE DESERTER.
See Military amusement, p. 16.

MARCH MAESTOSO.
(*In* [Moller & Capron's monthly numbers] The fourth number [Philadelphia,
1793] p. 29)

Pfte. 2 hds.
This is the well-known march from the opera *Henry the Fourth* by Martini.
          NN

MARCH OF THE THIRTY-FIFTH REGIMENT.
See Compleat tutor for the fife . . . p. 14.

MARCH TO BOSTON.
See Manuscript collection of hymns, songs, etc. (44).

THE FAVORITE MARCH IN FEUDEL [!] TIMES. Arranged for the piano
forte, violin and flute. New York, Sold by J. and M. Paff, No. 127 Broadway
[1799–1803] 1 l. 32½ cm.
(*With* The celebrated *March* in Blue Beard [M. Kelly] New York [ca. 1800])

Pfte. 2 hds. (violin and flute)
Feudal times, by Michael Kelly.   DLC

[248]

THE FAVORITE MARCH IN PIZZARRO. Composed by J. Hewitt. New York, Printed & sold at J. Hewitt's Musical repository, No. 23 Maiden Lane [ca. 1800] 1 l. 31½ cm.

Pfte. 2 hds.   DLC, NHi

THE FAVORITE MARCH IN PIZZARRO. New York, Published by John Paff [n. d.] 1 l. 31½ cm.

Pfte. 2 hds.
Not identical with the preceding.
Followed by: Waltz.   NN

From imprint, to be dated 1798, or after 1810. Since *Pizarro, or The Spaniards in Peru* was not performed in America until December, 1800, the former date seems out of the question. However, since Reinagle and Taylor composed the incidental music for the Philadelphia production as Hewitt did for New York (*cf. Pizarro in Peru*) it seems likely that this *March* was composed by one of them. In such case the later date of publication is hard to understand.

For further discussion of this confused authorship *cf.* Sonneck's "Early American Operas" in *Sammelbände der Internationalen Musikgesellschaft*, 1904–1905, p. 488; music, p. 494.

THE FAVORITE MARCH IN RAMAH DROOG. Composed by Mazzinghi & Reeve. New York, Printed & sold by G. Gilfert at his Musical magazine, No. 177 Broadway [1797–1801] 1 l. 31½ cm.

Pfte. 2 hds.   MWA

GRAND MARCH FROM THE OPERA OF THE PRISONER. Mozart.
(*In* The gentleman's amusement, ed. by R. Shaw. Philadelphia [1794–1796] p. 17)

Duet for flutes (or violins). Two staves.
In No. 2, May, 1794.   DLC, PHi

This is not a March from Attwood's opera, *The prisoner*, but appears in his score as "Where the banners of glory are streaming," which in turn is the aria "Non più andrai," from Mozart's *Le nozze di Figaro*. This march is a simplified and abbreviated arrangement of the above.

GRAND MARCH IN ALEXANDER THE GREAT. The music by A. Reinagle.
(*In* Mr. *Francis's ballroom assistant.* Philadelphia, ca. 1800. p. 6)
Pfte. 2 hds.   JFD, McD–W

MARCHE TURQUE. Par Crammer. New York, Published by J. Paff [n. d.] [2] p. 32½ cm.

Pfte. 2 hds.
Published possibly as early as 1798.
Crammer: J. B. Cramer.   DLC

———— The same.
[n. p., n. d.] [2] p. 32½ cm.

Pfte. 2 hds.
Sonneck gives date, ca. 1800.   DLC

[249]

THREE MARCHES. For the flute, violin or piano forte. Composed by
James Hewitt. [n. p., n. d.] 1 l. 20½ x 28 cm. (plate size)

Pfte. 2 hds.

Contents:
The New York Rangers march (Complete, four scores)
Governor Jay's march (incomplete)
Third march not given.
Published probably in New York, 179–.
John Jay: Governor of New York, 1795–1801.   NN

THREE NEW MARCHES. Philadelphia, Printed & sold by G. Willig, No.
185 Market street [1798–1804] [2] p. 33 cm.

Pfte. 2 hds.

Contents: Buonaparte's march, called the Pyrenees.—Buonaparte's march,
called the Mantuane.—Prussian march.   DLC, LSL

THE MARCH-GIRL.
See The match-girl.

MARIA ANTOINETTE'S COMPLAINT. In the temple after the execution
of Louis the 16th. Sung by Miss Pool at the oratorios, Mr. Walsh and
Miss Broadhurst at the Ladies' private subscription concerts. The music
by Mr. Percy. To be had at No. 163 North Third street, Philadelphia
[1793–95] 4 p. 33 cm.

Song, pfte. acc.
First line: Hush my soul for heav'n prepare.
This original edition may have been issued by Moller and Capron (or J. C.
Moller) in 1793; or by Willig in 1794–95. In the latter case Willig either
engraved the plate or purchased it from Moller.   NBuG

———— The same as preceding, except that part of the imprint was erased and
"No. 185 Market street" substituted. 1798–1804. This address confirms
Willig's eventual ownership of the above plate.   MWA

MARIAN OWNS HER LOVE. Written by a gentleman of this city. The
music by Haydn. Philadelphia, Printed by G. Willig [n. d.] 1 l. 34 cm.

Song, pfte. acc.
First line: Such passion in my bosom grew.
Published probably ca. 1800.   ABHu, PP–K

MARINE COLLECTIONS.
See Mr. Francis's ballroom assistant.

MARK, MY ALFORD, ALL THE JOYS.
See Songs, duets, and chorusses of "The Children in the wood."
See also The delights of wedded Love.

[MARK'D YOU HER EYE] Song by Mr. Sheridan. Set by Shield.
(In The universal asylum. Philadelphia, December, 1790. p. 412–414)

Song, pfte. acc.
Title from first line.   DLC (etc.)

[250]

THE MARKET LASS. Composed by Mr. Reeve. Price one quarter dollar.
New York, Printed and sold by G. Gilfert & co., at their Musical magazine,
No. 191 Broadway [1794–95] [2] p. 32 cm.

Song, pfte. acc.
First line: Tho' my dad I must own is but poor.   JFD, MWA, RPJCB

THE MARKET LASS. Composed by Mr. Reeve. Printed & sold by B. Carr
at his Musical repositories, New York & Philadelph. Price 20 cts. [1795–96]
[2] p. 33 cm.

Song, pfte. acc.
First line same as preceding.   MWA

MARLBOROUGH'S GHOST. Extracted from a late British publication. Set
to musick by E. Mann of Worcester.
(In The Massachusetts magazine, September, 1789. p. 587–588)

Song, pfte. acc.
First line: Awful hero, Marlb'ro rise.   DLC (etc.)

MARLBOROUGH'S GHOST.
(In The American musical miscellany. Northampton, 1798. p. 46–49)

Song, pfte. acc. Three staves.
First line same as preceding.   DLC (etc.)

LA MARMOTTE. Avec acompagnement de harpe ou forte piano. Philadelphia, Published by Mr. Trisobio [1797–98] [2] p. 33½ cm.

Song, pfte. acc.
First line: J'ai quitté la montagne.   CdeW, DLC, NN

THE MARQUIS OF GRANBY'S . . . march.
See Granby's march.

THE MARRIED MAN. A new song set to music.
(In The Boston magazine, January, 1784. Opposite p. 113)

Song, pfte. acc.
First line: I am married and happy.   DLC (etc.)

THE MARSEILLES HYMN in French & English. Price one quarter dollar.
Philadelphia, Printed for Carr & co., at their Musical repository, No. 136
High street [1793] [3] p. 34 cm.

Song, pfte. acc.
English text, p. [1]–[2]; French text, Marche des Marseillois, words and tune
only, p. [3].
First lines: Ye sons of France awake to glory.—Allons enfans de la patrie.
Composed by Claude Joseph Rouget de Lisle.   DLC, ES, McD–W, NN

"The Marseillois hymn in French and English" was advertised in December,
1793, as "published . . . printed singly" by "B. Carr & Co. Musical Repository, Southside of Market Street," Philadelphia. As to seeming inconsistency
in the address, cf. The match girl.

[251]

THE MARSEILLES HYMN in French and English. New York, Printed and sold by G. Gilfert & Co., No. 177 Broadway [1796] 3 p. 32½ cm.
Song, pfte. acc.
English text, p. 1-2; French text, Marche des Marseillois, words and tune, p. 3.
First lines same as preceding.   DLC

THE MARSEILLES HYMN. Philadelphia, Printed for G. Willig at his Musical magazin [!], No. 165 Market street [1795-97] [2] p. 33 cm.
Song, pfte. acc.
English text, p. [1]-[2]; French text, Marche des Marseillois, words and tune only, p. [2].
First lines same as preceding.
Sonneck's date: ca. 1796.   DLC, ES, JFD, PU

THE MARSEILLES HYMN.
See Evening amusement, p. 22.

THE MARSEILLES HYMN. Boston, Printed & sold by P. A. von Hagen, junior & cos. at their imported piano forte & music warehouse, No. 62 Newbury street [1798-99] [2] p. 32 cm.
Song, pfte. acc.
First line: Ye sons of France awake to glory.   JFD, MWA, N

MARSEILLES MARCH.
See Military amusement, p. 11.

MARTINI'S MARCH in Henry the IV.
See Evening amusement, p. 30.
See also March maestoso.

MARTINI'S OVERTURE.
(In [Moller & Capron's monthly numbers] The fourth number [Philadelphia, 1793] p. 23-28.)
Pfte. 2 hds.
This is Martini's Overture to the opera Henry the Fourth.
Martini: Giovanni Martini [Johann Paul Aegidius Schwartzendorf].   NN

*MARTIN'S [!] OVERTURE.
See Martin's [!] Overture.

MARY OF SUNBURY HILL. A new song. Sung by Mr. Dignum.
(In A collection of favorite songs, by Mr. Hook. New York [1799-1801] bk. [2], p. 4-5.)
Song, pfte. acc.
First line: Tho' the poets of yore tell of beauties a score.   DLC

MARY WILL SMILE. Sung by Miss Broadhurst. Written by a gentleman of Philadelphia. Composed by B. Carr. Printed & sold at B. Carr's Musical repository, Philadelphia; J. Carr's, Baltimore & J. Hewitt's, New York. (Price 25 cents)
(In Three ballads, by B. Carr. Philadelphia [1799] p. 4-5)
Song, pfte. acc.
First line: The morn was fresh and pure the gale.   JFD

[252]

—— Reprint (or one of the "seperate [!] sheets") ca. 1799.   ABHu, DLC

MARYLAND.
See United States country *Dances*, p. 12.

THE MARYLAND HORNPIPE.
See Mr. *Francis's ballroom assistant*, p. 12.

MARY'S BOWER.   Boston, Printed & sold at P. A. von Hagen & cos. imported
piano forte warehouse, No. 3 Cornhill.   And to be had at G. Gilfert, New
York.   Also where may be had Alone beside a stream & Adams march [ca.
1799]   [2] p.   32 cm.

Below imprint: For the piano forte, German flute or violin.

Song, pfte. acc.
First line: To Mary's bower haste away.   ES, JFD, MB, RPJCB

MARY'S DREAM, or Sandy's ghost.   Price 20 cents.   Philadelphia, Printed
for Carr and co., at their Musical repository, No. 136 High street [1793]   [2] p.
33½ cm.

Song, pfte. acc.   Arr. for "guittar" or flute, p. [2].
First line: The moon had climb'd the highest hill.
Composed by John Relfe.   ABHu, DLC, ES, LSL, MdHi

Advertised in December, 1793, as "published . . . printed singly . . . by
B. Carr & Co. Musical Repository.   Southside of Market Street," Philadelphia.

As regards inconsistency in address, *cf. The match girl.*

MARY'S DREAM, or Sandy's ghost.   Philadelphia, By G. Willig [n. d.]   p. 6.
31½ cm.

Imprint at foot of page.
Song, pfte. acc.
First line same as preceding.
Published probably 179–.   MWA

—— The same as preceding but without imprint, 179–.   DLC, PU

—— The same as preceding (without imprint) comprising the second page
(numbered 6) of a detached leaf from some collection.   On p. 5: *The smart
cockade.*   NN

—— The same.
Boston, Printed & sold by P. A. von Hagen, Junior & co. at their Musical
magazine, No. 62 Newbury street [1798–99]   1 l.   32 cm.

Song, pfte. acc.
First line same as preceding.   ES, MB, RPJCB

—— The same.
[n. p., n. d.]   1 l.   33 cm.

Song, pfte. acc.
First line same as preceding.
Published probably 179–.   DLC

[253]

MARY'S DREAM, or Sandy's ghost.
(*In* The American musical miscellany. Northampton, 1798. p. 195–198)
Melody and bass, with accompanying text.
First line: The moon had clim'd [!] the highest hill. DLC (etc.)

MASONIC DIRGE. Composed by the Rev. T. M. Harris, at the request of the Grand Lodge of Massachasetts [!]
(*In* Sacred dirges [Oliver Holden] Boston [1800] p. 22–23)
Air and chorus.
First line: While ev'ry orator and bard displays.
CSmH, DLC, ICN, MB, MH, MHi, MWA, NHi, NN, RPB

*MASONIC ODE BY JAMES HEWITT.
Advertised for performance "after the play" at New York, April 26, 1794, as "never performed in America. The music composed for the occasion by Mr. Hewit [!]."

*MASONIC ODE BY PETER VALTON.
On Monday, December 27, 1772, following St. John's Day, was performed at Charleston, S. C., an "Ode. [Words] by Sir Egerton . . . with voices and instruments . . . The music composed by Brother Peter Valton." The account of the occasion was given in the *South Carolina gazette*, December 31, 1772, with the words of the ode. It consisted of recitatives, airs, a duet and a chorus. The first recitative began: Behold the social band appears.

*MASONIC OVERTURE BY ALEXANDER REINAGLE.
A "new masonic overture" by Reinagle was to precede a "new pantomimical entertainment called Harlequin Freemason," at the New Theatre, Philadelphia, April 21, 1800.

MASONIC. Songs, oratorio, odes, anthems, prologues, epilogues, and toasts: adapted to the different degrees of Masonry. Waterford [New York], Compiled, printed & published by Brother James Lyon, in the Year of light vMDCCXCVII [1797] vii, [5]–140 p. 12½ cm.
Words only.
The Oratorio mentioned in the title is *Solomon's temple* [As it was performed for the benefit of sick and distressed Free Masons] p. [5]–15.
Odes, anthems, songs, p. 16–130; prologue and epilogues, p. [131]–137; toasts, p. [138]–140. DLC (lacks p. 19–26, 57–60, 115–122)

*THE MASQUE.
"The Masque, a new song book," was advertised without further particulars in Holt's *New York journal*, July 30, 1767, as "This day.—published, and sold, by Garrat Noel."

MASSACHUSETTS HOP.
See United States country *Dances*, p. 5.

MASSACHUSETTS MARCH. Composed by Mr. Frederick Granger of Boston.
(*In* The Massachusetts magazine, September, 1791. p. 579)
At head of title: For the Massachusetts magazine.
Pfte. 2 hds. DLC (etc.)

*MASSACHUSETTS MUSICAL MAGAZINE, by Oliver Holden.
We read in the *Massachusetts spy* (Worcester), March 14, 1793:

[254]

Proposal, for printing by Subscription, in monthly numbers, a new work, to be entitled, The MASSACHUSETTS MUSICAL MAGAZINE, intended principally, to furnish Musical Societies and other Practitioners in that pleasing art, with a choice and valuable collection of odes, anthems, dirges, and other favourite pieces of musick. Principally original American compositions. By Oliver Holden, author of the American Harmony.

As a work of this kind has never been attempted in this part of the Union, and as many have expressed a wish to see such a publication, it is presumed that it will be found exceeding useful, and meet a very general acceptance with all those who wish to possess themselves of a valuable collection of tunes, which are not to be found in musick books calculated only for schools and publick worship.

CONDITIONS

I. It shall be printed on fine paper, each number to contain eight pages octavo, sewed in blue covers.

II. The first number shall be ready for delivery the first week in April next, provided a sufficient number of subscribers can be obtained previous to that time.

III. The price to subscribers will be only six pence for each number, to be paid when the books are delivered.

IV. Those who subscribe for six sets, shall have a seventh gratis.

V. At the expiration of 12 months the volume will be completed, to which will be added a preface and index, and a list of subscriber's names.

As the price is set so exceedingly low the editor flatters himself that little persuasion will be necessary to effect a speedy and extensive subscription; he therefore wishes that those who hold subscription papers will return them to him before the middle of March, that he may determine on the number of copies to print. He also wishes that such gentlemen and ladies who have by them any favourite pieces of musick, of the above description, would favour him with correct copies of the same. Letters directed to the Editor in Charlestown, respecting this publication, will be gratefully received.

MASSACHUSETTS SONG OF LIBERTY.
See Liberty song.

MASTER HARRIS'S STRATHSPEY.
See Mr. *Francis's ballroom assistant*, p. 12.

*MASTER WALSH.
Song. Advertised in January, 1798, as "just published by J. Hewitt, No. 131 William st.," New York.

THE MATCH BOY. A favorite song. Sung by Mr. Dignum with great applause at Vauxhall Gardens. Composed by Mr. Hook. New York, Sold by J. and M. Paff [n. d.] [2] p. 32 cm.

After title: For the piano forte, flute or violin.
Song, pfte. acc.
First line: Ye wealthy and proud while in splendor ye roll.
Published probably 179–. An issue with identical title is listed in BM Cat. as ca. 1793. MB

THE MATCH GIRL.   A favorite song.   Composed by a lady.   Price 20 cents.
Philadelphia, Printed for Carr & co., at their Musical repository, No. 136
High street [1793]   [2] p.   33 cm.

Song, pfte. acc.   Arr. for "guittar," p. [2].
First line: Come buy of poor Mary good matches.

ABHu, ES, HFB, MWA, NBuG

As *The march-girl*, advertised in December, 1793, as "published . . . printed
singly" by "B. Carr & Co Musical Repository, No. 122   South side of Market
street," Philadelphia.

This inconsistency in address arose presumably from the fact that Carr & Co.
had recently moved from 136 High street to the address just given, and had
failed to make the corresponding change in their imprint.   It is to be noted
that *High* and *Market* refer to the same street.

THE MATCHLESS FAIR.   A favorite   sonnet.   Compos'd   by   Mr.   Hook.
Price 12 cents.   [Philadelphia] Publish'd by G. Willig, 163 North Third
street [1794–95]   1 l.   31½ cm.

Imprint at foot of page.
Song, pfte. acc., followed by arr. for guitar.
First line: Where could love the treasure steal.   PU

THE MATCHLESS FAIR.   Boston, Publish'd by P. A. von Hagen, No. 3
Cornhill & G. Gilfert, New York [ca. 1800]   1 l.   32 cm.

Imprint at foot of page.
Song, pfte. acc., followed by arr. for "guittar."
First line same as preceding.
Published possibly as early as 1799.   ES, N

MATILDA.   A favorite ballad.   Sung by Mrs. Chambers in the comedy of
Love's frailties.   Philadelphia, Printed and sold by G. Willig, Market street,
No. 185 [1798–1804]   [2] p.   29½ cm.

Song, pfte. acc.   Arr. for "guittar," p. [2].
First line: The rose had scarce bloom'd on Matilda's fair cheek.
                                                            JFD, RPJCB
MAY.   Alternative title of *Ode to May*, by James Fisin.

MAY.   A favourite pastoral.   Sung by Miss Leary.   Vauxhall.
(*In* A collection of favorite songs, divided into two books.   Arr. by A.
Reinagle.   Philadelphia [1789?]   bk. 2, p. 2–3.)

Song, pfte. acc.
First line: The hawthorn is sweetly in bloom.   CdeW, DLC, PU

*MAY DAY IN TOWN, or New York in an uproar.
This "comic opera, in 2 acts (never performed) written by the author of
'The Contrast' . . . the music compiled from the most eminent masters.
With an overture and accompaniments.   The songs of the opera to be sold
on the evening of the performance," was advertised for first performance on
May 18, 1787, at New York.   The author was Royall Tyler; the composer
is unknown.

[256]

MAY DAY MORN. A favorite sonnett. Composed by Mr. Hook. [New York] Printed for James Hewitt & sold at his Musical repository, No. 131 William street & by B. Carr, Philadelphia & J. Carr, Baltimore [1797–99] [2] p. 33½ cm.

Elaborately engraved caption.
Song, pfte. acc. Arr. for "guittar," p. [2].
First line: Sweet music wake the May day morn.   DLC, MB

———— The same as preceding.
(In A collection of new & favorite songs. [A] Philadelphia [ca. 1800] p. [80]–[81].   HFB

MAY I NEVER BE MARRIED. Alternative title of The kiss, by James Hook.

MAY MORNING. A new song. Written by the author of Anna and Gentle zephyr. The music composed by P. A. von Hagen. Boston, Printed & sold at P. A. von Hagen's piano forte warehouse, No. 4 Old Massachusetts bank, Head of the Mall & at the music store, No. 3 Cornhill. Also at G. Gilferts warehouse, N. York; David Vintons, Providence; W. R. Wilder, New-port; B. Macanulty, Salem; E. M. Blunt, Newbury-port; Isaac Stanwood, Portsmouth & E. A. Jenks, Portland. (Entered according to law) [n. d.] [2] p. 32 cm.

Below imprint: For the voice, P. F. flute & violin.
Song, pfte. acc. Arr. for guitar or clarinet, p. [2].
First line: The mellow lustre of the morn.
Published probably after 1800.   LSL, MB, RPB, RPJCB

MEDDLEY [!] with the most favorite airs and variations. Composed by I. C. Moller. Printed and sold at G. Willig? Musical magazin [!], No. 165 Market street, Philad. [1795–97] 2–6 p. 32 cm.

Imprint at foot of p. 2.
Pfte. 2 hds.
Sonneck gives date ca. 1796.
      DLC, JFD, NN, PPL, PP–K, RPJCB (lacks p. 4–5)

MEDLEY. New York, Printed and sold by G. Gilfert, No. 177 Broadway [1797–1801] [2] p. 33 cm.
Pfte. 2 hds.   DLC, NN

THE MEDLEY; or, New Philadelphia songster. Containing, A collection of the most approved songs among which are many of the most celebrated ballads, songs, duets, &c which were sung at the New theatre. Philadelphia: Printed by Neale & Kammerer, jun. 1795. 222 p. 9 x 17 cm.   NHi, RPB

A MEDLEY DUETTO adapted for two German flutes from the Federal overture, selected & composed by B. Carr.
(In The gentleman's amusement, ed. by R. Shaw. Philadelphia [1794–96] p. 42–45)

Duet for two flutes.
In Nos. 5 and 6, March 1, 1795.   DLC (lacks p. 45), PHi

A MEDLEY DUETTO, adapted from the overture to the Children in the wood.
Composed by Dr. Arnold.
(*In* The gentleman's amusement, ed. by R. Shaw. Philadelphia [1794–96]
p. 50–51)

Duet for flutes (or violins). Two staves.
In No. 6, 1795–96. DLC, PHi

*MEDLEY OVERTURE . . . by Alexander Reinagle.
See Medley *Overture* . . . by Alexander Reinagle.

*MEDLEY OVERTURE with variations by Chateaudieu [!].
See Medley *Overture* with variations by Chateaudieu.

MEG OF WAPPING. Written & composed by Mr. Dibdin & sung by him
in his Entertainment called ye General election. New York, Printed & sold
at J. Hewitt's Musical repository, No. 131 William street. Sold also by
B. Carr, Philadelphia & J. Carr, Baltimore. Pr. 25 cts.
(*In* A collection of new & favorite songs. [A] Philadelphia [ca. 1800] p.
[100]–[101])

Song, pfte. acc. Arr. for two flutes, p. [101].
First line: 'Twas landlady Meg that made such rare flip. HFB

Original issue advertised in December, 1797, as "published at Carr's Musical
Repository, Market-street," Philadelphia. Also advertised in January, 1798,
as "just published, by J. Hewitt, No. 131 William st.," New York. Possibly
both editions were identical.

MEGEN, OH! OH MEGEN EE. The much admired song in the Castle Spectre.
Boston, Printed & sold at P. A. von Hagen, junr. & cos. Musical magazine,
No. 55, Marlboro street. Where also may be had the favorite song of
Mounseer Nong Tong Paw & the latest published songs just received from
London [1799] 1 l. 31 cm.

Below title: For the piano forte, German flute or violin.
Imprint at foot of page.
First line: Sleep you or wake you, lady bright.
The castle spectre, by Michael Kelly. ES, JFD, MB, MWA, RPJCB

THE MEN ARE ALL ROVERS ALIKE. A new song. Sung by Miss Howells.
New York, Printed & sold at G. Gilfert's music store, No. 177 Broadway.
(*In* A collection of favorite songs, by Mr. Hook. New York [1799–1801]
bk. [1], p. 2–3)

Song, pfte. acc.
First line: To me yet in teens mama would oft say. DLC

————— Separate issue of preceding, 1799–1801. DLC

*THE MERMAID, or Nautical songster.
Advertised in April, 1793, as "for sale at the printing office of John Harrisson,
Yorick Head, No. 3 Peck-Slip," New York.

THE MERMAID: or Nautical songster. Being a new collection of favorite
sea songs. The sixth edition, with additions.
Here social mirth serenely smiles,
And joyful songs inspire the breast;

[258]

Music the weight of care beguiles,
And lulls each gloomy tho't to rest.

Copy right secured. New York, Printed and sold by J. Harrison, Yovick's
[!] head, No. 3 Peck-slip. 1798. 1, 82 p. 9 x 16 cm. RPB

THE MERMAID'S SONG. A canzonett by Haydn. Published & sold by G.
Willig, No. 185 Market street, Philadelphia [1798–1804] [2] p. 31½ cm.

Song, pfte. acc.
First line: Now the dancing sunbeams play.
NN, NRU–Mus, PHi, PP–K

THE MERMAID'S SONG.
(*In* Three . . . *Canzonetts* by Haydn. Philadelphia [1799] p. 2–3)

Song, pfte. acc.
First line same as preceding. NN

———— Separate issue of preceding, ca. 1799. ABHu, JFD, MB, McD–W, NN,
RPJCB

MERRILY DANCE THE QUAKER.
See Compleat tutor for the fife . . . p. 27.

MERRILY SINGS. Alternative title of *Away with melancholy*.

*THE MERRY COMPANION, containing twenty-six of the newest and most
approved songs, sung at the theatres in Boston, and other genteel places of
amusement. Boston, Printed and sold by J. White, near Charles River
Bridge. 1798. 16 mo.

THE MERRIMACK.
See No. 1 of a new sett of *Cotilions*.

THE MERRY PIPING LAD. A ballad in the Scots taste. Composed by R.
Taylor. Philadelphia, Printed for the Author, No. 96 North Sixth st. and
sold at B. Carr's Musical repositorys, Market st., Philadelphia; William st.,
N. York & at I. Carr's, Market st., Baltimore. Price ¼ of a dollar. [1795]
[2] p. 33 cm.

Song, pfte. acc.
First line: With the sun I rise at morn. CtY, DLC, ES, PP–K

Advertised for sale in March, 1795, "at Carr's Musical Repositories, Philadelphia and William street, New York . . ."

———— The same.
[n. p., n. d.] [2] p. 34 cm.

Song, pfte. acc.
First line same as preceding.
Published probably ca. 1795. NRU–Mus

MIDAS. A burletta in two acts by Kane O'Hara, esq. As performed at the
theatre in Boston. Printed at the Apollo Press in Boston by Belknap
rnd [!] Hall for William P Blake, No. 59 Cornhill, and William T. Clap,
No. 90 Newbury street [1794] 24 p. 17 cm.

Libretto.
Title-page. Verso, dramatis personae; text, p. [3]–24. MWA

THE MIDSHIPMAN. Sung by Miss Arnold of the New theatre with universal applause in the opera of the Rival soldiers. Philadelphia, Published by G. Willig, No. 185 Market street [ca. 1800] 1 l. 33 cm.

Song, pfte. acc.
First line: I'm here or there a jolly dog.

DLC, LSL, McD–W, MWA, NHi, PHi, PP–K

In first line of last stanza, the above edition gives the name *Barry*. The Von Hagen edition of similar date gives *Truxton*, both popular naval heroes. In original form: Royal William.

Miss Arnold sang in *The rival soldiers* at the New theatre, Philadelphia, December 6, 1799.

The rival soldiers, also known as *Sprigs of laurel*, by William Shield.

THE MIDSHIPMAN. Sung in the opera of Rival soldiers. Boston, Printed & sold at P. A. von Hagens music store, No. 3 Cornhill, and to be had at G. Gilfert's pianoforte ware house, No. 177 Broadway, New York [ca. 1800] 1 l. 30½ cm.

Song, pfte. acc.
First line same as preceding.
Published possibly as early as 1799.　　　　　　　　　　　　　　DLC, ES, NN

MILITARY AMUSEMENT. A collection of twenty four of the most favorite marches. Adapted for one or two German flute's, violin's, fife's, or oboe's, &c. Price 75 cents. Printed & sold at B. Carr's Musical repositories, Philadelphia and New York & J. Carr's, Baltimore [1796] 24 p. 15½ x 23 cm.

Title-page, verso numbered 2. Music, p. 2–23; index, p. 24.
For flutes, violins, fifes oboes, etc.
Two parts. Open score. Two staves throughout.

Contents:
　　p.　2　New French march. Le reviel [!] du peuple.
　　　　3　Presidents march [by Philip Phile].
　　　　4　Washingtons march.
　　　　5　Presidents new march.
　　　　6　General Knox's march.
　　　　7　Janizary's march.
　　　　8　Quick step in the Battle of Prague [by F. Koczwara].
　　8–9　Duke of Yorks march.
　10–11　Duke of Yorks troop.
　　　11　Marseilles march.
　　　12　Granbys march.
　12–13　Third Coldstream march.
　　　13　Duke of Gloster's march.
　　　14　Slow march in the Battle of Prague.
　　　15　Archers march.
　　　　　[Since this title is given in the Index (p. 24) as "March in the Archers" it is probable that we have here one of the few surviving numbers from Benjamin Carr's opera, *The archers*.]
　　　16　March in the Deserter [by Charles Dibdin].
　　　17　London march.
　　　18　General Waynes new march.
　　　19　General Wolfes march.

20 Belleisle march.
20 A Scotch reveilly [!].
21 Mozarts march. [Arr. of "Non più andrai" from *The marriage of Figaro*.]
22 Dead march [from *Saul*, by Händel].
23 Handels march ["See the conquering hero comes" from *Judas Maccabaeus*.]
23 Eugenes march.   DLC

Advertised in August, 1796, among "musical publications, printed by J. Carr, Music Store, No. 6 Gay street, Baltimore, and B. Carr's Musical Repositories, Market Street, Philadelphia and William street, New York."

THE MILITARY GLORY OF GREAT BRITAIN, an entertainment given by the late candidates for bachelor's degree, at the close of the anniversary commencement, held in Nassau Hall, New Jersey, September 29th, 1762. Philadelphia: William Bradford.   MDCCLXII.   15 p.   17½ x 13½ cm.

Title-page, verso blank.   Text, p. 3–15.
Contains four pieces of engraved music, consisting of choruses with instrumental accompaniments on five folding leaves.

Both the poet and the composer of this dramatic cantata seem to be unknown, but there are reasons for connecting James Lyon, the composer who took his degree of A. M. at Nassau Hall on the same day, with the curious "Entertainment."

A skeleton description of the work may follow:

INTRODUCTORY CHORUS [precedes p. 3].
Britain's Glory, sung at the Anniversary.
Allegro [in C maj.] "Triumphant fame ascends the skies."
Enter first Speaker; proclaiming Britannia Conqueror by way of Introduction to the next speech (p. 4–7).

CHORUS 2.   ALLEGRO.   Commencement in Nassau Hall in New Jersey, Sept. 29th, 1762.   [betw. p. 4–5, in C maj.]   "Gallia's sons shall vaunt no more."
Enter second Speaker; who enumerates several of the most important Conquests of Great Britain with encomiums on some of the principal generals (p. 4–7).

CHORUS 3d.   LARGO.   [in C. maj. betw. p. 8–9]   "Propitious Powers who guard our state."
Enter Eugenio; who, by way of Dialogue with Cleander, gives an account of the reduction of the Havannah (p. 8–12).

CHORUS 4th.   PIU ALLEGRO.   [in C. maj. betw. p. 12–13]   "Glory, triumph, vict'ry, fame forever crown Britannia's Name."
Enter fourth Speaker; suddenly transported, "What mean these Strains? these glad triumphant," (p. 13–14).

PART OF FOURTH CHORUS, "Glory, triumph, Vict'ry, Fame For ever crown Britannia's Name." [The music betw. p. 14–15 exactly the same as before except that the last five and a half measures are omitted in this later form.]
Enter fifth Speaker; who closes the whole with a solemn wish for the continued prosperity of the British nation.

CHORUS 5th to be sung in the tune of chorus 3d Allegro [on the same leaf
as Part of Fourth Chorus]:
"While mountains poise the balanced globe.

——— ——— ——— ——— ——— ——— ———

British Fame shall bear the prize;
And in a blaze of peerless glory rise."

    CSmH, CtY, DLC, NHi (lacks music), NN, PHi, Princeton U, RPB
See also Sonneck's *Francis Hopkinson . . . and James Lyon,* p. 129–131.

*MILITARY SYMPHONY by W. S. Morgan.
A "grand military symphony, accompanied by kettle drums," etc., composed
by Mr. Morgan, "was to be played at a 'grand concert,' " Boston, April 20,
1774.

THE MILITIA MARCH.
See Compleat tutor for the fife . . . p. 16.

A FAVORITE MINUET. Composed by G. C. Schetkey.
(*In* Twelve favorite pieces. Arr. by A. Reinagle. Philadelphia [1789?]
p. 15)

Pfte. 2 hds.
G. C. Schetkey: presumably J. George Schetky.   DLC

MINUIT [!] as danced at the theatres, Philadelphia & Baltimore.
(*In* Mr. *Francis's ballroom assistant.* Philadelphia, ca. 1800. p. 10)

Pfte. 2 hds.
Composed or arranged by Alexander Reinagle.   JFD, McD–W

MINUET DE LA COUR.
See Evening amusement, p. 31.

MINUETTO. By Pleyel.
(*In* The musical journal for the piano forte, ed. by B. Carr. Baltimore
[1800] v. 1, no. [12], p. (22)–(23).)

Pfte. 2 hds.
Pleyel: Ignaz Pleyel.   DLC, ES, LSL, NN, NRU–Mus

——— The same.

(*In* The musical journal for the flute or violin. Baltimore [1800] no. 12,
p. 24)

Duet for flutes or violins (or flute and violin).
Forms the first section of preceding.   DLC

MINUETTO & TRIO. By Pleyel.
(*In* The musical journal for the piano forte, ed. by B. Carr. Baltimore
[1800] v. 1, no. [12] p. (24).)

Pfte. 2 hds.   DLC, ES, LSL, NN, NRU–Mus

——— The same.

(*In* The musical journal for the flute or violin. Baltimore [1800] no. 12,
p. 22–23)

Duet for flutes or violins (or flute and violin).   DLC

[262]

MINUETTO WITH EIGHT VARIATIONS for the flute and violoncello. Composed by Geo. E⁴ Saliment. Printed by B. Carr & sold at his Musical respositories, New York & Phila⁴ Price ½ Dol.
(*In* The gentleman's amusement, ed by R. Shaw. Philadelphia [1794–96] p. 75–(77).)

Duet for flute and 'cello. "Flauto," p. 75–(77). Violoncello, separate leaf, unpaged.
In No. 10, ca. 1796.
PP–K copy has p. 75–(77) [*i. e.* the flute part] all eight variations complete, but lacks the 'cello part. So also PHi. DLC copy has 'cello part complete, but lacks p. (77), variations seven and eight for flute.   DLC, PHi, PP–K

MIRA OF THE VILLAGE PLAIN. French air. Written by G. Gray, esqʳ
(*In* Nine new songs, by I. B. Gauline. Philadelphia [ca. 1800] p. 17–18.)

Song, pfte. acc.
First line: On yonder spray the linnet sings.
I. B. Gauline: John B. Gauline.   ES, MdHi

THE MIRACULOUS MILL, or, the Old ground young.
Advertised for performance at Baltimore, November 21, 1795, as a "new pantomimical dance, composed by Mr. Francis . . . the music composed by Mr. De Marque."

MISCELLANEOUS AND INCOMPLETE [?] COLLECTION]
See [Miscellaneous and incomplete [?] *Collection*].

MISCELLANEOUS QUARTET by Alexander Reinagle.
A "miscellaneous quartett Mr. Reinagle" was to be played at the last City Concert, Philadelphia, March 16, 1793.

MISS ASHMORE'S CHOICE COLLECTION OF SONGS.
The new song book being Miss Ashmore's Favorite collection of songs, as sung at the theatres and public gardens in London and Dublin. To which are prefix'd the songs of the Padlock, Lionel and Clarissa, and many other opera songs, never before published. Containing in the whole, near three hundred: In which are many originals, and a variety of other songs, by different composers, which upon comparing, will be justly allowed (by every person) to be the best of the kind yet published, and may well be termed *"The Beauties of all the Songs selected."* The above mentioned book makes a neat small pocket volume, adorn'd with an elegant frontispiece of Miss Ashmore, & will be sold by the Publisher at the same Price they are sold for in Boston or Ireland.

Thus advertised in the *Boston evening post*, November 25, 1771, as "just published and to be sold by William McAlpine, in Marlborough street . . ."

In the *New York Mercury*, August 22, 1774, appeared an advertisement which is almost literally the same except that it begins, "Just published and to be sold at Mr. William Bailey's Store, in Beaver street [New York] Miss Ashmore's Choice collection of Songs, such as are sung etc. . . ."

Query: Were these two different reprints and did they contain music?

MISS SMITH'S WALTZ.
See Mr. *Francis's ballroom assistant*, p. 13.

[THE MOCK ITALIAN TRIO]   Sung by Miss Broadhurst, Mrs. Oldmixon
Mr. Marshall in the Critic.
(*In* The gentleman's amusement, ed. by R. Shaw.   Philadelphia [1794–9
p. 24–25)

Melody only, flute (or violin) with accompanying text.
First line: I left my country and my friends.
In No. 3, 1794–95.
Also called *Italian mock trio* and *Italian monk trio*.   DLC, PH

———— The Italien [!] mock trio.   Sung by Miss Broadhurst, Miss Brett & M
Tyler.   New York, Printed and sold by G. Gilfert & co., No. 177 Broadwa
[1796]   1 l.   33½ cm.

Song (or trio?), pfte. acc.
First line same as preceding.   DL

———— The same as preceding, except that in the imprint "& co." has been erase(
thus dating the present imprint as 1797–1801.   Probably issued about 179
                                                                JFD, MW

———— The Italian monk trio.   Sung by Mrs. Oldmixon, Mrs. Warrel and M
Marshall.   Printed and sold by G. Willig, Philadelphia, Mark. street, I
185 [1798–1804]   1 l.   33½ cm.

Song (or trio?), pfte. acc.
First line same as preceding.   DLC, PHi, MW.

The first performance of Sheridan's comedy *The critic* in which Miss Broad
hurst, Mrs. Oldmixon and Mr. Marshall took part was given in Philadelphia
December 22, 1794.   Mrs. Oldmixon and Miss Broadhurst were listed in th
cast as "Italian girls" and undoubtedly sang in this trio, although there ar
no "Italian girls" listed in the play proper and no such trio.   In point of fac
this is no real trio, but consists of a single voice part throughout, with th
following persistent though not particularly edifying refrain after each of it
three stanzas—"Which goes tang tang tang tang tang."   Perhaps each o
the three singers may have sung a single stanza, all joining in this refrain.

In the cast for a performance of *The critic* in New York, April 22, 179
Mr. Tyler, Miss Broadhurst and Miss A. Brett were listed as "Italian singers"
and presumably sang this same trio.   From *Minerva* (New York), May 17
1796, we learn that "the mock Italian trio, Ting ting tang ta" was to b
sung on the following evening by Miss Broadhurst, Miss Brett and Mr
Tyler, thus for the first time furnishing the title which was thenceforwar(
to cause so much confusion.   As we see from our entry, "Mock Italian" ha
already become "Italien [!] mock," with a still further transformation soo
to follow.

James Boaden's tragedy *The Italian monk* (perhaps with some of Arnold'
music) was first performed in America in 1798, and now our "Italian mock"
trio becomes the "Italian monk" trio, and hence associated with Arnold'
opera, *The Italian monk* and duly credited to him as its composer.   Thi
seems unwarranted, however, for we have seen that the Trio antedate
Arnold's opera by some two or three years (*cf. The Italian monk*) and probably
has no inherent connection with it—except its name.

Another interesting problem: Why was this trio so commonly introduced
into Sheridan's comedy of *The critic?*

THE MOCKING-BIRD: A collection of songs, a number of which are set to music. Philadelphia: Printed and sold by John M'Culloch, No. 1, North Third Street, 1793.

MODERN MUSIC.
(*In* The psalm-singers amusement, by William Billings. Boston, 1781. p. 72-77)

After title: N. B. After the audience are seated & the performers have taken the pitch slyly from the leader, the song begins.
Four-part chorus. Open score.

First stanza:
> To tickle the ear is our present intention,
> We are met for a concert of modern invention.
> The audience are seated
> Expecting to be treated
> With a piece of the best. CSmH, DLC, ICN, MB, MHi

MOGGIE, OR THE HIGHLAND BELLE. A parody on The Blue Bell of Scotland. Composed by R. Taylor. Printed and sold by R. Shaw at his music store, No. 13 South Fourth strc⁺ Philadelphia [n. d.] [2] p. 33 cm.

Song, pfte. acc. Arr. for the German flute, p. [2].
First line: Ah where and oh where is your Highland lassie gone.
Published possibly as early as 1800. DLC, ES, JFD, MB, RPJCB

MOLL IN THE WAD. A much admired duett. Sung in Larry's return. New York, Printed & sold at J. Hewitt's Musical repository. Price 12½ cents.
(*In* A collection of new & favorite songs. [A] Philadelphia [ca. 1800] p. [191])

Duet, pfte. acc.
First line: Miss Jenny don't think that I care for you. HFB

MOLLER & CAPRON'S MONTHLY NUMBERS]
Four issues have so far been found, and it seems unlikely that any more were published.

There were no title-pages, but each *Number* is preceded by a free leaf with an attractive ornamental design representing St. Caecilia playing the organ, an angel at her left playing the German flute. "B. Rebecca invt et delint— G. S. Facius sculp." Below this, "Printed for Moller & Capron, Philadelphia."

The year of publication becomes apparent from the following proposals which appeared in the *Federal gazette*, Philadelphia, March 13, 1793:

> MUSIC. The great scarcity of well adapted music for the pianoforte or harpsichord and particularly songs, has induced the subscribers to publish by subscription in monthly numbers, all the newest vocal and instrumental music, and most favourite songs, duets, catches and glees—as also by permission of the author, a set of canzonetti, composed by a lady in Philadelphia. [Mrs. Pownall?] . . . Moller & Capron.

1. Each subscriber to pay one dollar at the time of subscribing an three shillings on the delivery of each number.
2. Each number to contain six pages.
3. As soon as there is a sufficient number of subscribers, each sub scriber's name shall be inserted in the first number.
4. The first number to be delivered in March.

The first number. Printed and sold by Moller & Capron. Price to a sub scriber 3 shillings, to a none subscriber 6 shillings. Messrs. Moller ‹ Capron have for sale a great variety of music, pianofortis [!] ruled musi paper, as also all sorts of violin strings. [Philadelphia, 1793] 1 p. l 2–8 p. 33½ cm.

"The first number" contains on
p. 2–4 Sinfonia by I. C. Moller. [Arranged for pfte. in E-flat majoı Allegro spirituoso. Minuetto. Rondo. Minuet repeated.]
5 A favorite song by H. Capron. ["Softly as the breezes blowing'
6 A favorite hunting song. ["Hark hark from the Woodlands"]
7–8 A new favorite song by a lady of Philada. ["The cheerful sprin; begins to stay." Arr. for guitar, p. 8]

"The 2d number" contains on
p. 9–12 La Belle Catherine with variations. (In which is introduce the favorite air of the Yellow hair'd lady.) for the harpsichor or piano forte.
13 A lovely rose. [Song, followed by arr. for German flute.]
14–15 Delia. A new song by H. Capron. ["Soft pleasing pains."]

"Third number" contains on
p. 16–18 *Rondo.* By I. C. Moller. [For pfte. in F. major]
19–20 Ye Zephyrs where's my blushing Rose. A favorite song iı answer to the Mansion of peace. [Arr. for German flute oı guitar, p. 20]
21–22 Asteria's fields. By a lady of Philada. [Song, pfte. acc. "A. o'er Asteria's fields I rode."]
22 A new contredance. By H. Capron. [For pfte., in B-flat major 16 bars only]

"The 4ᵗʰ number" contains on
p. 23–25 Martini's overture.
26–27 [Lacking]
28 Martini's overture (concluded).
29 Andante.
March maestoso.
30 The shepherd. A new song. Com: by. H. Capron.

"Martini's overture" (p. 23–28) is his well-known overture to the opera, *Henry the Fourth.* "March maestoso" (p. 29) is the equally well-known march from the same opera. It would seem reasonable 'then to expect to find the "Andante" (p. 29) there also. However, a search through the score of the opera fails to locate it.

Hopk. (First three numbers complete); DLC (First three numbers, lack- ing p. 8 of First number and p. 1,. of Third number); PHi (Third number complete); NN (Third number, lacking p. 1.; Fourth number lacking p. 26–27).

MOLLER'S RONDO
See Moller's *Rondo.*

THE MOMENT.
See Twenty-four American country *Dances,* p. 19.

THE MONCKTON.
See Twenty-four American country *Dances,* p. 2.

MONEY MUSK.
See Evening amusement, p. 17.

A MONODY on the death of the much lamented, the late Lieutenant General
of the Armies of the United States (The music composed by Mr. R. Taylor
and Mr. Reinagle). The principal vocal parts by Mr. Darley, Miss Broadhurst, Mrs. Warrell and Mrs. Oldmixon. Assisted by Messrs. Warren, Cain,
Francis, Robbins, Warrell and Warrell, jun.

This monody on the death of Washington was advertised in *Claypoole's American daily advertiser,* Philadelphia, December 23, 1799, and performed at
the New theatre on the same date.

*A MONODY to the memory of the chiefs who have fallen in the cause of Am-
erican liberty. Accompanied with vocal incantations (the music of which is
entirely new) adapted to the distinct periods of the recital.

Thus advertised in the *Pennsylvania journal,* December 1, 1784, as the opening number of
"Lectures (Being a mixed entertainment of representation and harmony)"
. . . to "be opened on Wednesday the 7th instant."

The entertainment was to be closed by
"A *Rondelay* celebrating the Independence of America. Music, Scenery,
and other Decorations."
In the *Pennsylvania journal* for December 11, we read:
A few copies of the Monody, Rondelay etc. may be purchased at Mr.
Bradford's, or at the Theatre, price one shilling.

MONSIEUR MONG TONG PAW.
See Mounseer Nong Tong Paw.

*MONSTROUS GOOD SONGS FOR 1792. Boston, 1792.

MOORISH MARCH. In the opera of the Mountaineers.
(*In* The musical repertory. Boston [1796] No. I, p. (15).)

Pfte. 2 hds.
At top of page, last part of the song, "I sold a guiltless negro boy."
The mountaineers, by Samuel Arnold.   DLC, NRU–Mus

——— Separate issue of preceding, ca. 1796.   McD–W

MORN.
See Rosy morn.

THE MORN RETURNS IN SAFFRON DREST. In Rosina.
(*In* A collection of favorite songs, divided into two books.   Arr. by *I*
Reinagle.   Philadelphia [1789?] bk. 2, p. 11)

Song, pfte. acc.
First line same as title.
Rosina, by William Shield.   CdeW, DLC, P¨

THE MORNING.   A sonnet for the voice, harpsichord, violin or German flute
(*In* The American musical magazine.   New Haven, Daniel Read, 178◖
p. 16–17)

Song, pfte. (or harpsichord) acc.
First line: Come come my fair one, let us stray.
From *Hours of love*, by James Hook.   CtY, ICN, MB◖

[MORNING] SONNET I.
(*In* The hours of love, by J. Hook.   Philadelphia [ca. 1794] p. 2–3)

Song, pfte. acc.   Arr. for Ger. flute or "guittar," p. 3.
First line same as preceding.   DLC, JFD, LS◗

MORNING.   [Printed & sold by G. Willig, Philadelphia, 1795–97]   2–3 ◖
23½ x 34 cm.

At head of title: Sonnet I.
At foot of p. 2 and 3: C. Tiebout, Sculp., N. Y.
Song, pfte. acc.   Arr. for German flute or "guittar," p. 3.
First line same as preceding.
Imprint supplied from copy of *Evening*, apparently from same collection.

Obviously a detached leaf from a Willig edition of Hook's *Hours of love*.
                                                                NRU–Mu◗

THE MORNING.   Composed by J. Fisin.   New York, Printed & sold by G◖
Gilfert at his music store, Broadway [1797–1802]   [2] p.   31½ cm.

Song, pfte. acc.
First line: Hark, hark, hark, how sweet the milkmaid sings.   MWA

THE MORNING IS UP.   A favorite hunting song.   By William Shield.   New
York, Published by J. Hewitt, No. 131 William street.
(*In* A collection of new & favorite songs. [A] Philadelphia [ca. 1800]   p. [168]-
[169])

Song, pfte. acc.
First line same as title.   HFB

Original issue advertised in January, 1798, as "just published by J. Hewitt,
No. 131 William st.," New York.

MOSS ROSES.   A favorite ballad.   Composed by J. Moorehead.   Philadelphia,
Printed & sold by R. Shaw (music store) No. 13 South 4th street.   Also sold
by J. Carr, Baltimore & J. Hewitt, New York [n. d.]   [2]   p.   32 cm.

Song, pfte. acc.   Arr. for flute or guitar, p. [2].
First line: It was Ireland, sweet place where my daddy was living.
Published possibly as early as 1800.   ES, MB

IOTHER GOOSE'S MELODY; or sonnets for the cradle. In two parts. Part I. Contains the most celebrated songs and lullabies of the old British nurses, calculated to amuse children and to excite them to sleep. Part IId, Those of that sweet songster and nurse of wit and humour, Master William Shakespeare. Embellished with cuts, and illustrated with notes and maxims, historical, philosophical, and critical. The first Worcester edition. Worcester [Massachusetts]: Printed by Isaiah Thomas, and sold at his Book Store. MDCCLXXXV. 94 p., front. 9½ x 6½ cm.   MWA

———— The same. Second Worcester edition. Worcester [Massachusetts]: Printed by Isaiah Thomas and sold at his book store. MDCCXCIV. 94, [2] p. 9½ x 6½ cm.

Title-page identical with that of the first edition except that the phrase "old British nurses" is changed to "good old nurses."

CSmH, MWA

———— The same. Third Worcester edition. Printed at Worcester, Massachusetts, by Isaiah Thomas, jun. Sold wholesale and retail by him. 1799. 94, [2] p. 9½ x 6½ cm.

Title-page identical with that of the second edition.   MWA

The entire work (containing one page of printed music) is given in fac simile in William H. Whitmore's The original Mother Goose melody, Boston, 1892.

The first Worcester edition seems to have been the first American edition of the Mother Goose's melody though some have tried to trace it as far back as 1719 (Boston). Compare for instance Thomas' History of printing.

Isaiah Thomas probably reprinted his Mother Goose's melody from the publication of John Newbury, the English publisher, the first edition of which appeared about 1770, and the seventh in 1777.

MOUNSEER NONG TONG PAW. Written & composed by Mr. Dibdin and sung by him in his new Entertainment called the General election. Price 25 cts. N. York, Printed & sold by W. Howe at his music warehouse, No. 320 Pearl street [1798] 2–4 p. 32½ cm.

Song, pfte. acc. Three staves. Arr. for two flutes, p. 4. First line: John Bull for pastime took a prance. In imprint, "W. Howe" and "No. 320 Pearl street" seem to be of entirely different type from the rest.   MB

Advertised as Monsieur Mong Tong Paw in August, 1798, as "just published and for sale at Wm. Howe's wholesale and retail warehouse, 320 Pearl street," New York.

MOUNSEER NONG TONG PAW. Written & composed by Dibdin and sung by him in his new entertainment The General election. Philadelphia, Printed & sold by G. Willig, No. 185 Market st. [1798–1804] [2] p. 33 cm.

Song, pfte. acc. Arr. for flute or "guittar," p. [2]. First line same as preceding.   ES, PP–K

[269]

MOUNSEER NONG TONG PAW. A favorite song. Boston, Printed & sol at P. A. von Hagen, jun. & co's Musical magazine, No. 55 Marlboro stree Where also may be had the much admired song of the Little singing gir The same may also be had at G. Gilferts Musical magazine, N. York [179 2 p. 31½ cm.

Song, pfte. acc. Arr. for two flutes or violins, p. 2.
First line same as preceding. MB, MW

This "favorite song" as "sung by Mr. Hodgkinson last evening at the The atre, with the greatest applause," Boston, was advertised on March 30, 179 as "this day . . . published at P. A. Von Hagen, jun. and Co's, No. 5 Marlboro' Street."

MOUNSEER NONG TONG PAW. Boston, Printed & sold by P. A. von Hage at his piano forte warehouse, No. 3 Cornhill [ca. 1800] [2] p. 33 cm.

Song, pfte. acc. Arr. for 2 flutes or violins, p. [2].
First line same as preceding.
Published possibly as early as 1799. JFD, LSL, NRU–Mus, RPJCI

MOUNT VERNON. A solo.
(In Sacred dirges [Oliver Holden] Boston [1800] p. 14–15)

Song, pfte. acc. Two staves.
First line: From Vernon's mount behold the hero rise.
CSmH, DLC, ICN, MB, MII, MHi, MWA, NHi, NN, RPI

The "tributory honors" to George Washington, at the "Old South" Meeting House, Boston, in January, 1800, were to conclude with this composition by Oliver Holden.

MOUNT VERNON. L. M. by Jenks. Composed on the death of Gen'l Washington.
(In [The musical harmonist, by Stephen Jenks. New Haven, 1800] p. 9)
Four-part chorus. Open score.
First line: What solemn sounds the ear invade. ICN

THE MOUNTAINEERS, a comic opera. By George Colman, jun. As performed at the Theatre in Boston. Printed at the Apollo Press in Boston, by Joseph Belknap, for William P. Blake, No. 59, Cornhill, 1795. 44, [2] p. 18½ cm.

Libretto to Samuel Arnold's opera (1795).
Text followed by a 2 p. list of "plays and farces, for sale by Wm. P. Blake, No. 59 Cornhill." MB, MWA, NN

THE MOUNTAINEERS. A comic opera. By George Colman, junr, Esq. Author of 'Incle and Yarico,' 'Battle of Hexam' etc. etc. As performed at the Theatre in Boston. Second Boston edition. Printed at Boston by Thomas Hall. Waterstreet for William P. Blake at the Boston Bookstore. 1796. 44, [3] p. 17½ cm.

Libretto.
Title-page; dramatis personae, p. [2]; text, p. [3]–44; advertisement of plays and farces, p. [45]–[47].
MB, MH, MWA, NHi, NN (incomplete), PHi

The mountaineers was to be performed "with accompanyments" by Victor Pelissier at New York, March 30, 1796; with "a new overture composed by R. Taylor . . . The music of the songs, duets, glees, chorusses by Dr. Arnold. The accompaniments by Mr. Reinagle" at Philadelphia, April 18, 1796.

MOUNTAINEERS OF SWITZERLAND. Alternative title of *The archers.*

THE MOUTH OF THE NILE. Overture and four songs, by Thomas Attwood. New York, ca. 1799]   15 p.   34½ cm.

Title-page lacking.   Title supplied from contents.
Verso of p. 15 blank.

Contents:
    p.   1–7 Overture to the Mouth of the Nile.   Composed by T. Attwood.
        8–9 I'm as smart a lad as you'd wish to see.   Sung by Miss Simms.
      10–11 In the midst of the sea.   Sung by Mr. Fawcet.
      12–13 When the world first began.   Sung by Mr. Townshend.
      14–15 Success to Admiral Nelson.   Sung by Mr. Dibdin, Junr

In the *Overture*, title is followed by: New York, Printed & sold by G. Gilfert, Nº 177 Broadway and to be had at P. A. von Hagens Music store, Boston. At head of each song: In the musical entertainment the Mouth of the Nile. New York, Printed & sold by G. Gilfert, Nº 177 Broadway.
Below imprint, p. 8, 12: Attwood.
Below imprint, p. 10, 14: T. Attwood.
The mouth of the Nile was first produced in 1798; given in New York, May 13, 1799.   Its music was published in London in 1799 (*BM Cat.*)
Admiral Nelson's victory at the Battle of the Nile occurred August 1, 1798.

NRU–Mus

A FAVORITE MOVEMENT FOR THE PIANO FORTE by Vanhal.
    (*In* Twelve favorite pieces, arr. by A. Reinagle.   Philadelphia [1789?] p. 7–8)

Pfte. 2 hds.
In lower margin of p. 8: J. Aitken. Sculqt. [!]
Vanhal: J. B. Wanhal.   DLC

——— Separate issue of preceding, but without pagination, ca. 1789.   DLC

MOZART'S MARCH.
    See Military amusement, p. 21.

MR. FRANCIS'S BALLROOM ASSISTANT.
    See Mr. *Francis's ballroom assistant.*

MRS. CASEY.
    See Evening amusement, p. 29.

MRS. FRASER'S STRATHSPAY.
    See Evening amusement, p. 24.

MRS. LT. COL. JOHNSON'S REEL.
    See Twenty-four American country *Dances*, p. 8.

MRS. MADISON'S MINUET. Danced by Mrs. Green and Mr. Francis
Printed and sold at Carr's music store, Baltimore. A. Reinagle [n. d
1 l. 32 cm.

Pfte. 2 hds.
In lower r. h. corner: Ma. Min.
Published presumably ca. 1796, as Miss Willems and Mr. Francis were fellow
players in the New Theatre, Philadelphia, season of 1795–96. Miss Willem
became Mrs. Green in June, 1796. McD–V

MRS. POWNALL'S ADDRESS, in behalf of the French musicians, delivere
on her benefit concert night at Oeller's Hotel, Chestnut Street, Philadelphia
To which are added, Pastoral songs, written by herself at an early period o
life. Also the songs performed at the concerts.—New theatre. Philadelphia
Printed and sold at Story's office Fourth street, nearly opposite the India
Queen Tavern [1793] 4, 28 p. 12 mo.

The *Pastoral songs* have a special title-page, with imprint: Philadelphia
MDCCXIII [!]

Words only. NN

Advertised in March, 1793, as "published . . . printed on writing paper and
new type, containing 30 pages (Price 15 d.) . . ."

The songs referred to were "On by the spur of valeur"; "Kiss me now o
never"; "Poor Tom Bowling"; "Italian song"; "My Poll and my partne
Joe"; "A smile from the girl of my heart"; "Blythe Collin"; "Cottage boy."

The songs were not sung by Mrs. Pownall, but by other members of the
company on February 2. It does not necessarily follow from the above title
that these songs were published with their music or that Mrs. Pownall wrote
the words and the music of all the songs.

MRS. S. DOUGLAS' REEL.
See Twenty-four American country *Dances*, p. 10.

THE MUCH ADMIRED BALLAD OF THE WILLOW.
See The willow.

THE MUCH ADMIR'D DEATH AND BURIAL OF COCK ROBIN.
See Death and burial of Cock Robin.

THE MUCH ADMIRED SONG OF ARABELLA, THE CALEDONIAN
MAID.
See Arabella, the Caledonian maid.

MUIRLAND WILLY. New York, Printed at G. Gilfert & cos. Musical magazine, No. 209 Broadway near St. Pauls, where may be had a great choice of
music & musical instruments of the verry [!] first quality. As also piano
fortes let out on hire and if purchased within three months the hire abated.
[1795] [2] p. 33½ cm.

Song, pfte. acc.
First line: To yon lone cot out on the moor.
Composed by James Hook (*BM Cat.*) JFD, RPJCB

[272]

THE MULBERRY TREE.
Advertised in August, 1798, as "just published and for sale at Wm. Howe's wholesale and retail warehouse, 320 Pearl street," New York.

HE MULTIPLICATION TABLE. For the voice and pianoforte. Composed in a familiar style for juvenile improvement. By Dr. G. K. Jackson. [New York] Printed for the Author. Price 50 cents. Copyright secured [n. d.] 7 p. 33½ cm.
Song, pfte. acc.
First line: Twice 1 is 2.
Possibly published before 1800.   NN

HE MUNICHHAUSEN.
See Twenty-four American country Dances, p. 18.

HE MURM'RING STREAM. A favorite new song. Sung in the opera of Dimond cut dimond. Composed by Mr. Hook. New York, Printed & sold by G. Gilfert, No. 177 Broadway [1797–1801] 1 l. 34 cm.
Song, pfte. acc.
First Line: The murm'ring stream, the linnet's song.   JFD, MWA

MUSIC IS THE VOICE OF LOVE. Sung by Miss Bertles. Vauxhall.
(In A collection of favorite songs, divided into two books. Arr. by A. Reinagle. Philadelphia [1789?] bk. 2, p. 24)
Song, pfte. acc.
First line: Softly sweet the minutes glide.   CdeW, DLC, PU

"A MUSICAL ADDRESS, wrote by a citizen of Pennsylvania on the occasion" and sung by Mrs. Rankin in a "Concert of vocal and instrumental music" on August 9, 1792, at Vauxhall Gardens, was advertised in Dunlap's American daily advertiser, Philadelphia, of same date. First performed on the occasion of Mrs. Rankin's benefit, July 7, 1791.

*MUSICAL BAGATELLES, or 6 little ballads.
Advertised in August, 1799, Baltimore, as for sale at J. Carr's Music Store under "music lately published."

MUSICAL EXTRAVAGANZA in three parts, by R. Taylor.
See Nouvelle entertainment.

[THE MUSICAL HARMONIST, containing concise and easy rules of music together with a collection of the most approved psalm and hymn tunes, fitted to all the various metres. New Haven, Engraved and printed for the Author by A. Doolittle, 1800] 40 p. 13 x 21 cm.
By Stephen Jenks.
First issued in 1799 as New England harmonist.
Imperfect copy. Title supplied from ms. transcript.
Contains (p. 9): Mount Vernon. LM. By Jenks. Composed on the death of Gen'l Washington.   ICN

THE MUSICAL JOURNAL for the flute, or violin. Sold at the following Musical repositories, J. Carr's, Baltimore; J. Chalk's, Philadelphia and J. Hewitt's, New York [1800] 2 p. l., 48 p., 1 l., 48 p. 17 x 23 cm.
At head of title: Vol. [1] of. [The figure 1 is in ink.]
Title-page, verso blank.

On 2nd p. 1.: Musical journal for the flute or violin. Volume the 1st. Vocal section. Sold at J. Carr's Musical repository, Baltimore; J. Chalk's Philadelphia & J. Hewitt's, New York.

Music, p. [1]–47; pagination continuous, including title pages to each number except No. 9 (incorrectly numbered 8); odd numbers used throughout the Vocal section; Index to the Vocal section, p. 48.

This Vocal section is followed by the Instrumental section, with even numbers.

P. 1., with title (same as before, except Instrumental section instead of Vocal).

On p. [1]: No. 2 of a Musical journal for the flute or violin.

Instrumental section. Price to subscribers 18 cents. To non subscribers 25 cents. N. B. The numbers of the instrumental section are to be kept seperate [!] from the vocal.

Music, p. 2–47, pagination continuous, including title page to each number except Nos. 4, 14, 16, 18, 22, 24; index, p. 48.

In DLC copy, p. [1]–2 of the Vocal section are missing.

Contents: Vocal section—

No. [1]	p. 2–3	Rosa [p. 2 lacking in DLC copy].
	4	Pretty maids all in a row.
3	6–7	Poor Lima.
	8	Cupid benighted.
5	10–12	Canzonett by Jackson of Exeter.
7	14–16	Courteous stranger.
8 [i. e. 9]	17	Shakespeare's willow.
	18–19	Poor Mary.
	20	Little Boy Blew.
11	22–23	Ben & Mary.
	24	Portugueze hymn on the Nativity.
13	26–28	Two original Russian airs.
15	30–31	Ye lingering winds.
	32	Never doubt that I love.
17	34–36	A wandering gipsey.
19	38–39	The angler.
	40	By Baby Bunting.
21	42–44	Hurly Burly.
23	46–47	When the shades of night.
	48	Index. Vocal section.

Instrumental section—

No. 2	p. 2–4	Aria con variazione.
4	5–8	Thema con variazione. Pleyel.
6	10–12	Duo. Pleyel.
8	14–16	Sonate de Haydn.
10	18–19	Chantons l'Hymen.
	20	Air.
12	22–23	Minuetto & trio by Pleyel.
	24	Minuetto by Pleyel.
14	25–28	Six favorite German waltzen.
16	29–32	Duetto.
18	33–36	Six imitations.

[274]

No. 20   38–40 Andante d'Haydn.
    22   41–44 Andante d'Haydn (continued)
    24   45–47 Andante d'Haydn (concluded)
          48 Index.   Instrumental section.   DLC

MUSICAL JOURNAL for the pianoforte, selected and arranged by Benjamin Carr, of Philadelphia.

We read in the *General advertiser*, Philadelphia, January 20, 1800:

TO THE AMATEURS OF MUSIC

Joseph Carr, of Baltimore, respectfully informs the public that he intends publishing a MUSICAL JOURNAL, for the Pianoforte, selected and arranged by Benjamin Carr, of Philadelphia.

No. 1 will contain the much admired song in "The Secret," and a favorite "Nursery song." Particulars of this work may be seen at Mr. Chalk's Circulating Library, No. 75 North Third street, where subscriptions will be received.

Also on the same plan will be published a MUSICAL JOURNAL FOR THE FLUTE OR VIOLIN.

In the same paper, March 6, we read this advertisement signed August 6, instead of March 6:

A new Musical Repository is now opened at Chalk's Circulating Library, No. 75 North Third-street . . . Subscriptions received for the *Musical Journal* for the Piano Forte, and the Flute, or Violin; the first six numbers of which are already published, and may be purchased together or separately by non subscribers.

In the *Federal gazette* (Baltimore), on November 21, 1800, appeared the following advertisement of the second volume:

Music. Proposals for publishing by subscription the second volume of the Musical Journal for the piano forte (which will be continued annually.)

Selected and arranged by Benjamin Carr, of Philadelphia, and published by Joseph Carr, of Baltimore.

CONDITIONS

I. The Musical Journal will be in two sections, viz. one of vocal and one of instrumental music—a number of each section to be published alternately.

II. The vocal section to contain a collection of the newest and most esteemed songs, and, such, as have not, to the knowledge of the editor, been before published in this country; and the instrumental an elegant selection of those pieces, best calculated to delight the ear and improve the finger.

III. The second volume to be comprised in 24 numbers, to be published weekly, commencing on the first of December.

IV. Each number to contain 4 pages, neatly printed, price to subscribers 25 cents each, to be paid on delivery.

V. With the last number will be given, a general title page, complete indexes, and a list of subscribers. The volume to contain in all 100 pages of printing.

[275]

VI. Those subscribing, or procuring subscribers, for 6 copies, will have seventh gratis.

Subscriptions received at the following Musical Repositories—J. Carr's Gay street, Baltimore; J. Chalk's, North Third street, Philadelphia; and J. Hewitt's, Maiden Lane, New York—where may be had the first volum of the Musical Journal, complete, bound or unbound; or in sections, num bers, and single pieces or songs.

TO THE PATRONS OF MUSIC

The Subscription list, of the first volume of this work, contains the names o the most eminent teachers, and some of the first amateurs in Philadelphia who have sanctioned it by their approval, the vocal part, containing thos songs that the proprietor had the satisfaction of seeing become universa favorites; and the instrumental section; but here a remark would be imper tinent, as the names of Haydn, Pleyel, Boccherini etc speak for themselves The second volume, he hopes, in some instances, will be an improvement or the first; but this he promises, it shall not in any instance be inferior, and though the impossibility, in a work of this kind, of pleasing all, is evident, ye he faithfully pledges himself, that from the most simple ballad, to the most difficult sonata, it may contain, there shall be nothing to vitiate a musical taste.—The advantage of a work of this kind, under the editorship of a pro fessional person, and upon which the critical eyes of some eminent masters and amateurs among its subscribers, must act as guardians, will, it is pre sumed, raise its consequence with those who are desirous to forward the advancement of music in this country. The sources from which the Musical Journal will draw its materials, are some valuable libraries of music—regular communications from Europe, and occasional efforts of musical talents here: from these will be formed a collection of such songs most worthy of becoming favorites; and an elegant selection of Sonatas, Rondos, Airs, varied etc that shall be so arranged, that the proprietor trusts they will convey pleasure to the proficient, and improvement to the practitioner of every class. The weekly expense is trifling, scarce any song in England is now published under one shilling sterling, and in America, a quarter of a dollar for a song of two pages. But agreeably to the Proposals, the subscribers will have four pages of music, and that of the most select kind, for 25 cents—with these recom mendations, and a fervent wish, on the part of the publisher, to see the Musical Journal permanently established; and as he hopes it will be superior in its matter, to any other publication of a similar kind, he submits it to the patronage of the musical world, hoping that he may acquire thereby, some small share of fame and profit for himself, and for his subscribers, an annual addition of a valuable volume of music to their library . . .

JUST PUBLISHED

The new song of the Cottage on the moor. Music store, No. 6, Gay street, November 21.

In the *General advertiser*, Philadelphia, November 27, 1800, we read this advertisement by "J. Chalk, No. 75 North Third Street":

The second volume of the *Musical Journal* will comence on Monday, the first of December to be completed in 24 weekly numbers. Price to sub scribers 25 cents each number.

The first number will contain the much admired ballad of "The Blue Bell of Scotland." . . .

Consequently only the first volume and five numbers of the second were issued in 1800, and the present discussion is limited to these portions of the work.

ʹHE MUSICAL JOURNAL for the piano-forte in two sections, one of vocal and one of instrumental music. Selected and arranged by Benjamin Carr. Sold at the following Musical repositories. J. Carrs, Baltimore; J. Hewitts, New York & J. Chalks, Philadelphia. A musical journal for the flute or violin upon the same plan to be had as above. Engraved by I. E. Martin [1800] 2 p. 1., 54 p., 1 l., 48 p. 33 cm.

At head of title: Vol. [1] of. [The figure "1" is in ink.]
Above title, vignette, with open music book, lyre, etc.
Title page, verso blank; on 2nd p. 1., "Musical journal. Vol. [1] Vocal section. Sold at the following musical repositories, J. Carr's, Baltimore; J. Chalk's, Philadelphia and J. Hewitt's, New York."
Music, p. (2)–(53), pagination continuous, including title-page to each number except Nos. 11, 15, 19, 21, which have caption titles.
All page numbers are in parentheses at top center of page; odd numbers are used throughout the Vocal section; index to vocal section, p. (54).
Title-pages to individual numbers contain various lists of songs and instrumental pieces issued in this series; also the statement "Copyright secur'd according to law;" and at the foot of page, the imprint, "Baltimore, Publish'd by J. Carr and sold at J. Chalk's, Circulating library, No. 75 North Third street, Philadelphia; at J. Hewitts Musical repository, New York & J. Carr's music store, Baltimore." Numbers on title-pages, when given, are written in ink.

This Vocal section is followed by the Instrumental section with even numbers. P. 1. same as 2nd. p. 1., above, except *Instrumental* instead of *Vocal*. Music, p. (2)–(47), pagination continuous, including title-page to each number except Nos. 6, 8, 16, 22, which have caption titles, and No. 18 (blank). All page numbers are in parentheses at top center of page; index to instrumental section, p. 48.
Title-pages as in Vocal section, with numbers written in.
Identical imprint.

Contents: Vocal section—

No. [1] p.	2–3	Rosa.
	4	Pretty maids all in a row.
[3]	6–7	Poor Lima.
	8	Cupid benighted.
[5]	10–12	Death and burial of Cock Robin.
[7]	14–16	Courteous stranger.
[9]	18–19	Poor Mary.
	20–21	Little Boy Blew.
	22	Shakespeares willow.
11	23–26	The wood robin.
[13]	28–30	Two original Russian airs.
[15]	32–33	Ye ling'ring winds.
	34–35	Never doubt that I love.

[277]

No. [17] 38–39 A wandring gipsey.
          40   The angler.
     19   41–44 Ah! how hapless is the maiden.
     21   45–48 Ah! how hapless is the maiden (concluded).
     [23] 50–51 The widow.
          52   The faded lilly! or Louisa's woe.
          53   When the shades of night pursuing.
          54   Index.
Instrumental section—

No. [2] p. 2–4   Aria con variazione.
    [4]   6–8   Sonata by Pleyel.
     6   9–12   Sonata by Pleyel (concluded).
     8   13–16 Andantino Tiré de Boccherini.
    [10]   18–20 Lord Alexander Gordons reel.
    [12]   22–23 Minuetto by Pleyel.
           24   Minuetto & Trio by Pleyel.
    [14]   26–28 Six favorite German waltzen.
     16   29–32 Andante d'Haydn.
    [18]   34–36 3 Divertimentos by B. Carr.
    [20]   38–40 Six imitations by B. Carr.
     22   41–44 Rondeau de Viotti.
    [24]   46–47 Rondo by Pleyel.
           48   Index.

As noted above, the year 1800 carries us through Nos. 25–29 of the *Second volume*, as follows:

Vocal section—

No. 25 p. 2–4   The Blue Bell of Scotland.
    27   5–6   The death of Crazy Jane.
           7–8   L'amour interroge par un berger.
    29   9–11   The orphan's prayer.
           12   Adeste fideles.
Instrumental section—

No. 26 p. 2–4   Aria alla Tedesca.
    28   5–8   The lullaby of Correlli[!].

Sonneck adds:

"It is surprising that this publication, in a way the most important issued about 1800, should be so scarce. I have found of the earliest numbers 'No. 16' only and this possibly belonged to the second volume and was therefore published after 1800. The title reads:

ANDANTE D'HAYDN. No. 16 of a Musical Journal for the piano forte—Instrumental section.

4°. paged 29–32. It is the familiar c c e e / g g e."

It will be observed that our present report is somewhat more encouraging, though copies of complete volumes are still rare. Individual numbers are fairly numerous, as are certain reprints.

Above portions of Volumes 1 and 2, complete:

DLC (has t.-p., p. 47–48 photostat), ES, NN

[278]

The same, not complete but largely representative:

LSL, McD–W, MdHi, NRU–Mus (first volume complete), PP–K

THE MUSICAL REPERTORY, or The musical repository.

THE MUSICAL REPOSITORY by William Norman.

In the *Columbian centinel*, Boston, August 17, 1796, appeared the following:

Proposals of William Norman for publishing by subscription, every second month, a MUSICAL REPOSITORY, containing a variety of the most modern and favorite songs, as performed on the stage in Europe and America.

CONDITIONS

1. Each number shall contain 16 pages in folio. Copper plate engravings, on good paper, stitched in blue; and with the sixth number, will be given gratis, an elegant title page.

2. The tunes shall be judiciously arranged from the original operas, for the voice and the bass, and be fitted suitable for practice on the keyed instruments. Such airs in which the original pitch might not suit the German flute performers will be inserted in additional different and convenient pitch.

3. The price to subscribers will be one dollar, to be paid down on delivery— to non-subscribers it will be one dollar and 25 cents.

4. Those who subscribe for eleven, shall have a twelfth gratis. Subscriptions for this work received by the publisher at his book store, No. 75 Newbury-Street nearly opposite the sign of the Lamb.

On August 24, 1796, we then read:

Just published, by William Norman . . . No. I OF THE MUSICAL REPOSITORY containing the following pieces. [Then follows list of contents.]

On October 1, 1796, we read:

Just published . . . No. II OF THE MUSICAL REPOSITORY. [Again list of contents.]

In the *Columbian centinel*, June 26, 1799, appeared the following advertisement:

At the above place [William Norman . . . Bookstore, No. 75 Newbury street, or nearly opposite the Sign of the Lamb, Tavern, Boston] may be had THE MUSICAL REPOSITORY, as far as the fifth number, containing a great variety of songs and other pieces of music. As soon as opportunity offers, this Publication will be continued.

The sixth number of this collection was advertised in the *Columbian centinel*, for August 31, 1799, as follows:

MUSICAL REPOSITORY. Just published by William Norman . . . No. 6, of the Musical Repository. Containing the following pieces. "The Death of Anna"; "Ellin's fate deserves a tear"; "Sweet Little cottage"; "The Gipsy"; "The Girl of my heart"; "Ellen of the Dee"; "Hey dance to the fiddle and tabor"; "The Streamlet."

[279]

This number completes the first volume of the Musical Repository which for its size and the neatness of the work, is the cheapest instrumental music ever published in America, it being but 4d½ per page.

Sonneck adds, "I have not found a single number of this important collection!" Fortunately we are now able to make a more satisfying report.

Although advertised consistently throughout the three years of its existence as *The musical repository*, we find that the first two numbers issued in 1796 as *The musical repertory* are identical with those advertised as the first two numbers of *The musical repository*. Hence it becomes clear that while advertised under the name of *Repository*, the work, so far as we know it, was actually published as *Repertory*. Only as such has it ever been found. The first three numbers have been located, also fragmentary issues from the remaining three numbers. Through a reprint by Graupner in Boston, shortly after the turn of the century, it has been possible to piece together certain portions of these missing numbers.

The first three numbers are as follows:

THE MUSICAL REPERTORY. Boston. Printed and sold by William Norman, No. 75 Newbury street [1796]   16 p.   34½ cm.

Title on front cover.
Below title: Number I.   Containing the following pieces [here follows list of contents].   Vignette of musicians playing.
Below imprint: (Price to subscribers 1 Dollar, to nonsubscribers 1 Dollar 25 cents)
On fourth page of cover: William Norman . . . has constantly for sale [here follows list of books and music].

Contents:

p. (1)	When first to Helen's lute.
(2)–(4)	See sister see on yonder bough.
(5)	A favorite air.
(6)–(7)	A blessing on brandy & beer.
(8)	The rosary.
(9)	Walter's sweethearts.
(10)–(11)	The shipwreck'd seamans ghost.
(12)–(13)	Think your tawny moor is true.
(14)–(15)	I sold a guiltless Negro boy.
(15)	Moorish march.
(16)	Dear wanderer.

NUMBER II. [1796] p. 17–32.
Same cover as No. I except changed list of contents and of books on back cover.

Contents:

p. 17	When first I slipp'd my leading strings.
18–19	Rise Columbia.
20	Ah can I cease to love her.
21–23	An ode to sleep.
24–25	To me a smiling infant came.
25	Quick march.
26–27	Ye streams that round my prison creep.

[280]

28–29 A pastoral.
29–31 Zorade in the tower.
   32 Sterne's Maria.

NUMBER III. [1796–97] p. 33–48.

Cover same as preceding with changed list of contents.

Contents:

  p. 33 Resignation march.
  34–35 I that was once a ploughman.
     36 When bidden to the wake.
     37 The galley slave.
  38–39 Smalilou.
     39 Ere around the huge oak.
  40–41 Jem of Aberdeen.
  41–43 The jealous don.
     44 Finale [Oscar and Malvina].
  45–47 The capture.
     48 The sweet little girl that I love.

Of these three Numbers DLC has No. I complete.
                            No. II lacks t.-p.
                            No. III lacks p. 47–48.
MB has No. I incomplete, lacks p. 3, 4, 13–16.
NRU-Mus has No. I incomplete, lacks p. 1–4, 6–7.

What we know of the last three numbers is almost entirely derived from Graupner's reprints in his *Musical magazine*, Boston, 180–.

We have here visible evidence that the first 48 pages of *The Musical magazine* are direct reprints of the first 48 pages (*i. e.* the first three numbers) of Norman's *Repertory*. We have similar evidence in regard to Storace's "Lullaby," which occurs on p. 72–73 of what must have been the fifth number of the *Repertory*. Therefore, it is probable that up to p. 73, at any rate, Graupner reprinted Norman throughout, and there seems no reason to doubt that he also reprinted the few remaining pages of No. V.

So that taking the *Musical magazine* as our basis, we are able with reasonable accuracy to reconstruct Nos. IV and V of the *Repertory*.

The titles supplied in brackets have never been located in this particular form. The others have appeared either as reprints or as detached pages, presumably from the *Repertory*, although possibly from the later *Musical magazine*.

NUMBER IV.

  p. 49 [Oh ever in my bosom live]
  50–51 [Tom Tackle]
  52–53 O say bonny lass.
  54–55 Love soft illusion.
  56–57 Nancy, or the Sailor's journal.
  58–59 [A favorite song in . . . the Travellers in Switzerland]
  60–61 When nights were cold.
  62–64 [A favorite song in . . . the Spanish Barber]

NUMBER V.

p. 65 [The village holyday]
66–67 The silver moon.
68–69 [My bonny lowland laddie]
70–71 Ripe cherries.
72–73 Lullaby.
74–75 No that will never do.
76 Henry's cottage maid.
77 The primrose girl.
78–79 [The Scotch air . . . in the Pirates]
80 [The Jersey blue]

In No. VI we get little or no help from Graupner, for on p. 86–87 he gives "The attic bower . . . sung by Mrs. Graupner . . . on September 24th, 1802." Obviously this song could not have been taken from the *Repertory*. However, Graupner includes on p. 80–83 "The death of Anna" which is advertised as in No. VI of the *Repertory*, and there is a reprint of "Hey dance to the fiddle and tabor" similarly advertised. Unfortunately, these two titles are all that have been found of No. VI. For the remainder we must look to the advertisement quoted above.

THE MUSICAL SOCIETY.
(*In* The American musical miscellany. Northampton, 1798. p. 187–189)

Melody and bass, with accompanying text.
First line: Well met my loving friends of art. DLC (etc.)

MY BONNY LOWLAND LADDIE. A favorite Scotch song. Composed by Mr. Hook.
(*In* [Unidentified collection of instrumental and vocal music. New York] Hewitt & Rausch [1797] p. 9–10)

Song, pfte. acc.
First line: Of all the swains both far and near. DLC, ES

—————— The same as preceding.
(*In* A collection of new & favorite songs. [A] Philadelphia [ca. 1800] p. [90]–[91], numbered 9–10) HFB

—————— The same as preceding, but incomplete. Second page, numbered 9, of a detached sheet from above collection. Lacks p. 10. JFD

MY DAYS HAVE BEEN SO WONDROUS FREE.
(*In* [A volume of songs, etc., composed or copied by Francis Hopkinson. 1759–60] p. 63)

Song, harpsichord acc.
First line same as title.
Composed by Francis Hopkinson.

Sonneck adds:

Probably the earliest secular composition of a native American extant. A facsimile and a transcript of the pretty song (to Dr. Parnell's words), as also further historical data, are to be found in my book on "Francis Hopkinson . . . and James Lyon" (1905). DLC

[282]

MY FRIEND AND PITCHER. Poor soldier.
(*In* A collection of favorite songs, divided into two books. Arr. by A. Reinagle. Philadelphia [1789?] bk. 1, p. 13)

Song, pfte. acc.
First line: The wealthy fool with gold in store.
Poor soldier, by William Shield. CdeW, DLC, ES, Hopk.

[MY GEN'ROUS HEART DISDAINS] Song VII. Rondo.
(*In* Seven songs, by F. Hopkinson. Philadelphia [1788] p. 9–10)

Song, pfte. acc.
Title from first line. DLC, Hopk., MB, McD-W

*MY GRANDMOTHER.
Prince Hoare and Stephen Storace's "musical entertainment . . . never performed here" was advertised in the *Weekly museum* (New York) May 28, 1796, to be performed at Mr. Hodgkinson's benefit, May 30, 1796, with "orchestra accompanyments" by Victor Pelissier.

MY HEART IS DEVOTED DEAR MARY TO THEE. Alternative title of *The indigent peasant*, by James Hook.

MY HEAVY HEART. A favorite Scotch song. Sung by Miss Bertles. Vaux hall.
(*In* A collection of favorite songs, divided into two books. Arr. by A. Reinagle. Philadelphia [1789?] bk. 2, p. 21)

Song, pfte. acc.
First line: Blow on ye winds, descend soft rains. CdeW, DLC, PU

MY HEAVY HEART. A favorite Scotch song. New York, Published for P. Weldon. [ca. 1800] 1 l. 31½ cm.
Imprint at foot of page. Below imprint, letter "G."
Song, pfte. acc.
First line same as preceding. NN

MY HONOR'S GUARDIAN FAR AWAY. Sung by Mrs. Crouch in the opera of the Outlaws. Printed & sold by G. Gilfert, No. 177 Broadway, New York [ca. 1799] [2] p. 32½ cm.
Song, pfte. acc.
First line same as title.
The outlaws, by Michael Kelly, was first produced in 1798. DLC

MY JOURNEY IS LOVE. A celebrated new song. Composed by Mr. Reeve [n. p., 179–?] [2] p. 32 cm.
Song, pfte. acc.
First line: When I was at home as the lark I was gay.
From *Mirth's museum*. ABHu, DLC

[MY LAURA WILL YOU TRUST THE SEAS] A favorite song from the Agreeable surprise, an opera. The air by Chevalier Gluck.
(*In* The Massachusetts magazine, Boston, December, 1791. p. 769.)
Song, pfte. acc.
Title from first line.
The agreeable surprise, by Samuel Arnold. DLC (etc.)

[MY LOVE IS GONE TO SEA] Song II.
(*In* Seven songs, by F. Hopkinson. Philadelphia [1788] p. 2)

Song, pfte. acc.
Title from first line. DLC, Hopk., MB, McD-W

MY LOVE SHE'S BUT A LASSIE YET. Philadelphia, Published by G. Willig
[n. d.] p. 7. 33 cm.

Song, pfte. acc.
First line same as title.
Published probably ca. 1800. NBuG

MY MOTHER BIDS ME BIND MY HAIR.
(*In* Three . . . *Canzonetts* by Haydn. Philadelphia [1799] p. 6 [incomplete])

Song, pfte. acc.
First line same as title.
Lacks last page [7] NN

———— Separate issue of preceding, ca. 1799.
DLC, JFD, MB, McD-W, MdHi, MWA, RPJCB

[MY NATIVE LAND] Sung by Mr. Carr. in the opera of the Haunted tower.
(*In* The gentleman's amusement, ed. by R. Shaw. Philadelphia [1794-96]
p. 28)

Melody only, flute (or violin) with accompanying text.
Title from first line: My native land I bad [!] adieu.
In No. 4, February 1, 1795.
Benjamin Carr sang in *The haunted tower*, by Stephen Storace, New York,
January 9, 1795. DLC, PHi

MY NATIVE LAND. Price 12 cents. New York, Printed & sold by B. Carr
[ca. 1795] 1 l., numbered 3. 30 cm.

Song, pfte. acc.
First line: My native land I bade adieu. DLC

MY NATIVE LAND.
(*In* The favorite songs in the opera of [The haunted tower, by S. Storace]
New York [1795-96] p. 3)

Song, pfte. acc.
First line same as preceding. ABHu, JFD

MY NATIVE LAND. Arranged for two flutes.
(*In* Elegant extracts for the German flute or violin. Philadelphia [1796] bk.
2, p. 14-15)

Two flutes, with accompanying text. Two staves.
First line same as preceding. DLC, NN

MY NATIVE SHORE. New York, Printed & sold at J. Hewitt's Musical repository, No. 131 William street. Price 12½ cents.
(*In* A collection of new & favorite songs. [A] Philadelphia [ca. 1800] p. [155])

Song, pfte. acc.
First line: To fortune lost my native shore. HFB

—— Original issue of preceding.

Bound with *The poor sailor boy*, by Thomas Attwood.
Possibly published together.   DLC, NN
Advertised in January, 1798, as "just published."

MY POLL AND MY PARTNER JOE.
See Mrs. Pownall's address.

MY POOR DOG TRAY. A favorite song. Composed by J. Hewitt. Poetry
by T. Campbell. Price 25 cents. New York, Sold by J. Hewitt, No. 23
Maiden Lane [1799–1800] [2] p. 31½ cm.

Song, pfte. acc. Arr. for flute, p. [2].
First line: On the green banks of Shannon.   DLC, JFD, RPJCB

MY SOUL IS THINE SWEET NORAH. A favorite song. Sung by Mr.
Jonstone in Love in a camp, or Patrick in Prusia [!] Arranged for the piano
or harpsichord by A. Reinagle. [Thomas Dobson at the Stone House in
Second street, Philadelphia, 1789] [2] p. 33½ cm.

Song, pfte. acc.
First line: Away ye giddy smiling throng.
"My soul is thine, sweet Norah" forms the last line of the first stanza.
Love in a camp, by William Shield.   CdeW, ES, JFD, NN
Advertised in March, 1789, among other "songs and pieces, arranged for the
pianoforte or harpsichord by Alexander Reinagle," as "just published and
sold by Thomas Dobson, at the Stone House in Second Street," Philadelphia.

—— The same as preceding, but with pagination.
(*In* [A collection of favorite songs, arr. by A. Reinagle. Philadelphia,
1789 ?] p. 13–14)   ES

[MY TENDER HEART YOU STOLE AWAY] Sung by Mrs. Marshall.
(*In* The volunteers, by A. Reinagle. Philadelphia [1795 ?] p. 15)

Song, pfte. acc.
Title from first line.   DLC

[MY THOMAS IS THE KINDEST LAD] Sung by Miss Broadhurst.
(*In* The volunteers, by A. Reinagle. Philadelphia [1795 ?] p. 16)

Song, pfte. acc.
Title from first line.   DLC

MYRA.
(*In* The Philadelphia songster, ed. by A. Aimwell [pseud.] Philadelphia,
1789. p. 10–11)

Melody only, with accompanying text.
First line: The world my dear Myra.   NN

*THE MYSTERIOUS MARRIAGE, or, the Heirship of Roselva.
As "a play in three acts (never performed here) interspersed with music,
written by Harriet Lee, the music and accompanyments composed by Mr.
[James] Hewitt," this piece was to be given at New York, June 5, 1799.

[285]

*THE MYSTERIOUS MONK.
William Dunlap's tragedy was performed with "an Ode and chorusses, sung by monks, nuns and orphans . . . music by Mr. [Victor] Pelissier," in the third act at New York, October 31, 1796.

NANCY.   Sung in the opera of the Smugglers.
(*With* Lucy, or Selim's complaint.   New York [1797–99])
Song, pfte. acc.
First line: 'Twas where a willow's drooping branches.
The smugglers, by Thomas Attwood.   MB, PP–K

―――― The same as preceding.
(*In* A collection of new & favorite songs.   [A] Philadelphia [ca. 1800] p. [141])
                                                                                              HFB
*NANCY, CHINK A CHINK.
Advertised in August, 1798, as "just published and forsale (!) at Wm. Howe's wholesale and retail warehouse, 320 Pearlstreet (!)," New York.

NANCY DAWSON.
See Four excellent new *Songs*.

NANCY OF THE VALE.   A pastoral ballad.   Composed by R. Taylor. Philadelphia, Printed for the Author, No. 96 North Sixth street and sold at B. Carr's Musical repositorys, Market street, Philadelphia; William st., New York and at I. Carr's Market street, Baltimore.   (Price ¼ of a dollar) [1795]   [2] p.   33 cm.
Song, pfte. acc.
First line: Let fops with fickle falsehood range.
                                                            DLC, ES, NBuG, PP–K
Advertised in March, 1795, as for sale at "Carr's Musical Repositories, Philadelphia and William-street, New York . . . "

NANCY, OR THE SAILOR'S JOURNAL.   Composed by Mr. Dibdin [n. p., n. d.]   56–57 p.   32 cm.
Song, pfte. acc.
First line: 'Twas past meridian half past four.
From Dibdin's *Will of the wisp*.
Apparently a reprint from No. [IV] of *The musical repertory*, Boston, 1797–99.
                                                                                              MB

NANCY, OR THE SAILOR'S JOURNAL.   As sung by Mr. Williamson at The Theatre, New York, with universal applause.   New York, Printed & sold by G. Gilfert, No. 177 Broadway [1797–1801]   [2] p.   34 cm.
Song, pfte. acc.   Arr. for two flutes, p. [2].
First line same as preceding.
Sung by Mr. Williamson at Oeller's Hotel, Philadelphia, November 27, 1797.
                                                                                              JFD

THE FAVORITE SONG OF NANCY, OR THE SAILOR'S JOURNAL. As sung by Mr. Williamson at the Hay-market theatre, Boston, with universal applause.   Boston, Printed by Thomas & Andrews, Newbury-street. Price 25 cents.   [ca. 1798]   3 p.   33 cm.

Song, pfte. acc.   Three staves, voice part on middle staff.
Arr. for two flutes, p. 3.
First line same as preceding.
Printed from movable type.   MWA, NN, NRU–Mus

NANCY, OR THE SAILOR'S JOURNAL.
   (*In* The American musical miscellany.   Northampton, 1798.   p. 78–80)

Melody only with accompanying text.
First line same as preceding.   DLC (etc.)

—————— The sailors journal.   By Dibdin.   Printed at B. Carr's Musical repositories, New York & Philadelphia & at J. Carr's, Baltimore.   (Price 25 cents)
[1797]   2 p.   30½ cm.

At lower left hand corner, p. 2: Sailor's journal, p. 2.
Song, pfte. acc.   Arr. for two flutes, p. 2.
First line: 'Twas post meridian half past four.   DLC, MWA, NN

This song by Dibdin was advertised by J. Carr, Baltimore, among other
songs lately published in September, 1797.

—————— The same.
   (*In* Elegant extracts for the German flute or violin.   Philadelphia [1798]
bk. 3, p. 18)

Melody only, flute or violin, with accompanying text.
First line: 'Twas post meridian 2 [!] past 4.   DLC, NN

NAUTICAL SONGSTER.   Alternative title of *The Mermaid*.

NAUTICAL SONGSTER, or Seaman's companion.   To encrease [!] the joys
of Saturday night.   A collection of the newest and most approved songs
interspersed with many originals.   Baltimore, Printed for Henry S. Keatinge,
1798.   64 p., front.   13½ cm.

Title-page, verso blank; contents, p. 3–4; songs, p. [5]–64.
Words only, tunes occasionally mentioned.   DLC, RPJCB

*NAVAL AND MILITARY SONGS.
   See Songs.   Naval and military.

NAVAL MARCH.   Composed by M. Kelly.   New York, Printed & sold by G.
Gilfert, No. 177 Broadway.   And to be had at P. A. von Hagen's music
store, Boston [n. d.]   1 1.   31½ cm.

Pfte. 2 hds.
Published probably ca. 1800.
M. Kelly: Michael Kelly.   MWA

NAVAL OVERTURE, called "The Sailor's medley."
   See Poor Jack.

*THE NAVAL PILLAR; or, The American sailor's garland.
   Advertised in the *Federal gazette*, Baltimore, June 3, 1800, for performance
   on the same day as "A new musical entertainment (never performed here)
   . . . Altered from a celebrated piece of that name, written by Thomas Dibdin,
   author of the Jew and doctor . . . The music partly new and partly compiled by Moorhead . . . with accompaniments by Mr. [Alexander] Reinagle."

THE NAVAL VOLUNTEER. Alternative title of *American true blue.*

*NEEDS MUST, or, the Ballad singers.
According to Seilhamer (v. III, p. 79), this "musical trifle" was performed at New York on December 23, 1793. "For this piece," he says, "Mrs. Hatton, a sister of Mrs. Siddons, furnished the plot, which was slight, and wrote one of the songs; the whole of the dialogue was the work of Mrs. Pownall." The composer is not mentioned.
Mrs. Ann Julia Hatton, actress, poetess, playwright, came to New York in the winter of 1793–94.

THE NEGRO BOY.
See I sold a guiltless Negro boy.

NEGRO PHILOSOPHY. Written composed and sung by Mr. Dibdin in his new entertainment called the General election. New York, Printed & sold at J. Hewitt's Musical repository, No. 121 William street. Sold also by B. Carr, Philadelphia & J. Carr, Baltimore. Price 25 cents.
(*In* A collection of new & favorite songs. [A] Philadelphia [ca. 1800] p. [156]–[157])
Song, pfte. acc.
First line: One negro come from Jenny land.
It is quite evident that "121 William street" in the imprint should read "131."

The original issue is advertised August 23, 1797, as one of "two new songs" by J. Hewitt at his "Musical Repository, No. 131 William st.," New York.
HFB

NEIGHBOUR SLY. Dibdin.
(*In* The [gentleman's amusement, ed. by R. Shaw. Philadelphia [1794–96] p. 67)
Melody only, with accompanying text.
First line: The passing bell was heard to toll.
In No. [8], ca. 1796. DLC, PP–K

NEVER DOUBT THAT I LOVE. Composed by R. Taylor.
(*In* The musical journal for the pianoforte, ed. by B. Carr. Baltimore [1800] v. 1, no. [15] p. (34)–(35).)
Song, pfte. acc.
First line: Doubt the morning & evening dew.
DLC, LC, LSL, NN, NRU–Mus

———— The same as preceding. In separate issue of v. 1, no. [15] complete, ca. 1800. MdHi

———— The same.
(*In* The musical journal for the flute or violin. Baltimore [1800] no. 15, p. 32)
Melody only, flute or violin, with accompanying text.
First line: Doubt the morning and evening dew. DLC

NEVER TILL NOW I KNEW LOVE'S SMART.
(*In* The American musical miscellany. Northampton, 1798. p. 33–34)

Melody only, with accompanying text.
First line same as title.   DLC (etc.)

*THE NEW AMERICAN MOCK-BIRD.
See The American Mock-bird.

NEW [AMERICAN] PATRIOTIC SONGS . . .
See A collection of songs . . . Dibdin.

NEW ANACREONTIC SONG.
(*In* The American musical miscellany. Northampton, 1798. p. 107–109)

Melody only, with accompanying text.
First line: Anacreon they say was a jolly old blade.   DLC (etc.)

A NEW AND COMPLETE PRECEPTOR FOR THE VIOLIN, with a collection of cotillions, marches, etc. Philadelphia. Published & sold by Klemm & Brother. 30 p. obl. 4°.

Probably published after 1800.   CtY

*A NEW AND SELECT COLLECTION of the best English, Scots and Irish songs.
See A new and select *Collection* . . .

A NEW ASSISTANT FOR THE PIANO-FORTE, or harpsichord. Containing the necessary rudiments for beginners with twelve airs or short lessons progressively arranged, to which is added six sonatas, one of which is adapted for two performers. With preludes, rules for thorough bass, a short dictionary of musical terms &c. N. B. The lessons, sonatas & preludes have their fingering mark'd. Compil'd, compos'd and arrang'd by F. Linley, organist of Pentonville. Price 1 & ½ dollar. Baltimore, Printed & sold by I. Carr at his music store, Market street. And by B. Carr, at his Musical repositorys, Market street, Philadelphia & William st., New York. Where may be had Antoniotto's Treatise on the composition of music, 10s 6d Rameau's D°., 5s, Lamp's Thorough bass, 7s 6d, Twelve voluntaries selected from the works of eminent authors, 6s [1796] 1 p. l., 32 p. 32½ cm.

Title-page, verso blank; p. [1] blank; Rudiments, p. 2–5; Twelve airs, or lessons, p. 6–10; Six sonatas, p. 11–21; p. 22 blank; Preludes, p. 23–26; Second set of preludes, p. 27–29; Rules for thoro'bass, p. 30–31; Short dictionary of musical terms, p. 32 (numbered also 98).
Pfte. 2 hds.
The Six sonatas are unquestionably compositions of Benjamin Carr, and are as follows: Sonata I (F. major), p. 11.—Sonata II (B-flat major), p. 12–13.—Sonata III (G major), p. 14–15.—Sonata IV (C major, 4 hds.), p. 16–17.—Sonata V (D major), p. 18.—Sonata VI (B-flat major), p. 19–21.
The Dictionary of musical terms is identical with that appearing in The gentleman's amusement, p. 98, also published in 1796.
DLC, Harvard Musical Assn., LSL, McD–W (p. 23–30 only), PP–K (lacks t.-p., p. [1]–2).

Advertised in *The Federal gazette*, Baltimore, August 6, 1796, among "musical publications. Printed by J. Carr, music store, No. 6 Gay street, Baltimore

[289]

and B. Carr's Musical repositories, Market street, Philadelphia and William street, New York."

The seeming discrepancy in J. Carr's Baltimore address is probably due to the fact that it was at just about this time that he moved from Market to Gay street.

That the *Sonatas* here mentioned were composed by Benjamin Carr is established by the fact that they are included in a ms. list of Carr's compositions in the possession of Arthur Billings Hunt.

LINLEY'S ASSISTANT FOR THE PIANOFORTE. Containing the necessary rudiments for beginners and twenty four lessons progressively arranged with preludes, rules of thorough bass and a short dictionary of musical terms, &c. The lessons and preludes have their fingering marked. A new edition. Price one dollar fifty cents. Printed & sold by I. Carr at his music store, Market street, Baltimore. Where may be had Antoniotto's Treatise on the composition of music, Dls. 5 50, Rameau's ditto, 2 75, Lamp's Thorough bass, 3 25, Dr. Pepusch's Treatise on harmony, containing the rules of composing in 2, 3, and 4 parts, 2 50. Music engraved and printed [these last four words trimmed through the middle, and any possible further words gone] [1796] 1 p. l., 32 p. 31½ cm.

Title-page, verso blank; recto of p. 2, verso of p. 3 and recto of p. 4, blank, in Md Hi copy partially filled with ms. exercises; "Rudiments," p. 2–[5]; Lessons, p. 6–19; Walzer, p. 19; Life let us cherish, p. 20; Since then I'm doom'd, p. [21]; Fresh and strong the breeze is blowing, p. 22; Preludes, p. 23–29; Rules for thoro'bass, p. 30–31; Musical terms, p. 32.   MdHi

It will be noted that these two editions of what is essentially the same work differ only in their central section. In *A new assistant*, p. 6–22 contain twelve airs or lessons, together with six sonatas by Benjamin Carr. In *Linley's assistant* these same pages contain twenty-four lessons, followed by the various compositions listed above. Otherwise the two are identical.

Advertised September 30, 1796.

THE NEW BOW WOW.
See The new *Bow Wow.*

*A NEW BOW WOW SONG; the faithful dog, the knowing dog, the hearty dog, and many other dogs, in the character of an old dog by Mr. Hodgkinson; written by himself.

From 1793 on this was a *pièce de résistance* of John Hodgkinson, *e. g.*, sung by him at Mrs. Hodgkinson's benefit, New York, April 30, 1794. It does not appear whether he wrote both the words and the music.

THE NEW COLDSTREAM MARCH.
See Compleat tutor for the fife . . . p. 16.

*NEW CONSTITUTION MARCH AND FEDERAL MINUET.
Advertised in October, 1788, Philadelphia, as "composed by Mr. Sicard, adapted to the pianoforte, violin and German flute, etc. May be had of Mr. Rice in Market Street, and Mr. Atken opposite the City tavern. Mr. Sicard has also composed several new dances."

A NEW CONTREDANCE. By H. Capron.
See A new *Contredance* . . .

A NEW EDITION OF VIGUERIE'S FAVORITE SONATA for the piano forte·
See . . . Viguerie's favorite *Sonata* for the piano forte.

NEW ENGLAND GUARD'S MARCH. Composed by J. Hewitt. Boston,
Printed & sold at Hayt's Babcock & Appleton's music store, No. 6 Milk
street [n. d.] 1 l. 32½ cm.

Pfte. 2 hds.

Published probably ca. 1800. DLC

THE NEW ENTERTAINING PHILADELPHIA JEST BOOK.
See The new entertaining *Philadelphia jest book.*

*NEW FEDERAL OVERTURE. Composed by Mons. Leaumont.
See New *Federal overture* . . . Leaumont.

THE NEW FEDERAL OVERTURE. Selected and composed by James Hewitt.
See The new *Federal overture* . . . Hewitt.

NEW FRENCH MARCH. "Le reviel [!] du peuple."
See New *French march.*

NEW GLEE.
See New *Glee.*

NEW HAMPSHIRE. Allemande.
See United States country *Dances,* p. 4.

*THE NEW HIGHLAND LADDIE. Composed by Dr. Hayes, sung with
universal applause by Mr. Warrel in the Highland reel, at the New Theatre.
Thus advertised in May, 1794, New York, among "new music . . . published.—Philadelphia, printed for Shaw & Co. and sold by Harrison, No. 108
Maiden Lane, New York."

NEW INSTRUCTIONS FOR THE GERMAN FLUTE. Containing the easiest
and most modern methods for learners to play; to which are added a favourite
collection of minuets, marches, songs, tunes, duets, etc. Also, the method of
double tongueing, and a compleate scale and description of a new invented
German flute, with the additional keys, such as played on by two eminent
masters, *Florio* and *Tacet* [!]. Philadelphia, Printed & sold at G. Willig's
Musical magazine, Market street, No. 165 [1795–97] 31 p. 13½ x 21 cm.

Title-page, verso blank; instructions, p. 3–15; music, p. 16–29; description
of German flutes, p. 30–31.

For single flute, p. 16–21.

For two flutes, p. 22–29.

Contents:

    p. 16 The streamlet that flow'd.
    17–19 Selection from the Battle of Prague.
      20 Poor Jack, by Dibdin.
          Duke of York's march.
      21 Pleyel's German hymn with variations.
      22 President's march.
          God save Great Washington.
      23 The bed of roses.
          Duncan Davy.

Major Andre's complaint.
24 Ma belle coquette.
25 Duetto. Pleyel.
Cantabile.
26 Mr Depart [Duport] Cottillion [!].
Love forever.
27 See that pretty creature there in Don Juan.
Tell me babling [!] echo.
28-29 Romance by Haydn.   PPL

Advertised in *Rivington's Royal gazette*, New York, August, 1778, as "published and to be sold at the printer's . . . price 5 s. currency."
This evidently refers to the edition quoted by Evans (15925) but not located.

NEW JERSEY.
See United States country *Dances*, p. 9.

NEW KATE OF ABERDEEN. The music by H. Capron. Philadelphia,
Printed & sold by G. Willig, No. 185 Market street [1798–1804] 1 l.
31½ cm.

Song, pfte. acc.
First line: The rosy morning glads the plain.   PP-K

A NEW MEDLEY OVERTURE . . . selected and composed by J. Hewitt.
See A new medley *Overture* . . . J. Hewitt.

*THE NEW MINSTREL by William Selby.
We read in the *Boston evening post*, February 2, 1782:

PROPOSALS TO THE FRIENDS OF MUSIC AND THE FINE ARTS

Animated by the encouragement lately given in this young country, to certain of the sciences (and they have all a chain of union) the subscriber, professor of music, in Boston, begs leave to propose by printing by subscription, the NEW MINSTREL, intended to be a collection of original compositions in Music, one number to come out every month; and each number to consist of at least, one composition for the harpsichord, piano forte, or spinnett, one for the guittar, and one for the German flute, also of one song in French, and two songs in the English language.

The work to [be] amplified on large folio half sheets, sewed.

With the first number will be given an original frontispiece, and each composition displayed on copper-plate, all engraved with elegance and taste by an adept in the art and educated in Europe. [J. Norman ?]

Each number will be prefaced with about sixteen printed pages, of an essay on musical expression, by Mr. *Avison* [evidently his "Essay on musical expression," 1752] which pages may compose when the essay is compleat, a separate volume, according to the fancy of the professor.

As all the paper expended in this work must be of particular size and quality, and made for the purpose; as every plate will cost Mr. Selby more than eight dollars; and as each of the numbers could not be executed in London for less than five shillings, the price for each of the numbers is One Dollar and Half.

[292]

On the first of March next (if a sufficient number of subscribers appears) the first number will be delivered at Mr. Robert Bell's, Philadelphia; Messieurs Watson and Goodwin, Hartford; Mr. John Carret's, Providence; Mr. Bulkey Emerson's, Newbury; Mr. Samuel Hall's, Salem; Messieurs Fleet's in Cornhill; Mr. Gill's in Court Street; and Edward Powarr's, State Street, Boston, to each subscriber on his paying One Dollar and Half. The price of each number to a purchaser who does not subscribe will be Two Dollars.

WILLIAM SELBY

Mr. Selby conceives that he need not urge the literary and other benefits which might arise from a due encouragement of works of the above kind. At this age of general civilization, at this area of the acquaintance with a nation far gone in politeness and fine arts—even the stern patriot and lover of his country's glory, might be addressed on the present subject with not less propriety than the man of elegance and taste.

The promptness of this young country in those sciences which were once thought peculiar only to riper age, has already brought upon her the eyes of the world.

She has pushed her researches deep into philosophy and her statesmen and generals equalled those of the Roman name.

And shall those arts which make her happy, be less courted than those arts which have made her great? Why may she not be "In song unequall'd as unmatch'd in war"?

A cry has gone forth against all amusements which are but a step from Gothism.—The raisers of such a cry being unacquainted with distinctions, and little considering that "indulgences are only vices when pursued at the expence of some virtue" and that they intrench upon *No virtue*, they are innocent, and have in every age been acknowledged such by almost all moralists. *W. S.*

Note. The whole of the above work will be comprised in ten numbers.
Those that are inclined to encourage said work are earnestly requested to send their names as early as possible, to any of the above places, as it will enable the publisher to get them engraved and printed, ready to deliver by the said first of March. A list of the subscribers names will be printed alphabetically with the last number.

In spite of this remarkable "Selbst-Anzeige," as the Germans would say, Selby's "New minstrel" seems not to have been published.

NEW MISCELLANEOUS MUSICAL WORK. For the voice and piano forte. Consisting of songs, serenades, cantatas, canzonetts, canons, glees &c. &c. Composed by D^r. G. K. Jackson. Printed for the Author. Copyright secured. P. M. [n. p., n. d.] 20 p. 31 cm.

Title-page, verso numbered 1.
At head of t.-p.: N^o.

Contents:
    p.   1–2 The cricket.
          3 Song for two voices in canon.
          4 Huzza! for liberty.

    5–7 Sweet are the banks.
      8 American serenade.
      9 Cancherizante.
  10–13 A winters evening.
     14 New York serenade.
  15–16 Ah Delia.
  17–18 Dirge for General Washington.
     18 Dead march.
     19 The fairies.
     20 Glee. Gentle air.

In all cases except *The fairies*, p. 19, the caption title includes: Composed by Dr. G. K. Jackson. Printed for the Author. Copyright secured.

In the case of *The fairies*, "Copy right secured. Printed for the Author" is placed at foot of page.

The inclusion of the *Dirge for General Washington* and the *Dead March* would seem to indicate publication ca. 1800, although the actual date may have been considerably later. Issued probably in New York.

In MWA copy, "N⁰." on t.-p. is followed by the figure "1" in ink; in NN by the figure "2."   DLC, McD–W, MWA, NN

A NEW OCCASIONAL OVERTURE . . .
See A new occasional *Overture.*

A NEW PATRIOTIC SONG. The words and music by a gentleman of this city. New York, Printed & sold at J. Hewit's [!] Musical repository. Price 25 cents.
(*In* A collection of new & favorite songs. [A] Philadelphia [ca. 1800] p. [192]–[193])

Song, pfte. acc.
First line: O proud France you'll rue the day that you your independence sway.   HFB

NEW PHILADELPHIA JEST BOOK.
See Philadelphia jest book.

THE NEW PRESIDENT'S MARCH.
See Washington's march.
THE NEW PRESIDENT'S OR JEFFERSON'S MARCH.
See The new *President's or Jefferson's march.*

A NEW SCENA AND POLACCA. Composed for Madame Catalani. Adapted for the pianoforte and flute by G. G. Ferrari. Printed for and sold by J. & M. Paff, Broadway, New York [n. d.] 10 p. 33 cm.

Title-page. Music, p. 2–10.
Pfte. 2 hds.
Published possibly as early as 1799.   MWA

THE NEW SOMEBODY. Written by Mr. Bernard of the New Theatre. Composed by B. Carr. Printed & sold at B. Carr's Musical repository, Philadelphia; J. Carr's, Baltimore & J. Hewitt's, New York. (25 cents) (*In* Three ballads by B. Carr. Philadelphia [1799] p. 2–3)

Song, pfte. acc. Arr. for flute or "guittar," p. 3.
First line: To beg one boon or breath [!] one vow. DLC (incomplete), JFD

—— Reprint (or one of the "seperate [!] sheets"), ca. 1799. DLC, ICN, MWA

NEW SONG. Composed by a son of liberty.
See [That seat of science Athens]

NEW SONG. Set to music by A. Hawkins.
See [Throw an apple]

NEW SONG. Words and music by F. H. Esq.
See [Give me thy heart as I give mine]

NEW SONG FOR A SERENADE. By D. G. of Portland. The tune taken
from an air in the opera, Incle and Yarico, composed by Dr. Arne [!]
(*In* The Massachusetts magazine. Boston, August, 1791. p. [515]–516)

Melody and bass, with accompanying text.
First line: Rise my Delia, heav'nly charmer.
The "tune" is *Fresh and strong* by Samuel Arnold, not Arne.
D. G. of Portland: Daniel George.   DLC (etc.)

—— A new song for a serenade. By D. George.
(*In* The American musical miscellany. Northampton, 1798. p. 247–249)

Melody and bass with accompanying text.
First line same as preceding.   DLC (etc.)

THE NEW SONG BOOK.
See Miss Ashmore's choice collection of songs.

THE NEW SPINNING WHEEL. [n. p., n. d.] 1 l. 28½ cm.
Song, pfte. acc., followed by arr. for flute or guitar.
First line: One summer's eev [!] as Nancy fair.
Presumably American, 179–.
MWA copy is closely trimmed.   MWA

THE NEW VOLUNTEERS MARCH. [New York] I. and M. Paff [n. d.]
1 l. 33 cm.
Pfte. 2 hds.
Published possibly as early as 1799.   NN

—— The same as preceding, but with "Sold by I. and M. Paff" at foot of
page.   NBuG

NEW YANKEE DOODLE.
See Yankee Doodle.

NEW YORK.
See United States country *Dances*, p. 8.

THE NEW YORK PATRIOTIC SONG. Alternative title of *The Federal
constitution and Liberty forever.*

[295]

NEW YORK SERENADE. For two voices in canon. Composed by D
G. K. Jackson. Printed for the author. Copyright secured.
(*In* New miscellaneous musical work, by Dr. G. K. Jackson. [n. p., ca. 180
p. 14)
Duet, unaccompanied. Two staves.
First line: Oh my treasure crown my pleasure.   DLC, MW

THE NEW YORK SENERADING [!] WALTZ. Arranged for the piano fort
violin or flute [n. p., n. d.] [2] p. 32½ cm.
Below title, at left margin the letter "P"; at right margin the letter "W."
Pfte. 2 hds. (violin or flute)
Composed by Peter Weldon.
Sonneck gives: [New York, ca. 1800]   DL

———— The same as preceding except that the letters "P" and "W" have becon
the words "Peter" and "Weldon."
Sonneck gives: [New York, 180–].   DLC, McD–W, NI

NEWEST FASHION. The jovial songster containing a good collection of song
Boston, Printed by J. White, near Charles-river Bridge. 1800. 34 p. MW

NICOLAI'S FAVORITE SONATA.
See Nicolai's favorite *Sonata.*

NICOLAI'S 2 EASY SONATAS FOR THE PIANO FORTE.
See Nicolai's 2 easy *Sonatas* . . .

[NIGHT] SONNET IV.
(*In* The hours of love, by J. Hook. Philadelphia [ca. 1794] p. 8–9)
Song, pfte. acc. Arr. for Ger. flute or "guittar," p. 9.
First line: Night reigns around in sleep's soft arms.   DLC, JFD, LS

*THE NIGHT WAS DARK, the angry waves prepar'd.
This song by William Linley was advertised as "just published" among "ne
songs, sung at the theatres, New York," in the *Federal gazette*, Baltimor
June 25, 1798.

THE NIGHTINGALE.
(*In* The aviary. A collection of three sonnets by J. Hook.
Philadelphia [1798] p. (6)–(7).)
Song, pfte. acc. Arr. for "guittar," p. (7).
First line: Sweet nightingale, no more complain.
                          JFD, LSL, NN (lacks last page

THE NIGHTINGALE. Selected from the Aviary. A collection of sonnets.
Hook. Also just published

No. 1. The thrush.   No. 4. The robin red breast.
No. 2. The linnets.   No. 5. The nightingale.
No. 3. The goldfinch.   No. 6. The lark.
                and No. 7. The cuckoo.

New York, Sold by I. and M. Paff, No. 127 Broadway [1799–1803] [2] p
30½ cm.
At head of title: No. 5.
Imprint at foot of p. [2].
Song, pfte. acc.
First line same as preceding.   DLC, ES, NI

HE NIGHTINGALE. Boston, Printed & sold at P. A. von Hagen & cos. imported piano forte ware house, No. 3 Cornhill & G. Gilfert, New York. Where also may be had the much admired songs of Crazy Jane & Life let us cherish [ca. 1800] [2] p. 33 cm.

Below imprint: For the piano forte or guittar.
Song, pfte. acc. Arr. for German flute or violin, p. [2].
First line same as preceding.
Advertised in November, 1800, as "published." DLC, MB, N, RPJCB

HE NIGHTINGALE. A favorite cantata by Mr. Hook. New York, Printed for G. Gilfert, No. 177 Broadway [1797] 4 p. 31½ cm.

Song, pfte. acc.
Introduction and recitative, p. 1. First line: Sweet minstrel, sweet minstrel, sound those warbling notes again.
Song, p. [2]–4. First line: Sweet nightingale thy tunefull song.
JFD, McD–W, MWA, RPJCB

Advertised in March, 1797, to be published "in a few days."

——— A "cantata 'The nightingale'—Miss Huntley, bird accompaniments on the flageolet Mr. Shaw—[by Raynor] Taylor," was to be sung at a concert in Philadelphia, on April 21, 1796. No such composition by Raynor Taylor has been found.

'HE NIGHTINGALE. Arranged for the piano forte. With a flute accompaniment ad libitum. And as a dueet [!] for two performers on the piano forte. New York, Sold by J. & M. Paff, Broadway [1799–1803] 3 p. 32 cm.

Pfte. 2 hds. and flute, p. 1; pfte. 4 hds, p. 2–3.
This is not the melody of Hook's Nightingale.
Could it be Raynor Taylor's? MWA

THÉ NIGHTINGALE, or Charms of melody. Baltimore, Printed for Henry S. Keatinge. 1798.

THE NIGHTINGALE, or Songster's companion. Consisting of an elegant and polite selection of the most approved ancient and modern songs. [Two lines of verse] Philadelphia: Printed and sold by W. Woodhouse, at the Bible, No. 6, South Front-street. 1791.

'HE NIGHTINGALE OF LIBERTY: or Delight of harmony. A choice collection of patriotic, masonic, & entertaining songs. To which are added toasts and sentiments, moral, humorous, and republican. [Verses] New York, Printed by John Harrisson, And sold at his book-store, No. 3 Peck-slip, 1797. 83 p., front. 14½ cm.

Title-page; "Advertisement of books and stationary," p. [2]; Songs, p. [3]–80; Toasts and sentiments, p. 81; Contents, p. 82–83.
Words only, tunes occasionally mentioned.

NINA. Price 12 cents. Printed for B. Carr, Philadelphia [179–] p. 15. 33½ cm.

Song, pfte. acc.
First line: Near yonder murm'ring chrystal [!] stream.
Sung by Mrs. Melmoth in New York, March, 1794. MWA, NBuG

NINE NEW SONGS. Written by a young gentleman of Maryland. The mus.
by I. B. Gauline. Printed for the Author and sold by R. Shaw, No. 1
South Fourth street, Philadelphia and J. Carr's, Gay street, Baltimor
Harrison jun, sc [n. d.] 18 p. 33 cm.

Title-page.

Contents:

    p. [1]–2 The charms of music.
       3–4 The impatient lover.
       5–6 The male coquette.
       7–8 Answer to the Male coquett [!].
      9–10 Ah how sweet were those moments of love.
    11–12 Sweet is the balmy breath of spring.
    13–14 Ah were [!] are fled those hours.
    15–16 Adieu to all my heart holds dear.
    17–18 Mira of the village plain.

I. B. Gauline: John B. Gauline.
Published possibly as early as 1800.   ES, MdB

NO FLOW'R THAT BLOWS FROM SELIMA AND AZOR. Linley. [n. p
n. d.] (22)–(23) p. 31 cm.

Song, pfte. acc. Three staves, p. (23).
First line same as title.
Evidently a Carr imprint, 179–. *cf.* *Elegant extracts.*
Selima and Azor, by Thomas Linley, the Elder.   ABH

NO GOOD WITHOUT AN EXCEPTION. Written and composed by Charle
Dibdin for his new entertainment called Castles in the air. (20 cents
Sold by B. Carr at the Musical repository; H. & P. Rice, No. 50 Marke
st., Philadelphia; by J. Rice, Bookseller, Baltimore and by J. Harrison, No
108 Maiden Lane, New York.
(*In* The gentleman's amusement, ed. by R. Shaw. Philadelphia [1794–96
p. 14–15)

Song, pfte. acc.
First line: The world's a good thing.
In No. 2, May, 1794.   PH

———— Separate issue of preceding, 1796   LSI

Advertised in March, 1796, among other "new editions" as published "a
Carr's Musical Repository, William Street," New York.

———— The same as preceding.
(*In* A collection of new & favorite songs. [A] Philadelphia [ca. 1800
p. [188]–[189], numbered 14–15)   HFI

NO 'TWAS NEITHER SHAPE NOR FEATURE, as a duett.
(*In* Elegant extracts for the German flute or violin. Philadelphia [1798
bk. 3, p. 13)

Duet, flutes or violins (or flute and violin) with accompanying text.
First line same as title.
Composed by Johann Christian Bach.   DLC, NN

NO 'TWAS NEITHER SHAP [!] NOR FEATURE] A favorit [!] song. By Mr. Bach. Publish'd by G. Willig, No. 185 Market st. [1798–1804] 1 l., paged 1. 31½ cm.

Imprint at foot of page.
Song, pfte. acc.
Title from first line. DLC, ES, JFD, MWA, NN, PP–K

—— The same as preceding, but without imprint. DLC

NO LUCK ABOUT THE HOUSE.
See Manuscript collection of hymns, songs, etc. (43).

NO MORE HIS FEARS ALARMING. An admired new song. Composed by Stephen Storace & sung by Sr. Storace in the opera of the Pirates. [Philadelphia] Publish'd by G. Willig, 165 Market st. [1795–97] [2] p. 33 cm.

Song, pfte. acc.
First line same as title. DLC

NO MORE I'LL COURT THE TOWN BRED FAIR.
(*In* Young's vocal and instrumental musical miscellany. Philadelphia [1793–95] p. 35)

Song, pfte. acc.
First line same as title.
In No. 4, 1793.
From *The farmer*, by William Shield. DLC, Hopk.

—— Separate issue of preceding (without page number), ca. 1793. ES

NO MORE I'LL HEAVE THE TENDER SIGH. Sung by Mrs. Crouch in the new opera of the Seige [!] of Belgrade. Philadelphia, Printed by R. Shaw and sold at his music store, No. 13 South Fourth street [n. d.] [2]p. 33 cm.

Song, pfte. acc.
First line same as title.
The siege of Belgrade, by Stephen Storace.
Published possibly as early as 1800. DLC, McD–W, NN

NO NOT YET. A favorite song. Boston, Printed & sold by P. A. von Hagen & co. at their piano forte warehouse, No. 3 Cornhill and G. Gilfert, New York. Where also may be had the much admired song of Come buy my daffodillies [ca. 1800] [2] p. 32 cm.

Song, pfte. acc. Arr. for German flute or violin, p. [2].
First line; Young Willy lov'd me in his heart.
Published probably in 1799. RPB

NO SONG, NO SUPPER. An opera in two acts. With additional songs. As performed with great applause by the Old American company of comedians. Philadelphia, From the press of Mathew Carey, No. 118 Market street, 1792. 35 p. 16 mo.

Libretto by Prince Hoare to Stephen Storace's opera (1790).
Advertised in the *Federal gazette*, Philadelphia, December 6, 1792, as "just published." PHi

———— The same. Second Philadelphia edition. Philadelphia. From the pre
of Mathew Carey, Jan. 14, 1793. 32, [3] p. 17 cm.

Text is followed by a list of books printed by Mathew Carey, No. 118 Mark
street, p. [33]–[35]. MB, MWA, N

NO SONG, NO SUPPER. A comic opera in two acts. As performed wit
universal applause by the Old American company. Third American editior
With additions. New York, Printed by J. Harrisson for J. Reid, No. 1
Water street, 1793. 36 p. 16 cm.

Libretto.
Title-page; dramatis personae, p. [2]; text, p. [3]–36. DLC, M

NO SONG NO SUPPER. An opera in two acts. As performed at the theatr
in Boston. Printed at the Apollo Press in Boston for William P. Blak
No. 59 Cornhill. 1794. 29 p. 17½ cm.

Libretto.
Title-page; dramatis personae, p. [2]; text, p. [3]–29.
DLC, MB, MWA, NI

NO THAT WILL NEVER DO. A favorite song. Composed by Mr. Hool
[n. p., n. d.] 74–75 p. 32 cm.

Song, pfte. acc.
First line: When lovers are too daring grown.
Apparently a separate issue from *The musical repertory*, Boston [No. V, 1799]
DLC, E

NOBODY.
(*In* The American musical miscellany. Northampton, 1798. p. 252–254)

Melody only, with accompanying text.
First line: If to force me to sing it be your intention. DLC (etc.)

NOBODY. Composed by R. Taylor. Price 25 cents. Printed and sold a
B. Carr's Musical repository, Philadelphia; J. Carr's, Baltimore; & J. Hewitt's, New York [1797–99] [2] p. 32½ cm.

Song, pfte. acc.
First line: When as my swain began to woo. CSmH, NRU–Mus

NOBODY COMING TO MARRY ME. Composed by Mr. Cooke. Baltimore
Printed by Henry S. Keatinge [ca. 1798 ?] 1 l. 29½ cm.

Song, pfte. acc.
First line: Last night the dogs did bark.
Printed from movable type. LSL

[NOON] SONNET II.
(*In* The hours of love, by J. Hook. Philadelphia [ca. 1794] p. 4–5)

Song, pfte. acc. Arr. for guitar or Ger. flute, p. 5.
First line: Hush ev'ry breze [!] let nothing move. DLC, JFD, LSL

NOON. Sold by G. Willig, Philadelphia [1795–97] 4–5 p. 23½ x 33½ cm.

At head of title: Hush ev'ry breeze.
At head of first score: Sonnet II.

At foot of p. 4: I. Burger, jnʳ, Scᵗ., N. Y.
At foot of p. 5: I. Burger, Scᵗ.
Song, pfte. acc. Arr. for "guittar" or German flute, p. 5.
First line same as preceding.
Apparently a separate issue from some Willig publication of James Hook's
The hours of love. cf. similar issue of "Evening." DLC

—— Hush ev'ry breeze. From Hook's Hours of Love. Price 25 cents.
Philadelphia, Printed at Carr & cos. Musical repository [1793–94] [3] p.
32 cm.
Song, pfte. acc. Arr. for "guittar," p. [3].
First line same as title.
The same as [*Noon*] *Sonnet II.*
Sonneck gives date: 1794.
Sung in Philadelphia in 1792. ABHu, DLC, ES, JFD, MWA

—— Hush ev'ry breeze. Selected from the Hours of Love. Composed by
Mr. Hook [n. p., n. d.] [2] p. 32 cm.
Song, pfte. acc.
First line same as title.
Evidently considerably later than the preceding issue. Sonneck gives: ca.
1800. DLC, RPJCB

NORAH THE THEME OF MY SONG. Poor soldier.
(*In* A Collection of favorite songs, divided into two books. Arr. by A.
Reinagle. [1789 ?] p. 10)
Song, pfte. acc.
First line: Tho' Leixlip is proud of its close shady bowers.
Poor soldier, by William Shield. CdeW, ES, Hopk., (lacking in DLC copy).

NORTH CAROLINA JIGG [!]
See United States country *Dances,* p. 15.

THE NOSEGAY GIRL. Composed by Mr. Wilson. New York, Printed &
sold by Mrs. Howe, 320 Pearl street, Importer of all kinds of musical instruments. Price 25 cents. [1799–1800] [2] p. 33 cm.
Song, pfte. acc.
First line: When first I sold posies. ES

NOT MINE THE NARROW SOUL ASSUR'D. A favorite song. Sung in
the new opera of Abroad and at home. New York, Printed and sold by G.
Gilfert, No. 177 Broad Way [1797–1801] [2] p. 31½ cm.
Song, pfte. acc.
First line same as title.
William Shield's *Abroad and at home* was first produced in New York, Novem-
ber 10, 1797; in Philadelphia, January 12, 1798.
This issue probably ca. 1798. MWA

NOTHING LIKE GROG.
(*In* Elegant extracts for the German flute or violin. Baltimore [1794] bk. 1,
p. 10–11)
Melody only, flute or violin, with accompanying text.
First line: A plague of those musty old lubbers.
Composed by Charles Dibdin. DLC, NN

[301]

NOTHING LIKE GROG.
(*In* The American musical miscellany. Northampton, 1798. p. 55–58)

Melody only, with accompanying text.
First line same as preceding. DLC (etc.

*NOUVELLE ENTERTAINMENT, or, Musical extravaganza in three parts
composed by Raynor Taylor.
Under this title some sort of an *olio* "consisting of dialogue, comic, pastora
hunting and bacchanalian songs and duets . . . the whole of the musi
original and composed by Mr. Taylor," was to be "recited and sung by Mr
Taylor and Miss Huntley (his pupil) late of the Theatre Royal Coven
Garden" at Philadelphia, June 26, 1793.

[NOW ALL IN PREPARATION] Sung by Mr. Francis in the Haunted Towe
(*In* The gentleman's amusement, ed. by R. Shaw. Philadelphia [1794–96
p. 41)

Melody only, flute (or violin) with accompanying text.
Title from first line.
In No. 5, March 1, 1795.
Appears in the Storace score as "French tune." DLC, PH

NOW AT MOONLIGHT'S FAIRY HOUR. A duett for two voices. Compose
by Thomas Thompson. New York, Publish'd by J. and M. Paff, Broadway
[1799–1803] 7 p. 32 cm.

Title-page, with imprint at head of title.
Duet, harp or piano forte acc. Four staves.
First line same as title.
In lower margin of p. 7: W. P.

W. P.: William Pirsson. DLC, LSL, MB, NN, PH

In MB copy "Paff" has been erased from imprint and "Willson" substituted.
Also "62" follows "Broadway." Both written in ink [1812].
One NN copy has "J. & M. Paff" erased and "J. Willson, No. 16 Maïden
Lane" substituted [1815].

NOW'S THE TIME TO SING AND PLAY. A favorite song. Composed by
Mr. Hook. New York, Printed & sold by J. Hewitt, No. 131 William
street. Price 25 cents [1797–99] [2] p. 31½ cm.

Song, pfte. acc. Arr. for flute p. [2].
First line same as title. DLC, ES

———— The same as preceding.
(*In* A collection of new & favorite songs. [A] Philadelphia [ca. 1800] p.
[62]–[63]) HFB

NOW'S THE TIME TO SING AND PLAY. Boston, Printed & sold at P. A
von Hagen & cos. imported piano forte ware house, No. 3 Cornhill. And
to be had at G. Gilfert, New York. Where may be had Mary's bower &
Adams march [ca. 1799] [2] p. 33 cm.

Song, pfte. acc.
First line same as title. JFD, RPJCB

[302]

NOW LET RICH MUSIC SOUND] Written by Thomas Dawes, jun., esquire, and sung at the entertainment given on Bunker's Hill by the proprietors of Charles River Bridge at the opening of the same. To the foregoing tune. (*In* The American musical miscellany. Northampton, 1798. p. 133–134)

Words only.
Title from first line.
To be sung to the tune of "An ode for the Fourth of July" (*ibidem* p. 130–132).
The tune is that of "God save the King." DLC (etc.)

NO. 1. OF A NEW SETT OF COTILIONS [!]
See No. I of a new sett of *Cotilions* [!]

THE NYMPHS COMPLAINT. By Mr. Swan.
(In The songster's assistant, ed. by T. Swan. Suffield [ca. 1800] p. 11–13)
Song, pfte. acc.
First line: Why does the sun dart forth his cheerful rays. CtY, MB

) COME AWAY MY SOLDIER BONNY. Sung by Mrs. Warrell of the New Theatre with universal applause, in the opera of the Rival soldiers. Philadelphia, Published by G. Willig, No. 185 Market st. [1798–1804] [2] p. 32 cm.

Song, pfte. acc.
First line: O come away, come my soldier bonny.
Mrs. Warrell sang in Shield's *Rival soldiers, or Sprigs of laurel*, in Philadelphia, December 6, 1799. DLC, MWA, PP–K

[O COME SWEET MARY COME TO ME] Sung by Mr. Incledon in the new opera called Sprigs of laurel.
(*In* The gentleman's amusement, ed. by R. Shaw. Philadelphia [1794–96] p. 40–41)

Melody only, flute or violin, with accompanying text.
First line: When night & left upon my guard.
Title as given above forms last line of each stanza.
In No. 5, March 1, 1795.
Sprigs of laurel, or, The rival soldiers, by William Shield. DLC, PHi

O COME SWEET MARY COME TO ME. Sung by Mr. Hardinge of the New Theatre with universal applause, in the opera of the Rival soldiers. Philadelphia, Publish'd by G. Willig, No. 185 Market st. [ca. 1799] [2] p. 32 cm

Song, pfte. acc.
First line: When night and left upon my guard.
Title forms the last line of each stanza.
Mr. Hardinge sang in the first Philadelphia performance of *The rival soldiers*, April 5, 1799. DLC, MWA, PHi, PP–K

O COME SWEET MARY COME TO ME. Sung with great applause by Mr. Darley in Sprigs of laurel. New York, Printed & sold at J. Hewitt's Musical repository, No. [ ] Maiden lane [n. d.] [2] p. 32 cm.

Song, pfte. acc. Arr. for flute, p. [2].
First line same as preceding.
The Mr. Darley here referred to is presumably John Darley, Jr., who sang in the first New York performance of *Sprigs of laurel*, March 22, 1805. How-

ever, it is also possible from the imprint that reference is made to John Darley, Sr., who sang with Mr. Hardinge in the first Philadelphia performance of *The rival soldiers, or Sprigs of laurel*, April 5, 1799.   MW.

OH! COME TO MASON BOROUGH'S GROVE.
(*In* [A volume of songs, etc., composed or copied by Francis Hopkinson 1759–60] p. 163)

Song, harpsichord acc.
First line same as title.
Composed by Francis Hopkinson.   DLC

[OH DEAR DELIGHTFUL SKILL] Sung by Mrs. Oldmixon in the Prize, o 2. 5. 3. 8.
(*In* The gentleman's amusement, ed. by R. Shaw.   Philadelphia [1794–96 p. 60–61)

Melody only, flute (or violin) with accompanying text.
Title from first line.
In No. [8], 1796.
Mrs. Oldmixon sang in the first Philadelphia performance of Stephen Storace's *The Prize*, May 26, 1794, and several times in 1796.
                                                          DLC, PHi, PP-I

O DEAR WHAT CAN THE MATTER BE.   A favorite song or duett.   Price 20 cents.   Philadelphia, Printed for Carr and co. at their Musical repository No. 136 High street [1793]   [2] p.   33½ cm.

Song, pfte. acc., p. [1]; duet (three staves), p. [2].
First line same as title   ES, HFB, LSL, McD–W, NN

Advertised in December, 1793, as "published . . . printed singly" by "B Carr & Co. Musical Repository, No. 122 Southside of Market street," Philadelphia.   As regards seeming inconsistency in the address, *cf. The match girl.*

O DEAR WHAT CAN THE MATTER BE.
(*In* The gentleman's amusement, ed. by R. Shaw.   Philadelphia [1794–96 p. 28–29)

Duet for flutes or violins (or flute and violin) with accompanying text.
First line same as title.
In No. 4, February 1, 1795.   DLC, PHi

———— The same.
See Evening amusement [1796], p. 28.   Lacking in DLC copy.

O DEARLY I LOVE SOMEBODY.   Sung by Mrs. Mountain.   New York, Printed and sold by G. Gilfert & co., No. 209 Broadway near St. Pauls [1795]   [2] p.   32 cm.

Song, pfte. acc.
First line: Of all the swains both far and near.
Not identical (except as to its first line) with Hook's song "My bonny lowland lassie."   McD–W, MWA

DEARLY I LOVE SOMEBODY. Price 20 cents. Printed and sold at B. Carr's Musical repositories, Philadelphia and New York & J. Carr's, Baltimore [1797] [2] p. 30½ cm.

Song, pfte. acc.
First line: Of all the swains boht [!] far and near.   ABHu, LSL

Advertised September, 1797, as among other "songs lately published."

------ The same as preceding.
(*In* A collection of new & favorite songs. [A] Philadelphia [ca. 1800] p. [110]–[111])   HFB

) GENTLE BE THY SLUMBERS. Taken from the German Erato. New York, Printed & sold by G. Gilfert, No. 177 Broadway. And to be had of P. A. von Hagen, Boston [1797–1801] 1 l. 33 cm.

Song, pfte. acc.
First line same as title.   DLC

) GIVE ME THE LASS THAT I LOVE. A new song. Sung by Mr. Dignum.
(*In* A collection of favorite songs, by Mr. Hook. New York [1799–1801] bk. [2], p. 10–11)

Song, pfte. acc.
First line: How vainly you tell me I have not the art.   DLC

OH HAD IT BEEN MY HAPPY LOT. Sung by Miss Broadhurst in the farce of Flash in the pan. The words by Mr. Milns. Music by J. Hewitt. New York, Printed & sold at J. Hewitt's Musical repository, No. 131 William street. Price 25 cents.
(*In* collection of new & favorite songs. [A] Philadelphia [ca. 1800] p. [26]–[27])

Song, pfte. acc.
First line same as title.
Flash in the pan had its only performance in New York, presumably with Miss Broadhurst in the cast, on April 20, 1798.
The original issue was advertised as "just published" among "new songs, sung at the theatres New York" in the *Federal gazette*, Baltimore, June 25, 1798.   HFB

O INNOCENCE CELESTIAL MAID. Sung by Mrs. Warrel. Printed at B. Carr's Musical repositories Philadelphia & New York & J. Carr's, Baltimore (Price 25 cents) [1797] 2 p. 30½ cm.

Song, pfte. acc.
First line same as title.
In lower left-hand corner, p. 2: O innocence 2.   LSL, McD–W, NN, PP–K

Advertised by J. Carr, Baltimore, among other "songs, lately published," in September, 1797.

O TIS LOVE. Alternative title of *When first to Helen's lute*, by Samuel Arnold.

*O LET MY HARBOUR BE YOUR ARMS, PRETTY POLLY.
Advertised in March, 1797, as to be published "in a few days" by "G. Gilfert at his Musical Magazine, No. 177 Broadway," New York.

O LOVELY PEACE.   A favorite duet from Handel's oratorio of Judas Macca-
beus.   Philadelphia, Publish'd and sold at G. Willig's music store [179-?
2–4 p.   31½ cm.

Duet with bass.   Three staves.
First line same as title.   PP-I

Sung by Mrs. Pownall and Miss Wrighten in a sacred concert during Holy
Week at Charleston, March 24, 1796.

O NANCY WILT THOU GANG WI' ME.
(*In* The Universal asylum.   Philadelphia, March, 1790.   p. 189–192)

Song, pfte. acc.
First line same as title.
Air by Charles Thomas Carter.   DLC (etc.

――― O Nanny wilt thou gang with me.   A favorite song.   New York, Printed
for G. Gilfert & co., at their Musical magazine, No. 177 Broadway [1796
[2] p.   31½ cm.

Song, pfte. acc.   Arr. for flute, p. [2].
First line same as title.   MWA, PP-K, RPJCB

――― Oh Nanny.   Printed & sold at B. Carr's Musical repositories in New
York & Philadelphia & J. Carr, Baltimore.   Price 25 cents.   [1796?]   [2] p.
33 cm.

Imprint at foot of p. 2.
Song, pfte. acc.   Arr. for flute, p. [2].
First line same as preceding.   CdeW, LSL, MWA, NN

Probably the issue advertised (under the title *O Nancy will thou fly*) among
"new editions" of ". . . favorite songs, some of which never before published
in America," at Carr's Musical Repository, William Street, New York, in
March, 1796.

OH! NE'ER CAN I THE JOYS FORGET.   A ballad.   As sung by Miss
Stephens.   The words by I. R. Blanche, esqr.   Composed by Mr. I. Smith.
Printed for J. Carr, Baltimore.   Price 25 cts.   [n. d.]   [2] p.   32½ cm.

Song, pfte. acc.
First line same as title.
In lower margin of p. [2]: Oh! neer can I.
Possibly not 18th century.   MWA

O PITY A MAIDEN & PRAY TAKE HER PART.   Composed by Mr. Hook.
New York, Printed for G. Gilfert & co., No. 191 Broadway [1794–95]   [2] p.
33½ cm.

Song, pfte. acc.
First line: Ye youths wheresoever you wander.   JFD, RPJCB

Also as *O pitty* [!] *a maiden, and pray take her part* advertised in March,
1795, as "published and to be had at G. Willig's Musical Magazine, No. 165
Market street," Philadelphia.   This issue has not been located.

[306]

SAY BONNY LASS. A favorite Scotch song. New York, Printed and sold by G. Gilfert, No. 177 Broadway [1797–1801] 1 l. 31½ cm.

Song, pfte, acc.
First line same as title. **MWA**

SAY BONNY LASS. A favorite Scotch song in the opera of Incle and Yaricho [!] [n. p., n. d.] p. 52. 34½ cm.

Presumably a separate issue from *The musical repertory*, Boston. [No. IV, ca. 1797–99], p. 52.

Song, pfte. acc.
First line same as title.
Inkle and Yarico, by Samuel Arnold. **JFD**

As to the relation of "O say bonny lass" to Arnold's *Inkle and Yarico*, *cf.* "Oh say simple maid."

OH SAY SIMPLE MAID. A favorite dialogue in Inkle and Yarico to which is annex'd the original song of Oh say bonny lass. New York, Printed and sold at B. Carr's Musical repository. Price 12 cts. [1795–96] 1 l. 33 cm.

Duet, pfte. acc.
First lines: O say simple maid have you form'd any notion.—Oh say bonny lass will you live in a barrack.

At foot of page remainder of "Words in Inkle and Yarico" and "Original words." **LSL, McD–W, MWA, NN, RPJCB**

Samuel Arnold has made use of several ballad tunes in his *Inkle and Yarico*, among them "Oh say bonny lass." The title appears (in parenthesis) in the score at upper right hand corner of the first page of "Oh say simple maid."

Inkle and Yarico seems to have reached the peak of its popularity in America, ca. 1796, the probable date of this issue.

O SAY SIMPLE MAID.
(*In* Elegant extracts for the German flute or violin. Philadelphia [1796] bk. 2, p. 12)

Melody only, flute or violin, with accompanying text.
First line same as title. **DLC, NN**

OH SAY SIMPLE MAID. A duet in the comic opera of Incle and Yarico. (*In* The American musical miscellany. Northampton, 1798. p. 258–259.)

Melody only, with accompanying text.
First line same as title. **DLC**

OH SINCE I'VE FOUND YOU nothing grieves me. A favorite duett. Sung in the opera of the Outlaws. New York, Printed & sold at J. Hewitt's Musical repository. No 23 Maiden Lane. Pr. 25 cents.
(*In* A collection of new & favorite songs. [A] Philadelphia [ca. 1800] p. [54]–[55].)

Song, pfte. acc. Arr. for flute, p. [55].
First line same as title.
Original issue, 1799–1800.
The outlaws, by Michael Kelly. **HFB**

OH THE MOMENT WAS SAD. In the Surrender of Calais. New York Printed & sold at J. Hewitt's Musical repository, No. 131 William str [1797–99] 1 l. 31½ cm.

Imprint at foot of page.
Song, pfte. acc.
First line same as title.
The surrender of Calais, by Samuel Arnold. ABHu, DLC, ICN, NN

———— The same as preceding.
(*In* A collection of new & favorite.songs. [A] Philadelphia [ca. 1800] p
[194]) HFI

O WHITHER CAN MY WILLIAM STRAY. Composed by Mr. Hook. New York, Printed & sold at J. Hewitt's Musical repository, No. 131 William street. Sold also by B. Carr, Philadelphia & J. Carr, Baltimore. Price 25 cents. [1798] [2] p. 30½ cm.

Song, pfte. acc.
First line same as title. DLC, ES, NN, NRU–Mus

Advertised in January, 1798, as "just published by J. Hewitt, No. 131 William St.," New York; also in December, 1797, as "published at Carr's Musical repository, Market street," Philadelphia. These are undoubtedly identical.

———— The same as preceding.
(*In* A collection of new & favorite songs. [A] Philadelphia [ca. 1800] p.
[84]–[85]) HFB

*O WOULD I NE'ER HAD SEEN YOU.
Advertised in November, 1798, by "George Gilbert, at his music store, 177 Broadway, Apollo's Head," New York.

O YES SIR IF YOU PLEASE. Favorite song composed by I. Willson. 25 cts. New York, Publish'd by J. & M. Paff, Broadway [n. d.] [2] p. 33 cm.

Song, pfte. acc. Arr. for German flute, p. [2].
First line: As late I tripp'd it o'er the lea.
Published possibly as early as 1799. ES

OCCASIONAL OVERTURE.
See A new occasional *Overture*.

ODE (AIR, "THOU SOFT FLOWING AVON")
(*In* The Universal asylum, Philadelphia, July, 1790. p. 53–54)

Song, pfte. acc.
First line: Ye sages contending in virtue's fair cause.
Forms part of "An Exercise performed at the Public Commencement in the College of Philadelphia, July 17, 1790, containing an *Ode sacred to the memory of Dr. Franklin.*" This ode was reprinted from the *Universal asylum*, Philadelphia, in the *Massachusetts spy*, Worcester, September 2, 1790, with words and music. Sonneck adds: This is the only instance, as far as I could discover, that a piece of music was printed in our eighteenth century newspapers. DLC (etc.)

)DE AND CHORUSES.
See Mysterious monk.

)DE. As performed at the Stone chapel, Boston, before the President of the United States of America. Words by Mr. Brown of Boston.
(*In* [Unidentified collection (beginning with "A lesson")] Boston [?] ca. 1800. p. 7–8)

Song with chorus, pfte. acc.
First line: Behold the man whom virtue raise.   MHi

)DE. Composed by Mr. Low, for the 12th day of May, 1790, being the anniversary of the St. Tammany Society or Columbian order (For 1st verse see the annexed piece of music)
(*In* The New York magazine, May, 1790. p. 305)

Three-part chorus. Open score.
First line: Daughter of heav'n, thou gift divine.   DLC (etc.)

*AN ODE DESIGNED FOR A PUBLIC COMMENCEMENT in the College of Philadelphia. Contained in Francis Hopkinson's "Poems on several occasions" (v. III of his *Miscellaneous essays*), p. 89–91. Begins, "When heav'n spreads blessings." The music does not seem to be extant.

ODE FOR AMERICAN INDEPENDENCE, July 4th, 1789. By Daniel George. Set by Horatio Garnet.
(*In* The Massachusetts magazine, Boston, July, 1789. p. 452–453)

Melody and bass, with accompanying text, followed by three-part chorus. Open score.
First line: 'Tis done! the edict past.   DLC (etc.)

———— An ode for the Fourth of July. By Daniel George. Set to music by Horatio Garnet.
(*In* The American musical miscellany. Northampton, 1798. p. 142–147)

Melody and bass, with accompanying text, followed by three-part chorus. Open score.
First line same as preceding.   DLC (etc.)

Facsimile of this in Henry M. Brooks' *Olden time music* (Boston, 1888), p. 155–156.

ODE FOR INDEPENDENCE. Composed and set to music by Dr. Willard. Words given in Dunlap and Claypoole's *American daily advertiser*, August 7, 1794. The music does not seem to be extant.   DLC (etc.)

ODE FOR THE FESTIVAL OF ST. JOHN, Evangelist, in South Carolina, 1772. By the most worshipful the Honourable Sir Egerton Leigh, baronet, Grand Master, etc. etc. Set to music by brother Peter Valton.

Words printed under "Poetry" in the *Pennsylvania chronicle*, March 1–8, 1773, "from the South Carolina and American General Gazette—inserted by request of several of our readers." The music seems not to be extant. The ode begins: Behold the social band appears.

[309]

AN ODE FOR THE FOURTH OF JULY.
(*In* The American musical miscellany. Northampton, 1798. p. 130–132)

Four-part chorus. Open score.
First line: Come all ye sons of song.
Tune of "God save the King."
Facsimile in Louis C. Elson's *History of American music* (Boston, 1904), p
145–146.   DLC (etc.)

AN ODE FOR THE FOURTH OF JULY. By Daniel George. Set to music by
Horatio Garnet.
See Ode for American independence.

ODE FOR THE 4TH OF JULY, 1798.
(*In* New [American] patriotic songs, added to a collection of songs by C
Dibdin. Philadelphia, 1799. p. 323–325)

Words only.
First line: There's Ichabod has come to town.
                                                DLC, MWA, NHi, NN, RPJCB

ODE FOR THE FOURTH OF JULY, 1799. Written by Timothy Todd, esqr.;
set to music by the Revd. Chauncey Lee. Hudson, Engraved & sold by
G. Fairman. 1799. Broadside. 28 x 24 cm.

At head of title vignette of youthful Bacchus with lyre.
Engraved music for three-part chorus, with printed text below.
In the possession of H. V. Button, Waterford, N. Y.

ODE FOR THE NEW YEAR, JANUARY 1, 1789. Set to musick by Mr.
William Selby.
(*In* The Massachusetts magazine, Boston, January, 1790. p. 61–62)

Melody and bass, with accompanying text, followed by three-part chorus.
First line: Hark! notes melodious fill the skies.   DLC (etc.)

———— Ode for the New Year.
(*In* The American musical miscellany. Northampton, 1798. p. 189–195)

Melody and bass with accompanying text, followed by three-part chorus.
First line same as preceding.   DLC (etc.)

ODE FOR THE NEW YEAR, JANUARY 1, 1791. Words by Mr. G. Richards.
Musick by Mr. H. Gram.
(*In* The Massachusetts magazine, Boston, January, 1791. p. 55)

Song, pfte. acc.
First line: On the top of a mountain inscribed to fame.
H. Gram: Hans Gram.   DLC (etc.)

AN ODE FOR THE 22D OF FEBRUARY.
(*In* Sacred dirges [Oliver Holden] Boston [1800] p. 24)

Air (trio?).
First line: Now let your plaintive numbers gently rise.
                        CSmH, DLC, ICN, MB, MH, MHi, MWA, NHi, NN, RPB

*ODE FOR VOICES AND INSTRUMENTS by Benjamin Yarnold.
See Anthem and ode by B. Yarnold.

[310]

ODE FROM OSSIAN'S POEMS. The music composed by The Honourable Francis Hopkinson. Sold at Carrs music store, Baltimore [n. d.] 4, [1] p. 31 cm.

Song, pfte. acc.
First line: Pleasant is thy voice Oh Carrel.
Published probably 179–.   Harvard Mus. Assn., McD–W

*AN ODE IN HONOUR OF GENERAL WASHINGTON, composed by William Selby. Was to be performed at a concert in Boston, April 27, 1786.

ODE ON MUSIC. Words by Mr. Pope.
(*In* American harmony, by Oliver Holden, Boston, 1792. p. 13–17)

Three-part chorus, with treble solo. Open score.
First line: Descend ye nine descend and sing.
Composed by Oliver Holden.   CSmH, CtY, DLC, MH, MHi

ODE ON MUSIC. Words by Thaddeus M. Harris.
(*In* American harmony, by Oliver Holden, Boston, 1792. p. 3–4)

Treble, bass, and tenor soli and three-part chorus. Open score.
First line: 'Tis thine sweet pow'r to raise the thought sublime.
Composed by Oliver Holden.   CSmH, CtY, DLC, MH, MHi

*ODE ON PEACE.
An "Ode on peace" was sung at Nassau Hall (Princeton) during commencement, 1760. In Sonneck's book on "Francis Hopkinson . . . and James Lyon" he advanced arguments to attribute the musical authorship of this ode to James Lyon. The contention also is that this ode was identical with the one reported in the *New York Mercury*, October 1, 1759, as "set to music by Mr. James Lyon" and sung during commencement of 1759, on September 26. The ode begins, "Cheerful, fearless and at ease." The music seems not to be extant.

ODE ON SCIENCE.
Sonneck notes: Words and music by Jezaniah Sumner. Written in 1798, on the occasion of the first exhibition of the Bristol Academy, Taunton. Printed in *The Stoughton Musical Society's Centennial Collection* (Boston, 1878), p. 162. Is found also in the *Billings and Holden Collection of Ancient Psalmody* (Boston, 1836) p. 222.
First line: The morning sun shines from the East.
No copy of any original issue seems extant. Both reprints in DLC.

ODE ON SPRING. By Daniel George. Set to musick by Abraham Wood.
(*In* The Massachusetts magazine, May, 1789. p. 325–326)

Song, pfte. acc.
First line: Sweet Spring once more demands my song.   DLC (etc.)

ODE ON THE ANNIVERSARY OF INDEPENDENCE. Set to music by Mr. Selby.
Performed in Boston, July 4, 1787.

Words printed in the *Worcester magazine*, Worcester, Second week in July, 1787. p. 194.
William Selby's music seems not to be extant.   DLC (etc.)

ODE ON THE BIRTHDAY of his Excellency George Washington; celebrated by the Adopted Sons, at the Pennsylvania Coffee House, in Philadelphia, composed by a member of that society.
(*In* The Pennsylvania packet. February 24, 1786)
Words only.
First line: Parent of soothing airs and lofty strains. DLC (etc.)

*ODE ON THE LATE GLORIOUS SUCCESSES of his Majesty's arms, and present greatness of the English nation. Philadelphia: W. Dunlap. 1762. 14 p. 4°.
The ode is attributed in Sabin to Nathaniel Evans. It is doubtful if the ode called for music.
Nathaniel Evans (1742–1767). Born in Philadelphia; died in Haddonfield, New Jersey.

AN ODE SACRED TO THE MEMORY OF DR. FRANKLIN.
See Ode (Air: "Thou soft flowing Avon.")

ODE, sacred to the memory of our late gracious sovereign George II, written and set to music by Francis Hopkinson, 1761.
See An Exercise containing a dialogue and ode . . . 1761.

*ODE SET TO MUSIC, and sung by Mr. Bankson, accompanied with the organ, etc.
Mentioned as sixth number of the commencement exercises, College of Philadelphia, June 28, 1771, in the *Pennsylvania journal*, July 11.

AN ODE SET TO MUSIC, consecrated to the memory of the Rev. George Whitefield, A. M., who left this transitory life, in full assurance of the more glorious, September 30, 1770, aetatis 56.
By one of his friends in Boston, New England. 1 p. Broadside.
Words followed by music (11 bars engraved for "treble, counter, tenor and bass").
First line: As when the rising sun dispels the shades. MHi

AN ODE SET TO MUSIC on Mrs. B—s birthday. Hartlebury Castle, 1766.
The ode is contained in Francis Hopkinson's "Occasional poems." (v. III. of his *Miscellaneous essays*), p. 137–138. The recitative begins, "When Caesar's birthday glads Brittania's isle." The music seems not to be extant.

ODE TO COLUMBIA'S FAVORITE SON. Sung by the Independent Musical Society on the arrival of the President at the triumphal arch, in Boston, October 24, 1789.
(*In* The Massachusetts magazine, Boston, October, 1789. p. 659–660)
Solo voice and chorus.
First line: Great Washington, the hero's come.
Composed by Oliver Holden (Sonneck).
Reprinted in Louis C. Elson's *National music of America* (1900), p. 62.
DLC (etc.)

ODE TO HARMONY. Words by Garrick. Original.
(*In* The union harmony, by Oliver Holden. Boston, 1793. v. 2, p. 13–14)
Air, with instrumental acc. Three staves.
First line: Hail music, sweet inchantment [!] hail.
Composed by Oliver Holden. DLC, ICN, MH, MHi, MWA, NN

[312]

ODE TO MAY. The poetry by Dr. Darwin. The music composed by James
Fisin. New York, Printed & sold at J. & M. Paff's musical store, No. 127
Broadway [1799–1803] [2] p. 31½ cm.

Song, pfte. acc.
First line: Born in yon blaze of orient sky.
Followed on p. [2] by "Speed the plough" (three scores). Pfte. 2 hds.   NN

———— May. A favorite ballad. New York, Printed & sold by G. Gilfert, No.
177 Broadway [1797–1801] 1 l. 34 cm.

Below imprint: Composed by J. Fisin.
Song, pfte. acc.
First line same as preceding.   JFD, MWA

AN ODE TO SLEEP. Adapted to a favorite air in the opera, La rencontre
imprevue. Composed by Chevalier Gluck.
(In The musical repertory. Boston. No. II. [1796] p. 21–23)

Song, pfte. acc. Three staves.
First line: Come sweet sleep, the lab'rers blessing.   DLC

———— Separate issue of preceding, ca. 1796.   DLC, JFD, MB

*ODE TO THE NEW YEAR by Raynor Taylor.
An "Ode to the New Year, with a variety of other pieces . . . entirely
original by . . . Mr. Taylor, by whom the whole of the music is composed,"
was to be performed at Philadelphia on January 11, 1794.

ODE TO THE PRESIDENT OF THE UNITED STATES. By a lady. The
musick set by Mr. Hans Gram.
(In The Massachusetts magazine, Boston, October, 1789. p. 660–661)

Solo voice and chorus.
First line: The season sheds its mildest ray.   DLC (etc.)

TWO ODES . . . Commemorative of . . . [Washington] contained in: An
oration on the auspicious birth, sublime virtue and triumphant death of
General George Washington; pronounced Feb. 22, 1800; in Newbury second
parish—by Rev. Samuel Tomb. To which are annexed. Two Odes and an
Acrostic, commemorative of the birth and death of that illustrious personage;
composed by the same hand . . . Printed at Newburyport by Edmund M.
Blunt. 1800. 17, [3] p. 23 cm.

On p. 17: The two following odes were sung on the occasion with great
applause, by the musical band under the direction of Mr. Joseph Stanwood, jr.
Words only.
Nothing is known of the music to which these odes were sung.
        CSmH. DLC, MB, MBAt, MH, MHi, MWA, NHi, NN, PHi, RPJCB

OF PLIGHTED FAITH SO TRULY KEPT. A favorite duett sung by Mrs.
Hodgkinson and Mr. Tyler in the Siege of Belgrade. New York, Printed and
sold at J. Hewitt's Musical repository, No. 131 William street. Sold also
by B. Carr, Philadelphia & J. Carr, Baltimore [ca. 1797] [2] p. 31½ cm.

Duet, pfte. acc.
First line same as title.   LSL, NN

────── The same as preceding.
(*In* A collection of new & favorite songs. [A] Philadelphia [ca. 1800] p. [120]–[121]) HFB

Mrs. Hodgkinson and Mr. Tyler sang in the first New York performance of Stephen Storace's opera, *The siege of Belgrade*, on December 30, 1796.

OLD TOWLER. A favorite hunting song. Composed by Mr. Shield. Sung by Mr. Tyler at the New York theatre. New York, Printed and sold by G. Gilfert & co. at their Musical magazine, No. 177 Broadway [1796] [2] p. 31½ cm.

Song, pfte. acc. Arr. for guitar and flute, p. [2].
First line: Bright chanticleer proclaims the dawn. DLC, ES, NN

OLD TOWLER. Sung by Mr. Tyler.
(*In* Elegant extracts for the German flute or violin. Philadelphia [1798] bk. 3, p. 10–11)

Melody only, flute or violin, with accompanying text.
First line same as preceding. DLC, NN

────── Bright chanticleer. A favorite hunting song. New York, Printed by W. Howe, organ builder & importer of all kinds of musical instruments, No. 320 Pearl street [1797–98] [2] p. 32½ cm.

Song, pfte. acc.
First line same as preceding.
Composed by William Shield.
Sung at Norfolk, October 7, 1796. MB

*THE OLD WOMAN OF EIGHTY THREE.
A "comic burletta, never performed, called 'Old woman of eighty three' dressed in character . . . consisting of recitative, airs and duets . . ." was to be sung in Raynor "Taylor's Musical performance . . . the whole of the music original and composed by Mr. Taylor," at Annapolis on February 28, 1793.

*OLIO, composed by Raynor Taylor.
Advertised in *Dunlap's Daily American advertiser*, January 28, 1794, as being "similar in its nature but different with respect to the particular pieces" from a "Musical Performance" given at Philadelphia on January 18.

This consisted "of songs, duets, and trios; pastoral, serious and comic, entirely original . . . the whole of the music composed by R. Taylor." The "Olio" was to be performed on February 1.

ON BOARD THE VALIANT.
See And hear her sigh adieu.

ON BY THE SPUR OF VALEUR.
See Mrs. Pownall's address.

ON GENERAL WAYNE'S TAKING STONEY POINT.
See Liberty songs, p. 6–7.

[314]

ON MUSIC.
(*In* The American musical miscellany. Northampton, 1798. p. 297–300)

Two parts, with bass and accompanying text. Three staves.
First line same as preceding.   DLC (etc.)

ON MUSICK. Set by Mr. William Selby.
(*In* The Massachusetts magazine, Boston, April, 1789. p. 252–253)

Two parts, with bass and accompanying text. Three staves.
First line: To musick be the verse addrest.   DLC (etc.)

ON THE LIGHTLY SPORTIVE WING. A favorite song. Sung by Mrs.
Hodgkinson in the opera My grandmother. Composed by Storace. New
York, Printed for G. Gilfert & co. at their Musical magazine, No. 177 Broad-
way [1796] 3 p. 31½ cm.

Song, pfte. acc.
First line same as title.
Followed on p. 3 by "Say how can words a passion feign," from the same
opera.
Mrs. Hodgkinson sang in *My grandmother*, New York, May 30, 1796.
                                                           MWA, RPJCB

ONE KIND KISS. A favorite song. Composed by Dr. Jackson and sung by
Mrs. Hodgkinson. Price 20 cents. [n. p.] Printed at Carr's Musical
repositories [1796] [2] p. 32 cm.

Song, pfte. acc. Arr. for flute, p. [2].
First line: One kind kiss before we part.
Imprint implies Philadelphia and New York, perhaps also Baltimore.
                             McD–W, MH, MWA, NN, PHi, PP–K
Advertised as published in February, 1796.

ONE KIND KISS.
(*In* Elegant extracts for the German flute or violin. Philadelphia [1796]
bk. 2, p. 13)

Melody only, flute or violin, with accompanying text.
First line same as preceding.   DLC, NN

———— The same.
Boston, Printed & sold by P. A. von Hagen & cos. at their imported piano
forte warehouse, No. 3 Cornhill. And to be had of G. Gilfert, New York.
Where may be had To arms Columbia, How tedious alas are the hours,
Lillies & roses, Adams march, Mounseer Nong Tong Paw & Roslin castle.
[n. d.] 1 l. 35 cm.

Song, pfte. acc.
First line same as preceding.
Published probably in 1799.   JFD, MWA

ONE KIND KISS. Favorite song composed by Dr. G. K. Jackson. Copyright
secured. Boston. Published by the Author [n. d.] 3 p. 29½ cm.

Song, pfte. acc., with flute. Three and sometimes four staves.
First line same as preceding.
ca. 1800, or possibly later.   MB

[315]

ORPHAN BESS THE BEGGAR GIRL. A favorite new song. Composed by Thos Thompson. New York, Published by I. and M. Paff, No. 127 Broadway. Where may be had the Ladies musical journal published in numbers one every week. The numbers will be selected from the most fashionable new duetts, ballads and airs [1799–1803] [2] p. 31½ cm.

Song, pfte. acc.
First line: A poor helpless wand'rer. McD–W

THE ORPHAN BOYS TALE. Written by a gentleman. Composed by I. Blewitt. For the piano forte or harp. New York, Printed and sold by I. and M. Paff's music warehouse, No. 127 Broadway [1799–1803] [2] p. 32 cm.

Song, pfte. or harp acc.
First line: Ah! chide me not, sweet lady, pray.
I. Blewitt: Jonas Blewitt. DLC

THE ORPHAN'S PRAYER. A pathetic new song. Composed by Miss Abrams. Cts. 37½. New York, Printed for and sold by I. and M. Paff at their music warehouse, 127 Broadway [ca. 1800] 3 p. 31½ cm.

Song, pfte. acc.
First line: The frozen streets in moonshine glitter.
Miss Abrams: Harriet Abrams. DLC, NN, PP–K

THE ORPHAN'S PRAYER. A pathetic ballad. Words by M. G. Lewis. Music by Miss Abrams.
(*In* The musical journal for the pianoforte, ed. by B. Carr. Baltimore [1800] v. 2, no. 29, p. (9)–(11).)

At head of title: Decr 29, 1800. Journal No. 29. Vocal.
Song, pfte. acc.
First line same as preceding. DLC, ES, LSL, McD–W, NN

OUR COUNTRY IS OUR SHIP. New York, Printed & sold by G. Gilfert, No. 177 Broadway [1797–1801] 1 l. 32 cm.

In center of caption circular engraving of ship, encircled by the words, "Frigate United States."
Song, pfte. acc.
First line same as title. MWA, NRU–Mus

[OUR COUNTRY IS OUR SHIP] Song.
(*In* New [American] patriotic songs, added to a collection of songs by C. Dibdin. Philadelphia, 1799. p. 317–318)

Words only.
Title from first line. DLC, MWA, NHi, NN, RPJCB

OUR COUNTRY'S EFFICIENCY! Tune, To Anacreon in heaven.
(*In* New [American] patriotic songs, added to a collection of songs by C. Dibdin. Philadelphia, 1799. p. 226 [*i. e.* 326]–328)

Words only.
First line: Ye sons of Columbia determin'd to keep.
DLC, MWA, NHi, NN, RPJCB

OUR LORD IS RISEN FROM THE DEAD. A favorite hymn. Composed by
Dr. Arnold. New York, Printed for G. Gilfert & co., No. 191 Broadway
[1794-95]   4 p.   31½ cm.

Song and chorus, pfte. acc.
First line same as title   JFD, MWA

OUT OF MY SIGHT, or I'll box your ears. Duetto.
(*In* A collection of favorite songs, divided into two books.   Arr. by A.
Reinagle. Philadelphia [1789?]   bk. 1, p. 16)

Duet, pfte. acc.
First line same as title.
From *The poor soldier*, by William Shield.   CdeW, DLC, ES, Hopk.

OUVERTURE DE BLAISE ET BABET.
See Overture de Blaise et Babet.

OUVERTURE D'IPHIGENIE.   [Philadelphia]   Printed   and   sold   by   G.
Willig, No. 165 Market street [1795-97]   5 p.   31½ cm.

Imprint at top of p. 1.
Pfte. 2 hds.
Gluck's *Iphigénie en Aulide*.   DLC, Hopk., NN, PP-K

———— The same as preceding, except at foot of p. 1: d5; p. 2-5: aiphigenie 5.
                                                              DLC

OUVERTURE DE JULIE.   New York.   Printed for G. Gilfert & co., No. 209
Broadway.   Where may be had the greatest variety of vocal & instrumental
music, as also piano fortes [1795]   3 p.   33½ cm.

Pfte. 2 hds.
Julie, by N. Dezède.   RPJCB

OUVERTURE D'UNA COSA RARA.   [n. p., n. d.]   2-4 p.   33½ cm.

Pfte. 2 hds.
Composed by Vicente Martin y Solar.
Published probably ca. 1800.   DLC

OUVERTURE TO LA BELLE ARSENNE.   Opera.   Adapted as a lesson for
the piano forte. [n. p., n. d.]   [2] p.   31 cm.

Pfte. 2 hds.
Published perhaps ca. 1800.
La belle Arsène, by P. A. Monsigny.   RPJCB

[O'ER THE HILLS FAR AWAY]   Song VI.
(*In* Seven songs, by F. Hopkinson.   Philadelphia [1788] p. 7-8)

Song, pfte, acc.
First line same as above.   DLC, Hopk., MB, McD-W

*OVERTURE, 1ST OF.   M. A. Guenin.
Was to be performed at seventh City concert, Philadelphia, Feb. 11, 1792.
This rather cryptic title probably means: First overture of M. A. Guenin.

[317]

OVERTURE.   La buona figliuola.   [Philadelphia]   Published by G. Willig, 165
Market street [1795–97]   [2] p.   30 cm.

Pfte. 2 hds.
Composed by Nicolò Piccini.   MB, NN

OVERTURE.   La Schiava.
(*In* Twelve favorite pieces, arr. by A. Reinagle.   Philadelphia [1789?] p.
9–10)

Pfte. 2 hds.
Composed by Nicolò Piccini.   DLC

———— Separate issue of preceding, unpaged, 1789.   CdeW

Advertised in March, 1789, as "just published, and sold by Thomas Dobson,
at the Stone House, in Second Street," Philadelphia.

OVERTURE.   Marian.   Shield.
(*In* Twelve favorite pieces, arr. by A. Reinagle.   Philadelphia [1789?]   p. 19–
20)

Pfte. 2 hds.
In lower margin of p. 20: Philadelphia, Printed for A. Reinagle.   J. Aitken,
Scu.   DLC

———— Separate issue of preceding, unpaged, 1789.   CdeW, DLC

Advertised in March, 1789, as "just published and sold by Thomas Dobson,
at the Stone House in Second Street," Philadelphia.

OVERTURE.   Sofonisba.   [n. p., n. d.]   2–5 p.   33½ cm.
Pfte. 2 hds.
In lower margin of each page: Book 3d.
Paged both at top and bottom.
Sofonisba, by Mattia Vento.   DLC

OVERTURE.   The glorious first of June.   New York, Printed and sold at I. C.
Moller's music store.   Price 3 sʰ.   [n. d.]   3 p.   32 cm.

Pfte. 2 hds.
Composed by Stephen Storace.
Published probably 179–.   However, Sonneck has dated certain similar
issues ca. 1800.   MWA

*OVERTURE by Alexander Reinagle.
"A new overture Reinagle" was to be played at Mr. Juhan's concert, Philadelphia, May 29, 1787.   This was possibly identical with his "A new overture
in which is introduced a scots strathspey," performed at Reinagle's own
concert, Philadelphia, June 4, 1787.   It may or may not have been identical
with Reinagle's overture as performed at the Second Subscription concert,
New York, September 29, 1788.

A "New overture Mr. Reinagle" was to open a concert at the New Theatre,
Philadelphia, February 2, 1793.   Overtures of Reinagle appear frequently on
the concert-programs, but it is impossible to glean from the announcements
how many he composed or how to separate them.

*OVERTURE by F. Linley.
"A new overture composed for the occasion by Mr. F. Linley" was to precede
the performance of the "Castle spectre," Boston, November 28, 1798.

OVERTURE by Haydn.   Printed by G. Willig, Market st., Philadelphia [n. d.]
2–8 p.   31½ cm.

Pfte. 2 hds.

This *Overture* (so called) consists of the first movement of Symphony No. 32,
together with the second and third movements (Andante and Minuetto)
from Symphony No. 26, as listed in Pohl's Thematic Catalogue in vol. 2
of his *Joseph Haydn.*

Sonneck gives date, ca. 1800.   DLC, Hopk., JLH

———— Haydn's grand *Overture.*   [n. p., n. d.]   2–8 p.   32½ cm.

Pfte. 2 hds.

Sonneck suggests the following imprint: Philadelphia, G. Willig, ca. 1800.
Same combination as preceding.   DLC

*OVERTURE by John Christopher Moller.
In *Dunlap's American daily advertiser*, Philadelphia, January 12, 1792, we
read that an overture of Mr. Moller's "was to be played at the Fifth City
Concert under direction of Messrs. Reinagle and Moller at Mr. Oeller's Hotel,
January 14."

Also a "new" overture of his was to be played at a concert in New York in
February, 1798.

*OVERTURE by P. A. Von Hagen, jun.
A "new overture, composed by Mr. Von Hagen, jun." was to be played at
the Haymarket Theatre, Boston, October 25, 1797.

*OVERTURE by Philip Roth.
An "overture composed (for the occasion) by Philip Roth, Master of the
band, belonging to his Majesty's Royal Regiment of North British fusiliers,"
was to be played at a concert, Philadelphia, December 5, 1771.

*OVERTURE by Raynor Taylor.
In the Philadelphia *Minerva* for April 23, 1796, it is stated that a "new
overture" by R. Taylor was to precede a performance of The mountaineers,
"music . . . by Dr. Arnold, the accompaniments by Mr. Reinagle" at the
New Theatre, Philadelphia, April 25, 1796.

OVERTURE by the Earl of Kelly, adapted to the harpsichord by Mr. Jas.
Bremner.
Contained in a Ms. collection of "Lessons," p. 144–147.   Hopk.

*OVERTURE "CIRCE AND ULISSES," by Raynor Taylor.
Was to be played at a concert, Philadelphia, April 3, 1800.

OVERTURE DE BLAISE ET BABET.   Adapted for the pianoforte by A.
Reinagle.
(*In* Twelve favorite pieces, arr. by A. Reinagle. Philadelphia [1789?]
p. 21–24)

Pfte. 2 hds.
Blaise et Babet, by N. Dezède.   DLC

[319]

—— Separate issue of preceding.
Identical except paged 1–4.   ca. 1789.   DLC

OUVERTURE DE BLAIS [!] ET BABET.   Arrangee pour le clavecin ou le forte
piano.   Par C. Fodor.   Philadelphia, Printed and sold by G. Willig, Market
street, No. 185 [1798–1804]   Publ. no. 2.   7 p.   34½ cm.
Title-page.
Pfte. 2 hds.
Overture (p. 2–5) is followed on p. 6–7 by Andantino [originally a duet in
Act II, scene 4, of the opera].   DLC, McD–W, NN, PP–K, RPJCB

OUVERTURE DE BLAISE ET BABET.   Arranged for the piano forte by C.
Fodor.   Philadelphia, Published and sold at G. Willig's Musical magazine.
Pr. 62 c.   [n. d.]   7 p.   33½ cm.
Title-page.
Pfte. 2 hds.
Except t.-p. same plates as above.
Published probably about the same time.   PP–K

OVERTURE DE BLAISE ET BABET.   Pʳ 1ˢʰ 6ᵈ [n. p., n. d.]   5 p.   30 cm.
Pfte. 2 hds.
At foot of each page: Over de Blaise et Babet.
Sonneck's date, ca. 1800.   DLC

OVERTURE DE DÉMAPHON [!]   Arrangè pour le forte piano par Jacques
Hewitt.   Price 2/6.   Printed for B. Carr at his Musical repositorys in New
York & Philadelphia and by J. Carr, Baltimore [ca. 1796]   4 p.   34 cm.
Pfte. 2 hds.
Démophon, by Johann Christian Vogel.
Jacques Hewitt: James Hewitt.   DLC, Hopk., MB

OVERTURE DE LA CARAVANE.   Printed & sold by G. Willig, No. 185
Market st., Philadelphia [1798–1804]   Publ. no. 21.   2–5 p.   33 cm.
At head of title: Price 50 cents.
Pfte. 2 hds.
La caravane, by Grétry.   DLC, ES, MWA, PP–K

*OVERTURE IN 9 MOVEMENTS, expressive of a battle, etc., by James
Hewitt.   No. 1. Introduction.   2. Grand March; the army in motion.
3. The charge for the attack.   4. A National air.   5. The attack com-
mences, the confusion of an engagement is heard.   6. The enemy surrender
7. The grief of those who are made prisoners.   8. The conquerors quick
march.   9. The finale.

Thus advertised as to be played on September 26, 1792, at a "Subscription
concert" of "Messrs. Hewitt, Gehot, Bergman, Young and Phillips, professors
of music from the opera house Hanover Square, and professional concerts,
under the direction of Haydn, Pleyel, etc. London."

On June 18, 1793, the overture was to be played in New York with the introduction of "The Duke of York's celebrated March."

*OVERTURE IN 12 MOVEMENTS, expressive of a voyage from England to
America, by Jean Gehot.   No. 1. Introduction.   2. Meeting of the adven-
turers, consultation and their determination on departure.   3. March from

[320]

London to Gravesend. 4. Affectionate separation from their friends. 5. Going on board, and pleasure at recollecting the encouragement they hope to meet with in a land where merit is sure to gain reward. 6. Preparation for sailing, carpenters hammering, crowing of the cock, weighing anchor, etc. 7. A storm. 8. A calm. 9. Dance on deck by the passengers. 10. Universal joy on seeing land. 11. Thanksgiving for safe arrival. 12. Finale.

This programmatic overture was to be played at a Subscription concert, New York, September 21, 1792.

*OVERTURE OF YANKEE DOODLE.
On April 23, 1798, was to be performed at Charleston, S. C., Dibdin's opera "The Deserter . . . with the original overture of Yankee Doodle, composed by Degatie."

*OVERTURE to conclude with the representation of a Storm at sea, composed by James Hewitt.
This "new" overture was to open Hewitt's concert, New York, April 1, 1794.

OVERTURE [TO ROBIN HOOD]
See Robin Hood.

THE OVERTURE TO ROSINA. Philadelphia, Printed for and sold by G. Willig, No. 165 Market street.
(*In* [Miscellaneous and incomplete [?] collection] Philadelphia, G. Willig [ca. 1795] p. 1–4)

Pfte. 2 hds.
At foot of p. 4: C. S. Sculpt.
Rosina, by William Shield. DLC

OVERTURE TO ROSINA. Sheild [!] [n. p., n. d.] p. (34)–(37). 32 cm.

At head of title: Elegant extracts. Book the 2d.
Pfte. 2 hds.
Published probably by Carr, 179-. *cf.* *Elegant extracts.* NRU–Mus

OVERTURE TO THE CHILDREN IN THE WOOD. New York, Printed for G. Gilfert & co., No. 191 Broadway [1794–95] 4 p. 31 cm.

Pfte. 2 hds.
The children in the wood, by Samuel Arnold. JFD, MB, PP-K, RPJCB

*——— The same.
Advertised in March, 1795, as "published and to be had at G. Willig's Musical Magazine, No. 165 Market street," Philadelphia.

OVERTURE TO THE DESERTER.
(*In* Twelve favorite pieces, arr. by A. Reinagle. Philadelphia [1789?] p. 4–6)

Pfte. 2 hds.
In lower margin of p. 6: Philadelphia. Printed for A. Reinagle. I. Aitken. Sculpt.
Abbreviated and simplified form of the overture to *The deserter* (by Monsigny, Philidor and Dibdin). DLC

―――― Separate issue (identical except paged 1-3) ca. 1789.

CdeW, ES (incomplete)

OVERTURE TO THE DESERTER. Arranged for the pianoforte. [n. p., 179-?] [2] p. 33½ cm.

Pfte. 2 hds.   ABHu, MWA

OVERTURE TO THE LADY OF THE MANOR. Hook. [n. p., n. d.] (27)-(32) p. 34 cm.

Pfte. 2 hds.
On lower margin, p. (32): End of book the 1st.
Published probably by Carr, 179-. *cf. *Elegant extracts.*   PHi

OVERTURE TO THE MOUTH OF THE NILE. Composed by T. Attwood
New York, Printed & sold by G. Gilfert, No. 177 Broadway and to be had
at P. A. von Hagens Music store, Boston.
(*In* [The mouth of the Nile, by T. Attwood. New York, ca. 1799] p. 1-7)
Pfte. 2 hds.   NRU-Mus

OVERTURE WITH THE SONGS, chorus's, etc. etc. to Tammany, as composed and adapted to the piano forte by James Hewitt.
See Tammany, or the Indian chief.

THE CELEBRATED OVERTURE TO LADOISKA [!] Composed by Kreut-
zer.
(*In* [Unidentified collection of instrumental and vocal music. New York]
Hewitt & Rausch [1797] p. 2-7)

Pfte. 2 hds.
At foot of each page: Printed for Hewitt & Rausch.
Lodoiska, by Rudolph Kreutzer.   DLC, ES

―――― Separate issue of preceding, ca. 1797.   DLC, JLH, NN, RPJCB

THE CELEBRATED OVERTURE TO LODOISKA. Composed by Kreutzer.
New York,   Sold by J. and M. Paffs [n. d.] 6 p. 32½ cm.

Pfte. 2 hds.
Published possibly as early as 1799.   DLC, Hopk., McD-W

―――― The same as preceding with additional imprint at foot of p. 6: New York,
Printed & sold by J. & M. Paff.   DLC, RPJCB (lacks p. 3-4)

THE FAVORITE OVERTURE TO LODOISKA. As performed at the Theatre
Royal, Drury Lane. Composed by Mr. Krietzer [!] Price 6 sh. New
York, Printed for and sold at I. C. Mollers musical store [n. d.] 6 p. 31½ cm.

Pfte. 2 hds.
Followed by *Rondo*, by J. C. Moller.
Sonneck dates this imprint ca. 1800.   DLC, MWA

*MARTIN'S OVERTURE.
This undoubtedly refers to the popular *Grand overture to Henry I V*, by Martini
(Giovanni) il Tedesco [Johann Paul Aegidius Schwartzendorf].   Martini's

overture was advertised in April, 1795, as "published . . . and to be had of G. Gilfert & Co. at their Musical Magazine, No. 121 Broadway," New York. *See* Martini's Overture.

*MEDLEY OVERTURE to the pantomine Harlequin's invasion, by Alexander Reinagle. *cf.* Harlequin's invasion.

*MEDLEY OVERTURE with variations, by Chateaudieu.
A "medley overture with variations in which is introduced the favourite air of the President's march by Mr. Chateaudieu" was played at a concert in Philadelphia, February 26, 1799.

A NEW MEDLEY OVERTURE as performed at the Theatre with great applause. Selected & composed by J. Hewitt. New York, Printed for J. Hewitt's Musical repository, No. 23 Maiden Lane; B. Carr, Philadelphia and J. Carr, Baltimore [1799–1800]   8 p.   33½ cm.

Pfte. 2 hds.
At foot of p. 8: Engraved by W. Pirsson, No. 24 Rutgers street.
Contains many popular tunes, including *Hail Columbia*.   Closes with *Yankee Doodle* (unnamed) in ⅝ time.   ABHu, ES, PP–K

A later composition by James Hewitt, bearing this same title *The new medley overture*, and containing several of these same tunes, was published by Hewitt at 59 Maiden Lane, New York, ca. 1801.   In possession of ES

*"A NEW OCCASIONAL OVERTURE.   Composed by Mr. Reinagle" was advertised in Dunlap and Claypoole's *American daily advertiser*, March 17, 1794, to be given at the New Theatre, Philadelphia, in connection with a performance of "St. Patrick's day, or the Scheming Lieutenant" to be given on that date.

OWEN, OR THO' FAR BEYOND THE MOUNTAINS. A favorite Welch air. New York, Printed and sold by G. Gilfert, No. 177 Broadway [1797–1801] [2] p.   32½ cm.

Song, pfte. acc.   Arr. for German flute, p. [2].
First line: Tho' far beyond the mountains.
                                        DLC, ES, JFD, McD–W, RPJCB

OWEN. A favorite Welch air.   Printed and sold, Philadelphia, by G. Willig, Market street, No. 185.   [1798–1804]   [2] p.   31 cm.

Song, pfte. acc.   Arr. for flute, p. [2].
First line same as preceding.   DLC, NN, PP–K

OWEN. A favorite Welch air.   Price 25 cents.   Printed and sold at B. Carr Musical repository, Philadelphia; J. Carr, Baltimore and J. Hewitt, New York [1799]   [2] p.   33 cm.

Song, pfte. acc.   Arr. for flute, p. [2].
First line same as preceding.
                       ABHu, DLC, JFD, LSL, MB, MdHi, MWA, NN, PP–K

This "favorite Welch air, sung by Mr. Warrell at the Theatre and played to the new comedy of a Wedding in Wales," was advertised by B. Carr, Philadelphia, in March, 1799, as to be published shortly.

[323]

OWEN. A faorite [!] Welch air. Price 25 cents. New York, Printed & sold at J. Hewitt's Musical repository, No. 23 Maiden Lane [1799–1800] [2] p. 32 cm.

Song, pfte. acc. Arr. for flute, p. [2].
First line same as preceding. DLC, McD–W

———— The same as preceding.
(In A collection of new & favorite songs. [A] Philadelphia [ca. 1800] p. [136]–[137]) HFB

PADDY BULL'S EXPEDITION.
(In Young's vocal and instrumental musical miscellany. Philadelphia [1793–95] p. 32–33)

Song, pfte. acc.
First line: When I took my departure from Dublin's sweet town.
From A picture of Paris, by William Reeve (BMCat) or Shield?
In No. 4, 1793. DLC, Hopk.

PADDY'S RESOURCE. Being a select collection of original and modern patriotic songs, toasts and sentiments compiled for the use of all firm patriots. First American edition. Philadelphia, Printed for and sold by T. Stephens. 1796. 72 p., front. 17 cm.

At top of frontispiece: Tun'd to Freedom.
Below: Tear off your chains and let millions be Free.
Title-page verso blank; preface [in rhyme], p. [3]; contents, p. [4]; songs, p. [5]–72.
Words only. Tunes mentioned in practically all cases. DLC

PADDY'S RESOURCE. Being a select collection of original and modern patriotic songs. Compiled for the use of the people of Ireland. To which is added Arthur O'Connor's address. From the latest edition—with corrections. New York, Printed by R. Wilson, 149 Pearl street. At the request of a number of Hibernians in this country, who were desirous of having copies of them. 1798. 2 p. l., 48 p. 18 cm.

Title-page, verso blank; contents, second p. l. (verso blank); songs, p. [1]–37; Arthur O'Conner's address, p. 38–48. Words only. Tunes mentioned in all cases except one, viz., The united-men's march. Here the intended tune is apparently the Marseillaise. DLC

THE PADLOCK: a comic opera: as it is performed at the Theatre, Boston. Boston. Printed and sold by William Spotswood, No. 55. Marlborough street, 1795. 31, [5] p. 17 cm.

Libretto by Isaac Bickerstaff to Dibdin's opera (1768).
Title-page; advertisement and dramatis personae, p. [2]; text, p. [3]–31; list of books sold by W. Spotswood, p. [32]–[36]. MB, MWA, NN, PPL

*PANTOMIMICAL FINALE.
A "pantomimical finale with music, scenery, machinery and decorations entirely new" was to conclude "lectures moral and entertaining," Philadelphia, February 28, 1785. The author is not mentioned.

[324]

PAR SA LEGÉRETÉ. [Philadelphia, Filippo Trisobio, 1796–98] 1 l. 32½ cm.
Song, pfte. acc.
First line same as title.   CdeW, CSmH

——— The same as preceding.
(With Water parted from the sea, by Dr. Arne [Philadelphia, 1796–98]
p. [4])
Song, pfte. acc.
First line same as title.   NN

THE PARODY PARODIZED.
See Liberty song.

*PARSON UPON PAGE.
We read in the South Carolina gazette, April 20, 1738, "In a short time will be
published an excellent new ballad entitled Parson upon page. To the old
tune of Parson upon Dorothy. Price half a bitt."

PART OF FOURTH CHORUS.
See Military glory of Great Britain.

PARTHIE VII, VIII, X, XI, XII, XIII, XIV. For wind instruments by David
Moritz Michael.

MS. parts for 2 clarinets, 2 horns, and 1 or 2 bassoons in the Archives of the
Moravian Church, Bethlehem, Pa.

PARTITUR EINER FREUDEN MUSIC zum Friedens Dank Feste 21 Merz
1763. [by] Johann Friedrich Peter. t. p., 40 p. 8°.

Ten pieces (11 and 12 evidently missing) scored for 4-part chorus and strings,
2 flutes, 2 trumpets and fondamento.
In Peter's autograph (?).
The words are taken from chorals as "Lobe den Herrn meine Seele." The
whole cyclus, dated "d. 5ten Febr. 1774," in Archives of the Moravian
Church, Bethlehem, Pa.

The above is Sonneck's original entry. However, he seem to have been
mistaken; for Albert G. Rau in A catalogue of music by American Moravians,
Bethlehem, 1938, p. 18–19 says that this work was composed by Christian
Gregor and only copied by John Frederick Peter.

A PASTORAL by Metastasio.
See [Ah Delia] A pastoral.

THE PASTORAL NYMPH. A song tune for the voice, harpsichord and violin.
(In The American musical magazine. New Haven, 1786, p. 15)

Song, pfte. (or harpsichord) acc.
First line: On ev'ry hill, in ev'ry grove.   CtY, ICN, MBJ

PASTORAL SONGS by Mrs. Pownall.
See Mrs. Pownall's address.

[325]

THE PATENT COFFIN. Written & composed by Mr. Dibdin. New York, Printed & sold at J. Hewitt's Musical repository, No. 131 William street. Sold also by B. Carr, Philadelphia & J. Carr, Baltimore, Pr. 25 cts. [1797] [2] p. 34 cm.

Song, pfte. acc.
First line: Each age has boasted curious elves.   DLC, ES

Probably the same issue as that advertised in December, 1797, as "published at Carr's Musical Repository, Market street," Philadelphia.

———— The same as preceding.
(*In* A collection of new & favorite songs. [A] Philadelphia [ca. 1800] p. [160]–[161])   HFB

PATRICK IN PRUSSIA, or Love in a camp; a comic opera, in two acts, being the second part of the Poor Soldier. With all the songs, duets, etc. performed with universal applause by the American Company of Comedians. Written by John O'Keefe, Esq. Philadelphia: Printed and sold by E. Story, in Second Street, 4th door from Arch-street upwards. [1789] 34, [2] p. 17 cm.

Libretto to Shield's opera (1785).
Title-page; dramatis personae, p. [2]; text, p. [3]–34; "Books published and for sale by the printer thereof," p. [35]–[36].   LC, PPL

PATRICK IN PRUSSIA: or, Love in a camp: a comic opera, in two acts, being the second part of the Poor Soldier. With all the songs, duets, etc. Performed with universal applause by the American Company. Written by John O'Keefe, Esq. Philadelphia: Printed and sold by Henry Taylor, 1791. 39 p. 16½ cm.
Libretto.   MB, MH, NN, PPL

THE PATRIOT. A new song. Sung by Mr. Robins. The words by Mrs. Hatton.
(*In* Young's vocal and instrumental musical miscellany. Philadelphia [1793–95] p. 55–56)

Song, pfte. acc.
First line: While Europe strives with mad career.
In No. 7, ca. 1794.   DLC

*THE PATRIOT, OR LIBERTY ASSERTED.
This "play, interspersed with songs, in three acts, never acted here, . . . founded on the well known story of William Tell, the Swiss patriot, who shot an apple from his son's head, at the command of the Tyrant Grislor [!] which first gave liberty to the cantons of Switzerland . . . the songs and overture by Mr. [James] Hewitt," was performed at New York, June 4 (or possibly 5), 1794.

*"THE PATRIOT, OR LIBERTY OBTAINED. As altered from the play of Helvetic Liberty, and compressed into three acts by Mr. Bates. With a new medley overture and the music and songs, compiled and selected from the most popular tunes—by Mr. B. Carr of Philadelphia," was given for the first time at Philadelphia, May 16, 1796; at Baltimore, September 3, 1796.

ATRIOTIC MEDLEY, being a choice collection of patriotic, sentimental, hunting and sea songs, interspersed with Anacreontic & Cythrian poems, selected from the most approved authors. New York: Printed for Jacob Johnkin, Maiden lane. 1800. 208, [7] p. 14 cm. DLC

THE PATRIOTIC SONGSTER for July 4th, 1798. (Addressed to the volunteers of Baltimore) containing all the late patriotic songs that have been published.

Advertised on July 2, 1798, in Baltimore, as to be published "to-morrow" at "S. Sower's printing office, No. 67, Market street, at his book-store in Fayette-street and at Thomas, Andrews and Butler's bookstore (price eleven-pence)."

FAVOURITE PATRIOTIC SPANISH WALTZ. For the piano forte, violin or flute [n. p., ca. 1800] [2] p. 32½ cm.
Pfte. 2 hds. (violin or flute). DLC

ATTY CLOVER. From the opera of Marian.
(*In* The gentleman's amusement, ed. by R. Shaw. Philadelphia [1794–96] p. 4)

Melody only, flute (or violin) with accompanying text.
First line: When little on the village green.
In No. 1, April 1, 1794.
Marian, by William Shield. DLC, PHi

—— The same as preceding. On second page, numbered "4" of a detached portion (p. 3–6) from above collection. NN

AUL AND MARY. Taken from a fragment in Paul and Virginia. At the moment the vessel is on the wreck Paul discovers his mistress (standing on the stern) from the shore without the possibility of affording her any assistance. Words by A. A. H. Music by S. M. H. Philadelphia, Publis'd & sold by G. Willig, No. 185 Market st. [ca. 1800] 2–4 p. 32½ cm.

Song, pfte. acc.
First line: Chide on, chide on, ye foaming billows chide.
Even *BM Cat.* gives no clue to the identity of S. M. H. DLC, JFD, PP–K

AUL AU TOMBEAU DE VIRGINIE.
(*In* Six romances nouvelles, by R. Chateaudun. Philadelphie [ca. 1800] p. 2–5)
Song, pfte. (or harp) acc. Three staves.
First line: Repose en paix ma Virginie. DLC, LSL

AUVRE JAQUE. In French and English. Printed & sold at B. Carr's Musical repositories in New York & Philadelphia & J. Carr's, Baltimore. Pr. 20 cts. [1796] [2] p. 33½ cm.
Below imprint: N. B. The small notes with the tails downwards must be sung to the French words.
Song, pfte. acc.
First lines: Pauvre Jaque when I was near to thee.—Pauvre Jaque quand je tois pres de toi.
John W. Moore in his *Encyclopaedia of music*, Boston, 1854, names Madame B. de Travanet as composer of this song.
ES, LSL, McD–W, MWA, NN, PHi

[327]

Under the title of "Pauvre Jack," a "new edition" of this song, both French and English, was advertised in March, 1796, as published "at Carr Musical Repository, William Street," New York.

PAUVRE MADELON. A favorite dialogue and duett in the Surrender of Calai Price one quarter dollar. Phil₽., Printed for Carr & co. at their music stor No. 136 High st. Where may be had all the newest music reprinted fro European publications. An elegant assortment of piano fortes, guittar flutes, &c. [1793] [3] p. 33 cm.

Solo voice, pfte. acc., followed by Duetto, p. [2]. Arr. "for two flutes wit the original words" and "for the guittar," p. [3].
First line: Could you to battle march away.
The surrender of Calais, by Samuel Arnold.
ABHu, CtY, ES, HFB, JFD, McD–W, MWA, NBuG, NN, PHi, PP–K, PT
RPJC

PAUVRE MADELON. A favorite dialogue and duett in the Surrender of Calai Newᵏ, Printed for G. Gilfert & co., No. 191 Broadway. Where may be ha all the newest music reprinted from European publications [1794–95] [2]] 33½ cm.

Solo voice, pfte. acc., followed by "Duetto," p. [2].
First line same as preceding.   JFD, RPJC

———— The same.
New York, Printed & sold by G. Gilfert & co., No. 177 Broadway [179₠ [2] p. 32 cm.

Solo voice, pfte. acc., followed by "Duetto," p. [2].
First line same as preceding.   ES, NN, RPJC₧

———— Go with you all the world over. The much admired dialogue duett i the Surrender of Calais.
(*In* Young's vocal and instrumental musical miscellany.   Philadelphi [1793–95] p. 22–23)

Solo voice, pfte, acc., p. 22–23; Duetto, p. 23.   Three staves.
First line: Cou'd you to battle march away.
In No. 3, 1793.
The surrender of Calais, by Samuel Arnold.   DLC, Hopᵏ

*PEACE AND LIBERTY.
"A grand serenata, called Peace and liberty: consisting of recitation, recï tative, airs and chorusses. The parts recited . . . selected from the work of Thompson, Sterne, etc., etc. The music, vocal and instrumental, com posed by Handel, Arne, Tenducci, Fisher and Valentino, etc." was to b₽ performed "as never attempted before" at the theatre in Philadelphia July 29, 1795.

THE PEERLESS MAID OF BUTTERMERE. A ballad written and com posed by J. D. Winter. New York, Printed & published by I. & M. Paffs No. 127 Broad Way [1799–1803] 2 p. 31½ cm.

Song, pfte. acc.
First line: As late along the flow'ry side.   McD–W

[328]

EGGY PERKINS. Composed by Mr. Dibdin and sung by Mr. Gaudry at the Rotunda. [Philadelphia] Published by G. Willig, Market street, No. 165 [1795–97] 1 1. 33 cm.

Song, pfte. acc.
First line: Let bards relate of Sue and Kate.
From Charles Dibdin's *The oddities*.   CdeW, DLC, MWA

ENNSYLVANIA.
See United States country *Dances*, p. 10.

HE PENSIVE SHEPHERD. Written by G. Lathrop. Set to musick by Mr. S. Holyoke.
(*In* The Massachusetts magazine. Boston, September, 1789. p. 588–589)

Song, pfte. acc.
First line: How gloomy are the fields and plains.   DLC (etc.)

HE PERSIAN SLAVE. New York, Sold by I. and M. Paff, No. 127 Broadway [1799–1803] p. 7–8. 32 cm.

At head of title: (No. 4) Ladies musical journal.
Song, pfte. acc. Three staves.
First line: That I might prove my love sincere.
Imprint at foot of p. 8.   DLC

PETER PINDAR'S NEW GYPSY SONG, composed by Wright.
Advertised in December, 1793, by "B. Carr & Co. Musical Repository, 122 South side of Market Street," Philadelphia as "published . . . printed singly."

LA PETITE PIEDMONTESE, or the Travellers preserved.
This "serious pantomimical ballet . . . the music entirely new composed by R. Taylor," was to be performed at the New Theatre, Philadelphia, on June 19, 1795.

LE PETITTE BEAUTE DE MUSIQUE, or the Diletante's museum. Consisting of sonatas, concertos, rondos, the most favorite airs with variations for the piano forte from Haydn's, Pleyel's, Kozeluch's, Nicolai's, Clementi's, Schroeder's, Mozzart's [!], Moller's &c. Price 6/. New York, Sold by [J. C. Moller ?] [n. d.] 7 p. 32½ cm.

Title-page.
Imprint partially illegible; "6/" in ink.
Caption title, p. 2: Sonata I. Niccolai. Opera III.
Pfte. 2 hds.   DLC

——— Same t.-p., except n. p., n. d.
Pfte. 2 hds.
Contents: Sonata I, p. 2–5.—Sonata II, p. 6–8.
These sonatas are also by Nicolai, Op. XI, Nos. 1 and 2.   DLC

That these are probably Moller imprints is apparent not only from what can be seen of the original imprint on the first, but also because of the characteristic bass clef (particularly of the second, where it appears without dots) frequent in Moller imprints of about this period.
Sonneck dates both ca. 1800.

PHILADELPHIA ASSOCIATION QUICK MARCH.
See Compleat tutor for the fife . . . p. 28.

[329]

THE PHILADELPHIA HYMN. Composed by R. Taylor. Price 20 cent
[n. p., 179–?] [2] p. 31½ cm.

Song, pfte. acc. Arr. for two "guittars," p. [2].
First line: Oh Father of Heav'n to Thee we bend. DLC, Hopl

*PHILADELPHIA JEST BOOK, and cheerful witty companion. Being
choice collection of the most humorous and diverting jests, stories, anecdotes
bon-mots, repartees, new songs, and a curious variety of toasts, sentimen
and hob-nobs. Philadelphia: Printed and sold by William Woodhouse, 179(

*THE NEW ENTERTAINING PHILADELPHIA JEST-BOOK and chearfu
witty companion, &c. I love fun . . . Keep it up! G. A. Stevens
Philadelphia: Printed and sold by W. Woodhouse, at the Bible, No. (
South Front-Street. 1791.

THE PHILADELPHIA MEDLEY.
See Country *Dances.*

*THE PHILADELPHIA POCKET COMPANION for the German flute o
violin, being a collection of the most favourite songs, etc.—selected from th
European publications of the last twelve months. Likewise the same wor
for the guittar or clarinett. Price half a dollar.

"Vol. the first" thus advertised in *Dunlap's Daily American advertiser*
Philadelphia, April 28, 1794, where we read:
New Music. This day is published. To be continued annually, an
will for the future be published on each succeeding first of January . .
Printed and sold at Carr's and Co's Musical Repository, No. 122 Marke
street.

THE PHILADELPHIA POCKET COMPANION for the guittar or clarinett
Being a collection of the most favorite songs &c. Selected from the Europear
performances and publications of the last twelve month and as its con
tinuation will be annual it may be considered as a yearly journal of the mos
esteemd [!] lyric compositions. Vol. I for 1794. [Philadelphia] Printed a
Carr & cos. Musical repository. Price half a dollar. [1794] 40 p. 10 x 16 cm.

At head of title: To be continued annually.

Contents:

p. 2–3 The drummer. In the Prisoner.
    4–5 Lubin's rural cot.
    6–7 Air by Pleyel.
    8–9 Duett for two mandora's.
    10–12 Amynta.
    13–15 The pretty creature. In the Pirates.
    16–17 Louis XVI lamentation.
    18–19 Two bunches a penny primroses. Sung by Mrs. Franklin.
    20–21 Spring water cresses.
    22–23 Poor Richard. By B. Carr.
    24–27 The sea boys duett. In the Mariners.
    28 Ballad in Caernarvon castle.
    29 Ca ira.
    30–31 The seaman's home. Sung in the Midnight wanderers.
    32–33 Air. In the Pirates.
    34–37 Canzonett. With an accompanyment.
    38–40 Divertimento. MWA

'HE PHILADELPHIA SONGSTER. Part I. Being a collection of choice songs such as are calculated to please the ear while they improve the mind and make the heart better. By Absalom Aimwell, Esquire. Philadelphia, Printed and to be sold by John McCulloch in Third street, near the Market, Jan. 1789. 16 p. 15½ x 9½ cm.

Title-page, verso blank. Songs, p. 3-16.

Contents:

p.   3-4 God save America.
       5 A catch for three voices.
   6-7 Rosy Morn.
     7 Rose tree.
     8 Indian chief.
     9 Anna.
 10-11 Myra.
   11 Graceful move.
 12-13 Friendship.
   14 Glee for three voices [Drink to me only].
 15-16 Anna's urn.   NN

Ⅰ PIECE WITH VARIATIONS for the harpsichord or pianoforte etc.
By William Selby.
See Apollo and the Muses musical compositions.

*PIERRE DE PROVINCE and La Belle Magulone.
The "celebrated serious ballet, in two acts, told in action, (never performed in this country) . . . the new music entirely new, composed by Mr. [Alexander] Reinagle," was to be performed at the New Theatre, Philadelphia, May 2, 1796.

THE PIGEON. By the auther [!] of Auld Robin Gray. Philadelphia, Printed and sold by R. Shaw, N°. 13 South fourth street; J: Carrᵃ, Baltimore & J: Hewittᵃ, New York. (Price — [n. d.] 1 l. 32 cm.

Song, pfte. acc.
First line: Why tarries my love?
Composed by William Leeves (*BM Cat.*)
Published possibly as early as 1800.
Apparently published together with "The pigeon's return" (*q. v.*) since the price mark is carried across opposite outer margins of the two pieces. DLC

THE PIGEON'S RETURN. Philadelphia, Printed and sold by R: Shaw, N°. 13 South fourth street, and by J: Carr, Baltimore & J: Hewitt, New York.—25 cˢ) [n. d.] 1 l. 32 cm.

Song, pfte. acc.
First line: The dove flew around.
Published possibly as early as 1800.
Apparently published together with Leeve's "The pigeon" (*q. v.*) since the price mark is carried across opposite outer margins of the two pieces. DLC

PIONEERS MARCH.
See Compleat tutor for the fife . . . p. 23.

LA PIPE DE TABAC. A favorite French song with an English translation Arranged for the piano forte, violin and flute. New York, Printed and sol by I. and M. Paff, No. 127 Broadway [1799–1803] p. 2–3. 31½ cm.

Song, pfte. acc.
First lines: Hence the face of moping sorrow.—Contre les chagrins de la vi
McD–W, PP–1
From *Le petit matelot* by Pierre Gaveaux (1796).

——— The same as preceding, but without imprint.
Published probably ca. 1800. MNS

PIT A PAT. Sung by Mr. & Mrs. Marshall in Blue Beard. Printed & sold a B. Carr's Musical repository, Philadelphia; J. Carr's, Baltimore & J. Hewitt N. York (Price 25 cts.)
(*In* A collection of new & favorite songs. [C] Philadelphia [ca. 1799] p. 2–3

Duet, pfte. acc. Partially three staves.
First line: Twilight glimmers o'er the steep.

Mr. and Mrs. Marshall sang in the first American performance of Michae Kelly's *Blue Beard* in Philadelphia, May 24, 1799. ABHu, LSL, N]

——— Separate issue of preceding, ca. 1799. ABHu, MdH

PIT A PAT. A celabrated [!] duett as sung in the grand dramatic romance o Blue Beard. [New York] Sold by I. and M. Paff [ca. 1799] [2] p. 30½ cm

Imprint at foot of p. [2].
Song, pfte. acc.
First line: Twilight glimmers oer the plain.

Though performed in Philadelphia in 1799, Kelly's *Blue Beard* did not reach New York until 1802. It is possible, therefore, that this issue may not have appeared until about that time. NN

*PITY THE SORROWS OF A POOR OLD MAN, from the poem of the Beg- gar's petition.
Advertised in December, 1793, as "published . . . printed singly" by "B Carr & Co. Musical Repository, No. 122 Southside of Market street," Philadelphia.

*PIZARRO, OR, THE SPANIARDS IN PERU.
This "celebrated tragedy in 5 acts . . . written by Augustus von Kotzebue, and adapted to the English stage, by Richard Brinsley Sheridan . . . the music composed by Mr. [Alexander] Reinagle and Mr. [Raynor] Taylor," was first performed at Philadelphia, in December, 1800.

PIZARRO IN PERU, or The death of Rolla. A play in five acts. From the German of Augustus von Kotzebue. With notes marking the variations from the original. New York, Printed by G. F. Hopkins for William Dun- lap and sold at the office of the printer, No. 136 Pearl street; T. and J. Swords, No. 99 Pearl street; Gaine and Ten Eycke, No. 148 Pearl street; John Black, No. 5 Cedar street; Alex. Somerville, No. 114 Maiden Lane; and most other book-sellers in the U. States. 1800. iv, [2], [9]–92 p.

Title-page, verso blank; preceded by portrait of Mrs. Melmoth in the charac- ter of Elvira. Drawn by Dunlap. Tiebout Sculpt. Published for the

German Theatre by Wm. Dunlap; Preface, p. [iii]–iv; German Theatre, No. III. Pizarro in Peru, or The death of Rolla, p. [7]; Pizarro in Peru. As first performed at the New York Theatre, March 26, 1800. Characters . . . Performers . . . Music composed by Mr. Hewitt . . . , p. [8]; text, p. [9]–80; notes, [81]–92. CtY, DLC, MB, MH, MWA, RPB

As "The tragedy of Pizarro in Peru . . . the music composed by Mr. [James] Hewitt," performed at New York also in December, 1800.

HE PLAN OF A PERFORMANCE OF SOLEMN MUSICK, to be in the hall of the College of Philadelphia, on Wednesday evening April 10th, 1765, for the benefit of the Charity schools. 1765. 4 p. 12 mo.

Title-page, verso blank; text, p. 3–4.

    p. 3 Overture, Stamitz.
        Air.
        Solo on the violin.
        Overture, Earl of Kelly.
        Air.

    p. 4 Second overture, Martini.
        Overture in Artaxerxes. Arne.
        Sonata on the harpsichord.
        Chorus.

Sonneck adds: This is a concert program and not a play as Mr. Wegelin assumed. PPL

*LATO.
    See The select songster. New Haven, 1786. p. 65.

LATO'S ADVICE.
    (In The American musical miscellany. Northampton, 1798. p. 26–27)

Melody only, with accompanying text.
First line: Says Plato why should man be vain. DLC (etc.)

*THE PLEASING SONGSTER: or Festive companion: containing a . . . collection of songs . . . calculated for the entertainment of the social mind . . . Philadelphia: 1795.

*PLEYEL'S CELEBRATED CONCERTANTE.
    See Pleyel's celebrated Concertante.

*THE PLOWMAN'S ESCAPE FROM SEA.
    Song by Raynor Taylor. Was to be sung at his "musical performance . . . the whole of the music original and composed by Mr. Taylor," at Annapolis, Md., on February 28, 1793.

PLOW BOY.
    See Evening amusement, p. 16.

*A POCKET BOOK FOR THE GERMAN FLUTE containing necessary directions and remarks on that instrument, with an agreeable variety of celebrated airs, duets and songs, collected from the favourite opera entertain-

[333]

ments, etc. composed by the most admired authors in two parts, each is sol
separate at 12 s currency.

Advertised together with the two following titles in July, 1778, in *Rivington*
Royal gazette, New York, as published.

*A POCKET BOOK FOR THE GUITAR with directions, whereby every lad
and gentleman may become their own tuner.
Ibidem.

*A POCKET BOOK FOR THE VIOLIN. Embellished with curious remarks and
excellent examples by the late celebrated Signor Geminiani, etc. To which
are added a pleasing variety of songs, duets and airs, judiciously selected
from the most favorite operas, entertainments, etc.

Ibidem.

*A POCKET COMPANION FOR THE GERMAN FLUTE AND VIOLIN, by
F. C. Sheffer.

In the *Columbian centinel*, Boston, September 12, 1798, appeared the following
advertisement:

> *New Music.* Proposals for printing and publishing by subscription a
> POCKET COMPANION FOR THE GERMAN FLUTE AND VIOLIN
> containing a selection of airs, songs, duets, and trios, from the works o
> Haydn, Pleyel, Devienne, Hoofmaster (!), Doctor Arnold, Shield, Hook
> Dibdin, Linley, Carter, etc. together with correct and easy instructions
> for the flute, by F. C. Scheffer professor of music, teacher of the flute
> clarinet, violin, etc.

> The advantages of this undertaking to the musical world are so obvious as
> to preclude the necessity of further comment. Messrs. Linley and Co
> therefore, shall but add, that the public may rest assured, the whole work
> shall be executed in a stile superior to any hitherto published in this
> country.

> CONDITIONS

> The work shall be elegantly engraved, and will form a handsome pocket
> volume. The price to subscribers, one dollar and fifty cents to be paid
> on delivery, which shall take place on the first of January, 1799, after
> which time the price will be Two Dollars.

> * * * Subscriptions received at Messrs. Linley and Moore's Music
> Repository, No. 19 Marlborough street, Boston; Mr. Hewet [Hewitt],
> No. 131 William street, New York; Mr. B. Carr, Market street, Philadel-
> phia; and Mr. J. Carr of Baltimore.

THE POLITICAL DUENNA. A comic opera, in three acts, as it is performed by
the servants of his Britannic Majesty, with Lord North's recantation. To
which are added I. A letter to Mr. John Wesley on his calm address to the
Americans. Supposed to be written by the celebrated Junius. II. A letter
from an Irish gentleman in London to his friend and countryman, in his
Britannic Majesty's service, in America. Philadelphia: Printed and sold
by Robert Bell, next door to St. Paul's church, in Third street. 1778. 56
p. 21 cm.

Libretto with names of tunes to which the songs were to be sung. Title-
page, verso blank; *Personifications in the drama*, p. [5]; p. [6] blank; text, p.

[7]–45; p. [46] blank; "From the London Evening Post. On Lord North's Recantation . . . Chester, March 1, 1778," p. [47]–48; Letter to John Wesley, p. [49]–52; Letter from Irish gentleman, p. [53]–56.   PHi

HE POLLE.
See Favorite *Cotillions.*

OLLY PLY.
(*In* The American musical miscellany. Northampton, 1798. p. 265–267)
Melody only, with accompanying text.
First line: If ever a sailor was fond of good sport.
From *Castles in the air,* by Charles Dibdin.   DLC (etc.)

—— Jack's fidelity.
(*In* Elegant extracts for the German flute or violin. Philadelphia [1796]
bk. 2, p. 26–27)
Melody only, flute or violin, with accompanying text.
First line same as preceding.   DLC, NN

OLLY'S ANSWER.
See The select songster. New Haven, 1786. p. 12.

HE FAVORITE BALLAD OF THE POOR BLACK BOY. In the new musical farce of the Prize. Composed by Storace. Price 20 cents.
Philadelphia, Printed at Carr & cos. Musical repository [1794] [2] p. 33 cm.

Below and to the right of imprint: Jan. 13, 94.
At left of imprint: No. 2.
Song, pfte. acc. Arr. for flute or "guittar," p. [2].
First line: Your care of money, ah care no more.
Second number in Carr & cos. series of weekly issues. *cf.* "The Kentucky volunteer," by Raynor Taylor.   CdeW, CtY, ES, Hopk., MWA

—— The same as preceding.
(*In* A collection of new & favorite songs. [A] Philadelphia [ca. 1800]
p. [32]–[33])   HFB

OOR BLACK BOY. Sung by Miss Broadhurst in the Prize.
(*In* Young's vocal and instrumental musical miscellany. Philadelphia
[1793–95] p. 59)

Song, pfte. acc., followed by arr. for flute or guitar.
First line: You care of money, ah! care no more.
In No. 8, 1795.
Miss Broadhurst sang in the first American performance of Stephen Storace's
The prize at Philadelphia, May 26, 1794.   DLC

—— the same. Separate issue of preceding (unpaged) ca. 1795.   ES

POOR BLACK BOY. From the Prize. Sung by Miss Broadhurst and by Mr. Carr.
(*In* The gentleman's amusement, ed. by R. Shaw. Philadelphia [1794–96]
p. 48)

Melody (flute or violin) with accompanying text.
First line: You care of money ah care, no more.
In No. 6, 1795–96.   PHi

[335]

THE POOR BLIND GIRL. Written by Mr. C. I. Pitt. Composed by N
V. de Cleve. New York, Printed for G. Gilfert at his Musical magazi
No. 177 Broadway where may be had a great variety of musical instrumen
& music [1797] [2] p. 30 cm.

Song, pfte. acc.
First line: Though tender and young. RPJC

Advertised in January, 1797, as "just published by G. Gilfert, at his Music
Magazine, No. 177 Broadway," New York.

THE POOR BLIND GIRL. A favorite song. Written by Mr. C. I. Pit
Composed by Mr. V. Decleve. New York, Printed and sold by G. Gilfe
No. 177 Broadway [1797–1801] [2] p. 31½ cm.

Song, pfte. acc.
First line same as preceding. DLC, JFD, MW

THE POOR BLIND GIRL. Boston, Printed & sold by P. A. von Hagen juni
& cos. at their imported piano forte & music ware-house, No. 62 Newbu
street [1798–99] [2] p. 30½ cm.

Song, pfte. acc. Arr. for German flute or violin, p. [2].
First line same as preceding. DLC, RPJC

POOR EMMA. A celebrated new song. New York, Published by I. and M
Paff, No. 127 Broadway [n. d.] [2] p. 31½ cm.

Song, pfte. acc. Arr. for German flute, p. [2]. Three staves, upper sta
for lute.
First line: Keen blew the blast.
Published possibly as early as 1799. McD-V

*THE POOR FEMALE BALLAD SINGER, a pathetic song by Raynor Taylo
Was to be sung in an "Olio . . . entirely new" composed by R. Taylor, a
Philadelphia on February 1, 1794.

POOR JACK.
(In Elegant extracts for the German flute or violin. Baltimore, 179
bk. 1, p. 6–8)

Melody only, flute or violin, with accompanying text.
First line: Go patter to lubbers and swabs.
Composed by Charles Dibdin. DLC, N

POOR JACK.
(In The American musical miscellany. Northampton, 1798. p. 58–61)

Melody only, with accompany text.
First line same as preceding. DLC (etc.

POOR JACK BY DIBDIN. Price 25 cents. Philadelphia, Printed at Carr'
Musical repository [n. d.] [2] p. 32½ cm.

Song, pfte. acc. Arr. for flute, p. [2].
First line same as preceding.
Published possibly as early as 1794. LSL, NBuG

[336]

POOR JACK, or the Sailor's landlady.
This "pantomine interlude. With new music and a compiled Naval overture, called 'The sailor's medley' by Mr. [Benjamin] Carr," was to be performed at New York "after the play," on April 7, 1795.

POOR LIMA. A favorite ballad. Composed by Attwood & sung by Miss Broadhurst.
(*In* The musical journal for the piano forte, ed. by B. Carr. Baltimore [1800] v. 1, no. [3], p. (6)–(7).)

Song, pfte. acc.
First line: At early dawn from humble cot.
DLC, ES, MdHi, NN, NRU–Mus

POOR LIMA. Composed by Attwood.
(*In* The musical journal for the flute or violin. Baltimore [1800] no. 1, p. 6–7)

Melody only, flute or violin, with accompanying text.
First line same as preceding. DLC

THE POOR LITTLE CHILD OF A TAR. The much admired ballad sung by Mrs. Bland, Theatre royal, Drury lane. The words by Thomas George Ingall. The music by an amateur. New York, Published by I. and M. Paffs, No. 127 Brod Way [!] [1799–1803] 2 p. 32½ cm.

Song, pfte. acc.
First line: In a little blue garment all ragged and torn. DLC, McD–W

POOR LITTLE GYPSY.
See The little gipsey.

THE POOR MARINER.
(*In* Young's vocal and instrumental musical miscellany. Philadelphia [1793–95] p. 20)
Song, pfte. acc., followed by arr. for German flute.
First line: The winds whistled shrilly.
In No. 2, 1793. DLC, HFB, Hopk.

THE POOR MARINER. Price 25 cents. Printed and sold at B. Carr's musical repositories in Philadelphia and New York and J. Carr's, Baltimore [1796] [2] p. 33½ cm.

Song, pfte. acc. Arr. for flute, p. [2].
First line: The wind whistled shrilly. McD–W, NRU–Mus

Advertised in March, 1796, as published "at Carr's Musical Repository, William street," New York.

POOR MARY. Sung by Miss Broadhurst in the Italian monk. Composed by B. Carr.
(*In* The musical journal for the piano forte, ed. by B. Carr, Baltimore [1800] v. 1, No. [9], p. (18)–(19).)

Song, pfte. acc.
First line: Dark was the night the children slept.
DLC, ES, LSL, MdHi, NN, NRU–Mus, PP–K

————— Separate issue of preceding, ca. 1800. DLC

[337]

POOR MARY. Sung by Miss Broadhurst in the Italian monk at the New Yor
Theatre. Composed by B. Carr.
(*In* The musical journal for the flute or violin. Baltimore [1800] no.
[*i. e.* No. 9] p. 18–19)

Melody only, flute or violin, with accompanying text.
First line same as preceding.   DL

The Italian monk, with Miss Broadhurst in the cast, was first performed :
New York, June 5, 1798. This was apparently James Boaden's play (inte
spersed with music) founded on the novel by Mrs. Ann Radcliffe: *T*
Italian, or The confessional of the Black Penitents.

POOR MARY. New York, Printed & sold at J. Hewitt's Musical repositor
No. 23 Maiden Lane.
(*In* A collection of new & favorite songs. [A] Philadelphia [ca. 1800] p. [163

Song, pfte. acc.
First line: From cottage couch where slumbered Mary.
Original issue, 1799–1800.
Not identical with preceding.   HF

——— Separate issue ot preceding, ca. 1800.   DL

POOR RICHARD. By B. Carr.
(*In* The Philadelphia pocket companion for guittar or clarinett [Philadelphia
1794] v. 1, p. 22–23)

Melody only, with accompanying text.
First line: Poor Richard lov'd his Emma well.   MW.

POOR RICHARD. Written by Mr. John Carr. Composed by B. Carr . . .
(*In* Three ballads by B. Carr. Philadelphia [1799] p. 6–7)

Song, pfte. acc.
First line same as preceding.   JFI

*——— A different edition also issued by Carr was advertised in December
1793, as "published . . . printed singly" by "B. Carr & Co. Musical Repos
itory, No. 122 Southside of Market street," Philadelphia.

THE POOR SAILOR BOY. Composed by Mr. Attwood. New York, Printe
& sold at J. Hewitt's Musical repository, No. 131 William street.
(*In* A collection of new & favorite songs. [A] Philadelphia [ca. 1800] p. [202]

Imprint at foot of page.
Song, pfte. acc.
First line: Midst rocks and quick sands have we steer'd.   HFI

——— Original issue of preceding, ca. 1798.
Bound with: My native shore. Possibly published together. DLC, NM

THE POOR SOLDIER, a comic opera, in two acts, with the words, songs, duets
etc. As performed with universal applause, at the Theatre, New York.
Written by John O'Keefe, Esq. Philadelphia: Printed in the year 1787
29 p. 16½ cm.

Libretto to Shield's opera (1783).
Title-page; dramatis personae, p. [2]; text, p. [3]–29.   PPL

HE POOR SOLDIER. A comic opera, in two acts, with the words, songs, duetts, etc. as performed with universal applause by the American Company of Comedians. Written by John O'Keefe, Esquire. Philadelphia: Printed by T. Seddon, and W. Spotswood, 1787. 34, [2] p. 16½ cm.

Libretto.
Title-page; text followed by two page list of "plays & farces . . . Sold by Thomas Seddon." MB

HE POOR SOLDIER. A comic opera in two acts. With the words, songs, duets &c. As performed with universal applause by The American company. Written by John O'Keefe, Esq. Philadelphia, Printed and sold by Henry Taylor. M.DCC.XCI. 32 p. 18 x 10 cm.

Libretto. MB
See also "Songs, duets, etc. in the Poor soldier . . ." (words only).

THE POOR SOLDIER BOY.
"Song by Atwood." Advertised in January, 1798, as "just published by J. Hewitt, No. 131 William street," New York.

'OOR TOM BOWLING.
See Mrs. Pownall's address.

OOR TOM BOWLING, or the Sailor's epitaph. By Dibdin. Price 20 cents. Philadelphia, Printed at Carr & co's Musical repository [1794] [2] p. 33 cm.

Song, pfte. acc. Arr. for flute or "guittar," p. [2].
First line: Here a sheer hulk lies poor Tom Bowling.
From *The oddities.* CtY, LSL, MdHi, NN

Advertised February 3, 1794, as "this day" published.

'OOR TOM BOWLING.
(*In* Elegant extracts for the German flute or violin. Philadelphia [1796] bk. 2, p. 24–25)

Melody only, flute or violin, with accompanying text.
First line same as preceding. DLC, NN

'OOR TOM BOWLING, or the Sailor's epitaph. By Dibdin. Philadelphia, Printed by G. Willig, Market street, No. 185 [n. d.] [2] p. 31½ cm.

Song, pfte. acc. Arr. for flute or "guittar," p. [2].
First line same as preceding.
Published possibly as early as 1798. PP-K

'OOR TOM BOWLING, or the Sailor's epitaph by Dibdin. [n. p., n. d.] [2] p. 36 cm.

Song, pfte. acc.
First line same as preceding.
Published probably 179–. NRU–Mus

——— Tom Bowling, or the Sailor's epitaph by Dibdin.
(*In* Young's vocal and instrumental musical miscellany. Philadelphia [1793–95] p. 27)

Song, pfte. acc., followed by arr. for German flute.
First line same as preceding.
In No. 3, 1793. DLC, Hopk.

[339]

—— Poor Tom, or the Sailor's epitaph.
(*In* The American musical miscellany. Northampton, 1798. p. 31-33)

Melody only, with accompanying text.
First line same as preceding. DLC (et•

THE POOR VILLAGE BOY. Written and composed by the late Mr. Moul•
New York, Printed & sold at·J. & M. Paff's music store, No. 127 Broadw•
[1799-1803] [2] p. 33 cm.

Song, pfte. acc. Arr. for flute, p. [2].
First line: Soft blew the gale near yon bank's side.
Mr. Moulds: John Moulds. DLC, ES, N

POOR VULCAN, a burletta, in two acts, as performed at the New Theat•
Chestnut Street. Philadelphia: Printed by Wrigley & Berriman, No. 14
Chestnut Street. 1795. [Price one Eighth of a dollar.] 24 p. 17 cm.

Libretto by Dibdin.

Title-page; dramatis personae, p. [2]; text, p. [3]-24. PP•
"Poor Vulcan, or Gods upon earth" was advertised for first performance •
New York, on March 16, 1796, with "orchestra accompanyments by M
[Victor] Pelisier."

PORTUGUEZE HYMN ON THE NATIVITY. Alternative title of *Ades*
fideles.

THE POST CAPTAIN. Sung by Mr. Incledon at the Theatre Royal, Cove•
Garden, with unbounded applause. Composed by William Shield, Musicia•
in ordinary to His Majesty. New York, Published by I. and M. Paff, No. 12•
Broadway [1799-1803] 3 p. 33½ cm.

Song, pfte. acc.
First line: When Steerwell heard me first impart. DL•

—— The same as preceding, except that instead of being blank and unpage•
the fourth page is numbered "4" and contains the "3ᵈ verse" (seven scores).
DLC, McD-W, N•

POUR BIEN JUGER UNE MAITRESSE. Avec accompagnment de pian•
forte ou harpe [n. p., n. d.] [2] p. 32 cm.

At head of title: Air.
Song, pfte. (or harp) acc. Three staves. Voice part on upper staff.
First line same as title.
Because of its similarity to certain other issues it seems reasonable to assig•
its publication to Filippo Trisobio, Philadelphia, 1796-98. CdeV

THE POWER OF MUSICK. Words by Stoddard.
(*In* The harmony of Maine, by S. Belcher, Boston, 1794. p. 84-90)

Solo, trio and four-part chorus. Open score.
First line: Hark! some soft swell pants on the ev'ning breeze.
CtY, DLC, ICN, MB, MHi, MWA, NN•

[340]

RAYER OF THE SICILIAN MARINERS.
(*In* The gentleman's amusement, ed. by R. Shaw. Philadelphia [1794–96] p. 25)

Duet. Two staves.
First line: O sanctissima, o piissima.
In No. 3, 1794–95.   DLC, PHi

—— The same as preceding. On first page of separate sheet (p. 25–26) detached from original collection.   NN

RELUDES. In three classes. For the improvement of practitioners on the piano forte. Composed by A. Reinagle. Philadelphia, Printed at Carr & cos. Musical repository. Pr. 50 cents [1794] 4 p. 32½ cm.

Pfte. 2 hds.   LSL

Advertised in June, 1794, as published.

HE PRESIDENT.
See No. 1 of a new sett of *Cotilions.*

HE PRESIDENT OF THE UNITED STATES' MARCH. Composed by Mr. Sicard. Philadelphia, Printed by J. McCulloch [n. d.] 1 l. 32½ cm. Pfte. 2 hds.

Printed from movable type.
At foot of page: Cotillion minuet. Composed by Mr. Sicard.
Published probably in 1789.   DLC, NN

Above date is based on the fact that when Washington became President of the United States in 1789, Sicard was living in Philadelphia, and McCulloch was already publishing there. (*cf.* The Philadelphia songster.)

HE PRESIDENT'S MARCH.
This march has become immortal by furnishing the air to Joseph Hopkinson's *Hail Columbia.* It has generally been accepted that the march was composed in honor of George Washington's becoming President of the United States in 1789; but for many years its authorship remained in doubt. It was thought to be the work of one or the other of two well known musicians, Philip Roth or Philip Phile. Not until the discovery of a copy with its title followed by the words "By Pheil" was this question of its authorship answered.

In regard to this uncertainty of authorship, not then settled as we now know it, Sonneck notes:

> I would like to call attention to the remarkable fact that the program of Mrs. Grattan's benefit concert, as advertised in the *City gazette*, Charleston, S. C., November 8, 1798, for the same evening, shows as last number "Hail Columbia—Taylor." While this may mean at first glance that the music to "Hail Columbia," that is to say, "The President's march," was composed by Raynor Taylor, it probably and unfortunately does not. More likely, Taylor was to sing the national song, the audience joining in the chorus.

While the gist of this note is no longer entirely germane to our subject, Sonneck's point as to the ambiguity of early musical programs is still valid. As to which is the first edition of Phile's *President's march*, that honor would seem to go to the Carr & Co. issue which must have appeared between mi summer of 1793 and fall of 1794. However, it is possible that the issue f two flutes in *The gentleman's amusement* for April 1, 1794, may take prec dence. Other early (incidental) appearances of this march are to be not in the "Federal overture" by Benjamin Carr, 1794 (*q. v.*) and in the arrang ment of this Overture as a "Medley duetto adapted for two German flutes 1795. (*q. v.*)

PRESIDENT'S MARCH AND CA IRA. Price 12 cents. [Philadelphi
Carr & co. [1793–94] 1 l. 31½ cm.

Pfte. 2 hds.
President's march, by Philip Phile.
Published possibly as early as July, 1793.

CdeW, DLC, MdHi, MNSt, NHi, NN, PP, RPJC

THE PRESIDENT'S MARCH.
(*In* The gentleman's amusement, ed. by R. Shaw. Philadelphia [1794–9
p. 3)

For two flutes. Two staves.
In No. 1, April 1, 1794.   DLC, PI

——— The same as preceding. On first page, numbered "3" of a detache
portion (p. 3–6) from above collection.   N

THE PRESIDENT'S MARCH. Aranged [!] for two performers on one pian
forte by R. Taylor. Philadelphia, Engraved and published by Wm Pries
Sold at all the music stores in the United States. And by Preston and so
No. 97 Strand, London. Price 25 cents. [ca. 1795] [2] p. 34 cm.

Pfte. 4 hds.   CdeW, CSmH, DLC, ES, LSL, MB, NRU–Mu

Sonneck adds: When I examined the piece, "[182–?]" had been supplied a
date, but—

1. The whole appearance of the piece suggests the 18th century rathe than the 19th.

2. "The President's march" was more popular about 1795 than 1820, a least under its original name.

3. The *American daily advertiser*, Philadelphia, printed on January 7, 1795 the following advertisement: Music engraving. In all its branche correctly performed by Wm. Priest, musician of the New Theatre. Fo particulars inquire at No. 15 Apple Tree Alley between Fourth and Fift street.

4. Mr. Frank Kidson says in his "British music publishers, printers an engravers" (1900) on p. 106: In 1778, he [John Preston, the founder of th firm] had removed to 98 Strand, a mistake in the directory possibly for 97 for at this latter number the firm remains from before February, 1781 till about 1822 . . . In 1789 Preston . . . had just taken his son Thoma into partmership . . . Between 1798 and 1801, John Preston disappear from the firm, (though in some instances the old style, Preston & Son, i used) and Thomas alone remains . . .

For these reasons, I believe Raynor Taylor's arrangement of the march wa published about 1795.

PRESIDENTS MARCH.
See Military amusement, p. 3, August, 1796.

—— The same.
New York, Printed and sold by G. Gilfert, No. 177 Broadway [n. d.] 1 l.
32½ cm.
Pfte. 2 hds., followed by arr. for German flute or violin.
Published possibly as early as January, 1797.   DLC, JFD, MB, RPJCB

—— The same.
Boston, Printed & sold by P. A. von Hagen, junior & cos. at their Musical
magazine, No. 62 Newbury street [1798–99]. 1 l. 31½ cm.
Pfte. 2 hds., followed by arr. for German flute or violin.
Published possibly as early as May, 1798.   JFD, LSL

—— The same.
Boston, Printed & sold by P. A. von Hagen, Junior & cos. at their Musical
magazine, No. 62 Newbury street [1798–99] [2] p. 31 cm.
Pfte. 2 hds., followed by arr. for German flute or violin.
On p. [2], "Stamitz Air" and "A French march" (both pfte. 2 hds.).   MB

—— The same.
Philadelphia, Printed and sold by G. Willig, Mark. street No. 185 [1798–
1804] 1 l. 30 cm.
Pfte. 2 hds.
Followed by arr. for the flute.
Published probably ca. 1798.   DLC

—— The same.
New York, Printed and sold [n. d.] 1 l. 24½ x 15½ cm.
Imprint at foot of page.
Pfte. 2 hds.
Evidently a leaf from some collection or possibly from some magazine.
Published probably 179–.   DLC

—— The same.
See The instrumental assistant, p. 57.

THE PRESIDENTS MARCH. By Pheil [!] [n. p., n. d.] 1 l. 33 cm.
Pfte. 2 hds.
Followed by "March. By Moller."   DLC

Any exact dating of this important issue of *The President's march* seems impossible.   Perhaps, however, the fact that it has been the means of settling
the long disputed point of the authorship of the March may well offset this
deficiency.

For a time this issue was supposed to be from Moller & Capron in Philadelphia, and therefore dating as early as 1793–94.   But an examination of
Moller & Capron issues so far available has shown no bass clef like the very
characteristic one of this issue.   The same peculiar form of clef (often appearing without dots, as in this case) occurs in certain I. C. Moller, New
York, issues which Sonneck has dated ca. 1800.   Assuming this date to be
correct, then this present issue of *The President's march* (together with the
March. By Moller) should also be given as ca. 1800.

———— The President's march, followed by Washington's march [Philadelphia] B. Carr [1796].
See The new President's march.

———— The President's march, a new Federal song.
See Hail Columbia.

THE NEW PRESIDENT'S MARCH.
See Washington's march.

PRESIDENT'S NEW MARCH.
See Washington's march.

THE NEW PRESIDENT'S OR JEFFERSON'S MARCH.   As performed at the theatres, Philadelphia and Baltimore.
(*In* Mr. *Francis's ballroom assistant.* Philadelphia, ca. 1800.   p. 14.)
Pfte. 2 hds.
Composed or arranged by A. Reinagle.
Apparently not published until 1801.   JFD, McD–W

———— The same as preceding.   First page, numbered 14, of a detached leaf from above collection.   DLC

THE PRESSGANG DEFEATED.   Alternative title of *The American tar.*

THE PRETTY BRUNETTE.   Alternative title of *Dear Nancy I've sail'd the world all around,* by James Hook.
See also Then say my sweet girl can you love me.

THE PRETTY CREATURE.   In the Pirates.
(*In* The Philadelphia pocket companion for guittar or clarinett [Philadelphia, 1794]   v. 1, p. 13–15)
Melody only, with accompanying text.
First line: Oh! the pretty pretty creature.
The pirates, by Stephen Storace.   MWA

THE PRETTY LAD.   A favorite air in the Poor soldier.   Sung by Mrs. Tubbs. New York, Printed & sold at J. Hewitts Musical repository, No. 131 William street.   Sold also by B. Carr, Philadelphia & J. Carr, Baltimore.   Pr. 25 cents.   [1797–99]   [2] p.   30½ cm.
Song, pfte. acc.
First line: What days of fleeting pleasures past.
The poor soldier, by William Shield.   N, NN

———— The same as preceding.
(*In* A collection of new & favorite songs.   [A]   Philadelphia [ca. 1800]   p. [106]–[107])   HFB

Probably identical with the issue advertised in December, 1797, as "published at Carr's Musical Repository, Market street," Philadelphia.

PRETTY MAIDS ALL IN A ROW.   A favorite nursery song.   Composed by Mr. Hook.   For one or two voices.
(*In* The musical journal for the piano forte, ed. by B. Carr.   Baltimore [1800] v. 1, no. 1, p. (4).)
Song (or duet) pfte. acc.   Three staves.
First line: How does my ladys garden grow.
                          DLC, ES, LSL, McD–W, MdHi, NN, NRU–Mus, PP–K

[344]

PRETTY MAIDS ALL IN A ROW. A nursery song. Composed by Mr. Hook
(*In* The musical journal for flute or violin, Baltimore [1800] no. 1, p. 4)

Two parts. For flutes or violins (or flute and violin) with accompanying
text. Two staves.
First line: How does my lady's garden grow. DLC

PRETTY POLL & HONEST JACK. Printed for B. Carr & sold at his Musical
repositorys in Philadelphia & New York & by I. Carr, Baltimore.
(*In* The favorite songs, by Mr. Hook. Philadelphia [1794-95] p. 4-5)

Song, pfte. acc.
First line: When whistling winds are heard to blow.
McD-W and NN (complete), MWA and MdHi (lack p. 5)

———— Separate issue of preceding. Apparently from the same plate, but with
the following minor change in the imprint: "in Philadelphia and New York
and at J. Carr's Baltimore." DLC

Advertised in January, 1795, as "just published" by "B. Carr," New York.

———— 'Twas pretty Poll & Honest Jack. A favorite song. Sung by Mr. Dignum.
New York, Printed and sold by G. Gilfert & co. at their Musical magazine,
No. 191 Broadway [1794-95] [2] p. 33½ cm.

Song, pfte. acc.
First line: When wistling [!] winds are heard. JFD

Also advertised in March, 1795, as "published and to be had at G. Willig's
magazine, No. 165 Market street," Philadelphia. This issue has not been
located.

A PREY TO TENDER ANGUISH. A favorite song. Composed by Dr.
Haydn. Philadelphia, Printed & sold by G. Willig, No. 185 Market street
[1798-1804] [2] p. 33 cm.

Song, pfte. acc. Three staves. Voice part on upper staff.
Arr. for guitar or flute, p. [2].
First line same as title. DLC, ES, MWA, PP-K

———— The same.
Published by G. F. Weizsaecker and sold at G. Willig's Musical magazine,
No. 185 Market street, Philadelphia and G. Gilfert's Musical magazine,
New York [1798-1804] [2] p. 33 cm.

Below imprint, in brackets: Printed by Charles Cist, Philadelphia.
At head of title, vignette representing a reclining maiden with lyre.
Song, pfte. acc. Arr. for "guittar" or German flute (two staves with words
between), p. [2].
First line same as title.
Printed with movable type. NN

A PREY TO TENDER ANGUISH. Composed by Dr. Haydn. With an accompaniment for the harp or piano forte by J. F. Bohlius. Price 2 s. New
York, Publish'd by J. & M. Paff, Broadway [1799-1803] 2-3 p. 32 cm.

Song, pfte. acc. Three staves.
First line same as title.
On lower margin, p. 2: Engraved by E. Riley. ABHu, RPJCB

[345]

A discrepancy arises here in that J. and M. Paff were not on Broadway after 1803; E. Riley is not in the New York directory until 1806.

A PREY TO TENDER ANGUISH. Composed by Hayden [!] Philadelphia, Published by G. Willig [n. d.] p. 10. 32½ cm.

Song, pfte. acc.
First line same as title. PP-K

A PREY TO TENDER ANGUISH. Selected from the German Erato. Composed by Dᵣ Haydn. 12 cents. New York, Published for P. Weldon [n. d.] 1 l. 31½ cm.

Imprint at foot of page.
Song, pfte. acc.
First line same as title. McD-W

Although from their imprints the above issues might be considered as belonging to the eighteenth century, the fact that *BM Cat.* lists no earlier issue than 1800 makes it probable that they were all published after that date.

THE PRIDE OF OUR PLAINS. A new song. Written by the author of Anna, Gentle zephyr & May morning. The music composed by P. A. von Hagen. Boston, Printed & sold at P. A. von Hagen's piano forte ware house, No. 4 Old Massachusetts Bank, Head of the Mall & at the music store, No. 3 Cornhill. Also at G. Gilfert's warehouse, N. York; David Vinton's, Providence; W. R. Wilder, Newport; B. B. Macanulty, Salem; E. M. Blunt, Newbury Port; Isaac Stanwood, Portsmouth & E. A. Jenks, Portland [n. d.] [2] p. 33 cm.

Song, pfte. acc. Arr for guitar or "clarinett," p. [2].
First line: The blushing daughter of the thorn.
Published probably after 1800. LSL, MH, N, RPB, RPJCB

THE PRIMROSE. Composed by W. Langdon. Philadelphia, Printed for the Author, No. 70 Market street. Sold at B. Carr's Musical repository's, Market st., Philadᵉ; William st., N. York & at I. Carr's, Market street, Baltimore. Price ¼ of a dollar [1795] [2] p. 32 cm.

Song, pfte. acc.
First line: Ask, ask, me why I send you here. MdHi

Advertised in *Aurora* (Philadelphia), October 12, 1795, as "A new song."

THE PRIMROSE GIRL. Sung by Mrs. Pownall. Composed by J. Hewitt. (*In* Six songs, by Mrs. Pownall and J. Hewitt. New York [1794] p. 16)

Song, pfte. acc.
First line: Come, buy of poor Kate, primroses I sell. ES, HFB

———— The same as preceding.
(*In* A collection of new & favorite songs. [A] Philadelphia [ca. 1800] p. [144] numbered 16)

THE PRIMROSE GIRL. Sung by Mrs. Pownall [n. p., n. d.] 1 l. 29½ cm.
Song, pfte. acc.
First line same as preceding.
Published probably New York, ca. 1794. DLC

[346]

THE PRIMROSE GIRL. New York, Printed and sold by G. Gilfert & co., No. 191 Broadway [1794–95] 1 l. 34 cm.

Song, pfte. acc.
First line same as preceding.   DLC, JFD, NN, RPJCB

————The same.
(In The American musical miscellany. Northampton, 1798. p. 235–237)

Melody and bass, with accompanying text.
First line same as preceding.   DLC (etc.)

THE PRIMROSE GIRL. A favorite song [n. p., n. d.] p. 77. 31 cm.

Song, pfte. acc.
First line same as preceding.
Apparently a separate issue from The musical repertory, Boston [No. V, 1799].   ES

———— Primroses. A favorite song. Sung by Mrs. Pownall. With additions and alterations by a lady. New York, Published by J. Young & co. [ca. 1793–94] [21]–22 p. 32 cm.

Song, pfte. acc.
First line same as preceding.   NN

———— The same.
New York, Printed by James Harrison at his music ware house in Maiden Lane where may be had the greatest variety of new songs and music of all kinds [1794–95] [3] p. 33 cm.

Song, pfte. acc. Arr. for guitar, p. [3].
First line same as preceding.   MWA

———— Primroses. Sung by Mrs. Pownall.
(In Elegant extracts for the German flute or violin. Philadelphia [1798] bk. 3, p. 12)

Melody only, flute or violin, with accompanying text.
First line same as preceding.   DLC, NN

PRIMROSE HILL.
See Manuscript collection of hymns, songs, etc. (43).

PRIMROSES.
See The primrose girl.

PRIMROSES DECK. A favorite rondo. Sung by Mr. Carr at the amateur & professional concerts. Composed by Mr. Linley. Price 25 cents. Philadelphia, Printed & sold at Carr & cos. Musical repository. [1794] 4 p. 32½ cm.

Song, pfte. acc. Arr. for flute, p. 4.
First line: Primroses deck the bank's green side.
                                                      DLC, ES, Hopk., JFD, MWA

Advertised as published in April, 1794. Also advertised in January, 1795, by James Harrison, New York, as "published . . . with additional verses by a lady of this city." This latter issue has not been located.

PRINCE FERDINAND'S MARCH.
See Compleat tutor for the fife . . . p. 23.

THE PRINCE OF WALES'S MARCH.
See Compleat tutor for the fife . . . p. 23.

THE PRINCE OF WALES'S WALTZ.
(*With* The beggar girl. Ladies musical journal, No. 6 [New York, 1799–1803])

Pfte. 2 hds. DLC, NBuG

*THE PRISONER, OR FEMALE HEROISM.
This "comic romance in three acts . . . the music composed and adapted by Atwood. Orchestra accompanyments by Mons. [Trille] Labarre" was to be performed "for the first time" at the Federal Street Theatre, Boston, in March, 1797.

PRITHEE FOOL BE QUIET. Scotch song.
(*In* A collection of new & favorite songs. [A] Philadelphia [ca. 1800] p. [211])

Song, pfte. acc.
First line: Young Jockey sou* my heart to win. HFB

———— Separate issue of preceding, ca. 1800, or 179–. NN
Sung by Mrs. Hodgkinson at Columbia Garden, New York, July 6, 1798.

PROPITIOUS POWERS WHO GUARD OUR STATE.
See Military glory of Great Britain.

PRUSSIAN MARCH.
See Three new *Marches*.

THE PSALM-SINGERS AMUSEMENT. Containing a number of fuging [!] pieces and anthems. Composed by William Billings, author of the Singing master's assistant. Printed and sold by the Author at his house near the White Horse, Boston, 1781. I. Norman sculp. 103, [1] p. 12 x 19½ cm.

Title-page; advertisement, p. 2; music, p. 3–103; index, p. [104].
Four-part chorus. Open score.
The most important secular numbers are: Modern music, p. 72–77; Consonance, p. 81–89. CSmH, DLC, ICN, MB, MHi

PTALAEMON TO PASTORA. A new air by Mr. Wm. Selby.
(*In* The gentlemen & ladies town & country magazine. Boston, March, 1789. Opposite p. 104)

Song, pfte. acc.
First line: Farewell my Pastora, no longer yʳ swain. DLC (etc.)

THE PURSE, or, Benevolent tar. A musical drama, in one act, as performed at the Boston Theatre, Federal Street. By J. C. Cross. (The music by Mr. Reeve.) Boston. Printed for W. Pelham, No. 59 Cornhill. 1797. 24 p. 16 cm.

Libretto. CSmH, MB, MWA

First performed in the United States at the New Theatre, Philadelphia, January 7, 1795, with "accompaniments and new airs" by Alexander Reinagle.

[348]

Wegelin had "The purse" in mind when mentioning " 'American tars' ('The purse') Played at the Park Theatre, New York, January 29, 1798."
See also "Songs in the Purse . . ." (words only).

THE PURSUIT.
See How sweet in the woodlands.

THE PYRENEES.
See Three new *Marches*.

QUADRILL OR DOUBLE COTILLION.
See Quadrill or double *Cotillion*.

THE QUAKER; a comic opera in two acts as performed at the Theatre in Boston. Printed by P. Edes and S. Letheridge in Boston, for William P. Blake, No. 59 Cornhill, and William T. Clap, No. 90 Newbury street, 1794.   32 p.   17½ cm.
Libretto, by Charles Dibdin (1775).   MB, MH, MWA
As "The Quaker, or Benevolent friend.   The music by Dibdin; the accompaniments, with an introductory symphony, composed by R. Taylor," the opera was to be performed at Baltimore on September 28, 1796.

*QUARTET by Jean Gehot.
Was to be played at the City Concert, Philadelphia, December 1, 1792.

*QUARTET by John Christopher Moller.
A "quartetto, harmonica, 2 tenors and violoncello by Moller," was to be played at a concert, Philadelphia, May 5, 1795.   (The "harmonica" is, of course, Franklin's Armonica.)

*QUARTET by John Young.
A "quartetto Young" was to be played at the fifth City Concert, Philadelphia, on January 26, 1793.

*QUARTET by Petit.
A "quartetto (Petit) with variations for the clarinet" was to be played at a concert in Philadelphia, January 15, 1793.

*QUARTET by Victor Pelissier.
Was to be played at a concert in Philadelphia, May 31, 1792.

*QUARTETS by John Antes.
Although Sonneck states that a number of quartets by John Antes, a member of the Moravian congregation, Bethlehem, Pa., are said to be extant, it has been impossible to locate them.
However, NRU–Mus possesses the following interesting work undoubtedly by John Antes:
Tre trii per due violini e violoncello, obligato.   Dedicati a Sua Excellenza il Sigʳᵉ G. T. de Heidenstam, Ambassatore de Sa Maj. il Ri [sic!] de Suede a Constantinopel.   Composti a Grand Cairo dal Sigre.   Giovanni A–T–S. Dilettante Americano.   Op. 3.   London, Printed & sold by I. Bland at his music warehouse, No. 45 Holborn (ca. 1790).

QUEEN MARY'S FAREWELL TO FRANCE.
(*In* The American musical miscellany.   Northampton, 1798.   p. 30–31)
Melody only, with accompanying text.
First line: O! thou lov'd country.   DLC (etc.)

[349]

QUEEN MARY'S LAMENTATION.
See The select songster. New Haven, 1786. p. 27–28.

———— The same.
New York, Printed & sold at J. Hewitt's Musical repository, No. 23 Maiden Lane.
(*In* A collection of new & favorite songs. [A] Philadelphia [ca. 1800] p. [159])
Song, pfte. acc.
First line: I sigh and lament me in vain.   HFB

THE QUEEN OF FRANCE to her children just before her execution. The words by P. Pindar. The music by M. R. Chateaudun. [n. p., n. d.] [2] p. 33½ cm.
Song, pfte. acc. Three staves.
First line: From my prison with joy could I go.
Published probably by Carr, Philadelphia, ca. 1800.   PP–K

QUICK MARCH. In the pantomime of Oscar & Malvina.
(*In* The musical repertory, Boston [1796] No. II, p. 25)
Pfte. 2 hds
Oscar and Malvina, by William Reeve.   DLC

QUICK MARCH FROM THE BATTLE OF PRAGUE.
(*In* The gentleman's amusement, ed. by R. Shaw. Philadelphia [1794–96] p. 41)
Duet for flutes (or violins). Two staves.
In No. 5, March 1, 1795.
Composed by F. Koczwara.   DLC, PHi

QUICKSTEP.
(*With* Roslin Castle. Philadelphia [1798–1804] p. [2])
Pfte. 2 hds.   DLC, MWA

QUICK STEP.
(*With* The English naval dance. New York, I. and M. Paff [n. d.] p. [2])
Pfte. 2 hds.
Published probably ca. 1800   DLC, ES, NBuG, NN, RPJCB

QUICK STEP. Composed by R. Taylor.
(*With* Washington's march. Philadelphia, G. Willig [ca. 1795])
Pfte. 2 hds.   CSmH, MNSt, PPL

QUICK STEP IN THE BATTLE OF PRAGUE.
See Military amusement, p. 8.

*QUOD VIS.
Advertised in November, 1798, as "just published" by "George Gilbert at his musicstore, 177 Broadway, Apollo's Head," New York.

THE RACE HORSE.
(*In* Elegant extracts for the German flute or violin, Baltimore, 1794. bk. 1, p. 4–5)
Melody only, flute or violin, with accompanying text.
First line: See the course throng'd with gazers.   DLC, NN

THE RACE HORSE.
(*In* The American musical miscellany. Northampton, 1798. p. 152–155)

Melody only, with accompanying text.
First line same as preceding. DLC (etc.)

THE RAMBLE. A favorite duett. New York, Printed and sold by G. Gilfert & co., No. 177 Broadway [1796] [2] p. 31 cm.

Duet, pfte. acc.
First line: How sweet's the verdant vale. MWA

THE RANGERS COTILLON [!]
(*In* [Unidentified collection of instrumental and vocal music. New York] Hewitt & Rausch [1797] p. 8)

Pfte. 2 hds. DLC

———— The same as preceding. At foot of first page, numbered 8, of a detached leaf from above collection. JFD

———— The same as preceding.
(*In* A collection of new & favorite songs. [A] Philadelphia [ca. 1800] foot of p. [153] numbered 8) HFB

———— Separate issue of preceding, foot of page, numbered 8. MB

RECITATIVO E RONDO. Del Signor Giovanni Paisiello. Pubblicato in Filadelfia dal Sigr.Trisobio [ca. 1797] 8 p. 34½ cm.

Song, pfte. acc. Three staves.
First line: Ah! no mio bene non lasciar spaven tarti.
Filippo Trisobio, in Philadelphia, 1797. Died there, 1798. DLC

THE RECONCILIATION. Being a sequel to Damon and Clora. Composed by R. Taylor.
(*With* Damon and Clora. Philadelphia [1794] p. 4)

Duet, pfte. acc. Three staves.
First line: And art thou, Damon, faithles [!] grown. DLC, Hopk., LSL

THE RECONCILIATION, or the Triumph of nature. A comic opera, in two acts by Peter Markoe. [Verses] Philadelphia: Printed and sold by Prichard & Hall, in Market Street, between Front and Second streets, 1790. vi, [3], 10–48 p. 21 cm.

Libretto, with the tunes named to which the songs were to be sung.
Title-page, verso blank; dedication, p. [iii]; preface, p. [v]–vi; dramatis personae, p. [8]; text, p. [9]–48. DLC, PPL, RPB

Three airs were printed in the *Universal asylum*, Philadelphia, June, 1790, of which one ("Truth from thy radiant throne look down") is with music (tune: In infamy).

Peter Markoe informs us in the preface that "a revisal and correction of [Gessner's] 'Erastus,' literally translated by a native of Germany, lately arrived in Pennsylvania, gave rise to the following piece . . . A new character is added, songs are introduced, and the dialogue so modelled, as to be rendered (it is presumed) pleasing to an American ear." The author further narrates with some bitterness that "The reconciliation" was accepted by the

[351]

managers of the theatre in Philadelphia, but that he withdrew it after it had remained in their hands more than four months without having been performed though "approved of" by "his excellency Thomas Mifflin, Esq. President of the State of Pennsylvania," and "Thomas M'Kean, Esq. Chief Justice of the said State, in their official capacity according to law," to whom the work is dedicated.

For further particulars and a description of the libretto, see Sonneck's monograph on "Early American operas" (Sammelbände d. Int. Mus. Ges. 1904–05).

THE RECONSALIATION [!]   The words by a gentleman of Philadelphia. Music by I. Gehot.
(In Young's vocal and instrumental musical miscellany.   Philadelphia [1793–95] p. 3)
Song, pfte. acc., followed by arr. for German flute or violin.
First line: Pensive alone in yonder shade.
In No. 1, 1793.
I. Gehot: Jean Gehot.   DLC, ES, HFB, Hopk.

*THE RECRUIT.
This "musical interlude," written by the actor John D. Turnbull—the composer is unknown—was performed at Charleston, S. C., on March 12, 1796.

*THE REDEMPTION OF ENGLAND from the cruelties of the Danish invasion by Alfred the Great.   Written by the pious and philosophic Mr. Thompson, in conjunction with Mr. Mallet; and in the year 1751, altered and greatly improved by the latter.
This masque, composed by Arne and better known under the title of "Alfred the Great," was performed in January, 1757, at the College of Philadelphia with alterations and "near 200 new lines, besides a new prologue and epilogue . . . and a song of the Aerial Spirits . . . fitted to an excellent piece of new music by one of the performers." [Francis Hopkinson?]   An account of this extraordinary performance with reprint of most of the two hundred additional lines, etc., is to be found in the Pennsylvania gazette, Philadelphia, January 20, 27 and February 3, 1757.   See also Sonneck's book on "Francis Hopkinson . . . and James Lyon" (1905).

*THE REPUBLICAN HARMONIST; being a select collection of Republican, Patriotic, and Masonic songs, odes, sonnets etc.—American and European . . . By D. E., a Cosmopolite.
D. E.: Daniel Ebsworth.
From copyright records, Pennsylvania, May 7, 1800.

THE REQUEST.
(In [A collection of favorite songs, arr. by A. Reinagle.   Philadelphia, 1789 (?)] p. 5.)
Song, pfte. acc.
First line: Tell me babling [!] echo why.   ES

THE REQUEST.   An admired new song.   Composed by G. Vogler.
(In Young's vocal and instrumental musical miscellany.   Philadelphia [1793–95] p. 47)
Song, pfte. acc., followed by arr. for flute.   Three staves.
First line: Tell me babling [!] echo why.

[352]

In No. 6, 1794.

G. Vogler; Gerard Vogler, probably a brother of the better known Georg
Joseph Vogler, the Abbé.   ABHu, DLC, Hopk.

THE REQUEST. The same as preceding. First page, numbered 47 of a detached leaf from the above collection.   PHi

THE REQUEST. Composed by L'Abe Vogler. New York, Printed & sold by
G. Gilfert & co., No. 209 Broadway [1795] 1 l. 33½ cm.

Song, pfte. acc.
First line: Tell me babling [!] eccho [!] why.
Not composed by the Abbé Vogler. See preceding entry.   JFD, RPJCB

THE REQUEST. Published at B. Carr's Musical repositories, Philadelphia &
New York & J. Carr's, Baltimore. (Price 12 cents) [1796] 1 l. 32 cm.

Below imprint: N. B. The treble line is well adapted for the guittar.
Song, pfte. acc., followed by arr. for flute.
First line: Tell me babling [!] echo why.   DLC, LSL, MWA
Evidently the same issue as that advertised in August, 1796, as "reprinted"
among "Musical publications. Printed by J. Carr, Music Store, No. 6 Gay
street, Baltimore, and B. Carr's, Musical Repositories, Market street, Philadelphia and William street, New York."

—— The same.
New York, Printed & sold by G. Gilfert, No. 177 Broadway [1797–1801]
1 l. 31½ cm.

Song, pfte. acc.
First line same as preceding.   MWA, NN

—— The same.
New Yok [!] Printed and sold by I. C. Moller [n. d.] 1 l. 32½ cm.

Song, pfte. acc.
First line same as preceding.
Sonneck dates this issue ca. 1800.   DLC, RPJCB

THE REQUEST. Composed by L'Abe Vogler. Boston, Printed & sold at P.
A. von Hagen's imported piano forte ware house, No. 3 Cornhill [ca. 1800]
1 l. 31½ cm.
Song, pfte. acc.
First line: Tell me babbling echo why.
Not composed by the Abbé Vogler. See above.   ES, JFD, RPJCB

RESIGNATION MARCH. A French composition.
(*In* The musical repertory. Boston. [1796–97] No. III, p. 33)
Pfte. 2 hds.   DLC

THE RESOLUTION. A new song. Composed by Mozart. Published & sold
by G. Willig, No. 185 Market street, Philadelphia [1798–1804] [2] p. 32½ cm.

Song, pfte. acc.
First line: Ye gentle gales that careless blow.
                        ABHu, DLC, JFD, MWA, PP, RPJCB
The music is an arrangement for single voice of the duet in *Die Zauberflöte:*
Bei Männern welche Liebe fühlen. (Act I, no. 7). The text is entirely new.

[353]

THE RETREAT.
See Compleat tutor for the fife . . . p. 15.

LE RÉVEIL DU PEUPLE. In French and English. Printed & sold at B. Carr's Musical repositories in New York & Philadelphia & J. Carr's, Baltimore. Price 25 cents. [1796] [2] p. 33½ cm.

At head of title: "Vive la republique," the words grouped about a design consisting of the tri-color (two flags), a citizen's cap on a pole, sun's rays, &c.
Song, pfte. acc. Arr. for flute, p. [2].
First lines: People of France ye soul link'd people.—Peuple français peuple de freres. LSL, McD-W, MWA
Composed by Pierre Gaveaux (1795).
Advertised in March, 1796, as "a new patriotic French song, with the English translation . . . published, price 25 cents, at Carr's Musical Repository, William Street," New York.

LE RÉVEIL DU PEUPLE.
See Evening amusement [1796], p. 14.

———— The same.
See New French march *in* Military amusement [1796], p. 2.

RHODE ISLAND JIGG.
See United States country *Dances*, p. 6.

*RICHARD COEUR DE LION.
"(For the first time on the continent of America) the grand historical Romance, called Richard Coeur de Lion with all the original music, songs, and chorusses, composed by Gretry, the orchestra accompaniments entirely new, composed by Mons. [Trille] Labarre," was to be performed at Boston on January 23, 1797.

RIPE CHERRIES. A favorite song sung at Vauxhall Gardens. Composed by Mr. Hook. New York, Printed & sold by G. Gilfert, No. 177 Broadway [1797–1801] [2] p. 30½ cm.

Song, pfte. acc.
First line: Come buy my ripe cherries fair maidens come buy. NN

RIPE CHERRIES. A favorite song. Composed by Mr. Hook [n. p., n. d.] 70–71 p. 30 cm.

Song, pfte. acc.
First line same as preceding.
Evidently a separate issue from *The musical repertory*, Boston. [No. V, 1799]
ES MB

RISE COLUMBIA. An occasional song. Written by Mr. Thomas Paine of Boston. The air altered and adapted from the tune of Rule Brittannia [!] (*In* The musical repertory. Boston [1796] No. II, p. 18–19)

Song (with chorus), pfte. acc. Three staves (chorus part, five).
First line: When first the sun o'er ocean glow'd. DLC

———— Separate issue of preceding, ca. 1796. DLC, JFD, MH, RPJCB

RISE COLUMBIA. An occasional song. Written by Mr. Thomas Paine of Boston.
(*In* The American musical miscellany. Northampton, 1798. p. 103–105)

Melody only, with accompanying text, followed by three-part chorus. Open score.
First line same as preceding. DLC (etc.)

A fac simile of the above is given in L. C. Elson's *The national music of America*, Boston, 1924, p. 179–180.

RISE COLUMBIA. Boston, Printed & sold by P. A. von Hagen & co. Musical magazine, No. 3 Cornhill [ca. 1800] 1 l. 33 cm.

Song, pfte. acc.
First line same as preceding.
Probably published in 1799. ES

RISE CYNTHIA RISE. A favorite sonnet. Written by the Earl of Orford. Composed by Mr. Hook. Price one quarter dollar. Philadelphia, Printed for Carr & co., at their Musical repository, No. 136 High street [1793] [3] p. 31½ cm.

Duet, pfte. acc. Three staves. Arr. for two flutes and for the "guittar," p. [3].
First line same as title.
ABHu, DLC, ES, HFB, JFD, LSL, McD–W, MdHi, NRU–Mus, PP–K

Advertised in the *Daily American advertiser*, Philadelphia, for December, 1793, as published by "B. Carr & Co., Musical Repository, No. 122 Southside of Market street," Philadelphia. As to apparent inconsistency in address, *cf.* The match girl.

——— The same as preceding except [2] p. instead of [3] p. Lacks instrumental arrangements on p. [3]. McD–W

RISE, CYNTHIA, RISE. Printed & sold by G. Willig, Philadelphia [n. d.] [2] p. 33½ cm.

Duet, pfte. acc. Three staves. Arr. for "guittar," p. [2].
Published probably 179–. DLC, MWA, RPJCB

RISE, CYNTHIA, RISE. [n. p., n. d.] [2] p. 30 cm.
Duet, pfte. acc. Three staves. Arr. for "guittar," p. [2].
First line same as title.
Published probably ca. 1800 NBuG, PU

RISE CYNTHIA RISE. Composed by Mr. Shield. New York, Published for P. Weldon, No. 76 Chambers street [n. d.] 2 p. 31 cm.

Duet, pfte. acc. Arr. for two German flutes, p. 2.
First line same as title.
Published possibly as early as 1800.
Composed by James Hook, *not* by "Mr. Shield." ES, McD–W

RISE MY DELIA, HEAV'NLY CHARMER.
See New song for a serenade.

[355]

*THE RIVAL KNIGHTS, or La Belle Magalone.   New serious pantomime,
"the music by Reinagle."   Performed in Philadelphia, May 2 and June 27,
1796.

THE RIVER PATOWMAC.   An epicedium on the death of the august and
venerable General Washington.   Late Commander in chief of the armies of
the United States.   Written by Mr. Derrick.   The music composed by Mr.
Weizsaecker.   Philadelphia, Printed by G. Willig, No. 185 Market st. [ca.
1800]   [2] p.   32 cm.

Song, pfte. acc.
First line: O stream belov'd thy hallow'd wave.   McD–W, NRU–Mus

ROBIN A BOBBIN A BILBERY HEN.   From the Christmas box.   Composed
by Mr. Hook.   Price 12½ cents.   New York, Printed & sold at J. Hewitt's
Musical repository, No. 131 William street.   Sold also by B. Carr, Philadelphia & J. Carr, Baltimore [1797–99]   1 l.   32 cm.

Song, pfte. acc.
First line same as title.   MWA

*ROBIN HOOD, or Sherwood Forest.
    As "a comic opera . . . with the original overture by Baumgarten.   The
    rest of the Music and Accompaniments, composed by Shield, with addi-
    tional airs by Mr. [Alexander] Reinagle," Robin Hood was to be performed
    at Baltimore on November 6, 1794.

    As "the much admired comic opera . . . compressed in two acts, and per-
    formed for the first time here [in New York] as an afterpiece.   The music
    composed by Mr. [James] Hewitt," Robin Hood was given on December 24,
    1800.

THE ROBIN REDBREAST.   Selected from the Aviary.   A collection of sonnets.   Hook.   Also just published
                No. 1 The thrush.   No. 2 The linnets.
                No. 3 The gold finch.   No. 5 The nightingale.
                No. 6 The lark.   No. 7 The blackbird.
                         No. 9 The sonnet to beauty.
[New York] Sold by I. and M. Paff, No. 127 Broadway [1799–1803]   [2] p.
30½ cm.

At head of title: No. 4.
Imprint at foot of p. [2], followed by "No. 4."
Song, pfte. acc.
First line: Little bird with bosom red.   ES, NN

*ROBINSON CRUSOE, or, the Genius of Columbia.
    This "pantomimical romance in one act with entire new scenery, machinery,
    music etc." was to be performed by the Old American Company at Philadel-
    phia, February 10, 1790.   This probably was an adaptation of Thomas
    Linley's work.

    As "a new grand historical pantomime in 2 acts," adapted by the ballet
    dancer, Placide, "the music composed by Pellisier," Robinson Crusoe was
    performed at New York, on June 15, 1796.

[356]

ROMANCE AVEC ACCOMPAGNEMENT de harpe ou de piano. Musique de M. R. Chateaudun.
(*In* Six romances nouvelles, by R. Chateaudun. Philadelphie [ca. 1800] p. 6–7)

At head of title: No. 2.
Song, pfte. (or harp) acc. Three staves.
First line: Toi dont les accords enchanteurs.　　　　　　　　DLC, LSL

ROMANCE AVEC ACCOMPAGNEMENT de harpe ou de piano forte. Musique de M. R. Chateaudun.
(*In* Six romances nouvelles, by R. Chateaudun. Philadelphie [ca. 1800] p. 8–9)

At head of title: No. 3.
Song, pfte. (or harp) acc. Three staves. French and English text.
First lines: O toi! dont la penible enfance.—Oh thou whose prattling infancy.
　　　　　　　　　　　　　　　　　　　　　　　　　　　DLC, LSL

———— Separate issue of preceding (unpaged), 1799.　　　McD–W, NN

Advertised in *Aurora*, Philadelphia, March 26, 1799, among new and favorite songs published by B. Carr.

ROMANCE BY HAYDN.
(*In* The gentleman's amusement, ed. by R. Shaw. Philadelphia [1794–96] p. 33)

Duet for flutes (or violins). Two staves.
In No. 4, February 1, 1795.　　　　　　　　　　　　　　DLC, PHi

ROMANCE DE GONZALVE DE CORDOUE avec accompagnement de harpe ou piano forte. Musique de M. R. Chateaudun.
(*In* Six romances nouvelles, by R. Chateaudun. Philadelphie [ca. 1800] p. 12–13)

At head of title: No. 5.
Song, pfte. (or harp) acc. Three staves.
First line: Derobe ta lumiere.　　　　　　　　　　　　　　DLC, LSL

ROMANCE DE GONZALVE DE CORDOUE avec accompagnement de harpe ou piano forte. Musique de M. R. Chateaudun.
(*In* Six romances nouvelles, by R. Chateaudun. Philadelphie [ca. 1800] p. 14)

At head of title: No. 6.
Song, pfte. (or harp) acc. Three staves.
First line: Rosier, rosier, jadis charmant.　　　　　　　　DLC, LSL

ROMANCE GAULOISE AVEC ACCOMPAGNEMENT de harpe ou pianoforte, par M. R. Chateaudun.
(*In* Six romances nouvelles, by R. Chateaudun. Philadelphie [ca. 1800] p. 10–11)

At head of title: No. 4.
Song, pfte. (or harp) acc. Three staves.
First line: Ecoutez gente damoiselle.　　　　　　　　　　　LC, LSL

[357]

SIX ROMANCES NOUVELLES avec accompagnement de harpe ou de piano par R. Chateaudun. Se vend chez Carr à Philadelphie. Prix 1 dollar $^{25}\!/_{100}$ [ca. 1800] 14 p. 32 cm.

Title-page; music p. 2–14.
Songs, harp or pfte. acc. Three staves.
Contents:

    p. 2–5 [No. 1] Paul au tombeau de Virginie.
        6–7 No. 2 Romance.
        8–9 No. 3 Romance.
    10–11 No. 4 Romance gauloise.
    12–13 No. 5 Romance de Gonzalve de Cordoue.
    14 No. 6 Romance de Gonzalve de Cordoue.

May have been issued in 1799 (cf. No. 3, Romance). Sonneck, however, gives ca. 1800.   DLC, LSL

THE ROMP. A musical entertainment, in two acts. Altered from Love in the City, by Mr. Bickerstaff. As now performed with great applause by the Old American company at the theatre in Southwark. A new edition. Philadelphia: From the press of Mathew Carey. Oct. 31, 1792. 33, [1] p. 16½ cm.

Libretto to Dibdin's opera (1767).
Title-page; dramatis personae, p. [2]; text, p. [3]–33; advertisement, p. [34].
                                                                                          PHi, PP–L, PU
On p. [2]:

> The reader is requested to observe that some of the songs, and several pages in this entertainment, are omitted in the representation; and also that various alterations and additions are occasionally made by the Actors every time it is performed.

On p. 32–33:

> Song introduced by Mrs. Hodgkinson, in the first act:
> "What virgin or shepherd in valley or grove
> Can envy my innocent lays."

Mrs. Hodgkinson took part in the first American performance of The romp at Philadelphia, October 22, 1792.

THE ROMP, a musical entertainment, in two acts. Altered from Love in the city, by Mr. Bickerstaff. As performed with great applause by the old American company—second Philadelphia edition. Philadelphia. From the press of Mathew Carey. Jan. 19, 1793. 27, [1] p. 17½ cm.

Libretto.
Title-page; dramatis personae, p. [2]; text, p. [3]–27; advertisement of "books printed by Mathew Carey, and for sale at his store, No. 118 Market street, Philadelphia," p. [28].   MB, NN, PPL, RPJCP

ROMPING ROSY NELL.
See Rosy Nell.

[358]

ONDE CHANTEE a la Reine par Monseigneur le Dauphin. Philadelphia, Sold by H. & P. Rice, No. 50 Market street. Price twenty cents. Les paroles par M. de Curt. Musique de M. Martini. (*In* The gentleman's amusement, ed. by R. Shaw. Philadelphia [1794–96] p. 70–71)

Song, pfte. acc. Three staves.
First line: L'amour ici nons rassemble.
In No. [9], ca. 1796. PHi, PP–K

—— The same as preceding. Second and third pages, numbered 70 and 71, of a detached portion of above collection. PHi

—— Separate issue of preceding, p. 2–3. McD–W
Advertised in May, 1794, "Philadelphia, printed for Shaw & Co." Undoubtedly this issue. (*cf. The waggoner*, by Dibdin, with identical imprint, also advertised as published in May, 1794.) It is remarked of this song and a piece by Martini:

> Les suivans sont tirés d'une collection publiée à Londres par M. Curt, au profit de l'honourable infortune.

RONDEAU DE VIOTTI.
(*In* The musical journal for the pianoforte, ed. by B. Carr. Baltimore [1800] v. 1, no. 22, p. (41)–(44).)

At head of title: No. 22 of a musical journal for the piano forte. Instrumental section.
Pfte. 2 hds. DLC, ES, LSL, NN, NRU–Mus

A RONDELAY celebrating the Independence of America, 1784.
See A Monody, 1784.

RONDO by Francis Hopkinson.
See [My gen'rous heart disdains]

RONDO by Haydn.
(*In* The gentleman's amusement, ed. by R. Shaw. Philadelphia [1794–96] p. 58–59)

Duet for flutes (or violins). Two staves.
In No. 7, May 1, 1796. DLC, PHi (lacks p. 58), PP–K

RONDO by I. C. Moller.
(*In* [Moller & Capron's Monthly numbers] Third number [Philadelphia, 1793] p. 16–18)

Pfte. 2 hds.
At head of title: Third number. DLC, NN, PHi

—— Separate issue of preceding, ca. 1793. NN

—— Separate issue of preceding, paged 1–3, and with added imprint, "Publish'd by G. Willig, 185 Market street." Thus to be dated 1798–1804.
Imprint is placed at extreme upper right, between "Third number" and "By I. C. Moller." As to Willig's use of these early Moller & Capron plates, *cf.* Capron's song, *Delia.* PP–K

[359]

RONDO. By J. C. Moller.
(*With* The favorite *Overture to Lodoiska,* by Krietzer [!] New York [ca. 180
p. 2–4)

Pfte. 2 hds. MW

RONDO by Pleyel.
(*In* The musical journal for the pianoforte, ed. by B. Carr. Baltimore [180
v. 1, no. [24] p. (46)–(47).)

Pfte. 2 hds. DLC (lacks last page), ES, NN, NRU–Mu

RONDO FOR THE FORTE PIANO. Composed by R. Taylor. Philadelphi
Printed for the Author, No. 96 North Sixth street, and sold at Carr's Music
repository, Market st., and by I. Carr, Baltimore. (Price ½ of a dolla
[n. d.] 3 p. 33 cm.

Pfte. 2 hds.
Published possibly as early as 1794. DLC, N

THE FAVORITE RONDO BASQUE. Printed and sold at Carr's music store
Baltimore [179–?] [3] p. 33 cm.

Pfte. 2 hds. DL

FAVORITE RONDO by Garth.
(*In* Twelve favorite pieces, arr. by A. Reinagle. Philadelphia [1789?]]
11–12)

Pfte. 2 hds.
Composed by John Garth. DL

A FAVORITE RONDO for the piano forte. Composed by D. Steibelt.
No. [2]. Price [25] cents. Philadelphia, Published and sold at G. Willig
Musical magazine [n. d.] 3 p. 33½ cm.

Title-page; music, p. 2–3.
Pfte. 2 hds.
Foot of p. 2: S. R. No. 2.
Foot of p. 3: Rondo, Steibelt No. 2.
Possibly published after 1800. N]

A FAVORITE RONDO in the Gipsy style. Composed by Dr. Haydn. Pric
50 cts. Philadelphia, Published and sold at G. Willig's Musical magazin
[179–?] 5 p. 34½ cm.

Pfte. 2 hds.
The popular "Gipsy rondo" in Haydn's trio arranged for pfte. Publishe
probably before 1800. Hopl

A FAVOURITE RONDO. Composed by F. Staes.
(*In* Twelve favorite pieces, arr. by A. Reinagle. Philadelphia [1789?] ɪ
17–18)

Pfte. 2 hds.
F. Staes: Ferdinand Philippe Joseph Staes. DL(

*MOLLER'S RONDO.
Advertised among other music for the pfte. in April, 1795, as "publishe
and to be had of G. Gilfert & Co. at their Musical Magazine, No. 121 Broad
way," New York.

[360]

HREE RONDOS for the piano forte or harpsichord. Composed and humbly
dedicated to the Honourable Francis Hopkinson, Esq꞉ By William Brown.
Philadelphia, Printed and sold by the Author. Price two dollars. J. Aitken,
Sculp. [1787] 2 p. l., 6 p. 33 cm.

Title-page, verso blank; subscribers' names, second p. l. (verso blank);
music, p. [1]-6 (recto of p. [1] and verso of p. 6, blank).
Pfte. 2 hds. DLC, Hopk., MB, NN

OSA. Sung with great applause by Mrs. Merry in the comedy of the Secret.
Composed by A. Reinagle.
(In The musical journal for the piano forte, ed. by B. Carr. Baltimore
[1800] v. 1, no. [1], p. (2)-(3).)

Song, pfte. acc.
First line: Majestic rose the god of day.
Mrs. Merry sang in the first Philadelphia performance of *The secret*, Decem-
ber 30, 1799. DLC, ES, LSL, McD-W, MdHi, NN, NRU-Mus, PP-K

ROSA. Sung by Mrs. Merry in the Secret. Composed by A. Reinagle.]
(In The musical journal for the flute or violin. Baltimore, J. Carr [1800]
no. 1, p. 2-3)

Melody only, flute or violin, with accompanying text.
First line same as preceding. DLC (incomplete, lacks p. 2)

ROSA AND HENRY. The much admired song in the new comedy of the
Secret. Sung by Mrs. Merry. Printed & sold by G. Willig, No. 185
Market st. [1798-1804] 1 l. 32 cm.

Song, pfte. acc.
First line: Majestic rose the god of day.
Not to be confused with Reinagle's setting of the same text (cf. *Rosa* above).
BM Cat.: Music by a lady of fashion.
Published in London in 1799. This issue probably ca. 1800. DLC

ROSA AND HENRY [n. p., ca. 1800] 1 l. 32½ cm.

Song, pfte. acc.
First line same as preceding. DLC

THE ROSARY. Alternative title of *The cheering rosary*, by William Shield.

THE ROSE. A favorite song in the opera of Selima and Azor. Composed by
T. Linley.
(In [A collection of favorite songs, arr. by A. Reinagle. Philadelphia, 1789
(?)] p. 15-16)

At foot of p. 16: I. Aitken. Sculpt.
Song, pfte. acc.
First line: No flow'r that blows. ES

THE ROSE. [Philadelphia] Printed by G. Willig, Market st., No. 185 [1798-
1804] 8-9 p. 33 cm.

Song, pfte. acc.
First line: No flow'r that blows.
From *Selima and Azor*, by Thomas Linley, the Elder.
MWA, PP-K

———— The same as preceding, but without imprint.   RPJC

THE ROSE.
See Favorite *Cotillions.*

ROSE TREE
(*In* The Philadelphia songster, ed. by A. Aimwell [pseud.]   Philadelphia
1789. p. 7)

Melody only with accompanying text.
First line: A rose tree in full bearing.
From *Poor soldier,* by William Shield.   NY

A ROSE TREE.   Poor soldier.
(*In* A collection of favorite songs, divided into two books.   Arr. by A
Reinagle.   Philadelphia [1789?]   bk. 1, p. 15)

Song, pfte. acc.
First line: A rose tree full in bearing.   CdeW, DLC, ES, Hopk

THE ROSE TREE.
See Evening amusement [1796], p. 19.

A ROSE TREE.   A favorite song.   New York, Printed and sold by G. Gilfert
No. 177 Broad.Way [1797–1801]   1 l.   31½ cm.

Song, pfte. acc.
First line: A rose tree full in bearing.   DLC, MWA

ROSEDALE.
See Two new favorite *Cotillions.*

ROSETTE'S CELEBRATED "LA CHASSE."
See Book of songs . . . by M. A. Pownall and J. Hewitt.

ROSINA, a comic opera.   In two acts: as performed at the theatre, New York
By Mrs. Brooke, author of Julia Mandeville, etc.   [Design]   Philadelphia
Printed and sold by Enoch Story, in Second street, the corner of Walnut
street   [1787]   28 p.   17 cm.

Libretto to Shield's opera (1783).
Title-page; dramatis personae, p. [2]; text, p. [3]–28.
This copy contains the MS. mem. "James Cox Frontstreet Philada. May ye
27th 1791."
The libretto was advertised as "just published" in April, 1787.   PPI

ROSINA.   A comic opera, in two acts.   By Mrs. Brooke, author of Julia Mandeville, etc.   As performed at the theatre in Boston.   Printed at Boston, for
William P. Blake, at the Boston Bookstore, No. 59, Cornhill.   1795.   32 p
17 cm.

Libretto.
Title-page; dramatis personae, p. [2]; text, p. [3]–32.   MB, NHi, RPJCB

With "new orchestra accompanyments" by Victor Pelissier, the opera was
performed at New York, on February 17, 1796.

[362]

OSINA, or Love in a cottage. A comic opera in two acts. As performed with universal applause by the American company. Philadelphia, Printed and sold by Henry Taylor. 1791. 36 p. 18 cm.

Libretto.
Title-page, verso blank; advertisement, p. [3]; dramatis personae, p. [4]; text, p. [5]-36.
Same as preceding with slight textual differences.   MH, MWA, PPL

ROSINA'S HEART. Sung in the new opera the Castle of Sorrento. New York, Printed & sold at G. Gilferts music store, No. 177 Broadway [ca. 1800] 1 l. 32½ cm.

Song, pfte. acc.
First line: Together then we'd fondly stray.
The castle of Sorrento, by Thomas Attwood, first produced in 1799.   RPB

ROSLIN CASTLE.
See Liberty songs [178–?] p. 7–8.   (Words only)

—— The same.
See Evening amusement [1796] p. 16.

—— Roslin Castle. A favorit [!] death march. Published & sold by G. Willig, No. 185 Market street, Philadelphia [1798–1804] [2] p. 33½ cm.

Song, pfte. acc.
First line: 'Twas in that season of the year.
Foot of p. [2]: Quickstep. (For pfte. 2 hds.)   DLC, MWA

—— Roslin Castle. Boston, Printed & sold by P. A. von Hagen & co. at their imported piano forte and music warehouse, No. 3. Cornhill. Also by G. Gilfert, New York [ca. 1800] 1 l. 32 cm.

Song, pfte. acc.
First line same as preceding.
Probably published in 1799.   DLC, JFD, RPJCB

ROSLINE CASTLE. A favorite song.
(*In* The Boston magazine, November, 1783, opposite p. 34)
Song, pfte. acc.
First line: 'Twas in that season of the year.   DLC (etc.)

ROSLINE CASTLE. A favorite Scots song. New York, Printed and sold by J. and M. Paffs, No. 127 Broadway [1799–1803] [2] p. 33 cm.

Song, pfte. acc. Arr. for flute, p. [2].
First line same as preceding.   DLC, NN

ROSLINE CASTLE. A favorite Scots song. The words by Rd Hewit. New York. Printed & sold at J. Hewitt's Musical repository, No. 23 Maiden Lane. Pr. 25 cents.
(*In* A collection of new & favorite songs. [A] Philadelphia [ca. 1800] p. [64]–[65])

Song, pfte. acc. Arr. for flute, p. [65].
First line same as preceding.   HFB

———— Roslin Castle.
See Compleat tutor for the fife . . . p. 22.

ROSY MORN.
(*In* The Philadelphia songster, ed. by A. Aimwell [pseud.] Philadelphi.
1789. p. 6-7)

Two parts.
First line: When the rosy morn appearing.   N.

ROSY NELL. A new song, never before in print. Set by Philo-Musico.
(*In* The Massachusetts magazine. Boston, June, 1790. p. 377-378)

Song, pfte. acc.
First line: Let ev'ry pagan muse begone.   DLC (etc

———— Romping rosy Nell.
(*In* The American musical miscellany. Northampton, 1798. p. 155-157

Melody and bass, with accompanying text. Instrumental prelude an
postlude. Two staves.
First line: Let ev'ry Pagan muse be gone.   DLC (etc.

ROSY WINE.
(*In* The songster's assistant, ed. by T. Swan. Suffield [ca. 1800] p. 22-23

Song, pfte. acc.
First line: The wanton god who pierces hearts.   CtY, M

[ROUGH AS THE WAVES ON WHICH WE SAIL] Sung by Mr. Darley.
(*In* The volunteers, by A. Reinagle. Philadelphia [1795?] p. 17)

Song, pfte. acc.
Title from first line.   DL(

*RUDOLPH, or the Robbers of Calabria. A melodrama in three acts as per
formed at the Boston Theatre. Boston, 1799. 141 p. 18°.

Libretto by John D. Turnbull. Several editions.
Entry taken from Wegelin.

RULE NEW ENGLAND. A new patriotic song. Written by Thomas Paine
Esqr. A. M. The music composed by F. Schaffer. Boston, Printed & sol
at P. A. von Hagen's piano forte ware house, No. 4 Old Massachusetts bank
Head of the Mall & at the music store, No. 3 Cornhill. Also at G. Gilfert'
warehouse, N. York; D. Vinton's, Providence; W. B. Wilder, New Port
B. B. Macanulty, Salem; E. M. Blunt, Newbury Port; Isaac Stanwood
Portsmouth & E. A. Jenks, Portland [n. d.] [2] p. 35 cm.

Song, pfte. acc. Arr. for guitar or clarinet, p. [2].
First line: What arm a sinking state can save.
Published probably after 1800.   MWA, RPJCB

THE RURAL HARMONY. Being an original composition in three and fou
parts. For the use of singing schools and musical societies. By Jacob
Kimball, Jun. A. B. [Verses] Published according to Act of Congress.
Printed, typographically, at Boston, by Isaiah Thomas and Ebenezer T.
Andrews. Sold at their bookstore, No. 45 Newbury street; by said Thomas

in Worcester; and by the book sellers in Boston and elsewhere.   1793.   xvi, [17]–111, [1] p.   13 x 22 cm.

Title-page; preface, p. [2]; introduction to the art of singing, p. [3]–xvi; music, p. [17]–111; index, p. [112].
Three and four-part chorus.   Open score.

DLC, ICN (incomplete), MB, MH, MWA

In spite of the secular implications of its title, this work contains but one non-religious number.   The following is its lugubrious text, set to a fairly buoyant tune!

Ah lovely appearance of death,
No sight upon earth is so fair.
Not all the gay pageants that breathe
Can with a dead body compare.
With solemn delight I survey
The corps when the spirit is fled.
In love with the beautiful clay,
And longing to lie in its stead.   (p. 57–58)

▲ RURAL LIFE.   Composed by J. Hewitt.
(*In* Six songs by Mrs. Pownall and J. Hewitt, New York [1794]   p. 11)
Song, pfte. acc.
First line: How sacred and how innocent.   ES, HFB

―――― The same as preceding.
(*In* A collection of new & favorite songs. [A]   Philadelphia [ca. 1800] p. [152], numbered 11)   HFB

―――― Separate issue of preceding, paged 11, ca. 1794.   DLC

THE RURAL RETREAT.   Set by Mr. William Selby.
(*In* The Massachusetts magazine, Boston, October, 1789.   p. 657–658)
Song, pfte. acc.
First line: Shady groves and purling rills.   MB (etc.)

▸RURAL REVELS, or, the Easter holiday.
A "new Comic Pantomime Dance . . . called Rural revels . . . the music composed and selected by Mr. De Marque," was to be performed at the New Theatre in Philadelphia, on April 10, 1795.

THE RUSH LIGHT.   An additional song introduced and sung by Mr. Bates in Peeping Tom.   The words by G. Colman, Junᶜ Esqᶜ   Compos'd by Dr. Arnold.   Philadelphia, Printed at Carr & cos. Musical repository. Price twenty cents.   [1794]   [2] p.   31 cm.
Song, pfte. acc.   Arr. for flute, p. [2].
First line: Sir Solomon Simons when he did wed.   McD–W, MWA

Advertised in April, 1794, as "published . . . printed and sold at Carr's and Co's Musical Repository, No. 122 Market street," Philadelphia.

Under the title of *The little farthing rushlight*, advertised in *Aurora* (Philadelphia) to be sung by Mr. Bates at the New Theatre, May 20, 1795.

RUSSIAN DANCE.
See Evening amusement, p. 18.

*RUSTIC COURTSHIP, or the Unsuccessful love of poor Thomas, a crying song, with duet, trio etc. by Raynor Taylor.

Made part of an olio "entirely new," by R. Taylor, which was to be performed in Philadelphia, on February 1, 1794.

RUSTIC FESTIVITY. A new song composed by R. Taylor. Philadelphia Printed for the Author, No. 96 North Sixth street, and sold at B. Carr' Repository, Market st., and by J. Carr, Baltimore (Price ¼ of a Dollar [n. d.] [2] p. 33 cm.

Song, pfte. acc.
First line: Shepherd why this dull delay.
Sonneck date: ca. 1795.   CtY, DLC, ES, MWA

Advertised as "republished" in February, 1798, "by B. Carr at his Repository Marketstreet," Philadelphia.

SACRED DIRGES, HYMNS, AND ANTHEMS, commenorative of the death of General George Washington, the guardian of his country and the friend of man. An original composition by a citizen of Massachusetts. Printed at Boston by I. Thomas and E. T. Andrews, No. 45 Newbury street [1800] 24 p. 21 x 26 cm.

Cover-title and title-page.
On front cover: Funereal music, for 22d February. Published according to Act of Congress. Price, 50 cents single—40 cents by the dozen.
At head of cover-title, a design of flowers and musical instruments.
On last page of cover: Contents [nine numbers].
On title-page, an urn bearing the inscription: Born Feb. 22, 1732. Died at Mount Vernon, Dec. 14, 1799. Aged 68.
On pedestal of urn: The just shall be had in everlasting remembrance.
Below urn, verses and ms. note: By O. Holden [presumably an autograph].
Title-page, verso blank; dedication, p. [3]; preface, dated Jan. 27, 1800, p. [4]; music, p. [5]–24.

Contents:
    p. [5]–11 A funeral anthem [The sound of the harp ceaseth]
        12–13 Columbia's guardian sleeps in dust
        14–15 Mount Vernon [From Vernon's mount behold the hero rise]
        15–17 A dirge [Peace to his soul, the fatal hour is past]
        18–19 A hymn [And is th' illustrious chieftain dead]
        20–21 Anniversary dirge [Is this the anniversary so dear]
        22–23 Masonic dirge [While ev'ry orator and bard displays]
           23 A funeral hymn [Up to Thy throne Almighty King]   (Complete text on p. 19)
           24 An ode for the 22d of February [Now let your plaintive numbers gently rise]
Composed by Oliver Holden.
                    CSmH, DLC, ICN, MB, MH, MHi, MNSt, NHi, RPB, RPJCB
Certain copies (e. g. MNSt) have on front cover "30 cents by the dozen" instead of "40."

———— A second issue. The same as preceding with the addition of A dirge, or Sepulchral service, also by Holden. 1800.   MWA, NN

[366]

SAFE AND SOUND. A favorite polacca. Composed by James Hook. New York, Publish'd at I. and M. Paff music store, Broadway [1799–1803] [2] p. 32½ cm.

Pfte. 2 hds.   DLC, McD–W

THE SAILOR BOY. A favorite sea song. Introduced with great applause by Mr. Hodgkinson in No song no supper. Price 20 cents. Philadelphia, Printed for Carr & co. at their Musical repository, No. 136 High street [1793] [2] p. 34 cm.

Song, pfte. acc.
First line: Poll dang it, how d'ye do.

Mr. Hodgkinson took part in the first American performance of Stephen Storace's *No song no supper* at Philadelphia, November 30, 1792. This song does not appear in the score.   DLC, MWA, RPJCB

Advertised in December, 1793, as "published . . . printed singly" by "B. Carr & Co. Musical Repository, No. 122 Southside of Market Street," Philadelphia. As to apparent inconsistency in address *cf. The match girl.*

———— The sailor boy capering ashore.
(*In* Elegant extracts for the German flute or violin. Baltimore, 1794. bk. 1, p. 20–21)

Melody only, flute or violin, with accompanying text.
First line: Poll dang' it, how d'ye do.   DLC, NN

———— The sailor boy capering ashore.
(*In* The American musical miscellany. Northampton, 1798. p. 135–136)

Melody only, with accompanying text.
First line same as preceding.   DLC (etc.)

A SAILOR LOV'D A LASS. Composed by S. Storace for the Cherokee. Printed for and sold by B. Carr at his Musical repository's, Market st., Philadelphia & William street, New York and by I. Carr, Baltimore. Price 20 cents. [1796] [2] p. 32½ cm.

Song, pfte. acc.
First line same as title.
Advertised as published in 1796.   CtY, LSL, McD–W, MdIli, MWA, NN

A SAILOR LOV'D A LASS.
(*In* Elegant extracts for the German flute or violin. Philadelphia [1796] bk. 2, p. 6–7)

Melody only, flute or violin, with accompanying text.
First line same as title.
From *The Cherokee*, by Stephen Storace.   DLC, NN

THE SAILOR'S ALLEGORY.
(*In* Young's vocal and instrumental musical miscellany. Philadelphia [1793–95] p. 31–32)

Song, pfte. acc.
First line: Life's like a ship in constant motion.
In No. 4, 1793.   DLC, Hopk.

[367]

THE SAILOR'S CONSOLATION.
(*In* The American musical miscellany. Northampton, 1798. p. 137–139
Melody only, with accompanying text.
First line: Spanking Jack was so comely.
From *Private theatricals*, by Charles Dibdin.   DLC (etc.

—— The same.
(*In* Elegant extracts for the German flute or violin. Baltimore, [1794
bk. 1, p. 32–33)
Melody, flute or violin, with accompanying text.
First line same as preceding.   DLC, NN

THE SAILOR'S FAREWELL. A favorite new song. Composed by J. Fisin
New York, Printed & sold by George Gilfert, No. 177 Broadway [1797–1801
[2] p.   32½ cm.

Song, pfte. acc.
First line: As from the cheek of her I love.
J. Fisin: James Fisin.   DLC

THE SAILORS JOURNAL. Alternative title of *Nancy*, by Charles Dibdin.

THE SAILOR'S MAXIM. Written, composed & sung by Mr. Dibdin in his
entertainment of the General election. New York, Printed for W. Howe and
sold at his warehouse for music and musical instruments, No. 320 Pearl street.
Price 25 cents. [1797–98] [2] p.   32½ cm.

Song, pfte. acc. Arr. for two flutes, p. [2].
First line: Of us tars is reported again and again.
In NRU-Mus copy, advertisement of P. A. von Hagen, jun. & co., No. 62
Newbury sts., Boston (1798–99) is pasted over the original imprint.
                                                                                NRU–Mus

THE SAILOR'S MEDLEY. A collection of the most admired sea and other
songs. Philadelphia, Printed for Mathew Carey. 1800. 72 p., front.
17 cm.
(*Bound with* The syren. Philadelphia [ca. 1800])   NN, RPB

THE SAILOR'S ORPHAN BOY. A favorite new song. New York, Printed
and sold by I. and M. Paffs, No. 127 Broadway [1799–1803] [2] p.   33 cm.

Song, pfte. acc.
First line: Stay lady stay for mercy sake.   DLC

THE SAILOR'S ORPHAN BOY. A new song. New York, Printed & sold
at G. Gilfert's pianoforte ware house, No. 177 Broadway. And to be had of
P. A. von Hagen, No. 3 Cornhill, Boston [ca. 1800] [2] p.   33 cm.

Song, pfte. acc.
First line: Stay lady stay for mercy's sake.   DLC, JFD, NN, RPJCB

THE SAILORS RETURN. By Dibdin. Price 25 cents. Philadelphia, Printed
at Carr's Musical repository [1794] [3] p.   31 cm.

Song, pfte. acc. Arr. for flute or "guittar," p. [3].
First line: Bleak was the morn.
From *Private theatricals*.
Advertised in October, 1794, among "new songs never published in America."
                                                                                RPJCB

[368]

SAILOR'S SONG, by Raynor Taylor.
Made part of an *"Olio . . .* entirely new" by R. Taylor, which was to be performed in Philadelphia on February 1, 1794.

ST. BRIDES BELLS.
See Evening amusement.

THE ST. GEORGE.
See Twenty-four American country *Dances*, p. 20.

SALLY. A pastoral. Set by S. Holyoke.
(*In* The Massachusetts magazine. Boston, August, 1789. p. 523–526)

Song, pfte. acc.
First line: My Sally is fair as the flow'rs.   DLC (etc.)

SANDY'S GHOST. Alternative title of *Mary's dream*, by John Relfe.

SAPPHICK ODE.
(*In* The gentleman and lady's musical companion, by John Stickney. Newbury-Port, 1774. p. 47–48)

Four-part chorus.
First line: When the fierce North wind with his airy forces.
                                                         DLC, ICN, MB

SATURDAY NIGHT AT SEA.
(*In* The American musical miscellany. Northampton, 1798. p. 120–122)

Melody only, with accompanying text.
First line: 'Twas Saturday night the twinkling stars.   DLC (etc.)

SAVAGE DANCE.
See Evening amusement [1796] p. 16.
"Le sauvage", a dance by Pierre Landrin Duport, was advertised to be performed by his son, Master Louis, "not ten years of age," after a concert in Philadelphia, March 5, 1791. It was repeated at a benefit for Master Duport on July eleventh. It is possible, but not at all certain, that *Savage dance* is the dance here referred to.

*THE SAVOYARD, or, The Repentant seducer.
This "musical farce, in two acts . . . the music composed by Mr. [Alexander] Reinagle," was to have its first performance at Philadelphia, on July 12, 1797.

[SAY HOW CAN WORDS A PASSION FEIGN] Sung by Mrs. Oldmixon in the musical farce called My grandmother. Sold at Carrs Repository's, Philadelphia, N. York & Baltimore. Price 12 cents. [ca. 1795] p. 54. 31½ cm.

Song, pfte. acc.
Title from first line.
Followed by "Favorite country dance, compos'd by Dibdin," melody only.
                                                         ES, LSL, NN
Mrs. Oldmixon sang in Stephen Storace's *My grandmother* in Philadelphia, April 27, 1795.

SAY HOW CAN WORDS A PASSION FEIGN. Sung by Mrs. Hodgkinson in the opera My grandmother. New York, Printed for G. Gilfert & co. at their

Musical magazine, No. 177 Broadway [1796]   p. 3.   31½ cm.
(*With* On the lightly sportive wing, by Stephen Storace)

Song, pfte. acc.
First line same as title.
Mrs. Hodgkinson sang in *My grandmother*, New York, May 30, 1796.

MWA, RPJCB

SAYS JESSY ONE MORN.   Printed & sold by J. Carr, Baltimore.   Sigr.
Haibel [179– ?]   1 l.   30½ cm.

Song, pfte. acc.
First line same as.title.
In right-hand corner lower margin: E. T. C. 2.
Sigr. Haibel, presumably Jakob Haibel.

ABHu

*A SCALE FOR THE FLAGEOLET with favorite airs and the notes of birds.
Advertised in November, 1797, as "published at Carr's Musical Repository,"
Philadelphia.

[THE SCATTER'D CLOUDS ARE FLED AT LAST]
(*In* Harmonia Americana, by Samuel Holyoke.   Boston, 1791.   p. 43–45)

Three-part chorus.   Open score.
Title from first line.
Same text as *Spring* (*q. v.*) but different setting.

CSmH, DLC, ICN, MB, MH, MWA, NHi, NN, RPJCB

*THE SCORNFUL LADY, or, I wonder at you.   Song by Raynor Taylor.
Was to be sung in his "musical performance . . . the whole of the music
original and composed by Mr. Taylor," Annapolis, Md., January 20, 1793.

THE SCOTCH AIR in the comic opera of the Pirates.
See [As wrapt in sleep I lay]

SCOTCH MEDLEY in the overture to the Highland reel.
(*In* The gentleman's amusement, ed. by R. Shaw.   Philadelphia [1794–96]
p. 18–19)

Duet for flutes (or violins).   Two staves.
In Nos. 2 and 3, May [and June?] 1794.
The Highland reel, by William Shield.

DLC, PHi

A SCOTCH REVEILLY.
See Military amusement [1796], p. 20.

——— The Scotch reveilly.
See Compleat tutor for the fife . . . p. 11.

SCOTS AIR FROM THE HIGHLAND REEL.
See Evening amusement, p. 25.

*THE SCOTS MUSICAL MUSEUM, being a collection of the most favorite
Scots tunes, adapted to the voice, harpsichord, and pianoforte.   Advertised
in January, 1797, as "just published and to be sold at the bookstores . . .
and by John Aitkin, the editor, no. 193, South Second Street," Philadelphia

[370]

SCOTTISH MEDLEY OVERTURE by Alexander Reinagle to the opera of Auld
Robin Gray.
See Auld Robin Gray.

*SCUOLA DEL CANTO BY FILIPPO TRISOBIO.

TRISOBIO (Filippo) La Scuola del Canto; or a new . . . method of acquir-
ing perfection in Singing . . . to which are added six airs, four duets, and
two trios. Eng. and Ital. London [1820] obl. 4°.

This title Sonneck found in the British Museum Cat. under 557*e. 22 (2).
But the book must have been printed previous to 1800, as we read in Claypoole's *American daily advertiser*, Philadelphia, August 17, 1796:

> *To the Lovers of Music.* Signor Trisobio, from Italy, professor of vocal
> music, teacher and composer, respectfully informs the public, that he has
> composed a book entitled LA SCUOLA DEL CANTO, or, a new short,
> clear and easy method of acquiring perfection in singing, according to the
> most modern Italian stile, to which is added six airs, four duets, and two
> trios. This work is in consequence of the incessant observations made in
> three years, which he has been in Lisbon in the service of her majesty the
> queen of Portugal, where he was a member of a company of eighty of the
> best Italian professors. This book has had a favourite reception in
> London and Italy, he hopes for the same success in this famous metrop-
> olis . . .

It may serve as a clue to remark that Trisobio died at Philadelphia in 1798.

SE M'ABBANDONI. The favorite song in the opera La locandiera.
Composed by Sig^r Cimarosa and pub^d by Sig^r Trisobio. [Philadelphia, ca.
1797] 4 p. 34 cm.

Song, pfte. acc. Three staves: Vio. 1° con Voce, Viollino 2do, Basso.
First line same as title.
Sigr. Trisobio: Filippo Trisobio.   CdeW, NN

SE QUESTA O COR TIRANNO. Composed by Sig^r Sarti in Giulio Sabino and
published by Sig^r Trisobio. Philadelphia [ca. 1797] 1, [2] p. 34 cm.

Song, pfte. acc. Three staves, voice part on middle staff.
First line same as title.   CdeW, NN

THE SEA BOYS DUETT. In the Mariners.
(*In* The Philadelphia pocket companion for guittar or clarinett [Philadelphia,
1794] v. 1, p. 24–27)

Instrumental duet, with accompanying text.
First line: For compassion we implore.
Appears in the score of Thomas Attwood's *The mariners*, where it is ascribed
to Martini.   MWA

*THE SEABOY'S PILLOW from the last new afterpiece of the Mariners.
Advertised in December, 1793, as published by "B. Carr & Co. Musical
Repository, No. 122 South side of Market street," Philadelphia, among other
"last new songs from Britain."

[371]

THE SEAMAN'S HOME. Sung in the Midnight wanderers.
(*In* The Philadelphia pocket companion for guittar or clarinett [Philadelphia 1794] v. 1, p. 30–51)

Melody only, with accompanying text.
First line: O you whoes [!] lives on land are pass'd.
The midnight wanderers, by William Shield   MWA

THE SEASON OF LOVE IS NO MORE. A favorte [!] song. Composed by
Mr. Hindle. New York, Printed for G. Gilfert & Co., at their Musical
magazine, No. 177 Broadway, where may be had a great variety of musical
instruments & musick &c. [1796] [2] p. 31½ cm.

Song, pfte. acc. First stanza, three staves; second stanza, two.
First line: Yes, these are the meadows the shrubs and the plains.
Mr. Hindle: John Hindle.   McD–W, MWA

THE SEASONS MORALIZED.
(*In* The American musical magazine. New Haven, 1786. p. 3–6)

Duet, pfte. acc.
First line: Behold the changes of the skies.   CtY, ICN, MBJ

In Table of Contents given as "Composed by Dr. Dwight." It is possible,
however, that the word "composed" may refer to the text only.

THE SECOND GRENADIERS MARCH.
See Compleat tutor for the fife . . . p. 13.

THE SECRET.
See Country *Dances.*

SEE BROTHER SEE. A favorite song. Sung in the opera of the Children in
the wood. New York, Printed for G. Gilfert & co., No. 191 Broadway
[1794–95] [2] p. 33½ cm.

Song, pfte. acc.
First line: See brother see on yonder bough.
The children in the wood, by Samuel Arnold.
                                    DLC, JFD, MNSt, MWA, RPJCB

———— The same as preceding, except that the imprint reads, "Printed and sold
by" instead of "Printed for," and the song is completed on p. [3].   McD–W

Advertised in January, 1795, by G. Gilfert & Co., New York, as "just published at their magazine." Advertised also on March 19, 1795, in Philadelphia as "this day . . . published, and to be had at G. Willig's Musical
Magazine, No. 165 Market street." No copy of this last issue has been
located.

———— See sister see on yonder bough. A song in the opera of the Children in
the woods.
(*In* The musical repertory. Boston [1796] No. I, p. (2)–(4).)

Song, pfte. acc.
First line same as title.   DLC, MB (incomplete)

[372]

—— Separate issue of preceding, ca. 1796. Identical except that "Pr. 30 ct." follows title.   JFD

This is the same song as *See brother see* (the original form in the score) with the one word changed.

[SEE DOWN MARIA'S BLUSHING CHEEK]   Song V.
(*In* Seven songs, by F. Hopkins.   Philadelphia [1788]   p. 6)

Song, pfte. acc.
Title from first line.   DLC, Hopk., MB, McD–W

SEE SISTER SEE.
See See brother see.

A SELECT NUMBER OF PLAIN TUNES adapted to congregational worship.
By Andrew Law, A. B.   Joel Allen sculpt   [Boston, n. d.]   16 p.   16½ cm.

Four-part chorus.   Open score.   No text.
Contains on p. 8: Bunker Hill.   A Sapphick ode [music only].
Although supposedly compiled much earlier, this *Select number* . . . could
not have been published before 1775, when Law received his A. B. from
Rhode Island College, now Brown University.   DLC, ICN, RPB

—— The same as preceding, with the addition of: The American hero.   A
Sapphick ode.   By Nath. Niles, A. M.   Norwich [Connecticut] October . . .
1775.

This addition is apparently the text for Law's *Bunker Hill*.   *A Sapphick ode*,
music on p. 8.
First line: Why should vain mortals tremble at the sight of.
Both words and music are to be found also at MB and RPB.
                                                         CtY, CSmH

—— The same as preceding with a still different text for the tune *Bunker Hill*.
                                                              NN

THE SELECT SONGSTER, or A collection of elegant songs with music prefixed to each compiled by Philo. Musico.

"Music can soften pain to ease"
"And make despair & madness please."

[Engraved scene of boy and sleeping cupid]
Amos Doolittle, sculp. at N. Haven.

New-Haven: Printed by Daniel Bowen, in Chapel str. 1786.   66 p.   15 x
8½ cm.

Title-page, verso blank; preface, p. 3; contents, p. 3–66.   Unless otherwise
noted title of each song is followed by the melody and this by the text.

Philo. Musico: Chauncy Langdon.

Contents:
  p. 5–7   Damon and Clora. [Duet in canon form. "Go false Damon,
                your sighing is in vain."]
     8–9   The despairing damsel. [" 'Twas when the seas were roaring."]

[373]

Contents:

p. 62–64 The flowing bowl. ["Push about the bowl boys."]
  65 Plato. ["Says Plato why should man be vain?"]
  66 Index. [To names of songs.]   MWA, RPB

*THE SELECT SONGSTER: Being a cheap collection of new and elegant songs,
with tunes affixed to each.
  Advertised in Hudson and Goodwin's *Connecticut courant*, Hartford, Conn.,
in December, 1786, as "just published and to be sold by the printers hereof
and at D. Bowen's printing-office in New Haven."
  Probably identical with the preceding.

A SELECTION OF FAVORITE AIRS as performed at the Amphitheatre and
Charleston circus. Adapted for the piano forte. Charleston, S. C., Printed
and sold at P. Muck's music store, No. 52 Corner of Broad & King street [ca.
1800]. 7 p. 33½ cm.

Pfte. 2 hds.
In lower margin, p. 1: Thornhill.
Published probably after 1800 rather than before.
                              DLC, JFD (lacks p. 3–6), NBuG, RPJCB

A SELECTION OF THE MOST FAVORITE SCOTS TUNES with variations
for the piano forte or harpsichord. Composed by A. Reinagle. Philadelphia,
Printed for the Author; John Aitken, Sculpᵗ [1787] 28 p. 31½ cm.

Title-page.
Pfte. 2 hds.
Tunes given: Moss plate.—Lee rigg.—East nook of Fife.—Malt man.—
Lochell's march.—Mount your baggage.—Maggy Lauder.—Steer her up and
had her gawn.—Over hills and dales, &ᶜ—Dainty Davie.   CdeW, MB

  Advertised in the *Pennsylvania packet*, Philadelphia, August 28, 1787, as
"just published, Price three Dollars. Sold by T. Dobson & W. Young at
their respective Book Store's, Second Street."

SELIMA & AZORE. A new comic opera. Translated into English from the
Italian, by Mrs. Rigaud, the music by the most celebrated composer, Signor
Gretry. Performed by the American Company, Philadelphia [monogram
E. S.] Printed and sold by Enoch Story. [n. d.] 36 p. 17½ cm.

Libretto.
Title-page, verso blank; dramatis personae, p. [3]; setting of play, p. [4];
text, p. [5]–36.
                                        MH, PPL

  Sonneck adds: "Published probably in 1794, the year of performance at
Philadelphia." Since, however, it was performed at Philadelphia in 1787
and 1791, as well as in 1794, this does not seem conclusive. At best the dating of this rare issue is extremely difficult.

[SEND HIM TO ME] Sung by Mrs. Myrter in the Farmer.
  (*In* Young's vocal and instrumental musical miscellany. Philadelphia [1793–
95] p. 6–7)

Song, pfte. acc.
Title from first line.
In No. 1, 1793.
The farmer, by William Shield.   DLC, ES, HFB, Hopk.

[375]

THE FAVORITE SERENADING GERMAN WALTZ. Arranged for the piano forte, violin, or flute. [n. p., ca. 1800] [2] p. 32½ cm.
Pfte. 2 hds. (violin or flute). DLC

*A SET OF CANZONETTI composed by a lady of Philadelphia.
See [Moller & Capron's monthly numbers] Proposals.

SET OF MONS. LABASSES [!] QUADRILLES. Arranged for the piano forte by Mr. Mallet.

To quote Sonneck:
Labasse apparently stands for Labarre. This and the fact that "Mallet, Francis, musician," appears in the Boston directories for 1796 and 1800 renders it probable that the collection (in MWA) was published before the nineteenth century.

It is evident that Sonneck was not familiar with the complete imprint of this work, for had he been, he would have reached a different conclusion as to the date of its publication. This date is shown to be after, instead of before 1800. However, since Sonneck has called attention to the work, we give the following description:

SET OF MONS. LABASSES QUADRILLES, as danced at his Academy & quadrille parties, with their proper figures by M. Mann, arranged for the piano forte, by Mr. Mallet. Boston, Published by G. Graupner & sold for him by John Ashton, No. 197 Washington st. [180–] 1 p. l., 3 p. 35 x 25 cm.

Engraved ornamental title page.
Pfte. 2 hds. MWA

*A SET OF SIX SONATAS for the pianoforte or harpischord; and a book of twelve songs, with an accompaniment for the same instrument, composed by Alexander Juhan.

Proposals for publishing by subscription a set of six sonatas, etc., appeared in the City gazette, Charleston, S. C., June 13, 1792.

After a lengthy effusion in praise of arts and sciences in general, of music in particular, and especially of music in America, we read the following:

CONDITIONS OF SUBSCRIPTION

The Music will be engraved in Philadelphia. The first book, which is now in hand and advanced, will contain six sonatas; three with an accompaniment for the flute or violin, and three without, and will consist of fifty pages in folio. The Book of Songs, of eighteen pages as above, will be put in hand as soon as possible, after the delivery of the sonatas to the subscribers, a list of whom will be given with one of the books. The price to subscribers, Six dollars for both books; Two dollars to be paid the time of subscribing, Two on delivery of the sonatas, the remainder on the delivery of the songs.

N. B. The prices of these books are below those at which books of the same kind can be at present sold when imported from Europe. Subscriptions are received in Charleston, by Mr. Juhan, No. 108, Church street, and at Mr. Young's book store, No. 24 Broad street.

The same proposals were printed in other cities; for instance in Philadelphia, where subscriptions were taken in by the principal booksellers and "Mr. John Aitkins, who is the engraver."

Sonneck was unable to ascertain whether the six sonatas really appeared on the market. It is certain that a *Set of six songs* was published, for we read in the *City gazette*, Charleston, August 14, 1794:

Just arrived and for sale, at Mr. Young's book store, and at Mr. Cornet's in King street, next door to Kaiser's Tavern

A set of six songs, with an accompaniment for the pianoforte or harpsichord, composed by Alexander Juhan. The subscribers to Mr. Juhan's music are requested to send to Mr. Young's for their copies.

Aug. 11.

In the same number were printed the words of

A SONG ON GENERAL WASHINGTON, taken from Mr. Juhan's set of songs advertised for sale in this paper.

The song consists of a recitative, two airs and choruses. The recitative begins:

On the white cliffs of Albion, reclining sat Fame.

As to the actual publication of the six sonatas, we learn from a notice in Dunlap's *American daily advertiser*, Philadelphia, April 10, 1793, that there were "ready for sale at Thomas Dobson and Messrs. H. & P. Rice," Philadelphia, three sonatas for the piano forte or harpsichord, "one with accompaniment for flute or violin and two without," composed by Alexander Juhan. Subscribers are informed that "the remainder will make its appearance as soon as possible, and in the following manner, viz., 1st., Six songs with accompaniment of piano or harpsichord, 2nd., Six songs with a frontispiece for the book of 12, 3d., The three last sonatas with a frontispiece for six."

Here we have at least a partial answer to Sonneck's question, and know that three of the six sonatas were published, as well as the six songs.

It is much to be regretted that all trace of these publications seems to have been lost.

*A SET OF SIX SONGS, BY A. JUHAN.
See Set of six sonatas by the same author.

THE SETTE IN QUEEN MAB.
See Compleat tutor for the fife . . . p. 28.

SEVEN SONGS . . . by Francis Hopkinson.
See Seven *Songs* . . . By Francis Hopkinson.

THE SHADE OF HENRY. A favorite song. The words by M. P. Andrews, Esqr Set to music by Miss Abrams. Philadelphia, Printed & sold by G. Willig, No. 185 Market street. [ca. 1800] 2-4 p. 31½ cm.

Song, pfte. acc.
First line: Stranger do you ask me why.
Miss Abrams: Harriet Abrams.

PP-K

SHAKESPEARE'S WILLOW. Composed by B. Carr.
(*In* The musical journal for the piano forte, ed. by B. Carr. Baltimore [1800] v. 1, no. [9] p. (22).)

Below imprint: My mother had a maid call'd Barbarie; She was in love. And he she lov'd forsook her And she prov'd mad. She had a song of Willow. An old thing 'twas, but it express'd her fortune. And she died singing it.
Song, pfte. acc.
First line: A poor soul sat sighing.

DLC, ES, LSL, MdHi, NN, NRU–Mus, PP–K

———— The same.
(*In* The musical journal for the flute or violin. Baltimore [1800] no. 8 [*i. e.*, no. 9] p. 17)

At head of title: Copyright secur'd. No. 8 of A musical journal for the flute or violin. Vocal section.
Melody only, flute or violin, with accompanying text.
First line same as preceding. DLC

*THE SHAMROCK, or Saint Patrick's day in the morning.
This "new comic Irish dance . . . with an Irish medley overture composed by Mr. [Alexander] Reinagle," was to be performed at the New Theatre, Philadelphia, on March 18, 1796.

A SHAPE ALONE LET OTHERS PRIZE. A song set to musick by Mr. Hans Gram of Boston.
(*In* The Massachusetts magazine. Boston, October, 1790. p. 636)

Melody and bass, with accompanying text. Instrumental prelude.
First line same as title. DLC (etc.)

A SHAPE ALONE LET OTHERS PRIZE. Set to music by H. Gram.
(*In* The American musical miscellany. Northampton, 1798, p. 285–286)

Melody and bass, with accompanying text. Instrumental prelude.
First line same as title. DLC (etc.)

SHE DROPT A TEAR & CRIED BE TRUE. A favorite sea song. Composed by J. Moulds. New York, Printed for G. Gilfert & co., No. 209 Broadway near St. Pauls [1795] [2] p. 33½ cm.

Song, pfte. acc. Arr. for the German flute, p. [2].
First line: Ye ling'ring winds that feebly blow.
Title forms last line of first stanza. DLC, ES, JFD, RPJCB

———— Ye lingring winds.
(*In* The musical journal for the piano forte, ed. by B. Carr. Baltimore [1800] v. 1, no. [15], p. (32)–(33).)

Song, pfte. acc.
First line: Ye lingring winds that feebly blow.

DLC, ES, LSL, NN, NRU–Mus

———— The same as preceding in separate issue of v. 1, no. [15] complete, ca. 1800.
MdHi

———— Separate issue of preceding with p. [31] and [34] blank, ca. 1800.
DLC, McD–W

[378]

—— The same.
(*In* The musical journal for the flute or violin. Baltimore [1800] no. 15, p. 30–31)

Melody only, flute or violin, with accompanying text.
First line: Ye lingring winds that feebly blow. DLC

SHE'S QUITE THE THING. Boston, Printed & sold at P. A. von Hagen's piano forte ware house, No. 3 Cornhill, where may be had all the new published songs, music &c., just received from London. Also the best of Naples & Roman violin strings, of different prices & qualities [ca. 1800] [2] p. 30½ cm.

Song, pfte. acc. Arr. for the "guittar," p. [2].
First line: Pray young man, your suit give over.
Published possibly as early as 1799. DLC, JFD, LSL, RPJCB

SHE LEFT ME AH! FOR GOLD. A favorite song. New York, Printed for G. Gilfert & co. at their Musical magazine, No. 177 Broadway [1796] 1 l. 34 cm.

Song, pfte. acc.
First line: Tho' rude, thou art as northern blast.
                                        JFD, MWA, RPJCB

SHEEP IN THE CLUSTERS.
(*In* The American musical miscellany. Northampton, 1798. p. 68–70)

Melody only, with accompanying text.
First line: Her sheep had in clusters. DLC (etc.)

*SHELTY'S TRAVELS. A farce. Sequel to the "Highland reel."
Played at the John Street Theatre, New York, April 24, 1794.
In manuscript. By William Dunlap. Title taken from Wegelin.

THE SHEPHERD. A new song. Com: by H. Capron.
(*In* [Moller & Capron's monthly numbers] The fourth number [Philadelphia, 1793] p. 30)

Song, pfte. acc.
First line: My banks they are furnish'd with bees. NN

*THE SHEPHERD BOY. Song by Hook.
Advertised in March, 1797, as to be published "in a few days" by "G. Gilfert at his Musical Magazine, No. 177 Broadway," New York. Also advertised in April, 1798, as to be published "at Carr's Musical Repository," Philadelphia.

SHEPHERD I HAVE LOST MY LOVE.
See Anna.

SHEPHERD MARRY. A favorite ballad. Composed by James Fisin. New York, Printed & sold by G. Gilfert, No. 177 Broadway [1797–1801] [2] p. 31½ cm.

Song, pfte. acc.
First line: As rambling forth the first of May. DLC, MWA

THE SHEPHERD'S COMPLAINT. By Mr. Swan.
(*In* The songster's assistant, ed. by T. Swan. Suffield [ca. 1800] p. 14)
Song, pfte. acc.
First line: O nightingale! best poet of the grove. CtY, MB

THE SHEPHERD'S EVENING. A new song. Composed by R. Taylor.
(*In* Young's vocal and instrumental musical miscellany. Philadelphia
[1793–95] p. 41)
Song, pfte. acc.
First line: Now to pant on Thetis breast.
In No. 5, 1793. DLC, Hopk.

THE SHIPWRECK'D BOY.
(*In* [Unidentified collection of instrumental and vocal music. New York]
Hewitt & Rausch [1797] p. 25)
Song, pfte. acc.
First line: 'Twas near a rock within a bay. DLC, ES

———— The same as preceding.
(*In* A collection of new & favorite songs. [A] Philadelphia [ca. 1800] p. [179])
HFB
———— Separate issue of preceding, 1797. DLC

*THE SHIPWRECKED MARINER PRESERVED, or La Bonne petite fille.
This "serious pantomime, represented at the Philadelphia and Baltimore
theatres with universal applause. With original overture and music, composed by R. Taylor," was to be performed at the Federal Street Theatre.
Boston, on April 10, 1797.

THE SHIPWRECK'D SEAMANS GHOST. Philadelphia, Printed for Carr
& co. at their Musical repository, No. 136 High street
(*In* The favorite songs from the Pirates, by S. Storace. Philadelphia [1793]
p. (6)–(7).)
Song, pfte. acc. Arr. for German flute, p. (7).
First line: There the silver'd waters roam. HFB

———— Separate issue of preceding, 1793. ES, Hopk., LSL, MdHi, NN, PP–K

THE SHIPWRECK'D SEAMANS GHOST. A song in the Pirates. Composed
by Mr. Storace.
(*In* The musical repertory. Boston [1796] No. I, p. (10)–(11).)
Song, pfte. acc. Arr. for German flute, p. (11).
First line same as preceding. DLC, MB, NRU–Mus
In MB copy, after title: Pr. 25¢ This is in different type. Apparently
added later.

———— Separate issue of preceding, ca. 1796. DLC

SHOU'D HE THINK OF ANOTHER. Sung by Miss Leary at Vaux Hall.
(*In* [A collection of favorite songs, arr. by A. Reinagle. Philadelphia, 1789
(?)] p. 21–22)
Song, pfte. acc.
First line: Young Jocky calls me his delight. ES

THE SICILIAN ROMANCE, or The apparition of the cliffs. An opera. By Henry Siddons. As performed with universal applause. Philadelphia, Printed by Thomas Bradford, book-seller and stationer, No. 8 South Front street. 1794. 36 p. 17 cm.

Half-title: The Sicilian romance, or The apparition of the cliff. Libretto. Title-page; dramatis personae, p. [4]; text, p. [5]-36.   CSmH, DLC, MWA

Reeve's opera (1794), or rather Henry Siddon's libretto, was to be performed as a "musical dramatic tale in 2 acts," with "the music composed by Mr. [Alexander] Reinagle," at the New Theatre, Philadelphia, May 6, 1795.

*THE SIEGE OF BELGRADE.
Stephen Storace's opera (1791, libretto by Cobb), was to be performed for the first time in New York as "a comic opera in 3 acts, accompanyments by Pelisier," on December 30, 1796.

*THE SIEGE OF BELGRADE, a sonata for the piano forte.
Advertised in January, 1797, as "just published by G. Gilfert, at his Musical Magazine, No. 177 Broadway," New York.

THE SIEGE OF VALENCIENNES. A sonata for the harpsichord or pianoforte. By K. Kambra. New York, Printed for G. Gilfert & co., at their Musical magazine, No. 191 Broadway [1794-95]   13 p.   31½ cm.

Title page has design of wreath encircling title and surmounted by eagle, globe and shield.
Pfte. (or harpsichord) 2 hds.   MB, PU

SIGH NO MORE LADIES. For three German flutes or violins.
(In The gentleman's amusement, ed. by R. Shaw. Philadelphia [1794-96] p. 80-81)

Vocal trio (open score, three staves).
First line same as title.
In No. 10, 1796.   PHi, PP-K

THE SIGH OF REMEMBRANCE. In the new opera of Ramah Droog. Printed and sold by R. Shaw (Importer of music and musical instruments) Market street, No. 92, Baltimore. Price 25 cents. [1798-1800] [2] p. 31 cm.

Song, pfte. acc. Arr. for German flute, p. [2].
First line: Oft wealth or ambition will tempt us to dare.
The words of the title occur in the third line of each stanza.
Ramah Droog, by Joseph Mazzinghi and William Reeve, first produced in 1798.   LSL, MdHi

THE SIGH OF REMEMBRANCE. In the new opera of Ramah Droog. Printed and sold by R. Shaw, Importer of music and musical instruments, No. 13 South 4th st., Philadelphia. Price 25 cents. [n. d.] [2] p. 31½ cm.

Song, pfte. acc. Arr. for German flute, p. [2].
First line same as preceding.
Published possibly after 1800.   JFD, RPJCB

THE SIGNAL.
See Favorite Cotillions.

[381]

THE SILKEN SASH. Alternative title of *Little Taffline*, by Stephen Storace.

SILVAN, THE SHEPHERD SWAIN. Composed by R. Taylor. The words from the celebrated romance of the Knights of the swan. Written by Madame de Genlis. Price 25 cents. Printed and sold at B. Carr's Musical repository, Philadelphia; J. Carr's, Baltimore and J. Hewitt's, New York. Enter'd according to law. [1798] [2] p. 33 cm.

Song, pfte. acc.
First line: To be treated like a baby. DLC, MWA

Under the title of "Sylvan. The shepherd twain," this "new song, composed by R. Taylor. The words . . . taken from the 'Knights of the Swan.' Written by the Countess de Genlis," was advertised in February, 1798, as "published by B. Carr, at his Repository, Market street," Philadelphia.

THE SILVER MOON. Composed by Mr. Hook. New York, Printed for G. Gilfert & co., No. 209 Broadway [1795] [2] p. 33½ cm.

Song, pfte. acc.
First line: Where, where where shall I seek the lovely swain.
ES, DLC, JFD, MWA, NN, RPJCB
———— The same.
Printed and sold, Philadelphia by C. Hupfeld and Baltimore by H. S. Keating [ca. 1798] [2] p. 33 cm.

At head of title: (11)
Song, pfte. acc.
First line same as preceding.
As to date of publication, *cf*. Since then I'm doom'd. DLC, MWA, NN, PU

———— The same.
Printed and sold, Philadelphia by G. Willig, No. 185 Market street [1798–1804] [2] p. 33½ cm.

Song, pfte. acc.
First line same as preceding. Harv. Mus. Ass'n. DLC, LSL, PHi
This copy is apparently printed from the same plates as the Hupfeld and Keating issue. The only changes occur in parts of the imprint.

THE SILVER MOON. Boston, Printed & sold at P. A. von Hagen, junior & cos., No. 62 Newbury street [1798–99] [2] p. 30 cm.

Below imprint: For the piano forte, German flute, or violin.
Song, pfte. acc.
First line same as preceding. DLC, RPJCB

THE SILVER MOON. Composed by Mr. Hook. [n. p., n. d.] p. 66–67. 29 cm.
Song, pfte. acc.
First line same as preceding.
Evidently a reprint from *The musical repertory* [No. V, 1799] or possibly from Graupner's *Musical magazine* [180–], both published in Boston. *cf*. *The musical repertory*. NBuG

THE SILVER MOON. Composed by Mr. Hook. Price 25 cts. New York, Printed and sold at I. C. Moller's musical store [n. d.] 2 p. 32 cm.
Song, pfte. acc.
First line same as preceding.
Sonneck dates, ca. 1800. DLC, MWA

SILVIA.   By Mr. Clark.
(*In* The songster's assistant, ed. by T. Swan.   Suffield [ca. 1800] p. 17–18)
Song, pfte. acc.
First line: The glad'ning sun returns from rest.   MB

SINCE THEM I'M DOOM'D.   Sung by Mrs. Marshall in the Spoil'd child.
Published at B. Carr's Musical repositories, Philadelphia & New York &
J. Carr's, Baltimore.   (12 cts)   [1794–97]   1 l., paged 21.   32 cm.

Song, pfte. acc.
First line same as title.
Sonneck gives date, ca. 1796.
Not to be confused with the issue in *Linley's Assistant*, also p. 21, *q.v.*
Mrs. Marshall sang in *The spoil'd child*, in Philadelphia from March 19,
1794, to February 29, 1796.
Certain copies (*e. g.*, DLC) lack the apostrophe in "Spoil'd."
The plate is unquestionably the same.
                                        DLC, ES, LSL, McD–W, MdHi, NN

——— The same as preceding, but unpaged.   DLC

SINCE THEN I'M DOOM'D.
(*In* Linley's assistant for the pianoforte.   Baltimore [1796] p. 21)

Song, pfte. acc.
First line same as title.   MdHi

——— The same as preceding.   First page, numbered 21, of a detached leaf
from above work.   1796.   DLC

[SINCE THEN I'M DOOM'D]   Song in the Spoil'd child.
(*In* The American musical miscellany.   Northampton, 1798.   p. 293–294)

Melody only, with accompanying text.
Title from first line.   DLC (etc.)

SINCE THEN I'M DOOM'D.   Sung by Mr. [?] Marshall.   Philadelphia, by
C. Hupfeld and Baltimore, by H. S. Keating, Baltm. street, N. 158 [n. d.]
1 l.   32½ cm.

At head of title: (12).
Song, pfte. acc.
First line same as title.
Published probably ca. 1798, as Henry S. Keatinge is advertised as a pub-
lisher in Baltimore at that time.   DLC, PHi

SINCE THEN I'M DOOM'D.   A favorite song.   Philadelphia, Printed & sold
by G. Willig, No. 185 Market street [1798–1804]   1 l.   30 cm.

Song, pfte. acc.
First line same as title.
Sonneck gives date: ca. 1800.   DLC, JFD, MWA, RPJCB

SINCE THEN I'M DOOM'D.   A favorite song.   Sung in the Spoil'd child.
New York, Printed and sold by I. C. Moller's Musical store [n. d.]   1 l.
32½ cm.

Song, pfte. acc.
First line same as title.
Sonneck gives date: ca. 1800.   DLC, RPJCB

———— The same.
New York, Printed by G. Gilfert, No. 177 Broadway [1797–1801] 1 l.
31½ cm.

Song, pfte. acc.
First line same as title.   ABHu, DLC, MWA

[SINCE THEN I'M DOOM'D] Sung by Mrs. Jordan in the Spoil'd child.
(*In* [Two songs] Sung by Mrs. Jordan in the Spoil'd child [n. p., ca. 1800]
p. [1])

Song, pfte. acc.
Title from first line.   DLC

SINCE THEN I'M DOOM'D. A favourite air with variations for the piano
forte. [n. p., n. d.] 3 p. 33 cm.

Below caption: Je suis Lindor. Aria.
Pfte. 2 hds.
Published probably ca. 1800.   DLC

This popular farce, *The spoiled child*, has been variously ascribed to Mrs.
Jordan, Richard Ford and Isaac Bickerstaffe.

SINFONIA. By J. C. Moller.
(*In* [Moller & Capron's monthly numbers] The first number [Philadelphia,
1793] p. 2–4)

Pfte. 2 hds.   DLC

*SINFONIA BY GUENIN.
Was to be performed at a concert in Charleston, S. C., in April, 1795. Perhaps this Guenin was identical with the musician of the same name who
emigrated to the United States.

SING OLD ROSE AND BURN THE BELLOWS. A favourite glee for 3
voices. Sung by Mr. Bannister &c. in the Suicide [London] Printed for J.
Carr, Middle Row, Holborn [n. d.] [2] p. 32 cm.

Imprint at foot of p. [2].
Three-part chorus. Open score. Arr. for two German flutes, p. [2].
First line: Now we're met like jovial fellows.   DLC

———— The same as preceding.
(*In* A collection of new & favorite songs. [A] Philadelphia [ca. 1800]
p. [204]–[205])   HFB

Although issued in London, included here because it is a Carr imprint and
included in the above collection.

THE SINGING MASTER'S ASSISTANT, or key to practical music. Being
an abridgement from the New England psalm singer, together with several
other tunes never before published. Composed by William Billings, author
of the New England psalm singer [Verses] Boston (New England), Printed by
Draper and Folsom. 1778. (32), 104 p. 11½ x 19½ cm.

Title-page. Preface, p. [(2)]; Advertisement, p. [(3)]; To teachers of music,
p. [(4)]–(22); Musical dictionary, p. [(23)]–(27), To the Goddess of Discord,

p. [(28)]–(29), List of tunes and anthems, p. [(30)], An encomium on music, p. [(31)]–(32), Music, p. 1–104.

Four-part chorus. Open score.
Most important secular numbers: Chester, p. 12, Jargon, p. 102.

CSmH, DLC, ICN, MB, MH, MHi,ICN

SIX BALLADS, composed by Mrs. Pownall and J. Hewitt.
See Book of songs, by the same authors.

SIX EASY DUETTS for two violins or flute and violin . . . by I. Hewitt.
See Six easy Duetts . . . by I. Hewitt.

SIX FAVORITE GERMAN WALTZEN [!]
See Six favorite German waltzen.

SIX IMITATIONS of English, Scotch, Irish, Welch, Spanish & German airs.
By B. Carr.
(In The musical journal for the piano forte, ed. by B. Carr. Baltimore [1800] v. 1, no. [20], p. (38)–(40).)

Pfte. 2 hds.   DLC, ES, LSL, NN, NRU–Mus

——— The same.
(In The musical journal for the flute or violin. Baltimore [1800] no. 18, p. 33–36)

Melody only, flute or violin.   DLC

*SIX LITTLE BALLADS.
See Musical bagatelles.

*SIX NEW MINUETS with proper cadences for dancing, by Giovanni Gualdo.
Advertised in the Pennsylvania journal, November 8, 1770, as "composed for the Ball" on December 27.

SIX QUINTETTI À DUE VIOLINI, due viola è violoncello di John Friedr. Peter. d. 9. Jan. 1789.

Score and parts in Peter's autograph as No. 64–69 in the Archives of the Moravian Church at Bethlehem, Pa.

SIX ROMANCES NOUVELLES . . . par R. Chateaudun.
See Six Romances nouvelles . . . par R. Chateaudun.

*SIX SONATAS FOR THE HARPSICHORD or organ . . . By Peter Valton.
See Six Sonatas for the harpsichord or orgzn . . . by Peter Valton.

SIX SONATAS FOR THE PIANO FORTE or harpsichord . . . by Valentino Niccolai.
See Six Sonatas for the piano forte or harpsichord . . . by Valentino Niccolai.

SIX SONATAS FOR THE PIANO FORTE with an accompaniment for the flute . . . by Ignace Pleyel.
See Six Sonatas for the piano forte . . . by Ignace Pleyel.

*SIX SONATAS FOR THE PIANO FORTE with the accompanyment of a violin or flute . . . by an amateur.
See Six Sonatas for the piano forte . . . by an amateur.

[385]

SIX SONATINAS FOR THE PIANO FORTE . . . by I. A. K. Colizzi.
See Six *Sonatinas* for the piano forte by I. A. K. Colizzi.

SIX SONGS, composed by Mrs. Pownall and J. Hewitt.
See A book of songs . . . composed by M. A. Pownall and J. Hewitt.

THE SKY LARK: or gentlemen and ladies' complete songster. Being a collection of the most modern and celebrated American, English and Scotch songs [Verses] Worcester: From the press of Isaiah Thomas, jun. Sold at his book store and by the booksellers in Boston.—1795. x, [11]–228 p. 14 cm.

Title-page, verso blank; contents, p. [iii]–x; songs, p. [11]–228. Contains no music, and only once indication of tune: p. 56. "The Banks of Kentucke. Tune—Banks of the Dee." Very little, except the catch words of the title, taken from "The Sky Lark . . . London, 1772."

DLC, MB, MWA, NBuG (incomplete), PPL

———— The same.
Second Worcester edition. Worcester, From the press of Isaiah Thomas, jun. 1797. 310 p. 13½ cm.

Title-page same as in first Worcester edition, with the addition of "Together with an appendix; containing a number of celebrated Masonic songs, cotillions and countre dances. Being the second edition greatly enlarged and improved." MB (incomplete)

SLAVES IN ALGIERS; or, a Struggle for freedom: A play, interspersed with songs in three acts. By Mrs. Rowson, as performed at the new theatres in Philadelphia and Baltimore. Philadelphia: Printed for the author by Wrigley and Berriman, No. 149 Chestnut street, 1794. 2 p. l., ii, 72, [2] p. 15 cm.

On verso of title-page, "Copyright secured according to law." Recto of second p. l., inscription, verso blank; preface, p. [i]–ii; prologue, p. [1]–[2]; dramatis personae, p. [4]; text, p. [5]–72; epilogue, p. [73]–[74]. Certain copies (*e. g.*, PHi) have additional p. [75]: advertisement. DLC, PHi, PU, RPB

This play is entered here because it sometimes was called an opera and because in the preface Mrs. Susanna Rowson publicly acknowledged her obligation to Mr. Alexander Reinagle "for the attention he manifested, and the taste and genius he displayed in the composition of the music."

Susanna Haswell Rowson (1762–1824). Born in Portsmouth, England; died in Boston, Massachusetts. Once famous as a novelist ("Charlotte Temple," published early in 1791) and playwright. On account of the financial embarrassment of her husband, William Rowson, a musician, she went on the stage in 1792 at Edinburgh. From 1793 to 1797 she appeared on the American stage.

SLOW MARCH IN THE BATTLE OF PRAGUE.
See Military amusement [1796], p. 14.

*———— Slow march [in the Battle of Prague]
See Evening amusement [1796], p. 28 [lacking in DLC copy]

SMALILOU. A favorite Irish ballad in the opera, the Picture of Paris. Composed by Mr. Wᵐ Shield.
(*In* The musical repertory. Boston [1796–97] No. III, p. 38–39)
Song, pfte. acc.
First line: There was an Irish lad who lov'd a cloyster'd nun. DLC

THE SMART COCKADE. Philadelphia, By G. Willig, No. 185 Market st. [1798–1804] p. 5. 31½ cm.

Title placed between the words "Philadelphia" and "By."
Song, pfte. acc.
First line: On Entrick's green meadows.
BM Cat. lists: *On Entick's green meadows,* by James Hook. MWA, NN, PP

—— The same, p. 5., but without imprint. Verso blank. MWA

—— The same, p. 5, without imprint. Apparently a leaf from an unidentified collection. On p. 6: Mary's dream, or Sandy's ghost. NN

A SMILE & A TEAR. A favorite song. The words by M. P. Andrews, Esqr & set to music by Miss Abrams. New York, Printed & sold at J. & M. Paff's musical store, No. 127 Broadway [1799–1803] [2] p. 31½ cm.

Song, pfte. acc.
First line: You own I'm complacent, but tell me I'm cold.
Miss Abrams: Harriet Abrams. NN

—— The same as preceding, except that over the original imprint has been pasted the following: "New York, Printed for S. Terrett, No. 320 Pearl street." [1804–1805] DLC

A SMILE AND A TEAR. A favorite song. The words by M. P. Andrews, Esqr Composed by Miss Abrams. Philadelphia, Publish'd and sold at G. Willig's Musical magazine [ca. 1800] [2] p. 33½ cm.

Song, pfte. acc.
First line same as preceding.
Probably issued after 1800. MWA

A SMILE FROM THE GIRL OF MY HEART.
(*In* Young's vocal and instrumental musical miscellany. Philadelphia [1793–95] p. 26)

Song, pfte. acc., followed by arr. for flute or guitar.
First line: In the world's, in the world's crooked path where I've been.
Title forms the last line of each stanza.
From *The woodman,* by William Shield.
In No. 3, 1793. DLC, Hopk.

A SMILE FROM THE GIRL OF MY HEART. In the Woodman.
(*In* Elegant extracts for the German flute or violin. Philadelphia [1798] bk. 3, p. 5)

Melody only, flute or violin, with accompanying text.
First line same as preceding. DLC, NN
See also Mrs. Pownall's address.

A SMILE FROM THE YOUTH THAT I LOVE. Written by the author of the Marvellous pleasant love story and set to music by Thomas Wright. Philadelphia, Printed & sold by G. Willig, No. 185 Market street [1798–1804] [2] p. 31 cm.

Song, pfte. acc. Arr. for flute, p. [2].
First line: Tho' the language of friendship is sweet. DLC, RPJCB

THE SMILE OF BENEVOLENCE, by Dibdin.
(*In* Elegant extracts for the German flute or violin. Philadelphia [1798] bk. 3, p. 20)

Melody only, flute or violin, with accompanying text.
First line: Inspir'd by so grateful a duty.
From *Great news*, by Charles Dibdin.   DLC, NN

SNATCH FLEETING PLEASURES. Alternative title of *Life let us cherish*, by Hans G. Nägeli.

SO DEARLY I LOVE JOHNNY O. A favorite new song. Sung by Mrs. Franklin. New York, Printed & sold by G. Gilfert & co., No. 177 Broadway. Where may be had a general assortment of fine tuned piano fortes and other musical articles of superior quality [1796] [2] p. 33½ cm.

Song, pfte. acc.
First line: Young Sandy once a wooing came.   DLC, JFD, RPJCB

SO SWEET HER FACE, HER FORM DIVINE. Music by J. B. Gauline. Philadelphia, Printed by G. Willig, No. 185 Market st. [1798–1804] [2] p. 33½ cm.
Song, pfte. acc.
First line same as title.   DLC

—— The same as preceding, except below title: Written by a gentlemen [!] in Queen Ann's county. [1798–1804]   MdHi

SOCIAL HARMONY; or, The cheerful songster's companion. [Six lines of verse] New York: Printed by Samuel Campbell, No. 124 Pearl-street. 1795. 108 p. 24 mo.   MWA

[SOFTLY AS THE BREEZES BLOWING] A favorite song by H. Capron. (*In* [Moller & Capron's monthly numbers] The first number [Philadelphia, 1793] p. 5)
Song, pfte. acc.
Title from first line.   DLC

THE SOLDIER TIR'D. Compos'd by Dr. Arne.
(*In* A collection of favorite songs, arr. by A. Reinagle. Philadelphia [1789?] p. 14–16)
Song, pfte. acc.
First line: The soldier tir'd of wars alarms.
From *Artaxerxes*.   DLC

—— Separate issue (1789?) identical except that page numbers are here changed to 1–3.   CdeW, DLC, NBuG

Advertised in March, 1789, among other "Songs and pieces, arranged for the piano forte or harpsichord by Alexander Reinagle," as "just published, and sold by Thomas Dobson, at the Stone house, in Second street," Philadelphia.

THE SOLDIER TIRED. In Artaxerxes. New York, Printed at J. Hewitt's Musical repository, No. 131 William street. Sold also by B. Carr, Philadelphia & J. Carr, Baltimore. Price [ ] cents. [1797–99] [3] p. 32 cm.
Song, pfte. acc.
First line: The soldier tir'd of war's alarms.   DLC

THE SOLDIER'S ADIEU. By Dibdin. Price 20 cents. Philadelphia, Printed at Carr & co's Musical repository [1794] [2] p. 33 cm.

Song, pfte. acc. Arr. for flute or "guittar," p. [2].
First line: Adieu, adieu, my only life.
From *The wags.*　　　　　CtY, DLC, ES, LSL, McD–W, MWA, PP–K
Advertised February 3, 1794, as "this day published."

[THE SOLDIER'S ADIEU] Sung by Mr. Marshall. The words & music of this song by Dibdin.
(*In* The volunteers, by A. Reinagle. Philadelphia [1795?] p. 18–19)

Song, pfte. acc.
First line same as preceding.　　　　　　　　　　　　　　DLC

THE SOLDIER'S ADIEU.
(*In* Elegant extracts for the German flute or violin. Philadelphia [1796] bk. 2, p. 10–11)

Melody only, flute or violin, with accompanying text.
First line same as preceding.　　　　　　　　　　　　　DLC, NN

——— The same. Philadelphia, By G. Willig, No. 185 Market st. [1798–1804] [2] p. 33 cm.

Song, pfte. acc. Three staves, voice part on middle staff.
First line same as preceding.　　　　　　　　　　　　DLC, PP–K

——— The same as preceding except [3] p., with added arr. for two "fluttes" and for the guitar, p. [3]. [1798–1804]　　　　　　　　　　DLC

——— The same as preceding ([3] p.), but without imprint. Date probably the same as above.　　　　　　　　　　　　　　　　　　　PU

——— The same.
Boston, Printed & sold at P. A. von Hagen & cos. imported piano forte & music warehouse, No. 3 Cornhill. Also by G. Gilfert, New York [ca. 1800] [2] p. 30 cm.

Song, pfte. acc. Arr. for German flute, violin or "guittar," p. [2].
First line same as preceding.
Published probably 1799.　　　　　　　　　　DLC, LSL, RPJCB

——— Adieu, adieu my only life.
(*In* The American musical miscellany. Northampton, 1798. p. 118–120)

Melody only, with accompanying text.
First line same as title.
Composed by Charles Dibdin.　　　　　　　　　　　　DLC (etc.)

THE SOLDIERS EPITAPH. A favorite song. Composed by Ignace Pleyel. New York, Printed & sold by G. Gilfert, No. 177 Broadway [1797–1801] [2] p. 31 cm.

Song, pfte. acc. Arr. for flute or guitar, p. [2].
First line: Here full of scars lies brave Hal Brazen.　　　　　MWA

THE SOLDIERS FAREWEL [!] By Mr. Swan.
(*In* The songster's assistant, ed. by T. Swan. Suffield [ca. 1800] p. 33–34)

Song, pfte. acc.
First line: At length too soon, dear creature.　　　　　　CtY, MB

SOLDIER'S JOY.
See Evening amusement, p. 16.

*SOLO FOR THE VIOLIN, by A. Juhan.
A "Solo violin (newly composed) Juhan" made part of the program of "Mr. Juhan's concert," Philadelphia, April 10, 1787.

*A SOLO ON THE GRAND PIANOFORTE, composed by Dr. Berkenhead.
Was to be performed at a concert, Boston, on May 23, 1796.

*A SOLO ON THE VIOLONCELLO, composed by Mr. Demarque.
Was to be played by the composer at a concert, Baltimore, on November 25, 1793.

SOLOMON'S TEMPLE, an oratorio.
See Choice collection of Free Masons songs.
See also Masonic. Songs, oratorio, etc.

[SOME TELL US THAT WOMEN ARE DELICATE THINGS] Sung by Mr. Bates.
(In The volunteers, by A. Reinagle. Philadelphia [1795?] p. 8–9)
Song, pfte. acc.
Title from first line.   DLC

SOME TIME AGO. Sung by Mr. Johnson in the Siege of Belgrade. New York, Printed & sold by James Hewitt at his Musical repository, William street. By B. Carr, Philadelphia & J. Carr, Baltimore [1797–99] 1 1. 34 cm.

Song, pfte. acc.
First line: Some time ago I marry'd a wife.
Sung by Mr. Johnson in The siege of Belgrade, by Stephen Storace, New York, December 30, 1796.   DLC, NN

——— The same as preceding.
(In A collection of new & favorite songs. [A] Philadelphia [ca. 1800] p. [207])   HFB

SOMEBODY. Printed by B. Carr & sold at his Musical repositories, New York & Philadelphia & by I. Carr, Baltimore [1795–96] 1 1. 32 cm.

Song, pfte. acc., followed by arr. for "guittar."
First line: Were I oblig'd to beg my bread.
                                               ES, LSL, McD–W, MdHi, NN

——— The same.
Published by G. Willig at his Musical magazin [!], 165 Market street, Philad [1795–97] 1 1. 31½ cm.

Song, pfte. acc., followed by arr. for flute or guitar.
First line same as preceding.   MWA

——— The same.
(In American musical miscellany. Northampton, 1798. p. 172–174)
Melody and bass, with accompanying text.
First line: Was I reduc'd to beg my bread.
Differs somewhat, both in text and melody, from other editions. DLC (etc.)

[390]

SOMEBODY.
Boston, Printed & sold by P. A. von Hagen at his piano forte warehouse, No. 3 Cornhill [ca. 1800] 1 l. 32½ cm.

Song, pfte. acc., followed by arr. for "guittar."
First line: Were I oblig'd to beg my bred [!].
Published possibly as early as 1799.   JFD, RPJCB

[WERE I OBLIG'D TO BEG MY BREAD] Sung by Mrs. Warrell at the New Theatre.
(*In* The gentleman's amusement, ed. by R. Shaw. Philadelphia [1794-96] p. 59)

Melody only, flute (or violin) with accompanying text.
Title from first line.
In No. 7, May 1, 1796.   DLC, PHi, PP-K

*THE SON IN LAW.
Samuel Arnold's opera (1779. Libretto by O'Keefe) was to be performed "with accompanyments" by Victor Pelissier at New York, on February 7, 1798.

SONATA I.
(*In* Le petitte beaute de musique [New York, ca. 1800] p. 2-5)
Pfte. 2 hds.
In C Major, from Op. 11 by Valentino Nicolai.   DLC

SONATA I. By Niccolai. Printed by G. Willig, Philadelphia [179– ?] 2-7 p. 33 cm.
Pfte. 2 hds.
Manuscript note at foot of p. 2: Sold by I. and M. Paff, New York.
In C Major, from Op. 3.   DLC, Hopk., RPJCB

SONATA I. Niccolai. Opera III.
(*In* Le petitte beaute de musique. [New York, ca. 1800. p. 2-7)
Pfte. 2 hds.
In C Major.   DLC

SONATA II.
(*In* Le petitte beaute de musique [New York] ca. 1800. p. 6-8)
Pfte. 2 hds.
In D Major, from Op. 11 by Valentino Nicolai.   DLC

SONATA III. [n. p., ca. 1800] 6 p. 31 cm.
Pfte. 2 hds.
Page numbers at foot of page.
At foot of p. 1, 2, 5, 6: 3 Nicolai Op. 11.
At foot of p. 3, 4: 3 Nicolai 11.
No. 3, in C Major, of *Six sonatas* for the piano forte or harpsichord, Op. 11, by Valentino Nicolai, published in London, ca. 1797.   DLC, JFD

SONATA III. Printed & sold by G. Willig, Market st., Philadelphia [179– ?] 5 p. 35 cm.
At head of title: Sigʳ Haydn.
Pfte. 2 hds.
In C Major, No. 20 (Pohl), Breitkopf & Härtel, No. 5.
Sigʳ Haydn: Joseph Haydn.   DLC, MWA

[391]

SONATA IV. By Nicolai. [Philadelphia] Printed by G. Willig [n. d.] 7–10 p.
32½ cm.

Pfte. 2 hds.
No. 5, in G Major, of *Six sonatas* . . . Op. 3.
Published probably 179–.   DLC

SONATA VIII. By I. C. Moller. [n. p., 179–?] [2] p. 31½ cm.

Pfte. 2 hds.
I. C. Moller: John Christopher Moller.   MWA

Perhaps the sonata to be played by Moller at a City concert, Philadelphia,
December 1, 1792, as advertised in Dunlap's *American daily advertiser*,
Philadelphia, November 29, 1792.

SONATA & CHASSE FOR THE PIANOFORTE. Composed by D. Steibelt.
Price $1.50 cents. Published and sold at G. Willig's Musical magazine,
Philadelphia [n. d.] 15 p. 32 cm.

Title-page, verso blank; music, p. 3–15.
Pfte. 2 hds.
Published probably ca. 1800.   NN

SONATA BY PLEYEL.
(*In* The musical journal for the pianoforte, ed. by B. Carr. Baltimore [1800]
v. 1, nos. [4] and 6, p. (6)–(12).)

Below title: N. B. If a flute plays the accompaniment the small upper
notes where they occur are to be taken.
Pfte. and flute or violin. Three staves.
                    DLC, ES, McD–W (lacks p. 6), MdHi, NN, NRU–Mus

*SONATA composed by W. Langdon, music professor, Phila.
In *Aurora*, Philadelphia, October 7, 1795:

    Proposal for publishing by subscription an easy sonata for harpsichord
    or piano forte with an accompaniment for the violin or German flute.

*SONATA FOR BEGINNERS by John Henry Schmidt.
An advertisement by this musician in Claypoole's *Daily advertiser*, September
5, 1796, concludes:

    His easy Sonata for beginners, consisting in a largetto [!] minuet and trio,
    and Yankee Doodle, turned into a fashionable rondo, may be had of him
    at No. 50, Green street, where he has furnished rooms to let.

SONATA FOR THE PIANO FORTE with an accompaniment for a violin.
Composed by R. Taylor. Philadelphia, Printed for the Author, No. 96
North Six [ ], likewise at Carr's Musical reposit [ ]. Price one dol [ ]
[1797] 1 p. l., 2–6 p. 32½ cm.

Title-page, verso blank; p. [1] blank; music, p. 2–6.
Pfte. and violin. Separate staff for violin, no separate violin part.
Title-page torn, as above indicated, but intent of imprint clear.
                                                                    NRU–Mus

Advertised in October, 1797, as "published, price one dollar . . . printed for
the author, No. 96 North Sixth and to be had at the music stores," Philadelphia.

*SONATA FOR TWO VIOLINS and violoncello by William Selby.
See Apollo or the Muse's musical compositions.

A FAVORITE SONATA. By Niccolai. [Philadelphia] Publish'd by G.
Willig, No. 165 M⁵⁶; Price 75 cents. [1795–97] 7 p. 32½ cm.

Publ. no. 187.
Imprint above and at the right of title, apparently added later.
Pfte. 2 hds.
In C Major, but not identical with Op. 3, No. 1.
Niccolai: Valentino Nicolai.   DLC, McD–W, NN

— —— Nicolai's favorite Sonata. Printed and sold by J. Carr, music store,
Baltimore. Price 75 cents. [n. d.] 7 p. 32 cm.

Pfte. 2 hds.
Published possibly as early as 1796.   PP–K

A FAVORITE SONATA for the piano forte with an accompaniment for the
violin. Composed by Josʰ Willson. New Brunswick, Printed for the
Author & sold at the music shops, New York, &c. Copyright secured.
[n. d.] 4 p. 31½ cm.

Pfte. 2 hds. and violin. Three staves.
Published possibly as early as 1800.
Josʰ Willson: Joseph Willson.   DLC

VIGUERIE'S FAVORITE SONATA for the pianoforte. Price 50 cents.
Philadelphia, Printed for B. Carr [ca. 1800] 7 p. 31½ cm.

Title-page. At head of title: A new edition of.
Pfte. 2 hds.
Viguerie: Bernard Viguerie.   NN

SONATAS FOR THE PIANOFORTE by Alexander Reinagle.
DLC possesses in autograph a "Sonata Pianoforte A. Reinagle, Philadelphia," also three autograph pianoforte sonatas by the same composer in
one volume, the title page reading, "Sonata Pianoforte A. Reinagle."

Sonneck adds: Though nothing goes to show that these four sonatas were
written before 1800, nothing, on the other hand, allows us to infer that they
were written after 1800. Therefore attention is called here to these sonatas
which closely follow in the foot-steps of Ph. Em. Bach and the early Haydn
without being void of individuality. If the larger works of Reinagle all
were as fine and effective as these sonatas, he must have been a composer of
merit.

Presumably one of these sonatas was played by Reinagle at Miss Broadhurst's benefit concert, Philadelphia, April 3, 1800. (*Aurora,* Philadelphia,
March 31, 1800)

NICOLAI'S 2 EASY SONATAS for the pianoforte [n. p., n. d.] 8 p. 32 cm.

Title-page; music, p. 2–8.
Pfte. 2 hds.
Sonata I, p. 2–5.—Sonata II, p. 6–8.
Published probably ca. 1800.   NN

[393]

*SIX SONATAS FOR THE HARPSICHORD or organ; with an accompany-
ment for a violin: Composed by Peter Valton.

In the *South Carolina gazette*, Charleston, S. C., October 10, 1768, appeared
the following:

> Proposals for printing by subscription SIX SONATAS for the harpsichord
> or organ; with an accompanyment for a violin: Composed by Peter Val-
> ton, organist of St. Philip's, Charles Town, South Carolina. *Opera Prima.*
> To be printed on a good paper, and delivered to the subscribers some time
> this spring, if the plates can be engraved and sent by that time. Each
> subscriber to pay Four pounds Carolina currency the sett, on delivery of
> the books. Those who subscribe for six setts to have a seventh gratis.
> The subscribers names to be printed. Those who intend to encourage this
> work, are requested to send their names to the author, to Mr. Gaines or,
> to Mr. David Douglas, as soon as possible.

The same proposals appeared in other papers; for instance, under date of
"Charles Town, Jan. 10, 1769," in the *New York Mercury*, February 20, 1769.

SIX SONATAS FOR THE PIANO FORTE or harpsichord with an accompaniment for a violin. Composed by Valentino Niccolai. These sonatas are
composed for performers in general. Op. XI. Price 17s. 6d. Philadelphia, Printed by I. C. Moller (No. 163) North Third street. Where may be
had a great variety of vocal and instrumental music. [1793] 1 p. l., 31 p.
31½ cm.

Title-page, verso blank; music, p. 2–31.
Pfte. 2 hds. No separate violin part. NBuG, PU

—— Six Sonatas for piano forte or harpsichord. Composed by Valentino
Niccolai. These sonatas are composed for performers in general. Op. XI.
Philadelphia, Printed by G. Willig, Market street, No. 185. Where may be
had a great variety of vocal and instrumental music [n. d.] 31 p. 30½ cm.

Title-page.
Pfte. 2 hds.
Published possibly as early as 1798. McD–W, NN

SIX SONATAS FOR THE PIANO FORTE, with an accompaniment for the
flute. Composed and dedicated (by permission) to Her Majesty, the Queen
of Great Britain by Ignace Pleyel. Price 6 dolls. New York, Sold at I.
Paff's, Broadway [n. d.] 6 v. 33 cm.

At foot of title page: These sonatas single each 10ˢ/.
Title page for each volume, pagination continuous.
Pfte. and flute. Three staves, no separate flute part.
Sonneck's date, ca. 1800. But judging from the imprint, the date must be
1798 or 1811. Either is possible, but the evidence seems to point to the
later date.

> MWA and RPJCB, 6 Nos. complete, 101 p.
> DLC, Nos. 1–4, 67 p. (p. 3–4 mutilated)
> ABHu and MdHi, Nos. 1–2, 37 p.
> NBuG, No. 2, p. 20–37.

*SIX SONATAS FOR THE PIANOFORTE with the accompanyment of a
violin or flute, ad libitum.   Composed by an amateur.

The "proposals" for publishing the sonatas appeared in the *Federal gazette*,
Baltimore, September 22, 1796, where we read:

> The work will be published in monthly numbers; and the first No. appear
> on the first of January 1797—Price 4 dollars.   One half of the subscription
> to be paid at the time of subscribing and the residue on the delivery of the
> 4th number.

> After the appearance of the first sonata, subscribers shall be at liberty to
> erase their names from the list; or continue them at their option.   The
> money arising thereon, after deducting the charges, shall be remitted in
> Charleston, for the benefit of the unfortunate sufferers by the late fire.

> Subscriptions are received by Mr. Carr, Baltimore, Mr. Carr, at Phila-
> delphia and New York.   To non subscribers, each sonata will be delivered
> at one dollar.

*A SET OF SIX SONATAS.
See *A *Set* of six sonatas.

*THREE SONATAS FOR THE HARPSICHORD or pianoforte, by F. Linley.
Advertised in the *Salem gazette*, Massachusetts, November 21, 1800, as "for
sale by Thomas C. Cushing."   This title has been inserted as a musician by
the name of F. Linley was a resident of Boston about 1795–1800 (Sonneck).
There seems to be an error here as Francis Linley was still in England in 1795
and had returned to England in 1799.   Apparently he was in Boston only
ca. 1798.

THREE SONATAS FOR THE PIANO FORTE.   Composed and dedicated to
Miss Temple, by Jas. Hewitt.   Op. 5.   Pr. 10/.   New York, Printed for
the Author and sold at Carr's Musical repository, William street & at Gilfert
& co's.   Musical magazine, Broadway [1795–96]   17 p.   31 cm.

Pfte. 2 hds.   DLC

DLC has two other copies (incomplete), title-page identical with above, as
also are several pages.   The second and third pages, however, are from
entirely different plates from this, and p. 10 shows many typographical
variants.   Both copies have the composer's signature at foot of title-page.
One copy lacks p. 13–16, the other p. 5–17.

TWO SONATAS FOR THE PIANO FORTE.   With an accompanement [!] for
a violin.   Dedicated to the fair sex.   By D. Steibelt.   Op. 33.   Printed &
sold by G. Willig, No. 185 Market street, Philadelphia [ca. 1800]   8 p.   32 cm.

Pfte. 2 hds.
No separate violin part.   NN, PP–K

——— The same as preceding, but with imprint partially erased and "No. 12
South 4th street" substituted.   Incomplete (p. 1–4 only), to be dated not
earlier than 1805.   NBuG

SONATAS OR LESSONS FOR THE HARPSICHORD or piano forte by
William Selby.
See Apollo or the Muse's musical compositions.

SONATE DE HAYDN.
(*In* The musical journal for the flute or violin, Baltimore [1800]   no. 8, p. 14–16)

Duet for flutes or violins (or flute and violin).
Arranged from the first movement of Sonata in C Major, No. 20 (Pohl), Breitkopf & Härtel, No. 5.   DLC

SONATE MILITAIRE. Pour le piano forte. Composée par Jean Vanhal. Price 50 cents. Philadelphia, Published and sold at G. Willig's Musical magazine [ca. 1800?]   5 p.   31½ cm.

Pfte. 2 hds.
At foot of p. [1]: S. V.
At foot of other pages: S. Vanhal 5.
Jean Vanhal: J. B. Wanhal.   NBuG, NN

SONATINA A QUATRE MAINS. Par Fr. Rausch. [New York] Printed at G. Gilfert & cos. Musical magazine, No. 191 Broadway [1794–95]   2 p. 33½ cm.

Imprint at foot of p. 2.
Pfte. 4 hds.   RPJCB

SONATINA, composed by J. Haydn. Opera 71. Philadelphia, Printed & sold by G. Willig, No. 185 Market street [n. d.]   5 p.   32½ cm.

Pfte. 2 hds.
In C Major, listed in Pohl as "Thema mit variationen," No. 6 in *Kleinere clavierstücke.*
Published possibly as early as 1798.   DLC

———— The same as preceding, except in imprint, "Price 62½ cents," and with publication number 199.
Published 1798–1804.   DLC, Hopk., NN, PP–K

SIX SONATINAS FOR THE PIANO FORTE. Composed by I. A. K. Colizzi. New York, Printed for F. Rausch.   Price 1²⁵⁄₁₀₀ dol. W. Milns, Sc⸱ No. 29 Gold street [179–]   14 p.   31 cm.

Title-page; music, p. 2–14.
At foot of p. 14: Engᵈ. by W. Pirsson.
Pfte. 2 hds.
Probably published ca. 1795–98, as W. Milns was at No. 29 Gold street at that time. W. Pirsson was also active at about this same time.
                                                                                  DLC, ES, JFD, MB
I. A. K. Colizzi: John A. K. Colizzi.

THREE PROGRESSIVE SONATINAS for the piano forte with an accompaniment for a violin by J. Pleyel. Opera 35, Book I. Printed & sold by G. Willig, No. 185 Market street, Philadelphia [1798–1804]   7 p.   32 cm.

Publ. no. 76.
Title-page.
Pfte. 2 hds.   No separate violin part.
Contains Nos. I–III.
J. Pleyel: Ignaz Joseph Pleyel.   DLC

—— The same as preceding, with addition of "Price $1," and substitution of "No. 12 South 4th street" for "No. 185 Market street." There is partial erasure of the latter address. To be dated not earlier than 1805.　NBuG

THREE PROGRESSIVE SONATINAS for the pianoforte with an accompaniment for a violin, by J. Pleyel.　Opera 35, Book III.　Price [$1.25] Printed & sold by G. Willig, No. 185 Market street, Philadelphia [1798–1804] 13 p.　32½ cm.

Publ. no. 78.
Title-page.　Price figures in ink.
Pfte. 2 hds. and violin.　Separate violin part for No. VII only.
Contains Nos. VII–IX　　　　　　　　　　　　　　　　　　　NN

—— The same as preceding, but without price mark, and publisher's address changed to "No. 12 South 4th street."　To be dated not earlier than 1805. No separate violin part.　　　　　　　　　　　　　　　　　　　DLC

SONG.
See [Come all grenadiers]

SONG.
See [Come genius of our happy land]

SONG.
See [The heavy hours are almost past]

SONG.　Set by William Cooper.
See [When all the Attick fire was fled]

SONG.　Set to musick by a gentleman in the county of Worcester.
See [Ah, how needless is expression]

SONG.　. . . Set by *Philo-Musico.*
See [Bright Sol at length]

SONG.　Tune, Hearts of oak.
See [Whilst Europe is wrapt in the horrors of war]

SONG.　Tune, President's march.
See [Lo! I quit my native skies]

SONG.　Tune, Yankee Doodle.
See [Columbians all the present hour]

SONG ADAPTED TO THE PRESIDENT'S MARCH.
See Hail Columbia.

*A SONG BOOK.　Containing upwards of forty of the most modern and elegant songs now in vogue.　Amherst, Newhampshire, Printed by Samuel Preston. 1798.

*A SONG BOOK which contains all the new songs that have been published in England, to this time.
We read in the *New York Mercury*, March 16, 1761:

> James Rivington, Bookseller and Stationer over against the Golden Key, in Hanover Square . . . has this day published . . .

[397]

*SONG BY ALEXANDER REINAGLE.
A "Song (newly composed) Reinagle," but without any further information, was to be sung on January 25, 1787, at the eighth City Concert.

A SONG BY MR. SHERIDAN.
See [Mark'd you her eye]

SONG COMPOSED . . . By a Brother.
See [Ye gracious powers of chora [!] song]

*A SONG, composed by Mr. Kelly of the London theatres. Was "to be sung by Mr. Kelly" at the theatre in Baltimore, on August 2, 1793.

Mr. Kelly, English comedian and occasional composer, appeared in America first in 1792.

*A SONG FOR THE 4TH OF JULY, tune Hail Columbia, and many others that have never before appeared in print.

We read in the Federal gazette, Baltimore, July 2, 1798:

To-morrow will be published and for sale at S. Sower's printing office, No. 67, Market street, at his book store in Fayettestreet, and at Thomas Andrews and Butler's Book store . . . The Patriotic songster . . . also, a Song for the 4th of July . . .

SONG FOR TWO VOICES IN CANON.
See [Waft me some soft and cooling breeze]

SONG FROM THE WOODMAN.
See [When first I slipp'd my leading strings]

SONG IN SELIMA AND AZOR.
See [The storm is o'er]

SONG IN THE CASTLE SPECTRE.
"The much admired Song in the Castle Spectre," was advertised without further information in the *Columbian centinel*, Boston, March 30, 1799, as "This day published, at P. A. Von Hagen, jun. and Co's, No. 55 Marlboro' Street . . . "

SONG IN THE HAUNTED TOWER.
See [Hush, hush, such counsel do not give]

SONG IN THE OPERA OF THE CONJURER NO MAGICIAN.
See [A blessing on brandy and beer]

SONG IN THE SECRET.
See Rosa.

SONG IN THE SPOIL'D CHILD.
See [Since then I'm doom'd]

A SONG ON GENERAL WASHINGTON by Alexander Juhan.
See Set of six sonatas, by the same author.

[398]

SONG TO APOLLO. To be sung at the meeting of the Middlesex medical Association at Concord. Words by Mr. T. M. Harris. Musick by a gentleman of Boston.
(*In* The Massachusetts magazine. Boston. June, 1791. p. 380)

Song, pfte. acc.
First line: Kind father of the healing art. DLC (etc.)

*SONGS &c. IN THE COMET, or He would be a philosopher. A comedy in five acts. As performed by the Old American Company, New York. Written by William Milns. The music by J. Hewitt.
The above appears in the Copyright records of New York, under date of January 30, 1797.

In *The weekly museum*, New York, for January 13, 1798, the advertisement for that night's performance by the Old American Company reads as follows:
> Those ladies and gentlemen who wish to bid an Adieu to the John Street Theatre are respectfully informed this is the Last Night of ever performing in it. This evening will be presented a comedy, interspersed with songs called The comet, or He would be a philosopher. Written by Mr. Milns.

The songs referred to are undoubtedly these by James Hewitt, mentioned above.
The comet was first performed in New York, February 1, 1797.

*SONGS, COMIC, SATYRICAL, AND SENTIMENTAL. Philadelphia: Printed and sold by Robert Bell, in Third-street. 1777.
Written or compiled by George Alexander Stevens, 1710–1784.

SONGS, COMIC SATYRICAL AND SENTIMENTAL, by George Alexander Stevens. I love FUN!—Keep it up! Lecture on Heads. Philadelphia: Printed by R. Bell, Third street. 1778. [4]–9, [2]–12, 252 p. 17 cm.

Words only.
Alphabetical list of songs, p. 248–252. NHi, PHi

*SONGS composed by Dr. Berkenhead.
Two songs "composed by Dr. Berkenhead" were to be sung at a concert for his benefit at Boston, on February 25, 1796.

SONGS, DUETS, AND CHORUSSES, of the Children in the Wood. As performed by the Old American Company. Published, with permission of the managers, by William Humphreys, Asst. Prompter. New York: Printed by Samuel Loudon & Son, No. 82, Water Street, 1795. 16 p. 16°

Contains the words of the songs, etc., only.
On verso of title-page the *"Dramatis Personae"* with remark:
> The Music by Dr. Arnold, with Accompanyments and additional Songs, by Mr. Carr.

It seems as if only two were added.
> Number I. "When nights were cold." A favorite song. The words by Mr. Harwood, of the New Theatre, Philadelphia, composed by Mr. Carr, and
> Number VII. Helen. [Written by Mrs. Melmoth]:
> "Mark, my Alford, all the joys
> Attending on a wedded life." NN

[399]

SONGS, DUETS, ETC., in the Poor soldier, a comic opera, as performed with universal applause at the theatre, New York. Written by Mr. O'Keeffe. New York: Printed for Berry and Rogers, No. 35 Hanover Square. [n. d.] 24 p. 15½ cm.

Title-page; advertisements, p. [2]; dramatis personae, p. [3]; p. [4] blank; text, p. [5]–24.
Evans gives date of publication as 1790.
Contains the words only of the songs, etc., in Shield's opera.   PHi

SONGS, DUETS, TRIOS, ETC. in the Two misers. A comic opera, as performed at the New Theatre, Philadelphia . . . Printed by Wrigley & Berriman, No. 149, Chestnut-street, April, 1794. 12 p. 16 cm.

Title-page, with *dramatis personae* at head of imprint; text, p. [2]–12.
Contains the words only of the songs, etc., in Dibdin's opera.   DLC, PPL

*SONGS FOR THE AMUSEMENT OF CHILDREN. Middletown, Printed by M. H. Woodward, 1790.

SONGS IN BLUE BEARD.
See A collection of new & favorite songs. [C] [From the opera of Blue Beard

THE SONGS IN THE CASTLE OF ANDALUSIA, a comic opera, as performed at the New Theatre, Chestnut-Street. Corrected, with permission of the managers, by William Rowson, prompter. Philadelphia: Printed by Mathew Carey. 1794. (Price, an eighth of a dollar) 12 p. 16 cm.

Title-page; dramatis personae, p. [2]; text, p. [3]–12.
Contains the words only of the songs in Samuel Arnold's opera.   PPL

SONGS IN THE PURSE, or Benevolent tar. A musical drama in one act. As performed at the New Theatre, Philadelphia. Philadelphia: Printed by Wrigley & Berriman, No. 149, Chestnut Street. 1794. Price one-sixteenth of a dollar. 12 p. 8°.

Title-page.
Contains the words only of the songs in Reeve's opera.   PPL

*SONGS. NAVAL AND MILITARY.
In *Rivington's Royal gazette,* March 6, 1779, we read:

In a few days will be published in a pocket volume,
SONGS. NAVAL AND MILITARY. Printed by James Rivington.

On April 21, the collection was advertised as published.

THE SONGS OF TAMMANY, or the Indian chief. A serious opera. By Ann Julia Hatton.
See Tammany, or the Indian chief.

SONGS OF THE FARMER: a comic opera in two acts. As performed at the New Theatre, in Chestnut-street. By John O'Keefe, Esq. Philadelphia: Printed by Mathew Carey. March 12, 1794. Price, six cents. 12 p. 16 cm.

Title-page; dramatis personae, p. [2]; text, p. [3]–12.
Contains the words only of the songs in Shield's opera.   PPL

[400]

*[SONGS, published by James Harrison], New York, 1793.
In the *New York daily advertiser*, July 29, 1793, we read:

New Music. James Harrison, from London, begs leave to inform the ladies and gentlemen of New York and the public in general that he has opened a Music Store, at No. 38 Maiden lane, two doors from Queens st. . . . He has in preparation some of the NEWEST SONGS, now singing with the greatest applause, one of which he intends publishing every week—the first song will be ready for delivery in a few days, containing three folio pages of music, adapted to the piano forte, Violin, German Flute, and Guitar, price one shilling.

On July 13, Harrison had advertised in *The weekly museum*, New York, that he intended to publish "those much admired songs of Mr. Dibdin's, The rara avis, Roses and lilies, Virtue, and The lamplighter." Also, "those admired variations of Rosline Castle and Malbrouk, with a few favorite songs, to form one handsome volume folio with 30 pages of music intended as an entertaining set of lessons for the above instruments."

And on August 14, he informed the public

That two of his songs are now ready for delivery . . . and will be continued every week, to be ready for delivery every Monday morning.

*SONGS SET FOR THE VOICE AND HARPSICHORD, or pianoforte, etc. by William Selby.
See Apollo or the Muse's musical compositions.

THE FAVORITE SONGS from the last new opera called the *Pirates*.
Composed by S. Storace. Price one dollar. Philadelphia, Printed at Carr & cos. Musical repository, 136 High st. Where may be had all the newest music reprinted from European publications. Likewise and [!] elegant assortment of piano fortes, guittars, flutes, violins, and other musical articles of superior quality [1793] 16 p. 32 cm.
Title-page; music, p. (2)–(16). P. (2) is verso of t.-p.

Contents:

p. (2)–(4) Lullaby.
(5) Ah can I cease to love her.
(6)–(7) The shipwreck'd seamans ghost.
(8)–(9) The Scotch air in the comic opera of the Pirates.
(10)–(12) The capture.
(13)–(16) The jealous don.   HFB

Advertised in August, 1793, as "printed and sold at Carr & Co's Musical Repository, No. 136 High street." It is further remarked that

The principal beauties in this very favorite opera, now performing in London with the greatest applause, are comprised in this collection.

THE FAVORITE SONGS in the opera of [The haunted tower]. Price [5/7½].
Printed for B. Carr and sold at his Musical repositorys in New York and Philadelphia. And by I. Carr, Baltimore [1795–96] 6, 3 p. 33 cm.

Name of opera and price figures are handwritten.
Title-page; with elaborate wreath encircling title and imprint, bow at bottom, head in sunburst at top.

[401]

Contents:

p. 2 Tho' pity I cannot deny [Pleyel].
3 My native land [Storace].
4–5 Whither my love [Paisiello].
6 I sigh for the girl I adore [Hook].
[1]–3 Spirit of my sainted sire [Storace].

The songs by Pleyel and Paisiello are found in the score of *The haunted tower*. The song by Hook does not appear there.
The final pages, [1]–3, *Spirit of my sainted sire*, probably form a separate issue, bound in.

The haunted tower by Stephen Storace, with accompaniments by Victor Pelissier was first performed in New York, January 9, 1795.　　　ABHu

———— The same as preceding. (Title-page and p. 2–3 only)　　　JFD

THE FAVORITE SONGS SUNG AT VAUXHALL GARDENS. 179[4]. Composed by Mr. Hook. Price three quarters of a dollar. Printed and sold by B. Carr at his Musical repositorys, Market street, Philadelphia and William street, New York, and by I. Carr, Market street, Baltimore [1794–95] 10 p. 33 cm.

At head of title, elaborate spray of roses, also around "Price [　]" decorative sprays. In date on t.-p., figure "4" is in ink.

Contents:

p. 2–3 The Caledonian laddy.
4–5 Pretty Poll & Honest Jack.
6 Lucy Gray of Allendale.
7 I sigh for the girl I adore.
8–9 In the land of Hibernia.
10 Hark Eliza's tuneful voice.

McD–W and NN (complete); MWA and MdHi (lack p. 5–6)

This is presumably the collection advertised in January, 1795, by B. Carr, Philadelphia as "just published . . . a collection of the songs sung this last season at Vauxhall Gardens."
Possibly issued late in 1794.

*THE FAVORITE SONGS SUNG IN THE SHIPWRECK, arranged for the piano forte.

Thus advertised in February, 1799, as "just published by George Gilfert, at his musical store, No. 177 Broadway." The libretto of *The shipwreck* was written by Samuel James Arnold, the music composed by Dr. Samuel Arnold (1796).

[A VOLUME OF SONGS, ETC. (ms.) composed or copied by Francis Hopkinson. 1759–60] 2 p. l., 206 p. 24 x 30 cm.

On outside cover: Songs.
On first p. l., ms. note in ink, "Francis Hopkinson his Book," apparently not in Hopkinson's handwriting.
On second p. l., index, apparently in his own hand.
Of his own compositions (indicated by the initials "F. H." in upper left hand corner) there are the following:

[402]

My days have been so wondrous free, p. 63.—The garland, p. 111.—Oh come to Mason borough's grove, p. 163.—With pleasure have I past my days, p. 169. The 23ᵈ Psalm, p. 179.—An anthem from the 114ᵗʰ Psalm, p. 180–181.

This book was formerly in the possession of Mrs. Florence Scovel Shinn of New York, a descendant of Francis Hopkinson.   DLC

FOUR EXCELLENT NEW SONGS.   Called   Yankee   Doodle,   Death   of General Wolfe, Nancy Dawson, Guardian angels.   New York, Printed and sold by John Reid at his book and stationery store, No. 17 Water street. 1788.   8 p.   15 cm.

Title-page, with vignette of Mercury.
Words only.   Owned by Oscar Wegelin.

[FOUR SONGS FROM AN UNIDENTIFIED COLLECTION, ed. by B. Carr. New York, ca. 1795]   [4] p.   33 cm.

Song, pfte. acc.
Contents: The delights of wedded love, p. [1].—O 'tis love, p. [2].—The waxen doll, p. [3].—Dorothy Dump, p. [4].   Apparently these two leaves, without title-page, form a detached portion of a collection which may very probably have carried the familiar title of similar Carr issues—*The favorite songs in the opera of* [   ], the name of the opera being inserted in ink.   In this case it would seem to be *The children in the wood*, as all these songs are in some way connected with Samuel Arnold's opera of that name.   However, no complete copy of such issue has been located.
This hypothetical collection was presumably published by Carr in New York, ca. 1795.   *Cf.* imprint of *Dorothy Dump*, p. [4], and note *re* Hodgkinson's performance in *The children in the wood*.   NN

SEVEN SONGS FOR THE HARPSICHORD or forte piano.   The words and music composed by Francis Hopinkson.   Philadelphia, Publish'd & sold by J. Dobson; I. Aitken, Sculpᵗ   [1788]   2 p. l., 11, [1] p.   23 x 35 cm.

Title-page, verso blank.
On second p. l. (verso blank) Dedication: To His Excellency George Washington, Esquire . . . F. Hopkinson.   Philadelphia, Nov. 20, 1788.

The songs, with harpsichord or pfte. acc., are as follows:

p.   1 Song I [Come fair Rosina, come away]
    2 Song II [My love is gone to sea]
  3-4 Song III [Beneath a weeping willows shade]
    5 Song IV [Enraptur'd I gaze]
    6 Song V [See down Maria's blushing cheek]
  7-8 Song VI [O'er the hills far away]
9-10 Song VII Rondo.   [My gen'rous heart disdains]
   11 Song VIII [The trav'ler benighted and lost]

In vacant space at lower right hand corner of p. 11: For the remaining verses, see the printed songs.
On p. [12]: The songs.   [Words only]
At lower right hand corner of p. [12], following the text of Song VIII: N. B. This eighth song was added after the title page was engraved.
                                   DLC, Hopk., MB, McD-W

In McD–W copy, p. 1 is reversed, with verso blank instead of recto; p. [12] is lacking, and the second and third stanzas of Song VIII (otherwise not given) appear in ms. note pasted over the notation, "For the remaining verses, see the printed songs," in lower right-hand corner of p. 11.

The publication was thus advertised in the *Federal gazette*, Philadelphia, November 29, 1788:

> *New Music.* This day is published, and to be sold by Thomas Dobson at the Stone House in Second Street, between Chestnut and Market streets, A SET OF EIGHT SONGS. The words and music composed by the Honourable Francis Hopkinson.
>
> These songs are composed in an easy, familiar style, intended for young practitioners on the harpsichord or forte piano, and is the first work of this kind attempted in the United States. Price 7s 6.

In the dedication, after paying George Washington a high tribute and remarking that the songs are intended for "young Performers," F. Hopkinson writes:

> However small the reputation may be that I shall derive from this work, I cannot, I believe, be refused the credit of being the first native of the United States who has produced a musical composition.

It goes without saying that these words do not refer to the "Seven songs," as other extant compositions of Francis Hopkinson antedate them by thirty years. The songs were written, as was customary, without a separate system for the voice.

The words of the eight songs are to be found also among Francis Hopkinson's "Occasional poems," in v. III, p. 185–192 of his *Miscellaneous essays*. The words of songs VI, VII and VIII were printed in the *Federal gazette*, December 9, 1788; of Song VIII also, in the *Massachusetts magazine*, Boston, March, 1789, p. 186. The attractive "Rondo" (Song VII) is to be found in the appendix to Sonneck's book on *Francis Hopkinson . . . and James Lyon* (1905) where also a facsimile of George Washington's letter of acceptance and other interesting data are given.

[TWO SONGS] Sung by Mrs. Jordan in the Spoil'd child. Price 6d [n. p., n. d.] [2] p. 29½ cm.

Songs, pfte. acc.
Caption p. [2]: Act 2d.
First lines: Since then I'm doom'd (p. [1]). I am a brisk and sprightly lad (p. [2]).
Sonneck gives date, ca. 1800.   DLC

THE SONGSTER'S ASSISTANT containing a variety of the best songs, set to music in two parts. Most of the music never before published. By T. Swan. [Design] Suffield, Printed by Swan and Ely [n. d.] 36 p. 17 cm.

On verso of title-page: Index. [22 titles listed]
Songs, pfte. acc.
Contents:

p. 3–7 Hunting song. By Mr. Swan.
    8 The gentle shepherd. By Mr. Swan.
    9 The beauties of Spring.

[404]

p. 10–11 Lovely Spring. By Mr. Swan.
  11–13 The nymphs complaint. By Mr. Swan.
    14 The Shepherd's complaint. By Mr. Swan.
    15 Friendship. By Mr. Swan.
    16 The charms of Floremel.
  17–18 Silvia. By Mr. Clark.
  18–19 Freedom.
  20–21 Hunting song. By Swan.
  22–23 Rosy wine.
  23–24 Devonshire cut.
  24–25 Spring. By Mr. Swan.
  25–27 The happy wedding.
  27–28 The Dauphin.
  29–30 Strephon's farewel [!]. By Mr. Swan.
  30–31 The highland queen. By Swan.
  31–32 Advice to the fair. By Mr. Swan.
  33–34 The soldiers farewel [!]. By Mr. Swan.
  34–35 Faithless Damon.
  35–36 Capt. O'Blunder. By Swan.

The curious design consists of a canon for two voices by Swan, on a musical staff in form of a French horn, etc. Underneath we read "A. Ely, Sculpt."

CtY, MB, MWA

Sonneck adds: The little book contains twenty-two songs, the majority of them written by Swan. As Timothy Swan, who is better known as a psalmodist, was born in 1758, the undated "Songster's assistant" might have been published prior to 1800.

*THE SONGSTER'S MAGAZINE. Containing a choice collection of the most approved songs in the English language. Philadelphia: 1795.

SONNET I
  See [Morning] Sonnet I.

SONNET II
  See [Noon] Sonnet II.

SONNET III
  See [Evening] Sonnet III.

SONNET IV
  See [Night] Sonnet IV.

SONNET. For the fourteenth of October, 1793. When were entombed the Remains of his Excellency John Hancock, Esq., late Governor and Commander in Chief of the Commonwealth of Massachusetts. The music taken from an oratorio by the famous Graun, of Berlin. The lines written and adapted by Hans Gram, Organist of Brattle Street Church in Boston. [n. p., n. d.] [4] p. 14 x 21 cm.

Four-part mixed chorus. Open score.
First line: Columbia mourns, her pillars shake.
Published probably in 1793.

MB, MWA

[405]

SONNET TO TIME. Pleyel. [New York, Sold by I. and M. Paff, No. 127 Broadway, 1799–1803] [2] p. 33 cm.
At head of title: (No. 5) Ladies musical journal.
Song, pfte. acc.
First line: Capricious foe to human joy.
For supplied imprint *cf. Beauty.* A favorite sonnet . . . Pleyel. DLC

——— Time. [n. p., n. d.] p. 4. 31½ cm.
Song, pfte. acc.
First line same as preceding.
From some unidentified collection, probably ca. 1800. PHi

*SOPHIA OF BRABANT, or, the False friend.
This pantomime was to be performed for the first time at Philadelphia by the Old American Company at the Cedar Street Theatre, November 1, 1794 "with entirely new music, composed by Pelisier." [Dunlap and Claypoole's *American daily advertiser*, Philadelphia, of same date.]

SOPHRONIA.
(*In* The American musical miscellany. Northampton, 1798. p. 184–187)
Three-part chorus. Open score.
First line: Forbear my friends, forbear and ask no more. DLC (etc.)

*SOT POTPOURRI [!] with variations composed by Mr. Chateaudieu.
Was to be played at a concert in Baltimore, on July 13, 1796.

SOUTH CAROLINA.
See United States country *Dances,* p. 17.

*THE SPANISH BARBER, or, the Fruitless precaution, an opera in three acts, translated from the French of Beaumarchais, by G. Colemann, Esq. The music by Dr. Arnold and accompaniments by Carr, with additional airs by Messrs. Reinagle and Carr.
Thus advertised for performance at the New Theatre, Philadelphia, on July 7, 1794.
See Ah how hapless is the maiden.

*THE SPANISH CASTLE, or, the Knight of the Guadalquivir.
This "comic opera," the libretto by William Dunlap, composed by James Hewitt, had its first performance at New York, on December 5, 1800. According to Wegelin, Dunlap's libretto is extant in manuscript.
William Dunlap (1766–1839). Well known American painter, playwright (70 original plays and translations), theatrical manager, historian, founder and vice-president of the National Academy of Design, etc.

SPEED THE PLOUGH.
(*With* Ode to May, by James Fisin. New York, J. & M. Paff, 1799–1803)
Pfte. 2 hds.
Followed by directions for dancing. NN

——— The same.
See Country *Dances.*

[406]

SPENCERS FANCY.
See Evening amusement, p. 29.

THE SPINNING WHEEL.
(*In* The American musical miscellany.   Northampton, 1798.   p. 61–64)

Melody only, with accompanying text.
First line: To ease his heart and own his flame.   DLC (etc.)

SPIRIT OF MY SAINTED SIRE.   Sung by Hodgkinson.   Composed by Mr.
Storace.   Price 25 cents.   Printed by B. Carr at his Musical repository's in
New York & Philadelphia and by J. Carr, Baltimore [1795–96]   3 p.   33½ cm.

Song, pfte. acc.
First line same as title.
From *The haunted tower* by Stephen Storace, first performed in New York,
January 9, 1795.   John Hodgkinson was in the cast,
Sonneck dates this issue, ca. 1796.   ABHu, DLC, ES, JFD, LSL, NN

SPIRIT OF MY SAINTED SIRE.
(*In* The favorite songs in the opera of [The haunted tower, by S. Storace]
New York [1795–96]   p. 1–3   [following p. 6])

Song, pfte. acc.
First line same as title.   ABHu

*THE SPIRITS OF THE BLEST.
Song by Benjamin Carr.   Was to be sung by Miss Broadhurst at a concert in Philadelphia, April 11, 1799.   [*Aurora*, Philadelphia, April 10, 1799.]

THE SPOIL'D CHILD.   A farce in two acts.   As performed at the Theatre in
Boston.   First American edition.   Printed at Boston by Thomas Hall.
Sold at his office, Head of Water street.   1796.   28 p.   15½ cm.

Libretto.
Title-page; dramatis personae, p. [2]; text, p. [3]–28.   DLC, MWA

——— The same.
Printed at Boston, by Thomas Hall—Water street, for William P. Blake at
the Boston book store.   1796.   28, [3] p.   12 mo.   MH, MWA

Since both of the above are given as "First American editions," they must be
considered as variants of the same work.

SPORTING SONG.   From the Mysteries of the castle.   Sold at Carr's Musical
repository's, Philadelphia & N. York & by I. Carr, Baltimore.   Price 20
cents.   [1794–97]   [2] p.   32 cm.

Song, pfte. acc.
First line: Heigh lo! heigh lo!   The morning is up.
William Shield's *Mysteries of the castle* was first produced in 1795, but did
not reach America until May 12, 1798 (New York) and April 15, 1799
(Philadelphia).
This issue probably 1795–96.   RPJCB

[407]

SPRING.
(*In* The harmony of Maine, by S. Belcher, Boston, 1794. p. 63–64)
Four-part chorus. Open score.
First line: The scatt'red clouds are fled at last.
Same text as [The scatter'd clouds are fled at last] *q. v.*, but different setting.
CtY, DLC, ICN, MB, MHi, MWA, NN

SPRING, AN ODE. Words anon. Original.
(*In* The union harmony, by Oliver Holden. Boston, 1793. vol. 2, p. 10–11)
Three-part chorus. Open score.
First line: Old hoary Winter now has ceas'd his raging.
Composed by Oliver Holden.   DLC, ICN, MH, MHi MWA, NN

SPRING. By Mr. Swan.
(*In* The songster's assistant, ed. by T. Swan. Suffield [ca. 1800] p. 24–25)
Song, pfte. acc.
First line: Bright Sol is returning, the winter is o'er.   CtY, MB

SPRING WATER CRESSES.
(*In* The Philadelphia pocket companion for guittar or clarinett [Philadelphia. 1794] v. 1, p. 20–21)
Melody only, with accompanying text.
First line: When hoary frost hung on each thorn.   MWA

THE SPRING WITH SMILING FACE. Poor soldier.
(*In* A collection of favorite songs, divided into two books. Arr. by A. Reinagle. Philadelphia [1789?] bk. 1, p. 12)
Song, pfte. acc.
First line same as title.
Poor soldier, by William Shield.   CdeW, DLC, ES, Hopk

STAMITZ. Air.
(*With* Presidents march. Boston. P. A. von Hagen Jr. & co. [1798–99] p. [2])
Pfte. 2 hds.   MB

STERN'S [!] MARIA. Printet [!] for G. Willig, 165 Market street, Philadelphia [n. d.] p. 2. 31 cm.
Imprint at foot of page.
Song, pfte. acc.
First line: Twas near a thicket's calm retreat.
Composed by John Moulds.
Published possibly as early as 1795.   CtY, MWA, PU

STERNE'S MARIA. A pathetic song. Set to music by Mr. Moulds.
(*In* The musical repertory. Boston. [1796] No. II, p. 32).
Song, pfte. acc.
First line same as preceding.   DLC

———— Separate issue of preceding, ca. 1796.   JFD, MB, NN, NRU–Mus

[408]

STERNE'S MARIA.
(*In* The American musical miscellany. Northampton, 1798. p. 81–82)

Melody only, with accompany text.
First line same as preceding. DLC (etc.)

*STERNE'S MARIA, or the Vintage.
This opera in two acts (libretto by William Dunlap, composed by Victor Pelissier) had several performances in New York, the first occuring on January 14, 1799. No contemporary issues of its music have survived, but fortunately there are available three numbers from the opera in *Pelissier's Columbian melodies*, Philadelphia, °1811. These three excerpts are as follows: "I laugh I sing," sung by Mrs. Oldmixon; "Ah why on Quebec's bloody plain," sung by Mr. Tyler; and "Hope gentle hope," duet sung by Mr. Tyler and Mrs. Oldmixon.

According to Wegelin, Dunlap's libretto is extant in manuscript.

STILL THE LARK FINDS REPOSE. A favourite rondo. Sung by Miss Phillips.
(*In* Young's vocal and instrumental musical miscellany. Philadelphia [1793–95] p. 11–13)

Song, pfte. acc. Arr. for German flute, p. 13.
First line same as title.
In No. 2, 1793.
From *The Spanish rivals*, by Thomas Linley, the Elder.
DLC, HFB, Hopk.

STILL THE LARK FINDS REPOSE. Linley [n. p., n. d.] (14)–(16) p. 32½ cm.

Song, pfte. acc. Three staves.
First line same as title.
Possibly a Carr imprint 179–. *cf. *Elegant extracts.* PHi

Advertised also in November, 1798, as "just published" by "George Gilbert, at his Music Store, 177 Broadway, Apollo's Head," New York. This issue has not been located.

STILL TOSS'D TEMPESTUOUS ON THE SEA OF LIFE. The music by Mr. Labarte. Printed by G. Willig, No. 185 Market street. Philadelphia [1798–1804] 1 l. 31½ cm.

Song, pfte. acc.
First line same as title. MWA

THE STOLEN KISS. Composed by Mr. W. Wilson. New York, Printed for Mrs. Howe, No. 320 Pearl street, Importer of all kinds of musical instruments. Price 25 cents. [n. d.] [2] p. 32½ cm.

Song, pfte. acc.
First line: Tell me Maria, tell me true.
Published possibly as early as 1799. McD–W

STONEY POINT.
See Evening amusement [1796], p. 14.

———— The same.
See Compleat tutor for the fife. . . . p. 21.

LA STORACE.
See Evening amusement, p. 27.   Lacking in DLC copy.

THE STORM.
(*In* The American musical miscellany.   Northampton, 1798.   p. 52–55)
Melody only, with accompanying text.
First line: Cease rude Boreas.   DLC (etc.)

[THE STORM IS O'ER] Song in Selima and Azor.
(*In* The universal asylum.   Philadelphia, May, 1790.   p. 319–320)
Song, pfte. acc.
Title from first line.
Selima and Azor, by T. Linley, adapted from *Zémire et Azor* by André
E. M. Grétry.   DLC (etc.)

*THE STORM, OR THE AMERICAN SYREN: being a collection of the newest
and most approved songs.   Williamsburg: Printed by William Rind, and sold
by Edward Cumins, at the New Printing-Office.   1773.

Advertised in the *Virginia gazette*, Williamsburg, February 11, 1773, as
"just published . . . Price one pistareen."

STOUR LODGE.
(*In* The gentleman's amusement, ed. by R. Shaw.   Philadelphia [1794–96]
p. 9)

Flute (or violin).   Single staff.   Followed by directions for dancing.
In No. 1, April 1, 1794.   DLC, PHi

THE STRANGER.
See Country *Dances*.

TWO FAVOURITE STRATHPEY REELS introduced by Mr. Francis in the
Caledonian frolick.
(*In* The gentleman's amusement, ed. by R. Shaw.   Philadelphia [1794–96]
p. 3)

Flute (or violin).   Single staff.
In No. 1, April 1, 1794.   LC, PHi

——— The same as preceding.   On first page, numbered "3" of a detached
portion (p. 3–6) from above collection.   NN

THE STRAW BONNET.   Composed by Mrs. Pownall.
(*In* A collection of new & favorite songs.   [A] Philadelphia [ca. 1800] p.
[98]–[99] numbered 13–14)

Song, pfte. acc.
First line: When faries [!] are lighted by nights silver queen.   HFB

——— The same as preceding.
(*In* Six songs of Mrs. Pownall and J. Hewitt.   New York [1794] p. 13–14) ES

——— Separate issue from this collection, ca. 1794.   ES

[410]

THE STREAMLET. A favorite new song in the Woodman. Composed by W. Sheild [!]
(*In* A collection of favorite songs, arr. by A. Reinagle. Philadelphia [1789?] p. 9)

Song, pfte. acc.
First line: The streamlet that flow'd round her cot.   DLC

THE STREAMLET. A favorite new song in the opera of the Woodman.
(*In* Young's vocal and instrumental musical miscellany. Philadelphia [1793–95] p. 56)

Song, pfte. acc.
First line same as preceding.
In No. 7, ca. 1794.   DLC

THE STREAMLET THAT FLOW'D ROUND HER COT.
(*In* Elegant extracts for the German flute or violin. Baltimore [1794] bk. 1, p. 9)

Melody only, flute or violin, with accompanying text.
First line same as title.   DLC, NN

[THE STREAMLET THAT FLOW'D ROUND HER COT] Sung by Mr. Marshall in the Woodman.
(*In* The gentleman's amusement, ed. by R. Shaw. Philadelphia [1794–96] p. 25)

Melody only, flute (or violin) with accompanying text.
Title from first line.
In No. 3, 1794.   DLC, PHi

———— The same as preceding. On first page of separate sheet (p. 25–26) detached from original collection, 1794.   NN

Mr. Marshall sang in the first Philadelphia performance of William Shield's opera *The woodman*, June 18, 1794.

THE STREAMLET. New York, Printed & sold at J. Hewitt's Musical repository, No. 131 William street. Sold also by B. Carr, Philadelphia & J. Carr, Baltimore. Price 12 cents. [1797–99] 1 l. 32½ cm.

Song, pfte. acc.
First line same as preceding.   DLC, JFD, LSL, NN, PP–K, RPJCB

———— The same as preceding.
(*In* A collection of new & favorite songs. [A] Philadelphia [ca. 1800] p. [171])   HFB

THE STREAMLET THAT FLOW'D ROUND HER COT.
(*In* The American musical miscellany. Northampton, 1798. p. 181–182)

Melody only, with accompanying text.
First line same as title.   DLC (etc.)

*THE STREAMLET.
(*In* The musical repertory. Boston. [1799] No. VI)

No. VI, advertised August 31, 1799, as "just published" and containing *The streamlet*, has never been located.

STREPHON'S FAREWEL [!] By Mr. Swan.
(*In* The songster's assistant, ed. by T. Swan. Suffield [ca. 1800] p. 29-30
Song, pfte. acc.
First line: O! how shall I in language weak.   CtY, MI

STREW THE RUDE CROSSES OF LIFE O'ER WITH FLOWERS. *A*
favorite song. Sung at Vaux Hall Gardens. Composed by Mr. Hook
New York, Printed & sold by G. Gilfert, No. 177 Broadway [1797] [2] p
31½ cm.

Song, pfte. acc.
First line: Thro' life's rugged voyage each mortal must sail.   MWA

Advertised in March, 1797, among other "New songs for the Piano Forte"
as "just published by G. Gilfert at his Musical Magazine, No. 177 Broadway," New York.

STREW THE SWEET ROSES OF PLEASURE BETWEEN.
(*In* The American musical miscellany. Northampton, 1798.   p. 271-273)

Melody and bass, with accompanying text.
First line: If life's a rough path as the sages have said.   DLC (etc.)

STRONG THE BREEZE IS BLOWING.
See Fresh and strong the breeze is blowing.

A STRUGGLE FOR FREEDOM. Alternative title of *Slaves in Algiers.*

SUCCESS TO ADMIRAL NELSON. Sung by Mr. Dibdin, Junr in the musical
entertainment the Mouth of the Nile. New York, Printed & sold by G.
Gilfert, N⁰ 177 Broadway
(*In* [The mouth of the Nile, by T. Attwood. New York, ca. 1799] p. 14-15)

Below imprint: T. Attwood.
Song, pfte. acc.
First line: Now listen my Honeys.   NRU-Mus

SUCH PURE DELIGHT. Taken from the Highland reel.
(*In* Young's vocal and instrumental musical miscellany. Philadelphia
[1793-95] p. 14-15)

Song, pfte. acc.
First line same as title.
The highland reel, by William Shield.
In No. 2, 1793.   DLC, HFB, Hopk.

SUITE BY DAVID MORITZ MICHAEL.
For wind instruments (two clarinets, two horns, one bassoon). MS. parts
only. The first clarinet part bears the remark: D. M. M. Bey einer Quelle
zu blasen.

SUITE I

Pars. I. (in E flat maj.) consists of Allegro. Andante. Menuett. Presto.
Pars. II. (in B flat maj.): Pastorale. Menuett. Arioso. Presto.
Pars. III. (in E flat maj.): Allegro moderato. Menuett. Trio Andante.
Menuett da capo. Adagio. Presto. Moderato.

An "Introductio" precedes the three *partitas*, which means that they were suites within a suite.
In the Archives of the Moravian Church, Bethlehem, Pa.

*SUMMER, a pastorale song by Raynor Taylor.
Was to be sung in "Taylor's musical performance ... The whole of the music original and composed by Mr. Taylor," at Annapolis, on February 28, 1793.

"The favorite song of 'Summer'" was advertised in February, 1798, as "Republished ... by B. Carr, at his Repository, Market street" [Philadelphia] "with many others of the same author; ... to be had as above, and of J. Carr, Baltimore and J. Hewitt, New York."

SUNG BY MISS BROADHURST in the opera of Robin Hood.
See [I travers'd Judah's barren sand]

SUNG BY MISS BROADHURST in the Prisoner.
See [When the men a courting came]

SUNG BY MISS BROADHURST, Mrs. Oldmixon & Mr. Marshall in the Critic.
See Mock Italian trio.

SUNG BY MISS HARPER.
See [Sweet transports gentle wishes go]

SUNG BY MISS SOLOMONS in the character of Tom Thumb.
See [That pettyfogging Grizzle]

SUNG BY MISS SOLOMONS in the Prisoner.
See [Tears that exhale]

SUNG BY MR. BATES in Tom Thumb the Great.
See [We kings who are in our senses]

SUNG BY MR. CARR in the opera of the Haunted tower.
See [My native land]

SUNG BY MR. DARLEY in No song no supper.
See [How happily my life I led]

SUNG BY MR. FRANCIS in the Haunted tower.
See [Now all in preparation]

SUNG BY MR. INCLEDON in the new opera called Sprigs of laurel.
See [O come sweet Mary come to me]

SUNG BY MR. MARSHALL in the Woodman.
See [The streamlet that flow'd round her cot]

SUNG BY MR. MARSHALL in the Quaker.
See [I lock'd up all my treasure]

SUNG BY MRS. HODGKINSON in No song no supper.
See [Across the downs this morning]

SUNG BY MRS. HODGKINSON in the Archers.
See [There liv'd in Altdorf city fair]

SUNG BY MRS. MARSHALL in the comedy of She wou'd and she wou'd no**
See [Ye chearful virgins]

SUNG BY MRS. MARSHALL in the Highland reel.
See [Tho' I am now a very little lad]

SUNG BY MRS. MARSHALL in the Purse.
See [When a little merry he]

SUNG BY MRS. MARSHALL in the Spoil'd child.
See [I am a brisk and sprightly lad]

SUNG BY MRS. MYRTER in the Farmer.
See [Send him to me]

SUNG BY MRS. OLDMIXON in the opera of No song no supper.
See [Across the downs this morning]

SUNG BY MRS. OLDMIXON in the Noble peasant.
See [When scorching suns]

SUNG BY MRS. OLDMIXON in the Prize.
See [O dear delightful skill]

SUNG BY MRS. OLDMIXON in the Purse, or Benevolent tar.
See [How sweet when the silver moon is blinking]

SUNG BY MRS. SHAW in the opera of No song no supper.
See [Go George I can't endure you]

SUNG BY MRS. WARRELL at the New theatre.
See Somebody.

SUNG BY MRS. WARRELL in the Haunted tower.
See [Tho' pity I cannot deny]

SUNG BY MRS. WARRELL in the opera of Robin Hood.
See [The trump of fame]

SWEET ARE THE BANKS. A favorite canzonet. Composed by Dr. G. K.
Jackson. Printed for the Author. Copyright secured.
(*In* New miscellaneous musical work, by Dr. G. K. Jackson [n. p., ca. 1800]
p. 5–7)

Duet, pfte. acc. Three staves.
First line same as title.   DLC, MWA

SWEET AS SUMMERS FRAGRANT GALE. In the new opera the Cherokkee [!]
Composed by Mozzart [!] New York, Printed at G. Gilfert & cos.
Musical magazine, No. 209 Broadway. Where may be had an elegant assortement [!] of piano fortes, flutes, violins and other musical articles of
superior quality [1795] 1 l. 34½ cm.

Song, pfte. acc.
First line same as title.
The Cherokee, by Stephen Storace.
Probably an interpolation.   JFD, NRU–Mus

[414]

WEET BABES IN THE WOOD. A ballad. Founded on the well known legend. Price 25 cents. Printed and sold at B. Carr's Musical repository, Philadelphia; J. Hewitt's, New York and J. Carr's, Baltimore [1798–99] [2] p. 32½ cm.

Song, pfte. acc. Arr. for flute and for "guittar": p. [2].
First line same as title.   LSL, MWA, NN, NRU–Mus (torn)

WEET CHARITY. Printed at B. Carr's Musical repositories, New York & Philadelphia & J. Carr's, Baltimore (Price 12 cents) [1795–96] 1 l. 30½ cm.

Song, pfte. acc.
First line: In tatter'd weed from town to town.   NN

WEET ECHO. For the voice, violin and German flute.
(*In* The American musical magazine, New Haven, 1786. p. 17–18)

At head of title: An air.
Melody only. Instrumental parts cued in.
First line: Sweet echo, sweetest nymph that liv'st unseen.
From *Comus*, by Thomas A. Arne.   CtY, ICN, MBJ

WEET GIRL BY THE LIGHT OF THE MOON. [New York, Sold at I. and M. Paff's music store, No. 127 Broadway, 1799–1803] [2] p. 32 cm.

At head of title: No. 2 Ladies musical journal.
Imprint supplied from *Ladies musical journal.*
Song, pfte. acc.
First line: Twas a beautiful night.
Composed by James Hook.   DLC

SWEET GIRL BY THE LIGHT OF THE MOON. A favorite new song. Cents 25. [n. p., ca. 1800] [2] p. 32½ cm.

Song, pfte. acc.
First line same as preceding.   DLC

SWEET IS THE BALMY BREATH OF SPRING. (*In* Nine new songs, by I. B. Gauline. Philadelphia [ca. 1800] p. 11–12)

Song, pfte. acc.
First line same as title.
I. B. Gauline; John B. Gauline.   ES, MdHi

SWEET LAVENDER. Sung by Miss Broadhurst at Vauxhall. (*In* Elegant extracts for the German flute or violin. Philadelphia [1798] bk. 3, p. 6–7)

Melody only, flute or violin, with accompanying text.
First line: How happy was of late each morn.   DLC, NN

SWEET LILLIES OF THE VALLEY. Sung with great applause at Vauxhall Gardens. Composed by Mr. Hook. Price 20 cents. Philadelphia, Printed for Carr & co. at their Musical repository, No. 136 High street. Where may be had all the newest music, reprinted from European publications. Likewise an elegant assortment of piano fortes, guittars, flutes, violins, and othe musical articles of superior quality. [1793] [2] p. 33 cm.

Song, pfte. acc. Arr. for the "guittar," p. [2].
First line: O'er barren hills and flow'ry dales.

ABHu, DLC, ES, HFB, Hopk., JFD, LSL, MW.

In certain copies, e. g., one at DLC, "20" has been changed to "25" in pric given.

SWEET LILLIES OF THE VALLEY.
(In Elegant extracts for the German flute or violin. Baltimore [1794] bk 1, p. 14–15)

Melody only, flute or violin, with accompanying text.
First line same as preceding. DLC (lacks p. 15), NI

SWEET LILLIES OF THE VALLEY. Composed by Mr. Hook. New York Printed and sold by G. Gilfert & co. [1794–96] [2] p. 31½ cm.

Song, pfte. acc. Arr. for "guittar," p. [2].
First line same as preceding. MWA

SWEET LILLIES OF THE VALLEY.
(In The American musical miscellany. Northampton, 1798. p. 168–170)

Melody only, with accompanying text.
First line same as preceding. DLC (etc.)

Also advertised in March, 1795, as "published and to be had at G. Willig's Musica Magazine, No. 165 Market street," Philadelphia.
No copy of this issue has been found.

SWEET LITTLE BARBARA. A favorite duett in the Iron chest. Composed by Storace. Price 32 cents. Printed and sold at B. Carr's Musical repository, Philadelphia; J. Carr's Baltimore & J. Hewitt's New York [1799] 3 p. 32½ cm.

Duet, pfte. acc. (partly three staves).
First line same as title. ABHu, ICN, LSL, McD–W, NN

Advertised in March, 1799, as to be published shortly by "Benjamin Carr," Philadelphia.

THE SWEET LITTLE BIRD. The favorite echo song. Boston, Printed & sold at P. A. von Hagen's imported piano forte warehouse, No. 3 Cornhill. Sold also by G. Gilfert, New York [ca. 1800] [2] p. 33 cm.

Song, pfte. acc.
First line: 'Twas in May summer's queen.
Published possibly as early as 1799. DLC, N, RPJCB

*SWEET LITTLE COTTAGE.
(In The musical repertory. Boston [1799] No. VI)

No. VI, advertised August 31, 1799, as "just published" has never been located.

[416]

HE SWEET LITTLE GIRL OF THE LAKES. Sung by Master Broadhust [!] at the New Royal circus. Composed by W. Ware. New York, Published by I. and M. Paff, No. 127 Broadway [1799–1803] 2 p. 33 cm.

Song, pfte. acc.
First line: The breezes of morn shake the dew from the thorn.

DLC, RPJCB

HE SWEET LITTLE GIRL THAT I LOVE.
(In Elegant extracts for the German flute or violin. Baltimore [1794] bk. 1, p. 18–19)

Melody only, flute or violin, with accompanying text.
First line: My friends all declare.
Composed by James Hook.

DLC, NN

HE SWEET LITTLE GIRL THAT I LOVE. A favorite song. Price 20 cents. Printed and sold at B. Carr's Musical repositories in New York and Philadelphia and J. Carr, Baltimor [!] [1796] [2] p. 33 cm.

Song, pfte. acc. Arr. for "guittar," p. [2].
First line same as preceding.

DLC, JFD, McD–W, MH, MWA, NN, RPJCB

Advertised in March, 1796, among "new editions of . . . favorite songs some of which never before published in America" as published "at Carr's Musical Repository, William Street," New York.

THE SWEET LITTLE GIRL THAT I LOVE. A favorite song set to music by Mr. James Hook. [n. p., n. d.] p. 48. 32½ cm.

Song, pfte. acc.
First line same as preceding.
Evidently a reprint from The musical repertory, Boston [1796–97] No. III, p. 48.

LSL

THE SWEET LITTLE GIRL THAT I LOVE.
(In The American musical miscellany. Northampton, 1798. p. 106–107)

Melody only, with accompanying text.
First line same as preceding.

DLC (etc.)

SWEET LOVE I'LL MARRY THEE. A favorite Scotch song. Composed by Mr. Hook. New York, Printed for G. Gilfert & co. at their Musical magazine, No. 191 Broadway [1794–95] [2] p. 33½ cm.

Song, pfte. acc.
First line: When Donald first came wooing me.

JFD, RPJCB

Advertised in March, 1795, as "published and to be had of G. Gilfert & Co. at their Musical Magazine, No. 121 Broadway," New York. "121" is undoubtedly a misprint for "191."

SWEET MARTINDALE. Sung by Mr. Darley, junr at Vauxhall.
(In Elegant extracts for the German flute or violin. Philadelphia [1798] bk. 3, p. 16)

Melody only, flute or violin, with accompanying text.
First line: In Martindale a village gay.

DLC, NN

[417]

SWEET MYRA OF THE VALE. Sung by Mr. Tyler with great applause. Composed by J. Hewitt. New York, Printed & sold at J. Hewitt's Music repository, No. 23 Maiden Lane [1799–1800]   [2] p.   33 cm.

Song, pfte, acc.   Arr. for the "guittar," p. [2].
First line: When first I viewed the charming maid.
Sung by Mr. Tyler at Columbia Garden, New York, June 24, 1799.   DL

———— The same as preceding.
(*In* A collection of new & favorite songs. [A] Philadelphia [ca. 180€
p. [50]–[51])   HF]

SWEET NAN OF HAMPTON GREEN. An admired song. Composed b
Mr. Hook.
(*In* Young's vocal and instrumental musical miscellany. Philadelphi
[1793–95]   p. 63)

Song, pfte. acc., followed by arr. for guitar.
First line: With care I search'd the village round.
In No. 8, 1795.   DL(

———— Separate issue of preceding, but with page number changed to "2".
Otherwise identical.

Imprint to be supplied from similar issue of *Young Lubin was a shepherd bo*
"New York, Published by I. Young & Co.," apparently from some unidenti
fied collection published by John Young and probably dated 1792–93. ES

For other titles in this unidentified collection, *cf.* "Young Lubin was
shepherd boy."

SWEET NAN OF HAMPTON GREEN. [Philadelphia] Publisht [!] by G
Willig, where may be had a great variety of the newest vocal and instru
mental music. & &. [179–] [2] p. 32½ cm.

Song, pfte. acc.   Arr for guitar, p. 2.
First line same as preceding.   DLC, ES, PP–K, PU

Also advertised in April, 1795, as "published and to be had of G. Gilfert &
Co. at their Musical Magazine, No. 121 Broadway," New York. Nc
copy of this issue has been located.

SWEET PASSION OF LOVE. Composed by Dr. Arne. New York, Printed
& sold by G. Gilfert & co., No. 209 Broadway [1795] 1 l. 31½ cm.

Song, pfte. acc.
First line: This cold flinty heart it is you who have warm'd.
Title forms last line of each stanza.
Not by Dr. Arne as stated in title, but from *Cymon* by Michael Arne.
JFD, MWA, NRU–Mus, RPJCB

SWEET PASSION OF LOVE. From Cymon. Michael Arne. [n. p., n. d.]
p. (24)–(25). 32 cm.

Song, pfte. acc.
First line same as preceding.
Evidently a Carr imprint, 179–. *cf.* **Elegant extracts* . . .   LSL

[418]

WEET PASSION OF LOVE. Boston, printed & sold at P. A. von Hagen's imported piano forte warehouse, No. 3 Cornhill [ca. 1800] 1 l. 32 cm.

Song, pfte. acc.
First line same as preceding.
Published possibly as early as 1799.   JFD, LSL, MB, RPJCB

WEET POLL OF PLYMOUTH.
(*In* A collection of favorite songs, divided into two books. Arr. by A. Reinagle. Philadelphia [1789?] bk. 2, p. 10–11)

Song, pfte. acc.
First line: Sweet Poll of Plymouth was my dear.
From *The positive man*, by Michael Arne.   CdeW, DLC, PU

WEET POLL OF PLYMOUTH. Price 25 cents. Printed and sold at B. Carr's Musical repositories in Philadelphia & New York & J. Carr's, Baltimore [1796] [2] p. 32½ cm.

Song, pfte. acc. Arr. for "guittar," p. [2].
First line same as preceding.   LSL

Advertised in March, 1796, as published "at Carr's Musical Repository, William street," New York.

WEET ROSY SLEEP. Sung by Mrs. Hodgkinson in the School for greybeard's. Composed by B. Carr. Price 25 cents. [n. p., n. d.] 4 p. 33½ cm.

Song, pfte. acc. Arr. for "guittar" and for two flutes, p. 4.
First line: Sweet rosy sleep, oh! do not fly.
Probably published in New York, ca. 1795, as Mrs. Hodgkinson appeared in the cast for the first New York performance of *The school for greybeards*, April 20, 1795.   DLC, ES, MWA, NN

SWEET TRANSPORTS, GENTLE WISHES GO] Sung by Miss Harper.
(*In* Young's vocal and instrumental musical miscellany. Philadelphia [1793–95] p. 25)

Song, pfte. acc.
Title from first line.
From *Rosina*, by William Shield.
In No. 3, 1793.   DLC, Hopk.

SWEET TRANSPORTS. Sung in the opera of Rosina. New York, Printed & sold at J. Hewitt's Musical repository, No. 131 William street. Pr. 12½ cts. [1797–99] 1 l. 32½ cm.

Song, pfte. acc.
First line same as preceding.   MB, McD–W, NN

———— The same as preceding.
(*In* A collection of new & favorite songs. [A] Philadelphia [ca. 1800] p. [175])   HFB

SYLVAN. The shepherd twain.
See Silvan, the shepherd swain.

[419]

SYLVIA.
(*In* [Unidentified collection (beginning with "A lesson")] Boston [?] ca. 180
p. 4)
Song, pfte. acc.
First line: When from my Sylvia I remove. MI

SYLVIA.   A favorite canzonett.   Composed by T. Billington.
(*In* A collection of favorite songs, arr. by A. Reinagle.   Philadelphia [1789
p. 10).
Song, pfte. acc.
First line: Sylvia cou'd you know the passion.
In lower margin of p. 10: J. Aitken sculpt. DL

*SYMPHONY BY GIOVANNI GUALDO.
A "new symphony after the present taste, composed by Mr. Gualdo," we
to be played at a concert "directed by Mr. Gualdo after the Italian method,
at Philadelphia, on November 16, 1769.

*SYMPHONY BY RAYNOR TAYLOR.
A "new symphony composed by R. Taylor, of Philadelphia, to the gran
gala of song, dance and pantomime . . . called the Birthday, or Rural fete,
was to be played at the Federal Street Theatre, Boston, on February 2:
1797.   This was, of course, an overture, in accord with the terminology c
the period (Sonneck).

*A SYNOPSIS OF THE CONCERT to be performed to-morrow evening fo
the benefit of Mrs. Pownall with the words of the anthems, songs etc.
Thus advertised in the *City gazette*, Charleston, S. C., March 24, 1796, a
"published this morning and for sale, at the Columbian Herald Printin
Office . . . "
The concert consisted of selections from Händel's works, overtures, concerto
for different instruments, etc., a combination frequently styled "Oratorio
both in Europe and America.

THE SYREN: a choice collection of sea, hunting and other songs.   Philadelphia
Printed for Mathew Carey, No. 118 High Street [1800]   72 p., front
17 cm.
Words only. DLC, NN, RP
NN and RPB copies bound with *The sailor's medley*, Philadelphia, 1800.

THE SYREN, or Vocal enchantress, being a collection of the newest and mos
admired miscellaneous—pathetic and passionate—anacreontic and jovial,—
comic, ingenious, and witty,—sea, hunting and Masonic songs.   Selectec
from the most approved sentimental, humorous and ingenious publications
including all the best songs of Dibdin, Edwin, &c.   Wilmington, Printec
[by Bonsal & Niles] for and sold by James Wilson, bookseller and stationer
No. 5, High street, opposite the upper Market-house.   1797.   38, 36, 24
48, 28, [6] p.   12 mo. MH, RPB

TAKE OH! TAKE THOSE LIPS AWAY.   From Shakespear's Merchant o
Venice.   Composed by B. Carr.   Philadelphia, Printed & sold by Carr & co.
(*In* Four ballads by B. Carr.   Philadelphia [1794]   p. 4–5)
Song, pfte. acc.   Three staves.
First line same as title. DLC

[420]

AL LAL LA.
See Fal la la.

ALACOY. An Indian ballad as sung in the Algerine corsair. New York, Printed & sold at J. Hewitts Musical repository, No. 23 Maiden Lane. Sold also by B. Carr, Philadelphia & J. Carr, Baltimore. Price 25 cents [1799–1800] [2] p. 32 cm.

Song, pfte. acc. Arr. for flute: p. [2].
First line: When de thunder passa, passoo.
Algerine Corsair, by James Sanderson.   NN

—— The same as preceding.
(*In* A collection of new & favorite songs. [A] Philadelphia [ca. 1800] p. [116]–[117])   HFB

ALLY HO. Sung by Mrs. Pownall. New York, Printed & sold by G. Gilfert & co., No. 209 Broadway [1795] [2] p. 33 cm.

Song, pfte. acc.
First line: Ye sportsmen draw near.   JFD

This popular song was sung by Mrs. Pownall with the Old American Company at the Southwark Theatre in Philadelphia, January 4, 1793; at her benefits in New York, June 11, 1793, February 6, 1794, and September 4, 1794; and at her benefit in Boston, July 22, 1794.

TAMMANY, OR, THE INDIAN CHIEF.

The libretto to this "serious opera" was written by Ann Julia Hatton and the music composed by James Hewitt. The first performance, under the auspices of the Tammany Society, was thus advertised for March 3, 1794, New York:

An opera (a new piece, never before performed, written by a lady of this city) called Tammany, or the Indian chief. The prologue by Mr. Hodgkinson—the epilogue by Mr. Martin. The overture and accompanyments composed by Mr. Hewitt . . .

The second performance, March 6, was announced on March 5, with the N. B. Books with the words of the songs, will be sold at the doors—Price one shilling.

This refers to

THE SONGS OF TAMMANY, or the Indian chief. A serious opera. By Ann Julia Hatton. To be had at the Printing Office of John Harrison, No. 3 Peck Slip and of Mr. Faulkner, at the box office of the theatre. (Price one shilling.) 1794. 16 p. 12°. NHi (Two copies, one without title page)

Wegelin mentions, "In manuscript. Tammany. An opera," but remarks, "No trace can be found of the play itself being published. The prologue to Tammany was published in a volume of poems by R. B. Davis. New York, 1807, p. 120–121."

In the *New York daily advertiser,* March 29, 1794, appeared:

Proposals for printing by subscription, the overture with the songs, chorus's, etc etc to Tammany as composed and adapted to the pianoforte by Mr. Hewitt.

The price to subscribers 12 s. each copy, 4 s. to be paid at the time subscribing, and one dollar on delivery of the book, to non-subscribers will be two dollars. Subscriptions received by James Harrison, No. 1◖ Maiden-lane.

Sonneck was unable to ascertain whether the overture, etc., were publishe◖ For a description of "Tammany," *see* his monograph on *Early America◖ operas* (Sammelbände d. Int. Mus. Ges. 1904–5).

The question has been raised whether a "Tammany quick step" publishe◖ by Hewitt early in the nineteenth century and presumably composed by hi: (since it is issued in connection with his "Grand march as performd [!] at tℎ funeral procession at the Wallabout, Long Island") might not be a part ◖ the original music of *Tammany*. If so, it is the only known surviving excerp◖ In the possession of Elliott Shapiro.

*TANBERRY HUZZA.
Advertised in March, 1797, as to be published "in a few days" by "G. Gilfe: at his Musical Magazine, No. 177 Broadway," New York.

Can this refer to *Tantivy hark forward huzza*?

TANTIVY HARK FORWARD HUZZA. The favorite hunting song. Sung b◖ Mrs. Iliff at Vax [!] Hall. Philadelphia, Printed for A. Reinagle; J. Aitkeɪ sculpt. [1789] [2] p. 31½ cm.

Imprint at foot of p. [2].
Song, pfte. acc.
First line: No pastime, no sport can with hunting compare.　　　CdeW, DL◖

―――― The same as preceding, but with pagination.
(*In* [A Collection of favorite songs, arr. by A. Reinagle. Philadelphiℎ 1789 (?)] p. 17–18)　　　　　　　　　　　　　　　　　　　　　　　E:

In CdeW and ES copies "Vax" has been changed (in type) to "Vaux."

As *Tantive back forward*, advertised in March, 1789, as "just published an◖ sold by Thomas Dobson, at the Stone House in Second Street," Philadelphiℎ among "songs and pieces arranged for the pianoforte or harpsichord by Alex ander Reinagle."

THE TARTAN PLAIDDIE. Scotch song. Sung by Miss Leary. Vauxhal◖ (*In* A collection of favorite songs, divided into two books. Arr. by A. Reinagle◖ Philadelphia [1789?] bk. 2, p. 6–7)

Song, pfte. acc.
First line: By moonlight on the green.　　　　　　　　　　　CdeW, DLC, Pℓ

THE TARTAN PLAIDY.
(*In* Young's vocal and instrumental musical miscellany. Philadelphiℎ [1793–95] p. 42)

Song, pfte. acc.
First line: The low land lads think they are fine.
In No. 5, 1793.　　　　　　　　　　　　　　　　　　　　　　DLC, Hopk

―――― Separate issue of preceding, ca. 1793.　　　　　　　　　　　PH:

THE TEAR. A favorite song. Compos'd by J. Hook. Sung by Mrs. Leaver at Vauxhall.
(*In* A collection of favorite songs, arr. by A. Reinagle. Philadelphia [1789?] p. 5–6)

Song, pfte. acc.
First line: My heart from my bosom wou'd fly.
In lower margin of p. 6: J. Aitken. Sculpt. DLC

THE TEAR. Price 25 cents. Printed and sold at B. Carr's Musical repositories in New York and Philadelphia & J. Carr, Baltimore [1796,] [2] p. 31½ cm.

Song, pfte. acc. Arr. for flute, p. [2].
First line: My heart from my bosom would fly. DLC, RPJCB

Advertised in March, 1796, as published "at Carr's Musical Repository, William Street," New York.
The tear was sometimes mistakenly attributed to Godian.

———— The same as preceding.
(*In* A collection of new & favorite songs. [A] Philadelphia [ca. 1800] p. [126]–[127]) HFB

THE TEAR. A favorite song. New York, Printed for G. Gilfert & co., at their Musical magazine, No. 177 Broadway. Where may be had a great variety of musical instruments and musick &c. [1796] 1 l. 31½ cm.

Song, pfte. acc.
First line same as preceding. DLC, MWA

THE TEAR. Boston, Printed & sold by P. A. von Hagen, Junior & cos. Musical magazine, No. 62 Newbury street [1798–99] 1 l. 29½ cm.

Song, pfte. acc.
First line same as preceding. McD–W, N, RPJCB

THE TEAR. [n. p., n. d.] p. 7. 31½ cm.

Song, pfte. acc.
First line same as preceding.
Published probably 179–. HFB, NBuG, PU

THE TEAR. Sung by Mrs. Merry in the new play the Count of Burgundy. Printed by G. Willig, Philadelphia [ca. 1800] 1 l. 33½ cm.

Imprint at foot of page.
Song, pfte. acc.
First line same as preceding.
The Count of Burgundy, by Kotzebue, was performed in New York, March 3, 1800. DLC, PP–K, RPJCB

[TEARS THAT EXHALE FROM THE SPRING OF GOOD NATURE] Sung by Miss Solomons in the Prisoner. Attwood.
(*In* The gentleman's amusement, ed. by R. Shaw. Philahelphia [1794–96] p. 60)

Melody only for flute (or violin) with accompanying text.
Title from first line.
In No. [8], 1796. DLC, PHi PP–K

[423]

TELL ME FAIREST, TELL ME TRUE. Composed by F. Kotzwara. New York, Printed & sold by G. Gilfert, No. 177 Broadway, Opposite the Oswego Market [1798] 2 p. 34 cm.

Song, pfte. acc.
First line same as title. JFD, MWA

Advertised in November, 1798, as "just published" by "George Gilbert, at his Music Store, 177 Broadway, Apollo's Head," New York.

TELL ME IS IT LOVE. A new song. Composed by Mr. Hook. New York, Printed & sold by G. Gilfert, No. 177 Broadway [1797-1801] 1 l. 31½ cm.

Song, pfte. acc.
First line: Ah tell me why fond beating heart. JFD, MWA, RPJCB

TELL ME IS IT LOVE. Boston, Printed & Sold at P. A. von Hagen Junior & cos. Musical magazine, No. 55 Marlboro' street [1799] 1 l. 33 cm.

Song, pfte. acc.
First line same as preceding. LSL, RPJCB

TELL ME LOVELY SHEPHERT [!] WHERE. [n. p., n. d.] 2 p. 32½ cm.

Song, pfte. acc.
First line: Tell me lovely shephard [!] where.
From Solomon, by William Boyce.
The engraving of the music is exceptionally good, clean and clear, giving the impression of English origin. The engraving of the text, however, is very bad, rough and blurred—unquestionably eighteenth century American at its worst. To give even an approximate date to this very interesting issue seems impossible. DLC

TELL ME MY LOVE. A favorite song. Sung in the new opera of Abroad and at home. New York, Printed and sold by G. Gilfert, No. 177 Broadway [1797-1801] 3 p. 33½ cm.

Song, pfte. acc.
First line: Tell me my love, wouldst thou forego.
Abroad and at home, by William Shield was first performed in New York, November 10, 1797. DLC, MWA

TELL ME WHERE IS FANCY BRED. From Shakespear's Measure for measure. Composed by B. Carr. Philadelphia, Printed & sold by Carr & co.
(In Four ballads by B. Carr. Philadelphia [1794] p. 6-7)
Song, pfte. acc. Three staves.
First line same as title. DLC

——— Separate issue of preceding, ca. 1794. MWA

THE TEMPLE OF MINERVA. An oratorial entertainment performed in Nov. 1781, by a company of gentlemen and ladies in the hotel of the minister of France in presence of his Excellency George Washington and his lady.
Sonneck writes:
   The libretto of this very interesting entertainment appeared first, I believe, in the Freeman's journal, Philadelphia, December 19, 1781. We are in-

[424]

formed that this "Oratorio, composed and set to music, by a gentlemen whose taste in the polite arts is well known," made part of a concert given "on Tuesday evening of the 11th inst." by "his excellency the minister of France" in honor of "his excellency George Washington, and his lady, the lady of General Greene, and a very polite circle of gentlemen and ladies . . ."

The words of this "oratorial entertainment," which really was a kind of allegorical-political opera or dramatic cantata, with an overture, airs, ensemble numbers, and choruses in praise of the Franco-American alliance, reprinted in several newspapers as:

The TEMPLE OF MINERVA, a musical entertainment. Performed in Nov. 1781, by a band of Gentleman and Ladies at the hotel of the Minister of France, in Philadelphia.

The libretto was also printed on p. 391–392 of the *Columbian magazine,* Philadelphia, April, 1787, signed H. This signature and other circumstances left no doubt in my mind that Francis Hopkinson was the poet-composer of "The Temple of Minerva." This supposition was correct. Mrs. Florence Scovel Shinn, of New York City, a descendant of Francis Hopkinson, very kindly gave me access to her family papers. Among them are in the beautiful original bindings, and in the author's manuscript, two volumes of Francis Hopkinson's collected poems and prose writings. In the second volume I found on p. 18–22 a fragment of

THE TEMPLE OF MINERVA. America independent, an oratorial entertainment performed at the hotel of the Minister of France, February 1781.

These five pages are crossed out, in particular the words "America independent." We do not know Hopkinson's reasons for this, but apparently when, after his death, his writings were published in the form prepared by him for publication, it was this circumstance which led to the exclusion of "The Temple of Minerva." This, however, notwithstanding the fact that the work reappears perfect and without cross-marks on the unnumbered pages of the same volume under the title of this entry.

The music to the "oratorial entertainment" seems not to be extant. This is very much to be regretted, as "The Temple of Minerva" was Francis Hopkinson's most conspicuous musical effort. For further particulars, including complete text, *see* my book on "Francis Hopkinson . . . and James Lyon" (1905).

THE TENDER MOTHER. New York, Sold by J. and M. Paff, 127 Broadway [1799–1803] 1 l. 32 cm.

Song, pfte. acc.
First line: Bye, sweet baby, bye.   DLC

TENNESSEE.
See United States country *Dances,* p. 16.

TERRAMINTA. Words from "The Apollo." Set by S. Holyoke.
(*In* The Massachusetts magazine, Boston, May, 1790. p. 315–316)

Song, pfte. acc.
First line: When charming Terraminta sings.   DLC (etc.)

[425]

*THANKSGIVING ANTHEM, by William Tuckey.
In the *Boston evening post*, for December 15, 1760, we read:

New York, Decemb. 8.
The following Thanksgiving Anthem was on Sunday last performed to great Satisfaction, in Trinity Church, before his Excellency General Amherst, on his return to New York, from the conquest of Canada. Compil'd and set to Music by Mr. Tuckey.

This anthem consisted of soli and choruses. The first solo begins: Comfort ye my people, saith our God.

[THAT PETTY FOGGING GRIZZLE] Sung by Miss Solomons in the character of Tom Thumb.
(*In* The gentleman's amusement, ed. by R. Shaw. Philadelphiia [1794–96] p. 52)

Melody only, flute (or violin) with accompanying text.
Title from first line.
In No. 7, May 1, 1796.   DLC

[THAT SEAT OF SCIENCE ATHENS] A new song. Compos'd by a Son of Liberty and sung by Mr. Flagg at Concert hall, Boston, Feb. 13, 1770.
(*With* "The parody parodized, or The Massachusetts liberty song" in Edes & Gill's *North American almanack and Massachusetts register* for the year 1770. 17 x 19½ cm.)

Words only. Tune, "The British grenadier."
Title from first line: That seat of science Athens, & Earth's great mistress Rome.   DLC, MB, MHi

THE THEATRICAL SONGSTER or Amusing companion. Containing a choice collection of much admired songs sung at the theatres in Boston and other genteel places of amusement. Boston, Printed and sold by J. White, near Charles-river Bridge and by the booksellers. 1797. 24 p.   MH

THEMA CON VARIAZIONE. By Pleyel.
(*In* The musical journal for the flute or violin. Baltimore [1800] no. 4, p. 5–8)

At head of title: No. 4 of a Musical journal for the flute or violin. Instrumental section.
Duet for flutes or violins (or flute and violin).   DLC

THEN I FLY TO MEET MY LOVE. A favorite song. New York, Printed and sold at G. Gilfert's & co's Musical magazine, No. 209 Broadway near St. Pauls. Where may be had a great choice of music and musical instruments of the verry [!] first quality. As also pianofortes let out on hire. And if purchased within three months the hire abate [!] [1795] [6]–7 p. 32½ cm.

Song, pfte. acc. Arr. for german flute or "guittar," p. 7.
First line: When the bee at eve reposes.   DLC, RPJCB

THEN SAY MY SWEET GIRL CAN YOU LOVE ME, or the Pretty brunette. Sung by Mr. Darley at Vauxhall, 1793. Price 31 cents. Philadelphia, Printed at Carr & co's Musical repository [1794] 4 p. 33½ cm.

At foot of p. 1: Jan. 27. 94. No. 4.
Song, pfte. acc. Arr. for "guittar," p. 4.

First line: Dear Nancy I've sail'd the world all around.
Composed by James Hook. CtY, DLC, McD-W, MWA

Advertised by B. Carr & Co. in Dunlap and Claypoole's *American daily advertiser*, Philadelphia, January 31, 1794: This day is published a favorite Vauxhall song of this last season called "Then say my sweet girl can you love me or the Pretty brunette" composed by Mr. Hook.

THEN SAY MY SWEET GIRL CAN YOU LOVE ME.
(*In* Elegant extracts for the German flute or violin. Philadelphia, [1796] bk. 2, p. 28–29)

Melody only, flute or violin, with accompanying text.
First line same as preceding. DLC, NN

———— The same.
(*In* The American musical miscellany. Northampton, 1798. p. 200–202)

Melody only, with accompanying text.
First line same as preceding. DLC (etc.)

———— Dear Nancy I've sail'd the world all around, or the Pretty brunette.
Sung by Mr. Clifford. New York, Printed and sold by G. Gilfert & co., No. 209 Broadway [1795] [2] p. 33 cm.

Song, pfte. acc. Arr. for German flute, p. [2].
First line same as title.
Sung by Mr. Clifford in Boston, January 31, 1795. JFD

———— The same as preceding, except that the imprint reads, "Printed and sold at G. Gilfert & cos. Musical magazine, No. 209 Broadway." RPJCB

[THERE LIV'D IN ALTDORF CITY FAIR] A fragment. Sung by Mrs. Hodgkinson in the Archers.
(*In* Elegant extracts for the German flute or violin. Philadelphia [1796] bk. 2, p. 31)

Melody only, flute or violin, with accompanying text.
Title from first line.
The archers, by Benjamin Carr. DLC, NN

THERE WAS A JOLLY MILLER.
(*In* The American musical miscellany. Northampton, 1798. p. 109–111)

Melody only, with accompanying text.
First line same as title.
From *Love in a village*, by Thomas Arne. DLC (etc.)

THESPIAN CHAPLE inscribed to the memory of Mr. John P. Morton, late of the New Theatre, Philadelphia. The words by Mr. Derrick. Published by G. Willig, No. 185 Market street [Philadelphia, 1798–1804] 1 l. 30½ cm.

Song, pfte. acc.
First line: Beside the calm retreat.
Published probably 1798, the death-year of John Pollard Moreton, the popular "light comedian." DLC

[427]

THINK YOUR TAWNY MOOR IS TRUE. A song in the comic opera of the Mountaineers. Composed by Dr. Arnold.
(*In* The musical repertory. Boston [1796] No. I, p. (12)–(13).)

Song, pfte. acc.
First line: Think your tawny Moor is true, pretty Agnes?
DLC, MB (incomplete), NRU–Mus
In MB copy after title: Pr. 25 ᶜᵗ

THIRD COLDSTREAM MARCH.
See Third *Coldstream* march.

THOMAS AND SALLY, or the Sailor's return. Philadelphia, Henry Taylor. 1791. 24 p. 8⁰

Libretto by Isaac Bickerstaff of opera by Thomas A. Arne.   PPL

THOMAS JEFFERSON MARCH. Composed by Geo. Emrick. Printed and sold by G. Willig, 185 Market street, Philadelphia [1798–1804] 1 l. 32½ cm.

Pfte. 2 hds., followed by arr. for two flutes.   MNSt

THE THORN. Sung by Mr. Incledon at the Theatre Royal, Covent Garden. Composed by William Shield, musician in ordinary to His Majesty. New York, Sold by I. and M. Paff, No. 127 Broadway. Also now publishing a variety of the most celebrated songs, as singing at the nobilities public and private concerts in London [n. d.] 4 p. 31½ cm.

Below title: N. B. As some of the passages in this ballad may be to [!] high for many voices in the original key, the following transposition is added in order to render it more generally useful.
Song, pfte. acc.
First line: From the white blossom'd sloe.
"The Thorn, in its original key," p. 3–4.
Altho' possibly published as early as 1799, the fact that there are almost no examples in the whole song of the old (long) "s" makes an early nineteenth century date much more likely.   DLC, ES

THOU'RT GONE AWA FRAE ME, MARY. A favorite Scotch song. Sung by Mr. Dignum. New York, Printed & sold at G. Gilferts music store, No. 177 Broadway. And to be had of P. A. von Hagen, No. 3 Cornhill.
(*In* A collection of favorite songs, by Mr. Hook. New York [1799–1801] bk. [1], p. 4–5)

Song, pfte. acc.
First line same as title.   DLC

———— Separate issue of preceding, 1799–1801.   DLC, JFD, RPJCB

[THOU DEAR SEDUCER OF MY HEART] A favorite song. Translated from the Irish. New York, Printed & sold at J. Hewitt's Musical repository No. 23 Maiden Lane [1799–1800] 1 l. 33 cm.

Song, pfte. acc.
Title from first line.   ES, PH1

———— The same as preceding.

(*In* A collection of new & favorite songs. [A] Philadelphia [ca. 1800] p. [206])
HFB

THOU SOFT FLOWING AVON.
See Evening amusement, p. 17.

THOU SOFT'NING BALM. Sung in the new opera Wilmore Castle. New York, Printed & sold at G. Gilfert's piano forte warehouse, No. 177 Broadway [n. d.] 4 p. 32½ cm.

Song, pfte. acc.
First line same as title.
As James Hook's opera *Wilmore Castle* was first produced in 1800, it seems unlikely (though possible) that this issue could have appeared as early as that year.
CtY, DLC

THO' BACCHUS MAY BOAST, ETC. An admired new song.
(*In* The universal asylum, Philadelphia, November, 1790. p. 342–344)
Song, pfte. acc.
First line same as title.
Composed by William Shield (*BM Cat.*)
DLC (etc.)

THO' BACCHUS MAY BOAST OF HIS CARE KILLING BOWL.
(*In* The American musical miscellany, Northampton, 1798. p. 268–270)
Melody only, with accompanying text.
First line same as title.
DLC (etc.)

THO' FAR BEYOND THE MOUNTAINS. Alternative title of *Owen.*

[THO' I AM NOW A VERY LITTLE LAD] Sung by Mrs. Marshall in the Highland reel.
(*In* The gentleman's amusement, ed. by R. Shaw. Philadelphia [1794–96] p. 16–17)
Melody (for flute or violin) with accompanying text.
Title from first line.
In No. 2, May, 1794.
Mrs. Marshall sang in the first Philadelphia performance of Shield's opera *The Highland reel*, April 4, 1794.
PHi

[THO' PITY I CANNOT DENY] Sung by Mrs. Warrell in the Haunted tower.
(*In* The gentleman's amusement, ed. by R. Shaw. Philadelphia [1794–96] p. 40)
Melody only, flute (or violin) with accompanying text.
Title from first line.
In No. 5, March 1, 1795.
Sung by Mrs. Warrell in Philadelphia, February 18, 1795.
This song appears in the score of Stephen Storace's *The haunted tower*, where it is attributed to Pleyel.
DLC, PHi

THO' PITY I CANNOT DENY. Sung by Mrs. Pownall. New York, Printed & sold by B. Carr at his Musical repositories here & at Phila⁹
(*In* The favorite songs in the opera of [The haunted tower, by S. Storace] New York [1795–96] p. 2)
Song, pfte. acc.
First line same as title.
Sung by Mrs. Pownall in New York, January 9, 1795.
ABHu

—— Separate issue of preceding, 1795–96.   ES, MWA

—— Separate issue of the same, preceded by title-page of above collection, 1795–96.   JFD

THO' PRUDENCE MAY PRESS ME. New York, Printed & sold at J. Hewitt's Musical repository, No. 23 Maiden Lane [1799–1800] 1 l. 33 cm.

Song, pfte. acc., followed by arr. for "guittar."
First line same as title.
From *The deserter*, by Charles Dibdin (Monsigny and Philidor).   ES

—— The same as preceding.
(*In* A collection of new & favorite songs. [A] Philadelphia [ca. 1800] p. [186])   HFB

THO PRUDENCE. Deserter.
See Evening amusement [1796] p. 18.

THO' WEALTH IS ALLURING. A new song. Composed by Mr. Hook. New York, Printed & sold by G. Gilfert, No. 177 Broadway. And to be had at P. A. von Hagen's music store. Boston [1797–1801] [2] p. 31 cm.

Song, pfte. acc.
First line same as title.   MWA

THO' YOU THINK BY THIS TO VEX ME. A favorite duett. Sung by Mrs. Seymour & Mr. Jefferson in the Siege of Belgrade. New York, Printed and sold by James Hewitt at his Musical repository, No. 131 William street. And at B. Carr's, Philadelphia & J. Carr's, Baltimore [1797–99] [2] p. 31½ cm.

Duet, pfte. acc.
First line same as title.
Sung by Mrs. Seymour (Lilla) and Mr. Jefferson (Leopold) in *The siege of Belgrade*, by Stephen Storace, New York, December 30, 1796.
                                                DLC, LSL, MdHi, NN

—— The same as preceding.
(*In* A collection of new & favorite songs. [A] Philadelphia [ca. 1800] p. [78]–[79])   HFB

THREE BALLADS . . . by B. Carr.
See Three *Ballads.* Viz. The new somebody . . . Composed by B. Carr.

3 DIVERTIMENTOS. By B. Carr.
See 3 *Divertimentos.* By B. Carr.

*THREE DUETTS, FOR DIFFERENT INSTRUMENTS, composed by Mr. *Deaumont* [*recte* Leaumont].
Advertised in the *New York Minerva,* April 23, 1796, by "B. Carr, No. 131 William street," as "now publishing by subscription . . . The proposals may be seen at Mr. Carr's Musical Repository."

THREE DUETTS FOR TWO PERFORMERS . . . by Theodore Smith.
See Three *Duetts* for two performers on one harpsichord or piano forte. Composed by Theodore Smith.

THREE MARCHES . . . by James Hewitt.
See Three *Marches* for the flute, violin or piano forte.   Composed by James Hewitt.

THREE NEW MARCHES.
See Three new *Marches.*

THREE OF THE MOST ADMIRED CANZONETTS by Haydn.
See Three . . . *Canzonetts* by Haydn.

THREE PROGRESSIVE SONATINAS . . . by Pleyel.
See Three progressive *Sonatinas* for the piano forte . . . by Pleyel.

THREE RONDOS . . . by William Brown.
See Three *Rondos* for the piano forte or harpsichord . . . by William Brown.

*THREE SONATAS for the harpsichord . . . by F. Linley.
See Three *Sonatas* for the harpsichord or piano forte by F. Linley.

THREE SONATAS . . . by Jas. Hewitt.
See Three *Sonatas* for the piano forte.   Composed . . . by Jas. Hewitt.

THREE SWEETHEARTS I BOAST.   A favorite song.   New York, Printed for
G. Gilfert, No. 177 Broadway.   Where may be had: The nightingale, Ripe
cherries, The female cryer, How d'ye do, The way to get married, No that
will never do, Strew the rude crosses of life, The shepherd boy.   [ca. 1797]
[2] p.   33½ cm.

Song, pfte. acc.
First line: Three sweethearts I boast, pray who could wish more.
Re date, *cf.*   The nightingale, Female cryer, etc.   DLC, MWA

THE THRIFTY WIFE.   A favorite song.   Sung by Mr. Dignum.   New York,
Printed and sold by G. Gilfert & co. at their Musical magazine, No. 209
Broadway, near St. Pauls.   Where may be had a great variety of single
songs, lessons and alkinds [!] of musical instruments, strings &c.   [1795]
10–11 p.   31 cm.

Song, pfte. acc.
First line: I am a cheerful fellow.
Composed by James Hook.   MWA

THE THRIFTY WIFE, or Little waste.   A favorite song.   Composed by Mr.
Hook.   New York, Printed & sold by W. Howe, organ builder & importer
of all kinds of musical instruments, No. 320 Pearl street.   Price 25 cents.
[1798]   [2] p.   31½ cm.

Song, pfte. acc.
First line: I am a chearful [!] fellow.
Followed on p. [2] by "Coolun.   A celebrated Irish air."   MWA, NRU–Mus

Advertised in August, 1798, as "just published and for sale at Wm. Howe's
wholesale and retail ware house, 320 Pearl street," New York.

[THROW AN APPLE]   A new song.   Set to music by A. Hawkins.
(*In* The Boston magazine.   October, 1783, facing p. 33)

Song, pfte. acc.
Title from first line: Throw an apple up a hill.
Printed from movable type.   DLC (etc.)

THE THRUSH. [New York] Published by I. and M. Paff, Of whom may be
had—
    No. 2   The linnets.   No. 3.   The gold finch.
    No. 4   The robin red breast.   No. 5.   The nightingale.
                          No. 6.   The lark.
    [1799–1803]   [2] p.   30½ cm.

    At head of title: Selected from the Aviary, a collection of sonnets.   No. 1.
    Song, pfte. acc.
    First line: Sweet warbling thrush whose artless song.
    The aviary, by James Hook.   ES, NN

TILL NOAH'S TIME, ETC. A favorite song. Translated from the Danish
    by Mr. Hans Gram. The air a Gothick composition.
    (*In* The Massachusetts magazine. Boston, January, 1792. p. 53)

    Song, pfte. acc.
    First line: Till Noah's time men acted without meaning.   DLC (etc.)

TIME. A favorite rondo. Composed by James Hewitt. Printed by B. Carr
    & sold at his Musical repositories in New York & Philadelphia & at J. Carr's
    Baltimore [1795–96] [2] p. 31 cm.

    Song, pfte. acc. Arr. for "guittar," p. [2].
    First line: Speed the lazy foot of time.   DLC, NN

TIME. Alternative title of *Sonnet to Time.* by I. J. Pleyel.

TIME HAS NOT THIN'D MY FLOWING HAIR.
    See Canzonet.   Jackson.

THE TIMELY ADVISER.
    See The select songster. New Haven, 1786. p. 30–31.

TINK.A TINK. Sung by Mr. Bernard & Miss Arnold in Blue Beard. Printed
    & sold at B. Carr's Musical repository, Philadelphia; J. Carr's, Baltimore &
    J. Hewitts, New York (Price 25 cents)
    (*In* A collection of new & favorite songs. [C] Philadelphia [ca. 1799]
    p. 4–5)

    Duet, pfte. acc.
    First line: Yes Beda, thus Beda, when I melancholy grow.
    John Bernard and Miss Arnold took part in the first performance in Phila-
    delphia of Michael Kelly's *Blue Beard,* May 24, 1799.   ABHu, LSL, NN

———— Separate issue of preceding, ca. 1799.
                                  DLC, McD–W, MdHi, PP–K, RPJCB

THE FAVORITE DUETT OF TINK A TINK. New York, Printed & sold
    at G. Gilfert's music store, No. 177 Broadway [ca. 1799] 3 p. 29½ cm.
    Duet, pfte. acc.
    First line same as preceding.   DLC, JFD, MWA

THE TINKER. A favorite comic song in Merry Sherwood. Published at
    B. Carr's musical respositories, Philadelphia, New York & J. Carr's, Balti-
    more. Price 20 cents.

[432]

(*In* The gentleman's amusement, ed. by R. Shaw. Philadelphia [1794–96] p. (92)–(93).)

Song, pfte. acc.
First line: My father was a tinker's son.
In No. 12, ca. 1796.
Merry Sherwood, by William Reeve.   PHi, PP–K

———— The same as preceding.
(*In* A collection of new & favorite songs. [A] Philadelphia [ca. 1800] p. [184]–[185])   HFB

THE TIPLER'S DEFENCE.
See The select songster. New Haven, 1786. p. 61.

'TIS—AS FIRST WORD OF TITLE.
See It is . . .

TO ARMS COLUMBIA. A new patriotic song. Written for the Anniversary of the Massachusetts Charitable Fire Society, by Thomas Paine, A. M. The music composed by P. A. von Hagen, jun. Boston, Printed & sold at P. A. von Hagen & cos. Musical magazine, No. 3 Cornhill. Also by G. Gilfert New-York. Where may be had the greatest variety of warranted imported pianofortes & other musical instruments of superior quality. This day is published the new song of How tedious alas are the hours [1799] [2] p. 31½ cm.

Below imprint: For the pianoforte, German flute or violin.
In lower margin of p. [2], enclosed in oval wreath: Twenty five cents.
Song, pfte. acc.
First line: To arms, to arms when honor cries.

                                                        LSL, MWA, RPJCB

Advertised in the *Columbian centinel,* Boston, June 29, 1799, by "P. A. Von Hagen and Co. . . . Musical Magazine, No. 3 Cornhill," as "This day published . . ." Evidently identical with

TO ARMS, TO ARMS, a new patriotic song, written by Thomas Paine, A. M. . . . music by Mr. Von Hagen, jun.

as it was to be sung at a concert, Salem, Mass., on June 25, 1799.

TO ARMS COLUMBIA. A new patriotic song. Written by Thos. Paine & sung with great applause by Mr. Barrett at the Theatre on the 4th of July, 1799. New York, Printed & sold at J. Hewitts Musical repository, No. 23 Maiden Lane. Sold also by B. Carr, Philadelphia & J. Carr, Baltimore. Price 25 cents.
(*In* A collection of new & favorite songs. [A] Philadelphia [ca. 1800]   p. [176]–[177])

Song, pfte. acc. Arr. for two flutes, p. [177].
First line same as preceding.   HFB

TO ME A SMILING INFANT CAME. A favorite ballad. Printed at B. Carr's Musical repositories, New York & Philadelphia & J. Carr's, Baltimore. Price 12 cents. [1794–97] 1 l. 32½ cm.

Song, pfte. acc.
First line same as title.   CdeW, LSL

—— The same.

(*In* The musical repertory . . . Boston [1796] No. II, p. 24–25)

Song, pfte. acc.
First line same as title.
Sonneck ascribes this song to Sharp. *BM Cat.* lists same title as by J. Ambrose.
DLC

TO SOFTEN LIFE'S CARES. A favorite song. Sung in the new opera of Wilmore Castle. Composed by Mr. Hook. New York, Printed & sold at G. Gilfert's music warehouse, No. 177 Broadway [n. d.] [2] p. 33 cm.

Song, pfte. acc.
First line same as title.
As *Wilmore Castle* was first produced in England in 1800, it is doubtful, though possible, that this issue appeared as early as that year
DLC, JFD, RPJCB

TO THE MAID I LOVE BEST. A favorite song. Composed by Mr. Hook. [n. p., 179–] 2 p. 30½ cm.

Song, pfte. acc.
First line: Cupid lovely charming boy.
BM Cat. lists an English edition in 1796.
NN

Advertised in March, 1797, as to be published "in a few days" by "G. Gilfert at his Musical Magazine, No. 177 Broadway," New York. No copy with such imprint has been found.

A TOAST. Written and composed by Fra⁵ Hopkinson, esqʳ.
(*With* Brother soldiers all hail. Philadelphia, B. Carr [1799])

Song, pfte. acc.
First line: 'Tis Washington's health fill a bumper all round.
ABHu, DLC, LSL, MB, NN

THE TOBACCO BOX, or Soldier's pledge of love. New York, Printed & sold by G. Gilfert, No. 177 Broadway [1797–1801] [2] p. 31½ cm.

Song, pfte. acc. Arr. for guitar, p. [2].
First line: Tho' the fate of battle on tomorrow wait.
MWA

TOGETHER LET US RANGE THE FIELDS. A favorite duett introduced in the Woodman. Dr. Boyce. [n. p., n. d.] (62)–(64) p. 35 cm.

Duet, pfte. acc. Three staves.
First line same as title.
At foot of p. (64): End of Book the 2d.
The woodman, by William Shield.
Dr. Boyce: William Boyce.
Evidently a Carr imprint, 179–. *cf. *Elegant extracts.*
PHi

THE TOKEN. By Dibdin. Price 20 cents. [Philadelphia ?] Printed and sold at Carr's Musical repository [1794] [2] p. 32½ cm.

Song, pfte. acc. Arr. for flute, p. [2].
First line: The breeze was fresh, the ship in stays.
Advertised as published in October, 1794.
CtY, MWA

[434]

*TOLL DE ROLL DE ROLL.
Song by Storace. Advertised in January, 1798, as "just published by J. Hewitt, No. 131 William st.," New York. Also advertised in August, 1798, "just published and for sale at Wm. Howe's wholesale and retail warehouse, 320 Pearlstreet," New York.

TOLL TOLL THE KNELL. Composed by Storace. Sung by Mrs. Warrel. Printed & sold at B. Carr's Musical repository, Philadelphia; J. Carr's, Baltimore & J. Hewitt's, New York. (Price 25 cts.) [1797–1799] [2] p. 31½ cm.

Song, pfte. acc.
First line same as title. DLC, NN, RPJCB

As *Tell toll the knell* advertised in January, 1798, among "new songs. Published . . . at Carr's Musical Repository," Philadelphia. Carr added to the advertisement of this and *The willow:*

These two beautiful ballads are selected from the last productions of this much lamented genius.

———— The same.
(*In* A collection of new & favorite songs. [B] Philadelphia [1797–99] no paging) McD–W, PU

TOM BOWLING, or The sailor's epitaph.
See Poor Tom Bowling.

TOM PAINE'S JESTS; being an entirely new and select collection of patriotic bon mots, repartees, anecdotes, epigrams, observations &c. on political subjects. By Thomas Paine and other supporters of the rights of man. To which is added, A tribute to the swinish multitude; being a choice collection of patriotic songs. Speak truth and shame the Devil. Seria mixta jocis. Philadelphia, Printed for Mathew Carey, No. 118 Market-street. 1796. 72 p. 18 cm.

On p. 31–72: A tribute to the swinish multitude, being a choice collection of patriotic songs. Collected by the celebrated R. Thomson. Title-page (p. [31]) verso blank; "To the public, alias the 'Swinish multitude,' " p. [33]–37; p. [38] blank; songs, p. [39]–72.
Words only. Tunes mentioned for many of the songs.
DLC, MWA, NHi, NN, RPB, RPJCB

TOM STARBOARD. A favorite song in the opera of the Turnpike gate. Composed by J. Mazzinghi. New York, Printed & sold at J. and M. Paff's musical store, No. 127 Broadway [n. d.] 4 p. 32 cm.

Song, pfte. acc. Three staves.
First line: Tom Starboard was a lover true.
At foot of p. 4: Engrav'd by W. Pirsson, No. 417 Pearl street.
Published possibly as early as 1799. DLC

TOM TACKLE. A favorite song by Dibdin. Price 25 cents. Printed & sold by B. Carr at his Musical repository's in New York & Philadelphia & J. Carr, Baltimore [1795–96] [2] p. 32½ cm.
Song, pfte. acc.
First line: Tom Tackle was noble was true to his word.
From Dibdin's *Castles in the air*. ABHu, NN

[435]

TOM TACKLE.
(*In* Elegant extracts for the German flute or violin. Philadelphia [1796]
bk. 2, p. 3–5)

Melody only, flute or violin, with accompanying text.
First line same as preceding.   DLC, NN

———— The same.
(*In* The American musical miscellany. Northampton, 1798. p. 260–263)

Melody only, with accompanying text.
First line same as preceding.   DLC (etc.)

TOM TRUELOVE'S KNELL. A favorite song. Written and composed by
Mr. Dibdin. Price 20 cents. Printed at Carr's Musical repositories in
New York & Philadelphia & J. Carr's, Baltimore [1795–96] [2] p. 33 cm.

Song, pfte. acc. Arr. for flute, p. [2].
First line: Tom Truelove woo'd the sweetest fair.
From *Great news.*   MWA, NRU–Mus

TOM TRUELOVES KNELL, by Dibdin.
(*In* Elegant extracts for the German flute or violin. Philadelphia [1798]
bk. 3, p. 25)

Melody only, flute or violin, with accompanying text.
First line: Tom Truelove wood [!] the sweetest fair.   DLC, NN

*TOMMY THUMB'S SONG BOOK, for all little masters and misses, to be sung
to them by their nurses, until they can sing themselves. By Nurse Lovechild [Two lines] The first Worcester edition. Printed at Worcester,
Massachusetts, by Isaiah Thomas. 1788. 59 p. 32 mo.

Nurse Lovechild: Lady Eleanor Frere Fenn.

*———— Tom Thumb's song book, for all little masters and misses, to be sung
to them by their nurses. By Nurse Lovechild. To which is added a letter
from a lady, on nursing. Boston, Printed and sold by Samuel Hall, No.
53, Cornhill [1795] 48 mo.

TOMORROW. A favorite song. Boston, Printed & sold at P. A. von Hagen's
piano forte warehouse, No. 4 Old Massachusetts Bank head of the Mall & at
the Music store, No. 3 Cornhill. Also at G. Gilfert's ware house, N. York;
David Vinton's, Providence; W. R. Wilder, Newport; B. B. Macanulty
Salem; E. M. Blunt, Newburyport; Isaac Stanwood, Portsmouth and E. A.
Jenks, Portland [n. d.] [2] p. 31½ cm.

Below imprint: For the piano forte, guitar & clarinet.
Song, pfte. acc. Arr. for German flute, p. [2].
First line: In the downhill of life when I find I'm declining.
Published probably after 1800.   DLC, JFD, RPJCB

*TOMORROW.
Song by Raynor Taylor. Was to be sung in his "Musical performance . . .
the whole of the music original and composed by Mr. Taylor," at Annapolis,
Md., on February 28, 1793.

*THE TOUCHSTONE, or Harlequin traveller.
This "speaking pantomime entertainment . . . the music selected and composed by Mr. [John] Bentley," was to have its first performance at New York, on September 1, 1785.

TRAIN OR ARTILLERY GRENADIERS MARCH.
See Compleat tutor for the fife . . . p. 12.

TRANQUIL PLEASURES NEVER CLOY. Composed by J. Pleyel. Boston, Printed & sold by P. A. von Hagen & co. at their warranted imported piano fortes warehouse, No. 3 Cornhill. Also by G. Gilfert, N. York [n. d.] 1 l. 33 cm.

Below imprint: For the piano fortes & German flute or violin.
First line same as title.
Published probably in 1799.   JFD

[THE TRAV'LER BENIGHTED] Song VIII.
(*In* Seven songs, by F. Hopkinson. Philadelphia [1788] p. 11)

Song, pfte. acc.
Title from first line.   DLC, Hopk., MB, McD–W

*A TRIBUTE TO THE SWINISH MULTITUDE: being a choice collection of patriotic songs. Collected by the celebrated R. Thomson. London: Printed. New-York: Re-printed by Samuel Loudon & son, No. 82 Water-street. M, DCC, XCIV. 12 mo.

22d New York District Copyright, issued to John Goodeve, as Proprietor, 19 July, 1794.

A TRIBUTE TO THE SWINISH MULTITUDE: being a choice collection of patriotic songs. Collected by the celebrated R. Thomson. [Second edition.] London: Printed. New York: Re-printed by Samuel Loudon & son, No. 82, Water-street. M. DCC, XCV. x, [11]–96 p. 18 cm.

Half title; title-page, verso blank; "To the public," p. v–x; songs, p. [11]–96. Words only, tunes generally mentioned.   DLC, MWA

A TRIBUTE TO THE SWINISH MULTITUDE . . . 1796.
(*In* Tom Paine's jests . . . Philadelphia, 1796. p. 31–72)

Songs, words only.   DLC, MWA, NHi, NN, RPB, RPJCB

*TRIO BY GIOVANNI GUALDO.
A "trio composed by Mr. Gualdo" was to be performed at a "concert . . . directed by Mr. Gualdo after the Italian method," in Philadelphia, on November 16, 1769.

*A TRIP TO GRETNA-GREEN.
Song by Raynor Taylor. Was to be sung in his "Musical performance . . . the whole of the music original and composed by Mr. Taylor," at Annapolis, Md., on February 28, 1793.

TRIUMPHANT FAME ASCENDS THE SKIES.
See Military glory of Great Britain.

[437]

TRUE COURAGE. Written & composed by Dibdin. New York, Printed & sold at J. Hewitts Musical repository, Maden [!] Lane. Pr. 25 cents. Where may be had all new publications, likewise an asortment [!] of warranted patent piano fortes [n. d.] [2] p. 34 cm.

Song, pfte. acc.
First line: Why whats thats to you if my eyes I'm a'wiping.
Published possibly as early as 1799. McD–W

THE TRUMP OF FAME. Sung by Mrs. Warrell in the opera of Robin Hood (*In* Young's vocal and instrumental musical miscellany. Philadelphia [1793–95] p. 44–45)

Song, pfte. acc.
First line: The trump of fame your name has breath'd.
In No. 6, 1794. ABHu, DLC, Hopk.

[THE TRUMP OF FAME YOUR NAME HAS BREATH'D] Sung by Mrs. Warrell in the opera of Robin Hood.
(*In* The gentleman's amusement, ed. by R. Shaw [1794–96] p. 10)

Melody only, flute (or violin) with accompanying text.
Title from first line.
In No. 1, April 1, 1794.
Mrs. Warrell sang in the first Philadelphia performance of William Shield's opera *Robin Hood*, March 10, 1794. DLC, PHi

TRUMPET AIR BY MR. BREMNER.
Harpsichord piece in a MS. volume of "Lessons" in Hopk. on p. 119.
This was probably James and not Robert Bremner. Hopk.

*TRUMPET SONG BY RAYNOR TAYLOR.
Was to be sung by Miss Huntley (trumpet by Mr. Priest) at a concert of vocal and instrumental music, conducted by R. Taylor at Oeller's Hotel, Philadelphia, April 21, 1796.

TRUXTON'S VICTORY. A naval patriotic song. Sung by Mr. Hodgkinson. Written by Mrs. Rowson of Boston. Price 25 cents. [Boston, Printed by Thomas & Andrews. 1799 ?] 2 p. 39 cm.

Imprint in ink as above.
Song, pfte. acc.
First line: When Freedom, fair Freedom her banner display'd.
Printed from movable type.
Second page is numbered "[2]." MWA

Also advertised in March, 1799, as "published, at P. A. von Hagen, jun. and Co's, No. 55, Marlboro' street . . ." Boston.
No copy of this issue has been found.

A TURKISH RONDO. Composed by J. L. Dussek. Philadelphia, Printed & sold by G. Willig, No. 185 Market street [1798–1804] [4] p. 32½ cm.
Pfte. 2 hds. DLC, PP–K, RPJCB

TURKS MARCH.
See Compleat tutor for the fife . . . p. 12.

[438]

THE TURTLE DOVE COOS ROUND MY COT. Composed by Mr. Hook.
New York, Printed & sold at J. and M. Paff's music store, No. 127 Broadway
[1799–1803] [2] p. 32 cm.

Below imprint: Flauto solo.
Song, pfte. acc.
First line: Swift flew the day & merry pass'd the hours.

DLC, McD–W, MWA, NN

*TUTOR FOR THE VIOLIN. By C. Homan. Philadelphia.
Is "in the hands of the engraver and shortly will be published."
(*Aurora*, Philadelphia, February 6, 1796)

THE TWADDLE.
(*In* The American musical miscellany. Northampton, 1798. p. 111–114)
Melody only, with accompanying text.
First line: On sturdy stout Dobbin. DLC (etc.)

'TWAS—AS FIRST WORD OF TITLE.
See It was . . .

*TWELVE DUETS FOR 2 CLARINETS adapted from Pleyel by Mr. Priest of
the New Theatre, Philadelphia.
Advertised for sale by "Harrison, No 108 Maidenlane," New York, in May,
1794, among "new" music.

TWELVE FAVORITE PIECES. Arranged for the piano forte or harpsichord
by A. Reinagle. Philadelphia, Printed for A. Reinagle [1789?] 1 p. 1.,
24 p. 32½ cm.

Title-page, verso blank; music, p. 1–24.
Recto of p. 1, blank.
At foot of p. 6, 20: Philadelphia. Printed for A. Reinagle.
At foot of p. 3, 8: I. Aitken. Sculqt. [!]; of p. 20: I. Aitken, Scu.; of p. 14:
John Aitken, Sculpt.

Contents:
        p. 1–2 La chasse. Allegro. Del Sigr. Campioni.
          3 Brown's march.
        4–6 Overture to the Deserter.
        7–8 A favorite movement for the piano forte by Vanhal.
      9–10 Overture. La schiava.
    11–12 Favorite rondo. By Garth.
    13–14 Haydn's celebrated Andante for the piano forte.
      15 A favorite minuet. Composed by G. C. Schetkey.
      16 Faederal march. As performed in the grand procession
            in Philadelphia the 4th. of July, 1788. Composed and
            adapted for the piano forte, violin or German flute by
            Alex. Reinagle.
    17–18 A favourite rondo. Composed by F. Staes.
    19–20 Overture. Marian. Shield.
    21–24 Overture de Blaise et Babet. Adapted for the piano forte
            by A. Reinagle. DLC

This collection was probably printed by Thomas Dobson at the Stone House
in Second street, Philadelphia [1789]. *cf.* A collection of favorite songs,
divided into two books . . . [arr.] by Alexr. Reinagle.

TWENTY FOUR AMERICAN COUNTRY DANCES.
See Twenty four American country *Dances.*

TWENTY FOUR FASHIONABLE COUNTRY DANCES.
See Twenty four fashionable country *Dances.*

THE 23ᵈ PSALM.
(*In* [A volume of songs, etc., composed or copied by Francis Hopkinson.
1759–60] p. 179)

Three-part chorus. Open score.
First line: The Lord himself the mighty Lord.
Composed by Francis Hopkinson. DLC

THE TWINS OF LATONA. Poor soldier.
(*In* A collection of favorite songs, divided into two books. Arr. by A.
Reinagle. Philadelphia [1789?] bk. 1, p. 6–7)

Song, pfte. acc.
First line: The twins of Latona, so kind to my boon.
Poor soldier, by William Shield. CdeW, DLC, ES, Hopk.

TWO ANTHEMS FOR THREE AND FOUR VOICES . . . By William
Selby.
See Two *Anthems* . . . By William Selby.

TWO BUNCHES A PENNY PRIMROSES. Sung by Mrs. Franklin.
(*In* The Philadelphia pocket companion for guittar or clarinett [Philadelphia.
1794] v. 1, p. 18–19)

Melody only, with accompanying text.
First line: When nature first salutes the morn.
Composed by James Hook. MWA

TWO BUNCHES A PENNY PRIMROSES. An admired song. Composed
by Mr. Hook. [n. p.] Printed for Hewitt [ca. 1798] 1 l. 31½ cm.

Imprint at foot of page.
Song, pfte. acc.
First line: When Nature first salutes the Spring. NN

———— The same as preceding.
(*In* A collection of new & favorite songs. [A] Philadelphia [ca. 1800] p.
[190]) HFB

TWO BUNCHES A PENNY PRIMROSES. Philadelphia, Printed by G.
Willig, No. 185 Market st. [1798–1804] [2] p. 32 cm.

Imprint at foot of page.
Song, pfte. acc. Arr. for guitar, p. [2].
First line: When Spring returning decks the groves.
Differs from preceding, both in music and text. NRU–Mus

TWO BUNCHES A PENNY PRIMROSES. [n. p., ca. 1800] [2] p. 32 cm.

Song, pfte. acc. Arr. for guitar, p. [2].
First line: When Spring returning decks the grove. ES, NBuG

TWO FAVOURITE STRATHPEY REELS . . .
See Two favourite *Strathpey reels* . . .

THE TWO FRIENDS.
See Favorite *Cotillions.*

*TWO MARCHES, composed by Mr. Vidal.
Were to be played at a concert in Philadelphia, on June 17, 1774.

TWO NEW FAVORITE COTILLIONS.
See Two new favorite *Cotillions.*

TWO ODES AND AN ACROSTIC.
See Two *Odes* . . . commemorative of . . . [Washington]

TWO ORIGINAL RUSSIAN AIRS.
(*In* The musical journal for the flute or violin. Baltimore [1800] no 13, p. 26–28)

Air 1, p. 26–27.
Two parts. For flutes or violins (or flute and violin) with accompanying text.
First line: In constant Spring thy morn is wash'd.
Air 2, p. 28.
Two parts. For flutes or violins (or flute and violin) with accompanying text.
First line: Lend me thy saffron robe.   DLC

TWO ORIGINAL RUSSIAN AIRS.   Adapted to English words.
(*In* The musical journal for the pianoforte, ed. by B. Carr. Baltimore [1800]   v. 1, no. [13], p. (28)–(30).)

Air, p. (28)–(29).
"N. B.   This may be sung as a song, duett, or glee for three voices."
Song, pfte. acc.   Three staves.
First line: In constant Spring thy morn is wash'd.
Air 2, p. (30).
Song, pfte. acc.
First line: Lend me thy saffron robe.   DLC, ES, LSL, NN, NRU-Mus

———— Separate issue of preceding, 1800.   PP–K

TWO SONATAS FOR THE PIANOFORTE . . . By D. Steibelt.   Op. 33.
See Two *Sonatas* for the pianoforte . . . By D. Steibelt.

[TWO SONGS]   Sung by Mrs. Jordan in the Spoil'd child.
See [Two *Songs*] Sung . . . in the Spoil'd child.

THE UNFORTUNATE SAILOR.   A favorite song.   Composed by Mr. Hook.
New York, Sold by I. and M. Paff, No. 127 Broadway [n. d.]   [2] p.   33 cm.

Imprint at foot of p. [1].
Song, pfte. acc.   Arr. for flute, p. [2].
First line: Sam Sailyard loved Sally.
Published possibly as early as 1799.   ES, NN, RPJCB

THE UNFORTUNATE SAILOR.   Composed by Mr. Hook.   Sung by Mr. Fox.
New York, Printed & sold at J. Hewitt's Musical repository, No. 23 Maiden Lane.   Sold also by B. Carr, Philadelphia & J. Carr, Baltimore.   Price 25 cents.

(*In* A collection of new & favorite songs. [A] Philadelphia [ca. 1800 p. [72]–[73])

Song, pfte. acc. Arr. for flute, p. [73].
First line: Sam Sailyard lov'd Sally the girl of his heart.
Sung by Gilbert Fox at Vauxhall Garden, New York, August 27, 1800 HFB

———— Separate issue of preceding, ca. 1800.   DLC

UNFURL'D WERE THE SAILS. A new song. Composed by Mr. Hook
New York, Sold at J. Hewitt's Musical repository, No. 23 Maiden Lane.
Pr. 25 cents. [1799–1800] [2] p. 32½ cm.

Song, pfte. acc. Arr. for flute or "guittar," p. [2].
First line same as title.   NN

THE UNHAPPY SWAIN.
(*In* The American musical miscellany. Northampton, 1798. p. 179–181)

Melody and bass, with accompanying text.
First line: Cease ye fountains, cease to murmur.   DLC (etc.)

[UNIDENTIFIED COLLECTION (beginning with "A lesson")]
   See [Unidentified *Collection* (beginning with "A lesson")]

[UNIDENTIFIED COLLECTION OF INSTRUMENTAL AND VOCAL
   MUSIC. New York] Printed for Hewitt & Rausch.
   See [Unidentified *Collection* . . .] Printed for Hewitt & Rausch.

THE UNION HARMONY, or Universal collection of sacred music. In two
   volumes. Volume II. Containing a large and valuable collection of anthems, odes, and psalm and hymn tunes in three and four parts. Adapted
   to the use of American choirs and other practitioners; a great part of which
   were never before published. By Oliver Holden, author of the American
   Harmony. [Verses] Published according to Act of Congress. Printed
   typographically at Boston, by Isaiah Thomas and Ebenezer T. Andrews.
   Sold at their bookstore, No. 45 Newbury street; by said Thomas, in Worcester;
   by the editor at his store in Charlestown, and by the booksellers in Boston.
   1793. 175, [1] p. 12½ x 22 cm.

   Title-page; dedication, p. [2]; music, p. [3]–175; index to vol. II and table
   of first lines, p. [176].

   Three and four-part choruses. Open score.
   Most important secular numbers: Spring, an ode, p. 10–11.—Ode to harmony,
   p. 13–14.—Invocation to Charity, p. 61–65.
                            DLC, ICN, MH, MHi, MWA, NN

UNITED STATES.
   See Mr. *Francis's ballroom assistant.*

UNITED STATES COUNTRY DANCES.
   See United States country *Dances.*

THE VEIL. A favorite song. Sung in the new entertainment of Fashionable
   rallery [!] New York, Printed for G. Gilfert & co. at their Musical magazine,

[442]

No. [ ] Broadway.   Where may be had a great variety of musical instruments & musick &c.   [ca. 1796]   [2] p.   32½ cm.

Song, pfte. acc.
First line: With straw hat and spencer and tasty bandeau.
Listed in *BM Cat.* as composed by Jonas Blewitt and published in London, ca. 1796.   This is consistent with the American imprint.   **MWA**

VERMONT.   French country dance.
See United States country *Dances*, p. 3.

THE VERY POPULAR AND BEAUTIFUL SCOTCH BALLAD   . . .
See The Blue Bell of Scotland.

THE VETRANS [!] Written for the new entertainment called Great news, **or A** trip to the Antipodes.   Charles Dibdin.   Sold at Carr's Musical repository's, Philadelphia, New York & Baltimore.
(*In* The gentleman's amusement, ed. by R. Shaw.   Philadelphia [1794–96] p. 62–64).

Song, pfte. acc.   Arr. for two flutes, p. 64.
First line: Dick Dock a tar at Greenwich moor'd.
In No. [8], 1796.   **DLC, PHi, PP–K**

A VIEW OF THE TEMPLE—a Masonic ode.
(*In* The harmonist's companion, by Daniel Belknap.   Boston, Oct., 1797. p. 29–31)

Two-part chorus.   Open score.
First line: Sacred to heav'n behold the dome appears.   **DLC, MWA**

——— The same.
(*In* The Evangelical harmony, by Daniel Belknap.   Boston, Sept., 1800. p. 66–68)   **CtY, DLC, ICN, MB, MHi, MWA, RPJCB**

VIGUERIE'S FAVORITE SONATA.
See Viguerie's favorite *Sonata.*

THE VILLAGE HOLY DAY.   A favorite new air.   [Philadelphia]   Publish'd by G. Willig at his Musical magazin [!], No. 163 North Third street   [n. d.] 1 l.   31½ cm.

Imprint at foot of page.
Song, pfte. acc., followed by arr. for "Ger. flute" or guitar.
First line: Glimmring in the glowing West.
Published between November, 1794, and March, 1795.   **ES, MWA, PU**

——— The same as preceding, but without imprint, ca. 1795.   **ES**

——— The same.
(*In* Young's vocal and instrumental musical miscellany.   Philadelphia [1793–95]   p. 62)

Song, pfte. acc., followed by arr. for German flute or guitar.
First line same as preceding.
In No. 8, 1795.   **DLC**

Also advertised (as *The village holiday*) April, 1795, as "published and to be had of G. Gilfert & Co. at their Musical Magazine, No. 121 [*i. e.*, 191] Broadway," New York.   No copy of this issue has been found.

[443]

THE VILLAGE MAID.
(*In* The gentleman's amusement, ed by R. Shaw. Philadelphia [1794–95] p. 49)

Melody only for flute (or violin). Single staff.   DLC

*THE VILLAGE RECRUIT.
Advertised in November, 1798, by "George Gilbert, at his music-store, 177 Broadway, Apollo's Head," as "just published."

THE VILLAGE SPIRE. A celebrated song by Giordani.
(*In* Young's vocal and instrumental musical miscellany. Philadelphia [1793–95] p. 24–25)

Song, pfte. acc.
First line: Beneath yon mountain's shaggy cliff.
In No. 3, 1793.   DLC, Hopк.

*THE VINTAGE.
Opera. *See* Sterne's Maria.

*VIOLIN CONCERTO. By Giovanni Gualdo.
See Concertos.

*VIOLIN CONCERTO. By Philip Phile.
See Concertos.

*THE VIRGIN OF THE SUN.
This "play in 5 acts . . . being the first part of Pizarro in Peru, or the death of Rolla. Written by A. von Kotzebue," was to have its first performance at New York, on March 12, 1800. In act 4th "a desolate place, without the walls of the temple. Chorus of priests, who dig the grave of Cora. Music by M. [Victor] Pelissier."

VIRGINIA.
See United States country *Dances*, p. 13.

VIRGINIA REEL.
See Country *Dances*.

*VIRTUE OVER MUCH.
Comic song by Raynor Taylor. Was to be sung in his "Musical perform-ance . . . the whole of the music original and composed by Mr. Taylor," at Annapolis, Md., on February 28, 1793.

VIVE LA LIBERTÉ. A new song, composed by R. Taylor. Philadelphia, Printed for the Author, No. 96 North Sixth s treet, and sold at B. Carr's Musical repository's, Market street, Philadelphia; William street, New York and at I. Carr's, Market street, Baltimore. (Price ¼ of a dollar) [1795] [2] p. 33 cm.

Song with chorus, pfte. acc.
First line: When liberty to bless mankind.
Advertised as for sale in March, 1795.   DLC, NBuG, PP-K

*THE VOCAL CHARMER. Philadelphia: Printed and sold by William Spotswood. 1793.

Advertised in January, 1793, among "new books. American editions. For sale by William Spotswood . . . Song books . . . price sewed 3 s." It is remarked that

The above are embellished with engraved frontispieces, and will be found to contain the beauties of English poetry in that line.

Therefore "The vocal charmer" probably contained no music.

THE VOCAL COMPANION. Being a choice collection of the most approved songs, catches, duets, &c. Philadelphia, Printed for Matthew Carey, No. 118 Market street. 1796. viii, [9]–196 p., front. 16 cm.

Title-page, verso blank; index, p. [iii]–viii; songs, p. [9]–196. 217 numbered songs, words only. Tunes occasionally mentioned. DLC, MWA

*THE VOCAL ENCHANTRESS, or Town and country songster. A collection of the most celebrated new songs. Published by Rice & co., No. 50 Market street, Philadelphia.

Advertised in Dunlap's *American daily advertiser*, Philadelphia, April 9, 1791.

*THE VOCAL INSTRUCTOR, publish'd in numbers. No. 1. Containing the rules of vocal music, by principle in questions & answers;—remarks on the causes of its decline and hints for recovering its respectability. A morning and an evening hymn composed and set to music for this work;—and a sliding music scale, never before publish'd in which a moveable index points out the names and distances of the notes in all their variations; the other numbers of the work will contain sacred, moral or sentimental psalms, hymns, songs, etc. for the improvement and pleasure of youth. By Benjamin Dearborn.

Copyright records, Massachusetts District, February 28, 1797.

*THE VOCAL MAGAZINE OF NEW SONGS. For sale at Bell's book store, Third street, Philadelphia.

Advertised in the *Pennsylvania gazette*, Philadelphia, October 1, 1783. Whether this is American or English issue is not known.

*THE VOCAL MUSE, OR LADIES SONGSTER. Containing a collection of elegant songs. Selected from British and American authors.

Advertised in *Dunlap's American daily advertiser*, October 5, 1792, as "just published and to be sold at Messrs. T. Dobson and W. Young's book stores, Second Street, also at Mr. H. Kammerer's Store, No. 24, North Third street, [Philadelphia] (Price 3s 9. neatly bound)."

THE VOCAL REMEMBRANCER, being a choice selection of the most admired songs, including the modern. To which are added favourite toasts and sentiments. Philadelphia, Printed by William Spotswood. 1790. viii, 184 p., front. 17 cm.

Frontispiece: A pastoral scene. I. Smither, Sculp. Title-page; table of first lines, p. [ii]–viii; toasts and sentiments, p. viii; text, p. [1]–184.

Contains poetry only.   No tunes indicated.   MWA, NBuG (lacks front.)
NHi, PPI

"This book with the Apollo and Charmer will be found to contain as good a collection of songs as is extant in the English language." (William Spotswood's advertisement in the *Pennsylvania gazette*, September 29, 1790. Sonneck adds, possibly identical with

*THE VOCAL REMEMBRANCER.
Advertised in January, 1793, among "new books.   American editions.
For sale by William Spotswood . . . song books . . . price sewed, 4 s. 2."
It is remarked that

> The above are embellished with engraved frontispieces, and will be found to contain the beauties of English poetry in that line.

[A VOLUME OF SONGS, ETC. Composed or copied by Francis Hopkinson *See* [A volume of *Songs*, etc. . . . by Francis Hopkinson]

*VOLUNTARIES, or Fugues for the organ or harpsichord by William Selby.
See Apollo, and the Muse's musical compositions.

THE VOLUNTEERS.   A musical entertainment as performed at the New Theatre.   Composed by Alex^r Reinagle.   The words by Mrs. Rowson. Philadelphia, Printed for the Author and sold at the music shops [1795] [1], 4–20 p.   33½ cm.

Title-page.

Songs, duets, etc., pfte. acc.

Contents:

- p.   4 Here beneath our lowly cott.
-     5 We'll chearful our endeavours blend.
-     6 When I was a little lad.
-     7 When o'er the mountain's top we go.
-   8–9 Some tell us that women are delicate things.
-    10 Twas on a pleasant summer's eve.
- 11–12 Dear Yankoo, whither dost thou stray.
- 12–13 I'll talk of all my lover's charms.
-    14 When I've got the ready rhino wounds.
-    15 My tender heart you stole away.
-    16 My Thomas is the kindest lad.
-    17 Rough as the waves on which we sail.
- 18–19 Adieu, adieu, my only life (Dibdin).
-    20 Finale: Then haste the laurel wreath's entwine.   DLC

This "comic opera in two acts, (written by Mrs. Rowson) . . . the overture and music entirely new, composed by Mr. [Alexander] Reinagle," had its first performance at the New Theatre, Philadelphia, on January 21, 1795.

[VOUS L'ORDONNÉ JE ME SERAI CONNOITRE] A. favourite. French. song. (*In* [Miscellaneous and incomplete [?] collection] Philadelphia [ca. 1795] p. 10)

Song, pfte. acc.
Title from first line.
Attributed to Monsigny (*BM Cat.*)
Preceded on p. 9–10 by *The wedding day*, by James Hook.   DLC

[446]

—— Separate issue of preceding, 1795–97. DLC, MWA

VULCAN'S GIFT, or the Bower of Hymen. "With entirely new music and original overture" was to be performed in New York, June 25, 1796. (*Minerva*, New York, same date.)

What American composer furnished this "new music" and "original overture"?

WAFT ME SOME SOFT AND COOLING BREEZE] Song for two voices in canon. Composed by Dr. G. K. Jackson. Copyright secured.
(*In* New miscellaneous musical work, by Dr. G. K. Jackson [n. p., ca. 1800] p. 3)

Duet unaccompanied. Two staves.
Title from first line. DLC, MWA

THE WAGGONER. Written and composed by Dibdin (20 cents) Philadelphia. Sold by H. & P. Rice, No. 50 Market st., between Second and Front streets, (*In* The gentleman's amusement, ed. by R. Shaw. Philadelphia [1794–96] p. 38–39)

Song, pfte. acc.
First line: When I comes to town with a load of hay.
In No. 5, March 1, 1795. DLC, PHi

—— The same as preceding.
(*In* A collection of new & favorite songs [A] Philadelphia [ca. 1800] p. [180]–[181]) HFB

—— Separate issue of preceding, advertised as published in May, 1794. CtY

THE WALLS OF MY PRISON.
(*In* Young's vocal and instrumental musical miscellany. Philadelphia [1793–95] p. 37)

Song, pfte. acc.
First line: The walls of my prison are high.
Composed by Isabella Theaker More (*BM Cat.*)
In No. 5, 1793. DLC, Hopk.

WALTER'S SWEETHEARTS.
See Dorothy Dump, by Samuel Arnold.

THE WALTON.
See Twenty-four American country *Dances*, p. 7.

WALTZ.
(*With* The favorite march in Pizzaro. New York [1798?])
Pfte. 2 hds. Three scores. NN

THE WALTZ COTILLION.
See Favorite *Cotillions.*

THE WAMPUM BELT. Composed by James Hewitt.
(*In* [Unidentified collection of instrumental and vocal music. New York
Hewitt & Rausch [1797] p. 8)

Song, pfte. acc.
First line: The wampum belt no more can charm.
At foot of page: The rangers cotillon [!] (Pfte. 2 hds.)   DLC, ES

———— The same as preceding. First page, numbered 8, of a detached sheet
from above collection.   JFL

———— The same as preceding.
(*In* A collection of new & favorite songs. [A] Philadelphia [ca. 1800
p. [153] numbered 8)   HFE

———— Separate issue of preceding, ca. 1797.   MI

A WANDRING [!] GIPSEY. Composed by I. Percy. Words by P. Pindar
(*In* The musical journal for the piano forte, ed. by B. Carr. Baltimore
[1800] v. 1, no. [17], p. (38)–(39).)

Song, pfte. acc.
First line: A wand'ring gipsey, sir am I.
I. Percy: John Percy.   DLC, ES, LSL, NN, NRU–Mus

A WAND'RING GIPSEY. Composed by Percy.
(*In* The musical journal for the flute or violin. Baltimore [1800] no. 17,
p. 34–36)

Melody only, flute or violin, with accompanying text.
First line same as preceding.   DLC

For the same text (approximately) but different setting, *cf.* The gipsey,
by James Fisin.

THE WAND'RING VILLAGE MAID. Composed by R. Taylor. Philadelphia, Printed for the Author, No. 96, North 6th street. Sold at B. Carr's
Repository's, Market st., and William st., N. York. And by J. Carr, Market
st., Baltimore (Price ¼ of a dollar) [1795] [2] p. 33 cm.

Song, pfte. acc.
First line: Where roves my wand'ring Phoebe, where.
Advertised as published, "printed for the author" in March, 1795.

CtY, DLC, ES, PP-K

*THE WARBLING SONGSTER, or Cure for dullness. Philadelphia, 1795.

THE WARWICKSHIRE MARCH.
See Compleat tutor for the fife . . . p. 17.

WAS I A SHEPHERDS MAID. Philadelphia, Printed for A. Reinagle; I.
Aitken, Sculpt. [n. d.] [2] p.

Imprint at foot of p. [2].
Song, pfte. acc.
First line same as title.

[448]

Song in *The padlock*, by Charles Dibdin.
Probably printed by Thomas Dobson at the Stone House in Second street, Philadelphia, ca. 1789.   ES

—— The same as preceding, but with pagination.
(*In* [A collection of favorite songs, arr. by A. Reinagle.   Philadelphia, 1789?]
p. 19–20)   ES

*WASHINGTON.   A song by Mrs. Pownall.   Tune, Hearts of oak.
First line: To the earth's utmost verge, tho' Bellona is heard.

Words only appeared in Dunlap and Claypoole's *American Daily advertiser* (Philadelphia), July 29, 1794.
Was to be sung at a concert in Boston, on August 1, 1794.

WASHINGTON.   Set by S. Holyoke.
(*In* The Massachusetts magazine.   Boston, September, 1790.   p. 571–572)

Song, pfte. acc.
First line: When Alcides the son of Olympian Jove.   DLC (etc.)

WASHINGTON.   Set to music by S. Holyoke.
(*In* The American musical miscellany.   Northampton, 1798.   p. 274–277)

Melody and bass, with accompanying text.
First line same as preceding.   DLC (etc.)

WASHINGTON AND INDEPENDENCE.   A favorite patriotic song.   Composed by Victor Pelissier.   New York, Printed and sold by G. Gilfert, No. 177 Broadway   [1797–1801]   [2] p.   31½ cm.
Song, pfte. acc.
First line: When Freedom's son in these blest climes.   MWA

*WASHINGTON AND LIBERTY.
A "song in celebration of Washington and liberty.   Written and to be sung by Mrs. Pownall," was to be sung "after the play" at the City Theatre in Charleston, S. C., on February 22, 1796.

WASHINGTON GUARDS.   Written by John F. Wells, a member of the Third company of Washington Guards.   Copyright secured.   Philadelphia, Published and sold at G. Willig's music store   [n. d.]   [2] p.   33½ cm.

In lower right-hand corner, p. [2]: W. Guards.
Song, pfte. acc.   Tune, "Anacreon in heaven."
First line: To the brave sons of Freedom.
Since the text is set to the tune of "Anacreon in heaven," a tune very popular at the turn of the century, particularly ca. 1798–1800 (*cf.* "Adams and liberty") perhaps that date is as likely as any other, although the copyright notice and the absence of the long "s" might well suggest a somewhat later date.   DLC, PP–K

WASHINGTON GUARDS MARCH.   Composed by a member of the Washing
ton association.   Philadelphia, Published and sold at G. Willig's Music
magazine [n. d.] [2] p. 32 cm.

Pfte. and two flutes.

Followed on p. [2] by "Washington Guards quickstep."

Published probably ca. 1800.   DLC, MNSt, MWA, PP.

WASHINGTON GUARDS QUICKSTEP.

(*With* Washington Guards march. Philadelphia [ca. 1800] p. [2])

Pfte. and two flutes.   DLC, MNSt, MWA, PP.

*WASHINGTON'S COUNSEL FOREVER HUZZA!

This song was "written, composed and to be sung by Mr. Clifford" in th
comic opera of "The farmer," at the Charleston Theatre on January 22, 1794

WASHINGTON'S MARCH.

In his own annotated copy of this *Bibliography*, Sonneck has inserted a brie
article of his which appeared in *Zeitschrift der Internationalen Musikgesell
schaft*, for April, 1906.

Since this article is interesting in itself and practically covers the materia
in the original entry at this point, but (as the result of later research on Son
neck's part) tends to nullify much that he wrote earlier, it has seemed wise
to substitute it here.

As he suggests, his fullest earlier treatment of the entire subject is to be foun
in his book on *Francis Hopkinson . . . and James Lyon* (1905) where both
marches are reprinted in the Appendix.

The article from *Zeitschrift . . .* is as follows:

WASHINGTON'S MARCH

In my book on "Francis Hopkinson and James Lyon" (1905) a chapter had
to be devoted to this march as in certain—so to say—posthumous sources
Hopkinson's name is linked with it.   Simultaneously the tradition, vague
as it is, that the Washington's March was composed during our Revolu
tionary War (1775–1783) required a careful examination.   Research
brought not less than eight marches by that name to light and all eight
composed during the last decades of the eighteenth century.   I further
remarked that I ran across no reference to a Washington's March until the
year 1794.   The interesting historical puzzle was approached in my
"Bibliography of Early Secular American Music" (1905) with these words:

"Therefore, while a Revolutionary origin of one of the several marches
known by this or a slightly varying title is possible, it is by no means
certain, and in particular Francis Hopkinson's authorship is very
doubtful."

Since then, however, I have found two references to Washington's March
preceding the year 1794.   The one in newspapers of the year 1788, and the
other, which is by far more important, in the *Massachusetts Spy*, Worcester,
May 27, 1784.   There we read:

"Philadelphia

May 8.   On Saturday, the first of May, the sons of St. Tammany met
at Mr. Pole's seat, on Schuylkill, in order to celebrate the day . . . The
ceremony of the feast being ended, and the company seated on the

[450]

grass, thirteen toasts were drank, under the discharge of the artillery, with musick adapted to each, viz.

1. St. Tammany and the day—Musick, St. Tammany.
2. The United States—may the benign influence of the thirteen stars be shed on every quarter of the world.   Musick, Yankee Doodle.
3. Louis the XVIth, the defender of the rights of mankind.   May his people be as happy as he is great and good.   Broglio's march.
4. The United Netherlands.   Washington's March.
5. George Washington.   Clinton's retreat. . . ."

Consequently, the Revolutionary origin of Washington's March can no longer be doubted and even Francis Hopkinson's authorship now becomes more plausible.   It remains only to investigate to which of the eight marches the United Netherlands' toast was drank.   Applying the comparative method, six may immediately be eliminated and against the seventh beginning:

one of its several titles speaks convincingly: "President's New March," as our first president was inaugurated in 1789.   Therefore, we have to see in the Washington's March of Revolutionary origin the one beginning:

Washington.   O. G. Sonneck.

That Sonneck's conclusion in this matter (as he saw it) was sound, is self evident.   That still later research has shown he was mistaken as to the proper chronological sequence of the two marches is also entirely understandable, for early American music was notorious for its utter confusion in regard to the relation of a given title to a given piece of music.   In point of fact, if we *reverse the order of Sonneck's two musical quotations* we need not then alter a single syllable of what he has written.   His confusion arose from the fact that the title, "President's new march," as he used it, really referred to the second quotation and not to the first.   Evidently Sonneck had not seen the numerous other issues now available entitled "President's new march" or "New President's march," all of them opening with the phrase of this second quotation; whereas the vigorous upspringing leaps of the first quotation unquestionably belong to the Revolutionary "Washington's march" or "Washington's march at the Battle of Trenton"—which are identical.   It is unfortunate that in the one example of the "President's new march" here cited by Sonneck this title should have been given to the wrong music and thus precipitated an entirely false conclusion.

This later view of the matter holds in spite of the fact that (as we have seen)

[451]

the Revolutionary march is sometimes called "President's new march" an
the later march (contrariwise) is sometimes entitled "Washington's march
or "General Washington's march." Indeed if one knows these old work
merely by title he wanders in a hopeless maze. Only through examinatio:
of the music itself can he find his way out.

As to the much discussed question of Francis Hopkinson's authorship of th
Revolutionary "Washington's march" we need only say that while sucl
authorship seems entirely possible, it has not yet been fully established.

An interesting side light on the essential contemporaneousness of the thre
best known eighteenth century American marches is disclosed by the fac
that they all three appear together in *Military Amusement*, Philadelphia.
1796 (*q. v.*): on p. 3, "Presidents march"; on p. 4, "Washington's march;"
on p. 5, "Presidents new march."

Individual entries are as follows: First, Group I, those whose openin₣
measures are given in Sonneck's first musical quotation (*Washington's marcl
at the Battle of Trenton* and *Washington's march*); then, Group II, those represented by the second musical quotation (*Washington's march, General Washington's march, The new President's march* and *The President's new march*)

GROUP I

WASHINGTON'S MARCH at the Battle of Trenton.
(*With* Washington's march. Philadelphia. G. Willig [n. d.])

Pfte. 2 hds.
Possibly composed by Francis Hopkinson.
Published possibly as early as November, 1794.   MNSt, MWA, PPL

It is interesting to note that we have here, published simultaneously, both of
the Washington's marches which, individually and collectively, have aroused
so much discussion!

WASHINGTON'S MARCH.
(*With* The new president's march. [Philadelphia] B. Carr [1796])

Pfte. 2 hds.   CSmH, JFD, LSL

Advertised in the *American Minerva*, New York, February 23, 1796, under
"new musick" as "this day published . . . price 12 cents . . . printed and
sold by B. Carr."

──── The same.
See Military amusement [1796] p. 4.

──── The same.
New York, Printed for G. Gilfert, No. 177 Broadway [n. d.]   1 l.   30 cm.

Pfte. 2 hds., followed by arr. for German flute.
Published possibly as early as 1797.   PP–K

──── The same.
New York, Printed & sold by George Gilfert, No. 177 Broadway   [n. d.]
1 l.   32½ cm.

Pfte. 2 hds., followed by arr. for German flute.
Published possibly as early as 1797.   DLC, MB

—— The same.
(*With* The new President's march.   New York, J. Paff [1798 or 1811])

Pfte. 2 hds.
Published probably in 1798, although Sonneck notes that these marches were still popular at the time of our second war with Great Britain.

MB, MWA, NBuG, NRU–Mus

—— The same.
(*With* The new President's march.   New York, J. Hewitt [1799–1800])

Pfte. 2 hds.   DLC, ES, JFD
See also The instrumental assistant.

GROUP II

GENERAL WASHINGTONS MARCH.
(*In* The gentleman's amusement, ed. by R. Shaw.   Philadelphia [1794–96] p. 24)

For flute or violin.   Single staff.
In No. 3, June, 1794, to January, 1795.   DLC, PHi

WASHINGTON'S MARCH.   Philadelphia, Published and sold at G. Willig's Musical magazine [n. d.] 1 l. 32 cm.

Pfte. 2 hds.
Followed by "Washington's march at the Battle of Trenton"
Published possibly as early as November, 1794.   MNSt, MWA, PPL

WASHINGTON'S MARCH.   As performed at the New Theatre.   Philadelphia, Published and sold at G. Willig's Musical magazine [n. d.] [2] p. 34 cm.

Pfte. 2 hds.
"Quickstep composed by R. Taylor," p. [2].
Published possibly as early as November, 1794.   CSmH, DLC, MNSt, PPL
Sonneck adds: In 1793 concerts were given at the New Theatre, but the programs do not mention the march.   The first theatrical performance was given on February 17, 1794, and the march probably was then or afterwards played as incidental music.   However, Willig can not possibly have published the march before 1795 or very late in 1794, that is to say, before the foundation of his Musical magazine.

THE NEW PRESIDENT'S MARCH.   [Philadelphia] Printed by B. Carr. Price 12 cents.   [1796] 1 l. 33 cm.

Pfte. 2 hds.
Followed by "Washington's march."

Advertised in February, 1796, as "Published . . . printed and sold by Benjamin Carr," Philadelphia.   CSmH, JFD LSL

PRESIDENTS NEW MARCH.
See Military amusement [1796], p. 5.   DLC

GENERAL WASHINGTONS MARCH.
See Evening amusement [1796], p. 19

Melody only.   Single staff.   DLC

[453]

NEW PRESIDENT'S MARCH. Philadelphia, Printed and sold by G. Willi, Market street, No. 185. [n. d.] 1 l. 33 cm.

Pfte. 2 hds.
Published possibly as early as 1798.   DLC, P

THE NEW PRESIDENT'S MARCH. New York, Sold at J. Paff's music stor [1798 or 1811] 1 l. 32 cm.

Pfte. 2 hds.
Followed by "Washington's march."   MB, MWA, NBuG, NRU-Mu

——— The same.
New York, Printed & sold by J. Hewitt, No. 23 Maiden-lane Price 1 shillin [1799–1800] 1 l. 32 cm.

Pfte. 2 hds.
Followed by "Washington's march."   DLC, ES, JFl

It is a curious fact (to be observed above) that in every instance where bot marches are published together, it is the one from this second group tha invariably takes precedence! Was it more popular than the other?

WASHINGTON'S MARCH at the Battle of Trenton.
See Washington's march.

WASHINGTON'S MINUET AND GAVOTTE.
See United States country *Dances*, p. 1–2.

DIE WASSERFAHRT VON D. M. MICHAEL. 1. March. 2. Andantino 3. Menuetto. 4. Allegro. 5. Adagio. 6. Presto; choral-mässig. 7, Echo Allegretto. 8. Menuetto. Allegretto; Zusammenruf. 9. Retour march 10. Polonaise. 11. Rondo. Vivace. 12. Adagio; "Waldstück für 2 Hörne bey der Spring zu blasen." 13. Menuetto. Allegretto. 14. Andante; Allegro Presto. 15. Finale.

MS. orchestra parts to a suite (in E-flat maj.) for 2 clarinets, 2 bassoons 2 horns. In Archives of the Moravian Church, Bethlehem, Pa. First horn part missing [?]

Rufus A. Grider in his *Historical notes on music in Bethlehem, Pennsylvania from 1741–1871* . . . Philadelphia, 1873, mentions of Michael's "Parthien" for wind instruments in particular "Die wasserfarth" (or "The Boat ride") "It was composed for a diversion on the river on Whit Monday afternoon."

WATER PARTED FROM THE SEA. In Artaxerxes by D. Arne, and adorned with Italian graces by Mr. Trisobio. [Philadelphia, 1796–98] 3 p. 33½ cm Song, pfte. acc. Three staves, with voice part on middle staff.
First line same as title.
For supplied imprint *cf. Fair Aurora.*
Mr. Trisobio: Filippo Trisobio.
D. Arne: Dr. Thomas Augustine Arne.   CdeW, DLC, ES, PP-K

——— The same as preceding, except followed on p. [4] by "Par sa legéreté."
                                                                                          NN
*THE WATERMAN, or the First of August.
This "musical entertainment . . . music by Dibdin [1774], orchestra accompanyments by [Victor] Pelisier," was to be performed at New York, in October, 1796.

THE WAVING WILLOW. Sung in the Midnight wanderers. New York, Printed for James Hewitt. Pr. 2/ [n. d.] [2] p. 32 cm.

Song, pfte. acc.
First line: 'Twas at the hour of day's decline.
The midnight wanderers, by William Shield, was first performed in Philadelphia, June 1, 1796; in New York, May 3, 1797. Hence, the date of this issue would seem to be 1796–97, preferably 1797. However, as Hewitt was in partnership with Rausch in 1797, until taking over Carr's New York store in the fall of that year, the earlier date is probably, after all, the more reasonable one. ES, MWA

WAVING WILLOW. Sung by Miss Broadhurst. Published at B. Carr's Musical repositories, New York & Philadelphia & J. Carr's, Baltimore (12 cts.) [n. d.] p. (49). 34 cm.

At head of title: Musical journal, No. 23. Vocal section.
Imprint at foot of page.
Song, pfte. acc.
First line same as preceding.
Since p. 49 is lacking in No. 23 of Carr's *Musical journal for the piano forte*, Baltimore, 1800, it would seem at first sight that this must be a re-issue of the missing page. This deduction is disproved, however, by the publisher's address, which dates this issue as probably about 1796–97. This view is strengthened by the fact that Miss Broadhurst sang *Waving Willow* at her benefit concert in New York, November 15, 1796. It seems possible, then, that this issue is from an earlier collection published by Carr, of which all trace is lost; or it may be that while originally planned for the *Musical journal* (as we know it) this number was later discarded and issued separately. *See also* Lucy Gray of Allendale. PHi

WAVING WILLOW. Sung by Miss Broadhurst. Published at B. Carr's Musical repositories, New York & Philadelphia & J. Carr's Baltimore (12 cts.) [n. d.] 1 l. 32½ cm.

Song, pfte. acc.
First line same as preceding.
Published probably 1796–97. McD–W

THE WAXEN DOLL.
See When first I slipp'd my leading strings, by William Shield.

THE WAY TO GET MARRIED. A favorite song. Sung at Vauxhall Gardens. Composed by Mr. Hook. New York, Printed for G. Gilfert, No. 177 Broadway [1797] [2] p. 31 cm.

Song, pfte. acc.
First line: Come hither ye belles. MWA
Advertised in March, 1797, as to be published "in a few days" by "G. Gilfert at his Musical Magazine, No. 177 Broadway," New York.

THE WAY WORN TRAVELLER. In The Mountaineers. Composed by Dr. Arnold. Price 31 cents. Philadelphia, Printed at Carr & Cos. Musical repository [1794] 3 p. 32 cm.

Duet, pfte. acc.
First line: Faint and wearily the way worn traveller.
Advertised as published in February, 1794. NRU–Mus

———— The same as preceding, but with an additional page numbered "72." This page is headed "The way worn travellers. For two flutes," and is identical with page 72 of *The gentleman's amusement.* The date is therefore, ca 1796.

ABHu, CtY, DLC, ES, JFD, LSL, MB, McD–W, MNSt, MWA, NN

THE WAYWORN TRAVELLERS. For two flutes.
(*In* The gentleman's amusement, ed. by R. Shaw. Philadelphia [1794–96] p. 72)

Duet for two flutes.
In No. [9], 1796.   PHi, PP–K

———— The same as preceding. Fourth page, numbered 72, of a detached portion of the above collection. 1796.   PHi

[WE KINGS WHO ARE IN OUR SENSES] Sung by Mr. Bates in Tom Thumb the Great.
(*In* The gentleman's amusement, ed. by R. Shaw. Philadelphia [1794–96] p. 5)

Melody only, flute (or violin) with accompanying text.
Title from first line.
In No. 1, April 1, 1794.   DLC, PHi, PP–K

[WE'LL CHEARFUL [!] OUR ENDEAVOURS BLEND] Sung by Miss Broadhurst & Mr. Darley, Junʳ
(*In* The volunteers, by A. Reinagle. Philadelphia [1795?] p. 5)

Duet, pfte. acc.
Title from first line.   DLC

THE WEDDING DAY. A favorite song. Sung by Mrs. Hodgkinson. Price 20 cents. Philadelphia, Printed for Carr and co., at their Musical repository, No. 136 High street [1793] [2] p. 34 cm.

Song, pfte. acc. Arr. for flute or "guittar," p. [2].
First line: What virgin or shepherd of valley or grove.
Composed by James Hook.
Sung by Mrs. Hodgkinson in Bickerstaff's comedy, *The romp.*
Advertised as published in December, 1793.
In certain copies, *e. g.*, DLC, "20" has been changed to "25" in price given.
ABHu, CtY, DLC, ES, HFB, LSL, MdHi,MWA, N, NBuG, NN

THE. WEDDING. DAY. A. favourite. song. Publish'd by G. Willig, 165 Market street [Philadelphia]
(*In* [Miscellaneous and incomplete [?] collection] Philadelphia [ca. 1795] p. 9–10)

Song, pfte. acc.
First line same as preceding.
Followed on p. 10 by "A.favourite.French.song." [Vous l'ordonné je me serai connoitre] Attributed to Monsigny.   DLC

———— Separate issue of preceding, 1795–97.   DLC, MWA

[456]

THE WEDDING DAY. Boston, Printed & sold at P. A. von Hagen & co. at their warranted imported piano forte ware house, No. 3 Cornhill & G. Gilfert N. York [n. d.] [2] p. 31 cm.

Song, pfte. acc. Arr. for German flute or violin, p. [2].
First line same as preceding.
Published probably in 1799. DLC, ES, MWA, N, NN, RPJCB

THE WELCH [!] QUESTION. Alternative title of *Cymro oble.*

[WERE I OBLIG'D TO BEG MY BREAD]
See Somebody.

*WERTER TO CHARLOTTE, a favorite ballad.
Advertised in November, 1797, as "published at Carr's Musical Repository," Philadelphia.

WEST POINT PRESERVED. Alternative title of *The death of Major Andre and Arnold's treachery.*

WHAT A BEAU YOUR GRANNY WAS.
See Evening amusement, p. 14.

WHAT ARE THE BOASTED JOYS OF LOVE. Cavatina. Composed by Mr. Shield. Price 25 cents. Printed and sold at B. Carr's Musical repository, Philadelphia; J. Carr's, Baltimore & J. Hewitt's, N. York.
(*In* A collection of new and favorite songs. [B] Philadelphia [1797–99] 2 unnumbered p.)

Song, pfte. acc.
First line same as title. PU

———— Separate issue of preceding, 1797–98.
Advertised in January, 1798, as "published at Carr's Musical Repository," Philadelphia. ES, NN

WHAT CAN A LASSY DO. Sung by Mrs. Franklin at Vauxhall. Composed by Mr. Hook. New York, Printed & sold at J. Hewitt's Musical repository, No. 131 William street. Sold also by B. Carr, Philadelphia & J. Carr, Baltimore. Pr. 25 cts. [1797–98] [2] p. 32½ cm.

Song, pfte. acc.
First line: Young Jemmy's ganging after me.
DLC, ES, MB, MWA, NN, PP–K

Advertised in January, 1798, as "just published." Probably identical with issue advertised in December, 1797, as "published at Carr's Musical repository, Market street," Philadelphia.

———— The same as preceding.
(*In* A collection of new & favorite songs. [A] Philadelphia [ca. 1800] p. [94]–[95]) HFB

[WHAT MED'CINE CAN SOFTEN THE BOSOM'S KEEN SMART] A favorite song in the Chaplet. Composed by Dr. Boyce.
(*In* A collection of favorite songs, arr. by A. Reinagle. Philadelphia [1789 ?] p. 13)

Song, pfte. acc.
Title from first line. DLC

[457]

WHAT SHEPHERD OR NYMPH.
(*In* Young's vocal and instrumental musical miscellany. Philadelphia [1793–95] p. 46)

Song, pfte. acc.
First line same as title.
In No. 6, 1794.   ABHu, DLC, Hopk.

[WHEN A LITTLE MERRY HE] A favorite song. Sung by Mrs. Marshall in the new musical drama called the Purse. Engrav'd & published by J. Young & sold at Carr's Repository's. Phila⁹, N. York & Baltimore.
(*In* Young's vocal and instrumental musical miscellany. Philadelphia [1793–95] p. 57)

Song, pfte. acc.
Title from first line.
In No. 8, 1795.

The purse, or *Benevolent Tar,* by William Reeve, was first performed with Mrs. Marshall in the cast, January 7, 1795, at Philadelphia. Hence No. 8, of Young's *Miscellany* could not have been issued before that date.   DLC

——— The same as preceding. First page, numbered 57, of a detached leaf from above collection. 1795.   NN

——— Separate issue of preceding, but without pagination, ca. 1795.   ES, NN

——— Separate issue of preceding, but with "Lullaby" from Stephen Storace's *The pirates* on verso, paged 4. At top of page and preceding "Lullaby" is the final stanza of "When first this humble roof I knew" from *The lord of the manor,* by William Jackson of Exeter. ca. 1795.   DLC

[WHEN A LITTLE MERRY HE] Sung by Mrs Marshall in the Purse, or Benevolent tar.
(*In* The gentleman's amusement, ed. by R. Shaw. Philadelphia [1794–96] p. 36–37)

Melody only, flute (or violin) with accompanying text.
Title from first line.
In No. 5, March 1, 1795.   DLC, PHi

[WHEN A LITTLE MERRY HE] Sung by Miss Harding in the new musical drama cal'd the Purse, or Benevolent tar. Printed for & sold at Carr's Repository's, Philadelphia, New York, and by I. Carr, Baltimore [ca. 1795] 1 l. 32½ cm.

Song, pfte. acc.
Title from first line.
First New York performance with Miss Harding in the cast, February 23, 1795.   DLC, ES, LSL, MWA, RPJCB

[WHEN ALL THE ATTICK FIRE WAS FLED] Song. Set by William Cooper (*In* The Massachusetts magazine. Boston, August, 1790. p. 506–507)

Song, pfte. acc.
Title from first line.   DLC (etc.)

[458]

WHEN BIDDEN TO THE WAKE OR FAIR. Rosina.
(*In* A collection of favorite songs, divided into two books. Arr. by A. Reinagle. Philadelphia [1789?] bk. 2, p. 20)

Song, pfte. acc.
First line same as title.
Rosina, by William Shield. CdeW, DLC, PU

WHEN BIDDEN TO THE WAKE OR FAIR.
See Evening amusement [1796] p. 20.

WHEN BIDDEN TO THE WAKE. A favorite Scotch tune in the opera of Rosina.
(*In* The musical repertory. Boston [1796–97] No. III, p. 36)

Song, pfte. acc.
First line: When bidden to the wake or fair. DLC

———— Separate issue of preceding, 1796–97. DLC

WHEN BIDDEN TO THE WAKE.
(*In* The American musical miscellany. Northampton, 1798. p. 70–71)

Melody only with accompanying text.
First line same as preceding. DLC (etc.)

WHEN BIDDEN TO THE WAKE OR FAIR. A favorite song in Rosina.
New York, Printed & sold at J. Hewitt's Musical repository. Price 12½ cents. [n. d.] 1 l. 32½ cm.

Song, pfte. acc.
First line same as title.
Probably published ca. 1798, as MB copy is included in a group—all of which bear imprint, "131 William street." DLC, MB

———— The same as preceding.
(*In* A collection of new & favorite songs. [A] Philadelphia [ca. 1800] p. [187]) HFB

WHEN CAESAR'S BIRTHDAY GLADS BRITANNIA'S ISLE.
See Ode set to music on Mrs. B—s birthday.

WHEN DELIA ON THE PLAIN APPEARS. Composed by F. Kotzwara.
New York, Printed & sold by G. Gilfert, No. 177 Broadway [1798] 1 l. 34 cm.

Song, pfte. acc.
First line same as title. JFD

Advertised in November, 1798, as "just published" by "George Gilbert at his music store, 177 Broadway, Apollo's Head," New York.

WHEN EDWARD LEFT HIS NATIVE PLAIN. A new song. Composed by Mr. Hook. New York, Printed & sold at J. & M. Paff's music store, No. 127 Broadway [1799–1803] 4 p. 32 cm.

Song, pfte. acc.
First line same as title. DLC, NN

[459]

[WHEN FIRST COLUMBUS SOUGHT THIS STRAND] Song, set to music
by Mr. Reinagle.
(*In* The Philadelphia monthly magazine, February, 1798. p. 107)
Song, words only.
Title from first line.
The music seems not to be extant.   DLC (etc.)

[WHEN FIRST I SLIPP'D MY LEADING STRINGS] A favorite song from
the Woodman, a comic opera by Bate Dudley. The musick by William
Shield.
(*In* The Massachusetts magazine. Boston, October, 1791. p. 643)
Song, pfte. acc.
Title from first line.   DLC (etc.)

WHEN FIRST I SLIPP'D MY LEADING STRINGS. A song in the comic
opera of the Woodman. Composed by Mr. Shield.
(*In* The musical repertory. Boston [1796] No. II, p. 17)
Song, pfte. acc.
First line same as title.   DLC

WHEN FIRST I SLIPP'D MY LEADING STRINGS.
(*In* The American musical miscellany. Northampton, 1798. p. 76–78)
Melody only, with accompanying text.
First line same as title.   DLC (etc.)

———— The waxen doll. Sung by Miss Solomon in the Children in the wood.
(*In* The gentleman's amusement, ed. by R. Shaw. Philadelphia [1794–96]
p. 32)
Melody only, flute (or violin) with accompanying text.
First line: When first I slip'd my leading strings.
In No. 4, February 1, 1795.
Samuel Arnold's opera *The children in the wood*, with Miss Solomon in the
cast, was first performed in New York, December 26, 1794. This song from
William Shield's *The woodman* seems to have been persistently interpolated
in Arnold's opera.   DLC, PHi

———— The waxen doll. Sung by Miss Solomons in the Children in the wood.
Price 12 cents.
(*In* [Four songs, ed. by B. Carr. New York, ca. 1795] p. [3])
Song, pfte. acc.
First line: When first I slip'd my leading strings.   NN

———— Separate issue of preceding, ca. 1795.   DLC, LSL

The names *Solomon* and *Solomons* are used quite interchangeably throughout
this period.

———— The waxen doll. Sung by Miss Solomons in the Children in the wood.
Printed and sold at G. Willig's Musical magazin [!] No. 165 Market street,
Philadelphia. Price 12 cents [1795–97] 1 l. 31 cm.
Song, pfte. acc.
First line: When first I slip'd my leading strings.   MWA, NBuG, PHi

[460]

WHEN FIRST THIS HUMBLE ROOF I KNEW.
(*In* Young's vocal and instrumental musical miscellany. Philadelphia [1793–95] p. 51–52)

Song, pfte. acc.
First line same as title.
From *The lord of the manor,* by William Jackson of Exeter.
Followed on p. 52, by *Lullaby,* by Storace.
In No. 7, ca. 1794.   DLC

——— Separate issue of preceding, but with page numbers changed to 3–4, and with imprint at foot of both pages, "New York, Published by I. Young & co.," probably to be dated 1792–93.   ES

For other known titles in this second (unidentified) collection, *cf.* "Young Lubin was a shepherd boy."

Curiously enough DLC has also a copy of the "Lullaby," p. 4, preceded by [When a little merry he] by William Reeve (identical with p. 57 of Young's *Miscellany*) instead of "When first this humble roof I knew," as above.

WHEN FIRST THIS HUMBLE ROOF I KNEW. Price 12 cents [n. p., n. d.] 1 l. 32 cm.

Song, pfte. acc.
First line same as title.
From its marked similarity to B. Carr's New York issue of Storace's *My native land,* can reasonably be assigned to same imprint: New York, Printed & sold by B. Carr.   DLC

Presumably the issue advertised in March, 1796, among "new editions of . . . favorite songs some of which never before published in America," at "Carr's Musical Repository, William Street," New York.

WHEN FIRST THIS LITTLE HEART BEGAN. A favorite song. Sung in the opera of Zorinski. Composed by Dibdin. New York, Printed for G. Gilfert & c? at their Musical magazine, 177 Broadway [1796] [2] p. 34½ cm.

Song, pfte. acc.
First line same as title.
Zorinski, by Samuel Arnold, was first produced in 1795.
"When first this little heart began" is noted in the score as composed by Dibdin.   NRU–Mus

WHEN FIRST TO HELEN'S LUTE. A song in the opera of the Children in the woods [!]
(*In* The musical repertory. Boston [1796] No. I, p. (1).)

Song, pfte. acc.
First line same as title.
The children in the wood, by Samuel Arnold.   DLC, MB

——— O 'tis love. Sung by Mr. Carr.
(*In* [Four songs from an unidentified collection, ed. by B. Carr. New York, ca. 1795] p. [2])

Song, pfte. acc.
First line: When first to Helen's lute.
Title forms fifth line of second stanza.   NN

[461]

———— Separate issue of preceding, ca. 1795.　　　　　　　　　LSL
Benjamin Carr sang in the first American performance of Samuel Arnold's opera in New York, December 26, 1794.

[WHEN I'VE GOT THE READY RHINO WOUNDS]　Sung by Mr. Francis. (*In* The volunteers, by A. Reinagle.　Philadelphia [1795?]　p. 14)
Song, pfte. acc.
Title from first line.　　　　　　　　　　　　　　　　　DLC

WHEN I THINK ON YOUR TRUTH.　A favorite song by Mr. Delamain. [New York]　Sold by I. and M. Paff　[n. d.]　1 l.　32½ cm.
Song, pfte. acc., followed by arr. for flute or "guittar."
First line same as title.
Published possibly as early as 1799.
Mr. Delamain: Henry Delamaine (*Eitner*).　　　　　　　DLC

WHEN I WAS A CHIT.　Composed by Mr. Hook.　New York, Printed for G. Gilfert & co., No. 191 Broadway　[1794–95]　[2] p.　31 cm.
Song, pfte. acc.
First line same as title.　　　　　　　　　JFD, MWA, RPJCB

[WHEN I WAS A LITTLE LAD]　Sung by Mr. Francis. (*In* The volunteers, by A. Reinagle.　Philadelphia [1795 ?] p. 6)
Song, pfte. acc.
Title from first line.　　　　　　　　　　　　　　　　　DLC

WHEN ICICLES HANG BY THE WALL.　From Shakespear's Love's labour lost.　Composed by B. Carr.　Philadelphia, Printed & sold by Carr & co.
(*In* Four ballads by B. Carr.　Philadelphia [1794] p. 2–3)
Song, pfte. acc.　Three staves.
First line same as title.　　　　　　　　　　　　　　　DLC

———— Separate issue of preceding, ca. 1794.　　　　　　　　　ES

WHEN LUCY WAS KIND.　A favorite song sung at Vauxhall gardens. Printed for & sold by B. Carr at his Musical repository's, Philadelphia and N. York.　Sold also by J. Carr at his music store, Gay st., Baltimore (Price 20 cts.)　[1796]　[2] p.　32½ cm.
Song, pfte. acc.　Arr. for guitar or Ger. flute, p. [2].
First line same as title.
Composed by James Hook.
Advertised as published in March, 1796.　　　　　　CtY, ES, JFD

WHEN LUCY WAS KIND.
(*In* Elegant extracts for the German flute or violin.　Philadelphia　[1796] bk. 2, p. 22–23)
Melody only, flute or violin, with accompanying text.
First line same as title.　　　　　　　　　　　　　　DLC, NN

*WHEN MIGHTY MARS.
Advertised in Dunlap and Claypoole's *American daily advertiser*, Philadelphia, December 11, 1793, as published by "B. Carr & Co., Musical repository, No. 122 South side of Market street," among other "last new songs from Britain."

[462]

WHEN NICHOLAS. For three flutes or voices.
(*In* Elegant extracts for the German flute or violin. Philadelphia [1798] bk. 3, p. 22–23).

Trio, flutes or voices. Three staves.
First line: When Nicholas first to court began.
Composed by William Shield.   DLC, NN

WHEN NIGHTS WERE COLD. A favorite song. The words by Mr. Harwood. Set to music by Mr. B. Carr. Price [ ] Philadelphia. Printed by Carr & co., No. 122 Market street.
(*In* Four ballads by B. Carr. Philadelphia [1794] p. 8–9)

Song, pfte. acc. Three staves.
First line same as title.   DLC

———— Separate issue of preceding, ca. 1794.   DLC, MWA

WHEN NIGHTS WERE COLD. Introduced in the Children in the wood.
(*In* The gentleman's amusement, ed. by R. Shaw. Philadelphia [1794–96] p. 82)

Melody only, flute (or violin) with accompanying text.
First line same as title.
Composed by Benjamin Carr.
The children in the wood, by Samuel Arnold.
In No. 10, ca. 1796.   PHi, PP–K

WHEN NIGHTS WERE COLD. An original song. Composed by Mr. B. Carr, of Philadelphia. Introduced in the opera of the Children in the woods [n. p., n. d.] p. 60–61. 32 cm.

Song, pfte. acc.
First line same as title.
Apparently a reprint from *The musical repertory,* Boston, Number IV [1797–99].   JFD
See Songs, duets and choruses of The children in the wood.

WHEN NIGHTS WERE COLD. Sung by Mrs. Hodgkinson.
(*In* Elegant extracts for the German flute or violin. Philadelphia [1798] bk. 3, p. 19)

Melody only, flute or violin, with accompanying text.
First line same as title.   DLC, NN

WHEN ON A CLEAR AND CLOUDLESS NIGHT. Composed by Joseph Willson. Organist of Trinity Church. New York, Printed & sold at J. Hewett's Musical repository, No. [ ] Maiden Lane [n. d.] [2] p. 33 cm.

Song, pfte. acc.
First line same as title.
Published possibly as early as 1799.   ES

WHEN ON THE OCEAN. Sung by Miss E. Westray in the opera of the Shipwreck. New York, Printed and sold by George Gilfert, No. 177 Broadway [ca. 1799] [2] p. 32½ cm.
Song, pfte. acc. Arr. for German flute, p. [2].
First line same as title.   DLC, MWA

[463]

Samuel Arnold's opera *The shipwreck* had its first performance in New York February 18, 1799. Although the cast for the performance has never been found, Miss E. Westray was a member of the company at the time and presumably took part.

WHEN ONCE BY THE CLEAR GLIDING STREAM. A new song. Sung by Master Gray.
(*In* A collection of favorite songs, by Mr. Hook. New York. [1799–1801] bk. [2], p. 6–7)

Song, pfte. acc.
First line same as title. DLC

[WHEN O'ER THE MOUNTAIN'S TOP WE GO] Sung by Mr. Marshall.
(*In* The volunteers, by A. Reinagle. Philadelphia [1795?] p. 7)

Song, pfte. acc.
Title from first line. DLC

WHEN PENSIVE. Sung by Mrs. Marshall in Blue Beard. Printed & sold at B. Carr's Musical repository, Philadelpha[!]; J. Carr's, Baltimore & J. Hewitt's New York (Price 25 cents)
(*In* A collection of new & favorite songs. [C] Philadelphia [ca. 1799] p. 6–7)

Song, pfte. acc. Arr. for "guittar," p. 7.
First line: When pensive I thought of my love.
Blue Beard, by Michael Kelly had its first performance in Philadelphia May 24, 1799, with Mrs. Marshall as Fatima. ABHu, LSL, NN

—— Separate issue of preceding, ca. 1799.
ABHu, DLC, ICN (lacks part of p. 7), JFD, MdHi, MWA

WHEN PENSIVE I THOUGHT ON MY LOVE. A favorite new song. Sung in the grand dramatic romance of Blue Beard, or Female curiosity. New York, Printed & Sold by G. Gilfert, No. 177 Broadway [n. d.] [2] p. 32 cm.

Song, pfte. acc. Arr. for German flute, p. [2].
First line: When pensive I thought of my love.
Since Michael Kelly's *Blue Beard* seems not to have reached New York until 1802, this issue should probably be dated in reference to the Philadelphia performances, *i. e.*, ca. 1799. DLC, ES, JFD, MWA, RPJCB

WHEN PENSIVE. Sung by Miss Broadhurst in Blue Beard. Printed & sold by G. Willig, No. 185 Market st., Philadelphia [n. d.] [2] p. 34 cm.

Song, pfte. acc. Arr. for "guittar," p. [2].
First line: When pensive I thought of my love.
Published possibly as early as 1799. NN, PP–K

WHEN RURAL LADS AND LASSIES GAY. A favorite song. New York, Printed and sold by G. Gilfert & co., No. 209 Broadway [1795] [2] p. 33 cm.

Song, pfte. acc. Arr. for German flute, p. [2].
First line same as title. DLC, JFD

—— The same.
New York, Printed and sold by G. Gilfert, No. 177 Broadway [1797–1801] [2] p. 29½ cm.

Song, pfte. acc. Arr. for German flute, p. [2].
First line same as title. JFD, RPJCB

WHEN SANDY TOLD HIS TALE OF LOVE. A favorite song. Composed by Mr. Hook. Price 25 cts. New York, Printed and sold at I. C. Moller's musical store [n. d.] 2 p. 32½ cm.

Song, pfte. acc.
First line same as title.
Sonneck's date, ca. 1800. DLC, ES
DLC has also a second copy from same plate, but with imprint apparently erased. Sonneck has tentatively supplied the imprint "New York, James Hewitt, 1800," evidently with reference to its advertisement as "sung by Miss Brett at Mount Vernon" and "just published" in July, 1800, by "J. Hewitt, at the Musical Repository, No. 23 Maiden Lane," New York.

[WHEN SCORCHING SUNS THE THRIFTY EARTH] Sung by Mrs. Old-mixon in the Noble peasent [!]
(In The gentleman's amusement, ed. by R. Shaw. Philadelphia [1794–96] p. 64)
Melody only, flute (or violin) with accompanying text.
Title from first line.
In No. [8], 1796.
The noble peasant, by William Shield, was performed in Philadelphia with Mrs. Oldmixon in the cast, May 8, 1795. DLC, PHi, PP-K

WHEN SEATED WITH SAL. A favorite sea song. Sung by Mr. Harwood in the Purse, or Benevolent tar. Sold at Carr's Musical repository's, Philadelphia, N. York & Baltimore. (Price ⅛ of a dollar)
(In The gentleman's amusement, ed. by R. Shaw. Philadelphia [1794–96] p. 30–31)
Song, pfte. acc. Arr. for German flute, p. 31.
First line same as title.
In No. 4, February 1, 1795.
The purse, or Benevolent tar: William Reeve. DLC, PH

——— Separate issue of the preceding, 1795.
Advertised in January, 1795, as "just published" by "R. Shaw, No. 44 Seventh, near Mulberry st.," Philadelphia. ES, MWA
Mr. Harwood sang in the first Philadelphia performance of *The purse,* January 7, 1795.

WHEN SUMMER SWEET SUMMER. A favorite ballad. Written by Mr. Waldron. Composed by J. Sanderson. New York, Sold by I. and M. Paff [n. d.] 2, [1] p. 32½ cm.
Song, pfte. acc. Arr. for German flute, p. [3].
First line same as title.
Published possibly as early as 1799. DLC

WHEN THE HOLLOW DRUM. In the Mountaineers. Printed & sold by Carr at his Repository's, Philadelphia & N. York & by I. Carr, Baltimore. Price 25 cts. [1797] [3] p. 32 cm.
Song, pfte. acc. Arr. for flute, p. [3].
First line: When the hollow drum has beat to bed.
Advertised among other "songs lately published," September, 1797.
The mountaineers, by Samuel Arnold. DLC, JFD, LSL, MdHi, NN

[465]

WHEN THE HOLLOW DRUM. A favorite song. Sung in the Mountainneers [!] New York, Printed & sold by G. Gilfert, No. 177 Broadway [n. d.] [3] p. 30½ cm.

Song, pfte. acc.
First line same as title.
Followed on p. [3] by "Hope told a flatt'ring tale." (Song, pfte. acc.)
Published possibly as early as 1797.
The mountaineers was first performed in New York on March 30, 1796.
NN, PP–K

THE FAVORITE AIR, WHEN THE HOLLOW DRUM. Sung in the Mountaineers. Arranged as a rondo for the piano forte by T. Haigh. Boston, Printed & sold at P. A. von Hagen's imported piano forte warehouse, No. 3 Cornhill [n. d.] 4 p. 34 cm.

Pfte. 2 hds.
Published possibly as early as 1799. JFD, MWA, N, NBuG, RPJCB

[WHEN THE MEN A COURTING CAME] Sung by Miss Broadhurst in the opera of Robin Hood.
(*In* Young's vocal and instrumental musical miscellany. Philadelphia [1793–95] p. 43)

Song, pfte. acc.
Title from first line.
In No. 6, 1794.
Robin Hood, by William Shield, was first performed with Miss Broadhurst in the cast, March 10, 1794, at Philadelphia. Hence No. 6 of Young's *Miscellany* cannot be dated earlier than this. ABHu, DLC, Hopk.

WHEN THE MERRY BELLS. A new song. Sung by Miss Howells. The words by Bragshaw, junr. esqr.
(*In* A collection of favorite songs, by Mr. Hook. New York [1799–1801] bk. [2], p. 14–15)

Song, pfte. acc.
First line: As tripping o'er the new mown hay. DLC

WHEN THE MIND IS IN TUNE. Sung by Miss Broadhurst. Price 20 cents. Printed & sold at B. Carr's Musical repositories, New York and Philadelphia & J. Carr's, Baltimore [1794–97] [2] p. 33 cm.

Song, pfte. acc.
First line same as title.
Perhaps identical with the edition advertised by J. Carr, Baltimore, in September, 1797, among "songs lately published." ABHu, LSL, PHi

WHEN THE OLD HEATHEN GODS. Sung by Mr. Williamson in the farce of Flash in the pan. The words by Mr. Milns. Music by J. Hewitt. New York, Printed & sold by J. Hewitt at his Musical repository, No. 131 William st. Sold also by B. Carr, Philadelphia & J. Carr, Baltimore [1798] [2] p. 32 cm.

Imprint at foot of p. [2].
Song, pfte. acc.
First line same as title.

Of special interest because of reference to Washington in last line.
Only performance of *Flash in the pan*, New York, April 20, 1798.

MWA, NRU-Mus, PHi

Advertised in the *Federal gazette*, Baltimore, in June, 1798, as "just published" among "new songs sung at the theatres, New York."

———— The same as preceding.
(*In* A collection of new & favorite songs. [A] Philadelphia [ca. 1800] p. [104]–[105])

HFB

WHEN THE ORIENT BEAM.
See Hunting song, by Hans Gram.

WHEN THE ROSY MORN APPEARING. As a duett.
See Evening amusement, p. 15.

WHEN THE SHADES OF NIGHT PURSUING. Composed by J. Hewitt.
(*In* The musical journal for the piano forte, ed. by B. Carr. Baltimore [1800] v. 1, no. [23], p. (53).)

Song, pfte. acc.
First line same as title.

DLC, ES, LSL, NN, NRU–Mus

WHEN THE SHADES OF NIGHT. Composed by I. Hewitt.
(*In* The musical journal for the flute or violin. Baltimore [1800] no. 23, p. 46–47)

Melody only, flute or violin, with accompanying text.
First line: When the shades of night pursuing.
I. Hewitt: James Hewitt.

DLC

WHEN THE SHEPHERD ASKS MY HAND SIR. Sung in the favorite romance of the Captive of Spilberg. Composed by J. L. Dussek. New York, Printed & sold at J. Hewitt's, No. 23 Maiden Lane. Pr. 25 cents.
(*In* A collection of new & favorite songs. [A] Philadelphia [ca. 1800] p. [56]–[57])

Imprint at foot of p. [57].
Song, pfte. acc. Arr. for flute, p. [57].
First line same as title.
The captive of Spilberg (or *Spilburg*) was not performed in America until March 25, 1801 (New York).

HFB

WHEN THE STARS CAN BE TOLD. Boston, Printed & sold at P. A. von Hagen's imported pianoforte warehouse, No 3 Cornhill. Sold also by G. Gilfert, N. York; D. Winton, Providence; W. R. Wilder, New Port; B. B. Macanulty, Salem; E. M. Blunt, Newbury Port; I. Stanwood, Portsmouth & A. Jenks, Portland [n. d.] [2] p. 33 cm.

Song, pfte. acc.
First line same as title.
Composed by James Hook.
Published possibly as early as 1799.

RPJCB

[467]

WHEN THE STARS CAN BE TOLD. A favorite new song. Sung in the new opera of Dimond cut dimond [!]. Composed by Mr. Hook. New York, Printed & sold by G. Gilfert, No. 177 Broadway. And to be had at P. A. von Hagen's music store, Boston [ca. 1800] [2] p. 31 cm.

Song, pfte. acc.
First line same as title. MWA, NRU–Mus

Although first produced in 1797, Hook's *Diamond cut diamond* did not reach America in the eighteenth century.

WHEN THE WORLD FIRST BEGAN. Sung by Mr. Townshend in the musical entertainment the Mouth of the Nile. New York, Printed & sold by G. Gilfert, No. 177 Broadway.
(*In* [The mouth of the Nile, by T. Attwood. New York, ca. 1799] p. 12–13)

At right and below imprint: Attwood.
Song, pfte. acc.
First line same as title.
Thomas Attwood's *The mouth of the Nile* was performed in New York, May 13, 1799. NRU–Mus

—— Separate issue of preceding, ca. 1799. MWA

WHEN WE SAILOR LADS FIRST PUT TO SEA. A favorite song. Composed by Miss Bannister. Published by G. Willig, No. 185 Market st.; Philadelphia [1798–1804] [2] p. 33 cm.

Song, pfte. acc.
First line same as title.
This song appears in the score of Thomas Attwood's *The mariners* as "Compos'd by Miss Bannister." DLC

WHEN WILLIAM AT EVE.
(*In* A collection of favorite songs, divided into two books. Arr. by A. Reinagle. Philadelphia [1789 ?] bk. 1, p. 5)

Song, pfte. acc.
First line: When William at eve meets me down at the stile.
From *Rosina*, by William Shield. CdeW, DLC, ES, Hopk.

—— The same.
New York, Printed & sold by G. Gilfert, No. 177 Broadway [1797–1801] 1 l. 30½ cm.

Song, pfte. acc.
First line same as preceding. DLC, NN

WHEN WINTER ROBES THE HILLS AND PLAINS.
See Winter. Set by A. R.

WHEN YOU AND I LOVE MARRIED ARE. A favorite duetto. In the new opera of the Captive of Spilberg. Composed by I. L. Dussek. Printed and sold by R. Shaw (Importer of music and musical instruments) Market street, No. 92, Baltimore. Price 25 cents [1798–1800] [2] p. 33 cm.

Song, pfte. acc. Arr. for "guittar," p. [2].
First line same as title. LSL

[468]

———— The same as preceding, except that the address in imprint is changed to: No. 13 South Fourth st., Philadelphia.
Possibly published as early as 1800. **DLC**

Re Jan Ladislav Dussek's opera, *The captive of Spilberg*, *cf.* When the shepherd asks my hand sir.

WHERE'S THE HARM OF THAT. A favorite song. Composed by Mr. Hook. New York, Printed & sold at J. Hewitt's Musical repository, No. 131 William street. Sold also by B. Carr. Philadelphia & J. Carr, Baltimore. Price 25 cts. [1797–99] [2] p. 33½ cm.

Song, pfte. acc.
First line: Twas in the grove. **DLC, ES, NRU–Mus, PHi**

Probably identical with issue advertised in December, 1797, as "published at Carr's Musical Repository, Market street," Philadelphia, and in March, 1797, as to be published "in a few days" by "G. Gilfert. At his Musical Magazine, No. 177 Broadway," New York.

———— The same as preceding.
(*In* A collection of new & favorite songs. [A] Philadelphia [ca. 1800] p. [92]–[93]) **HFB**

WHERE LIFFEY ROLLS ITS SILVER STREAMS. A favorite song in the opera of Jack of Newbery. Composed by Mr. Hook. New York, Printed and sold at I. Hewitt's Musical repository, No. 131 William street. And at B. Carr's, Philadelphia and J. Carr's, Baltimore [1797–99] [2] p. 32 cm.

Song, pfte. acc. Arr. for "guittar," p. [2].
First line same as title. **NN, PHi**

Probably identical with issue advertised in December, 1797, as "published at Carr's Musical Repository, Market street," Philadelphia.

———— The same as preceding.
(*In* A collection of new & favorite songs. [A] Philadelphia [ca. 1800] p. [172]–[173]) **HFB**

WHILE MOUNTAINS POISE THE BALANCED GLOBE.
See Military glory of Great Britain.

WHILE THE MORN IS INVITING TO LOVE. A favorite song. Printed & sold at B. Carr's Musical repository, Philadelphia; J. Carr's, Baltimore, & J. Hewitt's, New York. Price 25 cents. [1797–99] [2] p. 32 cm.

Below imprint: Pianoforte, guittar & clarinett.
Song, pfte. acc. Arr. for flute or violin, p. [2].
First line: The sun when arising bespangles the dew.
Composed by Raynor Taylor.
ABHu, DLC, JFD, LSL, MdHi, NN, PP–K

[WHILST EUROPE IS WRAPT IN THE HORRORS OF WAR] Song. Tune, Hearts of oak.
(*In* New [American] patriotic songs, added to a collection of songs by C. Dibdin. Philadelphia, 1799. p. 321–322)

Words only.
Title from first line. **DLC, MWA, NHi, NN, RPJCB**

[469]

WHILST HAPPY IN MY NATIVE LAND.   Sung by Mr. Darley in the Farmer.
(*In* The gentleman's amusement, ed. by R. Shaw.   Philadelphia [1794–96]
p. (87).)

Melody only, flute (or violin) with accompanying text.
First line same as title.
In No. 11, 1796.
Mr. Darley sang in William Shield's opera *The farmer* in Philadelphia,
March 12, 1794, and January 8, 1796.   PHi, PP–K

WHILST WITH VILLAGE MAIDS I STRAY.   New York, Printed for and
sold at I. C. Mollers musical store, No. 58 Vesey street [1797] [2] p.   31 cm.
Song, pfte. acc.
First line same as title.
From *Rosina*, by William Shield.   DLC, JFD

WHILST WITH VILLAGE MAIDS I STRAY.   A favorite song in Rosina.
Philadelphia, Printed & sold by G. Willig, No. 158 [*i. e.*, 185?] Market st.
[n. d.]   [2] p.   32½ cm.
Song, pfte. acc.
First line same as title.
Published possibly as early as 1798.
                          DLC, ES, MWA, NRU–Mus, PHi, RPJCB

THE WHIM OF THE DAY.   The merry companion, containing twenty-six of
the newest and most approved songs sung at the theatres in Boston and other
genteel places of amusement.   Boston, Printed and sold by J. White, near
Charles River Bridge.   1798.   24 p.   16 mo.   MB

THE WHIPPOORWILL.
See Manuscript collection of hymns, songs, etc., (50).

THE WHITE COCKADE.
See Evening amusement, p. 19.

WHITE YOKE.
See Compleat tutor for the fife . . . p. 27.

WHITHER MY LOVE.   A favorite song in the Haunted tower.   Price 20 cents.
Philadelphia, Printed for Carr & co., at their Musical repository, No. 136
High street   [1793]   [2] p.   33 cm.
Song, pfte. acc.
First line same as title.
In certain copies, *e. g.*, DLC, "20" has been changed to "25" in price given.
Composed by Giovanni Paisiello and interpolated in Storace's opera *The
haunted tower.*   DLC, HFB, JFD, LSL, McD–W, MdHi, MWA, NBuG
Advertised in December, 1793, as "published . . . printed singly . . ."
by "B. Carr & Co. Musical Repository, No. 122 Southside of Market Street,"
Philadelphia.   As to apparent inconsistency in address, *cf.* The match girl.

WHITHER MY LOVE, FOR TWO FLUTES.
(*In* Elegant extracts for the German flute or violin.   Baltimore [1794] bk. 1,
p. 12–13)

Song, for two flutes with accompanying text.   Two staves.
First line same as title.   DLC, NN

WHITHER MY LOVE.
(*In* The favorite songs in the opera of [The haunted tower, by S. Storace] New York [1795–96] p. 4–5)

Song, pfte. acc.
First line same as title. ABHu

WHITHER MY LOVE. A favorite song in the Haunted tower. Boston, Printed & sold by P. A. von Hagen & cos. at their piano forte and music warehouse, No. 3 Cornhill. And also by G. Gilfert, New York. [n. d.] [2] p. 32 cm.

Song, pfte. acc.
First line same as title.
Published probably in 1799. DLC, JFD, RPJCB

WHO SO MERRY LIVES AS I. A favorite song. Composed by Metzger. Philadelphia, Published by G. Willig, No. 185 Market street [1798–1804] [2] p. 32½ cm.

Song, pfte. acc.
First line same as title. LSL, PP–K

[WHY COLLIN MUST YOUR LAURA MOURN]
See The select songster. New Haven, 1786. p. 16.

WHY HEeAVES MY FOND BOSOM]
See The select songster. New Haven, 1786. p. 18.

WHY, HUNTRESS, WHY.
See The archers, by Banjamin Carr.

WHY SLEEPS THE THUNDER.
See Air in the Reconciliation.

THE WIDOW. Sapphic by Southey. The music by B. Carr.
(*In* The musical journal for the piano forte, ed. by B. Carr. Baltimore [1800] v. 1, no. [23], p.(50)–(51).)

Song, pfte. acc.
First line: Cold was the night wind. DLC, ES, LSL, NN, NRU–Mus

Advertised in October, 1800, as "published at Chalk's Musical Repository and Circulating Library—No. 57, North Third Street," Philadelphia. Chalk's "Musical Repository" opened in 1800.

THE WILD GOOSE CHASE. A play in four acts; with songs, from the German of Augustus von Kotzebue; with notes, marking the variations from the original. By William Dunlap. Printed by G. F. Hopkins for William Dunlap, and sold at the office of the printer, No. 84 Maiden Lane [New York] . . . and most other Booksellers in the U. States. 1800. x, [2], [9]–104 p. 20 cm.

Title-page; frontispiece a portrait of Augustus von Kotzebue, "Engraved by Gilbert Fox;" also, in certain copies (*e. g.*, DLC), a portrait of Mr. Hodgkinson in the character of Baron Wellinghorst, drawn by Wm. Dunlap. The face engraved by C. Tvelmei (?). The drapery by G. Fox. "Published for the German Theatre by Wm. Dunlap." Title-page is followed by an "Advertisement" signed "W. Dunlap. New York, March 7, 1800." "The Life of Augustus von Kotzebue, written by himself. *My literary life,*" p. [iii]–x;

"German Theatre. No. [blank] The wild goose chase," p. [7]; "The wild goose chase as first performed at the New York Theatre, January 24, 1800. Characters . . . Performers . . . Music composed by Mr. Hewitt. Scenery by Mr. Ciceri," p. [8]; text, p. [9]–99; "Notes on the Wild goose chase" [in particular that "all the songs . . . are added by the translator . . ."], p. [100]–104.
Certain copies lack "By William Dunlap" on t.-p.
Certain copies show "No. I" on p. [7] after "German Theatre".
PU copy lacks portraits. NHi copy lacks portraits and first two pages.

CtY, DLC, MB, NHi, NN, PU

The play must soon have been altered, for it is called on February 19, 1800:

A Comic Opera, in three acts . . . The Music composed by Mr. Hewitt. As "The much admired Comic Opera of the Wild Goose Chase. Compressed in two Acts. The Music composed by Mr. Hewitt" it was to be performed in New York, on December 19, 1800.

In the mean time James Hewitt seems to have published the music, for Joseph Carr, when announcing his intention to publish the "Musical journal" (New York *Daily advertiser*, February 3) concludes the advertisement with

Next week, will be published, by J. Hewitt, the favourite songs in The Wild Goose Chase, as performed at the Theatre with great applause.

WILLIAM OF THE FERRY. Sung with the greatest applause at Vauxhall Gardens. (Price 20 cts.) Sold by Carr at his Musical repository's, Philadelphia & N. York & by I. Carr, Baltimore [1796] [2] p. 33 cm.
Song, pfte. acc.
First line: Oft as on Thame's banks I stray.
Advertised in March, 1796, as "published at Carr's Musical Repository, William Street," New York.

DLC, ES, LSL, McD–W, MWA, NN

THE MUCH ADMIRED BALLAD OF THE WILLOW. Composed by Storace. Sung by Mrs. Warrell. Price 25 cents. Printed and sold at B. Carr's Musical repository, Philadelphia; J. Carr's, Baltimore & J. Hewitt's, New York, &c. [2] p.
(*In* A collection of new & favorite songs. [B] Philadelphia [1797–99] no paging)
Song, pfte. acc. Arr. for "guittar," p. [2].
First line: Down by the river there grows a green willow.

PU

———— Separate issue of preceding, 1798.

DLC, NN

Advertised in January, 1798, as "just published by J. Hewitt, No. 131 William st.," New York. Possibly identical with the same song, also advertised in January, 1798, as published together with "Tell toll the knell" at "Carr's Musical Repository . . . Price one quarter dollar each, or in a collection with a neat title page annexed, one dollar fifty cents."

WILLY OF THE DALE. Composed by Mr. Hook. New York, Printed and sold by G. Gilfert & co., No. 209 Broadway near St. Pauls. Where may be had the greatest variety of vocal and instrumental music as also piano fortes [1795] [2] p. 33½ cm.
Song, pfte. acc. Arr. for "guittar," p. [2].
First line: When Spring dispensing sweets around.

DLC, JFD, RPJCB

[472]

THE WILTSHIRE MARCH.
See Compleat tutor for the fife . . . p. 13.

WINSOME KATE. Compos'd by Mr. Hook.
(*In* The gentleman's amusement, ed. by R. Shaw. Philadelphia [1794–96]
p. 61)

Melody only, flute (or violin) with accompanying text.
First line: Young Sandy's gone to kirk I ken.
In No. [8], 1796.   DLC, PHi, PP–K

———— He loves his winsome Kate. A favorite Scotch song. Composed by
Mr. Hook. New York, Printed & sold at J. Hewitt's Musical repository,
No. 131 William street. Sold also by B. Carr, Philadelphia & J. Carr,
Baltimore. Price 25 cts. [1797] [2] p. 33 cm.

Song, pfte. acc. Arr. for "guittar," p. [2].
First line: Young Sandy's gone to kirk I ken.   DLC, MB, NN

———— The same as preceding.
(*In* A collection of new & favorite songs. [A] Philadelphia [ca. 1800]
p. [200]–[201])   HFB

Advertised in December, 1797, as "published at Carr's Musical Repository
Market street," Philadelphia, but this was probably Hewitt's publication
for sale there.

WINTER.
(*In* The American musical miscellany. Northampton, 1798. p. 291–292)

Melody only, with accompanying text.
First line: Adieu ye groves, adieu ye plains.   DLC (etc.)

WINTER. Set by A. R.
(*In* The Massachusetts magazine. Boston, February, 1791. p. 117)

Song, pfte. acc.
First line: When Winter robes the hills and plains.
A. R., probably Alexander Reinagle.   DLC (etc.)

WINTER EVENING'S AMUSEMENT, or, Jovial companion. Containing a
choice collection of songs, much admired. And sung at most genteel places
of amusement. Boston, Printed and sold by J. White, near Charles. river
Bridg [!] and by W. T. Clap, in Fifth street. 1795. 24 p. 8 x 14 cm. RPB

A WINTER PIECE. Composed by S. Kleyser. Dedicated to J. Moses.
New York, Printed & sold at J. & M. Paff's musical store, No. 127 Broadway [n. d.] [2] p. 31½ cm.

Song, pfte. acc. Arr. for flute, p. [2].
First line: It was a winter ev'ning.
Published possibly as early as 1799.   NN

A WINTER'S EVENING. A favorite cantata. Sung by Mr. Hodgkinson.
Describing a forlorn mother & infant perishing in the snow. Composed by
Dr. G. K. Jackson. Printed for the Author. Copyright secured.
(*In* New miscellaneous musical work, by Dr. G. K. Jackson [n. p., ca. 1800]
p. 10–13)

Song, pftc. acc.
First line: It was a winter evening.   DLC, MWA

WISDOM'S FAVORITE.
See The select songster. New Haven, 1786. p. 51.

THE WISH, or the sequel to Henry's cottage maid. Composed by J. Hewitt. Price 20 cents. Printed and sold at B. Carr's Musical repositories in New York and Philadelphia and by J. Carr in Baltimore [ca. 1796] [2] p. 33½ cm.

Song, pfte. acc. Arr. for "guittar," p. [2].
First line: Sweet sounds that steal upon the pensive ear. DLC, MWA

THE WITCH. A favorite new song. New York, Printed and sold by G. Gilfert, No. 177 Broadway [1797] [2] p. 31½ cm.

Song, pfte. acc.
First line: As motley is thy fancied gear.
Composed by William Reeve.
Advertised in January, 1797, as "just published by G. Gilfert, at his Musical Magazine, No. 177 Broadway," New York. DLC, MWA

*THE WITCHES OF THE ROCKS, or, Harlequin everywhere. This pantomime, "with an entire new overture, songs, chorusses, and recitatives, composed by Mr. [Alexander] Reinagle" was performed at the New Theatre, Philadelphia, on February 26, 1796.

WITH A HEART LIGHT AND GAY. Sung by Mrs. Seymour in the Shipwreck. New York, Printed & sold by George Gilfert, No. 177 Broadway [n. d.] [2] p. 31½ cm.

Imprint at foot of p. [2].
Song, pfte. acc.
First line same as title.
Published probably ca. 1799. MWA

Samuel Arnold's opera The shipwreck was performed in New York many times in the season of 1799–1800. Mrs. Seymour was a member of the company at the time.

WITH LOWLY SUIT. From No song, no supper. Storace. [n. p., 179–?] p. (56)–(57). 34 cm.

Song, pfte. acc.
First line: With lowly suit and plaintive ditty.
Could this be from *Elegant extracts, (q. v.)? PHi
See also The ballad singer's petition.

WITH PLEASURE HAVE I PAST MY DAYS.
(In [A volume of songs, etc., composed or copied by Francis Hopkinson. 1759–60] p. 169)

Song, harpsichord acc.
First line same as title.
Composed by Francis Hopkinson. DLC

WITHIN A MILE OF EDINBURGH. A favorite Scotch song. Sung by Mrs. Pownall. New York, Printed for G. Gilfert & co., No. 209 Broadway near St. Pauls, where may be had an elegant assortment of piano fortes of the best makers in London [1795] [2] p. 33½ cm.

Song, pfte. acc. Arr. for German flute, p. [2].
First line: 'Twas within a mile of Edinburgh town.
Composed by James Hook (*BM Cat.*)   DLC, JFD

WITHIN A MILE OF EDINBURGH TOWN. A favrite [!] Scotch song. Sung by Miss Broadhurst. New York, Printed & sold by G. Gilfert & co., No. 209 Broadway near St. Pauls, where may be had a general assortment of fine tun'd piano fortes &c. [1795] [2] p. 33 cm.

Song, pfte. acc. Arr. for German flute, p. [2].
First line same as preceding.   DLC, MWA

WITHIN A MILE OF EDINBOURGH. Introduced & sung by Miss Broadhurst in the musical farce called My grandmother. Price 12 cents.
(*In* The gentleman's amusement, ed. by R. Shaw. Philadelphia [1794-96] p. 55)

Song, pfte. acc.
First line: 'Twas within a mile of Edinbourghtown.
In No. 7, May 1, 1796.
Sung by Miss Broadhurst in *My grandmother*, by Stephen Storace, at the New Theatre, Philadelphia, April 27, 1795.   PP-K

———— Separate issue of preceding, ca. 1796.   CdeW, DLC, ES, MdHi, RPJCB

WITHIN A MILE OF EDINBORO' TOWN.
(*In* Elegant extracts for the German flute or violin. Philadelphia [1798] bk. 3, p. 4)

Melody only, flute or violin, with accompanying text.
First line: 'Twas within a mile of Edinboro' town.   DLC, NN

WITHIN A MILE OF EDINBURGH.
(*In* The American musical miscellany. Northampton, 1798. p. 231-232)

Melody only, with accompanying text.
First line: 'Twas within a mile of Edinburgh town.   DLC (etc.)

WITHIN A MILE OF EDINBURGH TOWN. Boston, Printed & sold by P. A. von Hagen, Junior & cos., No. 62 Newbury street. Where may be had a general assortment of the best imported pianofortes &c. [1798-99] [2] p. 33 cm.

Song, pfte. acc. Arr. for German flute, violin or "clarinetti," p. [2].
First line: 'Twas within a mile of Edinburgh town.   RPJCB

WITHIN A MILE. New York, Printed & sold at J. Hewitt's Musical repository, No. 23 Maiden Lane [1799-1800] 1 l. 31 cm.

Song, pfte. acc.
First line same as preceding.   DLC, RPJCB

———— The same as preceding.
(*In* A collection of new & favorite songs. [A] Philadelphia [ca. 1800] p. [178])
                                                                        HFB

[475]

WITHIN A MILE OF EDINBORGH [!] With variations for the forte piano or violin. New York, Printed and sold at I. and M. Paffs music store, No. 127 Broadway [1799–1803] [3] p. 31½ cm.

Pfte. 2 hds.
At foot of each page: W.   ES

*———— 'Twas within a mile of Edinburgh town.
Advertised in March, 1796, "as sung by Miss Broadhurst" and "published at Carr's Musical repository, William street," New York. No such issue has been found.

WITHIN THESE SACRED BOWERS. A favorite song. Translated from the German. Composed by Mozart. New York, Printed & sold by G. Gilfert, No. 177 Broadway [1797–1801] 1 l. 34 cm.

Song, pfte. acc.
First line same as title.
An adaptation of "In diesen heil'gen hallen" from *Die Zauberflöte*.

DLC, JFD

THE WOLF AND THE PIKE. A patriotic song. Written by Andrew C. Mitchell. Philadelphia, Published and sold at G. Willig's Musical magazine [ca. 1800] [2] p. 33 cm.

In lower margin, p. [2]: Copyright secured.
Song, pfte. acc.
First line: A wolf once met a pike.   PP–K

THE WONDERFUL OLD MAN.
See The select songster. New Haven, 1786. p. 59–60.

*WOOD LARK SONG BOOK.
Advertised in the *Pennsylvania Gazette*, July 13, 1769, by

William Woodhouse, book-binder and stationer in Front-street near Chestnut-street and partly opposite Mr. John Bayly, Goldsmith, Philadelphia. Where merchants, shopkeepers and others may be furnished with . . . Wood Lark and Black Bird song books.

THE WOOD ROBIN. Boston, Printed & sold at P. A. von Hagen's Musical magazine, No. 3 Cornhill [n. d.] 1 l. 32 cm.

Song, pfte. acc.
First line: Stay sweet enchanter of the grove.
Composed by Reginald Spofforth.
Published possibly as early as 1799.   DLC, JFD, RPJCB

THE WOOD ROBIN. Composed by R. Spofforth. New York, Printed & sold by J. & M. Paff at their music store, No. 127 Broadway [1799–1801] 3 p. 30½ cm.

Song, pfte. acc. Three staves, upper staff for flute.
First line same as preceding.
At foot of p. 1: N. B. The flute part may be played on the upper part of the piano by a second person.
At foot of p. 3: Engraved by W. Pirsson, No. 417 Pearl Street.
William Pirsson was located at this address 1799–1801.

DLC, ES, MB, McD–W, N, RPJCB

———— The same.

(*In* The musical journal for the pianoforte, ed. by B. Carr. Baltimore [1800] v. 1, no. 11, p. (23)–(26).)

At head of title: No. 11 of a Musical journal for the pianoforte. Vocal section.
Song, pfte. acc. Three staves.
First line same as preceding. DLC, ES, LSL, MWA, MdHi, NN, NRU–Mus

THE WOOD ROBIN. A favorite song. Composed by Mr. R. Spofforth. Philad*, Published by John Aitken and sold at his Musical repository [ca. 1800] 3 p. 34½ cm.

After title: N. B. The flute accompaniment may be played on the upper part of the piano by a second person.
Song, pfte. acc. Three staves, upper staff for flute.
First line same as preceding. MWA

THE WOODMAN. A comic opera in three acts. As performed at the Theatre Royal, Covent Garden, with universal applause. By Mr. Bate Dudley. Philadelphia, Printed by Samuel Harrison Smith. 1794. 84 p. 18 cm.

Libretto to Shield's opera (1791).
Title-page, verso blank; dedication, p. [3]–[4]; advertisement, p. [5]; dramatis personae, p. [6]; text, p. [7]–84. MH, MWA, NIC, NN

Advertised on the last page of S. Harrison Smith's *American monthly review*, January, 1795:

Samuel Harrison Smith has just published to be sold by Mr. Stephens, No. 57 South Second Street . . . the comic opera of the Woodman . . .

*THE WOODMAN, or Female archery. With the original overture, etc. The words by the Reverend Bate Dudley, the music composed by Mr. Shield, and the accompaniments by Mr. Bradford of Charleston.

Thus advertised for second performance in America, on May 13, 1793, in Charleston, S. C.

THE WOODMAN. Written by Wm. Pearce, esqr Set to music by Mr. Linley. Price 25 cents. Printed and sold by R. Shaw at his music store, No. 13 South Fourth st., Philadelphia [n. d.] [2] p. 31½ cm.

Song, pfte. acc.
First line: Stay traveller tarry here tonight.
Mr. Linley: Thomas Linley, the Elder.
Published possibly as early as 1800. NN

THE WOODMAN'S FAIR DAUGHTER. New York, Printed & sold by G. Gilfert, No. 177 Broadway [1797–1801] [2] p. 34 cm.

Song, pfte. acc. Reproduction of the melody as if for instrumental performance, p. [2].
First line: 'Twas Spring when all nature look'd blooming and gay. JFD

WOOLF'S ADIEU.

(*In* The American musical miscellany. Northampton, 1798. p. 45–46)

Two parts, with accompanying text. Two staves.
First line: Too soon my dearest Sophia, pray take this kind adieu.
DLC (etc.)

[WOULD YOU GAIN THE TENDER CREATURE] In Acis and Galatea.
By Mr. Handel.
(*In* [Unidentified collection (beginning with "A lesson")] Boston [?] ca.
1800. p. 9–11)
Song, pfte. acc.
Title from first line.   MHi

WOULD YOU TASTE THE NOONTIDE AIR. From Comus. Dr. Arne [n.
p., n. d.] (14)–(15) p. 33½ cm.
Song, pfte. acc.
First line same as title.
Dr. Arne: Thomas Augustine Arne.
Possibly a Carr imprint, 179–.   PHi

THE WOUNDED HUSSAR. Composed by Mr. Hewitt. New York, Printed
and sold at J. Hewitt's Musical repository, No. 23 Maiden Lane [1800] [2]
p. 32 cm.
Song, pfte. acc. Arr. for flute, p. [2].
First line: Alone on the banks of the dark rolling Danube.
                    DLC, ES, JFD, MB, McD-W, MdHi, NN, RPJCB
Advertised in July, 1800, "as sung by Mr. Hodgkinson . . . just published."
Sung by Mr. Hodgkinson in New York, June 27, 1800.

———— The same.
Philadelphia, Printed & sold by G. Willig, No. 185 Market street [1798–1804]
[2] p. 33½ cm.
Song, pfte. acc. Arr. for flute or guitar, p. [2].
First line same as preceding.
Sonneck gives date, ca. 1800.   CSmH, DLC, JFD, MWA, RPJCB

THE WOUNDED SAILOR. Composed by R. Taylor of Philadelphia. Price
20 cents. Philadelphia, Printed at Carr's Musical repository [1794] [2] p.
33 cm.
Song, pfte. acc. Arr. for Ger. flute, p. [2].
First line: The vainly ambitious may proudly recite.
Advertised among "new songs, never published in America," in October, 1794
                                                                          Hopk.

THE WOUNDED SOLDIER. Composed by R. Taylor of Philadelphia. Price
20 cents. Philadelphia, Printed at Carr's Musical repository [1794] [2] p.
32½ cm.
Song, pfte. acc. Arr. for Ger. flute, p. [2].
First line: The vainly ambitious may proudly recite.
Advertised in Dunlap and Claypoole's *American daily advertiser*, Philadelphia,
December 1, 1794, among "new songs never published in America."
                                                     DLC, McD-W, PP-K

WULLY IS A BONNY LAD. [New York, I. and M. Paff, No. 127 Broadway
1799–1803] [2] p. 32½ cm.
At head of title: No. 9 Ladies musical journal.
Imprint supplied from *Ladies musical journal.*
Song, pfte. acc.
First line same as title.
Composed by James Sanderson.   DLC

[478]

THE YAGER HORN.
See Twenty-four American country *Dances.*

YANKEE DOODLE.

Neither the literary nor the musical history of this humorous patriotic song is clear. By tradition rather than by force of evidence the words are generally attributed to Dr. Shuckburgh, a surgeon in the army of either General Abercrombie or General Amherst; but when or where the tune originated remains an unsolved problem. This much, however, is certain: Yankee Doodle—see, for instance, Andrew Barton's opera *The Disappointment*—was popular in our own country for at least a decade before the Revolutionary War. Consequently all theories claiming that the air was imported by Hessians or others during our struggle for independence must be refuted. For an interesting glimpse into the labyrinth of conjectures surrounding the origin of "Yankee Doodle," consult Mr. Louis C. Elson's *National music of America* (1900).

However, Sonneck adds in his later *Report on . . . Yankee Doodle* (1909):

> Mr. Louis C. Elson, in his useful book on the "National Music of America," 1900, added in the main merely information received from Mr. Albert Matthews, of Boston. Nor does the amount of his original critical research rise above what may be expected from a book plainly designed and written in a style to satisfy the popular demand for more or less verified facts on our national songs.

Though the tune became very popular, Sonneck continues in the *Report:*

> "Yankee Doodle" did not appear in print in America until Benjamin Carr's "Federal Overture," a medley of patriotic songs, including "Yankee Doodle," and composed in 1794, was published "adapted for the piano-forte" by B. Carr, New York, in January, 1795. No copy of this appears to be extant, only a "medley duetto adapted for two German flutes" in the fifth number of Shaw and Carr's "Gentleman's amusement." Unfortunately the copy of the Library of Congress, the only one that has come to my notice, lacks the very pages where one could expect to find "Yankee Doodle" in the form given it by B. Carr. Nor have I as yet found a copy of John Henry Schmidt's "Sonata for beginners," 1796, in which our air was "turned into a fashionable rondo."

Fortunately, since the above was written, copies of both of these earlier issues have been located, leaving only the Schmidt "Sonata" unaccounted for.

As shown elsewhere, ES has a copy of Carr's "Federal overture," 1794, and PHi has a *complete* copy of "Medley duetto," 1795. For other early incidental appearances of *Yankee Doodle cf.* "The new Federal overture," 1797, and "The Federal constitution & liberty forever," ca. 1798.

The tune "Yanky Doodle" appears probably for the first time in print in James Aird's *A selection of Scotch, English, Irish and Foreign Airs*, vol. I. Glasgow, 1782. *cf.* Sonneck's *Report . . .* p. 121.

For Sonneck's very full discussion of the entire subject, *cf.* his *Report on "The Star Spangled Banner," "Hail Columbia," "America," "Yankee Doodle."* (1909), p. 79–156.

YANKEE DOODLE. An original American air. Arranged with variations for the piano forte. Sold at Carr's Musical repository's, Philadelphia & N. York & I. Carr, Baltimore. Price 38 cents. [1796] 4 p. 32 cm.

Pfte. 2 hds.
Advertised in the *Federal gazette*, Baltimore, in August, 1796, among "musical publications, printed by J. Carr, Music Store, No. 6 Gay street, Baltimore, and B. Carr's Musical Repositories, Market street, Philadelphia and William street, New York." MdHi, PP–K

YANKE [!] DOODLE.
(*In* Evening amusement, Philadelphia [1796] p. 18)

Melody only, for German flute or violin. DLC

NEW YANKEE DOODLE. Sung with great applause at the Theatre by Mr. Hodgkinson. New York, Printed & sold at J. Hewitt's Musical repository, No. 131 William street. Sold also by B. Carr, Philadelphia & J. Carr, Baltimore [n. d.] [2] p. 29 cm.

In caption, mounted oval portrait of "G. Washington."
Song, pfte. acc. Arr. for flute, p. [2].
First line: Columbians all the present hour.
Published possibly as early as 1797. CSmH, DLC, ES, LSL, MB

———— The same as preceding, but without portrait.
(*In* A collection of new & favorite songs. [A] Philadelphia [ca. 1800] p. [12]–[13]) HFB,

YANKEE DOODLE.
(*With* The Presidents march. A new Federal song. Philadelphia [1798])

Song, pfte. acc.
First line: Columbians all the present hour.
Presumably identical with the same song as advertised together with "The President's March" and "Washington's March," in June, 1798, in the *Federal gazette*, Baltimore, among "new musick. Just published."
DLC, MNSt, NHi, PP–K, PPL

NEW YANKEE DOODLE. Boston, Printed & sold at P. A. von Hagen & co. imported piano forte & music ware house, No. 3, Cornhill. Also by G. Gilfert, New York [1799–1800] [2] p. 33 cm.

Song, pfte. acc. Arr. for German flute or violin, p. [2].
First line: Columbians all, the present hour.
Published probably in 1799. ES, MB

YANKEE DOODLE.
(*In* Four excellent new *Songs*. New York, 1788)

Words only.
Owned by Oscar Wegelin.

See also Sonata for beginners, by John Henry Schmidt; Compleat tutor for the fife . . .; Federal overture, by B. Carr; Federal constitution; Overture of Yankee Doodle; The instrumental assistant.

YARRIMORE. An Indian ballad. Price 20 cents. Philadelphia, Printed at Carr & cos. Musical repository [1794] [2] p. 31 cm.

Song, pfte. acc. Arr. for "guittar," p. [2].
First line: My poor heart flutters like the sea.
Upper left hand margin: No. 5, Feb. 3, 1794.
Also advertised in Dunlap and Claypoole's *American daily advertiser*, Philadelphia, for February 3, 1794, as "this day . . . published."

ES, LSL, McD–W

YE CHEARFUL [!] VIRGINS HAVE YOU SEEN] Sung by Mrs. Marshall in the comedy of She wou'd & she wou'd not.
(*In* The gentleman's amusement, ed. by R. Shaw. Philadelphia [1794–96] p. 49)

Song, with flute (or violin) acc. Two staves.
Title from first line.
In No. 6, 1795–96. DLC

Mrs. Marshall took part in the first Philadelphia performance of Cibber's *She would and she would not* on May 26, 1794; again, March 6, 1795.

YE CRYSTAL FOUNTAINS. A favorite canzonett. Written by Mrs. Robinson. Composed by Sig.r Giordani. Printed for R. Shaw at his music store, Baltimore. Price 25 cents. [1798–1800] 2 p. 33 cm.

Song, pfte. acc.
First line same as title. McD–W, MdHi

YE FAIR POSSESSED.
See The select songster. New Haven, 1786. p. 39.

[YE GRACIOUS POWER OF CHORA [!] SONG] Song composed and sang [!] yesterday at the Festival of St. John the Evangelist by a Brother.

Words only; to be found in Dunlap's *American daily advertiser*, Philadephia, December 28, 1791.
Title from first line.
The music seems not to be extant.

YE JOVIAL TARS NOW LEND AN EAR.
See Captn. Truxton.

YE LING'RING WINDS.
See She dropt a tear.

YE LITTLE SONGSTERS. A much admired ballad. Composed by James Fisin. New York, Printed & sold at J. & M. Paff's Musical store, No. 127 Broadway [n. d.] [2] p. 32 cm.

Song, pfte. acc.
First line: Ye little songsters of the grove.
Published possibly as early as 1799. DLC

YE MORTALS WHOM FANCIES.
(*In* The American musical miscellany. Northampton, 1798. p. 295–296)

Melody only, with accompanying text.
First line same as title. DLC (etc.)

[YE SAGES, CONTENDING IN VIRTUES FAIR CAUSE]
See Ode (Air "Thou soft flowing Avon").

YE SLUGGARDS WHO MURDER.
See A hunting song . . . by Mr. Roth.

YE STREAMS THAT ROUND MY PRISON CREEP. A favorite song in the musical romance of Lodoiska. Composed by S. Storace.
(*In* The musical repertory. Boston [1796] No. II. p. 26–27)

Song, pfte. acc., with flute obbligato. Three staves.
First line same as title.
S. Storace: Stephen Storace. DLC

YE STREAMS THAT ROUND MY PRISON CREEP. Boston, Printed & sold by P. A. von Hagen at his imported piano forte & music warehouse, No. 3 Cornhill. Also by G. Gilfert, N. York [n. d.] [2] p. 31 cm.

After imprint: For the piano forte or guittar.
Song, pfte. acc. Arr. for German flute or violin, p. [2].
First line same as title.
Published possibly as early as 1799. ES, JFD, LSL, MB, RPJCB

YE ZEPHYRS, WHERE'S MY BLUSHING ROSE. A favorite song in answer to the Mansion of peace.
(*In* [Moller & Capron's monthly numbers] Third number [Philadelphia, 1793] p. 19–20)

Song, pfte. acc. Arr. for Ger. flute or guitar, p. 20.
First line same as title.
Composed by Sir John Andrew Stevenson (*BM Cat.*) DLC, Hopk., NN, PHi

THE YELLOW HAIR'D LADDIE. New York, Printed and sold by J. and M. Paffs, No. 127 Broadway [n. d.] [2] p. 31 cm.

Imprint at foot of p. [1].
Song, pfte. acc.
First line: In April when primroses paint the sweet plain.
On p. [2]: Kiss my lady (for pfte. 2 hds.).
Published possibly as early as 1799. DLC

*THE YORKSHIRE LOVE SONG.
Advertised in November, 1797, as "published at Carr's Musical Repository," Philadelphia.

[YOUNG CARLOS SUED A BEAUTEOUS MAID] Sung by Miss Broadhurst in the Prisoner.
(*In* The gentleman's amusement, ed. by R. Shaw. Philadelphia [1794–96] p. 65)

Melody only, flute (or violin), with accompanying text.
Title from first line.
In No. [8], 1796.
The prisoner, by Thomas Attwood, was performed with Miss Broadhurst in the cast, in New York, May 4, 1796. DLC, PHi, PP–K

YOUNG HENRY LOV'D HIS EMMA WELL. Sung with great applause in the opera of the Outlaws. Price 12½ cents. New York, Printed & sold at J. Hewitt's Musical repository, No. 23 Maiden Lane. (*In* A collection of new & favorite songs. [A] Philadelphia [ca. 1800] p. [183])

Imprint at foot of page.
Song, pfte. acc.
First line same as title.
The outlaws, by Michael Kelly, was first produced in 1798. HFB

THE YOUNG IRISH CAPTAIN'S THE HUSBAND FOR ME. A favorite song. Sung by Mrs. Franklin. New York, Printed & sold by G. Gilfert & co., No. 209 Broadway, near St. Pauls [1795] 8–9 p. 31½ cm.

Song, pfte. acc.
First line: Three lovers I boast. MWA, RPJCB

YOUNG JEMMY IS A PLEASING YOUTH. A favorite song. Boston, Printed & sold at P. A. von Hagen, junr. & cos. musical magazine, No. 3 Cornhill; also by G. Gilfert, New York. Where also may be had the new song, How tedious alas are the hours. Also a great variety of warranted imported piano fortes, flutes, hautboys, bassoons, trumpets, French horns, violins, guitars, fifes & other musical articles of superior quality [1799] [2] p. 31 cm.

Song, pfte. acc. Arr. for German flute, p. [2].
First line same as title. ES, MB, RPJCB

As *Young Gemmy is a pleasing youth*, advertised in June, 1799, as published by "P. A. Von Hagen, jun. and Co. Musical Magazine, No. 3 Cornhill," Boston.

THE YOUNG LOVER.
See The select songster. New Haven, 1786. p. 35–36.

YOUNG LUBIN WAS A SHEPHERD BOY.
(*In* Young's vocal and instrumental musical miscellany. Philadelphia [1793–95] p. 50)

Song, pfte. acc.
First line same as title.
In No. 7, ca. 1794. DLC
From *Carnival of Venice*, by Thos. Linley, the Elder.

——— Separate issue of preceding, but with page number changed to 5, and the following imprint at foot of page, "New York, Published by I. Young & co." Otherwise identical. ES, NN

Apparently from some unidentified collection published by John Young in New York, perhaps before leaving for Philadelphia, in which case to be dated 1792–93.

Other known titles in this collection are:

p. 2 Sweet Nan of Hampton Green.
3–4 When first this humble roof I knew.
4 Lullaby [Storace].

With this pagination these are found only as separate issues. No trace of the original collection has been discovered. However, they all appear with altered page numbers in *Young's* . . . *Miscellany*, Philadelphia (*q. v.*).

*THE YOUNG MASON'S MONITOR AND VOCAL COMPANION. An American production. (Entirely new) By Brother William M. Stewart. New York, Printed by Harrisson and Purdy, 1789.

[YOUNG SIMON IN HIS LOVELY SUE] The favorite duett sung in the opera of the Children in the wood. New York, Printed for G. Gilfert & co., No. 191 Broadway [1794–95] [2] p. 33½ cm.

Duet, pfte. acc.
Title from first line.
The children in the wood, by Samuel Arnold. JFD, McD–W, RPJCB

YOUNG WILLY FOR ME. Sung with great applause by Mrs. Seymour at the Ladies Concert. Price 25 cents. New York, Printed & sold at J. Hewitt's Musical repository, No. 131 William street. Sold also by B. Carr, Philadelphia & J. Carr, Baltimore [1797–99] [2] p. 33½ cm.

Imprint at foot of p. [2].
Song, pfte. acc.
First line: I've plenty of lovers. JFD, PHi

The Columbian Anacreontic Society, New York, ca. 1795–1800, presented each Spring a Ladies' Concert. In which one of these concerts Mrs. Seymour sang this song is uncertain.

———— The same as preceding.
(In A collection of new & favorite songs. [A] Philadelphia [1800] p. [66]–[67]) HFB

YOUNG'S VOCAL AND INSTRUMENTAL MUSICAL MISCELLANY. Being a collection of the most approved songs, duets, catches and glees. Adapted for the voice, piano-forte, violin and German flute. Printed in Philadelphia for the author and sold by him at No. 117 Race street, & by Mathew Carey, No. 118 Market street, and may be had in New York, at Dodds and Claus, Musical instrument makers, No. 66 Queen street. [1793–95] 2 p. l., 3–63 p. 31 cm.

Title-page, verso blank. "The names of the subscribers by whose encouragement the following work is published," 2nd p. l.
At head of title: No. [ ] To be continued monthly.
At upper right hand corner: Price one dollar.
Identical t.-p. as given above for eight separate issues, numbered in ink. "Price one dollar" written in ink on t.-p. of No. 1; on other title-pages, engraved.
Pagination of music continuous, title-pages and blank pages not counted.
To be first dated 1793, as evidently identical with

A collection of the choicest songs from the latest operas in Europe, adapted for the piano forte, violin and German flute.

Advertised in Dunlap's Daily American advertiser, February 14, 1793, as follows:

MUSIC. The subscriber proposes to publish in monthly numbers, a collection of the choicest Songs . . . Each number shall consist of six different songs.—The ladies and gentlemen who are disposed to become subscribers, are requested to apply or send their names to Mathew Carey, No. 118 in Market Street, between Third and Fourth streets, or to J.

Young, in Race street, etc. As soon as a certain number of subscribers appear, the work will be immediately commenced and executed with all possible dispatch. Such subscribers as send in their names with poetry which may be approved of, will have it set to music and introduced in the different numbers.

CONDITIONS

Subscribers to pay Half a Dollar on the delivery of each number.

John Young.

In the same paper on February 22, is added:

Subscribers names to be inserted in the first number.

There is no evidence to disprove a monthly issuance of the first five numbers as planned. At least they all seem to have been published in 1793. No. 6, however, could not have been issued earlier than March 10, 1794 (cf. [When the men a courting came] Sung by Miss Broadhurst) and No. 7 shows no evidence of being earlier than 1794. But No. 8 could not have appeared before January 7, 1795 (cf. [When a little merry he] A favorite song sung by Mrs. Marshall in . . . the Purse) and although the individual imprint of this song would seem to make possible a later date, there is no evidence in the remaining songs to support such a conclusion. Thus it becomes probable that the entire work was published between early 1793 and early 1795.

Of the eight numbers, DLC has 1–8; Hopk., 1–6; HFB, 1–2; ES, No. 1; ABHu, No. 6.

Contents:

No. 1.
p. 3 The reconsaliation [!]. The words by a gentleman of Philadelphia. Music by I. Gehot.
    4 Sung by Mrs. Hodgkinson in No song, no supper. [Across the downs this morning]
    5 Batchelors hall. By Dibdin.
  6–7 Sung by Mrs. Myrter in the Farmer. [Send him to me]
    7 Bonny Lem of Aberdeen as a country dance.
  8–9 The bleak wind wistles [!] o'er the main.
   10 From night till morn. A favorite duett.

No. 2.
p. 11–13 Still the lark finds repose. A favourite rondo sung by Miss Phillips.
  14–15 Such pure delight. Taken from the Highland reel.
  16–17 A favorite song in No song, no supper. Storace. [From aloft the sailor looks around]
   17 Cymro oble, or the Welch question.
   18 Lafayette. A new song.
   19 The lamplighter. Written and composed by Mr. Dibdin.
   20 The poor mariner.

No. 3.
p.   21 Bonny Charley. A favorite new Scotch song.
  22–23 Go with you all the world over. The much admired dialogue duett in the Surrender of Calais.

[485]

[486]

ZEPHYR, COME THOU PLAYFUL MINION. A favorite song in the Woodman. Composed by Mr. Shield and sung by Miss Moller at the concerts.
New York, Printed for and sold at J. C. Moller's musical store, No. 58 Vesey
st. Where may be had a great variety of music and musical instruments.
[1797] [2] p. 32½ cm.

Song, pfte. acc.
First line same as title.   DLC

ZEPHYR, COME THOU PLAYFUL MINION. Composed by Willᵐ Shield.
Boston, Published and sold at No. 6 Newbury street. Also at Mr. Mallet's
Musical repository, Devonshire street   [n. d.] [2] p. 32½ cm.

Song, pfte. acc.
First line same as title.
This imprint is very vague. If the "No. 6 Newbury Street" might be considered an error, and refer to "No. 62 Newbury street" instead, then we
might perhaps consider it a Von Hagen imprint, ca. 1798–99. But so far as
we know, Francis Mallet was not located at Devonshire street until 1805.
The issue would, however, seem to be distinctly an eighteenth century one.

                                                                    ES, NBuG

ZORADE IN THE TOWER.   A song in the opera of the Mountaineers.   Composed by Dr. Arnold.
(In The musical repertory.   Boston [1796] No. II, p. 29–31)

Song, pfte. acc.
First line: Bewailing, bewailing, she sunk heart broken on her pillow.   DLC

*ZORINSKI, OR FREEDOM TO THE SLAVES.
This "celebrated and highly esteemed play, interspersed with new and
elegant songs, the production of T. Mortion [!], esq. . . . the music by
Dr. Arnold. The accompaniments by Mr. Van Hagen of New York,"
probably P. A. von Hagen, senior, was to be performed at Hartford, Conn.,
on September 27, 1797.

First performed at New York, on March 30, 1798, with "accompaniments
by [Victor] Pelissier."

List of Articles and Essays Relating to Music

Locations are indicated of any books or pamphlets in this list. Magazines, however, should be located through the *Union List of Serials*.

AN ACCOUNT OF TWO AMERICANS of extraordinary genius in poetry and music.

> Printed in the *Columbian magazine*, Philadelphia, April 1788, p. 211–213. The poetical genius is "the late Robert Bolling, Esq., of Chellow, Va. in the county of Buckingham in Virginia;" the musical, "William Billings of Boston."

AN ADRESS [!] TO PERSONS OF FASHION containing some particulars relating to balls: and a few occasional hints concerning play-houses, card-tables etc. In which is introduced the character of Lucinda, a lady of the very best fashion, and of most extraordinary piety. [Two lines by Horace] Boston: Printed by W. M'Alpine in Marlborough street. 1757. 56 p. 8°.

DLC, MB, MHi

AN ARROW AGAINST PROFANE AND PROMISCUOUS DANCING. Drawn out of the quiver of the Scriptures by the ministers of Christ at Boston in New England. [Two lines from Judges 6:31. Two lines of Latin] Boston. Printed by Samuel Green and are to be sold by Joseph Brunning. 1684. 30 p. 14½ cm.

> The pamphlet was written by Increase Mather.
> Compare MHi Proc. 2d ser., v. ix, p. 460.

MB, MHi, NN

THE CONSTITUTION OF THE ESSEX MUSICAL ASSOCIATION. Established 28th March, 1797. Newberryport. Printed by Edmund M. Blunt. State street. 1798. 12 p. 12°.

MBAt

CRITICISM ON MODERN MUSICK by Dr. Franklin. Letter from Dr. B. Franklin to Mr. P. Franklin, at Newport.

> Printed in the *Universal asylum*, Philadelphia, August, 1790, p. 97–99; in the *Massachusetts magazine*, Boston, July, 1790, p. 412–414; and in the several editions of Benjamin Franklin's collected works. This interesting letter was probably written in 1765. Compare also Sonneck's article on "The Musical side of Franklin" in *Music*, November, 1900, and his "Benjamin Franklin's musical side" in *Suum cuique* . . . New York, 1916.

CRITIQUE OF THEATRICS.
Printed in the *Diary*, New York, April 16, 1796.
With special reference to recent performances of *The purse* and *The mountaineers.*

DANCES IN SPAIN.
Essay reprinted "From Townsend's travels," in the *Massachusetts magazine*, May, 1795, p. 106.

DANCING EXPLODED. A sermon shewing the unlawfulness, sinfulness, and bad consequences of balls, assemblies, and dances in general. Delivered in Charlestown, South Carolina, March 22, 1778. By Oliver Hart, A. M. Charlestown, South Carolina: Printed by David Bruce, 1778. 32 p. 17 cm. NHi

DESCRIPTION OF AN IMPROVED METHOD of tongueing the harpsichord or spinet, by F. H. esq.

See Improved method of quilling the harpsichord.

DESCRIPTION OF THE NORTH AMERICAN INDIAN DANCES.
Reprinted from Dr. William's history of Vermont in the *Massachusetts magazine*, January, 1796, p. 17–18.

DICTIONARY EXPLAINING SUCH GREEK, Latin, Italian and French words, as generally occur in music.

See Compleat instructor for the violin by H. B. Victor.

A DISCOURSE DELIVERED IN NEWMARKET, at the particular request of a respectable musical choir, to a numerous assembly convened for celebrating the birthday of the illustrious Washington, by James Miltimore, A. M., Pastor of a church in Stratham. Published by desire of the hearers Printed at Exeter, by Hrnry [!] Ranlet for the subscribers. 1794. 24 p. 8 vo. MWA

DISSERTATION ON SCOTTISH MUSIC. by James Tytler, 1800.
Mentioned in Moore's *List of modern musical works published in the United States*, 1876.

THE EFFECT OF MUSIC.
Printed in the *New York weekly magazine*, July 13, 1796, p. 12.

EFFECTS OF THE STAGE on the manners of a people: and the propriety of encouraging and establishing a virtuous theatre. By a Bostonian. Boston. Printed by Young & Etheridge, Market Square, sold by them and the several booksellers. 1792. 76 p. 8°.

Written by William Haliburton. DLC, MHi

AN ENCOMIUM ON MUSIC.
(*In* the singing master's assistant, by William Billings. Boston, 1778. p. [(31)]–(32).)

Closes with:
Great art thou O Music, and with thee there is no competitor, thy powers are far beyond the powers of—utterance.
CSmH, DLC, ICN, MB, MH, MHi, MWA

ESSAY ON MUSIC.
Printed in the *Columbian magazine*, Philadelphia, for March, 1790, p. 181–183; and May, 1790, p. 304–305.
Not continued as advertised.

ESSAY ON MUSICAL CRITICISM. From the third volume of Burney's General history of music.
Printed in *New York magazine*, March, 1793, p. 171–175.

ESSAY ON MUSICAL EXPRESSION by Mr. Avison.
See New minstrel, by William Selby.

AN ESSAY ON RYTHMICAL MEASURES by Walter Young, M. A. F. R. S.
Edin.
Reprinted from "the First vol. of Memoirs of science and arts," in the *New York magazine*, January, 1795.

AN ESSAY ON THE BEAUTIES and excellencies of painting, music and poetry.
Pronounced at the anniversary commencement at Dartmouth College, A. D. 1774. By John Wheelock, A. M. Tutor of said college. Published at the desire of the audience. Hartford: Printed by Eben Watson, near the Great Bridge. 15 p. 8°. MHi, NHi

——— Exactly the same title with addition of "Reprinted by S. Spear, Hanover." 10 p. 8°. MB

AN ESSAY TO SILENCE THE OUTCRY that has been made in some places against regular singing. In a sermon preach'd at Framingham by the Reverend Mr. Josiah Dwight . . . Boston, J. Eliot, 1725. 16 p. 17½ cm.
DLC (last leaf mutilated), MB, MHi

EXHIBITIONS OF PINDAR in the musical line.
Printed in the *Massachusetts magazine*, Boston, December, 1790. p. 715–716.

FAMILIAR DIALOGUES ON DANCING, between a minister and a dancer, taken from matter of fact, with an appendix containing some extracts from the writings of pious and eminent men against the entertainments of the stage and other vain amusements . . . By John Phillips . . . New York, Printed by T. Kirk, 1798. 39 p. 21 cm. DLC, MWA

THE GENERATION OF SOUND.
Printed in the *Pennsylvania magazine*, Philadelphia, January, 1775. p. 29–30.

AN IMPROVED METHOD of quilling the harpsichord, by F. Hopkinson, Esquire.
Papers read before the American philosophical society, Philadelphia, in 1783, 1784, 1786 and printed in the second volume (1786) of the "Transactions" of the society. The "Description of an improved method of tongueing the harpsichord or spinet, by F. H. Esq." as contained in the *Columbian magazine*, Philadelphia, May, 1787, p. 421–423, in part condenses the observations read before the American philosophical society, in part adds to them. The "Description" is also embodied in Hopkinson's "Miscellaneous poems and occasional writings," Philadelphia, 1792. Reprinted with historical observations in Sonneck's book on "Francis Hopkinson . . . and James Lyon" (1905).

INTRODUCTORY LESSONS practised by the Uranian society held at Philadelphia for promoting the knowledge of vocal music. Jan. 1, 1785. [Philadelphia, 1785] 2 p. l., iv, 20 p. pl. 11½ x 25½ cm.
Engraved throughout.
Probably compiled by Andrew Adgate, president of the society. DLC

*THE LAWFULNESS, EXCELLENCY AND ADVANTAGE of instrumental music in the public worship of God.
Advertised in the *Pennsylvania gazette*, Philadelphia, April 28, 1763, as "just published and to be sold by Wm. Dunlap, Philadelphia."

LETTERS ADDRESSED TO YOUNG MARRIED WOMEN. By Mrs. Griffith [Elizabeth, wife of Richard] (Verse) Philadelphia: From the press of John Turner. November, 1796. vi, [7]–126 p. 17 cm.
On p. 42–45: On music as one of the "most winning accomplishments . . . necessary to preserve the lover in the husband." DLC, MWA, NN

MEMOIRS OF THE CELEBRATED FARINELLI. From the Sentimental and Masonic magazine.
Reprinted in the *New York magazine*, June, 1795, p. 361–363.

MUSIC PHYSICALLY CONSIDERED.
This anonymous article, which recommends music for medical treatment, appeared on p. 90–93 of the *Columbian magazine*, Philadelphia, February, 1789.

MUSICAL DICTIONARY by Hans Gram and Oliver Holden.
Mentioned in Moore's *List of modern musical works published in the United States*, 1876, but Sonneck believed the dictionary merely formed part of some other publication. Probably Moore referred to the "Massachusetts compiler of . . . sacred vocal music together with a *musical dictionary*," by Gram, Holyoke, and Holden, Boston, 1795.

MUSICIAN MAINTAINS A PLEASANT DISPUTE on the dignity of his profession. In a letter from Aaron Monceca to Isaac Onis, Caraite [?] formerly a Rabbi at Constantinople.
Printed in the *American magazine and historical chronicle*, Boston, October, 1743. p. 65–68.

A NARRATIVE of his connection with the Old American Company from the fifth of September, 1792, to the thirty-first of March, 1797. By John Hodgkinson. New York: Printed by J. Oram, No. 33, Liberty street. 1797. 28, [1], p. 21 cm.
Hodgkinson's affidavit as to the accuracy of his narrative, p. [29]. NHi

NECESSARY DIRECTIONS.
Printed in *Worshipper's assistant*, by Solomon Howe, Northampton, 1799. p. [6].
A quaint and interesting article in which the author gives his "opinion concerning the mode of teaching in music." The book itself is "adapted to the weakest capacities and designed for extensive utility as an introduction to more critical and curious music." CSmH, CtY, DLC, MB, MWA, NN

OBSERVATIONS ON DANCING as an imitative art. (From Essays on philosophical subjects, by the late Adam Smith, L. L. D.)
Printed in the *Massachusetts magazine*, Boston, November, 1795, p. 519.

OF SACRED POETRY AND MUSIC. A discourse at Christ-church, Cambridge, at the opening of the organ on Tuesday, XXI August, MDCCLXIV. By East Apthorp . . . Boston, Printed by Green and Russell, 1764. vii, 22 p. 23½ cm. DLC, MWA

ON HARMONY.
Article signed "Harmonicus" in the *Boston magazine*, December, 1783. p. 64–65.

ON MUSIC AND DANCING.
Letter IX of the "Letters to a young lady. By the rev. John Bennet." In the *American Museum*, Philadelphia, March, 1792.

ON MUSICK.
Printed in the *Massachusetts magazine*, Boston, December, 1790. p. 755–756.

ON THEATRICAL ENTERTAINMENTS.
Printed in the *American magazine*, Boston, August, 1746. p. 356–357.

ON VOCAL MUSIC.
Printed in *Gentlemen and ladies town and country magazine*, Boston, November, 1789. p. 546.

ORATION ON MUSIC by Dr. H. Farnsworth. Cooperstown, 1795. 21 p. 12°.   MWA

AN ORATION ON MUSIC pronounced at Portland, May 28th, 1800, by Samuel Emerson, A. M. Published by special request from the press of E. A. Jenks, Portland. 1800. 20 p. 20 cm.   MH, MWA, NHi, NN, PHi

THE ORIGIN OF THE MUSICAL NOTES.
Reprinted from the *New London magazine* in the *Massachusetts magazine*, Boston, January, 1789. p. 31.

POWER OF MUSIC OVER ANIMALS and infants. From Eastcott's Sketches of the origin, progress and effects of music.

Reprinted in the *New York magazine*, June, 1794, p. 369–373.

THE POWER OF MUSICK.
Reprinted in the *American magazine*, Boston, February, 1745, p. 69, from the *Universal spectator*, No. 654.

POWER OF SOUND, or the influence of melody over the human heart; calculated for the advance of public religion.

Article signed "Maryland, Nov. 19. 1786. *Caecilius.*" Printed in the *Columbian magazine*, Philadelphia, December, 1786, on p. 160–163.

PROMISCUOUS SINGING no divine institution; having neither president [!] nor precept to support it, either from the musical institution of David, or from the gospel dispensation. Therefore it ought to be exploded, as being a humane invention, tending rather to gratify the carnal ears of men than to be acceptable and pleasing worship to God. By John Hammett . . . [n. p.] Printed in the year 1739. 1 p. l., iii, 29 p. 17 cm.

Evans (4366) suggests the imprint: [Newport ?, Printed by the Widow Franklin?]   DLC, MWA, RPB

REGULAR AND SKILFUL MUSIC in the worship of God . . . shewn in a sermon preached at the North Meeting-house, Newbury-Port, at the desire of the church and congregation, February 8th, 1774, by Oliver Noble, A. M., pastor of a church in Newbury. Printed at the desire of the Musical society in Newbury-Port. And of a number of gentlemen and ladies who heard it . . . Boston, Printed by Mills and Hicks, for Daniel Bayley in Newbury-Port, 1774. 46 p. 20 cm. DLC, MBAt, RPJCB

RELATIVE MERITS OF VOCAL AND INSTRUMENTAL MUSIC.
Printed in the *American magazine*, New York, June, 1788, p. 448–450. Signed "Orpheus." In the copy of the *American magazine* at NN an ink memorandum attributes the article to the pen of "N. Webster."

RELIGION PRODUCTIVE OF MUSIC. A discourse, delivered at Marlborough, March 24, 1773 at a singing lecture . . . By John Mellen. Boston, I. Thomas, 1773. 34 p. 19 cm. DLC, MWA

REMARKABLE CURE OF A FEVER BY MUSIC.
Printed in the *New York weekly magazine*, August 10, 1796, p. 44.

REMARKS ON MUSIC.
Printed in the *New York weekly magazine* from September 21, 1796–November 16, 1796. v. 2. p. 91, 103, 108, 124, 140, 156.

On p. 156: To be continued.
No continuation has been found.

REMARKS ON THE USE AND ABUSE OF MUSIC as part of modern education.
Article signed "Chiron," in the *New York magazine*, April, 1794, p. 224–229, and May, 1794, p. 265–268. Probably a reprint from an English magazine as the author refers to Purcell, Arne, Boyce as composers of "our" country.

THE RIGHTS OF THE DRAMA, or, an inquiry into the origin, principles and consequences of theatrical entertainment. By Philo Dramatis. [Verses] Boston. Printed for the author. 1792. 48 p. 8°. DLC, MHi

Advertised in the *Columbian centinel*, Boston, for August 25, 1792 as

The *Drama*. Now in the Press, and in a few days will be published The RIGHTS OF THE DRAMA . . .

In this pamphlet is contained a complete plan for the erection of a theatre, a calculation of Expense, and an accurate Balance drawn in favour of the proprietors or Managers.

As also the probable Emolution it would afford to Government if duly regulated . . .

RULES FOR JUDGING THE BEAUTIES of painting, music and poetry.
Printed in the *New York weekly magazine*, August 31, 1796, p. 65.

RULES OF THE ST. COECILIA [!] SOCIETY. Charlestown. Printed for the Society by Robert Wells, 1774. 11 p. 15 cm.

Title-page, verso blank; text, p. (3)–(11).
Contains twelve "Rules of the St. Coecilia [!] Society. Agreed upon and finally confirmed. November 22d, 1773."
Reprinted with notes in the *S. C. Hist. Mag.* I, p. 223–227 ScHi

A SCHEME for reducing the science of music to a more simple state, and to bring
all its characters within the compass of a common fount of printing-types;
especially calculated for the convenience of learners. By Benjamin Dearborn. Portsmouth, New Hampshire, 1785. 16 p. 8½ x 16 cm.
Contains several examples of the author's new style of printing music—
with letters instead of notes. NHi
Benjamin Dearborn was born in Portsmouth, New Hampshire in 1754;
died in Boston, 1838. For a detailed account of his many activities, musical
and non-musical, see article by Margaret E. Lippencott in the *New York
Historical Society Quarterly Bulletin,* for October, 1941.

THE SPEECH OF JOHN GARDINER, Esquire delivered in the House of Repre-
sentatives. On Thursday the 26th of January 1792; on the subject of the
report of the committee appointed to consider the expediency of repealing
the law against theatrical exhibitions within this commonwealth. [Verses
by Pope; quotation with translation from Cicero] Printed at the Apollo
Press, in Boston, for the author. 1792. 159 p., pl., 1 p. corrigenda. 8°
The speech proper ends on p. 101; "The letter to the author on the theatre,"
p. 103–108; "A dissertation on the ancient poetry of the Romans," p. 110–159.
DLC, MB, MBAt, MHi

STRIKING VIEWS OF LAMIA, the celebrated Athenian flute player, by Dr.
Burney.
Printed in the *Massachusetts magazine,* November, 1789, p. 684.

THOUGHTS ON MUSICK in a letter to a friend . . . G. H. M.
Printed in the *Universal asylum,* Philadelphia, July, 1790, p. 22–23.

THOUGHTS ON THE POWER OF MUSIC.
Article signed *"S."* on p. 85–89 of the *Monthly magazine and American review,* New York, February, 1800.

The author believes the real source of the pleasure we derive from music
to be more or less the "result of an association of ideas."

List of Composers

THIS LIST embraces all composers mentioned in the text as having had compositions published in the United States before or during 1800. Under each composer are listed all secular works known to have been so published (or advertised to be published) whether copies have been located or not. Also opera librettos issued under similar conditions are included.

Sonneck has also been followed in the inclusion of works by American composers (*i. e.*, composers living in the United States) which had appeared on concert programs, or had been performed at the theatre, or advertised to be performed during this period, whether these compositions were published or not.

No biographical sketches are here given of foreign composers appearing in such standard works as Grove, *Dictionary of music and musicians* (1940), *Baker's Biographical dictionary of music and musicians* (1940), Pratt, *New encyclopedia of music and musicians* (1929). Nor any extended notice (particularly as to the years after 1800) of composers in America who are listed in such easily accessible works as Grove, *American supplement* (1930), Baker (*above*, 1940), John Tasker Howard, *Our American music* (1939), F. J. Metcalf, *American writers and compilers of sacred music* (1925). Also, *Dictionary of American biography* and always, Sonneck, *Early concert-life in America* (1907) and *Early opera in America* (1915).

A., W.
  The beauties of friendship

ABRAMS, Harriet (1760–ca. 1825)
  Crazy Jane
  The orphan's prayer
  The shade of Henry
  A smile and a tear

ALEXANDER, ——
  Active in Boston, ca. 1792.

  Georgia Grenadiers march

ANTES, John (b. 1740)
  According to Rufus A. Grider in his *Historical notes on music in Bethlehem* (Philadelphia, 1873), John Antes was born in 1740, at Fredricktrop, Montgomery County, Pennsylvania, where the Moravians had a preaching station. He was ap- prenticed to a wheelwright in Bethlehem. Being a youth possessing much talent, he devoted himself also to the study of music, performing on all the stringed instruments; he also studied it as a science. Mr. Grider continues by saying that Antes went to Europe and was sent as a missionary to Egypt, where the Turks punished him with the *bastinado*, from the effects of which he never entirely recovered. While laid up in that country, he amused himself by composing quartets. When convalescent he returned to Europe. In Vienna, Antes made the acquaintance of Haydn, who, together with other musicians, is said to have performed his compositions.

  Quartets

ARNE, Michael (1741–1786)
Homeward bound
Sweet passion of love
Sweet Poll of Plymouth

ARNE, Thomas Augustine (1710–1778)
Bourville Castle
Columbia and Liberty
Fair Aurora
The soldier tir'd
Sweet echo
There was a jolly miller
Water parted from the sea
Would you taste the noontide air

ARNOLD, Samuel (1740–1802)
The agreeable surprise (libretto)
And hear her sigh adieu
Auld Robin Gray
Battle of Hexham (libretto)
The children in the wood (libretto)
Come Hope thou queen of endless smiles
Courteous stranger
Cupid benighted
The dead alive (libretto)
Dear Walter. *See* Dorothy Dump
Death and burial of Cock Robin
Dorothy Dump
An Easter hymn
Favorite songs . . . in The shipwreck
Finale to Inkle and Yarico
Fresh and strong the breeze is blowing
The gipsy's song
Go with you all the world over
Happy tawny Moor
If 'tis joy to wound a lover
In dear little Ireland
In the dead of the night. *See* Cupid benighted
Inkle (*or* Incle) and Yarico (libretto)
The Italian monk trio. *See* [The mock Italian trio]
The Italien [!] mock trio. *See* [The mock Italian trio]
The je ne scai quoi
The little gipsey
Little Sally
Love soft illusion

The maid of the mill (libretto)
A medley duetto
[The mock Italian trio]
Moorish march
The mountaineers (libretto)
My Laura will you trust the seas
O 'tis love. *See* When first to Helen's lute
O say simple maid
O the moment was sad
On board the Valiant
Our Lord is risen from the dead
Overture to The children in the wood
Pauvre Madelon
Poor Negro woman
The rush light
See brother (*or* sister) see on yonder bough
The son in law (libretto)
Songs, duets and chorusses of The children in the wood
Songs in The Castle of Andalusia
Songs sung in The shipwreck
The Spanish barber
Think your tawny Moor is true
Walter's sweethearts. *See* Dorothy Dump
The wayworn traveller
When first to Helen's lute
When on the ocean
When the hollow drum
With a heart light and gay
[Young Simon in his lovely Sue]
Zorade in the tower
Zorinski

ATTWOOD, Thomas (1765–1838)
The adopted child
Ah once when I was a very little maid
Ballad in Caernarvon Castle
The convent bell
The drummer
Each coming day
The favorite carol sung in The adopted child
Grand march from the opera of The prisoner (arr. from Mozart)
How charming a camp is. *See* The drummer
I'm as smart a lad as you'd wish to see

In the midst of the sea
Nancy
Overture to The mouth of the Nile
Poor Lima
The poor sailor boy
The prisoner
Rosina's heart
Success to Admiral Nelson
[Tears that exhale]
When the world first began
[Young Carlos sued]

B

BACH, Johann Christian (1735–1782)
Ah seek to know
Cease awhile ye winds to blow
No 'twas neither shape nor feature

BAILEY, Edward
English composer. Active from
ca. 1795.

Ella and Edwin

BANNISTER, *Miss*
When we sailor lads first put to sea

BARTHÉLEMON, Francois Hippolyte (1741–1808)
The boatman

BAUMGARTEN, Karl Friedrich (ca.
1740–1824)
Overture [to Robin Hood]

BELCHER, Supply (1751–1836)
Composer and compiler of hymn
tunes. Also violinist.

Friendship

BELKNAP, Daniel (1771–1815)
Composer and compiler of hymn
tunes. Also teacher (in Framingham, 1798).

Funeral ode
A view of the Temple—a Masonic
ode

BENTLEY, John
Harpsichordist and composer. First
mentioned in 1783 as manager of
the City Concerts, Philadelphia.
In 1785 he became the harpsichordist in the orchestra of the

Old American Company, for whom
he "selected and composed" several
pantomimes.

The cave of enchantment (pantomime *arr.*)

The touchstone (pantomime *arr.*)

BERGMAN, B.
Violinist and composer. First
mentioned in 1792, in New York
papers with Hewitt, Gehot, Young
and Phillips as "professors of music
from the Operahouse, Hanoversquare, and professional concerts
under the direction of Haydn,
Pleyel, etc., London." Resided at
New York until 1795, as member
of the theatre orchestra and actively
engaged in concert work. Later on
to be traced in Boston, Charleston,
S. C., etc.

The doctor & apothecary (*arr.* from
Storace)

BERKENHEAD, John L.
Blind musician. Very active as
organist, pianist and composer in
Boston.
First mentioned in 1795.

The demolition of the Bastile
Songs (unidentified)

BIGGS, Edward Smith (d. ca. 1820)
English composer and pianist.
Wrote many songs and glees; also
for piano forte.

A Hindustani girl's song

BILLINGS, William (1746–1800)
Wellknown composer and compiler
of anthems and hymn tunes. No-
table for his fuguing tunes, a novelty
at that time in America.

Consonance
Jargon

BILLINGTON, Thomas (ca. 1754–
1832)
Sylvia

BLEWITT, Jonas (d. 1805)
The lass of Humberside
The orphan boy's tale
The veil

BOCCHERINI, Luigi (1743–1805)
Andantino

BOIELDIEU, François Adrien (1775–1834)
Ouverture du Calife de Bagdad

BOULLAY, Louis
Violinist and composer. Probably one of the French musicians who fled to the United States from the West Indies in 1793. Appears first in that year as composer and violinist on concert programs at Philadelphia and Boston. Itinerant as member of several theatre orchestras; 1797 in Worcester, Massachusetts, as music teacher.

Bravoura song

BOYCE, William (1710–1779)
Tell me lovely shephert [!] where
Together let us range the fields
[What med'cine can soften the bosom's keen smart]

BRADFORD, Thomas
Composer and music publisher. A cellist by the name of Bradford appears as early as 1788 on New York concert programs. Possibly he was identical with this Thomas Bradford who came to Charleston, S. C., at the latest in 1791, when he founded a music store there under the firm of T. Bradford & Co. In 1795 firm without Co.

The duenna (arr. from Linley)
The woodman (arr. from Shield)

BREMNER, James (d. 1780)
Organist, music teacher, composer. A relative of Robert Bremner, the Scotch music publisher, composer and editor. Came to Philadelphia in 1763. In December of this year he opened a "music school . . . at Mr. Glover Hunt's near the Coffee House in Market Street" where he taught "young ladies . . . the harpsichord, or guitar" and "young gentlemen . . . the violin, German flute, harpsichord, or guitar." Bremner possibly became organist at St. Peter's in 1763, but all we know for certain is that he held a similar position at Christ Church in 1767, and that he is spoken of in the vestry minutes in December, 1770 as "the late organist." After an absence of several years he is again spoken of (in the diary of James Allen) as organist of Christ Church in 1774. He died near or at Philadelphia "on the banks of the Schuylkill" in September, 1780. The most prominent of his pupils seems to have been Francis Hopkinson who possessed several compositions of his teacher. Those still extant are a "Trumpet air," a "Lesson," a "March," "Lady Coventry's minuet with variations," all for the harpsichord. He was also the author of "Instructions for the sticcado pastorale, with a collection of airs," London, n. d. (mentioned by Fétis). See Sonneck, Early concert life in America, p. 66, n. 2.

Lady Coventry's minuet
Lesson
March
Overture (arr. from Earl of Kelly)
Trumpet air

BROWN, William
Flutist and composer. First mentioned in New York, where his concert in August, 1783, seems to have been the last given there under the British régime. October of the same year finds him in Philadelphia, with proposals for a series of subscription concerts. To be traced subsequently as flute virtuoso at Charleston, S. C., Baltimore, New York. Seems to have settled at Philadelphia in 1786, when he was one of the managers of the City Concerts.

In a manuscript note, Sonneck raises

the interesting question whether he may not have been the Braun noted in Eitner as a flutist who from 1770 to 1780 was connected with the Hofkapelle at Cassel, afterward coming to America. In 1806, mentioned as living in Hanau.

Three rondos

BUTLER, Thomas Hamley (1762–1823)
An Egyptian air

C

CALLCOTT, John Wall (1766–1821)
He sleeps in yonder dewy grave

CAMBINI, Giovanni Giuseppe (1746–1825)
Chantons l'Hymen

CAMPIONI, Carlo Antonio (b. ca. 1720)
La chasse

CAPRON, Henry
Violoncellist, composer, guitarist and singer. First mentioned in 1785, as one of the managers of the City Concerts, Philadelphia. Subsequently to be traced there and elsewhere as member of theatre orchestras and as concert performer. From 1788 to 1792, he seems to have resided at New York. November, 1792, finds him again in Philadelphia, where he finally settled in 1794, it seems, as principal of a French boarding-school. Of the many able musicians who emigrated to the United States in those years, Capron was one of the most prominent.
In *Early concert. life in America* (p. 80, note) Sonneck s t a t e s: He probably was identical with the "able violinist and one of the best p u p i l s of Gaviniés" who, according to Fétis, performed at the Concert Spirituel in 1768. Fétis and Eitner mention several of his published works . . .

Lionel de la Laurencie, however, in *L'ecole française de violon de Lully*

à Viotti, Paris, 1923, v. 2, p. 368–379, writes of him as Nicolas Capron. Therefore, unless there is confusion in regard to the name, Sonneck seems to be in error here.

Come, genius of our happy land
  Delia
Go lovely rose thy station choose
  Julia see
A new contra dance
New Kate of Aberdeen
[Softly as the breezes blowing]

CARR, Benjamin (1768/69–1831)
Composer, pianist, organist, singer, publisher. According to Virginia Larkin Redway (*The Carrs . . .*, in *Musical quarterly*, January, 1932) it would seem that the Carr family records indicate that Benjamin Carr was born in England, September 12, 1768, instead of 1769, as commonly given. He died in Philadelphia, May 24, 1831.

This prolific composer was connected with the "London Ancient Concerts" before he emigrated to New York in 1793. He was a favorite of the American public as a ballad singer and tried the operatic stage with some success in 1794–95. But his career as organist, pianist, concert manager, composer and publisher was of by far greater importance for the development of a musical life at Philadelphia. In fact, he had few, if any rivals in this respect. His compositions, both sacred and secular, are numerous. In addition to his published works, several manuscripts are extant; among them a miscellaneous collection of sacred music in Carr's handwriting, containing many original compositions, at the New York Public Library. Carr tried his hand successfully at almost every branch of composition. He was a thoroughly trained composer of the Ph. Em. Bach school and his works are distinguished by a pleasing softness of lines. He also

[501]

wrote a few instructive works. The Musical Fund Society of which he was a founder (1820) erected a monument to his memory after his death at Philadelphia.
See also under *Index of publishers.*

Ah! how hapless is the maiden
The archers (libretto)
Archers march
Bourville Castle (*arr.* from Arne)
The Caledonian frolic (*arr.*)
The children in the wood (*arr.* from Arnold)
Dead march and monody
The deserter (*arr.* from Dibdin)
Ellen arise
The Federal overture
Four ballads
A fragment (In the Archers)
How sweet is the morning
In vain is the verdure of spring
Little Boy Blew
The little sailor boy
Macbeth (*arr.* from Locke)
Mary will smile
A medley duetto . . . from the Federal overture
A Negro song
The new Somebody
The patriot (incidental music)
Poor Jack (incidental music)
Poor Mary
Poor Richard
Shakespeare's willow
Six imitations of English, Scotch, Irish, Welch[!], Spanish and German airs
The Spanish barber (*arr.* from Arnold)
The spirits of the blest
Sweet rosy sleep
Take oh! take those lips away
Tell me where is fancy bred
Three ballads
Three divertimentos
When icicles hang by the wall
When nights were cold
Why, huntress, why
The widow
The wreath of roses

CARTER, Charles Thomas (1734–1804)
O Nancy (*or* Nanny) wilt thou gang wi' (*or* with) me

CASSIGNARD, ——
Amateur guitarist and composer. Appears on Philadelphia concert programs in 1792.
Guitar compositions

CHATEAUDUN (Chateaudieu, Chatendun, Chattenden), R.
French violinst and composer. First mentioned in Baltimore papers in 1796. To be traced as late as 1799 in Philadelphia.

Adieu sweet girl
Medley overture
The Queen of France to her children just before her execution
Romance in French and English
Six romances nouvelles:
  [No. 1] Paul au tombeau de Virginie
  No. 2 Romance
  No. 3 Romance
  No. 4 Romance Gauloise
  No. 5 Romance de Gonzalve de Cordoue
  No. 6 Romance de Gonzalve de Cordoue
Sot potpourri [!]

CHEESE, Griffith James (1751–1804?)
Johnny was a piper's son

CIMAROSA, Domenico (1754–1801)
Se m'abbandoni

CLARK, ——
Silvia

CLEMENTI, Muzio (1752–1832)
Clementi's grand waltz

CLIFFORD, ——
Actor, singer, composer. Mentioned in the theatrical advertisements, Charleston, S. C., 1794, as "from the Bath theatre." Was a prominent member of West and Bignall's company.

Washington's counsel forever huzza!

COLIZZI, John A. K.
Active from ca. 1793.

Six sonatinas for the pianoforte

COOKE, ———
Nobody coming to marry me

COOPER, William
American composer and compiler of
hymn tunes, anthems, etc. Active
from ca. 1790.

An anthem designed for Thanksgiving Day
[When all the Attick fire was fled]

COPE, W. P. R.
English composer, active from ca.
1795.

Henry's departure

CORELLI, Arcangelo (1653–1713)
Corelli's Gavot
The Lullaby of Corelli

CORRI, Domenico (1746–1825)
As late by love
La belle Catherine (variations)

COSTELLOW, Thomas
English composer of songs; also for
harpsichord and pianoforte. Active
from ca. 1792.

The cherry girl
Henry's adieu
I know not why
The impudent creature stole from
    me a kiss

CRAMER, Johann Baptist (1771–
1858)
Marche turque

CROUCH, W. F.
The friendless boys tale

CUNNINGHAM, ———
Content

D

DAGUETTY (Daguettie, Daguitty,
Degatie)
Violinist and composer. Mentioned
as violinist in theatre orchestras,
Charleston, S. C., Savannah, Ga.,
1796–1798.

La fille a Simonette
Overture of Yankee Doodle

DAVY, John (1763–1824)
Crazy Jane

DEARBORN, Benjamin (1754–1838)
Vocal instructor

DECKER, I.
Funeral dirge

DE CLEVE, V.
English composer. Active from
1790.

The poor blind girl

DELAMAINE, Henry
Organist and composer. Active
1782–96 at Cork. (cf. Eitner)
When I think on your truth

DEMARQUE (De Marque), ———
Violoncellist and composer. Also
played violin and double bass.
Probably one of the musicians who
fled from Cape François to the
United States. First mentioned in
1793, on Baltimore concert programs. Was a prominent member
in the orchestra of Wignell and
Reinagle's company with headquar-
ters at Philadelphia. Member of the
City Theatre orchestra, Charleston,
S. C., 1798–99. His name is frequently met with on concert programs.

Concerto violincello [!]
Les deux chasseurs et la latière (arr.)
The elopement (arr.)
Harlequin shipwreck'd (arr.)
The miraculous mill
Rural revels (arr.)
A solo on the violoncello

DEVIENNE, François (1759–1803)
Air des deux Savoyards
The Battle of Gemappe

DEVONSHIRE, Georgiana (Spencer)
Cavendish, Duchess of, 1757–1806.
English composer. Active from
1798.

I have a silent sorrow here

DEZEDE, N. (1740/44–1792)
    Ouverture de Blaise et Babet
    Ouverture de Julie

DIBDIN, Charles (1745–1814)
    Adieu, adieu, my only life. *See*
      Soldier's adieu
    Anne Hatheaway [!]
    Batchelor's [!] Hall
    Ben & Mary
    Ben Backstay
    A collection of songs selected from
      Dibdin
    Comely Ned that died at sea
    Country dance
    Death or victory
    The deserter (libretto)
    Dibdin's fancy
    Dibdin's museum
    Father and mother and Suke
    The flowing can
    Home's home
    [I lock'd up all my treasure]
    I that once was a ploughman. *See*
      The lucky escape
    The invasion
    'Twas in the good ship Rover
    Jack at the windlass
    Jack Junk
    Jack's fidelity
    The jolly ringers
    The jubilee (incidental music)
    The labourer's welcome home
    The lamplighter
    Lionel and Clarissa (libretto)
    Lovely Nan
    The lucky escape
    Mad Peg
    Meg of Wapping
    Mounseer Nong Tong Paw
    Nancy, or The sailor's journal
    Negro philosophy
    Neighbour Sly
    No good without an exception
    Nothing like grog
    The padlock (libretto)
    The patent coffin
    Peggy Perkins
    Polly Ply
    Poor Jack
    Poor Tom. *See* Poor Tom Bowling
    Poor Tom Bowling

    Poor Vulcan (libretto)
    The Quaker (libretto)
    The romp (libretto)
    The sailor's consolation
    The sailor's journal. *Alternative title*
      of Nancy
    The sailor's maxim
    The sailor's return
    The soldier's adieu
    The smile of benevolence
    Tho Prudence may press me
    The token
    Tom Tackle
    Tom Truelove's knell
    True courage
    The vetrans [!]
    The waggoner
    The waterman
    Was I a shepherd's maid
    When first this little heart began

DIGNUM, Charles (1765–1827)
    Fair Rosale

DITTERSDORF, Karl Ditters von
    (1739–1799)
    The fields their wonted hues resume

DUBOIS, William
    French clarinetist, opera singer and
    composer. Emigrated to the United
    States about 1795. Appeared often
    on concert programs. Opened a
    music store at New York City after
    1800.

    Free Mason's march

DUPORT, Pierre Landrin (ca. 1755–
    ca. 1840)
    Dancing master and composer of
    dances. Emigrated to the United
    States in 1790.

    Cotillions
    Dance tunes, &c.
    No. 1 of a new sett of cotilions [!]
    Two new favorite cotillions
    United States country dances

DUPOUY, Alexr.
    Cotillions and country dances

DUSSEK, Jan Ladislav (1760–1812)
Aria alla Tedesca
Good night
Heigho
A Turkish rondo
When you and I love married are

DWIGHT, Timothy (1752–1817)
President of Yale College from 1795.

Columbia
Corydon's ghost (?)
The seasons moralized (?)

E

ELFORT, ――――
The Bastile

EMRICK, George
The invitation
Thomas Jefferson march

F

F., M.
The fortunate roam

FERRARI, Giacomo Gotifredo (1759–1842)
A new scena and polacca (*arr.*)
Three sonatas for the pianoforte

FISCHER (Fisher), Joh. Christian (1733–1800)
Fisher's minuet with new variations
Fisher's second minuet

FISIN, James (1755–1847)
English composer of songs, glees, sonatas, etc.

Gentle love
The gipsy
I felt the command and obey'd with a sigh
Loisa
May. *See* Ode to May
Morning
Ode to May
The sailor's farewell
Shepherd marry
Speed the plough
Ye little songsters

FLORIO, C. H.
English composer of songs, ballads, etc. Also an opera. Active from ca. 1795.

Far, far at sea

FOUCARD (Fouchard), ――――
Clarinetist and composer. Probably one of the French musicians who fled from Hispaniola to the U. S. in 1792. First mentioned in 1793 on concert programs in Boston, Philadelphia and Charleston, S. C., where he was a member of the City Theatre orchestra, 1796–1799.

General Pinckney's march

FOWLER, J.
An envious sigh

FRANCIS, William (1762–1827)
Ballet master and composer of dance music. In America from ca. 1794.

Mr. Francis's ballroom assistant
Mr. Francis' strathspey

FRITH, Edward
English composer. Active from ca. 1800.

The contented cottager

G

GALLI, Signora (d. 1804)
Graceful move

GARNET, Horatio
American composer. Active ca. 1789.

Ode for American independence
An ode for the Fourth of July. *See above* Ode for American independence

GARTH, John (1722–1810)
Favorite rondo

GAULINE, John Baptiste (1759–1824)
American composer. Native of Marseilles, but long a citizen of Maryland.

Adieu to all my heart holds dear

Ah how sweet were those moments of love
Ah were [!] are fled those hours
The American soldier
Answer to the male coquette
The charms of music
Crazy Emma
Crazy lain
The impatient lover
I strove but much I find in vain
The male coquette
Mira of the village plain
So sweet her face her form divine
Sweet is the balmy breath of Spring

GAUTIER, ———
Clarinetist and composer. First mentioned on Philadelphia concert programs in 1795.

Concerto on the clarinet

GAVEAUX, Pierre (1761–1825)
The dish of tea
Ladies answer to the "Pipe tabac."
Alternative title of The dish of tea
La pipe de tabac
Le réveil du peuple

GEHOT, Jean (b. ca. 1756)
Violinist and composer. Came to New York in 1792 with Hewitt, Bergman, Young and Phillips as "professor of music from the opera house, Hanover-square, and Professional concerts under the direction of Haydn, Pleyel, etc. London." During the following years his name very frequently appears on American concert programs. Gehot settled probably in Philadelphia as violinist in the orchestra of Wignell & Reinagle's company. Fétis mentions a Jean Gehot, violinist and composer who was born in Belgium about 1756, travelled in France and Germany after 1780, and lived in London in 1784. But he must have been there as early as 1781, as Pohl (*Mozart u. Haydn in London*, p. 370) traced him in London in that year as violin virtuoso. Eitner mentions numerous compositions by Gehot, 36 quartets, trios, etc. Of his theo-

retical works are known "A treatise on the theory and practice of music ..." London, 1784, and "The complete instructor for every instrument," London, 1790. That this Gehot is identical with the one who emigrated to the U. S. becomes evident from John R. Parker's "Musical reminiscences" in the *Euterpeiad*, 1822. It is there stated that he died in obscurity and indigent circumstances.

Overture in twelve movements
Quartet
The reconsaliation [!]

GELENIK, Joseph (1758–1825)
A popular Tyrolesian air

GILLINGHAM, George (d. 1823 ?)
Violinist and composer. Born in England, pupil of Giardini (John R. Parker). He came to the U. S. in 1793 or 1794 as leader in the orchestra of Wignell & Reinagle's company. In 1794 he was one of the directors of the "Amateur and Professional Concerts" at Philadelphia. He subsequently moved to New York, where he was still active as leader at "The New York Theatre" in 1822. A picture in the NHi shows him in this capacity. Gillingham seems to have been a violinist of unusual ability. Had played in the Handel Commemoration, London, 1784.

Harlequin's invasion (*arr.*)
The little Yankee sailor (*arr.*)
William and Lucy

GIORDANI, Giuseppe (1744–1798)
Altho' heav'ns good pleasure
The bleeding hero
A concerto for the pianoforte or harpsichord
Did not tyrant custom guide me
[Farewell ye friends of early youth]
I blush in the dark
Loose were her tresses
The village spire
Ye crystal fountains

[506]

GLUCK, Christoph Willibald (1714–
1787)
[Jai perdu mon Euridice]
Love, thou mad'ning power
My Laura will you trust the seas
    (arr. from Arnold)
An ode to sleep
Ouverture d'Iphigenie en Aulide

GRAEFF, J. C.
BM Cat. assigns the song *Lisbia*
to Johann George Graeff. This is
apparently the German flutist, J. G.
Graeff, who, according to Fétis,
spent the latter part of the eighteenth century in London, where he
published numerous works.

Lisbia

GRAM, Hans
American composer. Born in Den-
mark. Educated at Stockholm.
Seems to have settled at Boston as
early as 1789, where he was organist
of Brattle Street Church in 1793,
and for many years after. Is best
known as co-editor with Oliver
Holden and Samuel Holyoke of
"The Massachusetts Compiler,"
1795, the most progressive work on
psalmody which appeared in the
U. S. before 1800.

America. A new march
The death song of an Indian chief
A hunting song
Ode for the New Year
Ode to the President of the United
    States
A shape alone let others prize
Sonnet (arr. from Graun)

GRANGER, Frederick
Clarinetist and composer. Active,
Boston, from 1793.

Massachusetts march

GRAUN, Carl Heinrich (1703/4–
1759)
Oratorio. (Sonnet *arr.* from, by
    Gram)

GRAUPNER, Gottlieb (1767–1836)
Oboist, composer, music publisher.
Born in Germany, October 6, 1767,
died in Boston, April 16, 1836. Was
oboist in a Hanoverian regiment
until 1788, when he went to London.
There he played under Haydn.
From London he went to Prince
Edward's Island whence he arrived
at Charleston, S. C., in 1795. In
1797, he became oboist in the orchestra of the Federal Street Theatre,
Boston, where he settled definitely.
With some friends he founded a
"Philharmonic Society" which ex-
isted until 1824. He also was a
founder of the Handel and Haydn
Society and his importance in the
history of music at Boston has duly
been recognized by Dwight. About
1800 Graupner opened a music store.
He also engraved and published
music. *See also* Grove, Howard,
etc.

Columbia's bold eagle

GRÉTRY, André Ernest Modeste
(1741–1813)
Overture de la Caravane
Richard Coeur de Lion (arr.)
Selima and Azor (libretto)
The storm is o'er

GRIFFITH, John
Dancing master and composer. To
be traced in Providence, R. I.,
Boston, New York, Charleston, S.
C., and other cities.

A collection of . . . country dances

GUALDO, Giovanni (John), (d. 1771)
Musician and "wine merchant from
Italy, but late from London," who
came to Philadelphia in 1767, where
he is to be traced until 1771, teaching music, directing concerts "after
the Italian method" and performing
his compositions. Died December
20, 1771, of lunacy, in the Pennsylvania Hospital.
German flute concert
Six new minuets

Symphony
Trio

GUENIN (Genin), ──────

Composer and pianist. Probably one of the French musicians who fled from the West Indies to the United States. He first appears on Philadelphia programs in 1792, where we also find him as late as 1799.

Free Masons march (*arr.* from Dubois)
Overture, 1st of
Sinfonia

H

H., S. M.
Paul and Mary

HAGEN, Peter Albrecht von (*or* van) Sr.(1750[?]–1803)

Organist, music teacher, violinist, composer. Sittard in his history of concert-life at Hamburg, mentions a violin virtuoso by the name of Peter Albrecht von Hagen who gave a concert there in 1740. He probably was identical with the organist, composer and violinist at Rotterdam (pupil of Geminiani) whom Burney met in the seventies and of whom Enschedé speaks as still being there in 1776. Burney also mentions his son "who has been under M. Honaür at Paris." It was this son probably who came to Charleston, S. C., in 1774, calling himself P. A. van Hagen, jun., "organist and director of the City's Concert in Rotterdam. Lately arrived from London." In 1789, on New York concert programs, he changed the jun. into sen. in distinction from his son who then began his career as violin virtuoso. In the following year he called himself "organist, carilloneur and director of the City Concert at Zutphen." He resided at New York until 1796, from 1793 on as the principal manager of the Old City Concerts. Late in 1796 he removed to Boston with his family, where he opened a music school with his son and also a music store. For a while he was the leader in the New Theatre orchestra and his name appears frequently on concert programs. In 1800, he was organist at the Stone Chapel. In several of his advertisements he called himself "organist in four of the principal churches in Holland" with an "experience during 27 years as an instructor." On going to Boston in 1796, the family name was changed from *van* to *von* Hagen.

The adopted child (*arr.* from Attwood)
The Battle of Hexham. *See* The days of old (*arr.* from Arnold)
Columbus (incidental music)
Federal overture
Funeral dirge on the death of General Washington
Zorinski (*arr.* from Arnold)

HAGEN, Peter Albrecht von (*or* van) Jr. (1781–1837)

Music teacher, publisher, virtuoso, composer. Son of P. A. von Hagen, Sen.; first mentioned on New York concert programs in 1789 as pianist "eight years of age." Began his career as music teacher in 1792 at the age of eleven years. Late in 1796 the family moved from New York to Boston, where young Von Hagen continued his career as a concert performer.
See also under *Index of publishers.*

Adams and Washington
Anna
Gentle zephyr
How tedious alas! are the hours
I'm in haste
May morning
Overture
The pride of our plains
To arms Columbia

HAIBEL, Jacob (1761–1826)
Viennese singer and composer. (*cf.* Eitner)

Says Jessy one morn

HAIGH, Thomas (1769–1808)
English violinist, pianist and composer. Pupil of Haydn, 1791–92. (*cf.* Eitner)

Aria con variazione

HANDEL, George Frederic (1685–1759)
Duetto (*arr.*)
Handle's [!] celebrated water music
Handle's [!] water music
In Acis and Galatea. *See* [Would you gain the tender creature]
O lovely peace
[Would you gain the tender creature]

HARINGTON, Henry (1727–1816)
Damon and Clora
How sweet in the woodlands

HAWKINS, A.
English song composer. Active from ca. 1780.

[Throw an apple]

HAYDN, Franz Joseph (1732–1809)
Andante d'Haydn
A favorite rondo in the gipsey style
Haydn's celebrated Andante for the pianoforte
Haydn's grand overture. *See* Overture by Haydn
Hurly burly
Hymen's evening post
The knitting girl
Marian owns her love
The mermaid's song
My mother bids me bind my hair
Overture by Haydn
A prey to tender anguish
Romance
Rondo
Sonata III
Sonate de Haydn
Sonatina
Three canzonetts by Haydn

HEWITT, James (1770–1827)
Violinist, composer, publisher. Born in Dartmoor, England (June 4, 1770); died in Boston (August 1, 1827). Came to New York in 1792, with Gehot, Bergman, Young, and Phil-

ipps as "professors of music from the Operahouse, Hanoversquare, and Professional Concerts under the direction of Haydn, Pleyel, etc. London." Hewitt managed excellent subscription concerts at New York during the following years and was very active as virtuoso and leader in the orchestra of the Old American Company. He held an undisputed position as leading musician in New York and his social standing was excellent. Hewitt's career extended far into the 19th century and quite a few of his compositions are extant in our libraries though unfortunately only his minor works.
See also under *Index of publishers.*

Alknomook
The battle of Trenton
A book of songs (Pownall and Hewitt)
La chasse (*arr.* from Rossetti)
Collin's Ode on the passions (incidental music)
Columbus (incidental music)
The Federal Constitution and liberty forever (*arr.*)
How happy was my humble lot
How shall I my pain discover
The Indian chief. *See* Alknomook
'Twas in the solemn midnight hour
The lass of Lucerne lake
March in Pizarro
Mark my Alford
Masonic ode
My poor dog Tray
The mysterious marriage (incidental music)
New England guard's march
The new Federal overture
A new medley overture
Overture de Démaphon [!] (*arr.* from Vogel)
Overture in 9 movements
Overture to conclude with the representation of a Storm at sea
The patriot (incidental music)
Pizarro (incidental music)
The primrose girl

Robin Hood (*arr.* from Shield)
Six easy duetts (violin)
The Spanish castle
Sweet Myra of the vale
Tammany
Tammany quickstep
Three marches
Three sonatas
Time
The wampum belt
When the old heathen gods
When the shades of night
The wild goose chase (incidental music)
The wish
The wounded hussar

HINDLE, John (1761–1796)
English composer of songs and glees.

The season of love is no more

HOFFMEISTER, Franz Anton (1754–1812)
Duetto

HOLDEN, Oliver (1765–1844)
American composer and compiler of hymn tunes, anthems, etc. By trade a carpenter, Holden devoted his leisure hours to composition. His first collection, "The American Harmony," appeared in 1792. His most ambitious work was "The Massachusetts Compiler," 1795, which he co-edited with Hans Gram and Samuel Holyoke. In 1797, he was engaged by Isaiah Thomas as editor and reviser of "The Worcester Collection."

American harmony
Anniversary dirge
Columbia's guardian sleeps in dust
A dirge
A dirge or sepulchral service
A funeral anthem
A funeral hymn
A hymn
Invocation to Charity
Masonic dirge
Mount Vernon
Ode on music
Ode to harmony

Sacred dirges, hymns and anthems
Spring. An ode
The Union harmony

HOLYOKE, Samuel (1762–1820)
American composer and compiler of hymn tunes, anthems, etc. Also songs. Born at Boxford, Mass., October 15, 1762; died at East Concord, N. H., February 7, 1820.
Beneath the honors
The close of the year
Hark from the tombs
The pensive shepherd
Sally
[The scattered clouds are fled at last]
Terraminta
Washington

HOMAN, C.
Tutor for the violin

HOOK, James (1746–1827)
The Albion, the pride of the sea
All for pretty Polly
Alone by the light of the moon
And strew the sweet roses of pleasure between
Anna, or The adieu
As forth I rang'd the banks of Tweed
The aviary—A collection of sonnets
Contents: No. 1. The thrush.—No. 2. Linnetts.—No. 3. The gold finch.—No. 4 The Robin red breast.—No. 5. The nightingale.—No. 6. The lark.—No. 7. The black bird.—No. 8. The cuckoo.
The aviary. A collection of three sonnets.
Contents: The linnetts.—The gold finch.—The nightingale.
The black bird
Bonny Charley
Bright Phoebus
By Baby Bunting
The Caledonian laddie (*or* laddy)
A cent'ry ago
A collection of favorite songs sung at Vauxhall gardens
Come rouse brother sportsman
The contented shepherd
The cottage in the grove

[511]

Ripe cherries
Rise, Cynthia, rise
Robin a bobbin a Bilbery hen
She lives in the valley below
The silver moon
The smart cockade
Softly waft ye southern breezes
Strew the rude crosses of life o'er
  with flowers
Sweet girl by the light of the moon
Sweet lillies of the valley
The sweet little girl that I love
Sweet love I'll marry thee
Sweet Nan of Hampton Green
The tear
Tell me is it love
Then say my sweet girl can you love
  me
Thou'rt gone awa frae me, Mary
Tho' wealth is alluring
Thou soft'ning balm
The thrifty wife
The thrush
To the maid I love best
To soften life's cares
The turtle dove coos round my cot
Two bunches a penny primroses
The unfortunate sailor
Unfurl'd were the sails
The way to get married
The wedding day
What can a lassy do
When Edward left his native plain
When I was a chit
When Lucy was kind
When once by the clear gliding
  stream
When Sandy told his tale of love
When the merry bells
When the stars can be told
Where's the harm of that
Where Liffey rolls its silver streams
Whither can my William stray
William of the ferry
Willy of the dale
Winsome Kate
Within a mile of Edinburgh

HOPKINSON, Francis (1737–1791)
  Signer of the Declaration of Independence, our first Secretary of
  the Navy, Judge of the Admiralty

from Pennsylvania, satirist, poet,
inventor, painter, etc., in short, one
of the foremost men of Revolutionary times. He was also a
skilled musician with a decided gift
for composition. He spent much
time and thought on the improvement of the harpsichord and other
instruments, was proficient on the
organ and harpsichord, conversant
with the best music of his time, and
undoubtedly contributed more to-
ward the development of a musical
life at Philadelphia than any of his
contemporaries. Francis Hopkinson himself claimed to have been the
first native American composer and
the facts seem to bear out his claim,
James Lyon, of Newark, N. J., being
a close second and William Billings
of Boston, third. Strange to say
until fairly recently, Francis Hopkinson's interesting musical career
escaped the attention of our historians entirely. He was born at
Philadelphia, where he lived his
whole life long.

An anthem from the 114th Psalm
The garland. *See* A volume of songs
Give me thy heart as I give mine
In memory of Mr. James Bremner
My days have been so wondrous free.
  See A volume of songs
Oh come to Mason borough's grove.
  See A volume of songs
An ode designed for a public com-
mencement in the College of Phila-
delphia
Ode from Ossian's poems
Ode. (In an exercise containing a
dialogue and ode)
Ode (In an exercise containing a.
dialogue and two odes)
An ode set to music on Mrs. B——s
birthday
Seven songs—
  Contents:
  [Beneath a weeping willow's shade
    (III)]
  [Come fair Rosina, come away
    (I)]

[Enraptur'd I gaze (IV)]
[My love is gone to sea (II)]
[My gen'rous heart disdains (VII)]
[O'er the hills far away (VI)]
[See down Maria's blushing cheek (V)]
The trav'ler benighted and lost (VIII)]
The Temple of Minerva
A toast
The twenty third Psalm
Washington's march at the Battle of Trenton (attributed to)
A volume of songs (composed or copied by)
With pleasure have I past my days. *See* A volume of songs

HORSLEY, William (1774–1858)
The beggar boy

HOWARD, Samuel (1710–1782)
Farewell ye green fields

J

J., H.
The charming creature
The dawn of hope

JACKSON, George K.
Composer and organist. (*Grove*, 1745–1823, *Baker*, 1758–1822) Came to America 1796. Principally active in New York and Boston.

Ah Delia
American serenade
Cancherizante
The cricket
Dead march
Dirge for General Washington
The fairies
Gentle air
Huzza for liberty
The multiplication table
New miscellaneous musical work
New York serenade
One kind kiss
Song for two voices in canon
Sweet are the banks
[Waft me some soft and cooling breeze]
A winter's evening

JACKSON, William, of Exeter (1730–1803)
Canzonet [Time has not thin'd my flowing hair]
Canzonett [Love in thy eyes forever plays]
The heavy hours
When first this humble roof I knew

JENKS, Stephen (1772–1856)
American composer and compiler of hymn tunes, anthems, etc.

Mount Vernon
The musical harmonist

JORDAN, *Mrs.* (Dorothea Bland) (1762–1816)
Actress, singer. Probably composed little besides the popular *Blue Bell of Scotland.*

The Blue Bell of Scotland (attributed to)

JUHAN, Alexander (1765–1845)
Composer and violinist. "Alexander Juhan, junior, master of music," appears in Philadelphia in December, 1783, as "lately arrived." Probably the son of James Juhan, who came to Charleston, S. C., as a music teacher in 1771, and who, in 1783, advertised himself at Philadelphia as manufacturer of the "Great North American Fortepiano." This James Juhan is probably identical with the James *Juan* or *Joan* who was active in Boston, 1768–70. Alexander is believed to have been born in Halifax and brought to Boston in 1768. He is mentioned on Philadelphia concert programs, 1786, as violinist and as one of the managers of the City Concerts. His professional quarrel with Andrew Adgate in 1787, throws a peculiar light upon musical conditions at Philadelphia. He seems to have moved to Charleston, S. C., in 1791, where he is to be traced for a year or two. He then returned to Philadelphia.

A set of six sonatas

A set of six songs
Solo for the violin
Song on General Washington

K

KALKBRENNER, Christian (1755–1806)
Buonaparte's march

KAMBRA, Karl
German composer of songs, sonatas, chamber works, etc. Settled in London towards end of eighteenth century. Active from ca. 1780.

The siege of Valenciennes

KELLY, ——
English comedian and occasional composer. Appeared in America first in 1792.

Song

KELLY, Michael (1762–1826)

Blue Beard. A collection of new and favorite songs from
Chica cho
In the rough blast heaves the billow
March in Blue Beard
March in Feudel [!] times
Megen oh! Oh Megen EE
Naval March
Oh since I've found you
Pit a pat
Tink a tink
When pensive I thought on my love

KELLY, Thomas Alexander Erskine, *Sixth Earl of* (1732–1781)

Overture

KIMBALL, Jacob (1761–1826)
Composer and compiler of hymn tunes, anthems, etc.

[Ah lovely appearance of death]

KLEYSER, S.
A winter piece

KOTZWARA, Franz (d. 1791)
Ah Delia
As pendant o'er the limpid stream

The Battle of Prague
The gentle swan
Quick march from the Battle of Prague
Quick step in the Battle of Prague
Tell me fairest, tell me true
When Delia on the plain appears

KREUTZER, Rodolphe (*or* Rudolph) (1766–1831)
Fernando
Overture to Lodoiska

KRUMPHOLTZ, Johann Baptist (1745–1790)
Louisa's complaint

L

LABARRE (La Barre), Trille
Composer and teacher. First mentioned in November, 1793, in Boston papers as "professor and composer of music, lately from Paris." He taught "vocal music after the manner of Italian schools" and, for several years, played in the theatre orchestras of Boston. Possibly identical with Trille Labarre, the guitarist, who according to Fétis, lived in Paris towards the end of the eighteenth century and of whose works he mentions several with these imprint dates: Paris, 1787, 1788, 1793, 1794.

Latin oratorio
Lionel and Clarissa (*arr.* from Dibdin)
The prisoner (*arr.* from Attwood)
Richard Coeur de Lion (*arr.* from Grétry)
Set of Mons. Labasse's [!] quadrilles

LABARTE, ——
Still toss'd tempestuous on the sea of life

LANGDON, W.
"Music professor," Philadelphia, ca. 1795.

The primrose
Sonata

LAW, Andrew (1748–1821)
Composer and compiler of hymn tunes.

An American hero

LEAUMONT, R.
Composer. In 1796 leader of the band in concerts at Boston, still there in 1798, settled at Charleston, S. C., about 1801.

The maid of the mill (*arr.* from Arnold)
New Federal overture
Three duetts (Deaumont *recte* Leaumont)

LEEVES, William
English song composer. Active from ca. 1780.

The pigeon

LINLEY, Francis (1771–1800)
Composer and organist. Blind from birth. Came to America in 1796. First mentioned as composer in Boston papers of 1798, and as partner in the firm of Linley & Moore or Linley & Co. Returned to England in 1799.

Linley's assistant for the pianoforte
Linley's selection of country dances and reels
A new assistant for the pianoforte
Overture
Three sonatas

LINLEY, Thomas (senior) (1732/33–1795)
The duenna (with Thomas Linley, junior) (libretto)
Had I a heart
In my pleasant native plains
No flow'r that blows
Robinson Crusoe (pantomine)
The rose
Still the lark finds repose
The woodman (libretto)
Young Lubin was a shepherd boy

LOCKE, Matthew (1632/33–1677)
Macbeth (incidental music)

LOW, Samuel
American composer. Active as early as 1790.

An anthem . . . at the celebration of St. John's Day
Ode

LYON, James (1735–1794)
Composer and compiler of hymn tunes. Native of Newark, N. J. A close second to Francis Hopkinson for the title of first native American composer. Known to musical historians chiefly as compiler and editor of the psalm tune collection "Urania" (1761 or 1762), a book full of bibliographical puzzles and the most important and progressive of its kind and time published in America. To students of ecclesiastical history James Lyon is known as the first Presbyterian minister in Nova Scotia and to those of political history for his proposals to conquer Nova Scotia during the War of the Revolution.
Cf. Sonneck, *Francis Hopkinson . . . and James Lyon.*

A dialogue on peace [attributed to] Friendship
The military glory of Great Britain
Ode on peace [attributed to]

M

MALLET, Francis
Composer, singer, pianist, violinist, organist, etc. In Sonneck's original note regarding Mallet he writes: Probably one of the French musicians who fled to the U. S. from Hispaniola in 1793. First mentioned on Philadelphia concert programs in the same year. Seems to have belonged to the orchestra in Wignell and Reinagle's company. Settled in Boston about 1795, where he kept a music store besides being an active musician.

Later (in *Early concert life*, p. 291, n.1) Sonneck amends this statement as follows: Of Francis Mallet, who was destined to play a prominent part in Boston's musical life, General Oliver says in his "First Centenary of the North Church, Salem" (see Brooks, p. 167):

"Monsieur Mallet was a French, gentleman of much respectability who came to this country with Lafayette and served in the army of the Revolution to the end of the war. He then settled in Boston as a teacher of music, declining to receive any pension. He was among the earliest publishers of music in Boston, the friend and business partner of the celebrated Dr. G. K. Jackson and predecessor of Graupner, the famous double bass player, whose music store was in Franklin Street."

To this may be added that Mallet in 1798 is mentioned as organist to the "Rev. Mr. Kirkland's congregation." It is also clear that the biographical note in my *Bibliography* is a trifle incorrect as Mallet settled in Boston at least as early as 1793. Still I doubt that he came to Boston immediately after the war. It is more probable that he came to the United States as a refugee from Hispaniola(Sonneck).

Set of Mons. Labasses [!] quadrilles (*arr.*)

MANN, Elias (1750–1825)
Composer and compiler of hymn tunes. Teacher.

Andre's ghost
The grasshopper
Marlborough's ghost

MARKOE, Peter (1735–1792)
Poet, librettist. Born in Santa Cruz (St. Croix), West Indies; died at Philadelphia. Was educated at Trinity College, Dublin, read law in London, and settled at Philadelphia in 1783, where his "Miscellaneous poems" were printed in 1787. It is doubtful that Markoe

wrote any of the music for his comic opera *The reconciliation*. This seems rather to have been a sort of ballad opera, in which all musical numbers were assigned to well known tunes.

The reconciliation (libretto)

MARKORDT, J.
English composer. Active ca. 1780.
That petty fogging Grizzle
[We kings who are in our senses]

MARSHAL, Daniel
Ground Ivy

MARTIN Y SOLAR, Vicente (1754/56–1806)
Ouverture d'una cosa rara

MARTINI il Tedesco (Johann Paul Aegidius Schwartzendorf) (1741–1816)
A Son Altesse Royale Madame Elizabeth de France
March maestoso (Henry the Fourth)
Martini's overture
Ronde chantee a la Reine
The sea boys duett

MAZZINGHI, Joseph (1765–1839)
Ah could my fault'ring [!] tongue
A blessing on brandy & beer
Calm the winds
A favourite air grotesque
Happy were the days
The maid with the bosom of snow
March in Ramah Droog
The sigh of remembrance
Tom Starboard

METZGER, ———
Who so merry lives as I

MICHAEL, David Moritz (1751–1825)
Composer, violinist, player on wind instruments. Born in Germany. In America, 1795–1814, as music teacher at Bethlehem, Pa., and Nazareth, Pa., afterwards at Bethlehem, Pa., as class leader of the Single Brethren of the Moravian congregation.

Parthie VII, VIII, X–XIV

Suite
Die Wasserfahrt

MICHELE, Joseph
His Majesty's review of the volunteer corps of London

MOLLER, John Christopher (d. 1803)
Composer, organist, pianist, publisher. First mentioned on New
York concert programs of 1790 as
harpsichordist. End of the same
year he went to Philadelphia, where
(1792–93) he gave concerts with his
daughter, a musical prodigy. During the following years he resided at
Philadelphia as organist of Zion
Church, music teacher, concert performer, and (in 1792, with Reinagle
and Capron) as director of the City
Concerts. Moller was also a specialist on the Harmonica. In 1793
he and Capron kept a music store
and published music under the firm
of Moller & Capron, 163 North
Third St., combining therewith a
music school. In 1795, Moller
moved to New York and when P. A.
von Hagen, sen., moved to Boston,
late in 1796, he undertook the continuation of the Old City Concerts,
changing, in 1798, the name into
that of "Subscription Concerts."
As composer, Moller was not without talent, the symphony, for instance, mentioned in these pages
being harmless but pretty. Died in
New York, September 21, 1803.
Sonneck adds later: "Our John
Christopher Moller probably was
identical with the 'Moeller, J . . .
C . . .' of whose works several are
mentioned by Eitner." BM Cat.
also lists a group of works, some of
them identical with those given by
Eitner, as composed by "J. C. Moller" and ranging in date from 1775
to 1796. This latest date seems a bit
perplexing, as Moller had come to
America long before then.

La chasse
Concerto

Duetti (arr.)
A favorite new German waltz
March
Meddley [!] with the most favorite
airs and variations
Moller's rondo
Overture
Quartet
Rondo
Sinfonia
Sonata VIII

MONSIGNY, Pierre Alexandre (1729–
1817)
Ouverture to La belle Arsenne
Overture to The deserter
Tho prudence may press me
[Vous l'ordonné je me serai connoitre]

MOOREHEAD, John (d. 1804)
The lass of the lake
Moss roses
The naval pillar (arr.)

MORE, Isabella Theaker
English composer. Active ca. 1785.

The walls of my prison

MORGAN, W. S.
Violinist and composer. First mentioned 1770 in Boston paper as
"pupil of Signior Giardini, just arrived from England." Taught
music and played first violin, in
1771, in W. Turner's subscription
concerts. During the same year
he went to Newport, R. I., as organist. After having been discharged
for disorderly conduct and for con-
tracting debts and after an itinerant
career in several small towns, he
reappeared at Boston in 1773, and
is to be traced there until 1775,
mostly as violin virtuoso.

Hunting song
Military symphony

MOULDS, John
English song composer. Active from
ca. 1784.

The Caledonian maid
I sold a guiltless Negro boy

Jack Clueline
The poor village boy
She dropt a tear & cried be true
Sterne's Maria

MOZART, Wolfgang Amadeus (1756–1791)
Away with melancholy
Duetto
Fairy revels
Fischer's minuet. With variations by W. Mozart
Forget me not. *See* Schneider, Georg Lorenz
The fowler
Grand march. *Arr.* by Attwood, from Mozart
Last adieu
Let truth and spotless faith be thine
Merrily sings. *See* Away with melancholy
The resolution (*arr.*)
Sweet as summers fragrant gale. *Arr.* from Mozart
Within these sacred bowers

N

NÄGELI, Hans Georg (1773–1836)
Freut euch des Lebens. *See* Life let us cherish
Life let us cherish
Snatch fleeting pleasures. *See* Life let us cherish

NICOLAI (Niccolai), Valentino (d. 1798/99?)
Composer and pianist. Probably spent last years in London. Most popular works: Sonatas for piano forte or harpsichord, Op. 3 and Op. 11. Cf. *Fétis.*

A favorite sonata
Nicholai's favorite sonata
Nicolai's 2 easy sonatas for the piano forte
Six sonatas for the piano forte or harpsichord
Sonata I
Sonata II
Sonata III
Sonata IV

O

OSWALD, James (1710/11–1769)
Alloa house

OTT, David
Lob und Anbetung

P

PAGE, ——
A Christmas hymn

PAISIELLO, Giovanni (1741–1816)
The dream
For tenderness form'd
How can I forget
Recitativo e rondo
Whither my love

PELISSIER (Pelisier), Victor
French horn virtuoso, composer. First mentioned in 1792 on Philadelphia concert programs as "first French horn of the theatre in Cape François." After residing at Philadelphia for one year, he moved to New York as principal horn player in the orchestra of the Old American Company. His name is frequently met with on New York concert programs, and most of the arrangements and compositions for the Old American Company were written either by him or James Hewitt. Pelissier resided at New York for many years.

Sonneck adds: Possibly identical with the Pelissier of whom the Cons. Nat. at Paris possesses "Amusements variés avec accomp. de musette."

Ariadne abandoned (incidental music)
Bourville Castle (*arr.*)
The Castle of Otranto (*arr.* from Reeve)
The deserter (*arr.* from Dibdin)
Edwin and Angelina
The flitch of bacon (*arr.* from Shield)
La foret noire (*arr.* from Reinagle)
The Fourth of July (incidental music)
Harlequin pastry cook

[518]

The haunted tower (*arr.* from Storace)
The host that fights for liberty
Incle and Yarico (*arr.* from Arnold)
The jubilee (*arr.*)
The launch, or Huzza for the Constellation (*arr.*)
The lock and key (*arr.* from Shield)
The maid of the mill (*arr.* from Arnold)
The mountaineers (*arr.* from Arnold)
My grandmother (*arr.* from Storace)
The mysterious monk (incidental music)
Poor Vulcan (*arr.*)
Quartet
Robinson Crusoe
Rosina (*arr.* from Shield)
The siege of Belgrade (*arr.* from Storace)
The son in law (*arr.* from Arnold)
Sophia of Brabant
Sterne's Maria, or the Vintage
Sweetly in life's jocund morning
The virgin in the sun (incidental music)
Washington and independence
The waterman (*arr.* from Dibdin)
Zorinski (*arr.* from Arnold)

PERCY, John (1749–1797)
The captive
Marie Antoinette's complaint
A wandring [!] gipsey

PETER, John Frederick (1746–1813)
Composer, organist and violinist. Of the Moravian congreagtion in Bethlehem, Pennsylvania.
Six quintetti

PETIT, ———
Violinist and composer. Probably one of the French musicians who fled to the U. S. from the West Indies in 1793. Appears in this year on Philadelphia, Boston, and Charleston, S. C., concert programs as violinist. Seems to have settled at Charleston, S. C., where he is to be traced as member of the City Theatre orchestra in 1799.
Quartet

PHILE, Philip (d. 1793)
Violinist and composer. Name is variously given as Fyles, Pfeil, Pfylo, Philo, Phyla, Phyles, etc. First mentioned on Philadelphia concert programs in 1784 as violinist. In this or the following year he became the leader of the orchestra of the Old American Company. After an itinerant career, he settled at Philadelphia in 1789, and died there in 1793. Composer of *The President's march.*

Hail Columbia. *See* President's march
Harmony music
President's march (Hail Columbia)
Violin concerto

PHILLIPS, ———
Dancing master, violoncellist and composer. Came to New York in 1792 with Hewitt, Gehot, Bergman and Young as "professors of music, from the Operahouse, Hanoversquare, and Professional Concerts, under the direction of Haydn, Pleyel, etc." In one of his advertisements he called himself "dancing master from his academy, and the opera, London, director of the figures under the Earl of Aylesbury, at the Queen's Balls; master of ceremonies at the masquerades Pantheon, City Balls, London Taverns, Anacreontic Rooms, etc." To be traced for a few years on American concert programs as violoncellist.

Concerto violoncello

PHILO-MUSICO
The only definitely identifiable "Philo-musico" seems to be Chauncy Langdon, who according to Evans (19750) compiled *The select songster,* New Haven, 1786. That he may be the "Philo-musico" who contributed the following four titles to the *Massachusetts magazine* for 1790, is, of course, a possibility, but nothing more. These "Philo-" pseudo-

nyms were popular and plentiful in those days.

[Bright Sol at length]
The charms of nature
Columbia, a new country dance
Rosy Nell

PICCINNI, (Piccini), Nicola (1728–1800)
The accomplished maid
Overture. La buona figliuola
Overture. La schiava (*arr.* by Reinagle)

PICK, John (Jacobus)
Composer for the Harmonica. Mentioned in 1792 on Boston concert programs, later on in Southern papers. Seems to have settled at Boston in 1796 and remained for a few years.

Duet on the harmonica

PIERCY, H.
English song composer. Active from ca. 1798

The beggar girl

PIRSSON, William
Composer and engraver. Active in New York from ca. 1799.

A duetto for two flutes
Glide gently on thou murm'ring brook
Un jeu d'esprit

PLEYEL, Ignaz Joseph (1757–1831)
Air
Ah Mary shall thy heart
Beauty
Collins grave
Come blushing rose
Duetto
Henry's cottage maid
Hope thou source of ev'ry blessing
Minuetto
Minuetto and trio
Pleyel's celebrated concertante
Rondo
Six sonatas
The soldiers epitaph
Sonata

Sonnet to time
Thema con variazione
Tho pity I cannot deny
Three progressive sonatinas
Time. *See* Sonnet to time
Tranquil pleasures never cloy

POWNALL, *Mrs.* Mary Ann (1751–1796)
Actress, singer, poet and composer. Although the date of Mrs. Pownall's birth is commonly given as above, the Charleston *Gazette* in an obituary notice, published August 13, 1796, speaks of her as "aged 40 years." This however, is probably a mistake.

This great actress and singer was known in England as Mrs. Wrighten, of whom English critics said that she could not be equalled as *Lucy* in the Beggar's opera and Mr. Seilhamer claims that she was surpassed as a singer by Mrs. Billington and Mrs. Oldmixon only. She was also famous as Vauxhall singer. Mrs. Pownall came to America as a member of Hallam and Henry's Old American Company. She died in Charleston, S. C.

Address to the ladies of Charleston
Advice to the ladies of Boston
A book of songs(Pownall and Hewitt)
The happy rencontre
Jemmy of the glen
Kisses sued for
The labyrinth of love
Lavinia
Mrs. Pownall's address
The straw bonnet
Washington

PRIEST, William
Music engraver, arranger and publisher. He became a bassoonist and trumpeter in Wignell and Reinagle's company, Philadelphia, in 1794; returned after a few years to England, where his "Travels in America" were published in 1802.

Twelve duets for two clarinets (*arr.* from Pleyel)

R

R., F. (Frederick Rausch?)
Liberty's throne

RAUSCH, Frederick
Pianist, composer, teacher. Active
in New York as early as 1793.
See also under *Index of publishers.*

Sonatina a quatre mains

REEVE, William (1757–1815)
A favorite air in . . . Oscar and
   Malvina
All? from Oscar and Malvina
The desponding Negro
Finale (Oscar and Malvina)
Fishing duett
The galley slave
[How sweet when the silver moon]
The jolly gay pedlar
The lavender girl
March in Ramah Droog
The market lass
My journey is love
The new volunteers
Our country is our ship
Paddy Bull's expedition
The purse, or Benevolent tar (lib-
   retto)
Quick march (Oscar and Malvina)
The Sicilian romance
Songs in The purse, or Benevolent
   tar
The tinker
The wealth of the cottage is love
When a little merry he
When seated with Sal
The witch

REICHARDT, Johann Friedrich
(1752–1814)
The angler

REINAGLE, Alexander (1756–1809)
Pianist, composer, conductor, theatrical manager. Born in Portsmouth, England, he began his
musical career in Scotland, where
he received instructions both in the
theory and practice of music by
Raynor Taylor. He came to New
York in 1786, calling himself "member of the Society of Musicians in
London." His proposals to settle
in New York not meeting with
sufficient encouragement, he went
to Philadelphia after giving proof of
his abilities to the New Yorkers in
an excellent concert. In Philadelphia his talents were soon appreci-
ated, and he became music teacher
in the best families. He conducted
and performed in numerous concerts, besides presiding at the harpsichord in opera in several cities,
especially in Baltimore, before he
and Wignell founded the New
Theatre at Philadelphia in 1793.
This enterprise was in every respect
remarkable, but too great a preference was given to opera and the com-
mercial success was not in keeping
with the artistic. Reinagle developed an astonishing activity as
composer and arranger during these
years. He died at Baltimore, on
September 21, 1809. "During the
latter years of his life, he was
ardently engaged in composing
music to parts of Milton's Paradise
Lost, which he did not live to complete. It was intended to be performed in oratorio style, except that
instead of recitatives, the best
speakers were to be engaged in
reciting the intermediate passages."
(Parker, *Euterpeiad*, 1822.) The
manuscript of this work was extant
until about the turn of the century,
when it disappeared from the library
of Reinagle's grandson, Mr. Davis,
in Washington, D. C. The Library
of Congress possesses some really
fine sonatas of his in autograph.

Adieu thou dreary pile (*arr.*)
America, commerce & freedom
Arabs of the desert (*arr.*)
Auld Robin Gray (*arr.* from Arnold)
Blue Beard (*arr.* from Kelly)
La chasse
Chorus sung before Gen. Washing-
   ton . . . at Trenton
A collection of favorite songs divided
   into two books (*arr.* by Reinagle)

A collection of favorite songs (arr. by Reinagle)
Columbus (incidental music)
Concerto
Come hope thou queen of endless smiles (*Arr.* from Arnold)
Cousin John
Dear Anna
[Dear Yankoo whither dost thou stray]
Edwy and Elgiva
Fœderal march. *See* Federal march
Finale
La foret noire
Mr. Francis's ballroom assistant (*arr.*)
Harlequin's invasion (*arr.*)
Harlequin shipwreck'd (*arr.*)
[Here beneath our lowly cott]
I have a silent sorrow here
I'll talk of all my lover's charms
Indian march
In vain fond youth
'Tis not the bloom on Damon's cheek (*arr.*)
[Twas on a pleasant summer's eve]
The Italian monk (*arr.* from Arnold)
The lucky escape (*arr.* from Dibdin)
Masonic overture
Medley overture
Miscellaneous quartet
A monody on the death of . . . [Washington] (*with* R. Taylor)
Mrs. Madison's minuet
The mountaineers (*arr.* from Arnold)
My soul is thine sweet Norah (*arr.* from Shield)
[My tender heart you stole away]
[My Thomas is the kindest lad]
The naval pillar (*arr.*)
Occasional overture
Overture by Reinagle
Overture. La Schiava (*arr.* from Piccini)
Overture. Marian (*arr.* from Shield)
Pierre de Province
Pizarro (incidental music)
Preludes
The purse (*arr.* from Reeve)
Robin Hood (*arr.* from Shield)
Rosa
[Rough as the waves on which we sail]

The Savoyard
A selection of the most favorite Scots tunes with variations
The shamrock
The Sicilian romance (*arr.* from Shield)
Slaves in Algiers (incidental music)
Some tell us that women are delicate things
Sonatas for the pianoforte
The Spanish barber (Arnold. Additional airs)
Tantivy hark forward (*arr.*)
Twelve favorite pieces (*arr.*)
The volunteers
[We'll chearful [!] our endeavours blend]
[When I've got the ready rhino wounds]
[When I was a little lad]
[When o'er the mountain's tops we go]
Winter
The witches of the rocks

RELFE, John (1763–1837)
Mary's dream, or Sandy's ghost

RIMBAULT, Stephen (1773–1837)
English organist, pianist and composer. Active from ca. 1796. Father of the better known Edward Francis Rimbault.

At morning dawn the hunters rise

ROGERSON, *Dr.*
American singer and composer. Active ca. 1789.

Anthem sacred to the memory of his Excellency John Hancock. *See* Dr. Rogerson's anthem

ROSS, John (1764–1837)
Henry's return. The sequel to Crazy Jane
High o'er the grave where Mary sleeps
I ask not thy pity

ROSETTI, Francesco Antonio (Franz Anton Rössler) (1750–1792)
La chasse (*arr.*)

ROTH, Philip (d. 1804)
Teacher and composer. First mentioned in the papers of Philadelphia in 1771, as "Master of the band belonging to His Majesty's Royal Regiment of North British Fusiliers." He disappears for many years, but is to be traced as music teacher at Philadelphia from 1785 to 1804, the year of his death. He was well known to Philadelphians for his eccentricity and has been credited, but without proper evidence, with the composition of "The President's march" (Hail Columbia). This distinction now goes to Philip Phile.

A hunting song (wrongly attributed to)
Overture

ROUGET de l'ISLE, Claude Joseph (1760–1836)
The Marseilles hymn

S

$ $ $.
Hail patriots all

ST. VELLUM, *Mons.* (*perhaps* Vellum, St.)
A collection of country dances

SALE, W. R.
The faithful tar

SALIMENT, George Edward
Flutist and composer. First mentioned in 1791, in New York papers as "lately arrived." In the following year he was one of the managers of the Subscription Concerts. He resided at New York until 1800, when he disappears from the directories.

Minuetto with eight variations

SANDERSON, James (1769–1841)
The cottage on the moor
Talacoy
When summer sweet summer
Wully is a bonny lad

SARTI, Giuseppe (1729–1802)
Caro bene
Hush, hush such counsel do not give
Se questa o cor tiranno

SCHAFFER (Scheffer, Shaffer), Francis C.
Clarinetist and composer. First mentioned in 1796 on concert programs of Boston, where he resided for many years.

The bachelor's song
Concerto on the clarinet
A pocket companion for the German flute or violin
Rule New England

SCHETKY (Shetky), J. George (1776–1831)
The confusion in regard to the names J. G. C. Schetky (Johann Georg Christoff Schetky), J. George Schetky, George Schetky and G. C. Schetky, is somewhat relieved if we assume that George Schetky, J. George Schetky, and even G. C. Schetky are probably all one and the same—the "American" Schetky, son of J. G. C. Schetky.

Born in Edinburgh, June 11, 1776, Schetky died in Philadelphia, December 11, 1831. Nephew of Alexander Reinagle. Appeared as violoncellist on Philadelphia concert programs as early as 1787. In later years he became one of the prominent founders of the Musical Fund Society (1820). At one time (after 1800) he and B. Carr entered into partnership for publishing music.

Lord Alexander Gordon's reel (*arr.* J. G. C. Schetky)
A favorite minuet (G. C. Schetkey)

SCHMIDT, John Henry
Organist, pianist, composer, music dealer. First mentioned in New York papers in 1793, as "before his arrival in this country organist of the great church of Shiedam," Hol-

land. After an itinerant career in the South he settled at Philadelphia in 1796, where he was organist of St. Peter's in 1797. Perhaps he was identical with a Mr. Smith who gave "lectures interspersed with music and singing" at Philadelphia in 1788.

Sonata for beginners

SCHNEIDER, Georg Lorenz (b. 1765)
Composed operas, songs, instrumental works. Was still living in 1841. Cf. *Eitner* and *Fétis*.

Forget me not (wrongly attributed to Mozart)

SCHROEDER (Schroder), H. B.
English composer of songs, marches, sonatas, etc. Active from ca. 1790.

Everybody's march

SCHROETER (Schroetter), Johann Samuel (1750–1787)
Eitner assigns *The conquest of Belgrade* to the above composer. But BM Cat. calls attention to the fact that the fall of Belgrade (1789) occurred after J. S. Schroeter's death. Therefore it names J. H. Schroeter or H. B. Schroeder as the probable author.

The conquest of Belgrade (?)

SCHULZ, ———
Blossom lovliest flower
Holy nature heav'nly fair

SELBY, William (1738–1798)
Organist, harpsichordist and composer. First mentioned in 1771 on a Boston concert program as organist. Resided at Boston until his death. During the Revolution, when the musical life of Boston came to a stand-still, Selby made his living as a liquor dealer and grocer. With the year 1782 he started anew on his career as organist, teacher, musical editor, composer and arranger of excellent con-

certs. The rapid progress of music at Boston was largely prepared by him and it is unfair not to mention William Selby among the musical pioneers of Boston. He was organist at the Stone Chapel until his death, when he was succeeded by P. A. von Hagen.
See also Sonneck's *Early concert-life in America*, particularly p. 270 ff.

Anthems in four parts
A concerto for the organ or harpsichord
The lovely lass
The new minstrel
Ode for the New Year
An ode in honour of General Washington
On musick
A piece with variations for the harpsichord or pianoforte
Ptalaemon to Pastora
The rural retreat
Two anthems
Voluntaries

SEWELL, Jonathan M.
[Columbia's sons in song proclaim]

SHIELD, William (1748–1829)
Abroad and at home (Songs from)
Air
Amidst the illusions
The Arethusa
The bleak wind wistles [!] o'er the main
Bright Chanticleer
The bud of the rose
By this fountain's flow'ry side
The cheering rosary
Come smiling Hope
The contented dwarf
Dans votre lit
Dear wanderer
Distress me with these tears no more
Element of liquid beauty
Ere around the huge oak
Ere bright Rosina met my eyes
The farmer (libretto)
The flitch of bacon
From night till morn (?)

[524]

Good morrow to your night cap
The Green Mountain farmer
The heart that has ne'er tasted
  sorrow
The heaving of the lead
Henry cull'd the flow'ret's bloom
Her mouth which a smile
Hey dance to the fiddle & tabor
The Highland laddie
The Highland reel (libretto)
How can I forget
How happy the soldier
I've kiss'd and I've prattled
I travers'd Judah's barren sand
Johnny and Mary
Light as thistle down moving
The lock and key
Love in a camp. *See* Patrick in
  Prussia
The maid of Lodi
Mark'd you her eye
The midshipman
The morn returns in saffron drest
The morning is up
My friend and pitcher
My soul is thine sweet Norah
No more I'll court the town bred
  fair
Norah the theme of my song
Not mine the narrow soul assur'd
O come away my soldier bonny
O come sweet Mary come to me
Old Towler
Out of my sight or I'll box your ears
Overture to Rosina
Overture Marian
Patrick in Prussia (libretto)
Patty Clover
The poor soldier (libretto)
The post captain
The pretty lad
Robin Hood
The rosary. *See* The cheering rosary
A rose tree
Rosina (libretto)
Scotch medley
The seaman's home
[Send him to me]
Smalilou
A smile from the girl of my heart
Sporting song
The spring with smiling face

The streamlet that flow'd round her
  cot
Such pure delight
Sweet transports, gentle wishes go
Tell me my love
The thorn
Tho Bacchus may boast
The trump of fame
The twins of Latona
Waving willow
The waxen doll. *See* When first I
  slipp'd my leading strings
What are the boasted joys of love
When bidden to the wake or fair
When first I slipp'd my leading
  strings
When Nicholas
[When scorching suns the thrifty
  earth]
[When the men a courting came]
When William at eve
Whilst happy in my native land
Whilst with village maids I stray
The woodman (libretto)
Zephyr, come thou playful minion

SHUSTER, ———
A favorite lesson for the pianoforte

SICARD, ———
Composer and dancing master.
Came to Philadelphia about 1785.
Early in 1786, he advertised himself as "a pupil of the celebrated
Mr. Vestries, and assistant master
of Mr. Gardelle, the first dancing
master of the opera at Paris." To
be traced in Philadelphia for several
years.

Cotillion minuet
New constitution march and Federal
  minuet
The President of the United States
  march

SMITH, I.
Oh! ne'er can I the joys forget

SMITH, Theodore
English composer of songs and instrumental works. Particularly active 1770–1810.
Three duetts

SPOFFORTH, Reginald (1770–1827)
Ellen, the Richmond primrose girl
Hark the goddess Diana
The wood robin
The death of Anna
The death of Crazy Jane

SMITH, John Stafford (1750–1836)
Adams and liberty (Tune, "To Anacreon in heaven," attributed to)

STAES, Ferdinand Philippe Joseph (1748–1809)
Organist and composer at Brussels. Active as composer from ca. 1775. Cf. *Fétis* and *Eitner*.

A favourite rondo for the pianoforte

STANLEY, John (Charles) (1713–1786)
Arcadia

STEIBELT, Daniel (1765–1823)
A favorite rondo for the pinaoforte
Sonata & Chasse for the pianoforte
Two sonatas for the pianoforte

STEVENSON, John Andrew (1761–1833)
Louis XVI lamentation
Ye zephyrs, where's my blushing rose

STORACE, Stephen (1763–1796)
[Across the downs this morning]
Ah can I cease to love her
Air in The pirates
Are ye fair as op'ning roses
Captivity
The capture
The doctor & apothecary
Ever remember me
Fal lal la
The favorite songs from . . . The pirates
From aloft the sailor looks around
[Go, George, I can't endure you]
The haunted tower (libretto)
[How happily my life I led]
The jealous don
The little bird
Little Taffline, or The silken cord
Love from the heart
Lullaby
My native land

No more his fears alarming
No more I'll heave the tender sigh
No song, no supper (libretto)
Now all in preparation
Oh dear delightful skill
Of plighted faith so truly kept
On the lightly sportive wing
Overture. The glorious first of June
Poor black boy
The pretty creature
A sailor lov'd a lass
Say how can words a passion feign
The shipwrecked seaman's ghost
The siege of Belgrade
Some time ago
Spirit of my sainted sire
Sweet little Barbara
Tho pity I cannot deny
Tho you think by this to vex me
Toll, toll the knell
Toll de roll de roll
Welch air in The Cherokee
The much admired ballad of the willow
With lowly suit
Ye streams that round my prison creep

SUETT, Richard (1755–1805)
English singer and song composer. Active as composer from ca. 1793.

Canzonett

SUMNER, Jezaniah (1754–1836)
American composer. Lived in Taunton, Massachusetts. Cf. *The Stoughton Musical Society's Centennial Collection*, Boston, 1878, p. 304, for brief biographical note.

Ode on science

SWAN, Timothy (1758–1842)
American composer and compiler of both sacred and secular songs.

Advice to the fair
Capt. O'Blunder
Friendship
The gentle shepherd
The highland queen
Hunting song (1)
Hunting song (2)

Lovely spring
The nymphs complaint
The shepherd's complaint
The soldier's farewel [!]
The songster's assistant
Spring
Strephon's farewel [!]

T

TAYLOR, Raynor (1747–1825)

Organist, pianist and composer. Born in England; died in Philadelphia (August 17, 1825). According to John R. Parker (*Musical biography*, Boston, 1825), Taylor entered the King's singing-school as one of the boys of the Chapel Royal. After leaving the school, he was, for many years, established at Chilmesford, Essex county, as organist and music teacher. From there he was called to be the composer and director of the music to the Sadler Wells theatre. Taylor was a ballad composer of some renown in England before he, in October, 1792, appeared in Baltimore as "music professor, organist and teacher of music in general, lately arrived from London." He was appointed in the same year organist of St. Anne's at Annapolis, Md., but receiving no fixed salary he found himself obliged to move after a few months to Philadelphia. Here he was for many years organist of St. Peter's, and, in 1820, influential in founding the Musical Fund Society. His compositions are numerous and mostly of a secular character, but only his minor works have been preserved. As a specialty he cultivated burlesque musical olios, or extravaganzas, which came dangerously near being music hall skits. This strikingly illustrates the fact that the American public of those days was *not* horrified by secular tendencies in an organist, outside of the walls of the church. Taylor was also famous for his powers of improvisation. He, Alexander Reinagle, whose teacher he had been in England, and B. Carr undoubtedly were the most prominent musicians at Philadelphia about 1800.

Algerine captive
America and Brittannia [!]
L'amour interroge par un berger
Amyntor (Amintor)
The ancient tiplers
Ask why a blush
The beech tree's petition
The bells
Cease awhile ye winds to blow (*arr.* from Bach)
Chelmer's banks
Concert violin
De tout mon coeur
Ding dong bell
Divertimenti
Duncan Grey
An easy . . . lesson
The faded lilly
Fair Luna
A finale, "Spring", or Mirth and innocent festivity
Gay Strephon
Gray mare's the best horse
The happy shepherd and shepherdess
Hunting cantata
Hunting song
Independent and free
The Irish tailor
Jack the guinea pig
Jockey and Jenny
Jockey and Moggy
The Kentucky volunteer
The lass of the cot
Ma chere et mon cher
The maid of the grove
The march in Blue Beard (*arr.* from Kelly)
The merry piping lad
Moggie, or The highland belle
A monody on the death of . . . [Washington] (*with* Reinagle)
The mountaineers (*arr.* from Arnold)
Nancy of the vale
Never doubt that I love
The nightingale: a cantata

Nobody
Nouvelle entertainment
Ode to the New Year
The old woman of eighty three
The olio
Overture. Circe and Ulisses
Overture (The mountaineers)
La petite Piedmontese
The Philadelphia hymn
Pizarro (incidental music)
The ploughman's escape from the sea
The poor female ballad singer
The President's march (*arr.* from Phile)
The Quaker (*arr.* from Dibdin)
The queen of flowers
Quick step
The reconciliation (sequel to Damon and Clora)
Rondo for the forte piano
Rustic courtship
Rustic festivity
Sailor's song
The scornful lady
The shepherd's evening
The shipwrecked mariner preserved
Silvan, the shepherd swain
Sonata for the pianoforte
Summer
Symphony
Tomorrow
A trip to Gretna-Green
Trumpet song
Virtue over much
Vive la liberté
The wand'ring village maid
While the morn is inviting to love
The wounded sailor (*or* soldier)

THOMPSON, Thomas (b. 1777)
English organist, pianist and song composer. Pupil of Clementi and J. B. Cramer, also of Ries, Kalkbrenner and others. Cf. *Moore.*

Now at moonlight's fairy hour
Orphan Bess, the beggar girl

TRAVANET, *Madame* B. de
Poet and composer in Paris. Published two books of Romances (1797 and 1798) with original words

and music. Cf. *Gerber, Eitner* and *Moore.*

Pauvre Jaque

TRISOBIO, Filippo (d. 1798)
Singing teacher and composer. Came to Baltimore from London in July, 1796. After giving a concert he went to Philadelphia. Here he advertised his "Scuola del canto" and claimed to have been "in Lissabon in the service of her majesty the queen of Portugal, where he was a member of a company of eighty of the best Italian professors." As his "book has had a favourite reception in London and Italy" he hoped for the same in "this famous metropolis." He seems to have died there in poverty in 1798, for a James Ph. Puglia, a creditor of his, inserted in January, 1799, in Bache's *Aurora* an insulting "card" to "Jane Trisobio . . . widow and administratrix to the estate of Philip Trisobio, musician and song singer, late of the city of Philadelphia, deceased."

The clock of Lombardy
Scuola del canto

TUCKEY, William (1708–1781)
Born in Somersetshire, England; died at Philadelphia (September 14, 1781). First mentioned in the New York papers of 1753. From then until about 1774, he played an important part in the musical life of New York. He was organist of Trinity Church, taught music in the Free School belonging to this church, and gave concerts with good programs. He also inserted several proposals for printing by subscription some of his sacred compositions but seems not to have met with much encouragement. Several of his compositions found their way into our early hymn-books. In 1771, Tuckey advertised himself as "for some years a professor of the theory and practice of vocal music,

[528]

Vicar Choral of the Cathedral Church of Bristol and Clerk of the parish of St. Mary Port in said city." *Also see* Sonneck, *Early concert life in America,* p. 160–61, 176–181.

Thanksgiving anthem

V

VALTON, Peter
Organist and composer. Came to South Carolina from England in October, 1764, as successor to Benjamin Yarnold as organist of St. Philip's. Still active in Charleston in 1773.

Masonic ode
Ode for the Festival of St. John
Six sonatas

VANHAL (Wanhal), John Baptist (1739–1813)
A favorite movement for the pianoforte
Sonate militaire

VENTO, Mathia (1735/36–1776)
Overture. Sofonisba

VICTOR, H. B.
Composer, teacher, editor. From newspaper advertisements, we learn that he went from Germany to London in 1759, where he claimed to have been "musician to her late Royal Highness the Princess of Wales and organist at St. George in London." He came to Philadelphia in September, 1774, and remained there at least until 1778, teaching and editing music and giving concerts. In his advertisements he called himself inventor of "the tromba doppia, con tympana, on which he plays the first and second trumpet and a pair of annexed kettle drums with the feet, all at once," and of the "cymbaline d'amour, which ressembles the musical glasses played by harpsichord keys, never subject to come out of tune."

Favourite *collection of airs,* marches, minuets &c.
The compleat instructor for the flute
The compleate instructor for the guitar
The compleat instructor for the harpsichord
The compleat instructor for the violin

VIDAL, ——
Composer and performer. Appears at Philadelphia in 1774, claiming to have been "a musician of the chambers of the King of Portugal." He gave concerts in which he performed on the guitar, mandolin and psaltery. He seems to have combined music with the jewelry trade. Sonneck adds later: Possibly he was identical with the guitarist, B. Vidal, mentioned by *Fétis* and *Eitner.*

Two marches

VIGUERIE, Bernard (ca. 1761–1819)
Viguerie's favorite sonata

VIOTTI, Giovanni Battista (1753–1824)
Rondeau de Viotti

VOGEL, Johann Christoph (ca. 1756–1788)
Démophon (Overture)

VOGLER, Gerard
English composer, music seller and publisher. Possibly brother of Abbé Vogler. Active as composer from ca. 1775.

The request

W

WALSH (Master). *See* Welsh

WANHAL. *See* Vanhal

WARE, W.
The sweet little girl of the lakes

WEBBE, Samuel, *Sr.* (1740–1816)
Fair Rosale (*arr.,* Sr. or Jr.)
The mansion of peace

WEIZSAECKER, ———
The river Patowmac

WELDON, Peter
Pianist and composer. Active in
New York from ca. 1800.

The New York senerading [!] waltz

WELSH (Welch), Thomas (1780–
1848)
English singer and composer. As
"Master" Welsh (Walsh) he sang
in concert when only twelve years
old. Cf. *Grove*.

Crazy Henry to Crazy Jane
The death of poor Cock Robin
(Master Walsh)

WHEATLEY, William
English song composer. Active
from ca. 1760.

The cottager

WILLARD, *Dr.*
Ode for independence

WILLSON, Joseph
English composer of songs and works
for piano forte or harpsichord. Also
organist. Active from ca. 1796.
Apparently came to America about
the turn of the century. All of his
American issues, as far as their imprint is concerned, could have been
published as early as 1799, though
they may have been issued later.
In some of these issues he is referred
to as "Organist of Trinity Church."
Willson is mentioned in *Eitner*.

A collection of airs (*arr.*)
A favorite sonata for the pianoforte
Javotte, or The maid of the Alps
O yes sir, if you please
When on a clear and cloudless night

WILSON, ———
The nosegay girl

WILSON, William
English song composer. Seems to
have been active from ca. 1785. Is
mentioned in *Eitner*.

The stolen kiss

WINTER, J. D.
The peerless maid of Buttermere

WOLF, ———
Sonneck refers to the above as a
Moravian composer at Bethlehem,
Pennsylvania. It seems more probable that the manuscript here noted
was a copy of the work of some
foreign "Wolf"—perhaps Ernst Wil-
helm Wolf (1735–1792). The Moravians at Bethlehem are known to
have copied many foreign works.

Auf der Lüfte heil'gen Weben

WOOD, Abraham (1752–1804)
American composer and compiler of
hymn tunes, anthems, etc.

An anthem on peace. *See* a hymn on
peace
An elegy on the death of a young
lady
A funeral elegy on the death of
General George Washington
A hymn on peace
Ode on spring

WORGAN, James (the Younger)
English composer of songs and instrumental works. Active from ca.
1785.

Emma

WRIGHT, Thomas (1763–1829)
Peter Pindar's new gipsy song

Y

YARNOLD, Benjamin
Organist and composer. Came from
England to Charleston, S. C., in
November, 1753, as organist for St.
Philip's. When in 1764, Peter
Valton became his successor, Yarnold accepted the position of organist at St. Michael's and "agreed to
perform in that church at least for
one year." The year of his death
has not been ascertained, but it
seems that he died not long before
1791.

Anthem and ode

YOUNG, William

Flutist and composer. Came to New York in 1792, with Hewitt, Gehot, Bergman and Phillips as "professors of music from the Operahouse, Hanoversquare, and Professional Concerts under the direction of Haydn, Pleyel etc." After performing in concerts at New York, Young settled at Philadelphia in the same year and became flutist in the orchestra of Wignell and Reinagle's company.

Sonneck adds: According to Dunlap he was sentenced to death in 1797, for having killed in a desperate mood the constable who came to arrest him for contracted debts.

Sometimes confused with John Young, publisher.

Quartet

List of Songsters

In The Preparation of this *List* careful checking has been made with the *Chronological index of songsters, 1760–1875*, prepared by Robert Winslow Gordon, at the Library of Congress; also with a similar list in *American songsters of the eighteenth century*, by Alice Louise Thorpe, at Brown University. The researches in this particular field by Richard S. Hill of the Music Division of the Library of Congress have also proved most helpful.

An asterisk before a title indicates that no published copy of such title has been located.

*American academy of compliments, Wilmington, 1797
*The American cock robin, New York, 1764
*The American ladies pocket book, Philadelphia, 1798
*The American mock-bird, New York, 1760
*The new American mock-bird, New York, 1761
The American musical miscellany, Northampton, 1798
*American robin, New York, 1774
The American songster, New York, 1788
*The American songster, Portsmouth, 1790
*American songster, Boston, 1795
The American songster, Baltimore, 1799
The American songster, Baltimore, 1800
The amorous songster, New York, 1800
*The Apollo, Philadelphia, 1789
The Apollo, Philadelphia, 1791
Apollo, Philadelphia, 1793
*The Baltimore songster, Baltimore, 1798
*Blackbird songbook, Philadelphia, 1769
*The charmer, Philadelphia, 1790
*The charms of melody, Philadelphia, 1788
The Columbian songster, Brookfield, 1795
*The Columbian songster, Boston, 1795
The Columbian songster, New York, 1797
The Columbian songster and Freemason's pocket companion, Portsmouth,
    N. H., 1798
The Columbian songster [Wrentham, Mass], 1799
The companion, Providence, 1799
The Democratic songster, Baltimore, 1794
Dibdin's museum, Philadelphia, 1797
The echo, or Columbian songster, Brookfield, 1800
The echo, or Federal songster, Brookfield [1798]
Feast of merriment, Philadelphia, 1795
The festival of mirth, New York, 1800
Four excellent new songs, New York, 1788
The Freemasons monitor, Albany, 1797
*The Freemasons pocket book, New York, 1782
Freemason's pocket companion, Portsmouth, N. H., 1798

Gentlemen and ladies complete songster. *See* The skylark.
*Humming bird, Philadelphia, 1791
The humming bird, Boston, 1798
*Humming bird, Philadelphia, 1799
*Jemmy Carson's collection [of ballads ?], Philadelphia, 1762
*The jolly Hibernian, Philadelphia, 1790
*The jovial songster, Philadelphia, 1793
*Jovial songster, Baltimore, 1798
The jovial songster, Boston, 1800
Liberty songs, [n. p., 178–]
*Little Robin Red Breast, Worcester, Mass., 1786/87
*Loyal and humorous songs, New York, 1779
Masonic. Songs, oratorio &c., Waterford, N. Y., 1797
The medley; or, New Philadelphia songster, Philadelphia, 1795
*The mermaid, or Nautical songster, New York, 1793
The mermaid, or Nautical songster, New York, 1798
*Miss Ashmore's choice collection of songs, Boston, 1771
*The mocking-bird, Philadelphia, 1793
*Monstrous good songs for 1792, Boston, 1792
Mother Goose's melody, Worcester [Mass.], 1785
Mother Goose's melody. 2d Worcester ed., Worcester, 1794
Mother Goose's melody. 3d Worcester ed., Worcester, 1799
Nautical songster. *See* The mermaid
Nautical songster, or Seaman's companion, Baltimore, 1798
Naval and military songs. *See* Songs. Naval and military.
New [American] patriotic songs. Added to A collection of songs . . .
  Dibdin. Philadelphia, 1799
Newest fashion, Boston, 1798
*The nightingale, or Charms of melody, Baltimore, 1798
*The nightingale, or Songster's companion, Philadelphia, 1791
The nightingale of liberty, or Delights of harmony, New York, 1797
Paddy's resource, Philadelphia, 1796
Paddy's resource, New York, 1798
Patriotic medley, New York, 1800
*The patriotic songster for July 4th, 1798, Baltimore, 1798
*Philadelphia jest book, Philadelphia, 1790
*The new entertaining *Philadelphia jest-book*, Philadelphia, 1791
*The Philadelphia pocket companion, Philadelphia, 1794
The Philadelphia pocket companion, [Philadelphia], 1794
The Philadelphia songster, Philadelphia 1789
*The pleasing songster, Philadelphia, 1795
*The Republican harmonist, Pennsylvania, 1800
The sailor's medley, Philadelphia, 1800
*The Scots musical museum, Philadelphia, 1797
The select songster, New Haven, 1786
The skylark, Worcester, 1795
The skylark. 2d Worcester ed., Worcester, 1797
Social harmony, or The cheerful songster's companion, New York, 1795
*A song book, Amherst, 1798
*A song book, New York, 1761
*Songs, comic, satyrical and sentimental, Philadelphia, 1777
Songs, comic, satyrical and sentimental, Philadelphia, 1778

*Songs for the amusement of children, Middletown, 1790
*Songs.   Naval and military, [New York], 1779
The songster's assistant, Suffield [1800 ?]
*The songster's magazine, Philadelphia, 1795
*The storm, or the American syren, Williamsburg, 1773
The syren, Philadelphia, 1800
The syren, or Vocal enchantress, Wilmington, 1797
The theatrical songster, Boston, 1797
*Tommy Thumb's song book, Worcester, 1788
*Tom Thumb's song book, Boston, 1795
*A tribute to the swinish multitude, New York, 1794
A tribute to the swinish multitude, New York, 1795
A tribute to the swinish multitude (*In* Tom Paine's jests), Philadelphia,
   1796
*The vocal charmer, Philadelphia, 1793
The vocal companion, Philadelphia, 1796
*The vocal enchantress, Philadelphia [1791]
*The vocal instructor, Massachusetts, 1797
*The vocal magazine, Philadelphia, 1783
*The vocal muse, or Ladies songster, Philadelphia, 1792
The vocal remembrancer, Philadelphia, 1790
*The vocal remembrancer, [Philadelphia], 1793
*The warbling songster, or Cure for dullness, Philadelphia, 1795
The whim of the day, Boston, 1798
Winter evening's amusement, Boston, 1795
*Wood lark song book, Philadelphia, 1769
*The young Masons monitor, New York, 1789

List of First Lines

No Title is indicated when the first line and title are identical. A bracketed first line indicates that no title has been supplied by composer or publisher. As the entire *Bibliography* is based upon an alphabetical arrangement of titles, no page numbers for titles are given here.

First Line	Title	Composer
A		
[Across the downs this morning]		Storace
Adeste fideles. Hither ye faithful	Adeste fideles. *Also* Portuguese hymn on the Nativity	
Adieu, adieu my only life	Same as first line. *Also* The soldiers adieu	Dibdin
Adieu my Fernando	Fernando	Kreutzer
Adieu Philadelphia, dear Jenny adieu	The Kentucky volunteer	Taylor
Adieu sweet girl		Chateaudun
Adieu thou dreary pile		
Adieu to all my heart holds dear		Gauline
Adieu ye groves, adieu ye plains	Winter. *Also* The timely adviser	
Adieu! ye verdant lawns and bowers		
Ah! chide me not, sweet lady, pray	The orphan boy's tale	Blewitt
Ah Delia see the fatal hour	Same as first line. *Also* Ah Delia! *and* Delia	Kotzwara, *and* Jackson, G. K.
Ah how hapless is the maiden		Carr
[Ah how needless is expression]		
Ah how sweet were those moments of love		Gauline
[Ah lovely appearance of death]		Kimball, Jacob
Ah lovely Hannah do not slight	Lovely Hannah	
Ah Mary shall thy heart		Pleyel
Ah! no mio bene non lasciar spaven tarti	Recitativo e rondo	Paisiello
Ah once when I was a very little maid		Attwood
Ah seek to know		Bach, J. C.
Ah! tell me softly breathing gale		
Ah tell me why fond beating heart	Tell me is it love	Hook
Ah! tell me why should silly man	The contented dwarf	Shield
Ah tell me ye swains have you seen my Pastora	The cottagers daughter	
Ah where and oh where is our Highland lassie gone	Moggie, or The Highland belle	Taylor
Ah where are fled those hours	Ah were [!] are fled those hours	Gauline
Ah where can fly my soul's true love	Henry's cottage maid	Pleyel

[537]

First Line	Title	Composer
Ah why enveil that panting breast		
Ah why must words		
Ah will no chance [!] of clime	[tale	
Ah will no change of clime	Hope told a flatt'ring	
Ah woe is me, shou'd cuddy be	Ballad	Attwood
All in a lonely mossy cell	The fairies	Jackson, G. K.
Allons enfans de la patrie	The Marseilles hymn	Rouget de Lisle
Almighty God whose heav'nly pow'r		
Alone beside a stream		
Alone on the banks of the dark rolling Danube	The wounded hussar	Hewitt
Altho' heav'n's good pleasure		Giordani
Amidst the illusions that o'er the mind flutter	Amidst the illusions	Shield
L'amour ici nons rassemble	Ronde chantee a la Reine par Monseigneur le Dauphin	Martini
Anacreon they say was a jolly old blade.	New Anacreontic song	
And art thou, Damon, faithles [!] grown	The reconciliation	Taylor
And is th' illustrious chieftain dead	A hymn	Holden
Angels ever bright and fair		
Are ye fair as op'ning roses		Storace
Arm, arm ye brave and nobly join	The host that fights for liberty	Pelissier
Around the brim of the inspiring goblet		
As 'cross the fields the other morn	I'm in haste	Hook
As beside his chereful [!] fire	Lafayette	
As bringing home, the other day		
As Cupid in a garden stray'd	The bee	
As down on Banna's banks I strayed	Strephon and Polly	
As forth I rang'd the banks of Tweed		Hook
As frantic Henry his morning ramble took	Crazy Henry to Crazy Jane	Welch
As from the cheek of her I love	The sailor's farewell	Fisin, James
As late along the flow'ry side	The peerless maid of Buttermere	Winter
As late by love		Corri
As late I tripped it o'er the lea	Oh yes sir if you please	Willson, J.
As motley is thy fancied gear	The witch	Reeve
As on a lonely hill I stray'd	The cottager	Wheatley
As o'er Asteria's fields I rove	Asteria's fields	
As passing by a shady grove	The linnet	
As pendant o'er the limpid stream		Kotzwara
As rambling forth the first of May	Shepherd marry	Fisin
As 'tother day in harmless chat	The charming creature	J., H.
As tripping o'er the new mown hay	When the merry bells	Hook

First Line	Title	Composer
As when the rising sun dispels the shades	Ode set to music, consecrated to the memory of the Rev. George Whitefield	
[As wrapt in sleep I lay]		Storace
Ask, ask, me why I send you here	The primrose	Langdon
Ask why a blush		Taylor
Assembled round the patriot's grave	Funeral dirge on the death of General Washington	Von Hagen, P. A., Sr.
At early dawn from humble cot	Poor Lima	Attwood
At length too soon, dear creature	The soldiers farewel [!]	Swan
At morning dawn the hunters rise		Rimbault
At the close of the day, when the hamlet is [or was] still	The hermit	
At the dead of the night		Arnold
At the foot of yon mountain	The lass of the lake	Moorehead
Attention pray give while of hobbies I sing	The hobbies	
Away with melancholy	Same as first line. *Also* Merrily sings	Mozart
Away ye giddy smiling throng	My soul is thine sweet Norah	Shield
The awful day approaches fast	Louis XVI lamentation	Stevenson
Awful hero, Marlb'ro rise	Marlborough's ghost	Mann

B

First Line	Title	Composer
A bachelor leads an easy life	The bachelor's song	Schaffer
Banish sorrow, grief and folly	Wisdom's favorite	
Be hush my soul, for heav'n prepare	The captive	Percy
Begone dull care		
Behold array'd in light, and by divine command	A hymn on peace	Wood
Behold the changes of the skies	The seasons moralized	Dwight [?]
Behold the glorious day appears	Ode for Independence	Willard, *Dr.*
Behold the man whom virtue raise	Ode. As performed at The Stone Chapel, Boston	
Behold the social band appears	Masonic ode	Valton
Behold your honest little Ben	Little Ben	
Ben Backstay lov'd the gentle Anna	Ben Backstay	Dibdin
Beneath a green grove, a lovely young swain	Brays of Balendine	
[Beneath a weeping willow's shade]		Hopkinson
Beneath a willows pendant shade	Will not dare not tell	Von Hagen
Beneath the honors		Holyoke
Beneath yon mountain's shaggy cliff	The village spire	Giordani
Beside the calm retreat	Thespian chaple [!]	
Bewailing, bewailing, she sunk heartbroken on her pillow	Zorade in the tower	Arnold

First Line	Title	Composer
The bird that hears her nestling cry	The bird	
[The birds who wing their way through air]		
Bleak sweeps the wind	Edwy and Elgiva	Reinagle
Bleak was the morn	The sailors return	Dibdin
The bleak wind whistles [or wistles[!]] o'er the main		Shield
[A blessing on brandy and beer]		Mazzinghi
A blessing unknown to ambition and pride	The wealth of the cottage is love	Reeve
Blest on his own paternal farm	The Green Mountain farmer	Shield
Blest were the hours in which I stray'd	The happy dreamer	
Blithe Sandy is a bonny boy	The Caledonian laddy	Hook
Blossom lovliest flower		Schulz
Blow on ye winds, descend soft rains	My heavy heart	
The blushing daughter of the thorn	The pride of our plains	Von Hagen
A body may in simple way	If a body loves a body	Hook
Born in yon blaze of orient sky	Ode to May. Also May	
Breathe soft fair maid	The charms of music	Gauline
The breeze was fresh, the ship in stays	The token	Dibdin
The breezes of morn shake the dew from the thorn	The sweet little girl of the lakes	Ware
Bright chanticleer proclaims the dawn	Old Towler. Also Bright Chanticleer	Shield
Bright dawns the day		
Bright Phoebus has mounted the chariot of day	Bright Phoebus	Hook
Bright Sol at length by Thetis woo'd	Lovely Stella	
Bright Sol is returning the winter is o'er	Spring	Swan
Bring your vows to Cupid's shrine	American serenade	Jackson, G. K.
The broom bloom'd so fresh and so fair	She lives in the valley below	Hook
Brother soldiers all hail		
The butterfly flies round and round	On a beautiful butterfly burnt in a ball-room	
By Baby Bunting		Hook
By moonlight on the green	The tartan plaiddie	
By the side of a mountain	The contented shepherd	Hook
[By this fountain's flow'ry side]		Shield
Bye, sweet baby, bye	The tender mother	

C

First Line	Title	Composer
Calm the winds		Mazzinghi
Can hope now no pleasure restore	The impatient lover	Gauline
Le cannon vient de re'sonner	La carmagnole	
Capricious foe to human joy	Time. Also Sonnet to Time	Pleyel
Caro bene		Sarti
Ce regard plein de bien veillance	A Son Altesse Royale Madame Elizabeth de France, soeur du Roi	Martini
Cease awhile ye winds to blow		Bach

[540]

First Line	Title	Composer
Cease rude Boreas	The storm	
Cease ye fountains, cease to murmur	The unhappy swain	
The charms of Floremel		
Charming pleasing unseen wand'rer	Gentle Zephyr	Von Hagen
The cheek enros'd with crimson dye	The charms of nature	
Cheerful fearless and at ease	Ode on peace	Lyon
The cheerful spring begins today	Arise my fair. *Also* [The cheerfull Spring be-begins today]	
Chide on, chide on, ye foaming billows chide	Paul and Mary	H., S. M.
Cold was the night wind	The widow	Carr
Columbia, Columbia to glory arise	Columbia	Dwight
Columbia mourns, her pillars shake	Sonnet. For the four-teenth of October, 1793	Gram
Columbians all the present hour	New Yankee Doodle	
Columbians arise independence proclaim	The ladies patriotic song	
Columbia's brave friends with alertness advance	Adams & Washington	Von Hagen
Columbia's greatest glory	Immortal Washington	
Columbia's guardian sleeps in dust		Holden
[Columbia's sons in song pro-claim]		Sewell
[Come all grenadiers]		
Come all hands ahoy to the anchor	Jack at the windlass	Dibdin
Come all ye jolly sailors bold	The Arethusa	Shield
Come all ye sons of song	An ode for the Fourth of July	
Come all ye young lovers who wan with dispair [!]	Freedom	
Come blushing rose		Pleyel
Come buy my ripe cherries fair maidens come buy	Ripe cherries	Hook
Come buy of poor Kate, prim-roses I sell	The primrose girl. *Also* Primroses	Hewitt
Come buy of poor Mary good matches	The match girl	
Come buy, who'll buy	Little Sally	Arnold
Come Charity, come Charity, with goodness crowned	Invocation to Charity	Holden
Come come my fair one let us stray	[Morning] Sonnet I	Hook
Come, come, my love to the window come		
Come Emma dear and live with me	Emma	Worgan
[Come fair Rosina come away]		Hopkinson
Come fill your bumpers, fill them high	Independent and free	Taylor
[Come genius of our happy land]		Capron
Come hither ye belles	The way to get married	Hook
Come Holy Ghost, come Lord our God	Come Holy Ghost	

First Line	Title	Composer
Come hope thou queen of endless smiles		Arnold
Come join hand in hand, brave Americans all	Liberty song	
Come join my hearts in jovial glee	Huzza for the Constellation	
Come lads your glasses fill	Huzza for liberty	Jackson, G. K.
Come live with me and be my love.	The invitation	Emrick
Come loose ev'ry sail to the breeze	Homeward bound	Arne
Come my fair while blooming spring	The invitation	
Come now all ye social pow'rs		
Come rouse brother sportsman		Hook
Come smiling Hope		Shield
Come sweet sleep, the lab'rers blessing	An ode to Sleep	Gluck
Comfort ye my people, saith our God	Thanksgiving anthem	Tuckey, William
Contre les chagrins de la vie	La pipe de tabac	
Could [or cou'd] you to battle march away	Pauvre Madelon. *Also* Go with you all the world over	Arnold
Court me not to scenes of pleasure		
Courteous stranger, now free from danger	Courteous stranger	Arnold
A coward to love and manly duty	Henry's return	Ross
Cupid lovely charming boy	To the maid I love best	Hook
Cupid rambling once astray	L'Amour interroge par un berger	Taylor

D

First Line	Title	Composer
Dans votre lit that bright parterre	Dans votre lit	Shield
Dark was the night	Poor Mary	Carr
Daughter of heav'n, thou gift divine	Ode	Low, *Mr.*
A dawn of hope my soul revives	The dawn of hope	J., H.
The day is departed	Alone by the light of the moon	Hook
The day is gone and night is come	Ma chere et mon cher	Taylor
Dear Anna repine not the Gods bid us scorn	Dear Anna	Reinagle
Dear gentle Kate, oh! ease my care	Dear gentle Kate	
Dear is my little native vale		Hook
Dear Kathlean you no doubt find	Good morrow to your night cap	Shield
Dear Nancy I've sail'd the world all around	Same as first line. *Also* Then say my sweet girl can you love me, or, The pretty brunette.	Hook
Dear wand'rer, O whither thy steps shall I trace	Dear wanderer	Shield
[Dear Yankoo whither dost thou stray]		Reinagle

[543]

First Line	Title	Composer
Fair Aurora, prithee stay	Fair Aurora	Arne
The fair Eliza's living grace	Addressed to Miss D. by a lady, both of Boston	
Faithless Damon turn'd a rover	Faithless Damon	
Far o'er the swelling waves		Hook
Farewell my Pastora, no longer yʳ swain	Ptalaemon to Pastora	Selby
Farewel [!] to old England, thy white cliffs adieu	Dear Mary, or, Adieu to old England	Arne
Farewell ye friends of early youth		Giordani
Farewell ye green fields		Howard
The father of Nancy a forrester was	Lillies and roses	Hook
The fields their wonted hues resume		Ditters
The fields were gay, and sweet the hay	The gipsy's song	
The fields were green, the hills were gay	He stole my tender heart away	
Flocks are sporting, doves are courting	The beauties of Spring	
For compassion we implore	The sea boys duett	Martini
For England here [or when] with fav'ring gales [or gale]	Heaving of the lead	Shield
For tenderness form'd		Paisiello
For various purpose serves the fan		
Forbear my friends, forbear and ask no more	Sophronia	
Forever fortune wilt thou prove	Forever fortune	
Forget me not when friends & fortune smiling	Forget me not	Schneider
Fresh and strong the breeze is blowing		Arnold
Freut euch des lebens		Naegeli
Friendship, thou charmer of the mind	Friendship	Lyon
Friendship to ev'ry willing [or gen'rous] mind	Friendship	
[From aloft the sailor looks around]		Storace
From Chelmer's banks why flies my swain	Chelmer's banks	Taylor
From cottage couch where slumbered Mary	Poor Mary	
From maiden to maiden I rove	The male coquette	Gauline
From my prison with joy could I go	The queen of France to her children just before her execution	Chateaudun
From night till morn I take my glass	From night till morn	Shield (?)
From place to place I travers'd long	Dear little cottage maid	Hook
From thee Eliza I must go		
From the brook and the willow forsaking the plain	Eloisa's complaint	
From the seat of bliss above	An anthem . . . at the celebration of St. John's Day	Low

FIRST LINE	TITLE	COMPOSER
From the white blossom'd sloe	The thorn	Shield
From Vernon's mount behold the hero rise	Mount Vernon	Holden
From visions of eternal day	André's ghost	Mann
The frozen streets in moonshine glitter	The orphan's prayer	Abrams
Fy on the wars that hurried Willie from me	De'il tak the wars	

G

FIRST LINE	TITLE	COMPOSER
Gaily lads our friends are leaving	Gaily lads	
Gallia's sons shall vaunt no more	Military glory of Great Britain	Lyon (?)
Gather your rosebuds while you may	Gather your rosebuds	Hook
Gentle air thou breath of lovers	Gentle air	Jackson, G. K.
Gentle love this hour befriend me	Gentle love	Fisin
Gentle river, gentle river, lo thy streams are stain'd with gore	The bleeding hero	Giordani
The gentle swan with graceful pride	The gentle swan	Kotzwara
Give ear to me both high and low	Comely Ned that died at sea	Dibdin
[Give me thy heart as I give mine]		Hopkinson
The glad'ning sun returns from rest	Silvia	Clark
Glide gently on thou murm'ring brook		Pirsson
Glimm'ring in the glowing west	The village holyday	
The gloomy night stalked slow away	Mad Peg	Dibdin
Glory, triumph, vict'ry, fame forever crown Britannia's name	Military glory of Great Britain	Lyon (?)
Go gentle zephyr		
[Go George, I can't endure you]		Storace
Go lovely rose thy station choose		Capron
Go patter to lubbers and swabs	Poor Jack	Dibdin
Go tunefull bird that glad'st the skies	The lark	Hook
God save America free from tyrannic sway	God save America	
The gold finch swells his little throat	The gold finch	Hook
Great God thy energy impart	Hymn. On death	
Great news, great news I'm hither sent	Hymen's evening post	Hook
Great Washington, the hero comes	Ode to Columbia's favorite son	Holden
The groves, the plains, the nymphs	Cancharizante	Jackson, G. K.

H

FIRST LINE	TITLE	COMPOSER
Had I a heart		Linley
Hail! America, hail!		

[546]

First Line	Title	Composer
	I	
[I am a brisk and sprightly lad]		
I am a cheerful fellow	The thrifty wife, or Little waste	Hook
I am a fowler brisk and gay	The fowler	Mozart
I am a jolly gay pedlar	The jolly gay pedlar	Reeve
I am a poor youth in a distant land	The friendless boys tale	Crouch
I am a very little man	The little cot	
I'm as smart a lad as you'd wish to see		Attwood
I'm here or there a jolly dog	The midshipman	Shield
I'm in haste		Hook
I'm jolly Dick the lamplighter	The lamplighter	Dibdin
I am married and happy	The married man	
I am teaz'd to death from morn to night	I'll be married to thee	Hook
I'm told by the wise ones a maid I shall die	The friend and the lover	
I'm turned of twenty and a maid	The little singing girl	Hook
I ask not thy pity		Ross
I have a silent sorrow here		Duchess of Devonshire
I've kissed and I've prattled		Shield
I've plenty of lovers	Young Willy for me	
I've thought and I've said it	Home's home	Dibdin
I left my country and my friends	The mock Italian trio	
[I lock'd up all my treasure]		Dibdin
I lov'd so many maidens fair	Heigho	Dussek
I rise with the morn		
I sigh and lament me in vain	Queen Mary's lamentation	
I sigh for a damsel	The girl with a cast in her eye	
I sing the maid of Lodi	The maid of Lodi	Shield
I strove but much I find in vain		Gauline
I that once was a ploughman a sailor am now	The lucky escape	Dibdin
[I travers'd Judah's barren sand]		Shield
[I'll talk of all my lover's charms]		Reinagle
If ever a sailor was fond of good sport	Polly Ply. *Also* Jack's fidelity	Dibdin
If tis joy to wound a lover	Same as first line. *Also* A catch for three voices	Arnold
If life's a rough path as the sages have said	And strew the sweet roses of pleasure between	Hook
If to force me to sing it be your intention	Nobody	
If you're not too proud for a word of advice	Advice to the fair	
In a chariot etherial [!] from regions of light	Ode [*In* The Indian chief]	
In a little blue garment all ragged and torn	The poor little child of a tar	

[548]

First Line	Title	Composer
'Twas at night when the bell had toll'd twelve	Far, far at sea	Florio
'Twas at the hour of days decline	The waving willow	Shield
'Twas early on a holiday	The harmless shepherd	
'Twas in May summer's queen	The sweet little bird	
'Twas in that season of the year	Rosline [or Roslin] Castle	
'Twas in the blooming month of May	Come buy my daffodillies	
'Twas in the good ship Rover		Dibdin
'Twas in the green meadows so gay	How d'ye do	Hook
'Twas in the grove	Where's the harm of that	Hook
'Twas in the solemn midnight hour		Hewitt
'Twas in the sultry noontide hour		
It was Ireland, sweet place where my daddy was living	Moss roses	Moorehead
'Twas landlady Meg that made such rare flip	Meg of Wapping	Dibdin
'Twas near a rock within a bay	The shipwreck'd boy	
'Twas near a thicket's calm retreat	Sterne's Maria	Moulds
'Twas on a bank of daisies sweet	The black bird	Hook
'Twas on a pleasant summer's eve		
'Twas one day at Wapping	Jack Junk	Dibdin
'Twas post [or past] meridian, half past four	Nancy, or The sailor's journal	Dibdin
'Twas Saturday night the twinkling stars	Saturday night at sea	
'Twas Spring when all nature look'd blooming and gay	The woodman's fair daughter	
'Twas summer and softly the breezes were blowing	The banks of the Dee	
'Twas when the seas were roaring	The despairing [or dispairing [!]] damsel	
'Twas where a willow's drooping branches	Nancy	Attwood
Twas within a mile of Edinburgh town	Within a mile of Edinburgh	Hook

J

Jack Oakham was a gallant tar	Here's the pretty girl I love	Hook
[Jai perdu mon euridice [!]]		Gluck
J'ai quitté la montagne	La marmotte	Trisobio
The jealous don won't you assume when you marry	The jealous don	Storace
John Bull for pastime took a prance	Mounseer Nong Tong Paw	Dibdin
Johnny was a piper's son		Cheese
Julia see the rosy morning	Julia see	Capron

K

Keen blew the blast	Poor Emma	

First Line	Title	Composer
Kind father of the healing art	Song to Apollo	
The kiss that he gave when he left me behind	The kiss. *Also* May I never be married	Hook
Know ye not that a great man hath fall'n today	A funeral elegy on the death of General George Washington	Wood

L

First Line	Title	Composer
Last April morn as forth I walk'd	Ground ivy	Marshall
Last midsummer morning I gang'd to the fair	And a' for love of me	
Last night the dogs did bark	Nobody coming to marry me	Cooke
The lawland lads think they are fine	The Tartan plaidy	
Leander on the bay at Hellespont	Hero and Leander	
Lend me thy saffron robe	Air II, *of* Two original Russian airs	
Let bards relate of Sue and Kate	Peggy Perkins	Dibdin
Let ev'ry pagan muse be gone	Rosy Nell. *Also* Romping Rosy Nell	
Let ev'ry patriot hero sage	Let Washington be our boast	
Let fops with fickle falsehood range	Nancy of the vale	Taylor
Let horrid jargon split the air	Jargon	Billings
Let truth and spotless faith be thine		Mozart
Let tyrants shake their iron rod	Chester	Billings
Let's seek the bow'r of Robin Hood		
Life's like a ship in constant motion	The sailor's· allegory	
Life let us cherish		Naegeli
Light as thistle down moving		Shield
Lisbia live to mirth and pleasure	Lisbia	
Listen, listen to the voice of love		Hook
Little bird with bosom red	The robin redbreast	Hook
Little Boy Blew come blow me your horn	Little Boy Blew	Carr
Little inmate full of mirth	The cricket	Jackson, G. K.
Little insect that on high	The grasshopper	Mann
[Lo! I quit my native skies]		
Lo sorrow reigneth	A dirge, or Sepulchral service	Holden
Loose were her tresses		Giordani
The Lord hath done great things for us	An anthem designed for Thanksgiving Day	Cooper, William
The Lord himself, the mighty Lord	The twenty third Psalm	Hopkinson
The loud and clear ton'd nightingale		Ware
Love from the heart all its danger concealing	Love from the heart	Storace
Love in thy eyes forever plays	Canzonett	Jackson of Exeter
Love soft illusion, pleasing delusion	Love soft illusion	Arnold

[551]

First Line	Title	Composer
Love thou mad'ning power		Gluck
Lovely nymph now cease to languish		
Lovely nymph! O cease to grieve me	Lovely nymph	
A lovely rose my Henry brought	A lovely rose	
Lovely Spring is just returning	Lovely Spring	Swan
The lowland lads think they are fine	The highland laddie	
Ma belle coquette, ah why disdain	Ma belle coquette	Hook
Ma chere amie		Hook
Madame Veto avait promis	La Carmagnole	
Maidens listen I'll discover		Hook
Majestic rose the god of day	Rosa	Reinagle
	Also Rosa and Henry	Anon
Mark my Alford all the joys	The delights of wedded love	
[Mark'd you her eye]		Shield
The meads were all smiling, serene was the day	The lass of the cot	Taylor
The meadows look cheerful	The lassies of Dublin	
The mellow lustre of the morn	May morning	Von Hagen
Memory source of sweet employ	The emigrant	Hook
Midst rocks and quicksands have we steer'd	The poor sailor boy	Attwood
Miss Jenny don't think that I care for you	Moll in the wad	
The moon had climb'd the highest hill	Mary's dream, or Sandy's ghost	Relfe.
The moon was fair, soft was the air	The banks of Yarrow	
The morn returns in saffron drest		Shield
Morn shook her locks	The cottage boy	
The morn was fresh and pure the gale	Mary will smile	Carr
The morning is charming	Hunting song	Swan
The morning is up		Shield
The morning sun shines from the east	Ode on science	Sumner, Jezaniah
The morning was fair and the hamlet look'd gay	Anna	Von Hagen
A mountain maid, both rich and fair	Dilly dally, shilly shally	Hook
Mourn, mourn all ye winds	Dirge for General Washington	Jackson, G. K.
The murm'ring stream, the linnet's song	The murm'ring stream	Hook
My banks they are furnish'd with bees	The shepherd	Capron
My boys would know how our ship got her name	The Albion, the pride of the sea	Hook
My Collin is the kindest lad	The contented cottager	Frith
My cruel love to danger go	Poor negro woman	Arnold
My days have been so wondrous free		Hopkinson
My father was a tinker's son	The tinker	Reeve
My foes prevail, my friends are fled	Captivity	Storace

[552]

[553]

First Line	Title	Composer
Now Henry has left me to plough the salt sea	Henry's adieu	Costellow
Now's the time to sing and play [Now let rich music sound]		Hook
Now let your plaintive numbers gently rise	An ode for the 22d of February	Holden
Now listen my Honeys	Success to Admiral Nelson	Attwood
Now the dancing sunbeams play	The mermaid's song	Haydn
Now the happy knot is ty'd	The happy wedding	
Now the hilltops are burnished with azure and gold	The hill tops	
Now the sun is in the west	The cuckoo	Hook
Now to pant on Thetis breast	The shepherd's evening	Taylor
Now twilight's fairy hand	Collin's grave	Pleyel
Now wanton gales perfume the glade	The cottage in the grove	Hook
Now we're met like jovial fellows	Sing old rose and burn the bellows	

O

First Line	Title	Composer
O be joyful in the Lord [and] O praise the Lord all ye nations	Two anthems for three and four voices	Selby
O bright as the morning the maid of the wold	The maid with the bosom of snow	Mazzinghi
O come away, come my soldier bonny	O come away my soldier bonny	Shield
O come Louisa lovely fair	Crazy Iain	Gauline
Oh! come to Mason borough's grove		Hopkinson
[O dear delightful skill]		Storace
O dear what can the matter be		
O dearly do I love to rove	Bonny Charley	Hook
Oh farewell dear Erin	Drimendo	
O Father of Heav'n to thee we bend	The Philadelphia hymn	Taylor
O gentle be thy slumbers		
Oh had it been my happy lot		Hewitt
Oh happy tawny Moor	Happy tawny Moor	Arnold
O have you seen the blushing rose	Lucy Gray of Allendale	Hook
O hear a poor and shepherds tale	The death of Anna	Spofforth
O how I love to play	'Tis all a jest	Hook
O! how shall I in language weak	Strephon's farewell [!]	Swan
O innocence celestial maid		
O leave this barren spot to me	The beech tree's petition	Taylor
O lend dear maid thy patient ear	The lovely lass	Selby
O lilly! why so droops thy head	The faded lilly! or Louisa's woe	Taylor
O lovely peace		Handel
Oh my treasure, crown my pleasure	New York serenade	Jackson
O Nancy [or Nanny] wilt thou gang wi' [or with] me	Same as first line. *Also* Oh Nanny	
Oh! ne'er can I the joys forget		Smith
O nightingale! best poet of the grove	The shepherd's complaint	Swan

[554]

[555]

First Line	Title	Composer
On Richmond hill there lives a lass	The lass of Richmond hill	Hook
On sturdy stout Dobbin	The twaddle	
On that lone bank where Lubin dy'd [!]	Fair Rosale	Dignum
On the brink of the beach	I felt the command and obey'd with a sigh	Fisin
On the green banks of Shannon	My poor dog Tray	Hewitt
On the lightly sportive wing		Storace
On the top of a mountain inscribed to fame	Ode for the New Year	Gram
On the white cliffs of Albion reclining sat Fame	Song on General Washington	Juhan
On yonder spray the linnet sings	Mira of the village plain	Gauline
One kind kiss before we part	One kind kiss	Jackson, G. K.
One Negro come from Jenny land	Negro philosophy	Dibdin
One summer's eev [!] as Nancy fair	The new spinning wheel	
One summer's eve I chanc'd to stay	I know not why	Costellow
Tother day as I sat by the green willow tree	A cent'ry ago	Hook
The other day by sleep oppress'd	The dream	
Our country is our ship		Reeve
Our Lord is risen from the dead		Arnold
Out of my sight or I'll box your ears		Shield
O'er barren hills and flow'ry dales	Sweet lillies of the valley	Hook
O'er desert plain's and rushy meers	The desert plains	
O'er hill and valley, dell and glade	Hail happy warbler	Harrison
O'er moorlands and mountains	Content. *Also* The fortunate roam	
O'er the gloomy woods resounding	The death of Crazy Jane	Spofforth
[O'er the hills far away]		Hopkinson
Over the mountain and over moor	The beggar girl	Piercy

P

First Line	Title	Composer
Par sa legéreté		
Parent of soothing airs and lofty strains	Ode on the birthday of his Excellency George Washington	
The passing bell no longer toll'd	Loisa	Fisin
The passing bell was heard to toll	Neighbour Sly	Dibdin
Pauvre Jaque when I was near to thee *and* Pauvre Jaque quand je tois pres de toi	Pauvre Jaque	Travanet, *Mme.* B. de
Peace to his soul, the fatal hour is past	A dirge	Holden
Peaceful slumb'ring on the ocean	Lullaby	Storace
Pensive alone in yonder shade	The reconsaliation [!]	Gehot

First Line	Title	Composer
People of France ye soul link'd people [and] Peuple français peuple de freres	Le réveil du peuple	Gaveaux
A plague of those musty old lubbers	Nothing like grog	Dibdin
Pleasant is thy voice O Carrel	Ode from Ossian's poems	Hopkinson
The ploughman whistles o'er the furrow	The labourer's welcome home	Dibdin
Poets may sing of their Helicon streams	The Federal constitution & Liberty forever	Hewitt
Poll dang' it, how d'ye do	The sailor boy. *Also* The sailor boy capering ashore	
A poor helpless wand'rer	Orphan Bess the beggar girl	Thompson
A poor little gipsey, I wander forlorn	The little gipsey	
Poor Richard lov'd his Emma well	Poor Richard	Carr
A poor soul sat sighing	Shakespeare's willow	Carr
Poor suff'ring soul thy woe worn breast	Answer to the favorite song in the Stranger	
The poplar grove his presence grac'd	The poplar grove	Mazzinghi
Pour bien juger une maitresse		
Pray young man, your suit give over	She's quite the thing	
A prey to tender anguish		Haydn
The pride of ev'ry grove I chose	The garland	Hopkinson
Primroses deck the bank's green side	Primroses deck	Linley, T.
Propitious powers who guard our state	Military glory of Great Britain	Lyon (?)
Push about the bowl boys	The flowing bowl	

R

Rear'd midst the war empurpled plain	The death song of an Indian chief	Gram
Repose en paix, ma Virginie	Paul au tombeau de Virginie	Chateaudun
Return enraptur'd hours	Major Andre. *Also* Major Andre's complaint	
Returning home across the plain	Lubin's rural cot	
Rise, Cynthia, rise		Hook
Rise my Delia, heav'nly charmer	A new song for a serenade	
Robin a bobbin a Bilberry hen		Hook
The rose had scarce bloom'd on Matilda's fair cheek	Matilda	
A rose, a rose from her bosom stray'd	The mansion of peace	Webbe
A rose tree in full bearing	Rose tree	Shield

First Line	Title	Composer
Rosier, rosier, jadis charmant	Romance de Gonzalve de Cordoue. No. 6	Chateaudun
The rosy morning glads the plain	New Kate of Aberdeen	Capron
Rough as the waves on which we sail		Reinagle

S

First Line	Title	Composer
Sacred to heav'n behold the dome appears	A view of the Temple—A Masonic ode	Belknap, D.
Sad are the tidings rumuour [!] tells	Monody [In Dead march and Monody]	Carr
A sailor lov'd a lass		Storace
A sailor's life's a life of woe	The flowing can [or cann]	Dibdin
Sam Sailyard lov'd Sally	The unfortunate sailor	Hook
Say have you seen my Arabel	Arabella, the Caledonian maid	
Say have you seen young Sandy fair	The flower of Yarrow	Hook
Say how can words a passion feign		Storace
Say lads and lassies ha' ye seen	The lad wha lilts sae sweetly	Hook
Say will you leave your lowland haunts	The lass of Lucerne lake	Hewitt
Says Jessy one morn		Haibel
Says my father says he one day to I	Father and mother and Suke	Dibdin
Says Plato why should man be vain	Plato's advice. *Also* Plato	
Scarcely had the blushing morn	The capture	Storace
Se m'abbandoni		Cimarosa
Se questa o cor tiranno		Sarti
The sea was calm, the sky serene	The little sailor boy	Carr
The season sheds its mildest ray	Ode to the President of the United States	
See beneath yon bow'r of roses	Ella and Edwin	Bailey
See brother [or sister] see, on yonder bough	See brother [or sister] see	Arnold
[See down Maria's blushing cheek]		Hopkinson
See from yon cottage window plays	Ellen arise	Carr
See now the blust'ring Boreas blows	How cold it is	
See the course throng'd with gazers	The race horse	
See the morning star appear	A Christmas hymn	Page
[Send him to me]		Shield
Shady groves and purling rills	The rural retreat	
A shape alone let others prize		Gram
Shepherd I have lost my love		
A shepherd lov'd a nymph so fair [and] A shepherd wander'd we are told	Fal lal la	Storace
A shepherd once had lost his love	The little bird	Storace
Shepherd why this dull delay	Rustic festivity	Taylor

First Line	Title	Composer
Shepherds I have lost my love	Anna [*In* The Philadelphia songster]	
Should e'er the fortune be my lot	Little Taffline	Storace
Sigh no more ladies		
Silent, silent nymph	A glee	Pelissier
Since then I'm doomed		
Since Zeph'rus first tasted the charms of coy Flora	The hare hunt	
Sing to his shade a solemn strain	In memory of Mr. James Bremner	Hopkinson
Sir Solomon Simons when he did wed	The rush light	Arnold
Sit down neighbors all, and I'll tell a merry story	Bow wow wow	
Sleep you or wake you, lady bright	Megen oh! Oh Megen ee	Kelly
The smiling morn, the breathing Spring	The birks of Invermay	
Snatch fleeting pleasures		Naegeli
So fly our months and years	The close of the year	Holyoke
So sweet her face, her form divine		Gauline
Soft blew the gale near yon bank's side	The poor village boy	Moulds
Soft music let my humble lay	Canzonett	Suett
Soft pleasing pains unknown before	Delia	Capron
Soft Zephir [*or* Zephyr] on thy balmy wing	The mansion of peace	Webbe
[Softly as the breezes blowing]		Capron
Softly sweet the minutes glide	Music is the voice of love	
Softly waft ye southern breezes		Hook
The soldier tir'd of wars alarms	The soldier tir'd	Arne
Some men with rapture view no cheeks	I love them all	
[Some tell us that women are delicate things]		Reinagle
Some time ago, I marry'd a wife	Some time ago	Storace
The sound of the harp ceaseth	A funeral anthem	Holden
Spanking Jack was so comely	The sailor's consolation	
Speed the lazy foot of time	Time	Hewitt
Spirit of my sainted sire		Storace
Sprich sie! sprich sie, des Donners auf Sina, des Donners auf Sina dumpfe	Lob und anbetung	Ott
The spring with smiling face		Shield
The springtime returns	Alloa house	Oswald
Stay lady stay for mercy sake	The sailor's orphan boy	
Stay sweet enchanter of the grove	The wood robin	Spofforth
Stay traveller tarry here tonight	The woodman	Linley, the Elder
Stay ye fleeting moments stay	Last adieu	Mozart
Still the lark finds repose		Linley
Still toss'd tempestuous on the sea of life		Labarte
[The storm is o'er]		Grétry (Linley)
Stranger do you ask me why	The shade of Henry	Abrams

First Line	Title	Composer
Tell me my love, wouldst thou forego	Tell me my love	Shield
Tell me my lovely shepherd	The gentle shepherd	Swan
Tell me where is fancy bred		Carr
That I might prove my love sincere	The Persian slave	
[That petty fogging Grizzle]		Markordt
[That seat of science Athens & earth's great mistress Rome]		
Then haste the laurel wreaths entwine	Finale	Reinagle
There's Ichabod has come to town	Ode for the 4th of July, 1798	
[There liv'd in Altdorf city fair]		Carr
There the silver waters roam	Thes hipwreck'd seamans ghost	Storace
There was a frog liv'd in a well	The frog and mouse	
There was a jolly miller		Arne
There was an Irish lad who lov'd a cloyster'd [!] nun	Smalilou	Shield
There was an old man, and though 'tis not common	The wonderful old man	
There was Dorothy Dump	Dorothy Dump. _Also_ Dear Walter. _Also_ Walter's sweetheart	Arnold
They tell me I have grown too proud	All for pretty Polly	Hook
Think your tawny Moor is true, pretty Agnes?	Think your tawny Moor is true	Arnold
This cold flinty heart it is you who have warm'd	Sweet passion of love	Arne, Michael
Thou'rt gone awa frae me, Mary		Hook
Thou country unkind yet so dear	The American soldier	Gauline
[Thou dear seducer of my heart]		
Thou soft'ning balm		Hook
Tho Bacchus may boast of his care killing bowl	Tho Bacchus may boast	Shield
Though distant far from Jessy's charms	Her absence will not alter me	
Tho far beyond the mountains	Owen. _Also_ Tho' far beyond the mountains	
Tho I am in my teens, I have lovers in great plenty	I love to speak my mind	Hook
[Tho' I am now a very little lad]		Shield
Tho' tis fruitless to regret thee	Farethewell for ever	
Tho Leixlip is proud of its close shady bowers	Norah, the theme of my song	Shield
Tho' my dad I must own is but poor	The market lass	Reeve
Tho' oft we meet severe distress	The cheering rosary. _Also_ The rosary	Shield
Tho' pity I cannot deny		Pleyel
Tho' prudence may press me		Dibdin
Tho' rude thou art as northern blast	She left me ah! for gold	
Tho' scarce sixteen by men I'm told	Love shall be my guide	Hook

First Line	Title	Composer
Though tender and young, since my eyesight is gone	The poor blind girl	De Cleve, V.
Tho' the fate of battle on to-morrow wait	The tobacco box, or Soldier's pledge of love	
Tho' the language of friendship is sweet	A smile from the youth that I love	Wright
Tho' the muses ne'er smile by the light of the sun	The indigent peasant. *Also* My heart is devoted dear Mary to thee	Hook
Tho' the poets of yore tell of beauties a score	Mary of Sunbury Hill	
Tho' wealth is alluring		Hook
Tho' you think by this to vex me		Storace
Tho' youth and beauty grace the fair	The disappointed lover	
Three lovers I boast	The young Irish captain's the husband for me	
Three sweethearts I boast, pray who could wish more	Three sweethearts I boast	
Thro' forests drear I once did stray	Carol	Attwood
Thro' life's rugged voyage each mortal must sail	Strew the rude crosses of life o'er with flowers	Hook
[Throw an apple up the hill]		Hawkins
Thus for men the women fair	Fishing duett	Reeve
Thy influence love I needs must own	Come buy my wooden ware	
Till Noah's time men acted without meaning	Till Noah's time	Gram
Time has not thin'd my flowing hair	Canzonet	Jackson, Wm.
To arms, to arms, when honor cries	To arms Columbia	Von Hagen, Jr.
To Batchelor's hall, we good fellows invite	Bachelors [*or* Batchelors] Hall	Dibdin
To be treated like a baby	Silvan, the shepherd swain	Taylor
To beg one boon or breath [!] one vow	The new somebody	Carr
To ease his heart and own his flame	The spinning wheel	
To fair Fidele's grassy tomb	Fidele	
To fortune lost my native shore	My native shore	
To Mary's bower haste away	Mary's bower	
To me a smiling infant came		Sharp (?)
To me yet in teens mamma would oft say	The men are all rovers alike	
To musick be the verse addrest	On musick	Selby
To my muse give attention	Golden days of good Queen Bess	
To pleasure let's raise the heart cheering song	Hark forward tantivy huzza	Hook
To soften life's cares		Hook
To the brave sons of freedom	Washington guards	
To the earth's utmost verge, tho' Bellona is heard	Washington	
To the winds, to the waves, to the woods I complain	Ah weladay [!] my poor heart	Shield

First Line	Title	Composer
To tickle the ear is our present intention	Modern music	Billings
To yon lone cot out on the moor	Muirland Willy	Hook
Together let us range the fields		Boyce, Dr.
Together then we'd fondly stray	Rosina's heart	Attwood
Toi dont les accords enchant-eurs	Romance. No. 2	Chateaudun
Toll, toll the knell		Storace
Tom Starboard was a lover true	Tom Starboard.	Mazzinghi
Tom Tackle was noble	Tom Tackle	Dibdin
Tom Truelove woo'd the sweetest fair	Tom Truelove's knell	Dibdin
Too plain dear youth, those tell-tale eyes	The answer	
Too soon my dearest Sophia, pray take this kind adieu	Woolf's adieu	
Top sails aback the ship hove to	Jack Clueline	Moulds
Tother day as I sat by the green willow tree. *See* The other day as I sat		
Tranquil is Deaths happy slumber	A funeral hymn	
Tranquil pleasures never cloy		Pleyel
[The trav'ler benighted]		Hopkinson
Triumphant fame ascends the skies	Military glory of Great Britain	Lyon (?)
The trump of fame your name has breath'd	The trump of fame	Shield
Truth from thy radiant throne look down	Air in The reconciliation	Markoe
The tuneful lavrocks cheer ye grove	Jem of Aberdeen	Hook
The turban'd Turk who scorns the world	The Irishman	
Turn fair Clora—Go false Damon	Damon and Clora	Harington
Twice 1 is 2	The multiplication table	Jackson, G. K.
Twilight glimmers o'er the steep [*or* plain]	Pit a pat	Kelly
The twins of Latona, so kind to my boon	The twins of Latona	Shield

U

First Line	Title	Composer
Unfold Father Time, thy long record unfold	Freedom triumphant	
Unfurl'd were the sails		Hook
Up to thy throne, Almighty King, we raise our streaming eyes	A funeral hymn	Holden

V

First Line	Title	Composer
Vacation approaches with sadness I learn	Dear Whitelands adieu	
The vainly ambitious may proudly recite	The wounded sailor. *Also* The wounded soldier	Taylor
Vous l'ordonné je me serai connoitre	A favourite French song	Monsigny

First Line	Title	Composer
W		
[Waft me some soft and cooling breeze]		Jackson
The walls of my prison are high	The walls of my prison	More, I. T.
The wampum belt no more can charm	The wampum belt	Hewitt
A wand'ring gipsey, sirs am I	A wand'ring gipsey	Percy
A wand'ring gipsy, sirs, am I	The gipsy	Fisin
The wanton god who pierces hearts	Rosy wine	
Was I a shepherds maid		Dibdin
Was there ever a spark so confounded as I	I blush in the dark	Giordani
Water parted from the sea		Arne
[We kings who are in our senses]		
[We'll chearful [!] our endeavours blend]		Reinagle
The wealthy fool with gold in store	My friend and pitcher	Shield
Welcome mighty chief once more	Chorus sung before Gen. Washington . . . at Trenton	Reinagle
Well met my loving friends of art	The Musical society	
Were I obliged [or reduc'd] to beg my bread	Somebody	
What aileth thee, oh thou sea	An anthem from the 114th Psalm	Hopkinson
What are the boasted joys of love		Shield
What arm a sinking state can save	Rule New England	Schaffer
What can force the rending sigh	Un jeu d'esprit	Pirsson
What days of fleeting pleasures past	The pretty lad	Shield
What is beauty but a flow'r	Beauty	Pleyel
[What med'cine can soften the bosom's keen smart]		Boyce
What mournful strains invade our ears	Columbia's guardian sleeps in dust	Holden
What shepherd or nymph		
What solemn sounds the ear invade	Mount Vernon	Jenks
What sorrowful sounds do I hear	Corydon's ghost	Dwight [?]
What tho' the blooming genial year	Amyntor	Taylor
What virgin or shepherd of [or in] valley or grove	The wedding day	Hook
[When a little merry he]		Reeve
When a youth commences love	The young lover	
When Alcides, the son of Olympian Jove	Washington	Holyoke
[When all the Attick fire was fled]		Cooper
When as my swain began to woo	Nobody	Taylor
When at night the village swains	Cynthia's cottage	

First Line	Title	Composer
When bidden to the wake or fair		Shield
When Britain with despotic sway	Columbia and liberty	Arne
When Caesar's birthday glads Brittania's isle	An ode set to music on Mrs. B ——s birthday	Hopkinson
When charming Terraminta sings	Terraminta	Holyoke
When Cupid first his trade began	Donna donna donna Della	Hook
When de thunder passa, passoo	Talacoy	Sanderson
When Delia on the plain appears		Kotzwara
When Delia on the plains appears	Delia	
When Donald first came wooing me	Sweet love I'll marry thee	Hook
When Edward left his native plain		Hook
When fairies trip round the gay green	I sigh for the girl I adore	Hook
When faries [!] are lighted by night's silver queen	The straw bonnet	Pownall, *Mrs.* M. A.
When far from thee by adverse fortune drove	Crazy Emma	Gauline
[When first Columbus sought this strand]		Reinagle
When first I ken'd young Sandy's face	How sweet the love that meets return	Hook
When first I saw thee graceful move	Graceful move	Galli
When first I slipped [*or* slip'd] my leading strings	Same as first line. *Also* The waxen doll	Shield
When first I sold posies	The nosegay girl	Wilson
When first I viewed the charming maid	Sweet Myra of the vale	Hewitt
When first on the plain I began to appear	I'll die for no shepherd not I	Hook.
When first the sun o'er ocean glow'd	Rise Columbia	
When first this humble roof I knew		Jackson, Wm.
When first this little heart began		Dibdin
When first to Helen's lute	Same as first line. *Also* O 'tis love	Arnold
When first young Harry told his tale	Indeed young man I must deny	
When Freedom fair Freedom her banner display'd	Truxton's victory	
When freedom was banish'd from Greece & from Rome	Liberty's throne	R., F.
When Freedom's son in these blest climes	Washington and Independence	Pelissier.
When from my Sylvia I remove	Sylvia	
When heav'n spreads blessings	An Ode designed for a public commencement in the College of Philadelphia	Hopkinson
When hoary frost hung on each thorn	Spring water cresses	

First Line	Title	Composer
When I comes to town	The waggoner	Dibdin
When I drain the rosy bowl	Devonshire cut	
When I had scarcely told six-teen	I never would be married	
[When I've got the ready rhino wounds]		Reinagle
When I think on your truth		Delamain
When I took my departure from Dublin's sweet town	Paddy Bull's expedition	Reeve
When I was a chit		Hook
[When I was a little lad]		Reinagle
When I was at home as the lark I was gay	My journey is love	Reeve
When icicles hang by the wall		Carr
When liberty to bless mankind	Vive la Liberté	Taylor
When little on the village green	Patty Clover	Shield
When lovers are too daring grown	No that will never do	Hook
When Lucy was kind		Hook
When my fortune does frown	The jolly sailor	
When nature first salutes the morn [or Spring]	Two bunches a penny primroses	Hook
When Nicholas first to court began	When Nicholas	Shield
When night and left upon my guard	O come sweet Mary come to me	Shield
When nights were cold		Carr
When on a clear and cloudless night		Willson, J.
When on the ocean		Arnold
When once by the clear gliding stream		Hook
When one's drunk not a girl but looks pretty	A blessing on brandy & beer	Mazzinghi
[When o'er the mountain's top we go]		Reinagle
When pensive I thought of [or on] my love	When pensive	Kelly
When Phoebus the tops of the hill does adorn	Hunting song	Swan
When rural lads and lassies gay		
When Sandy told his tale of love		Hook
[When scorching suns the thrifty earth]		Shield
When seated with Sal		Reeve
When Spring dispensing sweets around	Willy of the dale	Hook
When Spring returning decks the grove [or groves]	Two bunches a penny primroses	
When Steerwell heard me first impart	The post captain	Shield
When Strephon appears how my heart pit-a-pat	Laughing song	
When summer sweet summer		Sanderson
When the anchor's weigh'd	Jack the guinea pig	Taylor
When the battle's rage is ended	Finale in Oscar and Mal-vina	Reeve
When the bee at eve reposes	Then I fly to meet my love	
When the fierce North wind with his airy forces	Sapphick ode	Stickney, John

First Line	Title	Composer
While o'er thy cheek desponding	He sleeps in yonder dewy grave	Callcott
[Whilst Europe is wrapt in the horrors of war]		
Whilst happy in my native land		Shield
Whilst with village maids I stray		Shield
Whither can my William stray		Hook
Whither my love days		Paisiello
Who kill'd poor Robin	The much admir'd Death and burial of Cock Robin	Arnold
Who so merry lives as I		Metzger
Why Collin must your Laura mourn		
Why does the sun dart forth his cheerful rays	The nymphs complaint	Swan
Why fair maid in ev'ry feature	Crazy Jane	Davy
Why heaves my fond bosom, ah! what can it mean		
Why oh why allmighty passion	The labyrinth of love	Pownall, *Mrs.* M. A.
Why should our joys transform to pain	The Indian philosopher	
Why should vain mortals tremble at the sight	The American hero	Law
Why sleeps the thunder in the skies		
Why steals from my bosom the sigh	Lavinia	Pownall, *Mrs.* M. A.
Why tarries my love	The pigeon	Leeves
Why thus do you treat us with scorn and disdain	Answer to the male coquett	Gauline
Why turns my Jen her head away	Air	Pleyel
Why whats thats to you if my eyes I'm a' wiping	True courage	Dibdin
Will you come to the bower		
Will you please gentle folks that little Javotte	Javotte, or The maid of the Alps.	Willson
The wind [*or* winds] whistled shrilly	The poor mariner	
With a heart light and gay		Arnold
With care I search'd the village round	Sweet Nan of Hampton Green	Hook
With down castlook and fault'-ring [!] heart	The faithful tar	Sale
With grief opprest and heaving sighs	Henry's departure	Cope
With lowly suit and plaintive ditty	With lowly suit	Storace
With pleasure have I past my days		Hopkinson
With straw hat and spencer and tasty bandeau	The veil	Blewitt
With the sun I rise at morn	The merry piping lad	Taylor
Within these sacred bowers		Mozart
A wolf once met a pike	The wolf and the pike	

First Line	Title	Composer
The women all tell me I'm false to my lass	The tipler's defence	
The world's a good thing	No good without an exception	Dibdin
The world my dear Myra	Myra	
Would ye be taught ye feather'd thronge [!]	Anne Hatheaway [!]	Dibdin
[Would you gain the tender creature]		Handel
Woud [!] you know true enjoyment	The black bird	Hook
Would you taste the noontide air		Arne
Wully is a bonny lad		Sanderson

Y & Z

First Line	Title	Composer
Ye banks and braes and streams around	Highland Mary	
[Ye chearful [!] virgins have you seen]		
Ye crystal fountains		Giordani
Ye fair possess'd of ev'ry charm	Ye fair possessed	
Ye gales that gently wave the sea	The boatman	Barthélemon
Ye gentle gales that careless blow	The resolution	Mozart (*arr.*)
Ye gentle winds that softly blow	Polly's answer	
[Ye gracious powers of chora [!] song]		
Ye jobbers, underwriters, ye tribe of pen and ink	The Jew broker	Dibdin
Ye jovial tars now lend an ear	Capt. Truxton, or Huzza for the Constellation	
Ye ladies who listen to fashions gay voice	The fashions	
Ye ling'ring winds that feebly blow	Ye lingering winds. *Also* She dropt a tear & cried be true	Moulds
Ye little songsters of the grove	Ye little songsters	Fisin
Ye mortals whom fancies		
Ye nymphs & swains attend my strains	The crops	Hook
Ye sages contending in virtue's fair cause	Ode	
Ye sluggards who murder your lifetime in sleep	Hunting song	Hook
Ye sons of Columbia determin'd to keep	Our country's efficiency	
Ye sons of Columbia who bravely have fought	Adams and liberty	Smith, John Stafford (?)
Ye sons of France awake to glory [*and* Allons enfans de la patrie]	The Marseilles hymn	Rouget de Lisle
Ye sons of Mars attend	The Dauphin	
Ye sportsmen draw near	Tally ho	
Ye streams that round my prison creep		Storace.
Ye tuneful linnetts bless my care	The linnetts	Hook

First Line	Title	Composer
Ye virgin souls whose sweet complaint	An elegy on the death of a young lady.	Wood
Ye wealthy and proud while in splendor ye roll	The match boy	Hook
Ye youths wheresoever you wander	O pity a maiden & pray take her part	Hook
Ye zephyrs where's my blushing rose		Stevenson
Yes Beda, thus Beda, when I melancholy grow	Tink a tink	Kelly
Yes these are the meadows the shrubs and the plains	The season of love is no more	Hindle
You [or your] care of money, ah! care no more	Poor black boy	Storace
You own I'm complacent but tell me I'm cold	A smile & a tear	Abrams
You tell me dear girl that I'm given to rove	I never lov'd any dear Mary but you	Hook
[Young Carlos sued a beautious maid]		Attwood
Young Damon has woot [!] me a monstrous long time	'Tis no fault of mine	Hook
Young Donald is the blithest lad	Donald of Dundee	
Young Henry lov'd his Emma well.		
Young Jammie [!] lov'd me weel and ask'd me for his bride	Auld Robin Gray	
Young Jemmy is a bonny boy	He stole my heart from me	Hook
Young Jemmy is a pleasing youth		
Young Jemmy's ganging after me	What can a lassy do	Hook
Young Jockey calls me his delight	Shou'd he think of another	
Young Jockey sout my heart to win	Prithee fool be quiet	
Young Lubin was a shepherd boy		Linley, the Elder
Young Lucy fair was lofty Devon's pride	William and Lucy	Gillingham
Young Myra is fair as spring's early flower	The beauties of friendship	
Young Sandy's gone to kirk I ken	He loves his winsome Kate. *Also* Winsome Kate	Hook
Young Sandy once a wooing came	So dearly I love Johnny O	
[Young Simon in his lovely Sue]		Arnold
Young Strephon met me on the green	Keep your distance	Hook
Young Teddy is an Irish lad	I've lost my heart to Teddie	Hook
Young Willy lov'd me in his heart	No not yet	
Your wise men all declare	The je ne scai quoi	Arnold
Zephyr come thou playful minion		Shield

List of American Patriotic Music

VOCAL AND INSTRUMENTAL PIECES LISTED IN THIS BIBLIOGRAPHY

Sᴏɴɢs without music are not included. An asterisk before a title indicates that no published copy of such title has been located.

VOCAL

Adams and liberty
Adams and Washington
America, commerce and freedom
The American soldier
Behold the man whom virtue raise. *See* Ode as performed . . . before the President of the United States
Boston patriotic song. *See* Adams and liberty
Brother soldiers all hail
Captain Truxton, or Huzza for the Constellation
Chester
Chorus sung before Gen. Washington
Columbia
Columbia and liberty
Columbians arise. *See* Ladies patriotic song
Columbians all. *See* New Yankee Doodle
Columbia's bold eagle
Columbia's brave friends
Come all ye sons of song
Come join hand in hand, brave Americans all. *See* Liberty song
Come swallow your bumpers. *See* Parody parodized
Dead march and monody
Death of General Wolfe
A dirge or sepulchral service
Dirge for General Washington
The Federal constitution & liberty forever
Freedom triumphant
Funeral dirge on the death of General Washington
A funeral elegy on the death of General Washington
God save America (Tune, "God save the king")

God save great Washington (Tune, "God save the king." No words)
Great Washington the hero's come. *See* Ode to Columbia's favorite son
Green Mountain farmer
Hail, America, hail
Hail Columbia
Hail Liberty
Hail patriots all
The host that fights for liberty
Huzza for liberty
Huzza for the Constellation
Immortal Washington
Independent and free
'Tis done, the edict's passed. *See* Ode for American independence
Jefferson and liberty
Kentucky volunteer
The ladies patriotic song
Lafayette
Let tyrants shake their iron rod. *See* Chester
Let Washington be our boast
Liberty song
Liberty's throne
Massachusetts song of liberty. *See* Liberty song
Mount Vernon
A new patriotic song
New Yankee Doodle
New York patriotic song. *See* Federal constitution
O stream belov'd, thy hallow'd wave. *See* The river Patowmac
Ode as performed . . . before the President of the United States
Ode for American independence
An ode for the Fourth of July
Ode for the 4th of July, 1798
Ode to Columbia's favorite son

INSTRUMENTAL

List of Opera Librettos

TITLE	LIBRETTIST	COMPOSER
The agreeable surprise	John O'Keeffe	Samuel Arnold
The archers	William Dunlap	Benjamin Carr
The Battle of Hexham	George Colman, Jr.	Samuel Arnold
The children in the wood	Thomas Morton	Samuel Arnold
Darby's return	William Dunlap	
The dead alive	John O'Keeffe	Samuel Arnold
The deserter	Charles Dibdin	Charles Dibdin
The disappointment	Andrew Barton	
The Duenna	Richard Brinsley Sheridan	Thomas Linley
Edwin and Angelina	Elihu Hubbard Smith	Victor Pelissier
The farmer	John O'Keeffe	William Shield
The fashionable lady	James Ralph	
The haunted tower	James Cobb	Stephen Storace
The Highland reel	John O'Keeffe	William Shield
Inkle and Yarico	George Colman, Jr	Samuel Arnold
Lionel and Clarissa	Isaac Bickerstaff	Charles Dibdin
Love in a village	Isaac Bickerstaff	Thomas Arne
The maid of the mill	Isaac Bickerstaff	Samuel Arnold
Midas	Kane O'Hara	
The mountaineers	George Colman, Jr.	Samuel Arnold
No song, no supper	Prince Hoare	Stephen Storace
The padlock	Isaac Bickerstaff	Charles Dibdin
Patrick in Prussia, or Love in a camp	John O'Keeffe	William Shield
The poor soldier	John O'Keeffe	William Shield
Poor Vulcan	Charles Dibdin	Charles Dibdin
The purse, or Benevolent Tar	James C. Cross	William Reeve
The Quaker	Charles Dibdin	Charles Dibdin
The reconciliation	Peter Markoe	
The romp	Isaac Bickerstaff	Charles Dibdin
Rosina	Mrs. Brooke	William Shield
Slaves in Algiers	Mrs. Susanna H. Rowson	James Hewitt
The son in law	John O'Keeffe	Samuel Arnold
Tammany	Ann Julia Hatton	James Hewitt
Thomas and Sally	Isaac Bickerstaff	Thomas Arne
The Woodman	Bate Dudley	William Shield

Index of Publishers, Printers and Engravers

IN PHILADELPHIA, NEW YORK, BOSTON, BALTIMORE AND ELSEWHERE

N THE United States before 1800 we find scarcely more than a baker's dozen of publishers of secular music, and all of these became active in the last decade. Before 1790 practically nothing but psalm and hymn books were published, with here and there an issue of secular character as in the various "Almanacks" and literary periodicals—also a very few songsters with music.

The most important of the bona fide publishing firms dealing exclusively (or at least predominantly) with musical publications were those of Benjamin Carr, Philadelphia and New York; George Willig, Philadelphia; George Gilfert, James Hewitt, J. and M. Paff, New York; Joseph Carr, Baltimore; P. A. von Hagen, Boston.

Of less importance, but still exclusively (or predominantly) music publishers were Moller & Capron, Filippo Trisobio, Philadelphia; J. C. Moller, John Young, Philadelphia and New York; R. Shaw, Philadelphia and Baltimore; William Howe (and his widow, Sarah), Peter Weldon, New York; William Norman, Boston.

Among the more important printers and general publishers more or less associated with musical interests during this period may be mentioned T. Dobson, H. and P. Rice, Philadelphia; James Harrison, New York; Henry S. Keatinge, Baltimore; W. P. (and L.) Blake, Linley and Moore, Thomas and Andrews, Boston.

It must also be borne in mind that the terms "publisher," "printer," "book-seller"—even "engraver"—were loosely employed at this time with the result that there is much overlapping and lack of clear definition in the use of these terms.

In order to give as vivid a picture as possible of these early publishing houses, and to indicate the basis on which many of the dates assigned to various issues in the preceding pages have been founded, the following lists are given. They, in turn, are based upon the study of newspaper advertisements and copyright records by both Sonneck and the present writer; on thorough examination of directories by the late Walter R. Whittlesey of the Library of Congress; on careful checking with the "Directory of early American music publishers" in *Early American sheet music*, by Harry Dichter and Elliott Shapiro,

New York, 1941; *Music directory of early New York City*, by Virginia Larkin Redway, New York, 1941; *One hundred and fifty years of music publishing in the United States*, by William Arms Fisher, Boston, 1931. Valuable assistance has also been given by Clarence S. Brigham of the American Antiquarian Society, and others.

The procedure adopted throughout this *Index* is as follows: Where a publisher's address is given as (*e. g.*)

> 131 William street, ca. August, 1797, to ca. February, 1799
> 23 Maiden Lane, ca. February, 1799 to late 1800

the meaning is that the publisher was *known* to be at 131 William street in August, 1797; that he was *known* to be at 23 Maiden Lane in February, 1799; and that late in 1800 he had changed to still another address. At just what time between these variously given limits he changed from one address to the other it is impossible to determine. In other words we are often compelled to deal with these stations along the path of his journeyings without knowing exactly whether they are way stations or terminal points. This is irritating to the devotee of exact scholarship, but perhaps after all not as serious as it might seem.

For the sake of textual economy, the date given above, *viz.*, "ca. August, 1797 to ca. February, 1799," when used in bibliographical entries in this work, is reduced to its lowest terms: 1797–99.

Also, only years of actual publishing are here taken into account. No record is ordinarily given of earlier (or later) years spent as teacher, silversmith, instrument maker, etc.

Sonneck's lead has been followed in not reporting in detail—except in certain important instances—the source of the data here given. And it must always be kept in mind that at any moment some obscure advertisement or musical notice may yet come to light and overturn our most plausible theories. Suffice it to say that the information here given, while admittedly tentative and in the nature of the case subject to change, is carefully based on such sources as are available, and is duly authenticated as far as any authentication can be obtained from the records of those days of comfortable, contented carelessness in all such matters as these.

As in the *List of composers*, any biographical material given here is based strictly on Sonneck's own biographical sketches, with only such additions as seem pertinent, or omissions designed to avoid unnecessary duplication. For fuller information as to certain publishers who were also composers, see *List of composers*.

☛ NUMBERS FOLLOWING A PUBLISHER'S NAME INDICATE THE PAGES IN THIS WORK ON WHICH HIS PUBLICATIONS ARE ENTERED.

CARR & CO. (B. Carr & Co., "Music printers and importers lately from London").
  136 High street, July into November, 1793.
    7, 33, 55, 106, 182, 213, 215, 243, 251, 253, 256, 304, 328, 355, 367, 380, 401, 415, 456, 470.
  122 Market (*or* High) street, November, 1793 to ca. October, 1794.
    10, 37, 56, 59, 60, 113, 144, 145, 184, 187, 189, 190, 219, 246, 301, 329, 330, 332, 335, 338, 339, 341, 347, 365, 371, 389, 420, 424, 426, 455, 462, 463, 481.
  Probably Benjamin Carr with his father, Joseph.

CARR, B. (Benjamin).
  122 High street, ca. October, 1794 to July, 1798.
    15, 96, 100, 104, 115, 122, 139, 153, 172, 177, 212, 235, 241, 336, 344, 366, 368, 370, 379, 382, 413, 434, 452, 453, 457, 478, 482. *Also* (probably same address) 191, 224, 297.
  138 High street, July, 1798 to March, 1799.
    No issues located.
  36 South Second street, March, 1799 through 1800.
    (However in 1800 listed only as "Instrument maker"—not as publisher.) 358(?), 393(?).

CARR, B. (Philadelphia and New York) and J. Carr (Baltimore), 1794 to 1797.
    10, 22, 30, 34, 38, 52, 61, 91, 92, 101, 112, 120, 123, 127, 129, 139, 140, 142, 144, 148, 157, 170, 176, 189, 193, 198, 206, 214, 224, 232, 239, 242, 245, 260, 287, 305, 306, 315, 320, 327, 337, 345, 346, 353, 354, 367, 369, 383, 390, 395, 401, 402, 407, 415, 417, 419, 423, 432, 433, 435, 436, 443, 455, 458, 462, 465, 466, 474, 480. *Also* "Printed for the Author" (R. Taylor), 23, 110, 207, 217, 225, 226, 259, 286, 360, 366, 392, 444, 448.

CARR, B. (Philadelphia), J. CARR (Baltimore) and J. HEWITT (New York), 1797 to 1799.
    35, 36, 38, 39, 44, 50, 54, 55, 62, 71, 82, 83, 92, 101, 103, 117, 121, 122, 132, 175, 177, 196, 199, 200, 214, 233, 234, 235, 252, 257, 294, 300, 323, 332, 415, 416, 432, 435, 457, 464, 469, 472.
  It seems safe to assume that most of the issues bearing either of the last two (composite) imprints given above were published in Philadelphia.
  See also New York.

MOLLER, J. C. (John Christopher).
  163 North Third street, ca. March, 1793 to ca. November, 1794.
    38, 60, 86, 116, 244, 394.

MOLLER & CAPRON (J. C. Moller and Henry Capron).
  163 North Third street, ca. March, 1793 to ca. November, 1794.
    265.

SHAW, R. (Probably *Ralph*, not *Robert* as Sonneck supposed).
  81 North Sixth street, ca. May, 1794 through 1794.
    No issues located.
  44 North Seventh street, ca. January, 1795 through 1796.
    160, 465.

13 South Fourth street, ca. November, 1800 (?).

52, 110, 144, 168, 177, 217, 225, 265, 268, 298, 299, 469, 477.

From Sonneck, however, it would seem that Shaw was at 197 Market street from ca. March, 1795 to ca. November, 1797, when his business failed. He then removed to Baltimore. Whatever the discrepancy here, Sonneck's date for the re-opening of Shaw's Philadelphia store at 13 South Fourth street in November, 1800, seems quite probable.

The uncertainties which have always surrounded R. Shaw as a music publisher are occasioned for the most part by confusing two contemporary R. Shaws— Ralph and Robert. The Philadelphia and Baltimore directories seem to have established, however, that the R. Shaw here referred to is Ralph.

The status of Shaw & Co. and Shaw & Price (John M. Price). mentioned by Sonneck, is still far from clear.

Shaw & Co., no address, 1794.
1, 42, 291, 359

Shaw & Price, no address, 1795.
No issues located.

See also Baltimore.

TRISOBIO, Filippo.

66 North Front street, 1796 to 1798.
65, 233. *Also* (probably same address) 108, 131, 251, 325, 340, 351, 371, 454.

WILLIG, G. (George).

163 North Third street ("in the house formerly occupied by Mr. Moller"), November, 1794 to ca. March, 1795.
81, 256, 443.

165 Market street, ca. March, 1795 through 1797.
11, 30, 31, 33, 36, 57, 62, 76, 81, 96, 114, 122, 146, 184, 186, 221, 225, 236, 237, 244, 257, 291, 299, 306, 317, 318, 321, 329, 345, 372, 390, 393, 408, 416, 456, 460.

185 Market street, 1798 through 1804.
6, 9, 10, 21, 32, 33, 38, 44, 45, 46, 49, 88, 91, 92, 93, 94, 101, 105, 113, 116, 119, 147, 149, 153, 154, 167, 173, 176, 185, 192, 193, 201, 203, 205, 206, 213, 225, 226, 228, 238, 239, 245, 247, 250, 256, 259, 260, 264, 269, 292, 299, 303, 320, 323, 327, 339, 343, 345, 353, 356, 359, 361, 363, 377, 382, 387, 388, 389, 394, 395, 396, 397, 409, 427, 438, 440, 454, 464, 468, 470, 471, 478.

[   ] Market street, 1795 through 1804.
61, 319, 391.

12 South Fourth street, 1805–, but originally issued before 1800.
84, 395, 397.

No address.
15, 35, 40, 45, 52, 65, 89, 116, 119, 127, 131, 150, 211, 216, 247, 250, 253, 268, 284, 300, 306, 320, 346, 355, 360, 387, 391, 392, 396, 418, 423, 449, 452, 453, 476.

YOUNG, J. (John).

117 Race street, 1793 through 1794.
484. *Also* (probably same address) 144, 458.

See also New York.

Important printers who issued musical works:

DOBSON, T. and W. YOUNG.
"Second street," 1787, 1792.
375, 445.

DOBSON, Thomas.
"Stone house in Second street," 1788–89.
403.   *Also* "Printed for A. Reinagle," 6, 66, 67, 69, 206, 212, 318, 422, 439,
448.   *Also* (probably the same) 59, 285, 388.

41 South Second street, 1791–.
377.

The well-known general publishing houses of Mathew Carey (Philadelphia) and William Spotswood (Philadelphia and Boston) published numerous opera librettos, songsters, etc., but apparently little or no music:

CAREY, Mathew.
118 Market street, 1792 to 1800.
7, 58, 111, 134, 231, 238, 299, 300, 358, 368, 400, 420, 435, 445.

SPOTSWOOD, William.
Front street, 1789 to 1793.
28, 29, 58, 237, 445, 446(?).
See also Boston.

General publishers in Philadelphia associated with musical interests and represented in this work—also printers and engravers:

PUBLISHERS

Aitken, John, no address, ca. 1800.   477.
Bader, S. R., no address, 1709.   37.
Birch, William Y., 17 South Second street, 1799.   16.
Campbell, Robert, 40 South Second street, 1795, 1790.   155, 218.
Chalk, John, 57 North Third street, ca. 1800.   91, 471.
Charless, Joseph, no address, 1797.   107.
Claypoole, David C., no address, 1796–99.   267, 371, 392.
Dunlap, William, Market Street, 1762–63.   130, 312, 492.
Dunlap and Claypoole, no address, 1793–94.   139, 176, 219, 309, 323, 406, 427, 462, 478, 481.
Hall and Sellers, no address, 1768.   227.
Hillegas, Michael, no address, 1776.   85.
Klemm and Brother, no address, ca. 1800.   289.
Neale and Kammerer, Jr., 24 North Third street, 1795.   138, 257.
Priest, William, 15 Apple Tree Alley, 1795.   342.
Rice, H., Market street, 1788–89.   9, 63, 67, 82, 290.
Rice & Co., 50 Market street, 1791.   445.

Rice, H. & P.:
    50 Market street, 1792–95/96. 1, 42, 359, 377, 447.
    16 South Second street, 1795/96–99. 74.
Seddon, Thomas, no address, 1788. 58.
Shallus, Francis, 40 Vine street, 1796. 110.
Stephens, Thomas, no address, 1796. 324.
Story, Enoch:
    Second street, 1787–89. 336, 362.
    Fourth street, 1793–94. 188, 272.
    No address. 99, 208, 375.
Taylor, Henry, no address, 1791. 237, 326, 339, 363, 428.
Weizsaecker, G. F., no address. 345.
Woodhouse, William, Front street, 1769, 1791. 43, 297, 330, 476.

PRINTERS

Aitken, Robert, 22 Market street, 1797. 107.
Bell, Robert, Third street, 1777–78. 1, 334, 399.
Bioren, John, no address, 1799. 74.
Bradford, Thomas, 8 South Front street, 1794. 181, 381.
Bradford, William, no address, 1762–3. 107, 261.
Cist, Charles, no address, ca. 1800. 345.
Cruikshank, Joseph, Market street, 1775. 130.
Dunlap, John, Market street, 1772. 129.
Dunlap, William, Market street, 1762–63. 130, 312, 492.
Goddard, William, Market street, 1767. 130.
Hupfeld, C., no address, ca. 1800. 149, 207, 382, 383.
Kammerer, H., no address, 1793. 218.
M'Culloch, John, Third street, 1789–93. 236, 265, 331, 341.
Ormrod, J., 41 Chestnut street, 1798. 175.
Prichard and Hall, Market street, 1790. 351.
Seddon, T. and W. Spotswood, no address, 1887. 339.
Smith, Samuel Harrison, no address, 1794, 1795. 477.
Stuart (Steuart), Andrew, Second street, 1762. 31, 76, 216.
Taylor, Henry, no address, 1790–91. 194, 218.
Turner, John, no address, 1796. 492.
Woodward, W. W., no address, 1794. 231.
Wrigley and Berriman, 149 Chestnut street, 1794–5. 340, 386, 400.

ENGRAVERS

Aitken, J. (John), no address, 1787–93. 6, 9, 37, 39, 49, 63, 67, 68, 69, 82, 144,
    181, 204, 206, 245, 361, 375, 403, 420, 422, 439, 448.
Burger, J., no address, 1795–97. 127, 301.
Facius, G. S., no address, 1793. 265.
Norman, John (*also* Boston), Third street, 1778. 83.
Priest, William, 15 Apple Tree Alley, 1795. 342.
Rebecca, B., no address, 1793. 265.
S., C., no address, ca. 1793–97. 38, 76, 321.
Smither, J., no address, 1775. 155.
Tiebout, Cornelius (*also* New York), no address, 1789. 63.

CARR, B. (Benjamin).

131 William street, late fall 1794 to ca. August 1797. (New York issues mostly 1795–96.)

95, 125, 140, 148, 166, 236, 284, 298, 307, 328, 395, 430, 461, 472, 476, 479. *Also* (probably same address) 191, 202, 216, 220, 233, 251, 263, 429.

Sonneck dates the opening of Carr's New York branch as "fall of 1794," and his dating of issues bearing this address as "1794–97" has been retained throughout this work. From Carr's announcement in the *Daily Advertiser* (New York), January 9, 1795, that "he has opened a Musical Magazine Repository at No. 131 William St.," it seems likely that this opening must have taken place rather late in the fall—in fact very near to, or at the beginning of 1795.

Sonneck's original belief that Carr had begun his publishing career in New York (instead of Philadelphia) in 1793 seems entirely disproved.

See also Philadelphia.

GILFERT, G., and Co. (George Gilfert and Frederick Rausch).

191 Broadway, ca. November, 1794 to April, 1795.

30, 81, 87, 112, 117, 184, 200, 212, 221, 224, 226, 237, 245, 251, 306, 317, 321, 323, 328, 345, 347, 360, 372, 381, 396, 417, 418, 443, 462, 484.

209 Broadway (near St. Paul's), ca. April, 1795 to ca. 1796.

10, 14, 22, 82, 88, 95, 111, 141, 190, 200, 201, 203, 207, 219, 225, 232, 238, 243, 272, 304, 317, 353, 378, 382, 414, 418, 421, 426, 427, 431, 464, 472, 475, 483.

177 Broadway, 1796.

14, 37, 56, 88, 102, 131, 152, 184, 187, 192, 201, 252, 264, 306, 314, 315, 328, 351, 369, 372, 379, 388, 423, 461. *Also* (probably same address) 442.

No address.

10, 416.

GILFERT, G. (Partnership dissolved at end of 1796).

177 Broadway, 1797 through 1801.

4, 8, 9, 12, 13, 25, 30, 33, 35, 38, 41, 43, 45, 46, 50, 62, 70, 82, 88, 89, 91, 93, 94, 95, 103, 107, 123, 131, 132, 133, 140, 141, 143, 155, 156, 164, 165, 174, 175, 176, 177, 178, 181, 182, 183, 185, 189, 191, 196, 198, 199, 200, 203, 205, 206, 213, 220, 221, 222, 224, 229, 233, 235, 244, 249, 257, 258, 271, 273, 283, 286, 287, 297, 301, 305, 307, 308, 313, 316, 322, 323, 336, 343, 350, 353, 354, 362, 363, 368, 379, 381, 384, 389, 403, 409, 412, 422, 424, 428, 429, 430, 431, 432, 434, 444, 449, 452, 455, 459, 463, 464, 466, 468, 469, 474, 476, 477. *Also* (probably same address) 1, 268.

HEWITT, J. (James).

Greenwich street, near the Battery, 1794.

47, 56.

1 Lumber street, 1795.

No issues located.

40 Gold street, 1796–97.

455.

131 William street, ca. August, 1797 to ca. February, 1799.

4, 9, 23, 24, 34, 49, 55, 78, 102, 111, 116, 138, 143, 153, 170, 178, 181, 186,

190, 198, 199, 204, 212, 217, 230, 231, 234, 242, 246, 255, 258, 268, 284, 288, 302, 305, 308, 313, 326, 338, 339, 344, 356, 388, 390, 411, 419, 430, 435, 457, 459, 466, 469, 472, 473, 480, 484. *Also* (probably same address) 440.

23 Maiden Lane, ca. February, 1799 to late 1800.
1, 43, 50, 60, 81, 151, 165, 193, 213, 227, 232, 249, 285, 307, 324, 338, 350, 363, 418, 421, 428, 430, 433, 441, 442, 454, 465, 467, 475, 478, 483. *Also* (probably same address) 303, 438, 463.

No address.
265, 294.

Sonneck: Though he [Hewitt] is to be traced as publisher as early as 1794, it was not until 1798 that he became important in this respect.

HEWITT & RAUSCH (James Hewitt and Frederick Rausch).[1]

Hewitt, 40 Gold street.
Rausch, 209 Broadway. } ca. March to August, 1797.
77, 143, 222.

An advertisement in *Minerva* (New York), March 10, 1797, mentions "new music to be published monthly by subscription by F. Rausch and J. Hewitt." So we know that their partnership was in existence at that time. Apparently it was dissolved in August of this same year. *See* J. Hewitt, above.

HOWE, W. (William).

320 Pearl street, 1797–98.
3, 9, 24, 102, 175, 205, 210, 221, 240, 269, 273, 286, 314, 368, 431. *Also* (possibly) 4.

HOWE, *widow* (Sarah).

320 Pearl street, 1799–1800.
132, 235, 301, 409.

MOLLER, J. C. (John Christopher).

58 Vesey street, 1797.
26, 52, 55, 238, 470, 487.

No address.
35, 38, 59, 88, 190, 212, 216, 318, 322, 353, 382, 465. *Also* (probably) 329, 343.

See also Philadelphia.

PAFF, John.

112 Broadway, 1798.
116, 179, 193, 249, 454. *Also* (possibly) 124.
149 Broadway, 1811.
156. *Also* (possibly) 394.

PAFF, J. and M. (John and M.).

112 Broadway, 1799.
No issues located.

---

[1] *No common address.*

127 Broadway, 1799–1803.

    34, 35, 40, 43, 44, 46, 53, 60, 88, 92, 94, 110, 124, 129, 132, 141, 144, 164, 167, 170, 182, 183, 188, 198, 205, 222, 228, 231, 236, 248, 296, 313, 316, 328, 329, 332, 336, 337, 340, 356, 363, 368, 387, 406, 415, 417, 425, 428, 432, 435, 439, 441, 459, 473, 476, 478, 481, 482. *Also* (probably same address) 145.

[ ] Broadway, 1799–1803.

    66, 86, 125, 133, 149, 229, 294, 297, 302, 345, 367, 462.

No address.

    6, 12, 14, 89, 124, 151, 175, 185, 197, 211, 215, 224, 255, 295, 308, 322, 332, 465.

RAUSCH, Frederick.

209 Broadway, 1794–99.

    396.

127 Broadway, 1800–1803.

No issues located.

With G. Gilfert and Co., ca. November, 1794, through 1796.

With James Hewitt, ca. March to August, 1797.

Evidently with J. and M. Paff, 1800–1803.

See Hewitt & Rausch.

WELDON, Peter.

76 Chamber street, 1800–1801.

    91, 92, 125, 242, 283, 346, 355.

YOUNG, I., & CO. (John Young).

No address, probably ca. 1792–93.

    243, 347, 418, 461, 483.

It is difficult to locate John Young in New York, either as to address or date—particularly as he is often confused with William Young (cf. *List of composers*).

See also Philadelphia.

GENERAL PUBLISHERS

Allen, Thomas, 16 Queen street, 1788. 21.

Berry and Rogers, 35 Hanover Square, 1786, 1790. 7, 400.

Campbell, Samuel, 44 Hanover Square, 1787–88. 105, 21.

Dunlap, William, no address, 1800. 332, 471.

Harrison, James, Maiden Lane, 1793–94. 65, 75, 347, 401.

Humphreys, William, no address, 1795. 399.

Jansen, Thomas B. & Co., 248 Pearl street, 1800. 141.

Johnkin, Jacob, Maiden Lane, 1800. 327.

Lewis and Horner, 17 Hanover Square, 1782. 147.

Noel, Garrat, no address, 1767. 254.

Pirsson, William, 417 Pearl street, ca. 1800. 166.

Reid, John, 17 Water street, 1788–93. 300, 403.

Rivington, James, Hanover Square, 1761; no address, 1779–80. 76, 397, 400.

Campbell, Samuel, 124 Pearl street, 1795.   388.
Erben, P., no address, ca. 1800.   124.
Gaine, Hugh, no address, 1761, 1779.   16, 240.
Harrisson, John, 3 Peck Slip, 1793–98.   187, 258, 259, 297, 300, 421.
Harrisson and Purdy, no address, 1789.   484.
Hodge, Allen and Campbell, no address, 1789.   99, 100.
Holt, John, "At the Exchange", 1764.   15.
Hopkins, G. F., 136 Pearl street, 1800.   332, 471.
   also 84 Maiden Lane.
Humphreys, James, Jr. and Valentine Nutter, no address, 1779.   114.
Kirk, Thomas, no address, 1798.   491.
Loudon, Samuel and Son, 82 Water street, 1794–95.   399, 437.
Morton, William, "Opposite Coffee House", 1786.   7.
Oram, James, 33 Liberty street, 1797.   492.
Robertson and Gowan, no address, 1795.   62.
Swords, T. & J., 99 Pearl street, 1796–97.   31, 118.
Wilson, Robert, 149 Pearl street, 1798.   324.

ENGRAVERS

Burger, J., Jr., no address.   301.
Dunlap, William, no address, 1789.   99.
Fox, Gilbert, no address, 1800.   471.
Hill, Samuel, no address, ca. 1797.   141.
Milns, William, 29 Gold street, ca. 1796.   396.
Pirsson, William, 417 Pearl street, ca. 1799.   4, 98, 149, 166, 323, 396.
Riley, E., no address, ca. 1800(?).   345.
Roberts, John, no address, 1800.   98.
Rollinson, William, no address, 1800.   90.
Scolex, no address, 1795.   62.
Tiebout, Cornelius (*also* Philadelphia), no address, ca. 1796, 1800.   127, 332.

BOSTON

BLAKE, W. P. (William Pinson).
   59 Cornhill, ca. 1792 to ca. 1796.
      7, 100, 106, 111, 134, 208, 259, 270, 300, 349, 362.   *Also* (probably same address) 407.

BLAKE, W. P. (and L.).
   1 Cornhill, ca. 1796 through 1799.
      2, 20, 188.   *Also* (probably same address) 106.
   Published numerous librettos, but little music.

HAGEN, P. A. von, Jr. & Co. (Peter Albrecht von Hagen and Benjamin Crehore).
   62 Newbury street, May, 1798 to March, 1799.
      5, 14, 30, 123, 174, 192, 201, 252, 253, 336, 343, 382, 423, 475.   *Also* (probably same address) 123, 244.

55 Marlborough street, March to May, 1799
81, 229, 230, 235, 258, 270, 398, 424, 438.

The firm did not begin to publish music before 1799 (Sonneck).

HAGEN, P. A. von & Co. (Also given as: P. A. von Hagen, Jr. & Co.).

3 Cornhill, May to June 28, 1799. (*Sonneck:* May, 1799 to November, 1800.)
3, 5, 14, 23, 27, 33, 48, 51, 55, 81, 91, 92, 103, 135, 152, 154, 185, 189, 194, 199, 223, 229, 234, 243, 253, 297, 299, 302, 315, 355, 363, 389, 433, 457, 471, 480, 483.

HAGEN, P. A. von.

3 Cornhill, June 28, 1799 through 1801. (*Sonneck:* November, 1800–.)
32, 45, 93, 126, 217, 231, 234, 238, 256, 260, 270, 353, 379, 391, 416, 419, 437, 466, 467, 476, 482.

3 Cornhill and 4 Old Massachusetts Bank, *also* 4 Old Massachusetts Bank (alone), 1802.
26, 156, 257, 346, 364, 436.

HAGEN, P. A. von, Jr.

4 Old Massachusetts Bank, 1803.

Sonneck states that "late in 1797, or very early in 1798, P. A. von Hagen, sen. and jun., opened a 'Musical Magazine and Warranted Piano Forte Ware House at 62 Newbury Street.' In May, 1798, Benjamin Crehore became a Partner and the firm became P. A. von Hagen, jun. & Co. . . . In November, 1800, the firm was dissolved by mutual consent and P. A. von Hagen (jun.) carried business on alone at the same address."

This latter statement is contradicted by the following announcement in the Boston *Columbian centinel* of July 3, 1799:

TAKE NOTICE

The Copartnership between P. A. von Hagen, senior, junior, and Benjamin Crehore, trading under the firm of P. A. von Hagen, jun. and Co. being this day, the 28th June 1799, dissolved by mutual consent: All persons having demands, will please to apply at P. A. Von Hagen's Musical Magazine, No. 3, Cornhill; and those indebted, are solicited to pay their respective ballance [!] to P. A. Von Hagen, he being duly authorised to settle the concerns of said Company.

*   *   *

This Day, is Published, by P. A. Von Hagen and Son, The New Song of "How tedious alas! are the hours." Also, the favourite Song and answer in the new Comedy of *The Stranger.*

Sonneck's position, however, seems to be somewhat borne out by the fact that various issues bearing the imprint of P. A. von Hagen & Co., 3 Cornhill, appeared during 1800, even as late as November of that year—*cf.* "Henry's return . . . Boston, Printed & sold at P. A. von Hagen & co. . . . No. 3 Cornhill." Advertised November 29, 1800, as "this day published."

Our only conclusion, then, can be that either the dissolution of the partnership failed to actually take place as announced, or (perhaps more likely) that the earlier imprint was retained despite the dissolution. This latter view seems strengthened by the fact that in the advertisement above, following the notice

[585]

of the dissolution of the partnership with Crehore, the form "P. A. von Hagen and Son" is used—a phrase which might easily be considered the equivalent of "P. A. von Hagen & co." However, because of this uncertainty, the present revision uses the expression "Published probably in 1799" in connection with the imprint: P. A. von Hagen & Co., 3 Cornhill; and "Published possibly as early as 1799" with the imprint: P. A. von Hagen, 3 Cornhill.

There is confusion also as to when the address "Old Massachusetts Bank, Head of the Mall" was added to "3 Cornhill," in connection with the firm name P. A. von Hagen—whether in 1800 or in 1802. As there seems to be authority for both views, it has seemed wise to use the expression "Published probably after 1800" in such case.

Again there is confusion in the use of the terms Senior and Junior. Sonneck states (*see* under *List of composers*) that P. A. von Hagen, Jr.—as he had styled himself since his arrival in Charleston in 1774—changed Jr. to Sr. on his New York concert programs in 1789, when his son appeared with him as singer, pianist, and somewhat later, violinist. However, he seems not to have continued this practice when establishing his business in Boston. For his earliest published music bears the imprint "P. A. von Hagen, Jr. and Co.," in which case it seems established that the term "Jr." refers to himself. This form of imprint lasted for one year only, and "Jr." never again appears in the imprint until von Hagen's death in 1803, when the business was taken over by his son.

LINLEY AND MOORE.
19 Marlborough street, 1798.
3, 169.
Published little music, but some important items.

NORMAN, William.
75 Newbury street, ca. August, 1796 to ca. September, 1799.
39, 98, 244, 279, 280.

GENERAL PUBLISHERS

Clap, William T., 90 Newbury street, 1794. 7, 134, 259, 349. Fifth street, 1795. 473.
Gerrish, Samuel, Cornhill, 1721. 170.
Hayts, Babcock & Appleton, 6 Mills street, ca. 1800. 291.
McAlpine, William, Marlborough street, 1771, 1757. 263, 489.
Mein and Fleeming, no address, 1768. 227.
Norman, William, 75 Newbury street, 1796–99. 39, 98, 244, 279, 280.
Pelham, William, 59 Cornhill, 1797. 348.
Spotswood, William (*also* Philadelphia), 55 Marlborough street, 1794–5. 21, 80, 194, 324.
Spotswood & Etheridge, no address, 1798. 195.
Thomas, Isaiah, no address, 1771. 494.
Thomas, Isaiah and Co., 45 Newbury street, 1789. 42.
Thomas, Isaiah and Ebenezer T. Andrews, 45 Newbury street, 1791–1800. 2, 16, 28, 104, 108, 113, 126, 152, 179, 180, 286, 364, 366, 438, 442.

PRINTERS

Belknap and Hall, no address, 1794. 7, 134, 259.
Belknap, Joseph, no address, 1795. 100.

Billings, William, no address, 1781. 348.
Boyles, John, no address, 1769. 1.
Draper and Folsom, no address, 1778. 384.
Edes and Gill, no address, 1770. 227.
Edes P. and S. Letheridge, no address, 1794. 349.
Eliot, J., no address, 1725. 491.
Franklin, J., no address, 1721. 170.
Green, Samuel, no address, 1684. 489.
Green and Russell, no address, 1764. 492.
Hall, Samuel, 53 Cornhill, 1795. 436.
Hall, Thomas, Water street, 1796. 270, 407.
Martin, Alexander, Quaker Lane, 1795. 63.
Mills and Hicks, no address, 1774. 494.
Russell, Ezekiel, no address, 1795. 79.
Russell, Jno. and Jos. N., Quaker Lane, 1795–96. 62, 63, 100.
White, James, "Near Charles River Bridge", 1795–1800. 219, 259, 296, 426, 470, 473.
Young and Etheridge, Market Square, 1792. 490.

ENGRAVERS

Allen, Joel, no address, 1793, ca. 1775. 78, 373.
C., J., no address, 1774. 188.
Norman, John (*also* Philadelphia), no address, 1781. 348.

BALTIMORE

CARR, J. (Joseph).
"Market St. near Gay St.", June, 1794 to ca. March, 1795.
23, 30, 120, 225, 286, 444, 448.
"No. 6 Gay Street," 1795 (Sonneck), 1796 (Evans), through 1802.
41, 53, 66, 90, 100, 124, 129, 133, 142, 149, 184, 190, 226, 230, 245, 261, 272, 273, 353, 393, 462, 480. *Also* (probably same address) 134, 289, 290, 306, 311, 360, 370.
First appears as publisher (in conjunction with B. Carr) in 1796 (Sonneck).

KEATINGE, George; Henry S.; and J.
All published songsters (words only).
Henry S. (158 Baltimore street, ca. 1798) seems to have published certain musical compositions also: 36, 287, 297, 300, 382, 383; George, 105; J., 36.

SHAW, R. (*probably* Ralph).
92 Market street (also given as 1 Light street), ca. November, 1797 to ca. November, 1800.
168, 177, 183, 217, 381, 468, 481.
There is still much uncertainty as to R. Shaw. Sonneck says of him, referring to the time between his failure in Philadelphia in November, 1797, and the re-opening of his Philadelphia store in November, 1800, "In the meantime, he travelled with theatrical companies through the South. He was also a fashionable ballad singer."
However, in *Early concert-life in America*, Sonneck speaks of Shaw's "well

[587]

supplied" music store in Baltimore, from 1797 through "the remaining years of the century."

Whether these two statements are contradictory to each other (involving two different R. Shaws) or whether they represent varied activities of one and the same man, it is hard to say.

See also Philadelphia.

GENERAL PUBLISHERS AND PRINTERS

Angell, James, no address, 1794. 105.
Hupfeld, C. and F. Hammer, 173 Market street, 179–. 123, 135, 218.
Sower, Samuel, 67 Market street, 1798. 327, 398.
Warner and Hanna, 2 North Gay street, 1799. 21.

ENGRAVERS

Edwin, David, no address, 1798. 53.
Martin. I. E.. no address. 1800. 277.

PUBLISHERS, PRINTERS, AND ENGRAVERS LOCATED ELSEWHERE

PUBLISHERS

Bayley, Daniel, Newburyport, Mass., 1774. 156, 494.
Cumins, Edward, Williamsburg, Va., 1773. 410.
Doolittle and Read, New Haven, Conn., 1786–87. 16.
Larkin, S., Portsmouth, N. H., 1798. 79.
Lyon, James, Waterford, N. Y., 1797. 254.
Macanulty, Bernard B., Salem, Mass., 1799. 57.
Spencer and Webb, Albany, N. Y., 1797. 147.
Thomas, Isaiah, Worcester, Mass. (*also* Boston), 1785–88. 233, 269, 436.
Thomas, Isaiah & Son, Worcester, Mass., 1800. 76.
Todd, Joseph J., Providence, R. I., 1799. 83.
Wilson, James, Wilmington, Del., 1797. 420.
Wright, Daniel and Co., Northampton, Mass., 1798. 16.

PRINTERS

Blunt, Edmund M.,Newburyport, Mass., 1798, 1800. 313, 489.
Bonsal and Niles, Wilmington, Del., 1797. 420.
Bowen, D., New Haven, Conn., 1786. 373, 375.
Bruce, David, Charlestown (Charleston), S. C., 1778. 490.
Brynberg, Peter, Wilmington, Del., 1797. 15.
Carter, John, Providence, R. I., 1788, 1779. 75, 76.
Dickman, Thomas, Greenfield, Mass., 1794. 76.
Doolittle, A., New Haven, Conn., 1800. 273.
Dunham and True, Hanover, N. H., 1796. 66.
Fry and Southwick, Albany, N. Y., 1797. 147.
Heaton, Nathaniel, Jr., Wrentham, Mass., 1799. 79.
Heaton, Nathaniel and Benjamin, Providence, R. I., 1799. 83.
Hudson and Goodwin, Hartford, Conn., 1786. 375.

Jenks, E. A., Portland, Maine, 1800.   493.
Melcher, John, Portsmouth, N. H., 1790, 1798.   21, 79.
Merriam, Ebenezer, Brookfield, Mass., 1800.   118.
Merriam, E. and Co., Brookfield, Mass., 1798.   118.
Muck, P., Charleston, S. C., ca. 1800.   375.
Neale, I., Burlington, Vt., 1795.   138.
Peirce, Charles, Portsmouth, N. H., 1800.   197.
Preston, Samuel, Amherst, N. H., 1798.   397.
Ranlet, H., Exeter, N. H., 1794–1800.   178, 209, 490.
Rind, William, Williamsburg, Va., 1773.   410.
Spear, S., Hanover, N. H., ca. 1774.   491.
Swan and Ely, Suffield, Conn., ca. 1800.   404.
Thomas, Isaiah, Jr., Worcester, Mass., 1795–99.   269, 386.
Thomas, Isaiah and David Carlisle, Jr., Walpole, N. H., 1795.   66.
Thomas and Waldo, Brookfield, Mass., 1795.   79.
Watson, Eben, Hartford, Conn., 1774.   491.
Wells, Robert, Charleston, S. C., 1774.   494.
Woodward, M. H., Middletown, Conn., 1790.   400.
Wright, Andrew, Northampton, Mass., 1798.   16.

ENGRAVERS

Doolittle, Amos, New Haven, Conn., 1800, 1786.   273, 373.
Ely, A., Suffield, Conn., ca. 1800.   405.
Fairman, G., Hudson, N. Y., 1799.   310.
Lynn, A., Alexandria, Va., 1799.   152.
Ruggles, E., Jr., *probably* Massachusetts, 1793.   78.

General Index

[For composers represented in this work, see separate *List of Composers*.]

A

Abercromby, General James, 154, 479
Abroad and at home (opera), 1, 82, 182, 301, 424
Accomplish'd maid (opera), 1
Acis and Galatea (serenata), 205, 478
Adams, John, 2, 3, 4, 5
Adde, ——, 174
Adgate, Andrew, 491
Adopted child (opera), 6, 56
Agreeable surprise (opera), 7, 100, 283
Aimwell, Absalom (pseud.), 331
Aird, James, 479
Alexander the Great, 249
Algerine Corsair (opera), 421
American citizen (New York), 74
American daily advertiser (Philadelphia), 355
American in London (musical entertainment), 16
American magazine (Boston), 492, 493, 494
American museum (Philadelphia), 78, 493
American patriotic songs (words only), 21
American tar, or The press gang defeated (ballet), 22, 207
American true blue (interlude), 22
Americana and Elutheria (masque), 22
Americana, or A new tale of the genii (masque), 22
Amherst, General Jeffry, 426, 479
Amintas (opera), 14
Amyntas (opera), 134
Anacreontic poems, 327
Anacreontic Society (Columbian), 78, 166, 178, 179, 216, 484
Anacreontic Society (London), 48
Anacreontic songs, 289
André, Major John, 25, 246, 457
Andrews, M. P., 377, 387
Anthems, 27, 28, 29, 87, 151, 180, 197, 366, 426, 442
Apollo, 29

Apollo press (Boston), 7, 100, 134, 208, 259, 270, 300, 495
Apotheosis of Franklin ("Allegorical finale"), 29
Apthorp, East, 492
Arabs of the desert (pantomime), 30
Arcadia (dramatic pastoral), 31
Archers (opera), 31, 427
Ariadne abandoned (musical piece), 32, 427
Arnold, Miss Elizabeth (singer), later Mrs. Poe, mother of Edgar Allan Poe, 62, 225, 260, 432
Arnold, Samuel James (playwright), 403
Artaxerxes (opera), 57, 388, 454
Atkins, Edward, 167
Atlanticus (pseud.), 155
Audin, jun., 29
Auld Robin Gray (opera), 35
Aurora (Philadelphia), 80, 173, 179, 195, 346, 357, 365, 407.
Avison, Charles, 292

B

Ballets (*See* Pantomimes).
Bankson, John (singer), 130, 312
Banksons, "The two master", 130
Bannister, Charles (singer), 384
Barrett, Giles L. (singer), 433
Barry, Captain John, 260
Barton, Andrew (playwright), 109
Bass viol, 143, 209
Bassoon, 142
Bates, William (singer), 365, 390, 456
Battle of Hexham (opera, *see* Days of old).
Battle pieces, 37, 38, 39, 55, 87
Beaumarchais, Pierre Augustin Caron de, 406
Beggar's opera, 135
Belle Arsène (opera), 317
Benda, Jiři (Georg) Antonin, 32
Bennet, Rev. John, 493
Bernard, John (actor), 217, 294, 432
Bertles, Miss (singer), 37, 273, 283

Claypoole's American daily advertiser (Philadelphia), 267, 371, 392
Clifford, —–— (singer), 427, 450
Cobb, James (playwright), 181
COLLECTIONS OF MUSIC (summary of titles):
American musical miscellany, 16
Apollo and the Muse's musical compositions, by W. Selby, 29
Aviary, by Hook, 35
Beauties of music published by W. Norman, 39
Book of songs (Six songs by Mrs. Pownall and James Hewitt), 47, 48
Book of twelve songs by A. Juhan, 48
Caledonian muse, 53
Canzonetti composed by a lady of Philadelphia, 54
Choice collection of Free Masons songs, 76
Clio and Euterpe, 65
Collection of airs, 66
Collection of contra dances, 66
Collection of country dances, 66
Collection of favorite songs, arr. by A. Reinagle, 66, 67
[Collection of favorite songs, arr. by A. Reinagle], 67–69
Collection of favorite songs, divided into two books, arr. by. A. Reinagle, 69–70
Collection of favorite songs by Hook, 70
Collection of new & favorite songs: [A], 71; [B], 74; [C], 74
Collection of songs by Dibdin, 74, 75
Collection of the newest and most approved songs, 75
Collection of the newest and most fashionable country dances and cotillions, 75
Collection of the newest cotillions . . . modern songs, 76
Compleat [!] instructor by H. B. Victor, 83
Compleat tutor for the fife (Willig), 84
Complete [!] tutor for the fife (1776), 85

COLLECTIONS OF MUSIC—Continued.
Dance tunes, etc., 96
Divertimenti by Raynor Taylor, 110
Elegant extracts, 31, 119
Elegant extracts for the German flute, 120–122
Evening amusement, 127
Favorite songs at Vauxhall Gardens, 402
Favorite songs from the Haunted Tower, 401
Favorite songs from the Pirates, 401
Favorite songs from the Shipwreck, 403
Favorite songs from the Wild goose chase, 472
Four ballads by B. Carr, 145
Four excellent new songs, 403
Four songs from an unidentified collection, 403
Gentleman's amusement (Paff), 156
Gentleman's amusement, by R. Shaw, 157–162
Hours of love, 190
The ladies' magazine, 222
Ladies' musical journal, 222, 316
Lady's musical miscellany, 223
Linley's assistant for the pianoforte, 290
Linley's selection of country dances and reels, 230
Manuscript collection of hymns, songs, etc., 247
Masque, 254
Massachusetts musical magazine, 254
Military amusement, 31
[Miscellaneous and incomplete (?) collection], 76
Miss Ashmore's choice collection of songs, 263
Moller & Capron's monthly numbers, 265
Mr. Francis's ballroom assistant, 146
Musical bagatelles, 54, 273
Musical journal (flute or violin), 273–275
Musical journal (pianoforte), 275–279

Lathrop, J., 211
Launch, or Huzza for the Constellation ("musical piece"), 226
Leary, Miss (singer), 204, 256, 380, 422
Leaver, Mrs. (singer), 423
Lee, Harriet (playwright), 285
Leigh, The honourable Sir Egerton, Baronet, 309
Lessons, 75, 144, 146, 226, 289, 290, 317
Lewis, Matthew Gregory (playwright), 93, 94, 316
Liberty, 2, 3, 4, 78, 85, 138, 174, 175, 215, 227, 228, 328
Librettos (*See* separate index of opera librettos, also individual titles).
Linn, John Blair (poet), 48.
Lionel and Clarissa (opera), 231
Lippencott, Margaret E., 495
Little Yankee sailor (musical farce), 235
Lloyd, Rev., 31
Locandiera (opera), 371
Lock and key ("musical entertainment"), 32, 186, 236
Lodoiska (opera), 141, 322, 482
Longman & Broderip (London publishers), 97
Lord of the manor (opera), 237, 243, 458, 461
Lossing and Winsor, 227
Louis XVI, King of France, 237, 250, 451
Love in a camp, or Patrick in Prussia (opera), 99, 285, 326
Love in a village (opera), 238
Love in the city (*See* The romp).
Love's frailties (comedy interspersed with music), 256
Low, Samuel, 309
Lucky escape (pantomime), 241

M

M., G. H., 495
Macbeth (incidental music), 245
McKean, Thomas. Chief Justice of Pennsylvania, 352
McKee, Thomas, 12
Madison, Mrs., 272
MAGAZINES (non-musical), newspapers, journals, etc.:
American citizen, 74

MAGAZINES—Continued.
American daily advertiser (*See also* Claypoole's American daily advertiser, Dunlap's American daily advertiser, and Dunlap and Claypooles' American daily advertiser), 355
American magazine, 492, 493, 494
American museum, 78, 493
Aurora, 80, 173, 179, 195, 346, 357, 365, 407
Boston chronicle, 227
Boston evening post, 263, 292, 426
Boston gazette, 227
Boston magazine, 6, 251, 363, 431, 493
City gazette, 376, 420
Claypoole's American daily advertiser, 267, 371, 392
Columbian centinel, 2, 20, 27, 29, 39, 105, 111, 174, 189, 194, 199, 223, 279, 334, 398, 433, 494
Columbian magazine, 50, 165, 489, 490, 491, 492, 493
Connecticut courant, 375
Diary, 489
Dunlap and Claypoole's American daily advertiser, 139, 176, 219, 309, 323, 406, 427, 462, 478, 481
Dunlap's American daily advertiser, 160, 238, 273, 314, 319, 330, 377, 392, 445
Federal gazette (Baltimore), 53, 91, 173, 275, 287, 289, 296, 305, 395, 398, 467, 480
Federal gazette (Philadelphia), 47, 265, 299, 404
Federal intelligencer, 145
Freeman's journal, 424
General advertiser, 275, 276
Gentlemen & ladies town and country magazine, 493
Massachusetts magazine, 8, 15, 24, 25, 39, 49, 57, 58, 78, 99, 104, 141, 145, 191, 194, 195, 211, 229, 239, 251, 282, 295, 309, 310, 311, 312, 313, 315, 329, 364, 365, 369, 378, 399, 404, 425, 430, 432, 449, 458, 460, 473, 489, 490, 491, 492, 493, 495
Massachusetts spy, 254, 308, 450

MAGAZINES—Continued.

Minerva (New York), 39, 161, 181, 220, 222, 264, 430, 438, 447
Minerva (Philadelphia), 319
Monthly magazine and American review, 495
New Jersey journal, 64
New London magazine, 493
New York daily advertiser, 47, 63, 140, 158, 401, 421, 472
New York gazette and Weekly Mercury, 240
New York gazette (Rivington's), 65
New York Historical Society quarterly bulletin, 495
New York journal, 254
New York magazine, 28, 99, 309, 490, 491, 492, 493
New York Mercury, 263, 311, 394, 397
New York weekly magazine, 494
Pennsylvania chronicle, 109, 309
Pennsylvania gazette, 43, 85, 130, 352, 445, 446, 476, 492
Pennsylvania journal, 267, 312, 385
Pennsylvania ledger, 83
Pennsylvania magazine, 155, 491
Pennsylvania magazine of history and biography, 171, 172
Pennsylvania packet, 63, 70, 312, 375
Philadelphia monthly magazine, 2, 139
Porcupine's gazette, 35
Public ledger, 139
Royal American magazine, 188
Royal gazette (Rivington's), 76, 147, 292, 334, 400
Salem gazette, 395
Sentimental and Masonic magazine, 492
South Carolina gazette, 254, 309, 325, 394
South Carolina historical magazine, 494
Trenton Sunday advertiser, 64
Universal asylum, 11, 88, 126, 134, 166, 183, 195, 196, 238, 250, 306, 308, 351, 410, 429, 489, 495
Universal spectator (London), 493
Virginia gazette, 410

MAGAZINES—Continued.

Weekly museum, 75, 283, 399, 401
Worcester magazine, 311
Magic flute (opera), 35, 225, 226, 353, 476
Magician no conjurer (opera, see Conjurer no magician).
Maid of the mill (opera), 165, 245
Mallet, ——— (English poet), 352
Mandora, 41, 115
Mann, Mrs., 234
MARCHES (summary of titles):
Adams march, 5
Admiral Nelson's march, 6
America, 15
Archers march, 31
Bedfordshire march, 40
Bellisle march, 41
Boston's.march, 48
Brown's march, 50
Buonaparte's march, 50, 51, 250
Burbank's march, 51
Burr's grand march, 51
Capt. Money's march, 54
Capt. Reed's march, 54
Coldstream march, 66
Congress, 87
Coronation march, 89
Count Brown's march, 92
Cumberland march, 95
Dead march, 100
Dead march and monody by B. Carr, 100, 101
Dorsetshire march, 112
Duke of Gloster's march, 116
Duke of York's march, 116
Duke's march, 116
Essex march, 126
Eugene's march, 126
Everybody's march, 129
Everybody's quick march, 129
Fœderal march, 139
Federals march, 140
Foot march, 144
Freemasons march, 147
French march, 148
Gen. Green's march, 154
General Knox's march, 154
General Pinckney's march, 155
General Washington's march, 453
Gen. Wayne's march, 155

North American almanack and Massachusetts register (Boston), 227, 426

Nurse Lovechild (Lady Eleanor Frere Fenn), 436

O

O'Hara, Kane (playwright), 259

O'Keefe (O'Keeffe), John (playwright), 7, 100, 134, 187, 188, 326, 338, 339, 391, 400

Oddities (entertainment), 143, 212, 224, 329, 339

Odes, 13, 16, 107, 129–130, 139, 140, 152, 174, 178, 180, 211, 227, 254, 286, 308–313, 352, 442

Offley, F., 132

Old woman of eighty three (burletta), 314

Oldmixon, Mrs., née George (singer), 2, 8, 10, 45, 81, 102, 122, 165, 166, 176, 193, 194, 204, 205, 215, 233, 235, 264, 267, 304

Olios, 12, 108, 195, 302, 314, 336, 366, 369

OPERAS (including burlettas, dramatic pastorals, musical farces, musical entertainments and pieces, masques, melodramas, pastoral operas, plays interspersed with music, etc. Summary of titles):

Abroad and at home, 1, 82, 182, 301, 424

Accomplish'd maid, 1

Acis and Galatea, 205, 478

Adopted child, 6, 56

Agreeable surprise, 7, 100, 283

Algerine Corsair, 421

American in London, 16

Americana and Elutheria, 22

Amintas, 14

Amyntas, 134

Arcadia, 31

Archers, 31, 427

Ariadne abandoned, 32

Artaxerxes, 57, 388, 454

Auld Robin Gray, 35

Battle of Hexham (*See* The days of old).

Beggar's opera, 135

Belle Arsène, 317

OPERAS—Continued.

Better sort, 42

Blaise et Babet, 319

Blockade, 44

Blockheads, 44

Blue Beard, 44, 62, 74, 248, 332, 400, 432, 464

Bourville Castle, 48

Buona figliuola, 318

Caernarvon Castle, 36

Capocchio and Dorinna, 54

Captive of Spilberg, 55, 168, 183, 467, 468

Caravane, 320

Carnival of Venice, 205, 483

Castle of Andalusia, 238, 400

Castle of Otranto, 56

Castle of Sorrento, 363

Castle spectre, 57, 258, 319, 398

Castles in the air, 135, 218, 298, 335, 435

Chaplet, 457

Cherokee, 133, 141, 367, 414

Children in the wood, 62, 105, 321, 372, 399, 460, 461, 463, 484

Columbus, 80, 207

Comet, 399

Comus, 478

Conjurer no magician, 44

Critic, 11, 264

Cymon, 418

Darby's return, 99

Days of old, 37, 100

Dead alive, 100

Démophon, 320

Deserter, 106, 248, 321, 430

Deux chasseurs et la laitière, 106

Diamond cut diamond, 273, 468

Disappointment, 109, 110, 479

Doctor and apothecary, 111

Double disguise, 112

Duenna, 114, 171

Edwin and Angelina, 118

Farmer, 125, 134, 299, 375, 400, 450, 470

Fashionable lady, 110, 134

Fashionable rallery [!], 442

Fast asleep, 9

Feudal times, 248

Flash in the pan, 305, 466

Flitch of bacon, 143

[613]

[614]

Universal asylum (Philadelphia), 11, 88, 126, 134, 166, 183, 195, 196, 238, 250, 306, 308, 351, 410, 429, 489, 495
Universal spectator (London), 493
Upton, William, 182, 203
Uranian Society, 491
Use and abuse of music, Remarks on, 494

V

Vancenza, or The dangers of credulity (novel), 237
Variations, 11, 32, 41, 48, 52, 69, 75, 115, 142, 144, 223, 257, 263, 329, 331, 384, 406, 426, 476, 480
Vernon, ——— (singer), 195
Violin music, 1, 13, 29, 34, 40, 48, 52, 53, 80, 83, 86, 87, 99, 101, 104, 106, 107, 115, 116, 120, 127, 141, 142, 151, 156, 164, 209, 258, 260, 289, 327, 334, 357, 359, 376, 390, 392, 439, 444, 480, 484
Violoncello music, 29, 87, 263, 390
Virgin of the sun (play with music), 444
Virginia gazette (Williamsburg), 410
Voluntaries, 29, 151, 446
Volunteers (entertainment), 102, 390, 446, 456, 462, 464
Vulcan's gift, or The bower of Hymen (pantomime), 447

W

Wags (entertainment), 389
Waldron,———465
Walsh, ——— (singer), 250
Waltzes, 12, 40, 65, 96, 140, 164, 263, 296, 327, 348, 376, 447
Warrell, ———(singer), 267, 291, 323, 429, 435, 438
Warrell, Junior (singer), 267
Warrell, Mrs. (singer), 187, 264, 267, 303, 305, 391, 472
Warren, ——— (singer), 267
Warren, Mrs. Mercy (playwright), 44, 227
Warriors welcome home (ballet), 111

Washington, George, 5, 14, 15, 25, 42, 50, 63, 64, 100, 101, 108, 152, 167, 172–173, 178, 204, 227, 267, 270, 273, 310, 312, 313, 356, 366, 377, 424, 434, 449, 467, 490
Washington, Mrs., 63, 223, 424
Washington Association, 449
Waterman, or The first of August (entertainment), 454
Watts, Dr., 149
Wayne, General Anthony, 155, 314
Webster, Noah, 494
Wedding day (comedy), 95
Wedding in Wales (comedy), 323
Weekly museum (New York), 75, 283, 399, 401
Wegelin, Oscar, 22, 44, 364, 379, 406, 409, 480
Weichsel, Mrs. (singer), 195
Welch, Master (singer), 24
Welsh music, 1, 95, 133, 323, 324, 457
Wells, John F., 449
Wesley, John, 334
West, ——— (singer), 4
Westray, Miss Ellen (singer), later Mrs. John Darley. (Her sisters, Elizabeth A. Westray, later Mrs. Twaits, and Juliana Westray, later Mrs. William B. Wood, were also well known performers), 74, 132, 212, 463
Wheelock, John, 491
Whitefield, Rev. George, 312
Whitmore, William H., 269
Wignell, Thomas (actor), 99
Wild goose chase (play interspersed with songs), 471
Will of the wisp (entertainment), 113, 245, 286
Willems, Miss (singer), later Mrs. Green, 272
Williams, Caleb (novelist), 211
Williams, Dr. (historian), 490
Williams, John, 108
Williamson, ——— (singer), 138, 174, 178, 233, 286, 460
Wilmore Castle (opera), 429, 434
Wind instruments, 325, 412, 454
Winter songs, 473
Witches of the rocks, or Harlequin everywhere (pantomime), 474